International Series in Operations Research & Management Science

Volume 161

Series Editor
Frederick S. Hillier
Stanford University, CA, USA

Special Editorial Consultant
Camille C. Price
Stephen F. Austin State University, TX, USA

For further volumes:
http://www.springer.com/series/6161

Marc Goetschalckx

Supply Chain Engineering

 Springer

Marc Goetschalckx
Georgia Institute of Technology
H. Milton Stewart School of Industrial & Systems Engineering
Ferst Drive NW., 765
30332-0205 Atlanta Georgia
USA
marc.goetschalckx@isye.gatech.edu

ISSN 0884-8289
ISBN 978-1-4419-6511-0   e-ISBN 978-1-4419-6512-7
DOI 10.1007/978-1-4419-6512-7
Springer New York Dordrecht Heidelberg London

Library of Congress Control Number: 2011930401

Springer is part of Springer Science+Business Media (www.springer.com)

Preface

The focus of this book is the engineering design and planning of supply chain systems. A supply chain system can be loosely described as a system that—through procurement, production, and distribution—delivers goods to satisfy the demands of customers. Most organizations have a supply chain supporting their missing, ranging from traditional business supply chains, to military logistics, to disaster relief or medical delivery systems. As a consequence, there exists a very large variety of supply chain system types with different goals, constraints, and decisions. But a systematic approach to the design and planning of any supply chain can be based on the principles and methods of system engineering. Systems engineering methodology uses three fundamental components: data, models, and solution algorithms.

This book is targeted at several audiences. The first target is a course for upper-level undergraduate students on supply chains. The second target is use in a capstone senior design project in the supply chain area. The third target is an introductory course on supply chains either in a master of engineering or a master of business administration programs. The last audience consists of students enrolled in logistics or supply chain postgraduate or continuing education courses.

The book can be roughly divided into four sections. The first section focuses on data management. Since most of planning and design requires making decisions today so that supply chain functions can be executed efficiently in the future, this section introduces forecasting principles and techniques. The next two sections treat decision making in the two primary areas of transportation and inventory. The second section of the book focuses on transportation systems. First, the characteristics of transportation assets and infrastructure are shown. Then four chapters focus on the planning of transportation activities depending on who controls the transportation assets. The third section of the book is focused on storing goods. The last section of the book is focused on supply chain systems that consider simultaneously procurement, production, transportation, and inventory, as well as the design of the supply chain infrastructure or network design.

In each chapter, first a model of the process being studied is developed followed by a description of practical solution algorithms. More advanced material is typically described in appendices. This makes it possible to use an integrated, breadth-first treatment of supply chain systems by using the initial material in each chapter. A more in-depth treatment of a specific topic or process can be found towards the end of each chapter.

Table of Contents

Chapter 1
Introduction

Learning Objectives After you have studied this chapter, you should be able to:

- Understand at a high level the domains of supply chains and logistics—their characteristics and components.
- Know various types of supply chain objectives, constraints, and costs.
- Know common supply chain definitions and acronyms.
- Know the various types and levels of supply chain planning.

The overall focus of this book is the application of engineering design and scientific management methodologies to the domains of supply chains and logistics. This introduction summarizes some of the definitions and characteristics of these domains. The general principles of engineering planning and design are discussed in the next chapter.

1.1 The Supply Chain and Logistics Domains

1.1.1 Logistics

Logistics is concerned with the organization, movement, and storage of material and people. The term *logistics* was first used by the military to describe activities associated with maintaining a fighting force in the field and, in its narrowest sense, describes the housing of troops. The term gradually spread to cover business and service activities. There exist a multitude of formal definitions. The Council of Supply Chain Management Professionals (CSCMP), formerly known as the Council of Logistics Management (CLM), is a large trade association in the United States that promotes the practice and education of logistics. Their definitions are probably the most widely used.

> Logistics Management is that part of Supply Chain Management that plans, implements, and controls the efficient, effective forward and reverse flow and storage of goods, services and related information between the point of origin and the point of consumption in order to meet customers' requirements.

M. Goetschalckx, *Supply Chain Engineering,* International Series in Operations Research & Management Science 161,
DOI 10.1007/978-1-4419-6512-7_1, © Springer Science+Business Media, LLC 2011

It identifies the following planning activities as part of logistics management:

> Logistics Management activities typically include inbound and outbound transportation management, fleet management, warehousing, materials handling, order fulfillment, logistics network design, inventory management, supply/demand planning, and management of third-party logistics services providers. To varying degrees, the logistics function also includes sourcing and procurement, production planning and scheduling, packaging and assembly, and customer service. It is involved in all levels of planning and execution—strategic, operational, and tactical. Logistics Management is an integrating function, which coordinates and optimizes all logistics activities, as well as integrates logistics activities with other functions including marketing, sales manufacturing, finance and information technology.

It is worthwhile to expand on some of the characteristics of logistics. Foremost is the fundamental principle that logistics takes a holistic view of all the activities that belong to its domain. Logistics is a mission-oriented discipline that will encompass and coordinate all the activities necessary to achieve its mission, which can be summarized as providing time and space utility to an organization.

A business organization has the goal of incorporating the following values into its products: form and function, time and space, and ownership. The form and function values are generated by both its research and design and its production activities. Providing customers with the right product, in the right place, at the right time, generates the time and space values, which is the domain of the logistics activities. Finally, the ownership value is created and enhanced by the marketing activities.

Logistics activities and systems have a significant impact on the economy and even on basic human existence. Numerous examples exist, but one of the most striking one occurred in 1990 when the former Soviet Union produced a bumper crop of potatoes, enough to feed its people, (*Atlanta Journal Constitution*, January 6, 1991), but at the same time a widespread shortage of potatoes was expected in the Soviet Union during the winter season of 1990–1991, (*Time* Magazine, December 3, 1990). In fact, most of the potato crop was stored in warehouses and railroad cars and rotted before it could be delivered to its intended customers. In this case, logistics systems and activities suffered a major breakdown.

Logistics focuses on three types of flows: material flows, information flows, and monetary flows. The most traditional flow is the physical "material flow," where the material can range from traditional products, through services, to livestock, and people. The "flows" can refer to material in motion, indicating the space utility typically associated with transportation, or to material at rest, indicating the time utility typically associated with storage and inventory.

The second important flow in logistic activities is the flow of information. Sharing information on the status of physical flows across various organizations executing the logistics functions can dramatically decrease the magnitude of the physical material flows. This has led to implementation of massive software packages for Enterprise Resource Planning (ERP) that provide such information first within a single organization and now among all the organizations in a supply chain. Finally, the increasingly global nature of trade and logistics has sharpened the focus on monetary flows in logistics. Currency fluctuations and fiscal regulations of trade associations such as the European Union (EU) and North American Free Trade Association (NAFTA) can dramatically change the feasibility and efficiency of the physical flows.

1.1.2 Supply Chain

Very closely related to logistics is the concept of a supply chain. A supply chain is a network of functional organizations that through their activities perform the logistics functions. Again many alternative definitions exist.

> A supply chain is a network of organizations that are involved through upstream and downstream linkages in the different processes and activities that produce value in the form of products and services in the hands of the ultimate customer. (Christopher 1998)

The CSCMP (2005) identifies the following planning activities as part of *Supply Chain Management* (SCM).

> Supply Chain Management encompasses the planning and management of all activities involved in sourcing and procurement, conversion, and all Logistics Management activities. Importantly, it also includes coordination and collaboration with channel partners, which can be suppliers, intermediaries, third-party service providers, and customers. In essence, Supply Chain Management integrates supply and demand management within and across companies. Supply Chain Management is an integrating function with primary responsibility for linking major business functions and business processes within and across companies into a cohesive and high-performing business model. It includes all of the Logistics Management activities noted above, as well as manufacturing operations, and it drives coordination of processes and activities with and across marketing, sales, product design, finance, and information technology.

The following definition is a distillation of several definitions: "A supply chain is an integrated network of resources and processes that is responsible for the acquisition of raw materials, the transformation of these materials into intermediate and finished products, and the distribution of the finished products to the final customers." It includes among others vendors, manufacturing and distribution facilities, forwarders, distributors, and wholesalers, third-party logistics providers, and all other entities involved with the sourcing, transformation, and transportation of products until they reach the customer. At the most elemental level, one can think of supply chain operations as production activities in addition to logistics operations.

The linkages consist of material, information, and financial flows. The supply chain is usually not a single or simple chain but a complex network with many divergent and convergent flows. Because of the current focus of companies on their core competencies, there are typically many different organizations in a supply chain. If all these organizations belong to the same (multinational) corporation, information flows usually are more complete and powerful and decision making is easier, but the fundamental nature of the supply chain remains unchanged. In other words, there is no difference in the definition of a supply chain depending on the fact if one or more corporations are involved.

For an organization to become part of a supply chain requires this to be a beneficial relationship or win–win situation in the long run for the organization and for the rest of the supply chain. There exist an enormous variety of supply chain implementations. In the manufacturing industries, examples are the manufacturing and distribution of consumer goods, the assembly of limited-quantity goods such as aircraft and locomotives, or the construction of telephone switching centers. In the service industries, supply chains take the form of hospital and provider networks, functionality and location of banking outlets, and hub-and-spoke networks by major airlines to offer seats on flights. In the defense organizations, supply chains correspond to personnel, equipment, and bases functions and locations. While many different manifestations and configurations exist, the underlying structure of any supply chain remains a network of capacitated production, storage, and transportation assets to provide customer service by the timely delivery of goods and services to the customers at the lowest possible cost.

Stadtler and Kilger (2008) define supply chain management as

> the task of integrating organizational units along a supply chain and coordinating materials, information, and financial flows in order to fulfill the demands of the ultimate customer with the aim of improving competitiveness of a supply chain as a whole.

1.1.3 Importance of Logistics

A snapshot of the size and importance of some components in the total business logistics costs in the United States for the years 2002–2006 is given by Trunick (2003, 2004, 2005, 2006), Wilson (2007), and Blanchard (2010), and shown in Tables 1.1 and 1.2.

Trends in logistics costs in absolute values and relative to the gross domestic product (GDP) are shown in Table 1.2 and in Figs. 1.1–1.3. Figure 1.1 shows the evolution of inventory costs; Fig. 1.2 shows the absolute costs for logistics activities in billion $ per year; Fig. 1.3 shows the relative importance of the logistics activities as a fraction of the GDP of the United States. Comparable figures for other areas of the world are difficult to obtain and validate.

In Fig. 1.1, the left axis shows the value of business inventory in billions of dollars and the right axis shows the inventory carrying rate on an annual basis.

The decline until 2004 in the absolute value of the inventory costs and the fraction of the GDP represented by inventory costs can be explained by three factors: (1) a downturn in the overall economic climate, e.g., the slowdown starting in 2001 after the bursting of the dot-com bubble; (2) continuing growth of low-inventory supply chain practices by corporations such as just-in-time part deliveries; (3) a low short-term interest rate that made holding inventory less expensive. The decline in transportation costs can be explained by the same downturn in the overall economic climate, but also by an erosion or net decrease of transportation prices due to very strong competition. However, due to the increased economic activity, carriers were able to introduce a price increase in 2004. Coupled with strongly increasing fuel

Table 1.1 U.S. business logistics costs 2002–2009

Category	2002 Costs	2002 Fraction	2003 Costs	2003 Fraction	2004 Costs	2004 Fraction	2005 Costs	2005 Fraction	2006 Costs	2006 Fraction	2007 Costs	2007 Fraction	2008 Costs	2008 Fraction	2009 Costs	2009 Fraction
Inventory																
Interest*	$23		$17		$23		$58		$93						$5	
Taxes, obsolescence, depreciation, insurance	$197		$205		$227		$245		$252						$233	
Warehousing	$78		$78		$82		$90		$101						$119	
Total inventory	$298	32.6	$300	32.1	$332	32.7	$393	33.2	$446	34.2		0.0		0.0	$357	32.6
(*Business inventory value)	$1,451		$1,492		$1,627		$1,763		$1,857							
Transportation																
Intercity motor carriage	$300		$315		$335		$394		$432						$542	
Local motor carriage	$162		$167		$174		$189		$203							
Rail carriage	$37		$38		$42		$48		$54						$50	
International water carriage	$21		$21		$22		$29		$32						$29	
Domestic water carriage	$6		$5		$5		$5		$5							
International air carriage	$7		$8		$9		$15		$15							
Domestic air carriage	$20		$21		$22		$25		$23						$29	
Forwarders	$14		$10		$18		$22		$27						$28	
Oil pipelines	$9		$9		$9		$9		$10						$10	
Total Transportation	$576	63.0	$594	63.5	$636	62.7	$736	62.2	$801	61.4		0.0		0.0	$688	62.8
Shipper costs	$6	0.7	$6	0.6	$8	0.8	$8	0.7	$8	0.6		0.0		0.0		0.0
Administration	$35	3.8	$36	3.8	$39	3.8	$46	3.9	$50	3.8		0.0		0.0	$51	4.7
Total logistics costs	$915	100.0	$936	100.0	$1,015	100.0	$1,183	100.0	$1,305	100.0	$1,396	100.0	$1,340	100.0	$1,096	100.0

Costs in B$, Fractions in %

Table 1.2 U.S. business logistics costs over a twenty-six year period

Year	GDP	Business inventory value ($B)	Inventory carrying rate (%)	Inventory costs	Transportation costs	Administration costs	Total logistics costs	Inventory cost % of GDP (%)	Transport costs % of GDP (%)	Logistics Cost % of GDP (%)
1981	3,130	747	34.7	259	228	19	506	8.3	7.3	16.2
1982	3,260	760	30.8	234	222	18	474	7.2	6.8	14.5
1983	3,540	758	27.9	211	243	18	472	6.0	6.9	13.3
1984	3,930	826	29.1	240	268	20	528	6.1	6.8	13.4
1985	4,210	847	26.8	227	274	20	521	5.4	6.5	12.4
1986	4,450	843	25.7	217	281	20	518	4.9	6.3	11.6
1987	4,740	875	25.7	225	294	21	540	4.7	6.2	11.4
1988	5,110	944	26.6	251	313	23	587	4.9	6.1	11.5
1989	5,440	1005	28.1	282	329	24	635	5.2	6.0	11.7
1990	5,800	1041	27.2	283	351	25	659	4.9	6.1	11.4
1991	5,990	1030	24.9	256	355	24	635	4.3	5.9	10.6
1992	6,320	1043	22.7	237	375	24	636	3.7	5.9	10.1
1993	6,640	1076	22.2	239	396	25	660	3.6	6.0	9.9
1994	7,050	1127	23.5	265	420	27	712	3.8	6.0	10.1
1995	7,400	1211	24.9	302	441	30	773	4.1	6.0	10.4
1996	7,810	1240	24.4	303	467	31	801	3.9	6.0	10.3
1997	8,320	1280	24.5	314	503	33	850	3.8	6.0	10.2
1998	8,780	1317	24.4	321	529	34	884	3.7	6.0	10.1
1999	9,270	1381	24.1	333	554	35	922	3.6	6.0	9.9
2000	9,870	1478	25.3	374	590	39	1003	3.8	6.0	10.2
2001	10,080	1403	22.8	320	581	37	938	3.2	5.8	9.3
2002	10,470	1451	20.6	300	577	35	912	2.9	5.5	8.7
2003	10,759	1494	20.1	300	600	36	936	2.8	5.6	8.5
2004	11,802	1627	20.4	332	644	39	1015	2.8	5.5	8.6
2005	12,216	1763	22.3	393	736	54	1183	3.2	6.0	8.6
2006	13,182	1857	24.0	446	809	50	1305	3.4	6.1	9.7
2007		1966					1396			9.9
2008							1340			10.1
2009				357	688	51	1096			

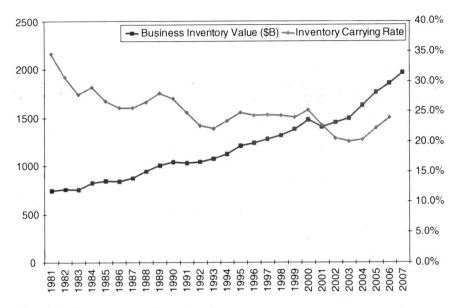

Fig. 1.1 Business inventory value and carrying rate

Fig. 1.2 Business logistics costs

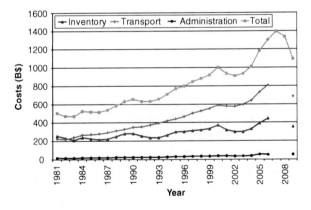

Fig. 1.3 Business logistics costs as fraction of the gross domestic product

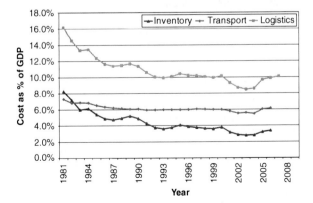

prices in 2005 and 2006 and the accompanying fuel surcharges, the fraction of the GDP attributed to transportation costs increased in 2005 and again in 2006. In addition, the inventory quantities and the interest rates and corresponding inventory carrying cost increased in 2005 and again in 2006. As a consequence, the fraction of the GDP attributable to logistics, after many years of decline, grew to close to 10% in 2005, nearly 10% in 2006, and fractionally higher than 10% in 2007. In 2006 the increase in transportation costs was mainly caused by the rise in fuel costs. The increase in inventory costs was due to an increase of inventory held, higher warehousing costs, and the increase in the interest rate for carrying inventory. The statistics for 2009 show a decrease of more than $244 billion and a combined decrease in 2008 and 2009 of $300 billion. These decreases are due to the severe recession of 2008–2009, indicating that logistics cost are strongly dependent on the overall economic level of the United States. Typically, annual logistics data become available in July or August of the following year.

The statistics on the importance of logistics costs for other areas of the world are much harder to obtain and validate. The following statistics have been collected from a variety of publications in the trade literature. Logistics cost are estimated to make up 14% of the GDP of the European Union. Vachine (2008) reports that logistics in India is a $100 billion industry in 2008, which is expected to reach $120 billion by 2010. Since the statistics may have been collected differently from statistics for the United States, any side-by-side comparison should be carefully validated.

1.1.4 Information Technology, Computers, and Communications

The fundamental physical technologies for transporting and storing materials have remained relatively unchanged during the last five decades. However, information technologies and especially the recent widespread use of the Internet have had a tremendous impact on the control and information flows in logistic systems. For the first time there exists a two-way and up-to-date communication between the end customers, their vendors, and logistics services providers. At the same time, the development of relatively inexpensive tags that can be placed in or on the product and that can be interrogated and updated without physical contact through radio waves (RFID) allow individual product items to store a variety of information on their supply chain history and future. This capability has created several new logistics tools and systems such as mass customization, yield management, end-to-end product and product history availability, and service auctions. For example, Fig. 1.4 illustrates the information presented to an end customer when the package, containing a single customer order, is shipped. The current location and the transportation history of the shipment are reported in detail. This allows the receiver to better plan its activities and provides detailed transactional data to the carrier to optimize its network and operations. In essence, the availability of accurate information has allowed the decrease of just-in-case material inventory without reducing the customer service level.

Fig. 1.4 UPS shipment tracking report over the internet

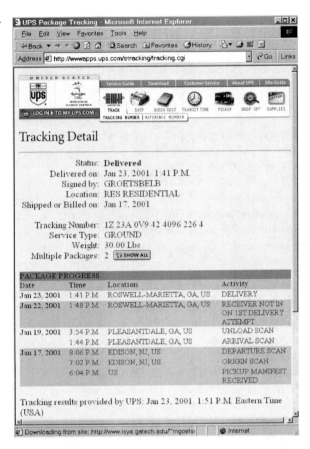

A *virtual logistics enterprise* temporarily combines various logistics service providers and requesters into a single organization for the execution of a particular logistics mission. After the mission has been completed, the component companies become independent again. A particular company may at the same time be a partner with another company for one logistics mission and a competitor for another mission. Such virtual enterprises have only recently become feasible because of the dramatic growth in information technology.

1.2 Logistics Planning and Decisions Support

1.2.1 Three Levels of Logistics Planning

To maximize the value along a supply chain, a large variety of planning decisions have to be made, ranging from the simple warehouse-floor decision of which item to pick next to fulfill a customer order, to the corporate-level decision to build a new manufacturing plant. Supply chain planning supports the full range of those decisions related to the design and operation of supply chains. The focus of this book is on the use of normative models and mathematical solution algorithms to support supply chain planning. Such models and algorithms require the identification and quantitative specification of objectives, constraints, and alternatives. In order for the solution generated by the algorithms to be implementable, it has to be based on accurate data for that particular problem instance. If either of the instance data, the decision support model, or the solution algorithm is incorrect, then the generated decisions will be of little practical value.

There exists a vast amount of literature, software packages, decision support tools, and design algorithms that focus on isolated components of the supply chain or isolated planning in the supply chain. Some examples are production planning in manufacturing, vehicle dispatching in transportation, and warehouse management systems in distribution operations. However, maximization of the potential for adding value along the supply chain requires an integrated and comprehensive planning approach. The supply chain considered should extend from the suppliers of the raw materials, through the various transformation stages, to the final consumers. In recent years, the recovery and recycling operations and processes of post-consumer products are also included in the supply chain and its planning.

In the last few decades, several companies have developed Enterprise Resource Planning (ERP) systems in response to the need of global corporations to plan their entire supply chain. Two major examples of such software vendors are Oracle and SAP. ERP systems integrate the data of one or more principal business functions such as accounting, human resources, production planning, and sales. In their initial implementations, the ERP systems were primarily used for the recording of transactions rather than for the planning of resources on an enterprise-wide scale. Their main advantage was to provide consistent, up-to-date, and accessible data to the enterprise.

In recent years, the original ERP systems have been extended with Advanced Planning Systems (APS). The main function of APS is the planning of enterprise-wide resources and actions. "The goal of APS is to find feasible, near-optimal plans across the supply chain as whole, while potential bottlenecks are considered explicitly" (Stadtler and Kilger 2008). This implies a coordination of the plans among several organizations and geographically dispersed locations. APS are responsible for planning, while ERP systems are still required as the transaction and execution system. APS use or extract data stored in the ERP to support algorithm-based decision making and then store the plans back into the ERP. APS do not substitute for ERP but supplement existing ERP systems.

APS typically comprise several planning modules ranging from strategic network planning, through intermediate demand planning and master planning, to operational material requirements planning (MRP), production planning, distribution requirements planning (DRP), and transportation planning. At the current time, the major emphasis in APS is on the operational planning and execution levels. The planning modules for strategic decisions are still in their infancy in current

Fig. 1.5 Organization of supply chain planning modules

Strategic	Stratetic Enterprise Planning			Strategic Demand Planning
Tactical	Master Production and Distribution Planning			Tactical Demand Planning
Operational	Material Requirem. Planning	Production Planning	Distribution Planning	Operational Demand Planning
Execution	Purchasing	Scheduling	Vehicle Dispatching	Demand Monitoring

implementations. The organization of the various planning modules in supply chain planning and the relations between them are shown in Fig. 1.5. More details on the hierarchy of planning tasks and on APS can be found in Stadtler and Kilger (2008) and Fleischmann and Meyr (2001). Software to plan the supply chain that has been created outside the ERP system many times is called Supply Chain Management software.

The individual planning tasks in an APS constitute in themselves very difficult planning problems. Sophisticated optimization algorithms, such as mixed integer programming (MIP), constraint programming techniques, and heuristic algorithms may be used. Since decisions are made at different times, by different decision makers, and in different locations, no single integrated and comprehensive planning model and corresponding planning algorithm exist. Most often, the overall planning task is solved using hierarchical decomposition or hierarchical planning.

Examples of major software houses offering APS or SCM are J. D. Edwards, and SAP. Several of these companies also provide the ERP system, while others rely on third-party ERP systems. The modules in these APS, their capabilities and functionalities, change continuously and dramatically. Many times, the only available information is based on marketing and promotional materials provided by the software vendors. The detailed assumptions, constraints, and objectives of the strategic models and algorithms are particularly hard to determine.

Previously, Anderson Consulting, in cooperation with the CLM annually compiled a database of software packages used for the planning and scheduling of logistics operations; see Haverly and Whelan (2000) for one of the most recent editions.

1.2.1.1 Strategic Planning

The decisions made at the strategic planning level are characterized by their permanence and importance to economic survival of the company. Examples in manufacturing are the construction of a manufacturing plant, the sizing and location of production capacity, the switch from company-owned to third-party logistics, the selection of distribution channels, and the identification and ranking of product–customer pairs. Examples in the service industry are the decision for two banks or hospitals to merge and again the identification of desirable product–customer pairs. Finally, examples in the defense sector are the configuration of the armed forces, the deployment of a new weapon system, and the decisions on location or closure of bases.

A third characteristic of strategic planning is the lack of quantitative and validated data for the full time horizon of the decision. A manufacturing plant typically has a useful life of twenty years or more, while the products manufactured in the facility may have a life cycle of less than a year. Many times the decision has to be based on external data that are forecasted with a huge amount of uncertainty, especially for time periods further and further into the future. Examples are the evolution of population and wages in various areas of the country or the world and the forecasts for the acceptance and use of technologies and products. The opportunities for success and the penalties for mistakes can mean the survival or demise of the corporation for several years or even permanently. Compared to tactical and operational planning, the strategic planning process is much more intermittent and much more decoupled from the data stored in ERP systems.

1.2.1.2   Tactical Planning

The decisions made at the tactical planning level typically have a permanence of three months to a year. Examples are the production schedule for the next three months, the long-term contract with a supplier or a transportation company, and the determination of the level of customer service. Tactical decisions are typically based on a mixture of internal and external data. Internal data may comprise sales forecasts based on historical sales and questionnaires. External data may include the overall health of the economy, the exchange rates between various currencies, and the season of the year. An external or corporate forecasting department typically creates the sales forecast in a periodic fashion. The configuration of the supply chain determined at the strategic level now translates into a number of constraints at the tactical level. The consequences of success or failure can have dramatic impact on the share price of the corporation.

1.2.1.3   Operational Planning

The decisions made at the operational planning level typically have a permanence of one day to one week. Examples are the weekly production schedule, the amount of product to be picked and shipped to a customer, and the amount of product purchased from a supplier. The data available to support operational planning is most often internal data which is known with great detail and accuracy. The more recent use of

ERP systems has provided planners with extensive operational data. The savings and penalties associated with operational decisions typically impact the performance measures of a facility or a department in a facility.

1.2.1.4 Execution

The decisions made at the execution level typically have a permanence of a few minutes to a few hours. Examples include which part to produce next, which part to pick next in a distribution center, or which customer is delivered to next by a vehicle. The data for the execution decisions is often known with certainty since it is based on direct observations of the physical world. The impact of a single execution decision is often very small or negligible, but since so many execution decisions are made, their aggregate impact determines the cost and resource consumption rates used at the higher planning levels.

In general, decisions made at higher planning levels transform into constraints at the lower planning levels. The result of planning at the lower levels in turn provides more accurate estimates or aggregate data for the characteristics of the operations. The engineering design and planning methodology uses those improved aggregate data in the next iteration of the higher level planning.

1.3 Summary and Conclusions

This chapter started off with the definition of supply chains, supply chain components, and various supply chain planning and design problems. One of the most important classifications of supply chain planning and design problems is their planning level. The higher level of the planning problem, the more comprehensive and the integrated the problem becomes, the more uncertain the data becomes, and the larger the variety of the design goals becomes. Uncertain data and multicriteria goals yield an especially complex engineering design problem.

1.4 Exercises

True/False Questions
1. Besides the material flow and the monetary flow, logistics is mainly concerned with the transportation flow in the logistics system (T/F) _____.
2. Strategic logistics planning is based on accurate transactional data (T/F) _____.
3. Tactical logistics planning can change the configuration of the logistics network (T/F) _____.
4. The sole focus of logistics planning is inventory management (T/F) _____.

World Trade Organization's Doha Round of Negotiations The negotiations in the framework of the current WTO Doha development round have proven to be very difficult, and progress towards reaching an agreement has been very slow because of the different goals of the different types of nations. Identify for each of the following nations, groups, or types of nations one area in which they want trade barriers lowered and free trade rules established and one area in which they prefer protectionist rules and regulations. The parties are the United States, the European Union, Japan, BRIC countries, and underdeveloped third-world countries. Explain in a single and succinct sentence why each of those countries wants to promote or obstruct free trade in areas that you have identified. Describe in a single paragraph the underlying principles that govern the global trade aspirations for the different types of nations and the different segments of their economy.

References

Blanchard, D. (2010). The state of the logistics market, 2010. *Material Handling Management, 7.*

Christopher, M. (1998). *Logistics and upply chain management: strategies for reducing cost and improving service* (2nd ed.). London: Pitman.

CSCMP. (2005). Council of supply chain management professionals. http://www.cscmp.org.

Fleischmann, B., & Meyr, H. (2001). Planning hierarchy, modeling, and advanced planning systems. In S. Graves & A. G. De Kok (Eds.), *Supply chain management handbook,* unpublished (Ch. 10).

Haverly, R. C., & Whelan, J. F. (2000). *Logistics software 2000 edition. Council of Logistics Management.* Illinois: Oak Brook.

Murphy, P. R., & Wood, D. F. (2008). *Contemporary logistics* (9th ed.). Upper Saddle River: Pearson, Prentice-Hall.

Stadtler, H., & Kilger, C. (2008). *Supply chain management and advanced planning* (4th ed.). Heidelberg: Springer.

Trunick, P. A. (2003). Time for a change. *Chief Logistics Officer, 8,* 25–29.

Trunick, P. A. (2004). How to beat the high cost of shipping? *Logistics Today, 45*(7), 26–29.

Trunick, P. A. (2005). Can we hold the line on logistics costs? *Logistics Today, 46*(8), 27–30.

Trunick, P. A. (2006). Good shippers hold the line on costs. *Logistics Today, 47*(8), 1–16.

Trunick, P. A. (2008). US logistics costs rise in 2007. *Outsourced Logistics, 1*(5), 41–42.

Wilson, R. (2007). 18th Annual The State of Logistics Report: The New Face of Logistics. CSCMP.

Chapter 2
Engineering Planning and Design

Learning Objectives After you have studied this chapter, you should be able to

- Know the general characteristics of systems design.
- Know the characteristics, advantages, disadvantages, and types of models.
- Know various types of supply chain objectives, constraints, and costs.
- Know the characteristics, advantages, disadvantages, and types of algorithms.
- Know various distance norms and understand their relationship with real-world distances.

The focus of this book is the application of scientific management and engineering design methodologies to the domain of supply chains and logistics. This chapter summarizes first the methodology of engineering design. It continues by providing a classification and characteristics of models and algorithms. The chapter concludes by describing models for the distance between two points at various levels of accuracy, which are some of the most fundamental models used in the management and design of logistic and supply chains systems.

2.1 Engineering Design and Design Process

2.1.1 Engineering Design

Industrial engineering, systems engineering, or industrial and systems engineering are engineering disciplines that focus on designing, planning, and managing complex systems using an engineering-based approach. Designing the "factory of the future" or the "supply chain for the twenty-first century" are complex tasks that require knowledge of a broad set of sciences, including engineering, mathematical, physical, computer and information, and behavior sciences as well as economics and business management. Systems engineering addresses both the structure and the behavior of the system to determine the system's performance. The principles and methodologies of system engineering apply to a large variety of systems, rang-

M. Goetschalckx, *Supply Chain Engineering,* International Series in Operations Research & Management Science 161,
DOI 10.1007/978-1-4419-6512-7_2, © Springer Science+Business Media, LLC 2011

ing from production systems such as factories and supply chains, to services systems such as health care delivery and transportation.

The goal of engineering design is the creation of an artifact. This artifact can be a physical object, a computer program, or a procedure. The artifact will have a function, i.e. a particular purpose. The following are examples of artifacts created by engineering design. An aircraft is a physical object with as its function transporting goods and people through the air. Quick sort is a computer program with as its function the efficient sortation of a collection of objects based on a single numerical attribute. The plan for the evacuation of a large city in anticipation of a disaster is a procedure with as its function the relocation of people from a particular geographical area. The artifact must function in the physical world and in particular in its physical environment. This environment poses constraints on the functioning of the artifact. During the execution of its function, the artifact will consume a number of resources. This consumption behavior is measured by the performance characteristics of the artifact.

In most engineering disciplines, engineering design has several stages. While the details will differ between various engineering disciplines, the following stages are commonly identified: (1) problem definition, (2) conceptual design, (3) detailed design, and (4) design specification and implementation. During each of these stages, engineering design decisions are made to progress towards the creation of the artifact. During the problem definition stage, decisions are made regarding the boundaries of the design domain, i.e. what can and cannot be controlled by the design effort, and the relevant performance criteria are identified. During the conceptual design, the different components of the artifact with their associated functions are defined. During the detailed design, the physical implementation of the components is determined, as well as their interactions and performance characteristics. During the design specification and implementation, documents are created that communicate the artifact in sufficient detail to other disciplines so that the artifact can be created according to the specifications. In many engineering disciplines, these documents are engineering blueprints. In software engineering these documents may be flow charts or pseudo code. Engineering documents that describe processes are often denoted as *standard operating procedures* or SOP.

Engineering design is one of the fundamental activities of engineers in any engineering discipline. However, engineering design is interpreted differently by the various engineering disciplines and is taught in vastly different ways in engineering colleges. The value of creativity and intuition, especially during the conceptual design stage, is widely accepted. The intuition of an experienced design engineer most often is not learned in an academic course but rather acquired through active participation in design projects. To start this process most engineering programs require a capstone design project as an essential component of an engineering education. This is further support for the contention that engineering design encompasses both elements of art and science. Good engineering design is based on a balanced combination of creativity and systematic methods. There exist a number of references on engineering design, e.g. Pahl and Beitz (1996), Hoare (1996), Ertas and Jones (1996), Park (2007) but they are relatively discipline specific.

A design procedure determines the various decision problems in the design project, in which sequence they are solved, and how they are related. In most of the engineering design projects, this design procedure is not a linear procedure from start to finish through the various phases or design problems. The current design of the artifact may violate some constraints or may have unacceptable or undesirable performance characteristics causing the design procedure to return to an earlier step in the procedure. The engineering design process is essentially an iterative process. However, the process has to progress towards the creation of the artifact; in other words, the engineering design process has to converge. Hierarchical design is an example of a standard decomposition design method, where decisions are divided based on their scope and time permanence into strategic, tactical, operational, and execution decisions. Decisions with longer time permanence function as constraints for decisions with shorter time permanence.

The different design problems solved during the design process have to be consistent. One way to ensure forward consistency is to interpret higher-level decisions as constraints for lower-level design problems. This is a natural mechanism and is often denoted as hierarchical decomposition. However, there exists a second consistency requirement which is called backward consistency. Backward consistency requires that performance criteria values, derived in the lower levels by more detailed models, are used in the higher-level design problems. This creates feedback loops that may cause the design procedure to solve an infinite loop of design problems. A fundamental challenge for any engineering design procedure is to ensure that (1) the various design problems are forward and backward consistent, and (2) that the design procedure converges.

2.1.2   Characteristics of an Engineered Artifact

2.1.2.1   Performance characteristics and feasibility

The terms artifact and engineered systems will be used interchangeably. A performance characteristic is a quantifiable and measurable property or characteristic of the designed system. The combination of all performance characteristics is called the quality of the designed system. A system is said to be feasible if its performance characteristics exceed certain minimally acceptable levels. Failure to do so will yield a defective artifact, which may lead to excessive costs, returns, loss of market share, recalls, and even liability law suits.

2.1.2.2   Total life cycle cost

The life cycle of a system is the time interval starting with its design and ending with its final disposition. A system has several time phases that are components of its total life cycle. With each phase there are associated types of cost. The major phases and associated cost types are given next.

1. The design time is the time necessary to design, but not to implement, the system. The time spent designing the system should be commensurate with the value of the system. Often there exists a decreasing quality benefit for spending more time during the design phase. A common principle in military planning states "a good plan today is better than a perfect plan tomorrow". The design cost is composed of all costs to design, but not implement, the system.
2. The production, construction, or implementation time is the time required to build the system. Large systems such as supply chains which involve capital assets, such as manufacturing plants, and logistics infrastructure, such as railroad tracks and ports, may take years or even decades to construct. Even reconfiguring a warehouse in a supply chain may require three to six months. The production, construction, or implementation cost is the cost to create or build the system, but not to operate the system.
3. The operational life time is the time the system is in operation. For most systems in supply chains and logistics this period has the longest duration in its overall life cycle. The operations or operational costs include the fixed and variable costs to operate the system.
4. The disposal time is the required to shut down and dismantle the system. Again large systems may require extensive periods to be shut down in an orderly fashion. The withdrawal of the United States forces from Western Europe in the late twentieth century required more than a decade. The disposal cost includes all the costs to shut down and dismantle the system.

The total life cycle cost is the total cost accrued during the total life cycle of the product. This cost sometimes also all the *total cost of ownership* or TCO.

2.1.3   Traditional Steps in the Engineering Design Process

There exists widespread consensus on the importance of good engineering design, but relatively few formal design methods have been developed. To our knowledge, none exist in the area of supply chains and logistics. The best approach appears to be to follow the traditional major stages in an engineering design process. These traditional steps in the engineering design process provide a framework on which tasks and decisions have to be executed in the various phases of the design project. One of the basic principles in the design methodology is that all the tasks in the current phase of the process have to be completed before the next phase can be started. The process aims to avoid "business-as-usual" designs by delaying the selection of the final design alternative early in the design process. The process also aims to avoid the selection of pre-conceived solutions by formalizing the steps in the process and making each step as much as possible science-based with specific deliverables. The following stages can be distinguished.

2.1.3.1 Formulate the problem

Formulation of the problem requires the definition of the function of the artifact and its physical environment. The more general or wider the problem is formulated, the more solutions are possible and the more diverse the solutions will be. Designing a local delivery system of packages to individual customers is a much more narrowly defined problem than designing a global supply chain for a new type of commercial aircraft. The formulation stage must create a least the following statements: a clear statement of the function of system, the goal of the system, the available budget in time and resources for design and implementation.

2.1.3.2 Collect data and analyze the problem

In the problem analysis stage there are three phases. The data on the current system must be collected, the constraints for the new system must be identified, and the evaluation criteria for the new systems must be defined. A formal description of the problem, including constraints and evaluation criteria, is often given in the *request for proposal* or RFP.

2.1.3.3 Generate alternative solutions

The key during this step is to generate as many as possible, high quality, creative solutions. This phase is commonly denoted as "brainstorming" or conceptual design. During brainstorming a group of design engineers and other participants generate as many proposals for solutions as possible within a given period of time. One of the main objectives during the conceptualization phase is to avoid business-as-usual solutions. Change of a system or product is inherently more difficult and risky than maintaining the status quo or use incremental engineering. The design engineers may also have vested interests in the current solution because they were instrumental in its design. Many engineers are risk averse and will try to minimize the resources required for the completion of a design project.

2.1.3.4 Evaluate design alternatives

During this step, the different alternative solutions are evaluated with respect to the different criteria. This involves computing the quality of each alternative with respect to each criterion as well as a structured method to assign relative importance to the different criteria. The performance assessment of any solution includes both a feasibility assessment and an economic evaluation. The feasibility assessment establishes if the proposed design solution satisfies the requirements. The economic evaluation determines the costs and benefits of the alternative solution.

2.1.3.5 Select the preferred design(s)

The best alternative is selected with a systematic method that integrates the scores of the various alternatives with respect to the various criteria. Since the ultimate selection decision often is made by executive people that are not part of the design team, a small number of diverse designs may actually be selected for further design in the next phase.

2.1.3.6 Specify the design

The detailed configuration specification is created. The typical result of this step is a set of detail oriented documents. Examples of such documents are: engineering blue prints, construction diagrams, standard operating procedures, disaster recovery plans, user's manuals, implementation plans and schedules, quality control and testing procedures. The importance of this step in the overall procedure cannot be underestimated. The famous quote by Thomas Edison that "genius is 1% inspiration and 99% perspiration" is often used to support this point.

2.1.3.7 Evaluate the design in use

Recall that the goal of engineering design is the creation of an artifact. In this step the selected design alternative is built. This allows the collection of all kinds of performance data on the implemented design under real-world conditions. The design process may start all over again by adjusting or redefining the objectives, parameters, and constraints. Changing the specification of the design will lead to *engineering change orders* or ECO that describe the modifications to the artifact being built in detail. Managing the engineering changes for a complex system consumes significant amounts of time and resources.

2.2 Modeling

2.2.1 Introduction

2.2.1.1 Modeling Definition and Model Usage

One of the most fundamental tools used in engineering design is a model. A (supply chain) model is a simplified representation or abstraction of a real-world (supply chain) system. Gass and Harris (1996) define a model as "*A model is an idealised representation—an abstract and simplified description—of a real world situation that is to be studied and/or analysed*". Williams (1999) defines a model as "*a structure which was built purposely to exhibit the features and characteristics of another object.*" Models are created because they are easier to manipulate than the real-world system or because they provide enhanced insight into the behavior of the real-world system. The enhanced insight may suggest new courses of action or decisions to achieve certain goals. Easier manipulation encourages more extensive experimentation with a variety of input factors. While there is an obvious cost associated with the development, construction, and maintenance of a model, models of various levels of complexity are used nearly universally in planning and design processes. The validity of using models as decision support aids differs significantly on a case-by-case basis. For example, one simple model predicts the rise and fall of the Dow Jones industrial stock market index for the coming year depending on whether the football team that wins the Super Bowl in January of that year belongs to the National or the American Football Conference. This is a very simple model to use, but it is difficult to argue its validity. At the opposite end of the modeling complexity spectrum with respect to supply chain systems, Arntzen et al. (1995) have developed a model for the global supply chain of a specific computer manufacturer that incorporates both spatial and temporal characteristics. Clearly, not all models are equally valid or suitable for supply chain design and a knowledgeable design engineer must carefully evaluate model use and model recommendations.

Models are used primarily to provide assistance when making decisions regarding complex systems. Ballou and Masters (1993) surveyed developers and practitioners in the logistics and supply chain industry to determine the most important characteristics and the state of the art in decision support systems for supply chain design. They found that model features and user friendliness were the most important characteristics of the models and design packages. Ballou and Masters (1999) repeated the survey six years later and observed that advances in computer hardware and software had allowed real-world strategic supply chain systems design projects to be completed using mathematical models that were incorporated in commercial software packages. They reported that specialized and efficient algorithms had been developed to solve the spatial and geographical location aspect of supply chain systems, but that specialized or general-purpose simulation models are used for the temporal aspects such as tactical inventory and production planning. Few models combine or integrate the spatial and temporal aspects of the supply chain. Based on a survey of active models and software packages, they found that the models are becoming more comprehensive and are beginning to include some tactical aspects. Global characteristics such as taxes, duties and tariffs, and exchange rates are included in only a few models. They reported that linear programming (LP), mixed-integer programming (MIP), and heuristics are the most commonly used techniques to find solutions. In the survey the practitioners responded with a large majority that modeling was used to configure their supply chain. In contrast with the 1993 result, in 1999 the practitioners ranked the optimality of the solution as the most important characteristic of the software. According to the practitioners, the best features of the models were their ability to represent the real-world system and to find an effective configuration. The worst features were the difficulty in obtaining the necessary data, the complexity of using the model, and the poor treatment of inventory costs, especially in connection to customer service levels. Finally, the authors observed that a consolidation trend is reducing the number of models and software applications.

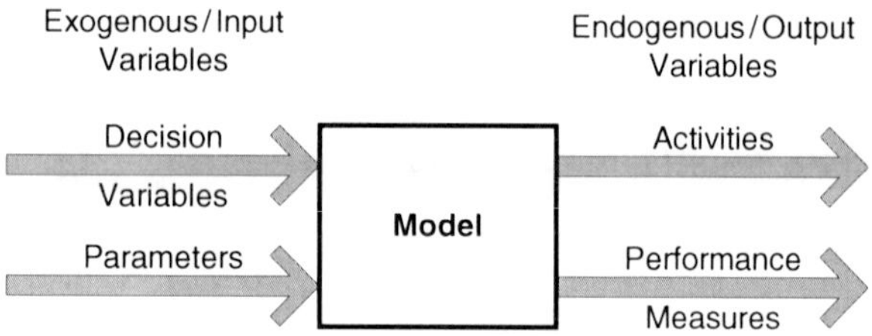

Fig. 2.1 Model input–output diagram

Fig. 2.1 Model input–output diagram

2.2.2 Modeling Terminology and Framework

The basic function of a model is to transform a number of known input variables into a number of output variables, whose values are sought. The input–output diagram of a model is shown in Fig. 2.1.

Exogenous or input variables are determined outside the model. They can be further divided into *parameters*, which are not controllable by the model and the decision maker, and *decision variables*, which are controllable. *Endogenous* or output variables are determined by the model. They can be further divided into *performance measures*, which quantify the behavior of the system with respect to one or more goals, and *activities*, which describe the configuration of the system being modeled and the intensity of activities in the system.

2.2.2.1 Modeling Process and Framework

The building of explicit models for the analysis, design, and management has traditionally been called *management science*. Most of the management problems are initially observed in the form of symptoms. A model is developed and used to aid in the decision-making. Based on the model recommendations, a number of decisions are made and implemented in the real-world system. The definition of a clear and comprehensive problem statement is part of the modeling process. This modeling process is most often not a single pass process but rather an iterative, successive refinement procedure, as illustrated in Fig. 2.2. If the decisions suggested by the model do not yield the anticipated results when they are implemented, then the model structure, the model data, or the solution algorithm has to be further refined.

2.2.2.2 Model Data

Even if the validity of the model has been established to a sufficient degree, obtaining correct and accurate data for use by the model is a difficult and time consuming process. The data required by the model usually correspond to some future time period and typically are forecasted based on historical data. Many times the historical data are simply not available or the forecasting methods have not been validated.

Fig. 2.2 Modeling
framework

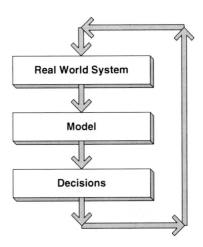

Recently, warehouse management systems (WMS), manufacturing execution systems (MES), and enterprise resource planning systems (ERP) have started to capture the status, actions, and performance of logistics systems in great detail. For example, a warehouse management system may have collected a detailed order history by individual customer and individual product or stock keeping unit (SKU) for the last few years. Typically, this raw data cannot be used directly in decision support models. A first transformation converts the detailed transaction data into aggregate statistics. For example, individual orders may be aggregated into average weekly demand and a demand distribution for a particular product is determined. The process of computing the statistics of historical orders is called *order profiling* and the process of computing statistics on the customers is called *customer profiling*. The aggregate statistics are then further synthesized and combined with general principles and characteristics to generate knowledge about the logistics system. For example, Pareto analysis may identify the products that account for the majority of the sales dollars and divide the products into fast, medium, and slow movers, compute the sales dollars for each class, and compute the Pareto parameter that indicates the skew of the products. This value of this skew quantitatively represents the knowledge if relatively few products make up most of the sales or if all products are approximately equally contributing to the sales.

The same transformation process occurs when modeling transportation systems. Detailed freight bills may have been retained for the transportation charges paid to trucking companies for the past year. This date is transformed into information by aggregating the customer destinations into regions based on their three-digit ZIP codes and by computing the average shipment quantity for each region. For each region the less-than-truckload (LTL) transportation cost is estimated using LTL freight rate tables based on the average shipment quantity for that region. Again Pareto analysis can be used to identify the regions that account for the majority of the outbound transportation charges. The location of each region can be found with help of a geocoding algorithm or database and the total transportation quantity to

Fig. 2.3 Data to knowledge
transformation

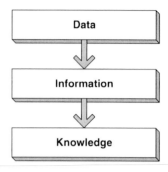

the regions can be used to compute the center of gravity to estimate the best location
for a distribution center. Figure 2.3 illustrates this transformation process from data
into information and knowledge.

One example of this transformation process is the computation of the required
length of roadway for waiting trucks for an interstate truck weight station. The data
collected consisted of the number of trucks passing the proposed location of the
weight station during different seasons of the year, days of the week, and hours of
the day. A second class of data consisted of the times required to weigh a truck at
other weight stations with the same technology. From this data, information was
obtained by statistical analysis which determined the average arrival frequency of
the trucks and the distribution of the interarrival times, the average time to weigh a
truck, and the distribution of the time to weigh a truck. Based on projected growth
rates the interarrival times for future periods were then computed. This information
was then inserted in the appropriate single-server queuing model to generate the
knowledge about the expected number of trucks waiting, the expected waiting time,
and the distribution of the waiting time. Finally, based on those waiting statistics,
the required length of roadway for waiting trucks was computed.

A second example is based on a real-world distribution system design project.
The objective of the project was to design a cost-efficient delivery policy to a group
of customers in the continental United States. The customers, the supplier, the products, their characteristics and the customers service policy were all considered to be
given and constraints to the distribution system to be designed. The customer and
aggregate product demand data were extracted from a corporate database, which
held detailed data on all sales orders for the last year. The data was then inserted into
a Microsoft Access relational database, which contained the customer identification, its city, state and ZIP code, and the product demand for the last year (Fig. 2.4).

The ZIP code of each customer was used to determine their geographical location expressed in longitude and latitude. This process is called *geocoding*, which is
defined in general as the process that assigns latitude and longitude coordinates to
an alphanumeric address. Geocoding can be performed with a variety of programs,
such as Microsoft MapPoint, and resources on the Internet, such as Yahoo Maps and
Google Earth. The alphanumeric address can be a street address or ZIP codes with
5 (ZIP), 7 (ZIP+2), or 9 (ZIP+4) digits. Once a latitude and longitude coordinates
are assigned, the address can be displayed on a map or used in a spatial search. The

Fig. 2.4 Relational database
with customer information
and demand

CUSTID	County	City	State	ZIP	TotalDemand
24069	PITTSYLVANIA	Sutherlin	VA	24594	125
24073	ROCKINGHAM	Hinton	VA	22831	1300
24074	ROCKINGHAM	Dayton	VA	22821	1075
24076	ROCKINGHAM	Dayton	VA	22821	100
24081	AUGUSTA	Weyers Cave	VA	24486	700
24089	FILLMORE	Lanesboro	MN	55949	1300
24090	STEARNS	Paynesville	MN	56362	1300
24094	MCLEOD	Plato	MN	55370	325
24095	OTTER TAIL	Fergus Falls	MN	56537	375
24098	STEARNS	Freeport	MN	56331	750
24105	TILLAMOOK	Nehalem	OR	97131	75
24116	JACKSON	Grass Lake	MI	49240	3950
24119	MONTCALM	Edmore	MI	48829	1225
24126	RUSSELL	Russell Springs	KY	42642	225
24128	BUCKS	Riegelsville	PA	18077	300
24133	COLUMBIA	Millville	PA	17846	1200
24134	LANCASTER	Stevens	PA	17578	650

Record: 1 of 15862

customers were then located on a map of the continental United States. This provided graphical information on the dispersion of the customers. It can be observed in the next figure that most of the customers were located in the Midwestern and the Northeastern areas of the country. The supply of the product had to be imported through a container port from Western Europe. Possible selections for the import port where ports located along the eastern seaboard with the Atlantic Ocean and in de Gulf of Mexico (Fig. 2.5).

Further data analysis runs were made to determine the aggregate product demand by state. It can be observed in the next figure that the states with the highest annual demand were California and Wisconsin. The transportation from the port to the distribution center occurred in a single intermodal container. The orders for the products by an individual customer corresponded to a small package. In this case

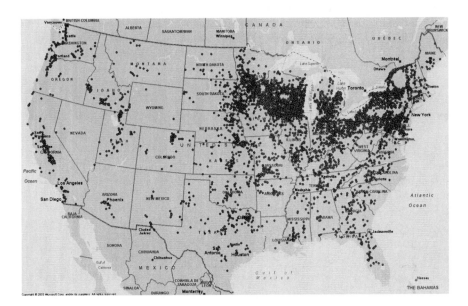

Fig. 2.5 Customer locations

Fig. 2.6 Total customer demand by state

the transportation cost from port to distribution center represented a small fraction of the delivery costs from the distribution center to the customers. Since the delivery transportation costs are roughly proportional to the quantities shipped multiplied by the shipping distance, a good distribution strategy would attempt to locate the distribution center closer to California (Fig. 2.6).

Finally, the logistics domain knowledge that the size of a customer order strongly impacts the delivery transportation cost caused the calculation of statistics on the average size of a customer order by state. The statistical analysis revealed that the state of California had the largest cumulative demand and that the customers in the state of Arizona placed the largest orders on average (Fig. 2.7).

Fig. 2.7 Average customer order size by state

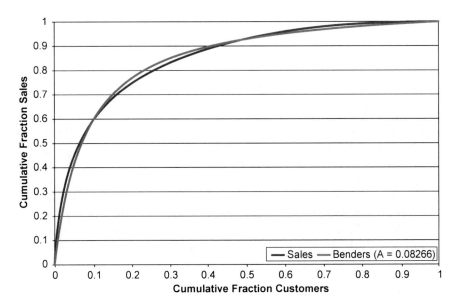

Fig. 2.8 Pareta curve for customer demands

To test the level of concentration of sales among the customers a Pareto analysis was executed. The following Pareto curve shows the cumulative fraction of sales by cumulative fraction of customers, when the customers are sorted by decreasing sales. The Pareto curve of the sales data was approximated by the Bender's curve with optimal parameter of 0.08266. This small parameter value indicates a strong concentration. Ten percent of the customers make up 60% of the demand and 5% of the customers make up 40% of the demand (Fig. 2.8).

This information was then used to develop the knowledge that for this logistics system a differentiated distribution strategy may be effective. A differentiated distribution strategy serves sub sections of the customers or of the products through distribution channels that have different structures. This is the opposite of a uniform or "one-size-fits-all" distribution strategy. In this particular project, customers in western states such Arizona, southern California, and New Mexico were serviced by a different transportation mode since their average order size was much larger than the orders from customers in the Midwest and the Northeast. A truck with a full truck load (FTL) was dispatched from the distribution center to a break bulk facility located in Arizona. There the full truck load was split into the individual orders of customers in Arizona, southern California, and New Mexico and the orders were then delivered to these customers by a parcel delivery company. Customers located in the other states were served directly by the parcel delivery company from the distribution center.

While the availability of transactional data has clearly enabled the modeling process, collecting, validating, and synthesizing the data is still a resource and time intensive activity that requires specific technical expertise, judgment, and insight into the logistics system.

2.2.2.3   Model Validation

The scientific validation method consists of the following steps: (1) formulate a hypothesis, (2) design and execute an experiment to test the hypothesis, (3) accept or reject the hypothesis with a certain level of confidence. This scientific validation method implies that you can control the input parameters to correspond to your experiment and test the outcome repeatedly.

It is often infeasible or impractical to validate a model for logistics or supply chain design in a scientific way. For example, to validate scientifically that one location for a major new manufacturing plant is better than another location is impossible, since only one plant can be built. Similarly, a frequent validation claim states that an organization saved a certain amount of expenses after having used a model for decision-making. Scientific validation would require the determination of expense reductions if no model had been used. In the following a number of validation approaches are described that are often used in practice to validate the models for logistics and supply chain systems.

One imperfect way to validate a model is to use the model to predict history. This activity is often called (historical) *benchmarking*. Historical data on parameters and actions for a particular problem instance are inserted into a model. The outcomes of the model are compared to the observed outcomes in the real-world system. The model is assumed to be valid if it mimics sufficiently closely the real-world behavior. In a second phase the model is allowed to optimize or set the value of the decision variables. The two outcomes, with and without the aid of the model for setting the decision variables, are compared. The yield of the improved decision-making process using the model becomes evidence for the value of the model. One would assume that the model is then used to support decision making for current and future problems. This, of course, assumes that historical validity implies future validity.

In the sensitivity validation method, one or more of the input parameters of the model are changed incrementally around a particular configuration. The changes in the output activities and performance measures are observed and tested to ascertain if the model makes rational changes. For instance, if the purchasing cost of components is increased, the total system cost to satisfy demand should also increase.

Component validation establishes the validity of components of the overall model. It is assumed that if valid components are combined in a valid way, the overall model will also be valid.

Finally, the weakest and most subjective method for model validation is relying on the judgment of experts in the field with respect to the validity of the model. Typically, the output activities and performance measures corresponding to several input scenarios are presented to the experts, who decide if the model outputs make sense. This type of validation is called *face validation* or *sanity check*. Clearly, the quality of the validation depends strongly on the level of expertise of the experts in the domain area and in modeling methodology.

2.2.3 Supply Chain Model Components and Supply Chain Meta Model

2.2.3.1 Supply Chain Model Components

Recall that supply chain operations is the aggregate term for the activities related to the movement, storage, transformation, and organization of materials. The planning of supply chain activities is divided into four categories depending on the planning time horizon: strategic, tactical, operational, and execution. When planning supply chain activities, there exist the following fundamental components of the supply chain system.

Time Periods

Logistics provides the time and space utility to the organization, while a supply chain provides the time and space and production utility. At the same time, the different planning levels are distinguished by their duration. A fundamental component is the time period(s) in the supply chain planning. If only a single time period exists the planning or model is said to be static. If multiple periods exist the model is said to be dynamic. For a strategic planning model often there are five periods of one year, corresponding to a five year strategic plan. For a tactical planning model the periods are often months, quarters, or semesters. For an operational planning level the typical periods are hours, days, or weeks. For an execution management task, the time periods are typically either seconds or minutes.

Geographical Locations

Supply chain components exist at a particular location in a geographical or spatial area. Typically, the geographical areas become larger in correspondence to longer planning periods. For a strategic model, the areas may be countries or states in the United States. If only a single country is defined then the model is said to be domestic, if more than one country exists the model is said to be global. For operational planning problems such as delivery routing the area may be restricted to a single city.

In strategic supply chain planning, the combination of a country and a period is used very often to capture the financial performance of a logistics system. This combination typically has characteristics such as budget limitations, taxation, depreciation, and net cash flow.

Products

The material being managed, stored, transformed, or transported is called a product. An equivalent term is commodity. It should be noted that the term material is here considered very loosely and applies to discrete, fluid, and gaseous materials, livestock, and even extends to people. If only a single material is defined, the model is said to be single commodity. If multiple materials are defined the model is said to be multi-commodity.

It is very important to determine the type of material being modeled. A first classification is into people, livestock, and products. The products are then further classified as commodity, standard, or specialty. A product is said to be a commodity if there are no distinguishable characteristics between quantities of the same product manufactured by different producers. Typical examples of commodities are low-fat milk, gasoline, office paper, and poly-ethylene. Consumers acquire products solely on the basis of logistics factors such as price, availability, and convenience. A product is said to be a standard product if comparable and competing products from different manufacturers exist. However, the products of different producers may have differences in functionality and quality. Typical examples are cars, personal computers, and fork lift trucks. Consumers make acquisitions based on tradeoffs between functionality, value, price, and logistics factors. A product is said to be a specialty or custom product if it is produced to the exact and unique specifications of the customer. The typical examples are specialized machines, printing presses, and conveyor networks. The product is typically described by a technical specification and the supplier is selected by reputation, price, and logistics factors.

If one or more products are transformed into or extracted from another product, the products are said to have a *Bill of Materials* or BOM. The corresponding material balance equations have more than one product. If the material balance equations can be written in function of a single product, the problem is said to be either single commodity or to have parallel commodities. For example, if based on the requirement for a quantity of the finished product of office paper all the required quantities of intermediate jumbo paper rolls and raw paper pulp can be computed, then all material quantities can be expressed in function of the finished product and a single commodity model would result. The existence of bill of materials equations makes the model significantly harder. Bill of materials can be converging or diverging. Assembly systems have a converging bill of materials where only a relatively few final products are produced from many components. Recycling and reverse logistics systems typically have a diverging bill of materials, when the source is a mixed stream of recyclable materials collected for individual consumers and sorted into separate commodities such as paper, glass, carton, and plastic.

Facilities

The locations in the supply chain network where material can enter, leave, or be transformed are called facilities and are typically represented by the nodes of the logistics network. Suppliers are the source of materials and customers are the sink for materials. The internal operation of suppliers or customers is not considered to be relevant to the planning problem. The other facilities are called transformation facilities.

Customers

The customer facilities in the network have the fundamental characteristic that they are the final sink for materials. What happens to the material after it reaches the customer is not considered relevant to the planning problem. The customer facilities can be different from the end customers that use the product, such as the single distribution center for the product in a country, the dealer, or the retailer.

For every combination of products, periods, and customers there may exist a customer demand. The demand can be classified as intermittent or regular. A regular demand has a pattern, be it constant, with linear trend, or seasonal. If a demand has no pattern it is said to be intermittent. For example, the demand for flu vaccines has a seasonal pattern, while the demand in developed countries for polio vaccines is said to be intermittent. Intermittent demand or demand for specialty products typically leads to a *make-to-order* or MTO production planning. Regular demand for standard or commodity products may yield a *make-to-stock* or MTS production planning.

Service level constraints are one of the complicating characteristics of customers in supply chain planning. Two prominent service level constraints are single sourcing and fill rate. The single sourcing service constraint requires that all goods of a single product group or manufacturer are delivered in a single shipment to the customer. Single sourcing makes it easier to check the accuracy of the delivery versus the customer order and it reduces the number of carriers at the customer facility where loading and unloading space often is at a premium. A customer may have a required fill rate requirement, which is the minimum acceptable fraction of goods in the customer order that are delivered from on-hand inventory at the immediate supplier to this customer.

Suppliers

The supplier facilities in the network have the fundamental characteristic that they are the original source of the materials. What happens to the material before it reaches the supplier and inside the supplier facility is not considered relevant to the planning problem. The supplier facilities can be different from the raw material suppliers that produce the product, such as the single distribution center for the product in a country.

For every combination of supplier facility, product, and time period there may exist an available supply.

Quantity discounts are one of the complicating characteristics of suppliers in logistics planning. A supplier may sell a product at a lower price if the product is purchased in larger quantities during the corresponding period. This leads to concave cost curves as a function of the quantity purchased for incremental quantity discounts.

Transformation Facilities

The transformation facilities in the network have the fundamental characteristic that they have incoming and outgoing material flow and that there exists conservation of flow over space (transportation) and time (inventory) in the facility. Major examples of transformation facilities are manufacturing and distribution facilities, where the latter are also denoted as warehouses.

For every combination of transformation facility, time period, and product there may exist incoming flow, outgoing flow, inventory, consumption of component flow, and creation of assembly flow. All of these are collectively known as the production and inventory flows. A facility may have individual limits on each of these flows.

Transformation facilities have two types of subcomponents: machines and resources. Machines represent major transformation equipment such as bottling lines, assembly lines, and process lines. A single facility may contain more than one machine. Each machine may have incoming, outgoing, component flow, and assembly flow for every combination of product and period. A machine may have individual limits on each of these flows. Machines, however, cannot have inventory. A resource represents a multi-product capacity limitation of the facility. Typical examples of resources are machine hours, labor hours, and material handling hours. Products compete with each other in facilities for resources and incoming material flows.

Several complicating factors in the modeling of transformation facilities exist. The first one is the binary nature of the decision to establish or use a facility or not. One can decide to build a manufacturing plant or not, but one cannot build 37.8% of a plant. The decisions for using a plant are thus of the binary type, which makes solving for them significantly harder. The second complicating factor is the related issues of economies of scale and diseconomies of scope. For many manufacturing processes there is a setup cost and a tuning or learning curve. The efficiency of the process grows if this start-up cost can be spread out over a longer steady-state production run. This phenomenon is called economies of scale. The opposite effect occurs when a facility must produce a large variety of products. Each of the products requires its own setup time, which decreases the overall capacity of the facility. Hence, allocation of many different products to a facility, which is known as facility with a large scope, reduces its capacity and increases the various production costs. This diseconomy of scope is also known as the flexibility penalty.

Transportation Channels

Transportation channels, or channels for short, are transportation resources that connect the various facilities in the logistics system. Examples are over-the-road trucks operating in either full truck load (FTL) or less-than-truck-load (LTL) mode, ocean-going and inland ships, and railroad trains.

For every combination of transportation channel, time period, and product there may exist a transported flow. A channel may have individual limits on each of these flows.

A major characteristic of a channel is its conservation of flow, i.e., the amount of flow by period and by product entering the channel at the origin facility equals the amount of flow exiting the channel at the destination facility at the same or future time period. A second conservation of flow relates channel flows to facility throughput flow and storage. The sum of all incoming flow plus the inventory from the previous period equals the sum of all outgoing flow plus the inventory to the next period. The channels represent material flow in space, while the inventory arcs represent material flow in time. Note that such inventory is extremely rare in strategic logistics models unless the models include seasonal tactical planning.

A channel has two types of subcomponents: carriers and resources. A carrier is an individual, moving container in the channel. The move from origin to destination facility has a fixed cost, regardless on the capacity utilization of the carrier, i.e. the cost is by carrier and not by the quantities of material moved on or in the carrier. Typical examples are a truck, intermodal container, or ship. A carrier may have individual capacities for each individual product or multi-product weight or volume capacities. A resource represents a multi-product capacity limitation of the channel. Typical examples of resources are cubic feet (meters) for volume, tons for weight, or pallets. Truck transportation may be modeled as a carrier if a small number of trucks are moved and cost is per truck movement, or it may be modeled as a resource if the cost is per product quantity and a large or fractional number of trucks are allowed.

There exist several complicating characteristics for modeling transportation channels. The first one is the requirement that an integer number of carriers have to be used. Typically a very large number of potential channels exist in a supply chain model so this requirement will create a large number of integer variables. The second is the presence of economies of scale for the transportation costs. Less common, is the third complicating factor, which requires a minimum number of carriers or a minimum amount of flow if the channel is to be used.

All of the logistics components described so far have distinguishing characteristics. These characteristics can be input data parameters or output performance measures. For example, most of the facilities, channels, machines and their combinations with products and periods have cost and capacity characteristics, which must be captured in data parameters. Sales have a revenue characteristic. The financial quantities achieved in a particular country and during a particular period are an example of output characteristics, which must be captured in performance variables.

Scenarios

So far all the logistics components described were physical entities in the logistics system. A scenario is a component used in the characterization and treatment of uncertainty.

Many of the parameters used in the planning of logistics systems are not known with certainty but rather have a probability distribution. If a parameter has a single value it is said to be deterministic, if it has a probability distribution it is said to be stochastic. For example, demand for a particular product, during a period by a particular customer may be approximated by a normal distribution with certain mean and standard deviation. In a typical logistics planning problem there may be thousands of stochastic parameters. The combination of a single realization or sample of each stochastic parameter with all the deterministic parameters is called a scenario. Each scenario has a major characteristic, which is its probability of occurring. However, this probability may not be known or even not be computable.

A large number of articles and books has been published on the management, design and modeling of supply chains and logistics systems. Some of the more recent books on supply chains that have a strong modeling component are De Kok and Graves (2003), Stadtler and Kilger (2004), Guenes and Pardalos (2005), Shapiro (2006), and Simchi-Levi et al. (2008).

2.2.3.2   Supply Chain Planning Meta-Model

A meta-model is an explicit model of the components and rules required to build specific models within a domain of interest. A logistics planning meta-model can be considered as a model template for the domain of activity planning for logistics systems. The following is a meta-model for the planning of logistics activities and systems. It lists the possible classes of decisions, objectives, and constraints in logistics planning.

Decide on

1. transportation activities, resources, and infrastructure;
2. inventory levels, resources, and infrastructure;
3. transformation activities, resources, and infrastructure;
4. information technology systems;
5. financial conditions for activities, such as transfer prices.

Objective

1. maximize the risk-adjusted total system profit based on the net present value of the net cash flow *NPV(NCF)* for strategic planning;
2. minimize the risk-adjusted total system cost for tactical and operational planning.

Subject to

1. capacity constraints such as demand, infrastructure, budget, implementation time;
2. service level constraints such as fraction of demand satisfied, fill rate, cycle times, and response times;

3. conservation of flow constraints in space, over time, and observing bill of materials;
4. additional extraneous constraints, which are often mandated by corporate policy;
5. equations for the calculation of intermediate variables such as the net income before taxes in a particular country and a particular period;
6. linkage equations that ensure that the components of the model behave in an internally consistent way, such as flows cannot traverse a facility that has not been established

Difficulties in Solving Supply Chain Models

There are several characteristics that make a logistic model hard to solve

1. A logistics model must be comprehensive and include the different major logistics activities of materials acquisition, transportation, production, and distribution.
2. The scope of a logistics model may include the supply chain from the original raw materials suppliers to the final destination of the products and even reverse logistics. This often implies bill-of-materials equations.
3. The scale of a logistics model, since it may include a very large number of logistics components and a large number of scenarios.
4. The accuracy or fidelity of the model may yield concave or general non-linear costs and constraints.
5. For strategic models, the treatment of uncertainty may yield non-linear and multiple objective functions.
6. Many logistics decisions are of go/no-go type which correspond to either binary or integer variables

Solution Approaches

Many different solution approaches have been applied to logistics models. Some of the more common ones are:

1. Exact mathematical optimization techniques can sometimes be used, but in general logistic models are large-scale, stochastic, non-linear, integer programming problems (LS SNLIP) which cannot be solved in a reasonable amount of time for realistic-size problem instances.
2. To make the problem more solvable it can be decomposed. Most often hierarchical decomposition is used to separate different levels of decision making. Mathematical decomposition techniques can be either primal or dual. Benders decomposition, see Benders (1962), is a typical primal decomposition and Lagrangean relaxation and decomposition is a common dual decomposition technique.
3. Stochastic simulation is often used for operational logistics models. Simulation is most often used when the model is of high fidelity and is less used for aggregate strategic models.

4. Various ad hoc heuristics or local search algorithms such as simulated annealing, genetic algorithms, and neural nets have been applied to logistics models.
5. For operational logistics models, constraint programming has been used successfully. Constraint programming is rarely applied to strategic models.

2.2.4 Classification of Models by Their Representation Form

2.2.4.1 Physical, Analog, and Mathematical Models

Models can be either physical (iconic), analog, or mathematical (symbolic). The three-dimensional scale models of military aircraft, automobiles, chemical molecules, a manufacturing plant with its machines, or a real estate development with its buildings and roads are just some of the examples of *physical* or *iconic* models. Physical models are homomorphic, which means they have the same appearance as the real system being modeled, but they usually have either a much smaller or much larger scale. Physical models of cars or airplanes manufactured out of wood or wax are used in wind tunnels to study their wind resistance and to determine their drag coefficient.

Analog systems do not physically resemble the real system they model but they exhibit connections between input parameters and output variables proportional to the relationships between the corresponding input parameters and output variables of the real system. A map is common example of an analog system. The location of two points and the distance between them are examples of input parameters and output variables in the analog model and the real system. If the distance on the map between a pair of points is twice as large as between another pair of points, then we expect the distance between the first pair in the real world also to be twice as large as between the second pair.

A dispatcher, when planning a truck trip from Chattanooga, TN to Jacksonville, FL, may measure the distances on a map of the interstate road network in the southeastern United States and then route the truck following the shortest path on the map. This would route the truck over the combination of I-75 and I-10 rather than I-16 and I-95 when traveling from Macon to Jacksonville (Fig. 2.9).

A classic example of an analog model used in logistics systems design is the Varignon frame. Weber described in 1909 the use of the model to determine the location of a new facility that minimizes the sum of weighted distances to existing facilities. Holes are drilled in the table at the locations corresponding to the customers. A thread is strung through each hole with a weight on one end and all the threads are tied together in a knot on the other end. The weights are proportional to the number of trips between the facility and its customers. The knot is raised above the table and then let go. The final location of the knot corresponds to the optimal location of the manufacturing facility. The optimal location of the knot and other interesting optimality conditions can be found based on the principles of the equilibrium on an object subject to static forces. This mechanical analog is illustrated in Fig. 2.10. It

Fig. 2.9 Road network map of the Southeastern United States as a printed analog model

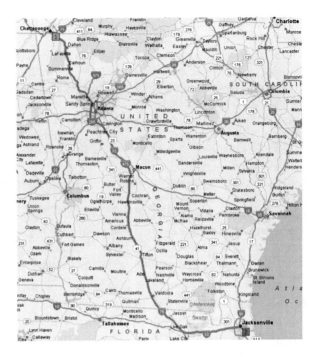

Fig. 2.10 Varignon frame as a mechanical analog model

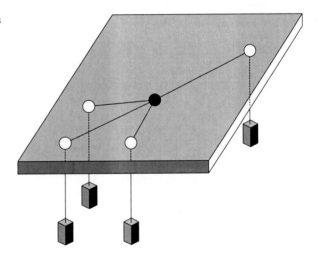

will be discussed in more detail in the chapter Supply Chain Models in the section on continuous location using Euclidean distances.

Mathematical or symbolic models incorporate the structural properties and behavior of the real system in mathematical relations. Because of the emergence of computers as powerful manipulators of symbolic relations, symbolic models have become the dominant type of models.

Models can be further divided into descriptive and normative models. *Descriptive* models predict the values or distribution of one or more output variables for a given set of parameters. *Normative* models determine the value of some decision variables to optimize one or more performance measures or objective functions. A widely used descriptive modeling tool in the design of material handling systems is digital simulation combined with animation. Descriptive queuing models are often used to predict the number of people and their expected waiting time in waiting line systems found in post offices, fast food restaurants, and amusement parks. Other common examples of descriptive models are regression, time series, and econometric models.

A widely used normative modeling tool in the design of strategic distribution systems is mixed-integer programming (MIP). The following notation is used in modeling transportation networks. The objective is to find a minimum cost set of flows (x) that satisfy the external flow requirements (b). Examples of external flows are customer demand (outflows) and vendor supplies (inflows). The notation shown is for a single commodity problem, so the subscript p indicating the commodity has been omitted:

x_{ij} Flow on the directed arc from node i to node j
c_{ij} Unit cost for one unit flow transported from node i to node j
b_i External flow for node i (positive for entering, negative for exiting the network, zero for intermediate nodes)
l_{ij} Lower bound of the flow on the directed arc from node i to node j (often zero)
u_{ij} Upper bound of the flow on the directed arc from node i to node j

Formulation 2.1 Minimum Cost Network Flow Formulation as a Normative Mathematical Model

$$Min \ \sum_{i}^{N}\sum_{j}^{N} c_{ij}x_{ij}$$

$$s.t. \ \sum_{h}^{N}x_{hi} - \sum_{j}^{N}x_{ij} = b_i \qquad \forall i \qquad\qquad (2.1)$$

$$l_{ij} \le x_{ij} \le u_{ij} \qquad\qquad \forall ij$$

To determine the decision variables in normative models, a solution method is required. This is often called "solving the model" and the solution method is referred to as the solution algorithm. An optimal solution is a decision that gives the best answer to a mathematical model, but it may not be the best answer to the original real-world problem. The normative mathematical models and their solution algorithms constitute the discipline of mathematical programming.

There exist a separation between the relationships that form the structure of the model and the data. For example, a strategic supply chain design model may contain customer objects that have as one of their characteristics monthly demand for a product. The requirement that customer demand is satisfied every month by shipments from the distribution center is a component of the model. The number of customers and their actual demands are data.

2.2.4.2 Deterministic versus Stochastic Models

A model is said to be *deterministic* if all its relevant data parameters are known with certainty, i.e., they are given as a unique values. For example, when scheduling our day we may assume that we know exactly how long it takes to drive to work in the morning. Of course, we realize the time it takes to drive to work varies from day to day. A model is said to be *stochastic* or *probabilistic* if some parameters are not known with certainty. Parameters that are not known with certainty are called *random variables* and they represent the ignorance and variability in the model. Usually, random variables are represented or modeled with probability distributions. Even though virtually all real-world problems are stochastic, deterministic models are still used very often because they may give an acceptable approximation of reality and they are much easier to construct and to solve than the corresponding stochastic models.

2.2.4.3 Deductive versus Inferential Models

A model is said to be *deductive* if it starts from the definition of variables, makes some assumptions, and then defines the relationships between the variables. For example, a simple deductive model to compute the average speed (v) at which corrugated cardboard boxes can be unloaded from the back of trailer is to assume that boxes are unloaded at a constant speed and to compute this speed by dividing the number of boxes on the trailer (n) by the total time it takes to unload the trailer (ΔT). This represents a top-down approach.

A model is said to be *inferential* if it determines the relationships between various variables by analyzing data from data streams or data warehouses. A typical example is the determination of relationships between variables with regression analysis. For example, you may collect total unloading times and number of boxes unloaded at the truck docks of a receiving department during a year and then determine a regression model to determine the relationship between those two data items. Based on the results of the regression analysis, you may then decide that those two items are linearly related and that boxes are unloaded at a constant speed.

2.2.5 Modeling Advantages and Disadvantages

2.2.5.1 Modeling Advantages

Probably the most significant advantage of using models to assist in the decision process of planning or configuring logistics systems results from the execution of the modeling process itself. Developing a supply chain model requires that the organization clearly articulates its business objectives, its standard or allowable business practices, the structure of the organization, and the business operating constraints and relations. This information can then be shared or presented to everybody involved with the supply chain such as employees, vendors, and customers.

The solution of the developed model requires that business parameter values and costs are defined consistently and have a numerical value agreed upon by all stakeholders in the supply chain. Again the process of defining and computing these parameters and costs is most likely more beneficial than their actual use in the model.

Since most models are solved by some form of optimization algorithm, the suggested configurations and activities typically will provide a higher quality solution than a manual decision process. The model results have the added benefit of being systematic and scientific, which may make their implementation more palatable or politically acceptable.

Developing the first supply chain model for an organization is a long and tedious process. However, once the model has been validated and gained acceptance, providing answers to the follow up supply chain questions becomes much faster, easier, and more accurate than would have been possible without modeling assistance.

2.2.5.2 Modeling Disadvantages

The major time and expenses in a modeling effort are usually associated with defining, collecting, validating, and correcting the model data, such as parameters and costs. Once these data have been accepted, they form a very valuable asset to the corporation.

The modeling process still requires specialized knowledge and computer software. The required powerful computer hardware has become less and less expensive. The recent advances in personal computer power and user friendly analysis software, such as spreadsheets and statistical analysis packages, have revolutionized modeling and brought the modeling process much closer to the practitioner and manager. However, this does not mean that the previously required analytical skills, mastery of advanced mathematics, computer programming, and algorithmic thinking are no longer required. Computer power and analysis software empower the knowledgeable modeler so that the modeling process can be performed faster and in greater depth. They do not guarantee by themselves that the appropriate model is applied or that the user understands the modeling assumptions and limitations of the software. Powerful analysis software is not unlike a chainsaw. With a chainsaw a logger can cut down a tree much faster than with a bow saw, but the use of a chainsaw does not guarantee that the right tree is cut down and significantly increases the risk of injury to an inexperienced logger. More than once simulation models have been developed with powerful and graphical digital simulation software and then decisions were based on a single model run.

The models for many supply chain problems are intrinsically hard to solve, be it either to find a feasible solution or to find the optimal solution. This often leads to very long computation times for the solution algorithms. It would not be unusual for a facilities design program to find a high quality layout in 24 h on a personal computer for a facility with no more than ten functional areas. The same computer program may then require more than 1 or 2 weeks of computing time to prove that this layout is within close range of the best possible layout.

2.2.6 Modeling Summary

2.2.6.1   Model Realism versus Model Solvability

There will always exist a tradeoff between model solvability and model realism. The more realistic the model is the more resources have to be allocated for model development, data collection, model maintenance, and model solving. Since all models involve some level of abstraction, approximations, and assumptions, the results of the models should always be interpreted with common (engineering) sense. Also, there is no such thing as a unique correct model. Just as two painters may create two vastly different views of the same landscape, different models can be developed to support decision making for a particular logistics problem.

Different models with different levels of detail and realism are appropriate and useful at different stages of the design process. Systematically increasing the level of model complexity for the same problem and evaluating their solutions and their consistency provides a way to validate the models. For example, a normative model based on queuing network analysis and simple travel time models may be used to determine the required number of cranes and aisles in an automated storage and retrieval systems (ASRS) to satisfy throughput requirements. A descriptive simulation model can then be used to verify and validate the performance of the system and investigate the behavior of the system during transient or exceptional events such as crane breakdowns. This successive refinement approach is a primal solution approach, which has the advantage that an approximately feasible solution exists if the solution process has to be terminated prematurely.

2.2.6.2   Decision Support versus Decision Making

There exist many examples of successful automated decision-making systems for operational decisions where the real world system is sufficiently simple so that it can be accurately represented and solved by a model. A prime example is the routing of a truck to deliver to a set of customers. Other examples are routing of an automated order-picking crane in a warehouse rack or building a stable pallet load with boxes that arrive on a conveyor belt. The more complex the real world system is, the more approximate any model will become. Models used to assist in strategic decision-making are infamous for not capturing many of the real world factors and subjective influences. Such strategic models should only be used as decision support tools for the design engineer. A healthy skepticism with respect to the results of any model is required. Just because a computer model specifies a particular decision, does not imply that this is the best decision for the real world system. One should be especially wary of experts that tout the infallibility of their computer models or the optimality of the generated decisions.

2.2.7 Distance Norms used as Simple Models

One of the most fundamental types of models used in the design, analysis, and operation of supply chains and logistics systems is the distance norm used to model the actual transportation distance. An example of actual distance is the over-the-road distance driven by trucks on the interstate highway system in national distribution systems. While recent computer advances have made it possible to use actual over-the-road distances in many models and solution algorithms, approximation of the real distance by a distance norm is still required in some algorithms because the actual distance is too expensive to compute or unknown. For instance, the location problem for which the Varignon frame is a mechanical analog may not place the new facility on the road network and thus any real distances need to be approximated.

The Euclidean, rectilinear, Chebyshev, and ring-radial distance norms are used to compute the distance between points in a plane. The great-circle distance norm is used to compute the distance between points on the globe.

2.2.7.1 Planar Distance Norms

A planar distance norm is the formula for computing the distance between two points in the plane. Let d_{ij} denote the distance between two points i and j in the plane with coordinates (x_i, y_i) and (x_j, y_j), respectively (Fig. 2.11).

Three norms are frequently used during supply chain analysis and design in the appropriate situations: Euclidean, rectilinear, and Chebyshev.

$$d_{ij}^E = L_2 = \sqrt{(x_i - x_j)^2 + (y_i - y_j)^2} \qquad (2.2)$$

$$d_{ij}^R = L_1 = |x_i - x_j| + |y_i - y_j| \qquad (2.3)$$

$$d_{ij}^C = L_\infty = \max\left\{|x_i - x_j|, |y_i - y_j|\right\} \qquad (2.4)$$

In the above formulas E, R and C denote the Euclidean, rectilinear, and Chebyshev norm, respectively. All the above norms are members of the family of L^n norms, defined as

$$d_{ij}^n = L_n = \sqrt[n]{|x_i - x_j|^n + |y_i - y_j|^n} \qquad (2.5)$$

Fig. 2.11 Distance between
two points

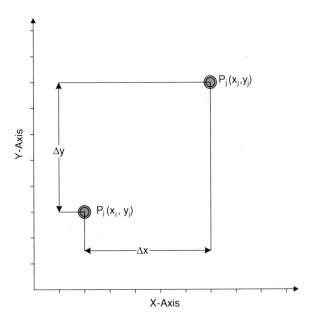

$P_j(x_j, y_j)$

Y-Axis

Δy

$P_i(x_i, y_i)$

Δx

X-Axis

where n is equal to 2, 1, and ∞, respectively, for the Euclidean, rectilinear, and Chebyshev norm.

2.2.7.2 Euclidean Norm

The *Euclidean* distance is also called the straight-line travel distance and is frequently used in national distribution problems and for communications problems where straight-line travel is an acceptable approximation. Multiplying the Euclidean distance with an appropriate factor, e.g. 1.2 for continental United States or 1.26 for the South Eastern United States, can then approximate the actual over the road distances. The Euclidean distance is the shortest distance between two points in a plane. However, the Euclidean distance may not follow a feasible travel path for a particular logistics system due to the internal structure in which case another appropriate distance norm has to be used. In those cases, the Euclidean distance is not the shortest (feasible) travel distance.

2.2.7.3 Rectilinear Norm

The *rectilinear* norm is primarily used in manufacturing and warehousing layout where travel occurs along a set of perpendicular aisles and cross aisles, and in cities with an orthogonal grid pattern such as New York. From this it derives its alternative name of Manhattan norm (Fig. 2.12).

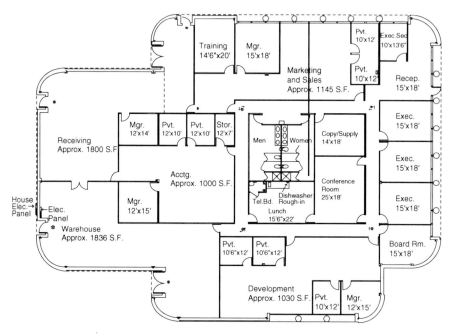

Fig. 2.12 Office layout with rectilinear travel

The rectilinear norm is also called the sequential travel distance for material handling devices that move only along one axis at the time. An example is the travel path used by a picker to retrieve cartons from shelves in a warehouse. The picker has to follow the pick aisles or cross aisles, which are arranged perpendicular in a ladder layout (Figs. 2.13, 2.14).

Fig. 2.13 Shelves in a ware-house with ladder layout

Fig. 2.14 Schematic of an order picking tour in a warehouse with ladder layout

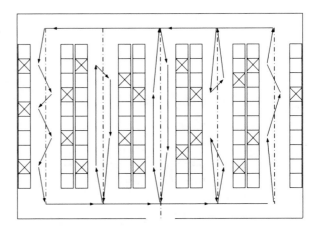

2.2.7.4 Chebyshev Norm

Finally, the *Chebyshev* norm is also called the simultaneous travel distance and is used with material handling equipment such as an automated storage/retrieval system or AS/RS and bridge cranes, where travel occurs simultaneously along two axes. In the following bridge example the bridge crane end truck and cross beam move independently from and simultaneously with the trolley and hoist. The end truck moves on a beam mounted on the side wall and supports the cross beam. The trolley moves on the cross beam and contains the hoist (Fig. 2.15).

2.2.7.5 Ring-Radial Distance

Other travel norms exist but are much less often used. One example is the ring-radial distance in old medieval cities such as the central districts of Paris and Moscow or the street plan corresponding to the canals in downtown Amsterdam (Fig. 2.16).

Fig. 2.15 Bridge crane example

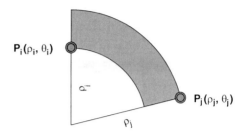

Fig. 2.16 Ring-radial distance illustration

The ring-radial distance between two points with radius and angular polar coordinates (ρ_i, θ_i) and (ρ_j, θ_j) is given by:

$$d_{ij}^{RR} = \min\left\{\rho_i, \rho_j\right\} \min\left\{\left|\theta_i - \theta_j\right|, 2\pi - \left|\theta_i - \theta_j\right|\right\} + \left|\rho_i - \rho_j\right| \quad (2.6)$$

The angular coordinate θ is expressed in radians. A variant of the ring-radial distance is used in generalized assignment algorithms for the vehicle routing problem to compute the estimated assignment cost of a customer or supplier facility to the sector that represents the vehicle route. The vehicle sector has its tip in the depot. For this variant the radius of the facility is always used, since the vehicle sector has no corresponding radius.

2.2.7.6 Great Circle Norm

A great circle of a sphere is defined by a plane cutting through the center of the sphere and the surface of the sphere. Examples of great circles on the earth are the equator and any meridian. The shortest distance between any two points on the surface of a sphere is measured along the great circle passing through them and is the shorter of the two arcs between the points on the great circle. Computing the distance between two points located on the surface of a sphere with the straight-line distance would imply digging a tunnel through the body of the sphere. The additional complexity of the great circle distance norm compared to the Euclidean distance norm is usually only warranted for intercontinental transportation models. A typical application is the curved routes of airplanes between two continents as seen on airline system maps.

The *great circle* distance norm computes the distance along a great circle on the surface of the earth between two points with latitude and longitude coordinates (lat_i, lon_i) and (lat_j, lon_j) with the following formula, where R denotes the world radius and where the latitude and longitude are expressed in radians:

$$d_{ij}^{GC} = R \cdot \arccos\left(\cos\left(lat_i\right)\cos\left(lat_j\right)\cos\left(lon_i - lon_j\right) + \sin\left(lat_i\right)\sin\left(lat_j\right)\right) \quad (2.7)$$

The earth radius is approximately 6371 km or 3959 miles. By convention the meridian running through Greenwich, England has a longitude that is equal to zero and is

Table 2.1 Coordinate conversion example

		Degrees	Minutes	Seconds	Decimal D.	Radians
Latitude						
Atlanta	GA	33	45	18	33.755	0.589136
Denver	CO	39	44	21	39.739	0.693579
Longitude						
Atlanta	GA	84	23	24	−84.390	−1.472883
Denver	CO	104	59	5	−104.985	−1.832329

Table 2.2 Great-circle distance calculations example

		Arc	Radius	Distance
Atlanta	Denver	0.305515	3957	1209

also called the zero meridian. The latitude of the equator is equal to zero. Finally, the full circumference of a circle corresponds to 360° or 2π radians. Usually, the longitude and latitude coordinates in geographical databases are expressed in degrees, minutes, and seconds. They have to be first converted to decimal degrees and then to radians. The range in radians of the longitude is $[-\pi, \pi]$ and of the latitude is $[-\pi/2, \pi/2]$.

As an example, the distance between the cities of Atlanta, Georgia and Denver, Colorado will be computed. The coordinates of Atlanta are 33°45'18"N and 84°23'24"W and of Denver are 39°44'21"N and 104°59'05"W. There are 60 min. and 3600 s per degree and the conversion to decimal degrees and radians is shown in the next table. Observe that the decimal degrees and radians are signed to indicate their relative position to the equator and zero meridian (Table 2.1).

The great circle distance calculation between these two cities is shown in Table 2.2, where the radius of the earth and thus also the final distance is expressed in miles.

2.2.7.7 Physical Distance versus Distance Norms

The adjustment factors to go from the Euclidean or great circle distance norm to the actual distance traveled over the road or rail network for developed countries were computed in Ballou (1999, pp. 557) and are summarized in the next table. The value of the adjustment factors depends on the density of the highway or railway network in area covered by the logistics model (Table 2.3).

Recent advances in computer and database technology have made it possible in the United States to get detailed driving instructions, distance, and estimated driving time between two locations based on their addresses. This route planning can

Table 2.3 Distance adjustment factors in developed countries

	Euclidean	Great circle
Road	1.21	1.17
Rail	1.24	1.20

be obtained from several inexpensive commercial software packages or from the Internet. The distances reported are actual over-the-road driving distances. An example for the route planned from the Georgia Institute of Technology to the Atlanta International airport is given next. Similar software is available for Western Europe. However, obtaining the corresponding reliable and up-to-date information for underdeveloped or developing areas of the world is very difficult. The availability and quality of such information has to be established on a case by case basis (Fig. 2.17).

The over-the-transportation network distance between the cities of Atlanta and Denver is computed based on the above adjustment factor and obtained from a mapping software. For this example Microsoft MapPoint was used. The results are shown in the following table. In this particular case, the difference between the adjusted and actual distance and between the average adjustment factor and the specific and derived adjustment factor for the two cities is 0.6% (Table 2.4).

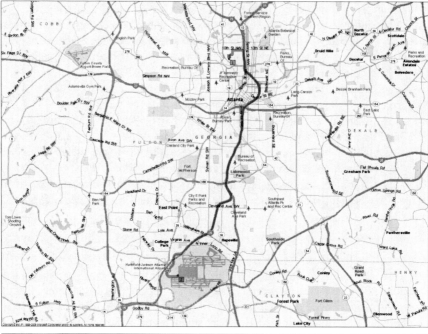

Time	Mile	Instruction	For	Toward
Summary:			13.7 miles (18 minutes)	
9:00 AM	0	Depart 755 Ferst Dr NW, Atlanta, GA 30318 on Ferst Dr NW (North)	0.3 mi	
9:00 AM	0.3	Turn LEFT (North) onto Dalney St NW	0.2 mi	
9:01 AM	0.5	Turn RIGHT (East) onto 10th St NW	0.5 mi	
9:02 AM	1	Take Ramp (RIGHT) onto I-75 [I-85]	6.9 mi	I-75 / I-85
9:10 AM	7.8	At exit 242, keep RIGHT onto I-85 [242]	3.7 mi	I-85 / Atl Airport / Montgomery
9:13 AM	11.5	At exit 72, turn RIGHT onto Ramp	0.4 mi	Camp Creek Pkwy / Atlanta Airport
9:14 AM	11.9	Road name changes to Airport Blvd	1.1 mi	
9:16 AM	13.1	Keep LEFT onto S Terminal Pkwy	0.6 mi	South Parking / Terminal South
9:18 AM	13.7	Arrive S Terminal Pkwy, Atlanta, GA 30320		

Fig. 2.17 Georgia Tech to Atlanta airport driving instructions

Table 2.4 Network distance calculations example

		Distance				
		Great circle	Factor	Adjusted	MapPoint	Factor
Atlanta	Denver	1209	1.17	1414	1406	1.16

In strategic and high-level logistics planning models, most often distances are approximated based on distance norms multiplied by the appropriate distance adjustment factor. This allows the computation of distances for a large variety of alternatives with minimal computational resources and the approximation accuracy is deemed acceptable. In operational and execution planning models, more accurate information is required and available. Distances are based on over-the-transportation network travel derived from mapping software. In general, the model and data accuracy should be appropriate for the level of logistics planning.

2.3 Algorithms

2.3.1 Algorithm Definition

To determine the decision variables in normative models, a solution method is required. This is often called "solving the model" and the solution method is referred to as the solution algorithm. An algorithm is a set of rules to determine the system activities and configuration in a normative model. This configuration can then be evaluated and yields a value for one or more performance measures.

2.3.2 Algorithm Characteristics

2.3.2.1 Efficient versus Effective

An algorithm is said to be *efficient* when it finds a solution in a short amount of computing time. More specifically, it is efficient if it runs in a polynomial time, i.e., its running time is not larger than a polynomial function of the size of the problem. The efficiency of an algorithm for large problem instances can be estimated by the order of the running time of the algorithm.

Order of the Running Time of an Algorithm

Suppose n is a measure of the problem instance size and the number of computational steps required by a certain algorithm is found to be

$$a_k n^k + a_{k-1} n^{k-1} + \ldots + a_1 n + a_0 \qquad (2.8)$$

where $a_k > 0$. Then we say that the algorithm is "of order of n^k", which is written as $O(n^k)$. The magnitude of the leading coefficient a_k is usually ignored, since for very large n, i.e. for very large problem instances, a lower order algorithm will always perform faster than a higher order algorithm. The actual performance on smaller problem instances may depend on the value of the different a coefficients.

The growth of the running time of an algorithm for the different types of algorithms is illustrated in the next table. The first two algorithms are said to be polynomial (P) and their running times grow relatively slowly. The last algorithm is said to be exponential or non-polynomial (NP) and its running time grows quickly to overwhelm the processing speed of any conceivable computer. Further details on the computational complexity of an algorithm can be found in Garey and Johnson (1976).

It is important to recognize during a supply chain design project if the algorithm that will be used to solve the model is easy or hard. Easy algorithms have a low polynomial growth of their running times. The most prominent examples are linear programming (LP) solvers. In linear programming the objective and all the constraints are linear equations and all the decision variables are continuous, which means that they can have fractional values. Very large linear programming models can be solved to optimality by current LP solvers. Many supply chain and logistics models focus on the flow of materials between facilities and they naturally correspond to a special subset of LP models called network flow models. The LP solvers can exploit the additional structure in the network flow models and solve instances faster or solve even larger problem instances. Hard algorithms typically have exponentially growing running times. This implies that optimal solutions can only be found in a reasonable amount of computing time for small problem instances. Many of the most commonly used models in supply chain and logistics belong to this class. Examples are vehicle routing, production planning and scheduling, distribution and supply chain system design, manufacturing and warehousing facilities layout, and fleet planning and scheduling. Many times, the problem becomes hard because certain configuration and activity decisions are restricted to have non-negative integer values. For example, a distribution center can be built in a particular location or not, but it cannot be partially built in a location. Similarly, a truck route will run from customer a to customer b, but it cannot continue half from customer a to customer b and half to customer c. These models belong to the class of either pure integer, where all decision variables are discrete, or mixed-integer programming (MIP) models, where there are both continuous and discrete decision variables. Pure and mixed-integer models usually are difficult to solve to optimality because the number of possible design configurations grows exponentially. For example, the number of possible combinations of building or not building N candidate distribution centers is 2^N. The computation time required to evaluate all these alternatives grows quickly beyond all reason, as illustrated in Table 2.5. Further information on integer and mixed-integer programming can be found in Nemhauser and Wolsey (1988).

Table 2.5 Algorithm running times

	Problem size			
	10	20	40	80
Run Time				
n	0.001 sec	0.002 sec	0.004 sec	0.008 sec
n^3	0.001 sec	0.008 sec	0.064 sec	0.512 sec
2^n	0.001 sec	1.024 sec	12.43 days	37.43 million millennia

In many instances of supply chain models, decision variables that are naturally discrete can be approximated with sufficient accuracy by continuous variables. For example, an LP solver may generate an optimal configuration for a logistics system that involves sending 5238.8 intermodal containers per year from Hong Kong to Long Beach, California. The error introduced by rounding the number of containers to 5239 is negligible. However, the effort required from the solver if all transportation flows of containers were restricted to be integer numbers of containers would be very significant.

2.3.2.2 Optimal (Exact) versus Heuristic (Approximate)

If the algorithm produces the mathematically best solution it is called an *optimal* or *exact* algorithm, if it produces a good, but not necessarily the best solution, is called a *heuristic* or *approximate* algorithm. An optimal solution is a set of configuration and activity decisions that gives the best answer to a performance measure of a mathematical model, but again it should be stressed that this is not necessarily the best configuration for the original real-world problem.

Worst Case Performance Bound of a Heuristic

Since a heuristic is not guaranteed to give the best possible configuration, decision-makers may be interested in the performance gap generated by the heuristic configuration compared to the best obtainable configuration. This performance gap can either depend on the particular problem instance or be the worst case bound for any instance. A heuristic algorithm for a minimization objective is said to have a worse case error bound of K, if for any problem instance the ratio of the heuristics solution to the optimal solution value is smaller than or equal to K and if there exist an instance for which this ratio is satisfied as an equality, i.e.

$$\min \ z \Rightarrow \begin{cases} \dfrac{z_{heuristic}}{z_{optimal}} \leq K \\ \exists p : \dfrac{z_{p,heuristic}}{z_{p,optimal}} = K \end{cases} \tag{2.9}$$

This is also called an a-priori performance bound since it does not depend on the execution of the heuristic for a particular problem instance. The asymptotic worst-case error bound of a heuristic is the worst-case error bound for very large problem instance, i.e., when the problem size grows to infinity. The asymptotic worst-case error bound is not larger and is usually strictly better than the worst-case error bound. Both performance bounds usually can only be computed for very simple heuristics and for very simple supply chain systems and operations problems and their value may be much worse than the average error bound on the performance of the heuristic. A more useful statistic is the average-case error bound but the average-case error bound is typically even more difficult to compute than the worse-case error bound.

The *optimality gap* is the worst-case performance bound of a heuristic solution for a particular instance. This gap is often of more interest to decision makers since it concerns their particular problem. For a minimization problem, the optimality gap is the difference between the solution generated by the heuristic and some lower bound value. Since the optimal solution value must fall between the lower bound and the heuristic solution, the optimality gap gives the maximum difference between the heuristic solution and the optimal solution. An algorithm is said to be *effective* if it produces a high quality solution or, equivalently, a small optimality gap.

2.3.2.3   Primal versus Dual

A primal algorithm initially creates and then maintains a feasible solution and improves the quality of the solution while it strives to reach optimality. A dual algorithm initially creates and then maintains an optimal solution for either a subset of the decision variables or of the constraints and strives to reach feasibility by adding either decision variables or constraints. The advantage of a primal algorithm is that on premature termination a feasible solution is available for implementation. In addition, the list of the best configurations found during the execution of the primal algorithm can be retained and considered for implementation based on other factors not included in the performance objective. The advantage of a dual algorithm is that on premature termination a bound on the optimal objective function value is available.

For example, consider the task of writing a research report before a given deadline. The report contains three sections: introduction, main body, and conclusions. A primal algorithm would create a rough draft of each section and then iteratively refine each section until the quality of the report is satisfactory. A dual approach would first create and refine the introduction until it cannot be improved any further. Then this process is repeated for the main body and finally for the conclusions section. Assuming the quality of the two final reports is the same, the primal approach at any time has a completed reported ready to be handed in.

Many solution algorithms for the design of complex supply chain systems are composite algorithms that have both primal and dual sub-algorithms embedded in them. The composite algorithm terminates when the gap between the solution value of the best-found primal feasible solution and the bound provided by the dual algorithm falls within an acceptable tolerance level.

2.3.2.4 Construction versus Improvement

A construction algorithm creates a feasible configuration for the supply chain based on the values of the data input parameters. An improvement algorithm requires a feasible solution or configuration in addition to the input parameters and attempts to improve the quality of the solution. Many improvement algorithms belong to the class of local search procedures. One, several, or all feasible solutions in the neighborhood of the current feasible solution are evaluated. A *first descent* algorithm will choose the first configuration it finds that has a better solution value than the current configuration. A *steepest descent* algorithm will choose the configuration with best solution value among all the configurations it evaluated around the current configuration. The process is repeated until the search algorithm cannot find a feasible solution with a better solution value in the neighborhood. All local search procedures may terminate at locally optimal solutions, i.e., there does not exist a better solution in the neighborhood of the current feasible solution but there may exist better solutions when considering the full solution space. First descent and steepest descent algorithms belong to the class of *deterministic* algorithms. Deterministic algorithms will always arrive at the same final configuration when they are started from a particular initial configuration. To find a different final configuration, deterministic algorithms must be started from a different initial configuration, which may be difficult or impossible to obtain. To avoid this phenomenon, Kirkpatrick et al. (1983) and Vechi and Kirkpatrick (1983) proposed a *non-deterministic* search algorithm called *simulated annealing*. This algorithm will evaluate random neighboring configurations and choose configurations with a better solution value but also choose configurations with a worse solution value with a decreasing probability during the execution of the algorithm. The algorithm is called simulated annealing because of its similarities with the behavior of energy levels in metal alloys during the annealing or cooling process.

2.3.2.5 Alternative Generating versus Alternative Selecting

An *alternative-generating* algorithm creates feasible solutions. An *alternative-selecting* algorithm selects the solution of the highest quality from a set of feasible candidate solutions provided to it as input parameters. A prominent example in the design of supply chains of an alternative-generating algorithm is the location-allocation problem, where the location of a given number of distribution facilities and the allocation of customers to these distribution facilities is to be determined. The decision space is the continuous area where the customers are located. Several optimal or heuristic algorithms exist that will generate the location of the distribution facilities. However, even the optimal location derived from the model may be infeasible for the real-world system. Typical examples are the location of a distribution center for the southeast region of the United States in the Gulf of Mexico or for the state of Georgia in downtown Atlanta. Because the algorithm has to describe the cost of the configuration in mathematical expressions, exceptions to cost or constraints can be difficult to incorporate. In addition, since the algorithm determines the solution, a method must be developed to evaluate all possible solution configurations. This typically implies that simplified and approximated cost functions will be used. All of these factors combined indicate that the application of alternative generating algorithms is usually reserved for problems that have a simple cost and constraint structure.

On the other hand, alternative selecting algorithms select a solution configuration from among a set of possible and feasible configurations. This implies that there exists an external mechanism to generate feasible configuration and evaluate the cost of these configurations. Typically this is a person or separate algorithm which is an expert for the problem domain. Since the solution algorithm picks a configuration from a set of feasible configurations, the proposed solution will always be feasible. It is assumed that the expert has the capability to recognize and incorporate exceptions and can compute accurate costs. Instead of a human expert, sometimes a secondary optimization problem, called the pricing problem, is used to find one or more alternatives that have the potential to improve the overall solution. The specific domain knowledge is imbedded in the pricing problem since it has the function of identifying potentially improving feasible alternatives. The solution algorithm to select the alternatives can then be of a general-purpose nature. Typically, variants of the set partitioning or the set covering algorithms are used. The prime application area of alternative selecting algorithms is usually for problems that have complex constraints or cost structures.

A second major class of alternative selecting algorithms is *simulation*. Simulation belongs to the class of descriptive algorithms, since all design and configuration occurs before the simulation is started and the simulation is used to evaluate the design. Almost all simulation applications today use digital Monte Carlo simulation methods, where realizations of input parameters are sampled randomly from prescribed probability distributions. These parameter values are then inserted in the simulation model of the logistics system under investigation and statistics on the performance measures of interest are collected. Simulation models typically have a very high level of detail or fidelity. Modern simulation applications are able to animate the results of simulation runs, which has proven to be very effective in debugging the simulation model and in marketing the proposed design. While simulation is a very powerful tool for the verification and validation of a design, it is limited in its design capabilities. Minor modifications to the configuration such as increasing the number of truck doors in a distribution center or changing the inventory level of a product can be made with little effort. However, a significantly different configuration of the supply chain requires the development of a new simulation model, which again has to be debugged and validated. In addition, simulation is a descriptive algorithm and relies on other programs or designers to generate good design

Fig. 2.18 Simulation with animation of a material handling system. (*Illustration courtesy of Retrotech*)

alternatives. These characteristics make simulation algorithms more useful in the later stages of the design, such as verification, validation, final tuning of the design, and acceptance testing, where the number of alternatives is limited but the required model fidelity is very high. Simulation can also be used to study off-line or in real time the effects of certain decisions on an existing logistics system, if the status of the simulation model and parameters is kept synchronized with the status of the real supply chain (Fig. 2.18).

Because many supply chains have a natural graphical and geographical representation, the combination of best characteristics of human designers and computerized models and algorithms into interactive and graphical design frameworks has proven to be very effective. The designer is responsible for higher- level decisions and the computer algorithms are responsible for the detailed computations. Communications between the designer and the computer algorithms is achieved through a graphical user interface. This user friendly and powerful interaction has now become a necessary requirement for the acceptance and use of logistics models and design algorithms. A typical screen of a program to design supply chains is shown in the next figure (Fig. 2.19).

2.3.3   Model Hierarchy and Corresponding Solution Technologies

2.3.3.1   Model Hierarchy and Associated Solution Technologies

Organizations typically start with simple models for a particular supply chain design or operations problem. Once the simple models and their configurations gain acceptance, the models are further refined and enhanced. When the models become more comprehensive and powerful, the corresponding solution algorithms

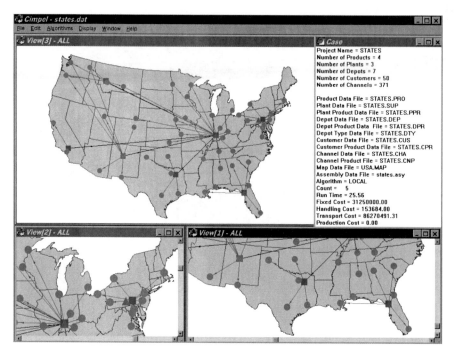

Fig. 2.19 Illustration of the graphical representation of a supply chain

become more complex and resource intensive. The first phase usually involves a deterministic and descriptive model. Examples are the computations to determine the cost, the distance, and duration of a vehicle route, or the computations to determine the cost for the warehousing personnel staffing for the next shift. In the next phase, organizations recognize that many parameters are not known with certainty and they develop stochastic descriptive models. The most prominent is digital simulation but queuing analysis is also sometimes used. Examples are the evaluation of the service levels for various levels of inventory in a hierarchical distribution system or estimation of waiting times experienced by truck for a dock at a distribution center. In the next phase, the decision makers attempt to improve the quality of the solution or to reduce the time and effort required to generate a solution by letting the computer models and algorithms make some decisions. The first step is typically a deterministic normative model and solution algorithm. Prominent examples are vehicle routing algorithms to determine the lowest distance or cost routes, or network flow models to minimize transportation costs. Much more demanding applications are the design of distribution and supply chain systems, which typically require mixed-integer programming models. Finally, the stochastic nature of the parameters is added to the models to create stochastic normative models. Examples are supply chain models that find the best inventory levels to achieve a required customer service level or supply chain models that find the most robust, flexible, and cost-efficient supply chain configuration for a variety of possible demand scenarios.

2.4   Summary and Conclusions

This chapter started off with a review of the definitions and characteristics of the engineering design methodology. Engineering design techniques are necessary to structure the engineering design process so that high-quality supply chains can be created. One of most prominent engineering design techniques is the use of models. The most important characteristics of models were summarized. A supply chain meta-model was presented that provides the structure for various supply chain models. The proper selection of the model, model fidelity and accuracy, and the validation of the model are necessary steps during the design process. Models for transportation distances in supply chain planning and design were used as an illustration of the various levels of models that can and should be used under different circumstances. Solving the model attempts to reach the goal for one or more performance characteristics of the model by determining values for decision variables. Most supply chain design or planning problems are too difficult to be solved by ad-hoc or manual techniques. The classifications and characteristics of solution algorithms were reviewed.

Supply chain planning and design is an especially complex variant of engineering system design. Only the proper application of engineering design methodology and tools can yield high-quality plans and designs in a systematic way in a reasonable amount of time. In order for system engineering methodology to be applicable it is required that all three of data, model, and planning algorithm have been developed for the system in question.

The value of accurate data for modeling-based engineering design was demonstrated repeatedly in this chapter. Most data for supply chain modeling is based on forecasting and this is especially true for tactical and strategic planning models. In the next chapter, forecasting techniques commonly used in supply chain planning and design are reviewed.

2.5   Exercises

True-False Questions

1. A "blue sky" design alternative indicates a design alternative generated without observing any external constraints such budgets or deadlines, (T/F) _____.
2. A model is stochastic if at least one of the input parameters is not known with certainty, (T/F) _____.

3. A significant cost associated with modeling is the cost to collect and validate data, (T/F)_____ .
4. An adjustment factor of 1.2 is a reasonable factor (with one significant digit after the decimal point) to approximate the relation between over the road distances in a developed network compared to Euclidean distances, (T/F) _____ .
5. An analog model is a replication of the real world system under investigation but generally at a different scale, (T/F)_____ .
6. Classic expert system algorithms are often used to assist during the design of strategic logistics systems, (T/F) _____ .
7. The process of attaching geographical or location coordinates to alphanumeric address data is known as geocoding, (T/F) _____ .
8. The acquisition costs of raw materials belongs to the class of variable costs in a logistics system, (T/F)_____ .
9. The fundamental objective of a model is to provide better insight or easier manipulation than can be gained from the real-world system, (T/F)_____ .
10. The sole focus of logistics planning is inventory management, (T/F) _____ .
11. The United States Census collects a variety of data useful for designing logistics systems in the United States, (T/F) _____ .

Emergency Trailers In 2006 in the aftermath of hurricane Katrina, the federal government through its FEMA administration owned and stored many thousands of home trailers. These trailers are to be used as temporary housing in case of disaster. The news story on the trailer storage given at http://www.newsobserver.com/102/story/411776.html states that 11000 trailers are being stored nationwide. Develop a decision support model for the number of trailers the federal government should own. Clearly identify all the members of the major components of the model (parameters, decision variables, activities, and performance measures) and how they are computed as well as the objectives and constraints.

References

Arntzen, B. C., Brown, G. G., Harrison, T. P., & Trafton, L. L. (1995). Global supply chain management at digital equipment corporation. *Interfaces, 25*(1), 69–93.
Benders, J. (1962). Partitioning procedures for solving mixed-variables programming problems. *Numerische Mathematik, 4*(1), 238–252.
Ballou, R. H., & Masters, J. M. (1993). Commercial software for locating warehouses and other facilities. *Journal of Business Logistics, 14*(2), 71–107.
Ballou, R. H., & Masters, J. M. (1999). Facility location commercial software survey. *Journal of Business Logistics, 20*(1), 215–233.
Ballou, R. H. (1999). *Business logistics management* (4th ed.). Englewood Cliffs: Prentice-Hall.
De Kok, A. G., & Graves, S. (Eds.). (2003). *Supply chain management: Design, coordination and operation.* Amsterdam: Elsevier.
Ertas, A., & Jones, J. C. (1996). *The engineering design process* (2nd ed.) New York: Wiley.
Garey, M. R., & Johnson, D. S. (1976). *Computers and intractability.* San Francisco: Freeman Press.

Gass, S. I., & Harris, C. M. (1996). *Encyclopedia of operations research and management science.* Boston: Kluwer Academic.

Guenes, J., & Pardalos, P. M. (Eds.). (2005). *Supply chain optimization.* Boston: Kluwer Academic.

Hoare, C. A. R. (1996). A theory of engineering design. Oxford University Computing Laboratory, pp. 331–335. http://www.comlab.ox.ac.uk.

Kirkpatrick, S., Gelat, C., & Vechi, M. (1983). Optimization by. simulated annealing. *Science, 220,* 671–680.

Nemhauser, G. L., & Wolsey, L. A. (1988). Integer and combinatorial optimization. New York: Wiley.

Pahl, G., & Beitz, W. (1996). In K. Wallace (Ed.), *Engineering design: a systematic approach* (trans: K. Wallace, L. Blessing, & F. Bauert). Springer: New York.

Park, G.-J. (2007). Analytic methods for design practice. New York: Springer.

Shapiro, J. F. (2006). *Modeling the supply chain* (2nd ed.). Pacific Grove: Duxbury Press.

Simchi-Levi, D., Kaminsky, P., & Simchi-Levi, E. (2008). *Designing and managing the supply chain: Concepts, strategies, and case studies* (3rd ed.). New York: McGraw-Hill.

Stadtler, H., & Kilger, C. (Eds.). (2004). *Supply chain management and advanced planning* (3rd ed.). Heidelberg: Springer.

Vechi, M., & Kirkpatrick, S. (1983). *IEEE Transactions on Computer Aided Design, CAD-2,* 215.

Weber, A. (1909). Uber den Standort der Industrien, Mohr, Turingen. English edition: Friedrich, C. (1929). *Alfred Weber's Theory of the Location of Industries* (trans: C. Friedrich). Chicago: University of Chicago Press.

Williams, H. P. (1999). *Model building in mathematical programming* (4th ed.). Chichester: Wiley. http://www.batchgeocode.com.

Chapter 3
Forecasting

Learning Objectives After you have studied this chapter, you should be able to:

- Understand the stochastic nature of a forecast and how to treat it in a scientific manner.
- Know the different types of forecasts and their main characteristics.
- Know the different types of forecasting methods and their main characteristics.
- Compute and interpret measures of forecast accuracy.

3.1 Introduction

3.1.1 Fundamental Requirement for Planning

Except for some planning at the operational level, supply chain planning and design involves making decisions now so that supply chain functions can be executed efficiently in the future. Modeling-based supply chain planning and design requires data that describe the future conditions accurately. Otherwise, analytical supply chain design would be futile. These data estimates are typically in the form of predictions and forecasts. Many forecasts and especially medium- and long-term forecasts are prepared by other departments in the organization, such as marketing or product development, rather than by the supply chain or logistics department. However, certain short-term forecasting is performed by logisticians, such as forecasting related to inventory control and individual user demand. In those cases, forecasting future conditions is often achieved by extrapolating the historical observations. The underlying pattern is often seasonal corresponding to the natural seasonality of many human and agricultural activities. The focus of this chapter will be on techniques for such relatively short-term forecasting, which are most often performed by logisticians. An often-used alternative term for these activities is demand planning—specifically tactical and operational demand planning.

Only in a few cases of operational supply chain planning are the activities that have to be performed already known. Examples are the routing and scheduling of

M. Goetschalckx, *Supply Chain Engineering,* International Series in Operations Research & Management Science 161, DOI 10.1007/978-1-4419-6512-7_3, © Springer Science+Business Media, LLC 2011

order pickers through a warehouse to collect customer orders after all orders have been received; the routing and scheduling of delivery trucks after the customer stops and quantities are known; and in manufacturing the scheduling of the assembly operations of computers after the customer orders for certain configurations have been received. In all other cases, the future activities have to estimated or forecasted.

The inherent difficulty of generating accurate predictions for future values, has led to the development of the production planning philosophy that avoids forecasts altogether. Production is only started after the complete order for a product has been received and is thus known with certainty. Such production planning is called *make-to-order* (MTO). The production planning that produces in anticipation of forecasted future demand is called *make-to-stock* (MTS). Even if the production or assembly of the final product is scheduled based on received orders in a MTO framework, the inherent time lags in the supply chain cause the inventory and production of subcomponents to be based on forecasts in a MTS framework.

Forecasting is an essential activity in any business and governmental organization since it provides the basic information for the planning and execution of all operational activities of the organization. In supply chain planning most forecasting is related to forecasting the demands of final and intermediate products on a repetitive basis. The forecast for the final products of an organization determines then the forecasts for intermediate products, parts, raw materials, and personnel.

3.1.2 *Demand Planning Structure*

The goal of demand planning is to predict the future consumption of "products," be it physical products, medical services, restaurant meals, or consumption of utilities such as electricity. Demand planning has to support aggregation and disaggregation along the following three dimensions: product family tree, geography, and planning horizon.

The product family tree is a hierarchical structure relating products to product groups, groups to families, and families to product lines. For example, an individual product or SKU may be a particular model of personal computer with specific processor, video, storage, and memory hardware. A product group may be based on all products with the same processor with different configurations for the other hardware. A product family may be all the product groups intended to be sold to a particular market segment such as the home user or the corporate user. Finally, the product line may be personal computers, which are separated from computer servers or personal digital assistants.

The geographical dimension is also hierarchically structured. It may be divided into areas, regions, countries, and world regions. The time dimension is typically structured in years, seasons or quarters, or months. If necessary it can be specified to the week or day level. Forecast quantities can be assigned to any intersection of product, geography, and time. Such three-dimensional databases grow very quickly in size even for small and mid-sized companies. Powerful database software and computer hardware have reduced the burden of collecting, maintaining, and processing such large amounts of data. A much more difficult problem has been to maintain the internal consistency between various levels and dimensions of the forecast data.

3.1.3 Pattern Classification

When forecasting a particular repetitive activity that is a component of supply chain, the most important requirement for generating high-quality forecasts is a fundamental understanding of the underlying pattern of the activity. Depending on its behavior over time, the underlying pattern can be classified as regular or irregular. If the pattern is regular the future values can be predicted based on past or historical values. Common regular patterns are a constant pattern, a trend pattern, seasonal pattern, or a combination of trend and seasonal pattern. Classic decomposition decomposes the pattern into a trend, seasonal, and random component. As long as the random variations are small compared to the underlying pattern, accurate forecasts can be obtained by popular mathematical forecasting techniques, such as regression and time series analysis. A pattern can also be irregular, when it is a singular occurrence, intermittent, or highly variable. The pattern is said to be "lumpy." Such variables are typically very difficult to forecast with any accuracy using popular mathematical models.

Finally, dependent or derived demand patterns constitute a special case when an independent variable causes predictable behavior for a number of other dependent variables. In this case the value of the demand for the final product is stochastic and forecasted with the techniques described above. But once the demand for the final product is known, the demand for all the subcomponents, raw materials, and resources is known with certainty. The derived demand is usually obtained by recursively exploding the *bill of materials* (BOM) of the final product to all of its individual product components. For example, the forecasted independent demand for a car model causes a dependent demand shifted back in time for the associated car engine. Most popular forecasting techniques are based on the assumptions of independent behavior with a random component. These methods are not applicable for forecasting dependent behavior.

The future logistics activities are subject to the actions of many different organizations in and outside the supply chain and to inherent uncertainty caused by truly random events. Therefore, the forecasting should be a collaborative effort among many groups in the supply chain. Marketing can provide advance estimates of the impact of future promotions and product introductions. The expertise of long-term employees may judge the impact that similar conditions have had in the past. The end result of the forecasting process should a consensus-based forecast that is used for all the planning by all organizations in the supply chain.

3.2   Classification of Forecasting Methods

Forecasting methods can be classified as quantitative or objective versus qualitative or subjective depending on the fact if an explicit model forms the basis of the forecasting method. Quantitative forecasting models can be further divided into causal and time series models.

3.2.1   Subjective or Qualitative Forecasting Methods

Subjective or qualitative forecasting methods use experts, subjective judgment, intuition, or surveys to produce quantitative estimates about the future. The information on which the forecasts are based is typically nonquantitative and subjective. Historical data may not be available or of little relevance to the forecast. The highly subjective nature of the forecast makes it very difficult to validate the accuracy and to standardize the methods. These methods are primarily used to predict the demand for a new product or a product in new areas, the impact of policy changes, or the impact of new technology. They are typically used for medium- to long-range forecasts.

Kurt Hellstrom, president of Ericsson, in an address to Comdex 2000 (*PC Magazine*, 16 Jan. 2000, p. 72) made the following statement regarding the adaptation of cell phones by consumers, which illustrates the difficulty of making long-term, strategic forecasts: "*Analysts predicted in 1980 that one million mobile phones would be used worldwide by the year 2000. They were wrong by 599 million.*" Saffo (2007) describes six rules for effective forecasting that are applicable to such strategic forecasts. His second rule advises to determine where the forecast is located on the S curve, which is a curve depicting the rate of change. In general, this curve is shaped as the curve of the cumulative normal distribution. An example of this curve is shown in the appendix on standard distributions. If the curve is extended to include the eventual declining use of the product or service, then it becomes the traditional life cycle graph. The early adoption corresponds to the bottom nearly horizontal section of the S, the explosive growth is represented by the vertical section, and the mature state of the product corresponds to the top nearly horizontal section of the S. The difficulty and one of the keys to effective forecasting identified by Saffo is to recognize where the current situation is located with respect to the inflection points of the life cycle curve.

The Delphi method is often used in qualitative forecasting. The Delphi method is an iterative procedure where forecasts are collected from a number of experts in the area and systematically reduced to a consensus forecast. During the next iteration, a statistical summary, usually presented anonymously, of the forecasts made during the previous iteration is provided to the experts. The experts are then asked if they want to revise their forecast. The goal of the Delphi method is to generate a consensus forecast from the group of experts. After a number of iterations the final forecast is generated by averaging the forecasts of the individual experts. According to Linstone and Turoff (1975), the Delphi method was originally developed at the RAND Corporation by Dalkey and Helmer (1951).

3.2.2 Quantitative or Objective Forecasting Methods

Objective or quantitative forecasting methods rely on a formalized underlying model to make predictions. They are divided into time series and causal methods.

3.2.2.1 Time Series Forecasting Models

Time series analysis is a forecasting method based on the fundamental assumption that future estimates are based on prior, historical values of the same variable. This implies that the historical pattern exhibited by the variable to be forecasted will extend into the future. In addition, it is implicitly assumed that historical data are available. The only independent variable in a forecasting model based on time series analysis is the time period. The future value of the variable is equal to the underlying pattern plus a random component. It is also assumed that the expected value of the random component is equal to zero and that the random component is normally distributed with variance σ^2. In other words, if D_t is the value of the variable in period t, Y_t is the value of the underlying pattern in period t, and ε_t is the random component in period t, then

$$D_t = Y_t + \varepsilon_t \tag{3.1}$$

$$\varepsilon_t = N(0, \sigma^2) \tag{3.2}$$

Time series forecasting methods are mostly used to forecast variables for the short to intermediate term. As such, time series methods are some of the forecasting techniques most often used by logisticians. The generic forecast model for time series computes the forecast F as a weighted linear combination of the past observations D using weights a,

$$F_{t+1} = \sum_{j=0}^{\infty} a_{t-j} D_{t-j} \tag{3.3}$$

Time series models and forecasting methods can be further divided into static models and adaptive models. A static method assumes that model parameters—such as the offset, trend, and seasonality factors and indicated by the a parameters in the previous formula—do not change during the forecasting process while new demand values become known. Equivalently, static methods do not change the underlying pattern based on new demand observations. The model parameters are estimated based on historical values and then the same values are used to compute all future forecasts. Examples of static forecasting methods are the average and regression. In adaptive forecasting, the values of the model parameters are updated after each demand observation becomes known. Examples of adaptive forecasting methods are moving averages and all the variants of exponential smoothing. Because it is the main forecasting technique used in the planning of logistic activities and supply chains, time series analysis is discussed in detail in the next chapter.

3.2.2.2 Box–Jenkins Methods

In the discussions and development so far, it has been assumed that the value of the forecasted variable only depends on the model parameters and historical data plus a random component. However, time series may exist where the values of the forecasted variable are related or correlated from period to period. In this case the data is said to be autocorrelated and formula (3.1) is no longer valid for such time series. Box and Jenkins (1970) developed a group of methods that are able to handle such autocorrelated data, such as the autoregressive integrated moving average, or ARIMA, method. The discussion of these advanced forecasting methods is beyond the scope of this book and the reader is referred to the book by Box and Jenkins.

Advanced forecasting methods such as the methods developed by Box and Jenkins are very powerful tools provided the forecaster has an extensive understanding of the underlying process and a large number of prior observations is available. It is recommended that no less than 72 observations be used to start the forecasting procedure. Because of their power, flexibility, and ease of use, the advanced methods can easily generate incorrect forecasts. It is always the responsibility of the forecaster to ensure that the assumptions used by a forecasting method are consistent with the real-world process, but this task is even more mandatory and important for advanced methods because of the complexity of the underlying assumptions. These advanced forecasting techniques can be used when there exists extensive historical data and to forecast the immediate future. Examples are forecasting the price of a stock on the exchange for the next 15 min. or forecasting the number of lightning strikes in a state for the next 10 min.

3.2.2.3 Causal Forecasting Models

A second major category of forecasting models consists of causal models. The basic assumption for a causal model is that the future value of the forecasted variable can be expressed as a mathematical function of the known current values of a set of different variables. For example, the historical sales of a product combined with the historical breakdown rates for this product allow the forecast of the number of breakdowns and required service parts during the coming year. Causal forecasting methods are often used in predicting future economic activity and future social and life science trends.

The known variables in the causal model are also called *leading indicators*, since they occur before or lead the forecasted variable and indicate the behavior of the forecasted variable. One such leading indicator often used in predicting supply chain activity is the purchased quantity of corrugated cardboard boxes. When companies expect an increase in sales, they purchase more shipping supplies such as cardboard boxes. Causal models can be quite good in predicting major changes and trends and are often used in the medium and long-range forecasts.

The major difficulty in applying causal models is of course the development of accurate cause-and-effect relationships, since the true causal relationship is often much more complex than the causal model. Causal models based on regression and economic techniques typically have substantial forecasting errors.

The causal relationship in general is given by the next formula, where Y is the forecasted variable computed in function of a number of know variables X.

$$Y = f(X_1, X_2, \dots X_N) \tag{3.4}$$

Econometric models are a subclass of causal models that use only linear causal relationships, as illustrated in the following expression.

$$Y = a_1 X_1 + a_2 X_2 + \dots a_N X_N \tag{3.5}$$

3.3 Forecast Quality and Performance Measures

3.3.1 Forecast Error and Forecast Performance

The *forecast error* is defined as the algebraic difference between the actual realized value for a particular time period and the forecast. The term *residual* is also used to indicate the difference between the observed value and the modeled or forecasted value. The forecasted value may have been computed during the prior period or in an earlier period.

The corresponding formulas to compute the forecast error are given next:

$$e_t = D_t - F_{t-\tau, t}$$
$$e_t = D_t - F_t \tag{3.6}$$

Expressions for the standard error of the forecast have been derived for static models such as regression and are incorporated in statistical packages and spreadsheets. The standard error for adaptive forecasting methods most often is estimated based on the calculation of the *root mean squared error* (RMSE) or the *mean absolute deviation* (MAD) of the series of forecasts made over time. These performance measures are defined below. Obviously it is desirable that the forecast error for a series of forecasts is as close to zero as possible.

A number of quality measures for forecasts have been defined in function of the forecast errors. The simplest measure sums the forecast errors to compute the *mean error* (ME). The sum of the forecast errors is also called the *bias*. The definition of the mean error has the disadvantage that large positive and negative forecast errors in different periods offset each other and give the false impression of a high-quality forecast because the mean error is small. To overcome this deficiency, the MAD computes the average of the absolute value of the forecast error. The *mean squared error* (MSE) method computes the average value of the squared forecast error. The MSE method also avoids offsetting positive and negative errors. However, the mean squared error has different units and dimensions than the forecast error, which makes its interpretation more difficult. To express the measure of the quality of the forecast error in the same units as the forecasted variable, the square root of the MSE is computed. This measure is called the root mean squared error (RMSE) and is equal to the standard deviation of the forecast error. The formulas for the various measures of forecast quality are given next:

$$ME = \frac{1}{n} \sum_{t=1}^{n} e_t \tag{3.7}$$

$$MAD = \frac{1}{n} \sum_{t=1}^{n} |e_t| \tag{3.8}$$

$$MSE = \frac{1}{n} \sum_{t=1}^{n} e_t^2 \tag{3.9}$$

$$RMSE = \sqrt{\frac{1}{n} \sum_{t=1}^{n} e_t^2} \tag{3.10}$$

All of the above quality measures are in absolute units, in other words, in the same units as the variable that is forecasted or those units squared. For example, if the units of the forecasted variable were changed from feet to meters, the absolute quality measures defined above would be roughly divided by three and the MSE would even be roughly divided by nine, while in reality the forecast quality has not changed at all. Therefore, many times it is more intuitive to express the forecast error as a percentage of the forecasted value. This is a called a relative forecast error. The quality measure most often used in function of the relative forecast error is the *mean absolute percentage error* (MAPE):

$$MAPE = \left[\frac{1}{n} \sum_{t=1}^{n} \left| \frac{e_t}{D_t} \right| \right] \cdot 100 \tag{3.11}$$

The MAPE computations can cause numerical difficulties if the realized value of the variable that is forecasted becomes equal to zero or very close to zero. If it is anticipated that the value of the forecast variable may become close to zero, then the MAPE quality measure should not be used.

Finally, the *tracking signal* is the ratio of the bias divided by the mean absolute deviation. If the tracking signal falls outside an interval centered at zero, then this is a signal that the forecast model is biased and the validity of the forecasting model or method should be investigated. The bias and tracking signal are discussed in further detail in the section on forecast monitoring.

3.3.2 Confidence Interval

The forecast F_t has a single numerical value and is called a *point estimate* or point forecast. The probability that the forecasted value F_t for the variable under consideration will be exactly equal to the expected value of the forecasted variable Y_t is very small. The point estimate is in effect the mean or expected value of a distribution of possible forecasted values. Hence, it is more useful to replace the point forecast with an interval forecast. An interval for which we can assert with a specified degree of certainty that it contains the expected value of the forecasted variable is called a *confidence interval*. Typically, a claim is made that with a probability of $1 - \alpha$ the interval

$$\left[F_t - z_{\alpha/2} \cdot \frac{\sigma}{\sqrt{n}}, F_t + z_{\alpha/2} \cdot \frac{\sigma}{\sqrt{n}} \right] \tag{3.12}$$

contains the expected value Y_t, where $z_{\alpha/2}$ is derived from the normal distribution. Since the expected value of the forecasted variable is either inside the above interval or not, speaking of a probability in this context seems inappropriate. What is really indicated is that in repeated sampling α percent of confidence intervals computed with the above formula will contain the expected value of the forecasted variable. Although the expected value of the forecasted variable will never be known nor will it be known if this expected value fell inside the computed interval, we can be assured that the method used to compute the interval is α percent reliable, that is, it is expected to work in α percent of the time.

The computation of the confidence interval requires the determination of the *standard deviation* of the random component of the forecasted variable. Again, since the standard deviation of the random component of the forecasted variable is not known, the forecast error is used as an estimate of the random component.

For static forecasting models, the derivation of the standard error is well established. The *sum of squared errors* (SSE), also called the *residual sum of squares* (RSS), is computed as

$$SSE = \sum_N (D_t - F_t)^2 = \sum_N e_t^2 \tag{3.13}$$

Under the assumption that the e_t's are uncorrelated random variables with mean equal to zero and common variance σ^2 an unbiased estimate of σ^2 is obtained by dividing SSE by its degrees of freedom, where the degrees of freedom is equal to the number of observations minus the number of parameters in the model. For the constant pattern model the number of parameters is one; for the linear trend model the number of parameters is two; for the additive seasonal model with cycle length P the number of parameters is $P+1$. The standard error is equal to the square root of the residual mean square. In the following formulas the number of parameters is indicated by k:

$$se = \sqrt{\frac{SEE}{N-k}} = \sqrt{\frac{\sum e_t^2}{N-k}} = \sqrt{\frac{\sum_{t=1}^{N}(D_t - F_t)^2}{N-k}} \qquad (3.14)$$

Note that this formula implies that the mean of the forecast error is assumed to be equal to zero. The built-in formulas in computer spreadsheets for computing the standard deviation of a sample will compute the sample mean and then will use this sample mean in the computation of the standard deviation. The formulas will then yield a smaller standard deviation if the computed sample mean is not zero. This implies that you cannot use either the built-in STDEV or the STDEVP functions of the Excel spreadsheet software. One way to compute the standard deviation in Excel spreadsheets is to use the following built-in functions

$$se = SQRT(SUMSQ(e_1 : e_N)/(COUNT(e_1 : e_N) - k)). \qquad (3.15)$$

The $1-\alpha$ percent confidence interval for a large number of observations can then be computed as

$$F_t \pm z_{\alpha/2} \cdot se_{F_t} \qquad (3.16)$$

The values of z in function of the probability $1-\alpha$ can be computed with the Excel function $NORMSINV(1-\alpha/2)$. The value of z for a number of commonly used probabilities is given in Table 3.1. Further information can be found in reference texts on probability and statistics for engineers, such as Hayter (1996).

Table 3.1 Confidence intervals for the standard normal distribution

$(1-\alpha)$	$\alpha/2$	z	$(1-\alpha)$	$\alpha/2$	z
0.5000	0.2500	0.6745	0.9250	0.0375	1.7805
0.6000	0.2000	0.8416	0.9500	0.0250	1.9600
0.6827	0.1587	1.0000	0.9545	0.0228	2.0000
0.7000	0.1500	1.0364	0.9750	0.0125	2.2414
0.7500	0.1250	1.1503	0.9800	0.0100	2.3263
0.8000	0.1000	1.2816	0.9900	0.0050	2.5758
0.8500	0.0750	1.4395	0.9950	0.0025	2.8070
0.9000	0.0500	1.6449	0.9973	0.0013	3.0000

3.3.3   Forecast Monitoring

3.3.3.1   Bias

After a forecast model has been constructed, it has to be monitored carefully to verify that model has not become invalid because of changes in the underlying data pattern. The forecasting models assume that the long-range expected value of the forecast error should be zero, since it corresponds to the random component in the data series. If the model consistently forecasts values that are either larger (or smaller) than the observed values, the expected value of the forecast will be different from zero and the forecast model is said to be *biased*. A valid forecast model should be unbiased. One way to determine if bias is present is to plot the forecast errors along the time axis. The points corresponding to the errors should be randomly distributed above and below the zero level:

$$bias_t = \sum_{i=1}^{t} e_i \tag{3.17}$$

3.3.3.2   Tracking Signal

A more systematic way to monitor a forecasting model is the tracking signal. Several variants of the tracking signal exist, but all of them compute the ratio of weighted algebraic sum of the forecast errors divided by the weighted sum of the absolute value of the forecast errors. This ratio should be close the zero. One way to compute the tracking signal is given as

$$ts_t = \frac{bias_t}{MAD_t} = \frac{\sum_{i=1}^{t} e_i}{\frac{1}{t} \sum_{i=1}^{t} |e_i|} \tag{3.18}$$

A large positive or negative value of the tracking signal indicates a biased forecast, which in turn indicates that the forecast model is no longer valid. There exists considerable discussion on what the acceptable boundary values of the tracking signal should be. Obviously, the numerical values of the acceptable extreme values depend on the exact method of computing the tracking signal. It is important not to use the extreme values of one definition with a different computation of the tracking signal. For the above variant of the tracking signal, extreme values of ± 6 have been suggested.

   An example of a large positive tracking signal occurs when the demand has a positive growth trend and a forecasting method for a constant pattern, such as moving averages, is used. Because the trend is not included in the forecasting model, the forecasted values will tend to systematically underestimate the real demand and the forecast errors will tend to be positive. After a sufficient number of periods, the tracking signal will become more and more positive and fall outside the allowable interval, which is a signal that the current forecasting model or method needs to be reevaluated.

Some software packages may automatically adjust the smoothing factors used in exponential smoothing procedures if the absolute value of the tracking signal becomes too large. This is called *adaptive smoothing*. Exponential smoothing methods are described in detail in the chapter on time series analysis. Adaptive smoothing gives the exponential smoothing forecasting methods additional power, but should be used with care since they change the responsiveness and stability of the forecasting method.

3.4   Forecasting Software

There exists a large variety of software applications for forecasting. Yurkiewicz (2003) provides a survey of the capabilities of such software packages. Spreadsheets such as Microsoft Excel also include forecasting functionality through a variety of statistical functions and its analysis tools.

3.5   Summary

Forecasting of future conditions is an essential planning activity for almost any organization. Strategic, long-range forecasts are based on qualitative data or quantitative data with very large uncertainties. Long-range forecasts may be obtained with qualitative or very simple quantitative forecasting methods. Shorter-term tactical and operational forecasts are usually based on historical data. Many powerful and highly mathematical forecasting techniques exist, such as regression, time series analysis, and forecasting methods for autocorrelated data. However, the most important requirement for the generation of a high-quality forecast is an understanding of the underlying data pattern of the forecasted variable. The correct forecasting method can then be selected for this underlying pattern. Applying correctly the wrong forecasting method for a data pattern will only generated wrong forecasts. One simple method to understand the underlying pattern is to graph the historical values over time. Since the underlying data pattern is almost never fully understood or remains unchanged for extended periods of time, most forecasts will have significant errors. Hence, it does not make much sense to report only the expected value of the forecasted variable. Based on the root mean square forecast error, confidence intervals can be established, which provide much more meaningful forecast information. A simple method to judge the quality of the forecast is to graph the forecast errors over time.

The generation of a high-quality forecast requires an understanding of the underlying pattern, the application of the correct method for that pattern, and reporting of the results with their stochastic characteristics. The forecasting results generated by the blind application of very sophisticated forecasting techniques should be highly suspect. The farther in the future the forecasts are, the easier it is to make very large forecasting errors.

In most supply chain planning, forecasting cannot be avoided because it describes the future conditions in which the supply chain has to operate. So logistics professionals should forecast with great care and avoid over-confidence in the forecast accuracy. This indicates that planning methods should be able to deal explicitly with uncertainty and the supply chain solutions should be robust.

3.6 Exercises

True/False Questions

1. Time series forecasting attempts to predict the future value of a variable based on the currently observed values of different variables (T/F) _____.
2. ARIMA models are used for forecasting autocorrelated data (T/F) _____.
3. Using forecasting techniques based on time series analysis, different forecasters will arrive at the same forecast if they use the same data (T/F) _____.
4. The confidence interval of a demand forecast is a critical datum when judging the quality of the short-term forecast of the future value of the demand (T/F) _____.
5. When the data are autocorrelated, they are assumed to be independent samples of a probability distribution (T/F) _____.
6. A professionally prepared forecast will include the expected value and a confidence interval for the forecast (T/F) _____.
7. A forecast of the weekly demand for products in a grocery store tends to be more accurate, as measured by the coefficient of variation, than the forecast for the daily demand for the same products (T/F) _____.
8. Given that all other parameters remain the same, a larger mean squared forecast error corresponds to a larger confidence interval (T/F) _____.
9. A forecast for the sales in a home improvement store of batteries of a single manufacturer tends to be more accurate, as measured by the coefficient of variation, than the forecast for the sales of batteries of all manufacturers combined (T/F) _____.

References

Ballou, R. H. (1998). *Business logistics management* (4th ed., Chap. 9). Englewood Cliffs: Prentice-Hall.

Box, G. E., & Jenkins, G. M. (1970). *Time series analysis, forecasting and control*. San Francisco: Holden Day.

Brockwell, P., & Davis, R. (1996). *Introduction to time series and forecasting*. New York: Springer.

Dalkey, N. C., & Helmer, O. (1951). The use of experts for the estimation of bombing requirements: a project Delphi experiment. Rand Corporation Report RM-727-PR, November 1951.

Gross, C. W., & Peterson, R. T. (1983). *Business forecasting* (2nd ed.). New York: Wiley.

Hayter, A. (1996). *Probability and statistics for engineers and scientists*. Boston: PWS Publishing Company.

Linstone, H., & Turoff, M. (Eds.). (1975). *The Delphi method: Techniques and applications*. London: Addison-Wesley.

Montgomery, D. C., & Johnson, L. A. (1976). *Forecasting and time series analysis*. New York: McGraw-Hill.

Montgomery, D., Peck, E., & Vining, G. (2001). *Introduction to linear regression analysis*. New York: Wiley.

Nahmias, S. (2000). *Production and operations analysis* (4th ed., Chap. 2). Boston: McGraw-Hill.

Saffo, P. (2007). Six rules for effective forecasting. *Harvard Business Review, 85*(7/8), 122–131.

Wilson, J. H., & Keating, B. (1990). *Business forecasting*. Homewood: Richard D. Irwin.

Yurkiewicz, J. (2003). Forecasting software survey. *ORMS Today*, pp. 44–51.

Chapter 4
Time Series Analysis

Learning Objectives After you have studied this chapter, you should be able to:

- Understand pattern decomposition of, and know the major patterns for time series variables.
- Match the appropriate forecasting method with the pattern of a time series variable.
- Know how to apply simple methods for time series forecasting such as moving averages and the three levels of exponential smoothing.
- Compute and interpret measures of forecast accuracy.

4.1 Time Series Characteristics

Recall that in the previous chapter objective or quantitative forecasting methods were defined as forecasting methods that rely on a formalized underlying model to make predictions. They are further divided into time series and causal methods. Time series analysis is a forecasting method based on the fundamental assumption that future estimates are based on prior, historical values of the same variable. This implies that the historical pattern exhibited by the variable to be forecasted will extend into the future. In addition, it is implicitly assumed that historical data are available. The only independent variable in a forecasting model based on time series analysis is the time period. Time series forecasting methods are mostly used to forecast variables for the short to intermediate term. As such, time series methods are some of the forecasting techniques most often used by logisticians and are developed in further detail in this chapter.

M. Goetschalckx, *Supply Chain Engineering,* International Series in Operations Research & Management Science 161,
DOI 10.1007/978-1-4419-6512-7_4, © Springer Science+Business Media, LLC 2011

4.1.1   Time Series

A *time series* is a set of observations x_t each being recorded at a specific time t. In a continuous-time time series, the observations are made continuously during a specified time interval. In a discrete-time time series, the observations are made at a discrete set of times. Often the observations are made at a fixed time interval and the time periods are renamed and scaled to the set of integer numbers $1, 2, ..., N$.

It is assumed that the value of the series variable in a particular period is equal to the sum of an underlying deterministic pattern and a random component. Furthermore, it is assumed that the expected value of the random component is equal to zero and that the random component is normally distributed with variance σ^2. In other words, if D_t is the series variable in period t, Y_t is the value of the underlying pattern in period t, and ε_t is the random component in period t, then

$$D_t = Y_t + \varepsilon_t \tag{4.1}$$

$$\varepsilon_t = N\left(0, \sigma^2\right) \tag{4.2}$$

$$E\left[D_t\right] = Y_t \tag{4.3}$$

$$Var\left[D_t\right] = Var\left[\varepsilon_t\right] = \sigma^2 \tag{4.4}$$

The pattern is also called the *systematic component*. When forecasting a time series, the first step, as always, should be to determine the underlying pattern of the variable, since it is this pattern that is assumed to extend into the future. Plotting the time series data allows one to determine if a trend, a seasonal component, a long-term cycle, any sudden changes, or any outliers are present. If sudden changes are present, different models may be constructed for each of the homogeneous segments of the series. If outliers are present, they should be further investigated to determine if there is any justification for discarding them. For example, an observation may have been recorded incorrectly or temporary promotion may have significantly increased customer demand.

Time series analysis uses the historical observations to determine the parameters of the underlying pattern. Specifically, the generic forecast model for time series computes the forecast F as a weighted linear combination of the past observations D using weights a. Depending on the assumed pattern and on the specific forecasting method different values of a are used.

$$F_{t+1} = \sum_{j=0}^{\infty} a_{t-j} D_{t-j} \tag{4.5}$$

Time series models and forecasting methods can be further divided into static models and adaptive models. A static method assumes that model parameters, such as the offset, trend, and seasonality factors, do not change during the forecasting process while new demand values become known. Equivalently, static methods do not change the underlying pattern based on new demand observations. The model parameters are estimated based on historical values and then the same values are used to compute all future forecasts. Examples of static forecasting methods are the average and regression. In adaptive forecasting, the values of the model parameters are updated after each demand observation becomes known. Examples of adaptive forecasting methods are moving averages and all the variants of exponential smoothing.

Any forecasting method for the underlying pattern can be interpreted as a low-pass filter that filters out the high-frequency oscillations of the random component. See Brockwell and Davis (1996) for an in-depth treatment of time series and forecasting from this point of view.

Following are simple but effective forecasting techniques for the most common data patterns, which are the constant, trend, and seasonal data patterns.

4.2 Constant Data Pattern

4.2.1 Constant Data Pattern Characteristics

A variable following a constant data pattern is assumed to have an unvarying or invariant expected value. This corresponds to a horizontal line in the time series graph. The actual realizations, which include the random component, are scattered around this horizontal line. The schematic of a constant data pattern is shown in Fig. 4.1.

A constant pattern has a single constant parameter, which is its mean μ. The forecasted values for all future periods are identical. The computation of the standard

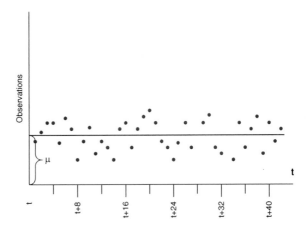

Fig. 4.1 Schematic of a time series following a constant pattern

deviation of the forecast error for static methods uses $N-1$ in the denominator since there is one model parameter. Since the mean of the forecast error is assumed to be zero, the computation of the standard deviation of the forecast error for adaptive methods uses N in the denominator, where N is the number of observations after the initialization of the model. This is equivalent to the computation of the *root mean squared error* (RMSE).

The value of N is different for the static and dynamic models, given the same number of historical observations. For static models, N is equal to the number of all historical observations. For dynamic models, historical observations are divided into an initialization phase and a training phase. For the dynamic models N does not include the observations in the initialization phase:

$$D_t = \mu_t + \varepsilon_t \tag{4.6}$$

$$F_{t+1} = F_{t+\tau} \qquad \forall \tau \tag{4.7}$$

$$\text{Static}: s_e = \sqrt{\frac{\sum_{t=1}^{N}(F_t - D_t)^2}{N-1}} = \sqrt{\frac{\sum_{t=1}^{N} e_t^2}{N-1}} \tag{4.8}$$

$$\text{Dynamic}: s_e = \sqrt{\frac{\sum_{t=1}^{N}(F_t - D_t)^2}{N}} = \sqrt{\frac{\sum_{t=1}^{N} e_t^2}{N}} \tag{4.9}$$

The forecasted values are illustrated in Fig. 4.2. Since the underlying pattern is assumed to be constant, the forecasted values for all the future periods are identical.

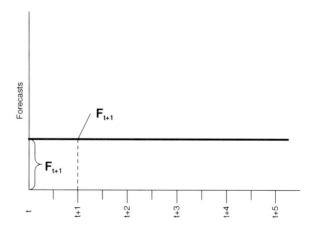

Fig. 4.2 Constant pattern forecasts

4.2.2 Forecasting Methods for a Constant Data Pattern

4.2.2.1 Naïve Method

Since the underlying pattern is assumed to be constant, the naïve method sets the next value of the forecasted variable equal to the current, last known value. This is clearly the simplest adaptive forecasting method.

$$F_{t+1} = D_t \tag{4.10}$$

4.2.2.2 Average and Moving Averages

Some of the simplest methods to forecast a variable with a constant data pattern are based on eliminating the random component by averaging the past observations, since the expected value of the random component is equal to zero. Several variants exist depending on the importance or weight attributed to the historical observations.

The *average* procedure assigns an equal weight to all prior observations:

$$F_{t+1} = \frac{1}{N} \sum_{i=0}^{N-1} D_{t-i} \tag{4.11}$$

where N is the total number of available observations for this variable.

One of the disadvantages of the average method is that the oldest observations have an equal weight in determining the forecast compared to more recent observations.

The *moving averages* procedure assigns an equal weight to a limited set of the most recent observations. The number of observations in this set is called the *interval* and is denoted by N. The weight of each observation is then equal to $1/N$ and the sum of all the weights is equal to one:

$$F_{t+1} = \frac{1}{N} \sum_{i=0}^{N-1} D_{t-i} \tag{4.12}$$

The *weighted moving averages* method assigns an unequal weight to a limited set of most recent observations. The sum of the weights is equal to one. Any observations outside the set can be thought of as having a weight equal to zero:

$$F_{t+1} = \sum_{i=0}^{N-1} w_i D_{t-i}$$
$$\sum_{i=0}^{N-1} w_i = 1 \tag{4.13}$$

The weighted moving averages method requires that, in addition to the interval N, the N different weights must also be determined. The weighted moving averages method may be used to forecast a variable with a growing or declining trend or with a seasonal behavior. Exponential smoothing methods for trend and seasonal patterns are also applicable in those cases and require fewer parameters or are easier to apply. As a consequence, the exponential smoothing methods are used more often than weighted moving averages methods.

4.2.2.3   Simple Exponential Smoothing

One of the most used methods for short-term forecasting of a variable with an underlying constant pattern is *exponential smoothing*. To differentiate this variant of exponential smoothing from later variants used for trend and seasonal patterns, this variant is also called *simple exponential smoothing* and the collection of all the variants is then called exponential smoothing. This nomenclature will be used from now on. Exponential smoothing has several significant advantages. It is mathematically simple, it requires a minimum amount of data, and it is self-adaptive to changes in the underlying data pattern.

In exponential smoothing, the past observations are not given equal weights. The more recent observations are given more weight than earlier observations and it will be shown that the weight decreases by a constant factor when going back further into the past.

There exist several equivalent expressions for the computation of the forecast in period $t+1$ based on the observed demand during period t and the forecast for time period t. The constant α in these expressions is commonly called the exponential *smoothing constant* and $(1-\alpha)$ is referred to as the *damping factor*. The impact of the most recent observation is dampened by the most recent forecast, which incorporates all the previous observations. Equivalently, the new forecast is equal to the previous forecast plus a smoothing term based on the forecast error. In this formula, the forecast for the previous period is adjusted or corrected based on its error with respect to the most recent data observation. The smoothing constant has a value strictly between 0 and 1. So the new forecast can also be interpreted as a convex combination of the most recent observation and the most recent forecast:

$$F_{t+1} = \alpha D_t + (1 - \alpha)F_t = F_t + \alpha (D_t - F_t) \qquad (4.14)$$

The following initial values are typically used to start the forecasting process. It should be noted that all exponential smoothing methods require a training phase after initialization and that the importance of the initialization values decreases over time as the process is used repeatedly:

$$\begin{aligned} F_2 &= D_1 \\ F_1 &= D_1 \end{aligned} \qquad (4.15)$$

By repeated substitution of the previous forecasts F_t with expression (4.14), we obtain the following expression for the next forecast. It shows that the weight for previous demand observations decreases geometrically with the constant factor $(1 - \alpha)$:

$$F_{t+1} = \sum_{i=0}^{t-1} \alpha(1 - \alpha)^i D_{t-i} + (1 - \alpha)^t D_1 \quad t \geq 1 \tag{4.16}$$

The limit of this expression for a large number of prior observations is defined for α strictly between zero and one and is equal to

$$F_{t+1} = \sum_{i=0}^{\infty} \alpha(1 - \alpha)^i D_{t-i} \tag{4.17}$$

Since α is strictly smaller than one, the sum of all the weights in the geometric series is defined and equal to one. The next forecast is thus a convex combination of all the previous observations.

$$\sum_{i=0}^{\infty} \alpha(1 - \alpha)^i = \frac{\alpha}{1 - (1 - \alpha)} = 1 \quad \alpha < 1 \tag{4.18}$$

using

$$\sum_{i=0}^{\infty} a^i = \frac{1}{1 - a} \quad a < 1 \tag{4.19}$$

However, we do not need to store all previous observations, since the impact of all previous observations is encapsulated in the value of the previous forecast F_t.

Choosing the appropriate value of the exponential smoothing constant requires a degree of judgment based on the understanding of the behavior of the underlying data pattern to balance the responsiveness versus the stability of the forecasting model. A higher value of the smoothing constant assigns more weight to the most recent observations. This allows the forecasting model to respond more quickly to changes in the underlying data pattern. However, if the value of the smoothing constant is increased too much then the model will start tracking the changes in the random component of the time series rather than in the underlying pattern. In this case, the forecast is said to be nervous.

Many times, a more stable forecast is desirable, which implies a smaller value of the smoothing constant. Low values of the smoothing constant provide very "stable" forecasts that are not likely to be influenced by the randomness of the time series. However, the more the smoothing constant is decreased the longer it takes for the forecasting model to adjust to fundamental changes in the underlying data pattern. Higher values of the smoothing constant may be appropriate if the underlying data pattern is likely to change more quickly such as for introduction of a new product, discontinuing of a product, start of a recession or economic boom, or a promotional campaign. These correspond to the inflection points of the S curve described in Saffo (2007).

However, if one expects that the underlying pattern is fundamentally a trend or seasonal pattern, the exponential smoothing methods appropriate for those cases should be used rather than a larger smoothing constant for the constant data pattern. Those exponential smoothing methods are discussed later in this chapter. The typical range of the exponential smoothing constant is [0.2, 0.4]. The exponential smoothing function implemented in the Excel spreadsheet uses 0.3 as the default value of the smoothing constant. If sufficient historical data is available, the smoothing constant can be chosen so that forecast error for the historical period is minimized. In this case, the smoothing constant is set to the value that minimizes the sum of squared errors over the historical period.

Assume that we want start forecasting the sales of a product. The underlying sales pattern for this product is assumed to be constant. The sales for period 1 were 62 units. Since this is the startup period, a smoothing constant of 0.4 was selected. The forecast for period 2 is 62 units, but the observed sales equaled 59 units. The forecast for the sales during the third period using exponential smoothing is then

$$F_3 = 0.4 \cdot 59 + (1 - 0.4) \cdot 62 = 60.8$$

The observed sales for period 3 are 68 and the forecast for sales during the fourth period is then

$$F_4 = 0.4 \cdot 68 + (1 - 0.4) \cdot 60.8 = 63.68$$

An example comparing the various forecasting methods for a constant underlying data pattern is given at the end of this section on the constant pattern.

4.2.2.4 Comparison of the Moving Averages and Exponential Smoothing Methods

The moving averages and exponential smoothing methods can be compared with respect to their treatment of outliers, data storage requirements, and responsiveness to changes. In the moving averages method an outlier is included in the average calculation with constant weight equal to $(1/N)$ until after N periods it is removed abruptly from the average calculation. In the exponential smoothing method the influence or weight of an outlier is systematically and gradually decreased but theoretically it never is removed from the calculations. In practice however, its influence or weight becomes so small that it becomes negligible.

The moving averages method must store an ordered list of N values for each forecasted variable and a method must be implemented to remove the oldest value and substitute it with the latest observation. The simple exponential smoothing method requires that the single value of the previous forecast is stored for each forecasted variable. While the differences in storage requirements and in the complexity of the update calculations are small for a single variable, they become significant when forecasting many hundreds of thousands of variables such as the demand in grocery or discount stores.

Both the moving averages and the simple exponential smoothing methods use a single parameter to control the responsiveness of the forecasting method to the changes in the observed values. One way to establish a relationship between the interval of the moving averages method and the smoothing constant of the simple exponential smoothing method is compute the average weighted "age" of the observations on which the forecast is based.

For the moving average method, the forecast is based on N observations with equal weight and with ages of $1, 2, \ldots, N$ periods. The *average weighted age* is then

$$\overline{a_{MA}} = \sum_{i=1}^{N} \frac{i}{N} = \frac{N+1}{2} \tag{4.20}$$

using

$$\sum_{i=1}^{N} i = \frac{N(N+1)}{2} \tag{4.21}$$

For the exponential smoothing method, the forecast is based on all the prior observations with geometrically declining weight. In the limit, the average weighted age is then

$$\overline{a_{ES}} = \sum_{i=1}^{\infty} i \cdot \alpha(1-\alpha)^{i-1} = \frac{1}{\alpha} \tag{4.22}$$

Using the following (Muther 1977, p. 357, or other tables of Z-transforms),

$$\sum_{i=1}^{\infty} i a^{i} = \frac{a}{(1-a)^2} \quad a < 1 \tag{4.23}$$

Making the average weighted age of both methods equal yields the following relationship between the smoothing constant and the interval length.

$$\frac{N+1}{2} = \frac{1}{\alpha} \tag{4.24}$$

Either constant can then be computed from the other with one of the following two formulas

$$\alpha = \frac{2}{N+1} \tag{4.25}$$

$$N = \frac{2-\alpha}{\alpha} \tag{4.26}$$

Table 4.1 Equivalent
parameters for moving
averages and exponential
smoothing

N	α	N	α
2	0.67	8	0.22
3	0.50	9	0.20
4	0.40	10	0.18
5	0.33	11	0.17
6	0.29	12	0.15
7	0.25		

The equivalent exponential smoothing constant for a number of interval lengths
of the moving averages method are shown in Table 4.1. Hence, a highly reactive
exponential smoothing constant of 0.4 is equivalent to a moving averages method
with an interval of 4 if we want the two methods to have the same average age of
data. Similarly, a more stable exponential smoothing constant of 0.2 is equivalent to
a moving averages method with an interval of 9.

4.2.2.5 Constant Pattern Forecasting Example

In this example we will determine the sales forecast for the next month of a product, which is assumed to have a constant sales pattern. The available data are the
monthly sales values for the past year. The numerical data are shown in Fig. 4.3 and
the graph of the historical data is shown in Fig. 4.4.

We will use four methods to forecast the next value based on the historical data:
moving averages with an interval of 2, denoted by MA(2); moving averages with an
interval of 4, denoted by MA(4); simple exponential smoothing with a smoothing con-

Period	Sales
1	62
2	59
3	68
4	37
5	48
6	38
7	60
8	53
9	50
10	46
11	49
12	41
13	
mean	50.92
std dev	9.83

Fig. 4.3 Historical data for
the constant pattern example

Fig. 4.4 Graph of the historical data for the constant pattern example

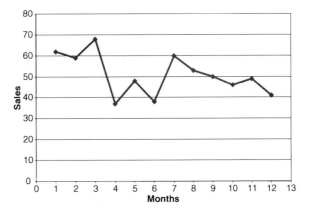

stant of 0.2, denoted by ES(0.2); and exponential smoothing with a smoothing constant of 0.4, denoted by ES(0.4). One of the alternative methods for the moving averages methods to start up their process is to use partial data during the initial periods of the forecasting process. The forecasts were computed with the formulas introduced above and collected in a spreadsheet, which is shown in Fig. 4.5. The graph of the forecasts is shown in Fig. 4.6. The computations for the first forecast are given next in detail:

$$F_3^{MA(2)} = \frac{62 + 59}{2} = 60.50$$

$$F_5^{MA(4)} = \frac{62 + 59 + 68 + 37}{4} = 56.50$$

$$F_3^{ES(0.2)} = 0.2 \cdot 59 + 0.8 \cdot 62 = 61.40$$

$$F_3^{ES(0.4)} = 0.4 \cdot 59 + 0.6 \cdot 62 = 60.80$$

Period	Sales	MA(2)	eMA(2)	MA(4)	eMA(4)	ES(0.2)	eES(0.2)	ES(0.4)	eES(0.4)
1	62								
2	59	62.00	3.00	62.00	3.00	62.00	3.00	62.00	3.00
3	68	60.50	−7.50	60.50	−7.50	61.40	−6.60	60.80	−7.20
4	37	63.50	26.50	63.00	26.00	62.72	25.72	63.68	26.68
5	48	52.50	4.50	56.50	8.50	57.58	9.58	53.01	5.01
6	38	42.50	4.50	53.00	15.00	55.66	17.66	51.00	13.00
7	60	43.00	−17.00	47.75	−12.25	52.13	−7.87	45.80	−14.20
8	53	49.00	−4.00	45.75	−7.25	53.70	0.70	51.48	−1.52
9	50	56.50	6.50	49.75	−0.25	53.56	3.56	52.09	2.09
10	46	51.50	5.50	50.25	4.25	52.85	6.85	51.25	5.25
11	49	48.00	−1.00	52.25	3.25	51.48	2.48	49.15	0.15
12	41	47.50	6.50	49.50	8.50	50.98	9.98	49.09	8.09
13		45.00		46.50		48.99		45.85	
Avg	50.92		2.50		3.75		5.91		3.67
St Dev	9.83		10.57		11.05		11.06		10.74
MSE			111.70		122.01		122.32		115.29
MAPE			17.06		19.52		19.69		17.69

Fig. 4.5 Numerical forecasts for the constant pattern example

Fig. 4.6 Graph of the forecasts for the constant pattern example

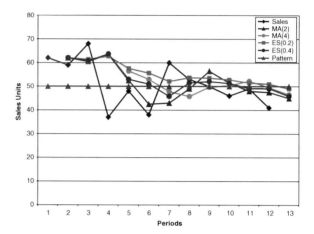

The forecasted values for period 13 range from 45 to 49 depending on the forecasting method used. The computations of the forecast for period 13 by the four different methods are given next:

$$F_{13}^{MA(2)} = \frac{49 + 41}{2} = 45.00$$

$$F_{13}^{MA(4)} = \frac{50 + 46 + 49 + 41}{4} = 46.50$$

$$F_{13}^{ES(0.2)} = 0.2 \cdot 41 + 0.8 \cdot 50.98 = 48.99$$

$$F_{13}^{ES(0.4)} = 0.4 \cdot 41 + 0.6 \cdot 49.09 = 45.85$$

The obvious question is which forecast is "correct" or the best? In the spreadsheet above the standard measures of forecast performance are computed based on the forecast errors for each method and period based on the formulas introduced above. The computations for the forecast errors for period 12 by the four different forecasting methods are shown next:

$$e_{12}^{MA(2)} = 47.50 - 41 = 6.50$$

$$e_{12}^{MA(4)} = 49.50 - 41 = 8.50$$

$$e_{12}^{ES(0.2)} = 50.98 - 41 = 9.98$$

$$e_{12}^{ES(0.4)} = 49.09 - 41 = 8.09$$

The forecasting method with the smallest mean square error (MSE) and mean absolute percentage deviation (MAPE) is the moving averages method based on two data points MA(2). This method also has the smallest average error. So all performance measures for this example indicate the selection of MA(2) as the preferred forecasting method. Note that MA(2) is equivalent to simple exponential smoothing with a smoothing constant of 0.67 for equal weighted average age of the data.

This does not imply that we should report that 45 as the forecasted value of the sales in period 13. We can, however, state that the expected value and median of forecasted sales is 45 and that there is a 68% chance that the sales in period 13 will fall in the one σ range 45 ± 10.6 or [34, 56], a 95% chance that sales will fall in the two σ range 45 ± 21.2 or [23, 67], and almost a 100% chance that the sales will fall in the three σ range 45 ± 31.8 or [13, 77].

The Excel spreadsheet includes in its analysis tools the moving averages and simple exponential smoothing methods. It also uses the term *damping factor* as the complement of the exponential smoothing constant. In other words, the sum of the smoothing constant and the damping factor is by definition equal to one. You must specify the damping factor as the parameter of the exponential smoothing method. Excel correctly suggest a range of 0.2–0.4 for the exponential smoothing constant, but it erroneously states that the default damping factor is 0.3, when in fact the default damping factor is 0.7 and the default smoothing constant is 0.3. The Excel spreadsheet computes the standard deviation of the forecast error only on the last three observations and forecasts for the exponential smoothing method and on the observations in the interval for the moving averages method.

As a final observation, the historical sales values were sampled from a normal distribution with a mean equal to 50 and a standard deviation of 10, which yields a coefficient of variation equal to 0.2. The exponential smoothing method ES(0.2), with smoothing constant equal to 0.2, generated a sales forecast closest to the true expected value of the sales in period 13. However, the underlying data pattern is almost never known in real-life forecasting projects.

4.3 Trend Data Pattern

A time series variable following a trend data pattern is assumed to have an unvarying or invariant initial value and invariant slope. This corresponds to a line with an non-negative slope in the time series graph. The actual realizations, which include the random component, are scattered around this line. An illustration of a trend data pattern is shown in Fig. 4.7.

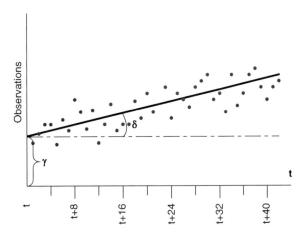

Fig. 4.7 Illustration of a time series following a trend pattern

4.3.1   Trend Data Pattern Characteristics

A trend pattern has two parameters—the offset of the trend at time zero, which is denoted by γ, and the slope, which is denoted by δ. The forecasted values for future periods are not identical. Since there are two model parameters, the computation of the standard deviation of the forecast error for static methods uses $N-2$ in the denominator. Since the mean of the forecast error is assumed to be zero, the computation of the standard deviation of the forecast error for adaptive methods uses N in the denominator, where N is the number of observations after the model initialization. Again, the value of N is different for the static and dynamic models, given the same number of historical observations. The forecasted values are illustrated in Fig. 4.8.

$$D_t = \gamma + \delta t + \varepsilon_t$$
$$\varepsilon_t = N\left(0, \sigma^2\right) \tag{4.27}$$

$$\text{Static}: s_e = \sqrt{\frac{\sum\limits_{t=1}^{N}(F_t - D_t)^2}{N-2}} = \sqrt{\frac{\sum\limits_{t=1}^{N} e_t^2}{N-2}} \tag{4.28}$$

$$\text{Dynamic}: s_e = \sqrt{\frac{\sum\limits_{t=1}^{N}(F_t - D_t)^2}{N}} = \sqrt{\frac{\sum\limits_{t=1}^{N} e_t^2}{N}} \tag{4.29}$$

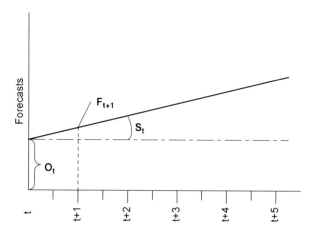

Fig. 4.8 Trend pattern forecasts

4.3.2   Forecasting Methods for a Trend Data Pattern

4.3.2.1   Polynomial Fitting

Polynomial fitting methods determine the coefficients of a polynomial that fits the observations most closely by minimizing the sum of squares of the deviations between the polynomial and the observed values. The methods are also known as *regression analysis* for polynomials and as *linear regression* for a straight-line or first-degree polynomial. All of these methods belong to the general class of *curve-fitting* methods.

If the quality of the fit were to be measured by the sum of deviations, large positive and negative deviations could offset each other and give a false measure of quality. If the absolute value of the deviations were used to measure quality, optimizing the coefficients would be much more difficult since the partial derivatives of the absolute value function are not defined everywhere. Hence, the sum of squares of the deviations is used to measure the quality of the fit. This method is called the *least squares method.*

In the case of an underlying trend pattern, a first-degree polynomial or line is used. This implies that two model parameters have to be determined, which are called the offset (O) and the slope (S). The term intercept is used interchangeably with offset.

$$F_t = O + t \cdot S \qquad (4.30)$$

The underlying pattern does not have to be a linear trend, since higher-level polynomials can be used. However, high-level polynomials increase the volatility or nervousness of the forecast and should be used with great care. Further information on polynomial fitting can be found in Montgomery et al. (2001). The Excel software can be used to perform linear curve fitting with the functions INTERCEPT and SLOPE that compute the intercept or offset and slope of the fitted line, respectively.

We will first derive the optimal parameters for the fitted line in function of general observations (x_i, y_i). Then the formulas will be specialized for the case of forecasting of a time series with successive, equal sized time periods. Using the following notation

$(x_i, y_i) =$	known pairs of independent x and dependent y variables
$N =$	number of known observation pairs
$\hat{y} =$	computed value of the dependent variable on the fitted line
$a =$	intercept of the fitted line on the y-axis
$b =$	slope of the fitted line
$x =$	independent variable
$\Sigma =$	summation over all observations, $i = 1...N$

the fitted line is described by the equation

$$\hat{y} = a + bx \qquad (4.31)$$

The sum of the squared deviations is expressed by

$$SSE = \sum \left(y_i - \hat{y}_i\right)^2 = \sum (y_i - a - bx_i)^2 \tag{4.32}$$

This sum can be minimized by setting the partial derivatives with respect to the line parameters equal to zero, which yields to the following system of two equations in two unknowns.

$$\frac{\partial SSE}{\partial a} = \sum 2\,(y_i - a - bx_i) = 0 \tag{4.33}$$

$$\frac{\partial SSE}{\partial b} = \sum 2\,(y_i - a - bx_i)\,x_i = 0 \tag{4.34}$$

$$Na + \left(\sum x_i\right) b = \left(\sum y_i\right) \tag{4.35}$$

$$\left(\sum x_i\right) a + \left(\sum x_i^2\right) b = \left(\sum x_i y_i\right) \tag{4.36}$$

Solving this system yields the optimal values for the offset and slope parameters

$$b = \frac{S_{xy}}{S_{xx}} = \frac{N \sum x_i y_i - \left(\sum x_i\right)\left(\sum y_i\right)}{N \sum x_i^2 - \left(\sum x_i\right)^2} \tag{4.37}$$

$$a = \bar{y} - b\bar{x} = \frac{1}{N}\left(\sum y_i - b \sum x_i\right) \tag{4.38}$$

These formulas can be simplified in the case of forecasting, where the independent variable t is assumed to be the index of the successive equal-size time periods, $t = 1$, $2,...N$. Recall that the line for the trend forecast is described by $F_t = O + t \cdot S$. Using the following expressions for the finite sums from 1 to N

$$\sum x_i = \sum i = \frac{N\,(N+1)}{2} \tag{4.39}$$

$$\sum x_i^2 = \sum i^2 = \frac{N\,(N+1)\,(2N+1)}{6} \tag{4.40}$$

the simplified formulas for linear trend forecast parameters become

$$S = \frac{S_{xy}}{S_{xx}} = \frac{N \sum i D_i - \frac{N(N+1)}{2} \sum D_i}{\frac{N^2(N+1)(2N+1)}{6} - \frac{N^2(N+1)^2}{4}} \tag{4.41}$$

$$O = \bar{D} - S\bar{t} = \frac{1}{N}\sum D_i - S\frac{N+1}{2} \tag{4.42}$$

For the static linear regression method for an underlying linear pattern, the variance of a forecast value is computed with the following formulas

$$se = \sqrt{\frac{SSE}{N-2}} = \sqrt{\frac{\sum_{t=1}^{N} e_t^2}{N-2}} = \sqrt{\frac{\sum_{t=1}^{N} (D_t - F_t)^2}{N-2}} \tag{4.43}$$

$$\bar{t} = \frac{1}{N} \sum_{i=1}^{N} t_i \tag{4.44}$$

$$\text{var}(F_t) = se^2 \left[1 + \frac{1}{N} + \frac{(t - \bar{t})^2}{\sum_{i=1}^{N} (i - \bar{t})^2} \right] \tag{4.45}$$

The standard error of the forecast is then

$$se_{F_t} = se \cdot \sqrt{1 + \frac{1}{N} + \frac{(t - \bar{t})^2}{\sum_{i=1}^{N} (i - \bar{t})^2}} \tag{4.46}$$

One of the major disadvantages of (linear) regression methods is that all the calculations have to be redone when new data become available. This occurs frequently when the actual sales in the next period become known. These calculations are relatively time consuming as compared to the calculations to update the corresponding adaptive exponential smoothing methods. The calculations can be simplified and the amount of data that has to be retained can be significantly reduced by storing and updating the values of the four sums $\sum i$, $\sum i^2$, $\sum i D_i$ and $\sum D_i$. The calculation and storage savings are even more pronounced in the general linear regression case, when the sums $\sum x_i$, $\sum x_i^2$, $\sum x_i y_i$, and $\sum y_i$ are stored.

A complete example using linear regression for an underlying data trend pattern is given at the end of this section on the trend pattern.

4.3.2.2 Double Exponential Smoothing (Holt's Method)

The *double exponential smoothing* method develop by Holt (1957) for data with a constant linear trend data uses two smoothing constants to adjust the intercept and slope. At the end of period t, when the real demand for this period is known, the parameters are updated based on the following formulas:

$$O_t = \alpha D_t + (1 - \alpha)(O_{t-1} + S_{t-1}) \tag{4.47}$$

$$S_t = \beta(O_t - O_{t-1}) + (1 - \beta)S_{t-1} \tag{4.48}$$

The following initial values are typically used to initialize the smoothing process. Again the importance of the initialization values decreases as the forecasting process is repeated over time.

$$O_1 = D_1$$
$$O_2 = D_2 \qquad\qquad (4.49)$$
$$S_2 = D_2 - D_1$$

The initialization requires that at minimum two observations or data points are available for initialization. If a larger number of observations is available, linear regression is typically used to estimate the slope and intercept of the underlying pattern. The forecasts are then computed with the following expressions

$$F_{t+1} = O_t + S_t \qquad\qquad (4.50)$$

$$F_{t,t+\tau} = O_t + \tau \cdot S_t \qquad\qquad (4.51)$$

The structure of the update process for the offset of forecast variable O_t and for the slope of the variable S_t is identical. The new value is computed as the sum of the last observed value multiplied by the corresponding smoothing constant and the previous value multiplied by one minus the smoothing constant or damping factor. The new forecast for the next period is equal to the offset plus one times the slope. The model parameters are updated for a number of periods during the training phase. At the end of the training phase, the model is then used to forecast in operational mode. The new forecast for periods further in the future is now different from the forecast for the next period and obtained by multiplying the slope with τ, the number of periods between the future period and the current time period.

Just as in the simple exponential smoothing method for the constant data pattern, the values of the two smoothing constants in the double exponential smoothing method should be based on careful judgment of the behavior of the underlying data pattern. Larger smoothing constants allow faster reaction of the forecasting model, which results in a smaller lag but a more "nervous" forecasting method. Smaller smoothing constants delay the reaction of the forecast model and provide for a more "stable" forecasting method. Typically, values for α are in the $[0.1, 0.4]$ range with 0.2 as a typical starting value. It is usually desirable to have more stable behavior of the slope, so 0.1 is often chosen as the starting value for β. The values of the smoothing parameters can also set to minimize the sum of the squared errors over a historical interval.

The double smoothing process requires a value for the initial offset and the initial slope. If enough historical data are available for the initialization phase, then these values can be computed with a linear regression model fitted through a subset of historical observations. The double exponential smoothing process is then used to update the offset and slope during the training phase and then to generate the next forecasts.

Consider the following small example of the update process. It is assumed that the underlying pattern follows a linear trend. The first four observations are 53, 47, 59, and 70 and will be used for the initialization phase. The linear regression through these 4 data points yields an intercept of 41.50 and a slope of 6.30. The offset of the line at period four is then equal to 66.70. The values of both smoothing constants were set equal to 0.2. The forecast for period 5 based on the offset and slope of period 4 is then

$$F_5 = O_4 + S_4 = 66.70 + 6.30 = 73$$

The new observed value is equal to 55, which implies that the forecast error for period 5 is equal to 18. The offset and slope for period 5 are now updated. Finally, the new forecast for period 6 is computed.

$$O_5 = \alpha D_5 + (1 - \alpha)(O_4 + S_4) = 0.2 \cdot 55 + 0.8 \cdot (66.70 + 6.30) = 69.40$$
$$S_5 = \beta(O_5 - O_4) + (1 - \beta)S_4 = 0.2 \cdot (69.40 - 66.70) + 0.8 \cdot 6.30 = 5.58$$
$$F_6 = O_5 + S_5 = 69.40 + 5.58 = 74.98$$

This process is repeated for all the periods in the training phase when future observations become available in the operational phase.

A complete example comparing double exponential smoothing methods with different smoothing constants for an underlying data trend pattern is given next. See Figs. 4.9 and 4.10 for the data table and graph.

Period	Sales
1	53
2	47
3	59
4	70
5	55
6	68
7	85
8	92
9	74
10	99
11	123
12	112
13	
mean	78.08
std dev	24.35

Fig. 4.9 Historical data for the trend pattern example

Fig. 4.10 Graph of the historical data for the trend pattern example

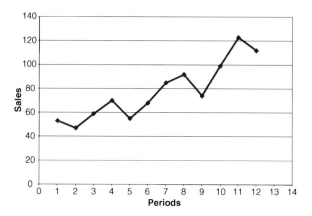

4.3.3 Trend Pattern Forecasting Example

We will first use the linear regression method to forecast the demand in period 13.

$$S_{xy} = N \sum i D_i - \frac{N(N+1)}{2} \sum D_i$$

$$= 12 \cdot 6971 - \frac{12 \cdot 13}{2} 937 = 10566$$

$$S_{xx} = \frac{N^2(N+1)(2N+1)}{6} - \frac{N^2(N+1)^2}{4}$$

$$= \frac{12^2 \cdot 13 \cdot 25}{6} - \frac{12^2 \cdot 13^2}{4} = 1716$$

$$S = \frac{S_{xy}}{S_{xx}} = \frac{10566}{1716} = 6.16$$

$$O = \frac{1}{N} \sum D_i - S\frac{N+1}{2}$$

$$= \frac{937}{12} - 6.16\frac{13}{2} = 38.06$$

We can then forecast the demand for any period in the future, starting with period 13. Note that for linear regression the offset computed above is the offset for time period 0.

$$F_{13} = O + S \cdot 13 = 38.06 + 6.16 \cdot 13 = 118.11$$

Using the INTERCEPT and SLOPE functions in Microsoft Excel, we find the same optimal values for the line-fitting parameters to be $S=6.16$ and $O=38.06$. The graph of the linear regression is shown in Fig. 4.11.

Next we will compute the forecast with the same four forecasting methods used for the constant pattern: moving averages with an interval of 2, denoted by MA(2),

Fig. 4.11 Graph of the linear regression curve for the trend pattern example

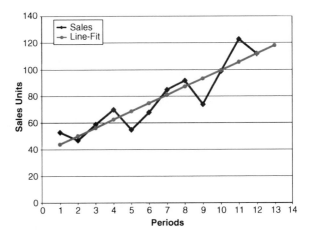

moving averages with an interval of 4, denoted by MA(4), simple exponential smoothing with a smoothing constant of 0.2, denoted by ES(0.2), and simple exponential smoothing with a smoothing constant of 0.4, denoted by ES(0.4). The forecasts with error statistics are shown in Fig. 4.12, the graph of the forecasts is shown in Fig. 4.13.

The MA(4) method has the smallest MAPE value and we will select this method to forecast the point value for period 13 and establish the confidence intervals. The 95% confidence interval is given by

$$CI_{0.95} = \left[102 \pm 1.96 \cdot \sqrt{305.74} \right] = [102 \pm 34.3] = [67.7, 136.3]$$

Next we will forecast the trend pattern with the double exponential smoothing method with a smoothing constant of 0.2, denoted by DES(0.2), and exponential

Period	Sales	MA(2)	eMA(2)	MA(4)	eMA(4)	ES(0.2)	eES(0.2)	ES(0.4)	eES(0.4)
1	53								
2	47	53.00	6.00	53.00	6.00	53.00	6.00	53.00	6.00
3	59	50.00	−9.00	50.00	−9.00	51.80	−7.20	50.60	−8.40
4	70	53.00	−17.00	53.00	−17.00	53.24	−16.76	53.96	−16.04
5	55	64.50	9.50	57.25	2.25	56.59	1.59	60.38	5.38
6	68	62.50	−5.50	57.75	−10.25	56.27	−11.73	58.23	−9.77
7	85	61.50	−23.50	63.00	−22.00	58.62	−26.38	62.14	−22.86
8	92	76.50	−15.50	69.50	−22.50	63.90	−28.10	71.28	−20.72
9	74	88.50	14.50	75.00	1.00	69.52	−4.48	79.57	5.57
10	99	83.00	−16.00	79.75	−19.25	70.41	−28.59	77.34	−21.66
11	123	86.50	−36.50	87.50	−35.50	76.13	−46.87	86.00	−37.00
12	112	111.00	−1.00	97.00	−15.00	85.50	−26.50	100.80	−11.20
13		117.50		102.00		90.80		105.28	
Avg	78.08		−8.55		−12.84		−17.18		−11.88
St Dev	24.35		16.84		17.49		22.82		17.67
MSE			283.50		305.74		520.98		312.23
MAPE			17.14		16.81		20.67		17.54

Fig. 4.12 Numerical forecasts for the trend pattern example

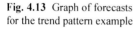 **Fig. 4.13** Graph of forecasts for the trend pattern example

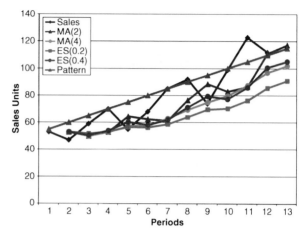

smoothing with a smoothing constant of 0.4, denoted by DES(0.4). The forecast and error statistics are shown in Fig. 4.14 and the graph of the forecasts is shown in Fig. 4.15.

The MAPE measures of forecast quality are 0.10 and 0.11 for the double expo-nential smoothing methods with smoothing constants of 0.2 and 0.4, respectively. This should be compared with the MAPE values of the simple exponential smooth-ing method, which are equal to 20.7 and 17.6 corresponding to smoothing constants 0.2 and 0.4, respectively. The forecasting methods for an underlying trend pattern clearly have a much better quality than the forecasting methods for an underlying stationary pattern. This reemphasizes the principle, that the most important require-ment for a high-quality forecast is to correctly identify the underlying pattern and then to apply a forecasting method developed for that pattern.

Period	Sales	DES(0.2)	eDES(0.2)	offset(0.2)	slope(0.2)	DES(0.4)	eDES(0.4)	offset(0.4)	slope(0.4)
1	53								
2	47								
3	59								
4	70			66.70	6.30			66.70	6.30
5	55	73.00	18.00	69.40	5.58	73.00	18.00	65.80	4.86
6	68	74.98	6.98	73.58	5.30	70.66	2.66	69.60	4.65
7	85	78.88	−6.12	80.11	5.55	74.24	−10.76	78.55	5.51
8	92	85.65	−6.35	86.92	5.80	84.05	−7.95	87.23	6.14
9	74	92.72	18.72	88.98	5.05	93.38	19.38	85.63	4.59
10	99	94.03	−4.97	95.02	5.25	90.22	−8.78	93.73	5.30
11	123	100.27	−22.73	104.82	6.16	99.03	−23.97	108.62	7.21
12	112	110.98	−1.02	111.18	6.20	115.83	3.83	114.30	6.91
13		117.38				121.21			
Mean	78.08		0.31				−0.95		
Std Dev	24.35		12.96				13.93		
MSE			167.91				193.98		
MAPE			0.10				0.11		

Fig. 4.14 Numerical trend forecasts for the trend pattern example

Fig. 4.15 Graph of trend forecasts for the trend pattern example

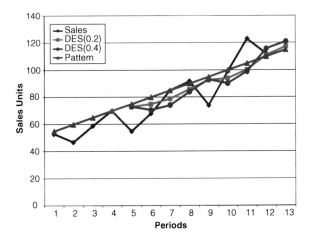

It can be observed in the above figure that the exponential smoothing with 0.4 as smoothing constant reacts quicker to the changes in the observed values than the exponential smoothing with 0.2 as smoothing constant. For example, at period 11 both forecasts are nearly identical. However, the observed value for period 11 is much larger than both forecasted values. The forecast by DES(0.4) for period 12 is then larger than the forecast by DES(0.2).

The DES(0.2) and DES(0.4) have virtual identical MAPE values, but the DES(0.2) has a smaller MSE and we will select this method to forecast the point value for period 13 and establish the confidence intervals. The 95% confidence interval is given by

$$CI_{0.95} = \left[117.4 \pm 1.96 \cdot \sqrt{167.9} \right] = [117.4 \pm 25.4] = [92.0, 142.8]$$

Finally, it should be noted that the sales data was generated by a pattern with an offset of 50 and a slope of 5 units and that the standard deviation of the random component was 15 units. The expected value of the sales during period 13 is then equal to $50 + 5 \times 13 = 115$. The 95% confidence interval of the probability distribution has the boundary values $115 \pm 1.96 \cdot 15 = 115 \pm 29.4 = [85.6, 144.4]$. Obviously, the true parameters for the underlying pattern are almost never known.

4.4 Seasonal Data Pattern

4.4.1 Seasonal Data Pattern Characteristics

A seasonal data pattern is the assumed to be the combination of a nonseasonal component and seasonal fluctuations. The *periodicity* or cycle length is the number of periods after which the seasonal cycle repeats itself and it will be denoted by P.

Fig. 4.16 Historic values of U.S. durable goods shipments

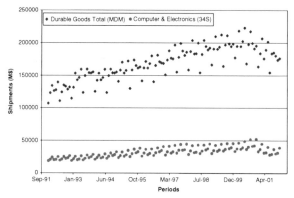

The next two figures illustrate the seasonality present in many supply chains. In Fig. 4.16 the value of monthly shipments of all durable goods (MDM) and of computers and electronics (34S) in the United States are shown, as collected by the U.S. Commerce Department. This figure illustrates the long-term trends of the shipments. In Fig. 4.17, the same values are shown on a monthly basis. This figure illustrates that the shipments have clear and systematic monthly variations. Recognizing and exploiting these monthly variations allows for a better forecast of shipment value in future months.

The first task in forecasting seasonal variables is to determine the season or cycle length. The cycle length should be based on the intrinsic properties of the forecasted variable and the process that generates the variable, which can be determined by consulting with the problem domain experts. The periodicity can also be estimated

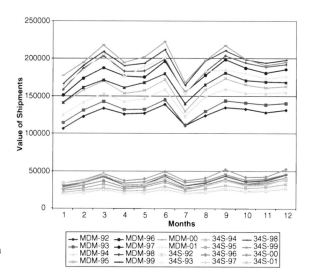

Fig. 4.17 Value of U.S. durable goods shipments on a monthly basis

from the data points by counting the number of periods between successive top values and successive bottom values. However, because of the inherent random nature of the data, examining the data points may yield more than one value for the periodicity. Many supply chain variables follow a yearly pattern generated by the yearly agricultural or yearly socio-cultural cycles. Other common patterns exist that are related to the days in a month or the weeks in a quarter.

The classic *additive decomposition* method assumes that the data are generated by the following process

$$D_t = Pat_t + C_t + \varepsilon_t$$
$$\sum_{t=1}^{P} C_t = 0 \tag{4.52}$$
$$\varepsilon_t = N\left(0, \sigma^2\right)$$

where Pat_t is the trend component, C_t is the seasonality component with a known periodicity P, and ε is the random component with a zero expected value. The data is "deseasonalized" by subtracting the seasonal component, applying a forecasting method for a trend based pattern, and then "reseasonalized" by adding the forecast of the seasonal component.

The *multiplicative decomposition* method assumes that the data are generated by the process in which the pattern is multiplied by the seasonal effect, where C_t is the seasonality factor with a known periodicity P. The data is "deseasonalized" by dividing by the seasonal factor, applying a forecasting method for a trend based pattern, and then "reseasonalized" by multiplying by the forecast of the seasonal factor.

$$D_t = Pat_t \cdot c_t + \varepsilon_t$$
$$\sum_{t=1}^{P} c_t = P \tag{4.53}$$
$$\varepsilon_t = N\left(0, \sigma^2\right)$$

In the additive variant, the amplitude of the seasonal variations stays constant over time, while in the multiplicative variant the amplitude of the seasonal variations is proportional to the amplitude of the underlying linear trend. The additive and multiplicative seasonal patterns are illustrated in Figs. 4.18 and 4.19.

There exists also a multiplicative variant which assumes which the underlying process is given by

$$D_t = Pat_t \cdot c_t \cdot \varepsilon$$
$$E\left(\varepsilon\right) = 1 \tag{4.54}$$

Further information on forecasting based on classic time series decomposition for this last underlying seasonal pattern can be found in Ballou (1998).

Fig. 4.18 Additive seasonal pattern illustration

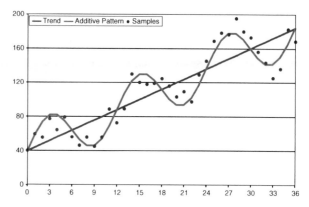

Fig. 4.19 Multiplicative seasonal pattern

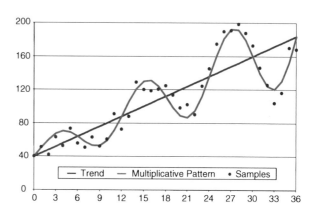

4.4.2 Seasonal Pattern Forecasting Example

The example in Fig. 4.20 will be used to illustrate the various forecasting methods for a seasonal pattern.

As the first step in understanding the underlying pattern, the numerical data is displayed graphically. The pattern appears to be seasonal with an upward trend. It is not clear from the graph if the amplitude of the seasonal oscillations increases with the linear trend. In real-life cases this indicates the simultaneous use of both the additive and multiplicative variants. The example in Fig. 4.21 will continue using seasonal regression and both the additive and multiplicative variants.

The first task is to determine the cycle length or periodicity of the underlying seasonal pattern. In this particular example this task is not difficult. The time interval between two successive high values or peaks is four periods and the time interval between two successive low values or valleys is also four periods. So we assume that the underlying seasonal pattern has a cycle length of four periods.

Fig. 4.20 Historical data for the seasonal pattern example

Period	Demand
1	19
2	26
3	19
4	11
5	23
6	30
7	22
8	13
9	27
10	35
11	26
12	16
Avg.	22.3
Std. Dev.	7.0

Fig. 4.21 Graph of historical data for the seasonal pattern example

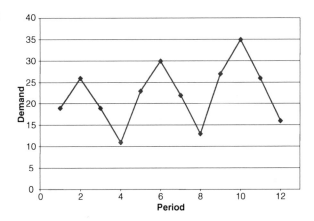

4.4.3 Forecasting Methods for a Seasonal Data Pattern

4.4.3.1 Seasonal Linear Regression

As all linear regression methods, seasonal regression is a static method that assumes that the underlying pattern remains unchanged and uses all the data to determine the model. Seasonal regression assumes that the seasonal variations are additive to the underlying trend. The seasonal regression model uses indicator variables δ_{it}, which are binary variables indicating whether a particular time period corresponds to the i-th period in the seasonal cycle or not. For example, in forecasting monthly demand data that have a yearly seasonal pattern, there would be 12 indicator variables that indicate if a particular month is the first, second, ..., twelfth month in the cycle. The forecast model is then given by

$$F_t = O + S \cdot t + \sum_{i=1}^{P} \delta_{it} \cdot C_i \tag{4.55}$$

Since the underlying model is linear, the standard regression tools in statistical packages or spreadsheets can be used to determine the optimal value of the model parameters. There are $P+2$ model parameters, consisting of the offset, slope, and P seasonality terms. However, the seasonality terms and the offset are linearly related, so there are only $P+1$ independent model parameters and the residual degrees of freedom are equal to $N-P-1$. The computations of the standard error and of the standard deviation of the forecast error use $N-P-1$ in the denominator.

$$\text{Static: } se = \sqrt{\frac{SSE}{N - P - 1}} = \sqrt{\frac{\sum_{t=1}^{N} e_t^2}{N - P - 1}} = \sqrt{\frac{\sum_{t=1}^{N} (D_t - F_t)^2}{N - P - 1}} \tag{4.56}$$

with

$$\bar{t} = \frac{1}{N} \sum_{i=1}^{N} t_i \tag{4.57}$$

$$\text{var}(F_t) = se^2 \left[1 + \frac{1}{N} + \frac{(t - \bar{t})^2}{\sum_{i=1}^{N} (i - \bar{t})^2} \right] \tag{4.58}$$

The standard error of the forecast is then

$$se_{F_t} = se \cdot \sqrt{1 + \frac{1}{N} + \frac{(t - \bar{t})^2}{\sum_{i=1}^{N} (i - \bar{t})^2}} \tag{4.59}$$

The standard error of the forecast increases for forecasting periods that are further into the future. The lines corresponding to the lower and upper confidence limits in the forecast graph will not stay parallel but will diverge. These diverging lines are sometimes called the *cone of uncertainty*. However, for well-tuned models the differences for periods in the immediate future are small and often the standard error is used to compute confidence intervals.

The model parameters, consisting of the offset, slope, and P seasonality terms, are determined once based on all the available data by minimizing the residual sum of squared errors. After they have been determined they are assumed to remain constant. A detailed example of the application of seasonal regression is shown next for the common seasonal pattern example.

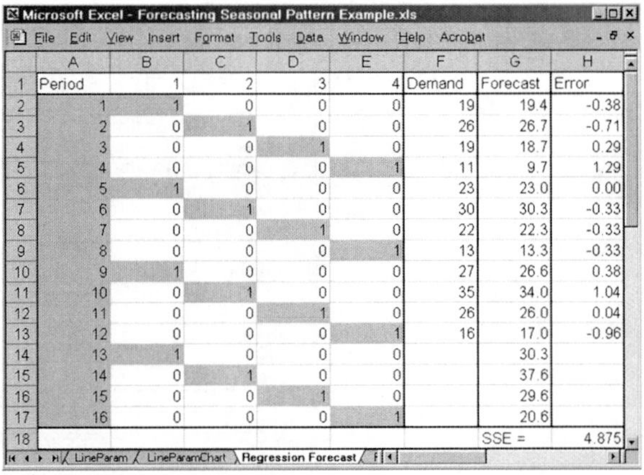

Fig. 4.22 Forecast with seasonal regression for the seasonal pattern example

Microsoft Excel - Forecasting Seasonal Pattern Example.xls

Period	1	2	3	4	Demand	Forecast	Error
1	1	0	0	0	19	19.4	-0.38
2	0	1	0	0	26	26.7	-0.71
3	0	0	1	0	19	18.7	0.29
4	0	0	0	1	11	9.7	1.29
5	1	0	0	0	23	23.0	0.00
6	0	1	0	0	30	30.3	-0.33
7	0	0	1	0	22	22.3	-0.33
8	0	0	0	1	13	13.3	-0.33
9	1	0	0	0	27	26.6	0.38
10	0	1	0	0	35	34.0	1.04
11	0	0	1	0	26	26.0	0.04
12	0	0	0	1	16	17.0	-0.96
13	1	0	0	0		30.3	
14	0	1	0	0		37.6	
15	0	0	1	0		29.6	
16	0	0	0	1		20.6	
						SSE =	4.875

LineParam / LineParamChart \ Regression Forecast

Seasonal Regression Example

For a static forecasting method such as regression, all the available data are used to determine the model parameters. The forecast results based on 12 periods of data are shown in Fig. 4.22, the regression options for Microsoft Excel are shown in Fig. 4.23, and the model parameters derived with seasonal regression in Fig. 4.24. Finally, the demand and forecasts based on seasonal regression are shown in Fig. 4.25. The 95% confidence intervals for the forecasts are also shown in this figure.

The independent variables for the seasonal regression are given in columns A through E, with column A corresponding to the time index and columns B through E correspond to the indicator variables. The cells in Fig. 4.22 are shown as shaded when they contain a nonzero element and the columns of the indicator variables show the characteristic staircase pattern. Observe that the offset or constant in the

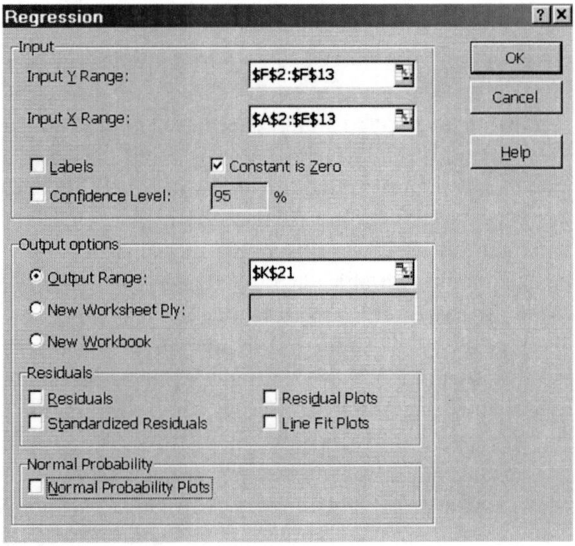

Regression

Input

Input Y Range: $F$2:$F$13

Input X Range: $A$2:$E$13

☐ Labels   ☑ Constant is Zero

☐ Confidence Level: 95 %

OK

Cancel

Help

Output options

⦿ Output Range: $K$21

○ New Worksheet Ply:

○ New Workbook

Residuals

☐ Residuals   ☐ Residual Plots

☐ Standardized Residuals   ☐ Line Fit Plots

Normal Probability

☐ Normal Probability Plots

Fig. 4.23 Seasonal regression model excel options

Fig. 4.24 Seasonal regression model parameters and performance measures for the seasonal pattern example

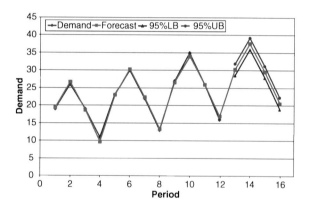

	K	L	M	N	O	P	Q
21	SUMMARY OUTPUT						
22							
23	*Regression Statistics*						
24	Multiple R	0.995528					
25	R Square	0.991076					
26	Adjusted R Square	0.843119					
27	Standard Error	0.834523					
28	Observations	12					
29							
30	ANOVA						
31		*df*	*SS*	*MS*	*F*	*gnificance F*	
32	Regression	5	541.375	108.275	155.4718	2.92E-06	
33	Residual	7	4.875	0.696429			
34	Total	12	546.25				
35							
36		*Coefficients*	*andard Err*	*t Stat*	*P-value*	*ower 95%*	*Upper 95%*
37	Intercept	0	#N/A	#N/A	#N/A	#N/A	#N/A
38	X Variable 1	0.90625	0.073762	12.28612	5.43E-06	0.73183	1.08067
39	X Variable 2	18.46875	0.606765	30.43805	1.07E-08	17.03398	19.90352
40	X Variable 3	24.89583	0.654227	38.0538	2.25E-09	23.34883	26.44283
41	X Variable 4	15.98958	0.706218	22.64113	8.3E-08	14.31964	17.65952
42	X Variable 5	6.083333	0.761812	7.98535	9.22E-05	4.281936	7.884731

Fig. 4.25 Forecast graph based on seasonal regression for the seasonal pattern example

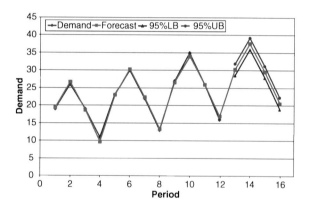

Excel options was forced to zero to eliminate the linear dependency between the seasonality terms and the offset.

The SSE indicated by the Residual value in the above figure is 4.875, which is significantly smaller than the variability of 541.375 captured by the regression model. This indicates that the regression is highly accurate. The same is also demonstrated by an R-square value of 99%.

Since the seasonality terms are measured with respect to the linear trend, each of the seasonality variables can be increased by an amount without impacting the fit of the regression, if at the same time the intercept is decreased by the same amount. Graphically, this is equivalent to moving the linear trend line up or down the y-axis, as illustrated in Fig. 4.26. This implies that either the offset or one of the seasonality variables can be set arbitrarily. The determination of the regression parameters shown above was executed with the offset or intercept forced to zero. Alternatively, the regression could have been performed excluding one of the indicator variables, which is equivalent to setting the seasonality variable for that period equal to zero.

Fig. 4.26 Effect of normalization for the additive seasonal model

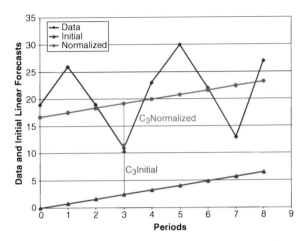

Table 4.2 Forecasts and confidence intervals for the seasonal example by seasonal regression

Period	Forecast	95%LB	95%UB
13	30.25	28.6	31.9
14	37.58	35.9	39.2
15	29.58	27.9	31.2
16	20.58	18.9	22.2

In the updating procedure for the seasonality terms in the additive variant of Winter's method, the seasonality terms are normalized in such way that they sum up to zero, which implies that the offset also has to be updated as part of the normalization process (See Fig. 4.26).

The standard error is computed as follows

$$se = \sqrt{\frac{SSE}{df_{res}}} = \sqrt{\frac{\sum_{j=1}^{N} e_t^2}{N - 1 - P}} = \sqrt{\frac{4.875}{12 - 5}} = \sqrt{0.696} = 0.835$$

The 95% confidence intervals for the forecasts for the next cycle are then computed as shown in Table 4.2.

The MAPE for the seasonal regression is 2.8% at the end of period 12.

4.4.3.2 Additive Triple Exponential Smoothing (Winter's Method)

There exist several variants of the triple exponential smoothing method developed by Winters (1960) depending on the assumption about the behavior of the underlying process. In each variant, the triple exponential smoothing method uses three smoothing constants to adjust the intercept, slope, and *seasonality term C_t* or *seasonality factor c_t* corresponding to the current period.

For the additive variant the trend and the seasonal terms are added together and the underlying process is assumed to be

$$D_t = Pat_t + C_t + \varepsilon = O + t \cdot S + C_t + \varepsilon_t$$
$$\varepsilon_t = N\left(0, \sigma^2\right)$$

$$(4.60)$$

At the end of period t, when the real demand for this period is known, the parameters are updated based on the following formulas:

$$O_t = \alpha\left(D_t - C_{t-P}\right) + (1 - \alpha)(O_{t-1} + S_{t-1})$$

$$(4.61)$$

$$S_t = \beta(O_t - O_{t-1}) + (1 - \beta)S_{t-1}$$

$$(4.62)$$

$$C_t = \gamma\left(D_t - O_t\right) + (1 - \gamma)C_{t-P}$$

$$(4.63)$$

As an adaptive method, triple exponential smoothing requires historical data to initialize the model parameters, followed by more recent historical data to adjust the model parameters. The adjustment phase is sometimes also called the seasoning or training phase.

The starting values of the model parameters can be computed with several methods. The minimum number of observations required to start the method is equivalent to one full cycle plus one additional observation of historical data or $P + 1$. With this initialization method the initial model parameters are computed as

$$O_t = D_t$$

$$(4.64)$$

$$S_t = (D_t - D_{t-P})/P$$

$$(4.65)$$

$$C_i = D_i - (D_t + (i - t) \cdot S_t) \quad i = 1 \ldots P$$

$$(4.66)$$

Observe that this implies that the initial estimate of C_p equals zero before normalization.

All the seasonality terms are then normalized so that their sum equals zero. To compensate for this linear translation of the demand values, the offset is also adjusted by this normalization process. The forecast for the next and future periods is then computed based on the normalized offset and the normalized seasonality terms. It should be noted that normalization does not change the forecast or improve the forecast quality; rather normalization standardizes the forecasting results to eliminate possible ambiguity.

$$C_t = C_t - \left(\frac{1}{P}\sum_{j=1}^{P} C_j\right)$$

$$(4.67)$$

$$O_t = O_t + \left(\frac{1}{P}\sum_{j=1}^{P} C_j\right)$$

$$(4.68)$$

If data for more periods is available, seasonal regression with indicator variables can be used to estimate the initial parameter values. The triple exponential smoothing process is then used to update the offset and slope and generate the forecasts for future periods. The forecasts for the next periods are then computed with

$$F_{t+1} = O_t + S_t + C_{t+1-P} \tag{4.69}$$

$$F_{t,t+\tau} = O_t + \tau S_t + C_{t+\tau-P} \tag{4.70}$$

Just as in the simple exponential smoothing method for the constant data pattern, the values of the three smoothing constants in the triple exponential smoothing method should be based on careful judgment of the behavior of the underlying data pattern. Typically, values for α are in the $[0.1, 0.4]$ range with 0.2 as a typical starting value. It is usually desirable to have a more stable behavior of the slope and seasonality factors or components, so 0.1 is often chosen as the starting value for β and γ. The values of the smoothing parameters can also set to minimize the sum of the squared errors over an historical interval.

Additive Triple Exponential Smoothing Example

Both variants of triple exponential smoothing are adaptive forecasting methods. The first decision to be made is how much of the data to allocate to the estimation of the initial parameter values (initialization phase) and how much of the historical data to allocate to the training or adaptation process (adjustment phase). The multiplicative variant requires at least two full cycles to estimate the initial parameters, so we will use the data from the first two cycles or eight periods to estimate the initial parameters and then the data from the last cycle to train the model. For the additive variant, we will use three different initialization methods that have different data requirements: (1) using one cycle plus one period of data, (2) using two cycles of data, and (3) using seasonal regression for many cycles of data (See Figs. 4.27 and 4.28).

Period	Demand
1	19
2	26
3	19
4	11
5	23
6	30
7	22
8	13
Avg.	20.4
Std. Dev.	6.3

Fig. 4.27 Initial data for the seasonal pattern example

Fig. 4.28 Graph of historical data for the seasonal pattern example

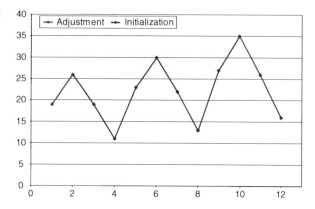

The next task for this method is to compute the initial estimates of the underlying trend. To illustrate the first alternative manual method for initializing the additive method, assume we only had data available for periods 4–8 for the initialization process and retained data for periods 9–12 for training the smoothing method. This is an example of the "cycle plus one" initialization method that requires only one cycle plus one additional data point, which is the fewest possible number of initial data points. The initial linear forecast is derived by connecting the demands in periods 4 and 8. This implicitly assumes that the seasonality terms for period 4 and 8 are equal to zero. The initial values are then

$$C_8 = C_4 = 0$$
$$O_8 = 13$$
$$S_8 = \frac{13 - 11}{4} = 0.5$$

Based on this initial estimate of the trend line, the seasonality terms for the other periods in the cycle can now be computed. Based on all the seasonality terms in a full cycle, the adjustment constant for normalization can then also be computed.

$$C_1 = 23 - (13 - 3 \cdot 0.5) = 23 - 11.5 = 11.5$$
$$C_2 = 30 - (13 - 2 \cdot 0.5) = 30 - 12 = 18.0$$
$$C_3 = 22 - (13 - 1 \cdot 0.5) = 22 - 12.5 = 9.50$$
$$\frac{1}{4} \sum_{i=1}^{4} C_i = \frac{1}{4} (11.5 + 18.0 + 9.50 + 0.00) = \frac{39}{4} = 9.75$$

The normalized seasonality terms and offset are then computed as follows. It should be noted that the slope remains the same. The normalization process is graphically equivalent to moving the linear trend line up or down parallel to itself by the adjustment constant. In other words, the normalization executes a translation transformation.

Fig. 4.29 Initial linear forecast parameters graph based on cycle plus 1 initialization

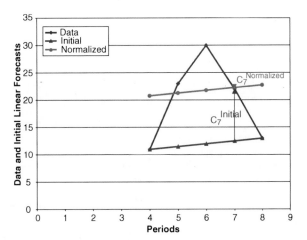

$$C_1 = 11.5 - 9.75 = 1.75$$
$$C_2 = 18.0 - 9.75 = 8.25$$
$$C_3 = 9.50 - 9.75 = -0.25$$
$$C_4 = 0.00 - 9.75 = -9.75$$
$$O_8 = 13 + 9.75 = 22.75$$

The initialization calculations are illustrated in Fig. 4.29.

Next we will use an initialization method that uses exactly two cycles. It averages the seasonal variations inside a cycle to compute two trend points that represent the average demand in each cycle. The trend line is then constructed through these two points. Cycle one covers periods 1–4 and its average time coordinate is thus 2.5; cycle 2 covers periods 5–8, and its average time coordinate is thus 6.5. The computations for the average demand for each cycle and the slope and offset in period 8 are shown next and are illustrated in Figs. 4.30 and 4.31.

$$\overline{x_{C1}} = \frac{1+4}{2} = 2.5$$

$$\overline{y_{C1}} = \frac{19 + 26 + 19 + 11}{4} = 18.75$$

$$\overline{x_{C2}} = \frac{5+8}{2} = 6.5$$

$$\overline{y_{C2}} = \frac{23 + 30 + 22 + 13}{4} = 22$$

$$S_8 = \frac{22 - 18.75}{6.5 - 2.5} = 0.81$$

$$O_8 = 22 + (8 - 6.5) \cdot 0.81 = 23.22$$

Fig. 4.30 Initial linear forecast parameters

Initial Linear Forecast		
	Period	Demand
Cycle 1	2.5	18.75
Cycle 2	6.5	22.00
Slope 8		0.81
Intercept	8.0	23.22

Fig. 4.31 Initial linear forecast parameters graph for the
seasonal pattern example

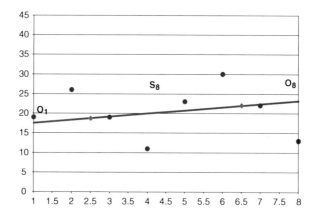

The initial and normalization adjustment value for the four seasonality terms can
then be computed as follows. Because the linear trend line was computed based on
the average demand of two full cycles, the adjustment factor for the normalization
must be zero.

$C_1 = 19 - (23.22 - 0.81 \cdot 7) = 1.47$ $C_2 = 26 - (23.22 - 0.81 \cdot 6) = 7.66$

$C_5 = 23 - (23.22 - 0.81 \cdot 3) = 2.22$ $C_6 = 30 - (23.22 - 0.81 \cdot 2) = 8.41$

$\bar{C}_1 = \frac{1}{2}(1.47 + 2.22) = 1.84$ $\bar{C}_2 = \frac{1}{2}(7.66 + 8.41) = 8.03$

$C_3 = 19 - (23.22 - 0.81 \cdot 5) = -0.16$ $C_4 = 11 - (23.22 - 0.81 \cdot 4) = -8.97$

$C_7 = 22 - (23.22 - 0.81 \cdot 1) = -0.41$ $C_8 = 13 - (23.22 - 0.81 \cdot 0) = -10.22$

$\bar{C}_3 = \frac{1}{2}(-0.16 - 0.41) = -0.28$ $\bar{C}_4 = \frac{1}{2}(-8.97 - 10.22) = -9.59$

$$\frac{1}{4}\sum_{i=1}^{4} C_i = \frac{1}{4}(1.84 + 8.03 - 0.28 - 9.59) = 0.0$$

Based on those two parameters the linear forecast can be computed, which is shown
in column C of the next figure. The initial eight estimates of the seasonality terms
are computed as the difference between the demand and the linear forecast and
are shown in column 4. The terms for the corresponding periods are averaged and
shown in column 5. The computations for the calculation of seasonality term of the

Period	Demand	Forecast Linear	Seasonal Term	Seasonal Term	Normed S. Term	Normed L. Forec.	Forecast Seasonal	Forecast Error
1	19	17.53	1.469	1.844	1.844	17.53	19.38	–0.38
2	26	18.34	7.656	8.031	8.031	18.34	26.38	–0.38
3	19	19.16	–0.156	–0.281	–0.281	19.16	18.88	0.13
4	11	19.97	–8.969	–9.594	–9.594	19.97	10.38	0.63
5	23	20.78	2.219			20.78	22.63	0.38
6	30	21.59	8.406			21.59	29.63	0.38
7	22	22.41	–0.406			22.41	22.13	–0.13
8	13	23.22	–10.219			23.22	13.63	–0.63
Sum	163	163.0		0.000	0.000		163.00	0.00

Fig. 4.32 Initial parameters for the additive model for the seasonal pattern example

fourth period in the cycle are shown next. In this particular example we used the normalized seasonality terms to start the process, so they already sum to zero and the normalization process does not change the seasonality terms or offset. Because of the linear dependency between the offset and the seasonality terms, the initial regression can return many different values for the seasonality terms and the offset. However, the normalization process always yields a unique set of seasonality terms and offset (See Fig. 4.32).

$$C_4 = 11 - 19.97 = -8.969$$
$$C_8 = 13 - 23.22 = -10.219$$
$$\overline{C_4} = \frac{(-8.97) + (-10.22)}{2} = -9.594$$
$$O_8 = 23.22$$
$$F_8 = 23.22 - 9.594 = 13.63$$

Next, we will use seasonal regression based on eight time periods to determine the initial parameters. The regression method can be used when there are two or more cycles of data available for the initialization process. The regression yields a slope equal to 0.81 and an offset for period 8 equal to 23.22 after normalization of the seasonality terms. The normalized offset, slope, and normalized seasonality terms and are shown in the last row of Fig. 4.33.

	Period	1	2	3	4	Demand	Forecast	Linear Forecast
	1	1	0	0	0	19	19.38	17.53
	2	0	1	0	0	26	26.38	18.34
	3	0	0	1	0	19	18.88	19.16
	4	0	0	0	1	11	10.38	19.97
	5	1	0	0	0	23	22.63	20.78
	6	0	1	0	0	30	29.63	21.59
	7	0	0	1	0	22	22.13	22.41
	8	0	0	0	1	13	13.63	23.22
16.719		0.813	1.844	8.031	–0.281	–9.594		

Fig. 4.33 Seasonal regression based on two cycles for the seasonal pattern example

If more data points are available, it is beneficial to use initial estimates based on all the data points. The remainder of the calculations for the additive variant of Winter's method are based on initial estimates obtained using two-cycles, which in this case is equal to the initialization by seasonal regression since both use the same eight historical data points. We next will train or season the model by adjusting the offset, slope, and seasonality terms using forecasts for the periods 9 through 12 for which the historical demand is known.

The forecast for period 9 is then computed and the offset, slope, and seasonality term for period 1 are then updated with the exponential smoothing formulas. Seasonality term one is shaded in the row for period 9 to indicate it is adjusted during that period. Next, all the seasonality terms have to be normalized so that they again sum to zero and the offset has to be normalized as well.

$$F_9 = O_8 + S_8 + C_{9||4} = 23.22 + 0.81 + 1.844 = 25.88$$
$$O_9 = \alpha\,(D_9 - C_1) + (1 - \alpha)\,(O_8 + S_8)$$
$$= 0.2\,(27 - 1.844) + 0.8\,(23.22 + 0.81) = 24.26$$
$$S_9 = \beta\,(O_9 - O_8) + (1 - \beta)\,S_8$$
$$= 0.1(24.26 - 23.22) + 0.9 \cdot 0.81 = 0.83$$
$$C_1 = \gamma\,(D_9 - O_9) + (1 - \gamma)\,C_1$$
$$= 0.1\,(27 - 24.26) + 0.9 \cdot 1.844 = 1.934$$

$$\sum_{t=1}^{P} C_t = 0.09$$

$$C_1 = C_1 - \left(\frac{1}{P}\sum_{t=1}^{P} C_t\right) = 1.934 - (0.09/4) = 1.911$$

$$O_9 = O_9 + \left(\frac{1}{P}\sum_{t=1}^{P} C_t\right) = 24.26 + (0.09/4) = 24.28$$

The computations for the forecasts made at the end of period 12 for all the periods in the next cycle are shown next and forecasts for the next cycle are shown in Fig. 4.36.

$$F_{12,13} = (O_{12} + S_{12}) + C_{13||4} = (26.90 + 0.84) + 1.907 = 29.65$$
$$F_{12,14} = (O_{12} + \tau S_{12}) + C_{14||4} = (26.90 + 2 \cdot 0.84) + 8.155 = 36.74$$
$$F_{12,15} = (O_{12} + \tau S_{12}) + C_{15||4} = (26.90 + 3 \cdot 0.84) + (-0.313) = 29.11$$
$$F_{12,16} = (O_{12} + \tau S_{12}) + C_{16||4} = (26.90 + 4 \cdot 0.84) + (-9.749) = 20.51$$

The standard error is computed as follows

$$RMSE = \sqrt{\frac{\sum_{i=1}^{N} e_i^2}{N}} = \sqrt{\frac{1.13^2 + 1.88^2 + 0.06^2 + 1.61^2}{4}} = 1.36$$

Period	Demand Actual	Demand Forecast	intercept	slope	error	Average error	Std.Dev error	Abs. Rel error	MAPE	Lower Bound CI	Upper Bound CI
1	19	19.38									
2	26	26.38									
3	19	18.88									
4	11	10.38									
5	23	22.63									
6	30	29.63									
7	22	22.13									
8	13	13.63	23.22	0.81							
9	27	25.88	24.26	0.84	−1.13	−1.13	1.13	4.17%	4.17%		
10	35	33.12	25.49	0.87	−1.88	−1.50	1.55	5.36%	4.77%		
11	26	26.06	26.39	0.87	0.06	−0.98	1.26	0.22%	3.25%		
12	16	17.61	26.94	0.84	1.61	−0.33	1.36	10.03%	4.95%		
13		29.65								27.0	32.3
14		36.74								34.1	39.4
15		29.11								26.4	31.8
16		20.51								17.9	23.2

Fig. 4.34 Forecast by the additive model for the seasonal pattern example

Period	Seasonality Terms					Normalized Seasonality Factors					Normed Intercept
	C1	C2	C3	C4	sum	C1	C2	C3	C4	sum	
1											
2											
3											
4											
5											
6											
7											
8	1.844	8.031	−0.281	−9.594	0.000	1.844	8.031	−0.281	−9.594	0.000	23.22
9	1.934	8.031	−0.281	−9.594	0.090	1.911	8.009	−0.304	−9.616	0.000	24.28
10	1.911	8.159	−0.304	−9.616	0.150	1.874	8.121	−0.341	−9.654	0.000	25.53
11	1.874	8.121	−0.346	−9.654	−0.005	1.875	8.123	−0.345	−9.653	0.000	26.39
12	1.875	8.123	−0.345	−9.781	−0.128	1.907	8.155	−0.313	−9.749	0.000	26.90

Fig. 4.35 Seasonality terms normalization in the additive model for the seasonal pattern example

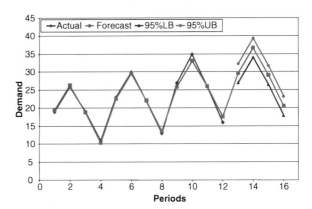

Fig. 4.36 Graph of forecast with the additive model for the seasonal pattern example

The 95% confidence intervals for the forecasts for the next cycle are then computed as follows and are summarized in Table 4.3. Finally, the demand and forecasts based on additive triple exponential smoothing are shown in Fig. 4.36. The 95% confidence intervals for the forecasts are also shown in the figure.

Table 4.3 Forecasts and confidence intervals for the seasonal example by the additive triple smoothing method

Period	Forecast mean	Lower bound CI	Upper bound CI
13	29.65	27.0	32.3
14	36.74	34.1	39.4
15	29.11	26.4	31.8
16	20.51	17.9	23.2

$$CI = F_t \pm z \cdot \sigma = 29.65 \pm 1.96 \cdot 1.36 = [27.0, \ 32.3]$$

The MAPE by this forecasting method is 4.95%.

4.4.3.3 Multiplicative Triple Exponential Smoothing

The multiplicative variant of the triple exponential smoothing method for seasonal data assumes that the data are generated by a process in which the pattern is multiplied by the seasonal effect.

$$D_t = Pat_t \cdot c_t + \varepsilon_t \tag{4.71}$$

At the end of period t, when the real demand for this period is known, the parameters are updated based on the following formulas, where $\|$ indicates the modulo operator:

$$O_t = \alpha \left(D_t / c_t \right) + (1 - \alpha)(O_{t-1} + S_{t-1}) \tag{4.72}$$

$$S_t = \beta(O_t - O_{t-1}) + (1 - \beta)S_{t-1} \tag{4.73}$$

$$c_{t\|P} = \gamma \left(D_t / O_t \right) + (1 - \gamma)c_{t-P\|P} \tag{4.74}$$

All the seasonality factors are then normalized so that their sum equals the number of periods in the cycle. The offset and slope are then also normalized and the forecast for the next and future periods is then computed based on the normalized offset, slope, and seasonality factors.

$$c_t = c_t \cdot \frac{P}{\sum\limits_{j=1}^{P} c_j} \tag{4.75}$$

$$O_t = O_t \cdot \left(\frac{1}{P} \sum\limits_{j=1}^{P} c_j \right) \tag{4.76}$$

$$S_t = S_t \cdot \left(\frac{1}{P} \sum\limits_{j=1}^{P} c_j \right) \tag{4.77}$$

$$F_{t+1} = (O_t + S_t)\, c_{t+1\|P} \tag{4.78}$$

$$F_{t,t+\tau} = (O_t + \tau S_t)\, c_{t+\tau\|P} \tag{4.79}$$

To compute the initial values of the intercept, slope, and seasonality factors, at least two full cycles of historical data are required. If data for more periods is available, seasonal regression with indicator variables can be used to estimate the initial parameter values. But it should be noted that seasonal regression is an additive model.

Multiplicative Triple Exponential Smoothing Example

The number of periods to determine the initial parameter values was set equal to two cycles. The number of periods remaining for the adaptive or training phase is then equal to one cycle. The next task is to compute initial estimates of the underlying trend. We will compute an average value for each of the two cycles and fit a straight line through those points. The detailed calculations have been shown in the application of the additive variant to the example.

If more than two cycles of data are available for the determination of the initial parameters, the slope and intercepts can be computed with linear regression techniques. If the number of periods is equivalent to a number of full cycles, linear regression can be performed on the average demand per cycle (See Fig. 4.37).

The next task is to compute the initial seasonality factors. There exists one factor for each of the time periods in the cycle. The factors are computed as the ratio of the observed value divided by the linear forecast. The computations for the calculation of seasonality factor of the fourth period in the cycle are shown next, including the normalization of the seasonality factors so that all factors in a cycle sum up to the number of periods in the cycle. The calculations must be based on consistent values, i.e., we can use the normalized seasonality factors with the normalized slope and normalized offset or we can use the original seasonality factors with the original slope and offset. To normalize the offset and slope we must divide by the same normalization factor we used for the seasonality factors. In other words, the normalization executes a scaling transformation.

Fig. 4.37 Initial linear forecast parameters for the seasonal pattern example

Parameters			Initial Linear Forecast		
			Period	Demand	Regress.
N	4				
α	0.2	Cycle 1	2.5	18.75	
β	0.1	Cycle 2	6.5	22.00	
γ	0.1	Slope 8		0.81	0.81
Conf.	0.95	Intercept 8	8.0	23.22	23.22
z	1.96				

$$c_4 = \frac{11}{18.75 + 1.5 \cdot 0.81} = 0.551$$

$$c_8 = \frac{13}{23.22} = 0.560$$

$$\overline{c_4} = \frac{0.551 + 0.560}{2} = 0.555$$

$$\sum_{t=1}^{4} c_t = 4.041$$

$$c_4 = 0.555 \frac{4}{4.041} = 0.550$$

$$S_8 = 0.81 \frac{4.041}{4} = 0.82$$

$$O_8 = 23.22 \frac{4.041}{4} = 23.46$$

The computations for the seasonal forecast for period 8 are shown next, and the seasonal forecast for all periods and the corresponding errors are shown in Fig. 4.38.

$$F_8 = O_8 \cdot c_{8||4} \quad = 23.46 \cdot 0.550 = 12.90$$
$$= 23.22 \cdot 0.555 = 12.90$$
$$e_8 = D_8 - F_8 = 13 - 12.9 = 0.1$$

Period	Demand	Forecast Linear	Seasonal Factor	Avg. S. Factor	Normed S. Factor	Forecast Seasonal	Forecast Error
1	19	17.53	1.084	1.095	1.084	19.20	−0.20
2	26	18.34	1.417	1.403	1.389	25.74	0.26
3	19	19.16	0.992	0.987	0.977	18.90	0.10
4	11	19.97	0.551	0.555	0.550	11.09	−0.09
5	23	20.78	1.107			22.76	0.24
6	30	21.59	1.389			30.30	−0.30
7	22	22.41	0.982			22.11	−0.11
8	13	23.22	0.560			12.90	0.10
Sum	163	163.0		4.041	4.000	163.0	−0.01
Standard Error							0.314

Fig. 4.38 Initial forecast for the seasonal pattern example

Fig. 4.39 Graph of initial forecast for the seasonal pattern example

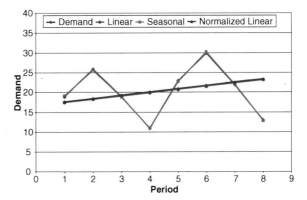

The forecast of the historical values using the linear trend and seasonality factors computed above is shown in Fig. 4.39. The forecasted values match the observed values very closely, which is numerically demonstrated by a standard error of 0.314.

The computations for the forecast and for the updates of the trend parameters and seasonality factor for period 9 are shown next. Observe that only the seasonality factor associated with this period is updated directly based on the new observed value, but that the normalization of the seasonality factors may also changes the other factors.

$$F_9 = (O_8 + S_8) \cdot c_{9\|4} = (23.46 + 0.82) \cdot 1.084 = 26.32$$

$$O_9 = \alpha \left(D_9/c_1 \right) + (1 - \alpha) \left(O_8 + S_8 \right)$$
$$= 0.2 \left(27/1.084 \right) + 0.8 \left(23.46 + 0.82 \right) = 24.40$$

$$S_9 = \beta \left(O_9 - O_8 \right) + (1 - \beta) S_8$$
$$= 0.1(24.40 - 23.46) + 0.9 \cdot 0.82 = 0.83$$

$$c_1 = \gamma \left(D_9/O_9 \right) + (1 - \gamma) c_1$$
$$= 0.1 \left(27/24.40 \right) + 0.9 \cdot 1.084 = 1.086$$

$$\sum_{t=1}^{P} c_t = 4.002 \qquad \frac{P}{\sum\limits_{t=1}^{P} c_t} = \frac{4}{4.002} = 0.9995$$

$$c_1 = c_1 \frac{P}{\sum\limits_{t=1}^{P} c_t} = 1.086 \cdot 0.9995 = 1.086$$

$$O_9 = \frac{24.40}{0.9995} = 24.42$$

$$S_9 = \frac{0.86}{0.9995} = 0.83$$

Period	Demand Actual	Demand Forecast	intercept	slope	error	Average error	Standard error	Abs.Rel error	MAPE	Lower Bound	Upper Bound
1	19	19.20									
2	26	25.74									
3	19	18.90									
4	11	11.09									
5	23	22.76									
6	30	30.30									
7	22	22.11									
8	13	12.90	23.22	0.81							
9	27	26.32	24.40	0.83	−0.68	−0.68	0.68	2.52%	2.52%		
10	35	35.06	25.24	0.83	0.06	−0.31	0.48	0.16%	1.34%		
11	26	25.46	26.18	0.84	−0.54	−0.39	0.50	2.09%	1.59%		
12	16	14.85	27.46	0.89	−1.15	−0.58	0.72	7.18%	2.98%		
13		30.77								29.4	32.2
14		40.56								39.1	42.0
15		29.44								28.0	30.9
16		17.13								15.7	18.5

Fig. 4.40 Forecast for the seasonal pattern example

Period	Seasonality Factors					Normalized Seasonality Factors					Normalized	
	c1	c2	c3	c4	sum	c1	c2	c3	c4	sum	Offset	Slope
1												
2												
3												
4												
5												
6												
7												
8	1.095	1.403	0.987	0.555	4.041	1.084	1.389	0.977	0.550	4.000	23.46	0.82
9	1.086	1.389	0.977	0.550	4.002	1.086	1.388	0.976	0.549	4.000	24.42	0.83
10	1.086	1.388	0.976	0.549	4.000	1.086	1.388	0.976	0.549	4.000	25.24	0.83
11	1.086	1.388	0.978	0.549	4.002	1.085	1.388	0.978	0.549	4.000	26.20	0.84
12	1.085	1.388	0.978	0.553	4.003	1.085	1.387	0.977	0.552	4.000	27.48	0.89

Fig. 4.41 Seasonality factors for the seasonal pattern example

The normalization factor is equal to 0.9995, which is nearly 1.0, so the normalization will change the slope, offset, and seasonality factors very little. The displayed values before and after normalization are thus often identical in Figs. 4.40 and 4.41.

After the first training period, the standard error will be computed as the RMSE based on the errors of the training periods. So an initial (degenerate) value of the RMSE for the first training period is the error of the first training period itself. In this example

$$se_9 = RMSE_9 = e_9 = 0.68.$$

In practical situations the standard error of the first training period will never be used in calculations to determine the confidence interval for a forecast. Since the initialization phase uses a static model, it would be more correct to compute the standard error of the first training period with the formula based on the static model. The number of observations would be the number of periods in the initialization phase. The errors would be summed for all the observations in the initialization

Fig. 4.42 Graph of forecast for the seasonal pattern example by multiplicative triple exponential smoothing

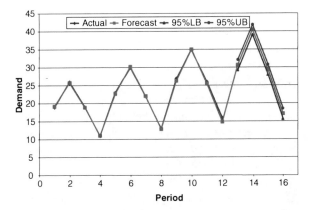

phase and the denominator would be $(N-1-P)$ for a pattern with linear trend and seasonality and P periods in a season. One of the purposes of the adjustment phase is to generate a better estimate of the standard error based on all the errors of the adjustment phase.

The adjustment calculations are repeated for periods 10–12 and the adjustment phase ends with period 12. The computations for the forecasts made at the end of period 12 for all the periods in the next cycle are shown next and forecasts for the next cycle are shown in Fig. 4.42.

$$F_{12,13} = (O_{12} + S_{12})\, c_{13||4} = (27.48 + 0.89) \cdot 1.085 = 30.78$$
$$F_{12,14} = (O_{12} + \tau\, S_{12})\, c_{14||4} = (27.48 + 2 \cdot 0.89) \cdot 1.387 = 40.58$$
$$F_{12,15} = (O_{12} + \tau\, S_{12})\, c_{15||4} = (27.48 + 3 \cdot 0.89) \cdot 0.977 = 29.46$$
$$F_{12,16} = (O_{12} + \tau\, S_{12})\, c_{16||4} = (27.48 + 4 \cdot 0.89) \cdot 0.552 = 17.13$$

Finally, the computations for the confidence intervals for the forecasts for the periods in the next cycle with a 95% confidence level are shown next using 0.72 as the standard error.

$$RMSE = \sqrt{\frac{\sum_{i=1}^{N} e_i^2}{N}} = \sqrt{\frac{(-0.68)^2 + 0.06^2 + (-0.54)^2 + (-1.15)^2}{4}} = 0.72$$

$$CI = F_\tau \pm z \cdot \sigma = 30.77 \pm 1.96 \cdot 0.72 = [29.37,\ 32.19]$$

The forecast and confidence intervals are shown in Table 4.4.

The MAPE generated by this forecasting method is equal to 2.9%.

Table 4.4 Forecasts and confidence intervals for the seasonal example by the multiplicative triple smoothing method

Period	Forecast mean	Lower bound	Upper bound
13	30.8	29.4	32.2
14	40.6	39.1	42.0
15	29.4	28.0	30.9
16	17.1	15.7	18.5

4.5   Summary

Short-term tactical and operational forecasts are usually based on historical data. Many powerful and highly mathematical forecasting techniques exist, such as regression, time series analysis, and forecasting methods for autocorrelated data. However, the most important requirement for the generation of a high-quality forecast is an understanding of the underlying data pattern of the forecasted variable. The correct forecasting method can then be selected for this underlying pattern. Applying correctly the wrong forecasting method for a data pattern will only generated wrong forecasts. One simple method to understand the underlying pattern is to graph the historical values over time. Since the underlying data pattern is almost never fully understood or remains unchanged for extended periods of time, most forecasts will have significant errors. Hence, it does not make much sense to report only the expected value of the forecasted variable or point forecast. Based on the root mean square forecast error, confidence intervals can be established, which provide much more meaningful forecast information. A simple method to judge the quality of the forecast is again to graph the forecast errors over time.

The generation of a high-quality forecast requires the understanding of the underlying pattern, the application of the correct method for that pattern, and the reporting of the results with their stochastic characteristics. The forecasting results generated by the blind application of very sophisticated forecasting techniques should be highly suspect. The farther in the future the forecasts are, the easier it is to make very large forecasting errors.

4.6   Exercises

True/False Questions

1. A cyclic demand pattern has cycles of varying length and magnitude (T/F) _____ .
2. Time series forecasting attempts to predict the future value of a variable based on the currently observed values of different variables (T/F) _____ .
3. A forecast created by the moving averages method lags any trend the forecasted variable may have (T/F) _____ .
4. In exponential smoothing the weights of the different historical values form a geometrically decreasing pattern when the values go farther back in time (T/F) _____ .
5. In exponential smoothing a larger smoothing constant will create a forecast that more rapidly tracks a current trend in the forecasted variable (T/F) _____ .
6. Using forecasting techniques based on time series analysis, different forecasters will arrive at the same forecast if they use the same data (T/F) _____ .

7. Using the moving averages forecasting method, only the last observation or realized demand needs to be kept (T/F) _____.
8. A higher value of the alpha parameter in exponential smoothing forecasting increases the stability of the forecast (T/F) _____.
9. The sum of the normalized seasonality factors in the multiplicative variant of Winter's exponential smoothing method must add up to the number of periods in the cycle (T/F) _____.
10. Holt's exponential smoothing method requires three smoothing constants (T/F) _____.
11. At least two full cycles of data are required to use the multiplicative variant of Winter's exponential smoothing method (T/F) _____.
12. The moving averages forecasting technique is the appropriate forecasting method when the underlying data exhibits a linearly growing trend (T/F) _____.

Soccer Balls Seasonal Forecasting The Soccer Ball Company (SBC), Inc. manufacturers and sells introductory level soccer balls to sports retailers. The following statistics in Table 4.5 have been collected on the amount of sales in the United States on a quarterly basis and reported in thousands of balls. You are asked to forecast the amount of future sales with the additive variant of Winter's seasonal method. Execute all calculations and display all results with three significant digits beyond the decimal point.

The result of your calculations has to be inserted in the following four tables that have identical structure to the tables used in class. The last two tables are components of one single large table, but are shown sequentially to fit the width of the page. Corresponding lines in both tables are identified by the period index. The fields that you have to complete are shown as shaded.

In Table 4.6, compute the average demand for each cycle and compute the slope and intercept of the trend. Also compute the standard deviate corresponding to the 80% confidence limits.

In Table 4.7, compute the missing linear forecasts and the missing values for the seasonality factors.

In Table 4.8 summarize the values that you have computed so far. Compute the forecast for period 9.

Table 4.5 Sales data (in thousands of balls)

Quarter	Period	Demand
Q1-2003	1	17
Q2-2003	2	48
Q3-2003	3	31
Q4-2003	4	50
Q1-2004	5	15
Q2-2004	6	39
Q3-2004	7	25
Q4-2004	8	43

Table 4.6 Calculation on the initial forecast trend

Parameters			Initial Linear Forecast		
P	4			Period	Sales
α	0.2		Cycle 1		
β	0.1		Cycle 2		
γ	0.1		Slope	8	
Conf.Lim.	0.8		Intercept	8	
z					

Table 4.7 Calculation on the initial seasonal forecast

Period	Demand	Forecast Linear	Seasonal Factor	Avg. Seas Factor	Normed S. Factor
1	17				
2	48	37.25	10.75		
3	31	35.75	-4.75		
4	50	34.25	15.75		
5	15	32.75	-17.75		
6	39	31.25	7.75		
7	25				
8	43	28.25	14.75		

At the end of period 9, additional data have been collected and the amount of sales was 6,000 balls.

Give the formulas for updating the intercept and slope of the linear forecast and compute the updated values.

Give the formulas for updating and then normalizing the seasonality factors and intercept and compute the updated values.

Give the formulas for computing the forecasts on the sales amount in future periods and compute the updated values for next four periods.

Give the formula for the standard error of a static additive forecasting model in function of N observations and P periods per season. Compute the forecast error with the formula for the standard error for period 9 and insert the results in Table 4.8.

Give the formula to compute the confidence interval for the demand forecast. Compute the number of standard deviations corresponding to the confidence limits of 80%, and the boundaries of the confidence interval for the forecast for period 10 only.

Give the formula to compute the MAPE in function of N observations. Compute the MAPE for the forecast for period 9.

PPC Triple Exponential Smoothing This question has the additional purpose to familiarize you with the structured answers you would need to provide to a similar question during an examination.

The Polychromatic Paper Company (PPC) produces high-quality, glossy, wrapping paper for gifts. They sell primarily to discount merchandisers and drugstore

Table 4.8 Calculation on the seasonal forecast

Period	Demand Actual	Demand Forecast	Lower CI Bound	Upper CI Bound	intercept	slope	error	Standard error	MAPE
1	17								
2	48								
3	31								
4	50								
5	15								
6	39								
7	25								
8	43								
9	6								
10									
11									
12									
13									

Period	Seasonal. Factors					Normaliz. Seasonal Factors					Normal.
	C1	C2	C3	C4	sum	C1	C2	C3	C4	sum	Intercept
1											
2											
3											
4											
5											
6											
7											
8											
9											

chains. They have collected quarterly data on the sales of their top-of-the-line paper grade, expressed in millions of rolls. The data for the last two years are given in Table 4.9. You are asked to provide a sales forecast for the same product for the next year, periods 9–12, with an 80% confidence interval. Use two significant digits after the decimal point in all your calculations.

Identify the underlying data pattern and write down the algebraic expression for it. Provide a concise and complete definition of the variables that are used in the algebraic expression.

Use the appropriate exponential smoothing method for this underlying data pattern to forecast the demand for the next year. Use the standard values for the smoothing constant(s). Compute the forecast offset (or intercept), the slope, the linear forecast, the seasonality factors, and the seasonal forecast based on the data.

Table 4.9 Historical sales data

Period	Demand
1	8
2	12
3	15
4	32
5	6
6	8
7	9
8	22

Summarize your calculations in the following table. Not all the rows, columns, or cells of the table have to be used. Show the computations to derive the intercept and slope at end of period 8.

Period	Demand	Linear forecast		Seasonality factor	Seasonal forecast	Forecast error
1	8					
2	12					
3	15					
4	32					
5	6					
6	8					
7	9					
8	22					

Compute the forecasts for the next year. For each period you must show the linear forecast, the seasonality factor used, and the expected value, lower and upper bound of the confidence interval of the seasonal forecast. Summarize your calculations in the next table. Compute and show the standard deviation of the forecast error, the number of standard deviations corresponding to the confidence limits, and the size of the confidence interval.

Period	Linear forecast	Seasonality factor	Seasonal Forecast	Lower conf. int.	Upper conf. int.
9					
10					
11					
12					

At the end of period 9 the company contacts you again with the new sales data for this period and asks you to update your forecast for the next four periods (periods 10–13). The actual sales for period 9 were 4 million rolls. Compute the updated values for the slope, intercept, seasonality factors, and standard deviation of the forecast error. Give the formulas for the computation of the update intercept, slope, and seasonality factors. Compute the updated values for the intercept, slope, and seasonality factors, standard deviation of the forecast error, and the size of the confidence interval. Finally, show your computations for the update forecasts in the next table.

Period	Linear forecast	Seasonality factor	Seasonal forecast	Lower conf. int.	Upper conf. int.
10					
11					
12					
13					

Assume that the company reported to you that the sales for period 9 were 7 million rolls. In other words, the actual sales of 4 million rolls never happened and the actual sales were 7 million rolls. What would be your forecasting report to PPC state in this case?

Retail E-Commerce Sales The U.S. Department of Commerce reported in November 2002 on the quarterly online sales by e-commerce retailers as shown in the following table.

Quarter	2000 ($)	2001 ($)	2002 ($)
1Q	5.81	8.26	9.88
2Q	6.35	8.25	10.27
3Q	7.27	8.24	11.06
4Q	9.46	11.18	

Online sales reported in billion $

Compute the forecasts for the online sales for the next four quarters with a 90% confidence interval. Use two significant digits after the decimal point in all your calculations. For each quarter you must show the linear forecast, the seasonality factor used, and the expected value, lower, and upper bound of the confidence interval of the seasonal forecast. Summarize your calculations in a table. Compute and show the standard deviation of the forecast error, the number of standard deviations corresponding to the confidence limits, and the size of the confidence interval.

High-Voltage Electrical Consumption The Industrial Metals Foundry is in the process of budgeting for their energy costs during the next year. Their energy costs are primarily related to their consumption of high-voltage electricity for their electric arc smelters. They have recorded their energy costs for the past three years on a quarterly basis. They have asked you to provide them with a forecast of their energy costs for the next year with a 90% confidence level. Clearly explain your general approach and state the assumptions that you have used to arrive at this forecast. Use the answer structure provided in the previous exercise to provide the details of your response to their request. The data is shown in the next table.

Period	Demand
1	27,000
2	70,000
3	41,000
4	13,000
5	30,000
6	73,000
7	48,000
8	15,000
9	34,000
10	82,000
11	51,000
12	16,000

References

Ballou, R. H. (1998). *Chapter 9 in Business logistics management* (4th ed.). Englewood Cliffs: Prentice-Hall.

Brockwell, P., & Davis, R. (1996). *Introduction to time series and forecasting.* New York: Springer.

Hayter, A. (1996). *Probability and Statistics for Engineers and Scientists.* Boston: PWS Publishing Company.

Holt, C. C. (1957). Forecasting seasonal and trends by exponentially weighted moving averages. Office of Naval Research Memo, No. 52.

Kutner, M., Nachtschiem, C., Wasserman, W., & Neter, J. (1996). *Applied linear statistical models.* Boston: McGraw-Hill.

Montgomery, D. C., & Johnson, L. A. (1976). *Forecasting and time series analysis.* New York: McGraw-Hill.

Montgomery, D., Peck, E., & Vining, G. (2001). *Introduction to linear regression analysis.* New York: Wiley.

Muther, E. (1977). *Transform methods with applications to engineering and operations research.* Englewood Cliffs: Prentice-Hall.

Neter, J., Kutner, M. H., Nachtsheim, C. J., & Wasserman, W. (1996). *Applied linear statistical models.* Boston: McGraw-Hill.

Weisberg, S. (1985). *Applied linear regression.* New York: Wiley.

Winters, P. R. (1960). Forecasting by exponentially moving averages. *Management Science, 6,* 324–342.

Chapter 5
Transportation Systems

Learning Objectives After you have studied this chapter, you should be able to

- Know the major definitions of the actors, transportation modes, and services
- Know the major performance characteristics of transportation modes
- Know the major transportation modes and their main performance characteristics
- Know the principal documents used in transportation services
- Know the definitions of incoterms and free trade zones

5.1 Introduction

5.1.1 General Characteristics of Transportation Services

5.1.1.1 Transportation Expenditures in the United States

Transportation costs represent the single largest cost element in logistics operations. Estimates range from 50–65% of the total logistics cost is accounted for by transportation. So the management of transportation services is clearly an important task for logistics and supply chain engineers. The goal of this chapter is to identify the major characteristics of transportations services and to list the major transportation modes and their respective characteristics. The trends of the total transportation cost and the transportation cost as a fraction of the total logistics costs are shown in Fig. 5.1. The data is based on Trunick (2003, 2004, 2005, 2006) and Wilson (2007).

5.1.1.2 Effect of Transportation Services on World Trade

The lack of readily available transportation necessitates that the production and consumption of products occurs in relative proximity so that goods can be deliv-

M. Goetschalckx, *Supply Chain Engineering,* International Series in Operations Research & Management Science 161, DOI 10.1007/978-1-4419-6512-7_5, © Springer Science+Business Media LLC 2011

Fig. 5.1 Transportation cost
and relative fraction trends

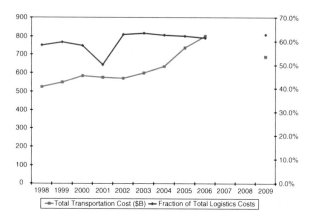

ered to the customers within an acceptable time limit. As a consequence the total amount produced in any one location is limited. This in turn causes the production infrastructure to be at the crafts level because the customer base cannot support large concentrated production facilities. For the same reason there will be only a few production facilities per geographical area. As a consequence the customers have limited choices available to them. The existence of relative inexpensive and sufficiently speedy transportation services change this economic pattern completely. The large area of potential customers now allows large production facilities with specialized production techniques and the associated economies of scale. This lowers unit production costs and allows the producers to expand their competitive area. As a consequence more than one producer may now compete in a particular area which tends to lower the purchase costs for the consumers. Finally, the concentration of large numbers of customers in large cities is made possible because supplies can be transported to the city from a wide area with many different suppliers.

The availability of fast, reliable, and affordable transportation services typically yields a richer product offering at lower consumer prices. Consumers consider these definite advantages of transportation and trade. However, simultaneously the inefficient producers are no longer protected by the geographical barriers of distance. Very large and very efficient producers may now compete for the consumer demand and as a consequence profit margins may become very thin or non-existent. Local producers may go bankrupt or just stop producing, which negatively impacts the local employment. Political entities such as countries may want to protect their local producers by erecting new trade barriers such as duties, product standards, and local content laws. Organizations such as the World Trade Organization or WTO have as their goal the elimination of these trade barriers to promote unrestricted world trade. Meetings of the WTO attract many active opponents of globalization and free trade that have been economically disadvantaged by competitors that may be located in other regions of the world.

5.1.1.3 Transportation Definitions

A shipper is any person or organization that needs to transport goods or people. A carrier is a person or organization that provides transportation services of people or freight as part of a commercial enterprise. Carriers can range from a single self-employed driver operating their own truck to large, international trucking, shipping, or airline companies.

Carriers are typically divided into three types depending on who owns the transportation assets and the transported goods. A *common carrier* is a corporation or organization that provides a specific transportation service to the general public at an established price and must carry everybody or everything compatible with that service. A common carrier thus has no right to reject particular compatible passengers or freight from shippers that are willing to pay the price. The doctrine of common carriage was originally developed with respect to stagecoaches, ships, and trains. More recently, it has been applied to pipelines and aircraft and even to communication networks such as telephone and internet networks. A *contract carrier* is an organization that has entered into a specific legal agreement with a shipping organization to provide contractually agreed upon transportation services for an agreed upon price. This allows the contract carrier to be more selective with respect to the shippers it serves and more responsive to its customers than a common carrier. If the contract extends over several months, the transportation assets, such as trucks, may be painted with the color scheme and trademarks of the shipper even though they belong to the carrier. A *private carrier* is a transportation organization who transports its own goods using transportation assets that it owns or leases. These assets are called a *private fleet*. For private carriage the shipper and carrier are the same organization.

There exist five basic modes of transportation: pipeline, water, rail, road, and air. The water-based transportation are sometimes further divided into inland water and ocean-going transportation. Finally, any permanent presence of humankind in orbit around the earth in the space station or possible at other locations in the solar system will require some form of space transportation. To satisfy a transportation service request a single transportation mode may be used exclusively or several modes may be combined. The main characteristics of a transportation service are: availability, capacity, price, average transit time, transit time variability, and loss and damages. To select a service the tradeoff must be made between the characteristics of the various alternative services.

5.1.2 Performance Measures of Transportation Services

5.1.2.1 Costs

Transportation costs are traditionally divided into fixed and variable costs. Fixed costs are independent of the intensity of the (transportation) activity such as terminal facilities, administration, roadways and tracks. Variable costs are dependent on intensity of the activity, such as labor, fuel, maintenance, and handling. Variable cost in transportation services may be based on a either distance or volume or a combination of both.

Transportation costs vary significantly in size and structure from one transportation service to another. Ballou (1999) provides statistics showing that the fastest transportation modes are generally also the most expensive. The relative ratios may change over time. The average costs are usually expressed as costs per ton-mile. Average costs can be used for general comparisons. However the selection of a particular transportation service should be based on the actual charges which often depend on the commodity shipped, the origin and destination, the distance between the end points, the quantity shipped, and the time of the year. The transportation of goods typically is subject to significant economies of scale, which leads in turn to large quantity discounts. Quantity discounts can be either incremental or full discount. In the first case, the discount is only given for the additional freight and the resulting total cost curve is a piecewise linear concave cost curve. In the second case, the discounted rate is given for all the freight and the resulting total cost curve may have discontinuities. The two types of cost curves are shown in Fig. 5.2. Quantity discounts imply that $c_1 > c_2 > c_3$.

Many freight transportation costs are very asymmetric, i.e., the cost for shipping freight from location A to location B is significantly different from the cost for shipping the same quantity of freight from location B to location A. This is usually caused by a large one-directional flow. For example, the shipment of large quantities of fresh fruits and vegetables from countries in the Caribbean basin to the cities of the Northeastern United States in reusable containers creates a large flow of empty containers back to the Caribbean basin. This significantly reduces the price for shipping freight in that direction.

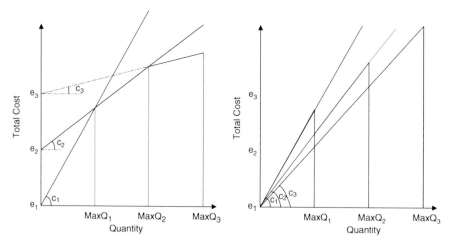

Fig. 5.2 Total cost curves for incremental and full-quantity discounts

The carrier incurs the transportation costs and the shipper has to pay transportation charges. The difference between its costs and charges contributes to the profit (or loss) of the carrier.

5.1.2.2 Transit Time

The transit time is the elapsed time between the moment the goods are picked up at the door or dock of the supplier until the moment the goods are delivered to the dock or door of the designee. This is also called the door-to-door transit time. The complete transportation service may use several different transportation modes but this is largely irrelevant to the shipper who is primarily interested in the overall characteristics of the service. The transit time has a strong influence on the configuration of a supply chain. For example, before the full implementation of the free flow of goods between the member countries of the European Union (EU) it was not unusual for shipments between the densely populated countries of Western Europe to spend more time waiting for document processing at border crossings than actually moving on the highway. To guarantee speedy delivery most companies had at least a single distribution center in each major country. When the EU eliminated these time consuming documentation operations at the borders, many companies changed their supply chain configuration from a distribution center per country to a few strategically located distribution centers for the whole EU. The shorter transit times allowed the economies of scale for the distribution center facility and operations to outweigh the larger delivery distance.

5.1.2.3 Transit Time Variability

Companies maintain safety inventory to buffer against the variability in the transit times from their suppliers to their distribution centers. A higher variability increases the required safety inventory to achieve the same level of customer service. The higher inventory levels tie up capital, require larger warehouses, and increase the risk of product obsolescence.

5.1.3 Transportation Units

The units of transportation were originally defined in historically separated countries, measurement systems, and industries. In recent times, an effort has been made to standardize these units, but many local units are still being used. Great care should be taken that all the organizations involved in a transportation request and service use the same or consistent units.

A common unit of transportation quantity is the *hundredweight* or *cwt*. The English version is often called the *long hundredweight* and is equal to 112 pounds. The

American version is called the *short hundredweight* and is exactly equal to 100 pounds or approximately 45.36 kg. The *c* in the *cwt* abbreviation is the symbol for the Roman numeral 100. One of the most confusing units in freight transportation is the ton, since so many different variants exist. The *ton* is a traditional unit of volume used for measuring the cargo capacity of a freight transportation vehicle such as a ship, train, or truck. *Gross tonnage* (GT) is the volume of the ship measured at its outer hull and is expressed as a multiple of 100 ft^3 or 2.83 m^3. *Net tonnage* (NT) is the volume of a ship available for carrying cargo. Harbor fees are usually based on either gross tonnage or net tonnage. A *freight ton* is exactly 40 ft^3 or approximately 1.13 m^3. However a *ton* also expresses the weight of the transported freight and is exactly equal to 20 hundredweights. The American version is called a *short ton* and there are 2000 pounds in a short ton, which is approximately equal to 907.2 kg. The British version is called a *long ton* and there are 2240 pounds in a ton, which is approximately equal to 1016 kg. The *deadweight ton* or *dwt* is used to indicate the cargo capacity of ships in long tons and is equal to 2240 pounds. Finally, the *metric ton* expresses the weight of the transported freight and is exactly equal to 1000 kg. All of this confusion can be avoided by expressing quantities in the metric SI system, i.e., express volume in cubic meters and weight in metric tons. But great care must be taken when interpreting quantities and sizes described on transportation documents, especially when abbreviations are used.

5.1.4 Transportation Structures

Freight transportation operations often either show a hub-and-spoke structure or a point-to-point structure. In the point-to-point structure goods are transported directly from the origin to the destination point. The total number of transportation legs is large. The advantage of this direct shipping method is a reduced travel time and travel distance for the goods. The disadvantage is that the frequency of the service between a pair of points may be lower because of low traffic volume between the points, which in turn may yield higher transportation costs. In the "hub-and-spoke" system, goods are first transported to a local consolidation hub, then shipped by long-haul freight carrier to a destination hub, and finally delivered from the destination deconsolidation hub to the final destination. The total number of transportation legs is smaller, since each end point is only connected to a single hub. The advantage of hub-and-spoke is the higher frequency of service between a point and its serving hub and between hubs. This consolidation may also reduce the transportation cost because of the economies of scale in transportation. The disadvantages are the longer trip time for the goods and the possible congestion at the hubs. To avoid waiting times for the carriers at a hub, incoming and outgoing carriers are scheduled for peak interchange periods, which may lead to significant congestion and delays. Hub-and-spoke systems are used in LTL trucking, international intermodal container transportation, and also for air transportation of passengers. Often hybrid networks are used, where the origin and destination points with the highest pair wise traffic volume are served by direct point-to-point transportation and the traffic on the legs with lower volume are routed over the hub-and-spoke network. The local delivery transportation is also known as peddling or "milk runs".

Finally, transportation networks can also lack any structure but route the transportation carriers in an opportunistic manner. Two examples are the full truck load transportation and tramp trade. For the full truck load example, drivers call in to the main office or into an exchange after the delivery of a load to its destination to find the next load that originates close to their current location. The truck route then becomes a concatenation of origin-to-destination legs and the driver may not return to its home base for weeks at a time. Ships that are engaged in tramp trade do not have a fixed schedule or sequence of ports of call and are called tramp freighters. Both trucks and ships are the transportation assets and part of the transportation infrastructure that execute the transportation requests via the spot market. One equivalent for the transportation of people is the operation of taxi cabs in a metropolitan area.

5.2 Transportation Modes and Infrastructure

5.2.1 Introduction

A map showing the major transportation channels in the United States is shown in Fig. 5.3. It clearly illustrates the different interstate densities in the eastern and western parts of the country.

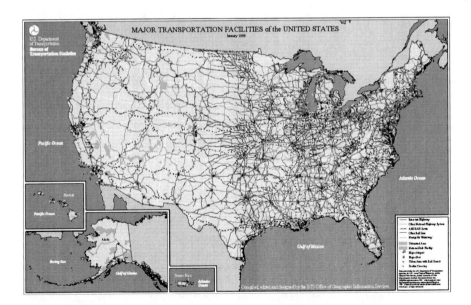

Fig. 5.3 Major transportation infrastructure in the United States, 1996

The relative cost importance of the major transportation modes and their five-year trends are shown in Fig. 5.4. The data is based on Trunick (2003, 2004, 2005, 2006), Wilson (2007), Blanchard (2010). It shows that local and long-haul intercity road transportation account for more and three fourths of the overall transportation costs. It is rumored that a Teamster's Union President boasted that "*Except for the basic utilities such as water, electricity, and natural gas, everything you consumed today has been transported to you on a truck.*"

The various transportation modes have different cost and performance characteristics. Table 5.1 shows the number of miles than can be transported using different modes using a single gallon of fuel (Trunick 2008). The strong rise of the cost of fuel at the end of 2007 and beginning of 2008 caused fuel to surpass labor as the largest cost for motor carriers.

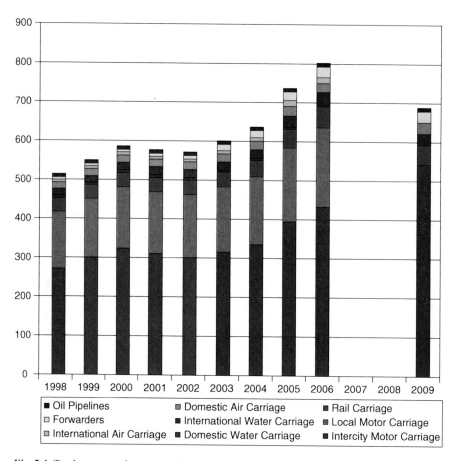

Fig. 5.4 Total transportation cost and transportation mode costs trends

Transport mode	Distance (miles)
Barge (inland water)	576
Rail	413
Motor Carriage	155

Table 5.1 Ton-miles per gallon of fuel. (Source: Outsourced Logistics, July 2008)

Distance: one ton freight carriage per gallon

5.2.2 Pipeline

A pipeline is a system of connected pipes for the transportation of liquids, gasses, and slurries. Slurries are fine solid particles suspended in a liquid. Pumps, valves, and other control devices control the flow. Products may be stored temporarily in storage tanks. Pipeline diameters can vary from a few inches in chemical refineries and oil gathering lines to more than 30 ft in water and sewage collection systems. Larger diameters are much more efficient. The Trans-Alaskan crude oil pipeline has a diameter of 48 inches. Pipelines can be used inside the facilities, on campus environments such as chemical refineries, or for long-distance transportation. Pipelines inside the facilities are usually suspended from the ceiling and pipelines used for long distance transportation are usually laid underground, although the Trans-Alaskan pipeline is suspended on columns above the ground to avoid damaging the permafrost. Pipelines usually consist of sections of pipe made of metals, such as steel, cast iron or aluminum, concrete, or plastics.

Pipelines have a very high initial construction cost, but once installed are highly cost efficient. The cost characteristics are similar to those for rail transportation. The variable cost include the cost for operating the pumping stations and the cost of moving the products. The ratio of fixed cost to total cost is highest among all the transportation modes. Rates for pipeline transportation are competitive with inland waterways and are three to four times smaller than for rail transportation. The average transportation speed of 3–5 miles per hour is not very large, but this is compensated for by the 24 hours a day, 7 days a week continuous operation. Pipelines form a highly dependable form of transportation since there are few interruptions that may cause transit time variability. Because of the nature of the products and the underground construction, weather does not significantly affect operations. Based on the above characteristics, pipelines are most suited to the transportation of high volume liquids and gasses. The most common examples of pipelines are the transportation of crude oil and refined petroleum products such as gasoline, natural gas, and coal slurries.

The costs of moving a product consist mainly of the power consumed in the pumping stations. The pumps must overcome the frictional resistance in the pipe, which is proportional to the circumference of the pipe. The volume capacity is proportional to the cross section of the pipe. So larger diameter pipes are much more efficient from the marginal cost point of view, provided there is enough product volume to justify the fixed cost of the larger diameter pipe.

Most pipelines are privately owned and are associated or affiliated with major oil companies. The pipeline companies own the pipe, terminals, and pumping stations and either own or lease the right of way for the pipe. The pipeline companies are classified as common carriers since they carry the products of all shippers.

In 2006, the British Petroleum Company (BP) was forced to close sections of the pipeline feeder system to the Alaska pipeline, which connects the oil field of Prudhoe Bay with the shipping port of Valdez, because rust had corroded the pipelines and could potentially cause a massive spill. This separated Prudhoe Bay, the largest oil field at that time in the United States, from its market in the continental United States. Prudhoe Bay was at that time responsible for 8% of the nation's consumption and more than 30% of the consumption on the west coast of the United States. The very large economies of scale for pipeline transportation typically result in an extremely concentrated infrastructure. This is a disadvantage for pipeline operations, since a single natural or man-made calamity may block all the freight transportation. The prime examples of natural calamities are earthquakes. Man-made calamities include sabotage and government-ordered shutdowns.

The Atlanta metropolitan area is serviced by two pipelines operated by the Colonial and Marathon companies. The Colonial pipeline has a diameter of 36 inch and runs from Houston to New York. It carries a variety of gasoline types as well as other fuels such diesel and jet fuel and home heating oil. The minimum batch size is 75000 barrels or 3.2 million gallons and fills the pipeline for more than 11 miles and can fill the 16-gallon gas tanks of 200000 cars according to the AJC (2008). The various products are not separated in the pipeline so they mix together at the boundaries between different products. These mixes can either be downgraded or sold for re-refining. The pipeline carries generic commodity fuel types. At the junctions, such as the Atlanta junction, the distributors add their special ingredients to create the gasoline of a particular brand with distinct qualities. The gasoline is then transported by truck to the various gas stations.

5.2.3   Rail

Rail or rail transport is the transportation of goods and passengers along a system of rails or tracks. The vehicles traveling on the tracks are arranged in a train, which is a sequence of individually powered or un-powered vehicles that are linked together and move as a unit. A locomotive is rail vehicle that has as its single function to push or pull the un-powered vehicles, which are typically called cars or wagons. For traditional railroads, the tracks consist of two parallel rails. The gauge is the distance between the tracks. Different countries may operate railroad systems with different gauges created by independent historical development. For electrified tracks, the locomotives have electric engines that draw and return electric energy from and to the high-voltage electricity lines running parallel to the track. Again, different countries may operate electrified tracks at different voltages caused by independent development. In the United States, most freight trains are propelled by diesel engines.

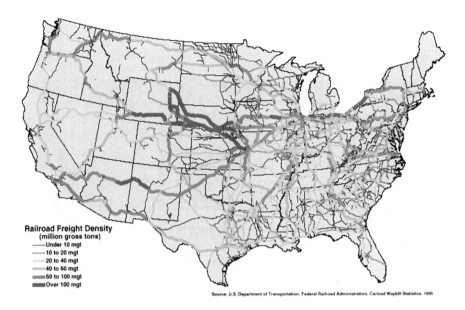

Source: U.S. Department of Transportation, Federal Railroad Administration, Carload Waybill Statistics, 1995

Fig. 5.5 Railroad freight volumes in the United States, 1995

In Fig. 5.5, the freight intensities are shown for the United States. In 1995, the major rail transportation was coast-to-coast. This trend has further increased in recent years due to the increased volume of intermodal containers coming from Asia that are offloaded on the west coast and then transported by rail to the population centers on the east coast. Again the density of the tracks decreases significantly once the midpoint of country is passed when traveling from east to west.

Railroad transportation is highly efficient with respect to marginal costs, but is a very capital intensive mode of transportation. This is especially true if the company that owns and maintains the tracks is a non-governmental corporation. The main capital investments of a railroad are the tracks, switching yards, and rolling stock. A switching yard is freight facility that functions as a node in a railroad network where trains are assembled and disassembled out of individual wagons. Rolling stock refers to the vehicles that move on the tracks. Rolling stock is composed primarily out of locomotives and cars, but also includes several specialty vehicles.

A unit train consists of cars that all have the same destination, so that no assembly and disassembly of the train (switching) has to be executed during the trip, which allows for a significant reduction of the total trip duration. Typically all the cars in the train contain the same commodity, such as the trains that supply electrical power plants with coal. A typical unit train traveling from the west coast to the east cost may consist of four locomotives and flatbed cars with double-stacked intermodal containers. A unit train may consist of up to 100 cars. A unit train with 100 hopper cars, each carrying 100 tons of coal, holds about 10000 tons of coal, sufficient fuel for 1.5 days for an electric power plant. The largest unit trains on earth are operated privately by two mining corporations in north-western Australia to transport iron ore from the inland mining area to ports on the coast with final destinations such as China, Japan, and Korea. A train may consist of up to 300 freight cars propelled by six locomotives and stretch up to 3 km long and transport up to 26000 tons of ore (Economist 2009).

If the train cars carry intermodal containers, this is called "container-on-flat-car" (COFC) and if two containers are placed on top of each other this is know as double-stack. If the train cars carry truck trailers, this is known as "trailer-on-flat-car" (TOFC) or "piggyback". Double-stack trains can carry more freight per train than piggyback trains, but require special cars with a lowered central section so that the double stacked containers can pass underneath gages and bridges. The bridges over the railroad tracks in Europe do not allow the use of double stacked containers, significantly reducing the load carrying capacity of the trains. This is an example of a volume-based capacity constraint.

High-speed rail transportation systems have been built in Europe and Japan to serve mostly passenger traffic. The implementation of such systems in the United States has been prevented by the high costs of track construction or upgrades and the difficulties of acquiring the right-of-way for new tracks. The Federal Railroad Administration (FRA) performed a commercial feasibility study of high-speed rail for passenger traffic. In this study and similar studies, the estimated costs to upgrade existing railroad tracks to operate at 90, 110, 125, and 150 mph are $300,000, $550,000, $3,000,000, and $5,000,000 per mile, respectively (FRA 2003). The main target area for such systems is passenger traffic between major metropolitan areas up to 400 miles apart. The main challenges, according to FRA, are the control systems to ensure safe and efficient mixed passenger and freight traffic at these high speeds, non-electric locomotives to avoid expensive railroad electrification, and cost effective and safe crossings to avoid expensive grade separations. The only implemented high-speed rail system in the United States consists of the Acela trains that operate in the northeast corridor. However, technical difficulties prevent the Acela trains to travel at their rated top speed of 150 mph. A completely different technology for rail transportation is maglev, where trains can use magnetic levitation for propulsion and support. These trains do not have wheels but float on a magnetic force field. It is estimated that the cost to construct a magnetic levitation track is in excess of $100 million dollars per mile. In 2008 the only commercially operated maglev train connects the airport of Shanghai with the city center.

The high-speed railroad network for passenger rail in Europe is constantly being expanded. Most of the rail tracks are located inside France and are denoted by "tres grande vitesse" (TGV) or "very high speed". Other lines indicate newly constructed international TGV tracks, and others lines enable high speed rail service on previously existing intercity tracks. The trains can achieve 300 km/h, or about 186 mph, on TGV tracks, the second generation of trains can reach a top speed of 320 km/h or about 200 mph. The trains running between Paris and Marseilles are double-deckers (TGV-duplex). In April 2007, a specially equipped double-decker TGV train set a new speed record for a train on wheels by reaching 357 mph or 575 km/h. This is roughly equivalent to 160 m/s. The train consisted of two engine cars and three passenger cars and the engines were rated at 19.6 MW or more than 25000 horsepower, Alstom (2007).

The Atlantique serves inside France, the Eurostar connects England with the continent through the tunnel under the English Channel and the Thalys connects France with other countries on the continent. Each train is painted in distinctive colors. The trains are 200 m long. The time it takes for two trains going opposite ways to pass each other is about 1.2 s.

5.2.4 Roadway

Road freight transportation uses trucks to move goods over the network of roads. Trucks roll on wheels equipped with rubber tires. The wheels are mounted on a number of axles. Trucks can be categorized by their load-carrying capacity into light trucks, medium trucks, and heavy trucks. Off-road trucks form an additional class of trucks but are not further considered in this book. Light trucks are roughly the same size as a passenger car and are used by individuals and commercial enterprises. In the United States, they are called pickup trucks. The full-size pickup truck models of the Ford Motor and General Motors companies are the most popular model for their respective companies. Medium trucks have a load-carrying capacity between that of light and heavy trucks. The cabin and cargo space form integral parts of the truck and the wheel axles are in permanent parallel alignment. A medium truck is typically used for city delivery. A heavy truck typically consists of a tractor and trailer combination. Heavy trucks are used primarily in inter-city transportation. The tractor is responsible for the propulsion and control of the truck and the trailer holds the transported goods. The trailer is often called a semi-trailer because half of the load is supported by the tractor or a detachable dolly. The tractor-trailer combination is sometimes denoted as a semi. The tractor and trailer can be disconnected and may be managed separately. Examples of a long-haul tractor-trailer truck and of local delivery trucks are shown in Figs. 5.6, 5.7, 5.8, 5.9 and 5.10.

Depending on the type of goods transported, over-the-road vehicles can be capacitated because of their volume, also called cubed-out, or capacitated because of their weight-carrying limit, also called weighted-out.

Increasing the volume or weight capacity of a truck reduces shipping costs moderately and is desirable from the carrier and shipper point of view. However, damage to the road surface and the corresponding maintenance costs increase with the weight per axle. Furthermore, an increase in the total allowable weight of a truck increases the construction costs of bridges and thus of the highways. In the United States, the federal government has placed limitations on the size and weight of trucks that use the interstate highway system. The standard tractor-trailer combination has five axles and the current federal limit is 80000 pounds (40 short tons). Individual states may have different limits that apply to their state and local highways. So trucks exceeding the federal weight or size limits have to avoid the federal interstate highway system and use smaller secondary state roads. In Europe the limitations on weight per axle have led to the use of six and seven axle tractor-trailer trucks. Trucks of this type often have the capability to raise some of their axles and

Fig. 5.6 Tractor-trailer inter-city truck example

Fig. 5.7 Tractor-trailer truck cabin

Fig. 5.8 Local delivery truck with lift gate

Fig. 5.9 Postal local delivery truck

Fig. 5.10 LTL truck with double trailer

wheels when they are carrying little or no load to save on tire wear and tear. In 2006 the German state of Niedersachsen conducted a test to allow Riesenlaster or giant-trucks, also called gigaliners in the UK, which consist of a tractor, a trailer, and secondary shorter trailer. The total length is 25.25 m long compared to the length of 16.5 m for a standard tractor trailer. The load-carrying capacity of one giant-truck is equivalent to that of 1.5 standard tractor-trailer trucks and the transportation by 2 giant-trucks is more economical in fuel and labor costs than 3 standard long-haul trucks. It also reduces congestion on the interstate highways since two giant-trucks require 130 m while three standard trucks require 172 m, including all safety distances between the trucks.

For local delivery trucks, the amount of goods on a trip may also be limited by the amount of time it takes to pickup and deliver and to travel. For example, the postal trucks delivering residential mail are almost never limited by either the weight or the volume of the mail but rather by the time it takes to deliver the mail. The U.S. Postal Service is the largest fleet operator in the United States. Most of its fleet consists of local delivery vehicles.

Vachini (2008) states that challenges for India are related to infrastructure. He estimates that 60–70% of the freight in India moves by road but that the average speed of a truck carrying cargo is about 20 km per hours, which means it covers about 200 km in a day. The government has started the Golden Quadrilateral project to connect four large metropolitan areas, New Delhi in the north, Mumbai in the west, Chennai in the south, and Kolkata in the east, with four to six-lane highways.

5.2.5 Inland Water

Water-based transportation can be classified as ocean-going and inland water based. The vessels transporting freight on inland water ways are called barges. A large variety of inland barges exist. They may be self-propelled or pushed by a tug or tow-boat. The arrangement of barges lashed together and pushed by a towboat is called a *tow*. Inland waterway transportation is highly efficient to transport large volumes of bulk commodities moving over long distances. Their main disadvantage is their limited accessibility. The majority of inland waterways consist of the great rivers and their tributaries and of major lakes.

In the United States the primary inland water ways are the Great Lakes and the Mississippi River system, which includes the Mississippi river and its connecting waterways. There exist few navigable waterways in the Western United states due to the mountainous geography. "The U.S. inland navigation system consists of 8200 miles of rivers maintained by the Corps of Engineers in 22 states, and includes 276 lock chambers with a total lift of 6100 ft. The highly adaptable and effective system of barge navigation moves over 625 million tons of commodities annually, which includes coal, petroleum products, various other raw materials, food and farm products, chemicals, and manufactured goods." (US Corps of Engineers 2006).

One of the main island water transportation arteries in the United States is the Mississippi river. In a typical tow arrangement on the lower Mississippi, barges are arranged in a tow of five barges wide in strings of eight barges long. Each barge has a capacity of 1500 tons, so the capacity of a single tow is 60000 tons. The usual draft of a loaded barge is 12 ft. Such a tow arrangement measures 175 ft wide and 1600 ft long. In the summer of 2006, the Mississippi was dangerously low due to drought conditions in its upper basin. As a consequence the draft of loaded barges had to be reduced to 9 ft, with a corresponding reduction in weight capacity to 900 tons, and the width of a tow had to be reduced by a single string of barges because of the narrower navigable channel, Talbot (2006). These measures reduced the capacity of a single tow to 28800 tons. These measures significantly increased the transportation costs of the goods and also reduced the total transportation capacity of the Mississippi since there is a limited number of towboats and pilots.

Vessels that carry trucks are categorized as roll-on, roll-off (RORO) if the tractor remains connected to the trailer, or as "fishyback" if only the trailers are transported. In general, roll-on, roll-off indicates that the cargo vehicles drive on the vessel at the origin and drive off the vessel at the destination. An international ocean-going

Fig. 5.11 Map of the inland navigable waterways in the eastern United States (Source: US Corps of Engineers 2006)

example of roll-on, roll-off is the delivery of finished cars to the United States from Japan.

5.2.6 Ocean Going

The vast majority of ocean-going cargo vessels carry crude oil and petroleum products, bulk and ore, or intermodal containers. The class of vessels that delivers assembled cars to the United States is an example of another relatively rare type. The current generation of supertankers that carry crude oil between major oil fields and refinery ports has a cargo capacity of more than 320000 dwt and are denoted as Ultra Large Crude Carriers or ULCC.

In October 2000, the USS Cole was being ferried from Yemen to the United States. The carrier had to take the roundabout route around the Cape Point, at the southern tip of Africa, because it would not fit through the Suez Canal. The largest ships that can traverse the Suez Canal are denoted as SuezMax. The limiting factor for the Suez Canal, which has no locks, is the allowable draft or depth below the waterline of the ships. A similar situation exists with respect to the Panama Canal, where some ships are so large that they cannot fit in the various locks when crossing the Panama Canal. Such ships are called "Post-PanaMax" ships since they cannot be used for an "all water" route via the Panama Canal between the Atlantic and Pacific Ocean. Ships that are built to fit exactly in the locks of the Panama Canal are called PanaMax. Ships that cannot fit through either the Panama or the Suez Canal are called Capesize, since they have to take a route around the Cape of Good Hope at the southern tip of Africa and Cape Horn at the southern tip of South America. Other major chokepoints for large oceangoing ships are the Straits of Malacca between Malaysian peninsula and the island of Sumatra and the English Channel between England and the European continent. The depth of one of the shallowest sections of the Straits of Malacca is only 25 m and this limits the allowable draft of the ships. Sometimes the term Malacamax is used to denote ships that can traverse the straits. The ULCC Knock Nevis has a draft of 24.6 m and cannot traverse the Straits of Malacca or the English Channel. It has a length of 458 m and a width of 69 m. It is the largest ship ever built and is currently used as a floating storage and off-loading (FSO) platform in the port Qatar. One of the largest bulk carriers is the Berge Stahl or "Steel Mountain", with a cargo capacity of 365000 dwt. The ship is 343 m long, has a width of 65 m, and a draft of 23 m. It is used for the transport of iron ore on regular schedule from the mining terminal of Ponta da Madeira in Brazil to the port of Rotterdam in the Netherlands.

Some of the largest containerships when coming in from Europe to North America will discharge first in the Halifax port, because it is a very deep port. After discharging some of their containers, the ships will not lie as deep in the water as when fully loaded and then the ships can continue to the more shallow harbors further south along the US East Coast.

A list of the largest seaports is given in Table 5.2. The Port of Rotterdam is ranked first in 2003 because of its combined volume of crude oil and intermodal containers but it dropped to third place in 2005 because of the spectacular growth of the economies of Southeast Asia and China. The ports of southern Louisiana and Houston also derive a significant fraction of their total tonnage from crude oil handling.

DP World is seeking approval for London Gateway, a container hub port and logistics park, 25 miles from London. It would be the country's and Europe's largest logistics park. The proposed port would be able to handle 3.5 million TEU annually along 2.3 km of container docking berths at an estimated cost of $3 billion. The port would also include other terminals, free trade zones, and logistics facilities, (Outsourced Logistics 2008).

5.2.7 Intermodal Transportation Systems

Intermodal freight transportation refers to the transportation of freight in containers by multiple transportation modes, such as ship, train, and truck, without handling of the freight inside the containers. This containerization reduces the handling and associated handling cost of the freight, improves security, reduces damage and loss, and reduces the transit time of the freight. The two main disadvantages of the use of these standardized and reusable containers are the requirement of transportation

Table 5.2 Largest seaports in the world 2008 (millions of tons). (Source: AAPA www.aapa-ports. org)

Rank	Port	Country	Measure	2008 Tons (M)	Metric Tons (M)
1	Singapore	Singapore	FT	515	524
2	Shanghai	China	MT	508	508
3	Rotterdam	Netherlands	MT	421	421
4	Tianjin	China	MT	365	365
5	Ningbo	China	MT	362	362
6	Guangzhou	China	MT	347	347
7	Qingdao	China	MT	278	278
8	Hong Kong	China	MT	259	259
9	Qinhuangdao	China	MT	252	193
10	Dalian	China	MT	246	246
11	Busan	South Korea	RT	242	246
12	Nagoya	Japan	FT	218	222
13	Shenzhen	China	MT	211	211
14	South Louisiana	US	MT	203	203
15	Houston	US	MT	192	192
16	Antwerp	Belgium	MT	189	189
17	Ulsan	South Korea	RT	170	173
18	Chiba	Japan	FT	165	168
19	Port Hedland	Australia	MT	159	159
20	Port Kelang	Malasyia	FT	152	155
21	Rizhao	China	MT	151	151
22	Yingkou	China	MT	151	151
23	Kaohsiung	Taiwan	MT	147	147
24	Inchon	South Korea	RT	142	144
25	Yokohama	Japan	FT	142	144

MT metric ton, *FT* freight ton, *RT* revenue ton (conversions to metric tons estimated)

quantities corresponding to full containers and the management and transportation of empty containers to balance the container flows.

Figure 5.12 shows an example of the required material handling equipment to unload an ocean-going container ship in a semi-automated manner. The tall cranes in the left picture are the quay cranes that unload the containers from the ship. The schedule of unloading operations is computer-generated, but the movements are controlled by human operators. The containers are then placed on the orange automated guided vehicles (AGVs), of which one is shown in the foreground. The AGVs are fully computer controlled. The AGVs transport the containers to the yard cranes. The yard cranes pick up the containers from the AGVs and put them in stacks of up to three containers for temporary storage. Later the yard cranes will pick up the containers again and take them to waiting trucks, railroad cars, or again to the AGVs for further transportation by container ship. The yard cranes are also fully computer controlled. Maximizing the throughput and responsiveness of the combined material handling systems requires extensive computer support for the execution and planning of material handling moves and stores. The feasibility and

Fig. 5.12 Material handling equipment in an intermodal container port (Photo of Europe Combined Terminal (ECT), Rotterdam, The Netherlands)

efficiency of the scheduling rules are tested by a large simulation model of the combined material handling devices. The system shown is installed at the container port of Rotterdam in the Netherlands. Similar automated container unloading operations are also under consideration in the ports of Singapore, Hong Kong, and Inchon in South Korea. One of the most modern and automated container ports to date is the port of Hamburg (CTA) that uses AGVs and a system of twin gantry cranes in the yard. Each set of twin yard cranes serves the same container storage locations in the yard and are constructed so that they can pass each other. One of the driving forces for the automation is the desire to operate the port facilities 24 hours a day, seven days a week so that the time in port of container ships is minimized.

The trend in ocean-going container ships is towards ever increasing ship size and capacity. It is impossible for a printed publication to remain up to date in listing the largest ships or ship to port visits. The following provides a brief list of benchmarks in container shipping. In 1998 the Sovereign Maersk was launched and became the world's largest container vessel, able to carry over 6500 20 ft-long containers (TEU or Twenty-foot Equivalent Unit). A less frequently used unit of container capacity and throughput is Forty-Foot Equivalent Unit or FEU. In 2003 a new class of vessels was deployed with a capacity of 8000 TEUs. The OOCL vessel Shenzhen was the first vessel of this class, later joined by its sister ship the Rotterdam. In 2005 the CMA CGM Otello ship with a capacity of 8488 TEUs was placed into service and it became the largest container ship to enter the Belgium port of Zeebrugge. Also in 2005, the sister ships MSC (Mediterranean Shipping Company) Susanna and Pamela, each with a capacity of 9200 TEUs and a length of 336.7 m, were the largest container ships ever to dock at the port of Antwerp, Belgium. Currently vessels with a 10500 TEUs capacity are being built and ships with capacity of up to 12000 TEUs are being planned.

For the container ship Shenzhen, the containers are stacked seven high above the deck and nine high below deck. The containers above and below the deck are separated by deck plates. The containers are arranged in 17 rows across the deck.

The annual throughput of the largest container ports is shown in Table 5.3. Only the ports of Los Angeles and Long Beach on the west coast and the combined ports of New York and New Jersey on the east coast are ranked in the top twenty. The

Table 5.3 Largest seaport container ports in 2008. (Source: AAPA (2008) www.aapa-ports.org)

Rank	Port	Country	2008
1	Singapore	Singapore	29.918
2	Shanghai	China	28.006
3	Hong Kong	China	24.494
4	Shenzhen	China	21.416
	Los Angeles/Long Beach	United States	14.200
5	Busan	South Korea	13.446
6	Dubai Ports	UAE	11.827
7	Ningbo	China	11.226
8	Guangzhou	China	11.001
9	Rotterdam	Netherlands	10.784
10	Qingdao	China	10.024
11	Hamburg	Germany	9.737
12	Kaohsiung	Taiwan	9.677
13	Antwerp	Belgium	8.663
14	Tianjin	China	8.503
15	Port Kelang	Malasyia	7.974
16	Los Angeles	US	7.850
17	Long Beach	US	6.350
18	Bremen/Bremerhaven	Germany	5.488
19	Tanjung Pelepas	Malasyia	5.466
20	New York/New Jersey	US	5.265
21	Laem Chabang	Thailand	5.128
22	Xiamen	China	5.035
23	Dalian	China	4.526
24	Tanjung Priok	Indonesia	3.984
25	Nhava Sheva	India	3.953

Freight in M TEUs.

Europort of Rotterdam, the Netherlands, (ECT) has become the largest container terminal in Europe, with over 10 million containers shipped in 2008.

5.2.8 Air

International air cargo is carried most often by wide-body aircraft called jumbo jets. The biggest jumbo jet currently in use is the Boeing 747, which can carry about 125 tons or 273000 pounds. One major package carrier company has placed orders for the super-jumbo Airbus 380 airplane, which carry a list price of $280 million. The Airbus 380 has a freight capacity of 150 tons or 330000 pounds. The planes are scheduled to be delivered starting in 2008 (FedEx) but the delivery of the planes has been repeatedly delayed. The planes will be able to fly nonstop between the sortation hubs of the package carriers and China. The planes were purchased to provide additional transportation capacity, given the sharply growing trans-pacific

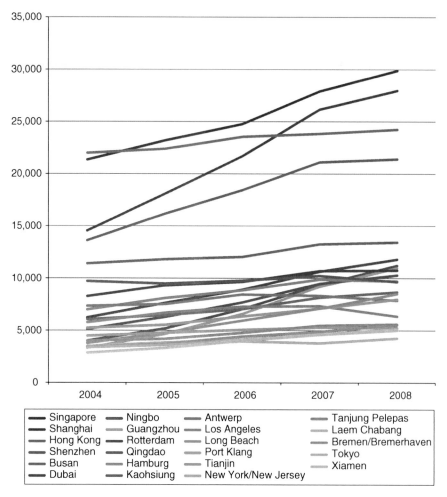

Fig. 5.13 Growth of largest seaport container ports 2004–2008. (Source: AAPA (www.aapa-ports. org))

trade volumes while at the same time flights and gates are strictly limited by international aviation treaties. The large planes will enable the package carriers to get larger volume and efficiencies out of their existing take-off and landing slots.

The Antonov 225 is used to transport the Russian space shuttle between air fields. Finally, Boeing uses the 747 Large Cargo Freighter to transport parts for its new Dreamliner 787 plane from various component suppliers in the world to its assembly plant.

The largest airports with respect to handling air cargo are shown in Table 5.4. Memphis and Louisville are the sortation hubs of the two major package carriers, FedEx and UPS, respectively. Anchorage is a refueling stop for the flights from the two package sortation hubs in the United States to China.

5.2.9 Space

Increasingly the transportation operations into space and in particular into low orbital space are evaluated by the same criteria of performance and price as the more traditional transportation operations. Building the international space station, that will circle the earth in the twenty-first century, will require numerous space carrier trips from earth to a low orbit. According to the Atlanta Journal and Constitution the average cost of launching one pound into earth orbit at the end of 1999 was about $5000 (AJC, 19 September, 1999, pp. G4). During 2004, while the space shuttle fleet was grounded, the international

Table 5.4 Largest cargo airports in 2009. (Source: Airports Council International (ACI) www. airports.org)

Rank	Airport	Airport code	Country	Total tons	% Change
1	Memphis	MEM	USA	3,697,185	0.4
2	Hong Kong	HKG	Hong Kong	3,384,765	(7.5)
3	Shanghai	PVG	China	2,539,284	(2.3)
4	Incheon	ICN	South Korea	2,313,001	(4.6)
5	Anchorage	ANC	USA	1,990,061	(14.9)
6	Louisville	SDF	USA	1,949,130	(1.3)
7	Dubai	DXB	Arab Emirates	1,927,520	5.6
8	Frankfurt	FRA	Germany	1,887,718	(10.6)
9	Tokyo (Narita)	NRT	Japan	1,851,972	(11.8)
10	Paris	CDG	France	1,818,503	(10.8)
11	Singapore	SIN	Singapore	1,660,851	(11.8)
12	Miami	MIA	USA	1,557,401	(13.8)
13	Los Angeles	LAX	USA	1,506,295	(7.6)
14	Beijing	PEK	China	1,420,977	4.0
15	Tapei	TPE	Taiwan	1,358,304	(9.0)
16	London	LHR	Great Brittain	1,349,574	(9.2)
17	Amsterdam	AMS	Netherlands	1,314,938	(17.9)
18	Chicago	ORD	USA	1,150,027	(14.1)
19	New York	JFK	USA	1,135,043	(21.8)
20	Bangkok	BKK	Thailand	1,045,194	(10.9)
21	Guangzhou	CAN	China	955,271	39.3
22	Indianapolis	IND	USA	900,583	(9.0)
23	Tokyo	HND	Japan	779,103	(8.3)
24	Newark	EWR	USA	767,668	(13.5)
25	Luxembourg	LUX	Luxembourg	628,641	(20.2)
26	Osaka	KIX	Japan	608,871	(28.0)
27	Shenzhen	SZX	China	606,013	1.3
28	Dallas/Fort Worth	DFW	USA	601,780	(8.6)
29	Kuala Lumpur	KUL	Malaysia	601,409	(9.7)
30	Mumbai	BOM	India	568,007	1.6

Loaded and unloaded freight and mail in metric tons.

space station had to be supplied by conventional unmanned Russian rockets. The load carrying capacity of the cargo rockets was not sufficient, so that at one time the inventory of food on the space station ran dangerously low.

It is instructive to compare the payload capacities of the carriers used by the various transportation modes. A standard over-the-road tractor-trailer truck with an approximate capacity of 25 metric tons for packaged goods and 35 metric tons for bulk and liquid goods will be used as reference. The Alaska pipeline transported in 2006 on average 64 million liters a day or 64000 m^3 per day. This is roughly equivalent to 2000 tanker trucks per day. The space shuttles can carry 22 tons into orbit, which is roughly equivalent to one truck. The large cargo airplanes can carry up to 150 tons of freight, which is equivalent to 6 trucks. A bulk railroad car can hold up to 100 tons. A unit train can contain up to 100 cars, so its total payload is 10000 tons, which is equivalent to 300 trucks. A unit train with double stacked intermodal containers can transport 200 containers, which is equivalent to 200 trucks. A barge tow on the lower Mississippi is configured as five barges wide by eight barges long. Each barge can hold 1500 tons, so the total payload of a tow is equal to 60000 tons, which is equivalent to 1800 trucks. A large container ship holds 17 parallel rows of containers, 15 containers high, and 19 containers long, for a total load of about 4500 FEU or 9000 TEU containers. This is equivalent to 4500 trucks. The largest ULCC crude carrier can hold up to 560000 deadweight tons of crude petroleum, which is equivalent to 17000 trucks. A typical ULCC crude carrier with a capacity of 415000 deadweight tons of crude petroleum is equivalent to 12500 trucks. The largest bulk carrier has a capacity of 365000 freight tons of iron ore, which is equivalent to 11000 trucks.

5.3 Transportation Documents and Contract Terms

The terms of the international sales contract between buyer and seller that specify the transportation and duty obligations are called Incoterms (**International Commercial Terms**). These terms can be set on a contract by contract basis and a large variety of Incoterms are used in practice. The most current definitions of 13 standardized Incoterms are published by the International Chamber of Commerce (ICC) (2000).

FOB or *Free On Board* indicates that the seller pays the freight costs to deliver the goods past the ship's rail in the port of export. However, many variations and ambiguities exist depending on exactly where the goods are made available to buyer at the seller's expense. If the carrier is a not a ship, the Incoterms FCA, *Free Carrier*, should be used. EXW at the sellers dock, also known as *Ex Works*, transfers the ownership and cost and duty responsibilities as soon as possible to the buyer. CIF or *Cost, Insurance, and Freight* indicates that the seller will pay the costs, freight, and insurance to deliver the goods past the ship's rail to a specified port of import. Again, many variations exist depending on exactly where the goods are made available to the buyer. If the carrier is not a ship, the Incoterms CIP, *Carriage and Insur-*

Table 5.5 ICC incoterms 2000 list

Label	Name
CIP	Carriage and Insurance Paid To (location)
CPT	Carriage Paid To (location)
DAF	Delivered At Frontier (location)
DDP	Delivered Duty Paid (at location)
DDU	Delivered Duty Unpaid (at location)
EXW	Ex Works (at location)
FCA	Free Carrier (at location)
	Following terms apply to ocean carriage
FAS	Free Alongside Ship (at port)
FOB	Free On Board (at port)
CFR	Cost and Freight (at port)
CIF	Cost, Insurance, and Freight (at port)
DES	Delivered Ex Ship (at port)
DEQ	Delivered Ex Quay (at port)

ance Paid, should be used. DDP at the buyers dock, also known as *Delivered with Duty Paid*, delivers the goods to the buyer's receiving dock with any import duties already satisfied. EXW and DDP are the two extremes of the range of Incoterms, where EXW represents the minimum obligation for the seller and DDP represents the maximum obligation for the seller. In all but one of the standard Incoterms the buyer pays the duties. The exception is "Delivered with Duty Paid" (DDP), where the seller pays the duties. The ICC recommends that any use of Incoterms references both "Incoterms 2000" and the explicit location of the transfer of obligations between seller and buyer. An example of the correct usage is "CIF Port of Singapore Incoterms 2000."

The *bill of lading* (BOL) is the most important document in the shipping process. A BOL is required for each shipment, and acts as a receipt and a contract. A properly completed BOL legally shows the shipper that has ownership of the goods, that the carrier has received the freight as described, and is obligated to deliver that freight in good condition to the destination (consignee). A closely related document is the freight bill. A *freight bill* is a multiple copy document issued by a commercial carrier which generally contains the name of the carrier, the name and the location of the shipper and the consignee, the shipping date, a description of the commodity to be transported, the rate, the total freight charge, and whether the freight charge is collect or prepaid. The freight bill should consist of at least three copies. The original, which is delivered to the shipper and serves as the carrier's invoice; the consignee's copy, which is retained by the recipient who signs for the delivery of the shipment; and the delivery receipt copy, which is retained by the carrier as proof of delivery.

A *foreign trade zone* (FTZ), also called a *free trade zone* is a commerce site set up in or near customs ports of entry where merchandise is considered legally outside the country's territory. Duties or taxes only have to be paid when the goods leave the foreign trade zone and are imported into the country. Goods do not have to be imported into the country but may be held or processed in the foreign trade zone and then exported to a third country without incurring duties. A common example of free trade zone is the duty-free shop area in international airports.

Foreign trade zones have the following main benefits. Duties are deferred and may be reduced since merchandise in inventory within an FTZ may be held indefinitely without paying customs duty. Duties are only paid when the merchandise is brought into country. If a corporation combines domestic and foreign goods in an FTZ, duty is paid only on the foreign content of the finished product imported. Goods may be stored, processed, and assembled, displayed, or destroyed while in the zone. Goods imported and stored in a Foreign Trade Zone may be re-exported without ever incurring duties, avoiding lengthy duty drawback procedures. Goods imported and held in an FTZ are not subject to state and local value-added taxes. Most state and county tax authorities exempt all merchandise in an FTZ from inventory taxation. To obtain this favorable status, the operations in a free trade zone are subjected to additional documentation requirements and the free trade zone infrastructure, such as warehouse facilities, has to be physically separated from the surrounding area.

5.4   Exercises

True-False Questions
1. A first order approximation of the weight capacity of an over-the-road trailer for bulk goods is 20 metric tons, (T/F) _____.
2. A freight bill for a shipment does not include prices and rate information for that shipment, (T/F) _____.
3. A freight bill is a legal contract between the shipper and the carrier for the movement of the designated freight between the indicated sites, with reasonable dispatch, and without damage, (T/F) _____.
4. A slurry is transportation technology where solid products are suspended in liquid and then pumped through a pipeline between different locations, (T/F) _____.
5. A transport broker functions as the middleman between the carrier and the shipper and assumes liability for the timely transportation of the goods, (T/F) _____.
6. Consolidation will yield relative greater benefits if the original shipment size is larger, (T/F) _____.
7. Contract carriers hire themselves out to service all shippers that want to use their services, (T/F) _____.
8. Demurrage refers to the penalty charges imposed on a shipper if it retains a transportation carrier beyond an allowed free time period, (T/F) _____.
9. Empty container management, movement, and storage are significant costs for the logistics systems using intermodal containers, (T/F) _____.
10. F.O.B. pricing means that the sales price includes the transportation costs to the final customer, (T/F) _____.

11. Low variable costs and high fixed costs create significant economies of scale in railroad transportation costs, (T/F) _____.
12. Piggyback refers to the shipment of over the road containers in a convoy of trucks, (T/F) _____.
13. Railroad corporations have a higher fixed cost but lower operating cost than a highway transportation corporations that can handle equivalent transportation requests, (T/F) _____.
14. The average amount of goods in a LTL shipment is larger than in a CL shipment, (T/F) _____.
15. The average delivery time is inversely related to the cost per flow unit per mile in the major transportation modes, (T/F) _____.
16. The fundamental principle of freight consolidation is to reduce costs by achieving economies of scale on the transportation moves, (T/F) _____.
17. The rates for first class mail in the United States are an example of uniform or distance-invariant rates, (T/F) _____.
18. The relatively low fixed costs of highway motor carriers tend to create a larger turnover of carrier corporations than for other transportation modes, (T/F) _____.
19. The standard size for a full size intermodal container is 8 (w) by 8 (h) by 40 (l) feet, (T/F) _____.

Giant Trucks A recent development in over-the-road freight transportation is the use of so called "giant trucks", also called "gigaliners" in the UK and "riesenlaster" in Germany. Give the definition of a giant truck, including its dimensions and numerical characteristics relevant to freight transportation. Describe the main advantages and disadvantages of using this type of trucks. Finally, identify product groups for which or geographical regions where the use of such giant trucks may become a common occurrence. Finally, compare giant trucks with tractor-trailer trucks with an extra trailer with respect to their dimensions and operating characteristics and give advantages and disadvantages of each type.

References

AAPA. (2008). American Association of Port Authorities. www.aapa-ports.org. Accessed Sep 2010.
Alstom. (2007). http://www.record2007.com/site/index_en.php.
Atlanta Journal-Constitution. (2008). Why did gasoline supplies go south. Atlanta Journal-Constitution. 05-Oct-2008, p. A8.
Ballou, R. H. (1999). *Business logistics management* (4th ed.). Englewood Cliffs: Prentice Hall.
Blanchard, D. (2010). The state of the logistics market, 2010. *Material Handling Management, 7.*
Economist. (2009). Steel and Brass. *Economist,* 13-Jun-2009, p. 70.
Federal Railroad Administration (FRA). (2003). High-speed rail technology development. http://www.fra.dot.gov/us/content/201.
Outsourced Logistics. (2008). The UK's new $3 billion port gets the go-ahead. *Outsourced Logistics, 1*(2), 10.

Talbot, C. (2006). Mississippi dangerously low. *Atlanta Journal-Constitution,* 30-Aug-2006, p. C3
  from the Associated Press.
Trunick, P. A. (2003). Time for a change. *Chief Logistics Officer, 8,* 25–29.
Trunick, P. A. (2004). How to beat the high cost of shipping. *Logistics Today, 7,* 26–29.
Trunick, P. A. (2005). Can we hold the line on logistics costs? *Logistics Today, 8,* 27–30.
Trunick, P. A. (2006). Good shippers hold the line on costs. *Logistics Today, 47*(8), 1–16.
Trunick, P. A. (2008). US Logistics Costs Rise in 2007. *Outsourced Logistics, 1*(5), 41–42.
United States Corps of Engineers. (2006). http://www.tec.army.mil/echarts/inlandnav/.
Vachini, P. (2008). Coping with India. *Outsourced Logistics, 1*(2), 8–9.
Wilson, R. (2007). 18th Annual The State of Logistics Report: The New Face of Logistics. CSCMP.

Chapter 6
Single Flow Routing Through a Network

Learning Objectives After you have studied this chapter, you should:

- Know the classification system for vehicle routing problems and algorithms.
- For the class of single-flow routing problems you should know:

  - The characteristics of the base problem and various variants.
  - The mathematical formulation.
  - Dijkstra's solution algorithm.
  - How to solve problems of modest size with a computer program.

6.1 Vehicle Routing Systems Classification

The classification of vehicle routing applications, formulations, and algorithms is based on three characteristics. The first characteristic is if either one or more vehicles are used. If only a single vehicle is used, there is no assignment decision regarding which task is to be executed by which vehicle. This is clearly an easier problem than if multiple vehicles are present and assignment decisions have to be made. The second characteristic is if the decisions have to consider the status of the vehicles before and after the execution of the transportation services. The first class does not consider the status of the vehicle before the origin of the transportation task or the status of the vehicle after the completion of the task at the destination of the transportation task. If the prior and posterior statuses of the vehicles do not have to be considered, the transportation tasks can be thought of as performed by different and independent vehicles. This class of problems is called origin-destination routing or also flow routing. These problems are easier to solve than problems where the transportation requests have to be jointly served by one or more vehicles. Transportation tasks are jointly served when service of one request changes the status of the vehicle so that it impacts the service of other transportation requests. Examples include the case where the location at the end of servicing one request impacts the costs for starting the service of another request and the case where there is a cost associated with moving the empty vehicle after all requests have been satisfied.

M. Goetschalckx, *Supply Chain Engineering*, International Series in Operations Research & Management Science 161,
DOI 10.1007/978-1-4419-6512-7_6, © Springer Science+Business Media, LLC 2011

Fig. 6.1 Transportation
models classification

Number of Vehicles	Single	Multiple
Vehicle Status		
Request-Only (Flow)	Single Flow (SPP)	Multiple Flows (NFP)
Prior & Post (Vehicle)	Single Vehicle Roundtrip (TSP)	Multiple Vehicles Roundtrip (VRP)

It should be noted that the term "vehicle" here is used as the generic term for a transportation asset that performs transportation tasks, such as trucks, planes, ships, taxis, buses, etc. The first class considers the transportation tasks more from the shipper's point of view since it does not consider the status of the vehicle after the transportation request has been completed. The second class considers the tasks more from the carrier's point of view since they have to consider the status of the vehicle. The classification system is illustrated in Fig. 6.1 and the acronym for a prominent problem in each class is also shown. The acronyms are defined below in their respective sections.

The third characteristic is whether the problem explicitly considers multiple time periods. If a problem ignores the time periods, has only a single period, or if the transportation decisions in the different time periods are independent, then the problem is said to be static. A problem is dynamic if it considers multiple time periods and the decisions in each time period are dependent.

6.2 Single Vehicle Origin–Destination Routing

This problem is more often called the shortest path problem (SPP). It should be noted that the set partitioning problem is another frequently used problem in transportation models that has an identical acronym, so the SPP acronym has to be carefully interpreted. The set partitioning problem is discussed in the framework of single and multiple vehicle roundtrip routing.

6.2.1 Shortest Path Applications

6.2.1.1 Driving Instructions

You can request driving directions between any two addresses in the continental United States from a variety of websites. To respond to your query, the software must find the shortest path between two points on the underlying street network in the United States. The street network is based on the TIGER files, which are published by the U.S. Census Bureau and are completely revised every 10 years on a rotating basis for different areas of the country. Driving directions produced by a popular personal computer application for the trip from state road Georgia 400 to the Atlanta airport are shown in graphical and text format in Figs. 6.2 and 6.3.

Conceptually, the physical road network is abstracted to a mathematical network, where the road intersections correspond to the nodes in the network and the road

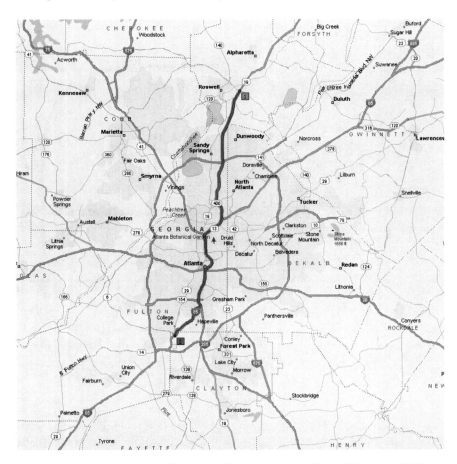

Fig. 6.2 Route-planning software illustration. (Map generated by Microsoft MapPoint 2010)

Time	Mile	Instruction	For
Summary: 30.3 miles (31 minutes)			
9:00 AM	0	Depart near Roswell on US-19 [SR-400] (South-West)	7.9 mi
9:08 AM	7.9	At exit 4B, road name changes to SR-400 [N Fulton Expy]	0.4 mi
9:08 AM	8.2	At exit 3, turn RIGHT onto Ramp	0.3 mi
9:08 AM	8.6	Keep LEFT to stay on Ramp	0.7 mi
9:09 AM	9.3	*Toll road* Merge onto SR-400 [Turner McDonald Pkwy]	1.1 mi
9:10 AM	10.4	*Toll road* Keep LEFT onto Local road(s)	0.3 mi
9:11 AM	10.7	*Toll road* Merge onto SR-400 [Turner McDonald Pkwy]	1.9 mi
9:13 AM	12.6	Stay on SR-400 [Turner McDonald Pkwy] (South)	2.5 mi
9:15 AM	15.1	Merge onto I-85 [SR-403]	2.8 mi
9:18 AM	17.9	Merge onto I-75 [I-85]	7.3 mi
9:26 AM	25.3	At exit 242, keep RIGHT onto I-85 [242]	3.7 mi
9:29 AM	28.9	At exit 72, turn RIGHT onto Ramp	0.4 mi
9:30 AM	29.4	Road name changes to Airport Blvd	0.9 mi
9:31 AM	30.3	Arrive near College Park	

Fig. 6.3 Route planning driving instructions

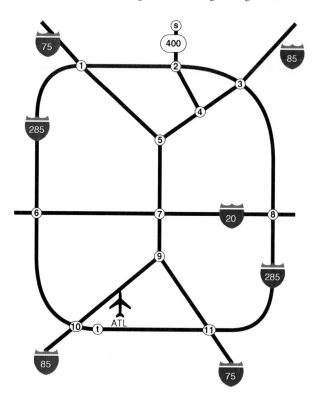

Fig. 6.4 Major road network to abstract network transformation

segments between intersections corresponds to edges in the network. In Fig. 6.4, the network based on the interstates and some of the major state roads for the Atlanta metropolitan area is shown. It can be used to plan a trip from the starting point in the northern suburbs of Atlanta, denoted by the start node s, to the destination node corresponding to the Atlanta airport, denoted by the terminal node t. The example network consists of 13 nodes and 25 edges, but a real network would contain many more nodes and edges.

Finding the shortest path or directions between two locations is a typical example of the engineering modeling approach. The map and the origin and destination locations correspond to the data. The abstracted road network with its edges, intersections, and travel lengths forms the information. Finally, after executing a solution algorithm, the shortest path between the origin and destination locations is known and this corresponds to the knowledge how to travel with the shortest travel distance from the origin to the destination.

6.2.1.2   Equipment Replacement

A typical decision to be made in equipment replacement planning is when to replace a particular vehicle or machine with a newer model. This decision is usually based on the tradeoff between the leasing cost and maintenance cost, where it is assumed that the newer equipment will have a higher leasing cost but a lower maintenance cost and that the used equipment will have the opposite cost characteristics. It is also assumed that a vehicle must be available during the entire planning horizon.

The corresponding network has a node for each time period during the planning horizon. Each decision for machine deployment can be represented as an arc from the starting period to the end period of the usage of that machine. The length of the arc is equal to sum of the leasing and maintenance costs over the corresponding lifetime of the vehicle discounted to the present time. The least cost equipment replacement schedule can then be found as the shortest path from the start node to the end node of the planning horizon.

6.2.2 Shortest Path Problem (SPP)

In all of the above examples and applications, the real world planning problem is reduced to an abstract network, consisting of nodes and undirected edges or directed arcs. Transportation can only occur over the network links between the network nodes and travel starts at the start node s and ends at the terminal node t. The network links have a length corresponding to a real-world travel length, travel duration, or cost. The objective is to find the shortest path from start node s to terminal node t.

When solving a real world problem with the SPP two major tasks have to be completed. The first task is the abstraction of the real world problem to a SPP. This task requires the identification of the real world entities corresponding to the nodes and the edges of the network and the determination of the cost computation method for the cost on each edge. The second task is the solution of the abstracted SPP. This task requires the identification of the proper variant of the SPP and of the solution algorithm best suited for this variant. If no implementation of the algorithm is available, the algorithm has to be implemented and tested. Finally, the problem instance has to be solved and the obtained solution has to be validated. The first task is task-specific and different for every problem and requires problem understanding and an engineering design methodology. The second task is generic since it is executed for a standardized problem formulation. It requires techniques from computer science and software development. Solution algorithms have been described in the literature and standard solver implementations are available.

6.2.2.1 Shortest Path Formulation

The SPP can be thought of as finding the minimum cost path for sending one unit of flow from the origin to the destination node. The SPP is thus a sub class of the minimum cost network flow problem, or MCNFP. The following notation was introduced for describing minimum cost network flow problems. The objective is to find a minimum cost set of flows (x) that satisfy the external flow requirements (b). There is also one constraint for each node that ensures the conservation of flow in that node.

x_{ij} Flow on the directed arc from node i to node j

c_{ij} Unit cost for one unit flow transported from node i to node j

b_i External flow for node i (1 for the source node, -1 for the destination node, zero for intermediate nodes)

Formulation 6.1 Shortest Path Formulation as a Minimum Cost Network Flow Formulation

$$
\begin{aligned}
Min \quad & \sum_{i}^{N} \sum_{j}^{N} c_{ij} x_{ij} \\
s.t. \quad & \sum_{h}^{N} x_{hi} - \sum_{j}^{N} x_{ij} = b_i \quad \forall i \\
& 0 \le x_{ij} \qquad\qquad\quad \forall ij
\end{aligned}
\tag{6.1}
$$

Since SPP is a subproblem of the MCNFP, it can be solved with standard network flow algorithms. This will be discussed further in detail below. However, because of its simple structure, the SPP can be solved very efficiently with a greedy algorithm provided that none of the edge costs are negative. This algorithm was originally proposed by Dijkstra (1959).

6.2.3 Dijkstra's Shortest Path Algorithm

6.2.3.1 Algorithm Description

Algorithms for determining the shortest path are based on the notion of one or more labels associated with each node. At the start of the algorithm all labels are called temporary. Temporary labels are upper bounds on the length of the shortest path from the starting node to the corresponding node. Label setting algorithms convert one temporary label to a permanent label during each iteration. A permanent label is the exact shortest path length from the starting node to the corresponding node. Dijkstra's algorithm belongs to this class of label setting algorithms.

The following notation is used in the description of Dijkstra's algorithm

N, D Set of all nodes and destination nodes, respectively

T, P Set of nodes with temporary and permanent labels, respectively

$l(k)$ Label of node k

c_{kj} Length of the edge between nodes k and j

$\Gamma(k)$ Set of successor nodes of node k, also called the forward star of node k, which is the set of nodes for which an edge or arc from node k to this node exists

$pred(k)$ The predecessor node on the current shortest path to node k

The algorithm has an initialization phase and then a main iterative phase. In the initialization phase, all the node labels are set to infinity and are set to temporary. The label of the origin node s is set to zero and is set to temporary. The main phase iteratively executes the following four steps.

1. Find the node p with the minimum temporary label $l(p) = \min_{x \in T}\{l(x)\}$
2. For all the successor nodes of node p with temporary labels, update their labels if necessary to indicate a reduced shortest path length to those nodes. The update formula for the temporary labels is

$$l(x) = \min\{l(x), l(p) + c_{px}\}$$

   If the temporary label was reduced, then the predecessor node on the current shortest path to node x is set to the node p, i.e. $pred(x) = p$
3. Since node p is the node with the smallest temporary label and all edge costs are nonnegative, no shorter path to node p can exist. So $l(p)$ is the exact length of the shortest path to node p and the label of node p can be marked as permanent
4. If all destination nodes have permanent labels stop, else go to step 1

Dijkstra's algorithm can be described very compactly in pseudo-code. Such description is useful as the communication mechanism between the operations research analyst and the computer science programmer, since it describes all the steps in the algorithm uniquely and completely, but without describing the low level details, execution steps, and data structures.

Algorithm 6.1. Dijkstra's Shortest Path Algorithm for Dense Graphs in Pseudo-Code

$P = \varnothing, \ T = N, \ l(i) = \infty \ \ \forall i \in N, \ l(s) = 0, pred(i) = s \ \ \forall i \in N$
$while \ D \ I \ T \neq \varnothing \ \{$
$\qquad k \leftarrow l(k) = \min\{l(j) : j \in T\}$
$\qquad P \leftarrow P \cup \{k\}, \ T \leftarrow T - \{k\}$
$\qquad for \ j \in \Gamma(k) \cap T$
$\qquad\qquad if \ l(j) > l(k) + c_{kj}$
$\qquad\qquad\qquad l(j) = l(k) + c_{kj}, \ pred(j) = k$
$\qquad \} \ endwhile$

6.2.3.2 Shortest Path Algorithm Illustration

The SPP algorithm is illustrated in the following small network shown in Figs. 6.5 and 6.6. The number on each edge indicates the length or cost of this edge. The callout for each node gives the label of that node and its predecessor node if it has

Fig. 6.5 Shortest path problem SPP1

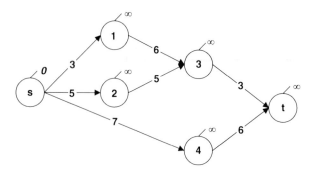

Fig. 6.6 Shortest path problem SPP1 solution

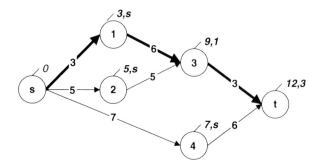

been determined. The first figure shows the network after the initialization phase, the second figure shows the network after the algorithm has completed. The shortest path length to node t is equal to 12 and it reaches node t from node 3. The complete shortest path can then be found by back tracing through the predecessor nodes. For example, the shortest path to node 3 has a length of 9 and it reaches node 3 from node 1. The shortest path is shown by bold edges in the second network.

6.2.3.3 Dijkstra's SPP Algorithm Characteristics

Dijkstra' algorithm is a classic example of forward dynamic programming. It bases the optimality of its final path on the principle of optimality and the property of nonnegative arc or edge lengths. The result of the algorithm is a directed tree rooted at the origin node s.

Computationally, the most expensive step is the identification of the node with the lowest temporary label. Finding the lowest temporary label involves testing a maximum of n nodes and this process has to be repeated for n iterations. Hence, the total algorithm complexity is $O(n^2)$ for this implementation.

The maximum size problem that can be solved in a reasonable amount of time depends on the speed of the computer, but problem sizes from 100,000 to 1,000,000 nodes are feasible with contemporary personal computers.

The density of a graph is the number of edges or arcs present in the graph divided by the total number of edges or arcs possible, which is equal to $n(n-1)$ for edges and $2n(n-1)$ for arcs. If every node is connected with every other node, the graph is called a *complete graph* and its density equals one. So the density of a graph is a number between 0 and 1. The implementation described above is only efficient for high-density graphs.

A graph is said to be sparse if it has a low density. For sparse graphs the above implementation is inefficient. Assume the temporary labels are stored in an ordered sequence by increasing value. Since, during each iteration only a few temporary labels may change, the ordered sequence of temporary labels may change only in a few locations. It would be inefficient to examine the whole sequence during each iteration to find the minimum temporary label. For sparse graphs it is more efficient to store and maintain the temporary labels in a heap structure. Finding the temporary label with the lowest value then involves just removing the label at the top of the heap. Several heap implementations exist, such as binary, Fibonnaci, and radix heaps. The computational complexity for the SPP algorithm is $O(m + n \cdot \log n)$ for the Fibonacci heap and $O((m + n) \cdot \log n)$ for the binary heap. The reduced execution times have to be balanced against the significantly longer implementation times. Two of the main advantages of Dijkstra's algorithm are its simple data and execution structures, while heap implementations are significantly more intricate. Even using the standard type library (STL) to implement the heap, programs based on the heap implantation will be hundreds of times larger and more complex than Dijkstra's algorithm. The corresponding implementation effort is only justified if the SPP will be solved repeatedly or has to be solved for extremely large problem instances. Dijkstra's algorithm would not be a good choice of algorithm to find the shortest path over a road network to determine driving directions between two addresses or locations.

6.2.3.4 SPP2 Algorithm Example

A somewhat larger example of the SPP is given next. Table 6.1 gives the asymmetrical distances between the nodes and Fig. 6.7 shows the network with the data. Figure 6.8 shows the solution of SPP2 from node *1* to node *4*.

Table 6.1 Shortest path example SPP2 distance matrix

From/To	1	2	3	4	5	6	7	8	9
1		10					3	6	12
2	10		18				2		13
3		18		25		20			7
4			25		5	16	4		
5				5		10			
6			20		10		14	15	9
7		2		4		14			24
8	6				23	15			5
9	12	13				9	24	5	

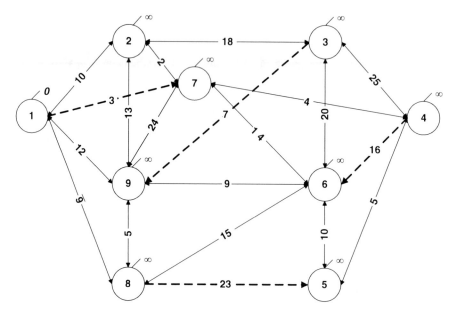

Fig. 6.7 Shortest path example SPP2 network

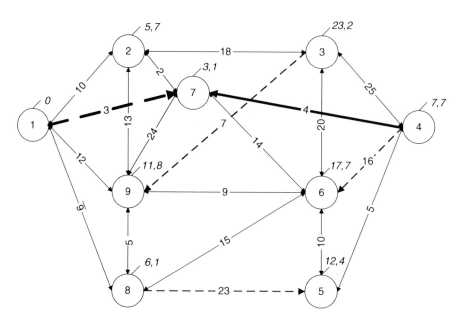

Fig. 6.8 Shortest path example SPP2 solution

The solid edges indicate bidirectional connectors with identical symmetric distances in both directions, the dashed edges indicate asymmetric, one-directional connectors.

Because of the theoretical interest and the simplicity of the SPP and Dijkstra's algorithm for it, it has been discussed widely in reference publications and on the Internet. Among others, Athanasios (2006) created a JAVA applet implementing Dijstra's shortest path algorithm that nicely illustrates the dynamic programming progression. This applet is located on the personal home page of this student in computer science, so the applet may not be available in the future.

6.2.3.5 Shortest Path Problem (SPP) Variants

A large number of applications can be abstracted to the either the classic SPP or one of its variants. Some of the most frequently used variants are described next.

One Source to One Sink (s to t)

This is the classic and original variant described above. Dijkstra (1959) was one of the first to propose an optimal algorithm for solving this problem, which is based on forward dynamic programming. Each node has a single label. All nodes start out as having a temporary label. The algorithm converts during each iteration the label of one node from temporary to permanent. This classic algorithm is easy to implement and relatively efficient, so that problems that have up to 1,000,000 nodes can be solved in reasonable time on contemporary computers.

One Source to All Sinks (s to all)

This variant determines the shortest path from one source to all possible destination nodes. When solved with Dijkstra's algorithm, this problem requires very little additional computations. In essence, the computations continue after the label of the first destination node has become permanent until the labels of all destination nodes have become permanent.

All Pairs

This variant determines the shortest path from all source nodes to all possible destination nodes.

k Shortest Paths

This variant determines not just the shortest path between an origin and destination node, but also the next $k-1$ shortest paths. It is primarily used when one is interested in performing sensitivity analysis on the shortest path, since the incremental cost or regret between the first and second shortest path to a node will be known at the completion of the algorithm.

General Costs

All the variants described above rely on the property that no edge or arc exists that has a negative cost. This implies that the cumulative cost along the edges of a path is non-decreasing. The algorithms used to solve these problems belong to the class of *label setting* algorithms. If edges with negative costs exist, the problem is said to have general costs. The algorithms used to solve the general cost problem belong to the class of *label correcting* algorithms. These algorithms are much less efficient than label setting algorithms, so much smaller problems can be solved to optimality. All labels are converted from temporary to permanent in the last iteration.

Finally, if a monotonically nondecreasing status variable along the path exists, then negative arc costs are allowed. Each node no longer will a have a single label, but may have multiple labels in function of the nondecreasing status variable. During every iteration a single label of a node, but not the node itself, is converted from temporary to permanent. While the algorithm is executing, a node will have a number of labels, some of which may be permanent and some of which may be temporary. An example of this variant with general costs is the pricing subproblem of the set partitioning formulation and algorithm for roundtrip vehicle routing. In this example, the nondecreasing status variable is the cumulative amount of goods to be delivered by the vehicle on its route. When a vehicle visits a node, the amount of goods delivered by the vehicle always increases and total amount is limited by the vehicle capacity, so the number of nodes visited on a route is limited. This variant is discussed later in detail in the set partitioning problem (SPP) algorithm for vehicle routing problems (VRP).

Longest Path in Acyclic Graphs

In all the variants described so far the objective has been to find the shortest path between the origin and destination node. In project management, one is often interested in finding the minimum total duration of the project. A project network is a type of network used to represent the activities and events in project scheduling and management. A node in the network corresponds to an event and an arc to an activity or task. Possible events are (1) the start of the project, (2) the completion of a project, and (3) the completion of one or more task or activities to be executed in the project. The activities may have precedence relationships, i.e., one activity cannot be started until one or more other activities have been completed. The existence of an arc from node i to node j implies that task i has to be completed before task j can be started and the length of an arc is the duration of the task. A path is a sequence of activities satisfying the precedence constraints, i.e., a feasible sequence. The tasks on the longest path from start to end node are called *critical* since they determine the minimum total project length. Tasks that are not on the critical path may have some slack time and the reduction of the duration of those tasks will not reduce the overall project duration. Two historical project management methods that use the longest path algorithm are the critical path method (CPM) and the program evaluation and review technique (PERT). PERT was first used in the 1950s to manage the building process of the Polaris, which was the first nuclear ballistic submarine of the U. S. Navy. PERT is used to manage large-scale and complex projects. CPM was used by the Dupont Company to manage industrial construction projects. CPM has been used extensively both in paper-and-pencil implementation as well as in contemporary project management software such as Microsoft Project for the management of projects in construction, product development, and software development.

Note that the standard shortest path algorithm by Dijkstra has to be modified in two ways. First, the maximum operator is used to determine the new label of the successor nodes. Second, if the successor node had permanent label and this label value is increased, i.e. there is a net change, then the label of this successor node has to be made temporary again. The modified Dijkstra's algorithm to find the longest path is shown below in pseudo code. Other algorithms for determining the longest path have been developed, but the above modification is very simple to implement even though the computational complexity increases as compared to the standard Dijkstra's algorithm. Note that if a directed cycle exists in the graph, the algorithm will never terminate execution. The existence of a directed cycle indicates there is no feasible solution to the project management problem since at least two tasks exist that are mutually dependent, i.e., each task has to be completed before the other task can start.

Algorithm 6.2. Longest Path Algorithm for Dense Graphs in Pseudo-Code

$P = \varnothing,\ T = N,\ l(i) = \infty\ \ \forall i \in N,\ l(s) = 0, pred(i) = s\ \ \forall i \in N$
$while\ D\ I\ T \neq \varnothing\ \{$
$\quad\quad\quad k \leftarrow l(k) = \min\{l(j) : j \in T\}$
$\quad\quad\quad P \leftarrow P \cup \{k\},\ T \leftarrow T - \{k\}$
$\quad\quad\quad for\ j \in \Gamma(k)$
$\quad\quad\quad\quad\quad if\ l(k) + c_{kj} > l(j)\ \{$
$\quad\quad\quad\quad\quad\quad l(j) = l(k) + c_{kj},\ \ pred(j) = k$
$\quad\quad\quad\quad\quad\quad if\ j \in P\ then\ P \leftarrow P - \{j\}, T \leftarrow T + \{j\}$
$\quad\quad\quad\quad\quad\quad \}$
$\quad\quad \}\ endwhile$

State Transition Diagram

Often problems can be reduced to finding the optimal path through a state transition diagram. A state transition diagram is a network, where each node corresponds to a feasible state of the system and where the arcs correspond to feasible transitions from one state to another state. The optimal path may be the shortest or longest path from the initial state to the final state. Reducing the problem involves the determination of a concise and complete characterization of the state of the system and the determination of all the feasible states and feasible transitions.

Consider the classic puzzle of three water jugs. An 8-gallon jug is filled with water. In addition, one empty 5-gallon and one empty 3-gallon jug are also given. Your task is to find a sequence of pours to divide the 8 gallons of water into two equal parts of 4 gallons using only the three containers. No other measuring devices are allowed. What is the smallest number of transfers or pours that are needed to achieve this division.

One solution method consists of constructing a state transition diagram for this problem and finding the shortest path through the network, where the length of each arc is equal to one. The nodes of the network correspond to all the feasible states of the water in the containers. The arcs correspond to possible transitions between those states. The state of the system is encoded in a 3-tuple; corresponding to the amount of water in the 8-, 5-, and 3- gallon jug, respectively. The start node is indicated by $(8,0,0)$ and the end node is indicated by $(4,4,0)$ since only the two largest containers can hold 4 gallons. From the start node, only two feasible nodes can be reached, namely $(3,5,0)$ and $(5,0,3)$.

The corresponding network with all feasible states and feasible transitions is shown in Fig. 6.9. The arcs are drawn as dashed lines and their direction is indicated by an arrowhead. Bidirectional edges are drawn as solid lines. Executing an edge more than once will only increase the total number of pours without reaching a new state, so in the optimal pouring plan no edge will be executed more than once. The index of each feasible state is shown in the circle next to the node. Based on this network, the smallest number of pours required to divide the water in half is equal to seven.

6.2.4   Minimum Cost Network Flow Formulation of the SPP

Earlier the SPP was formulated as a minimum cost network flow problem (MCNFP) in (6.1). The SPP is equivalent to finding the flow path with the minimum cost from the origin node s to the destination node t for a single unit of flow. The external inflow (supply) at node s is thus one and the external out-flow (demand) at node t is negative one, and all other nodes have no external flows. The flow variables will never be larger than one, since the only required flow to the outside is equal to one. Hence, there are no upper or lower bounds besides the nonnegativity constraints

Fig. 6.9 Water pouring
puzzle network

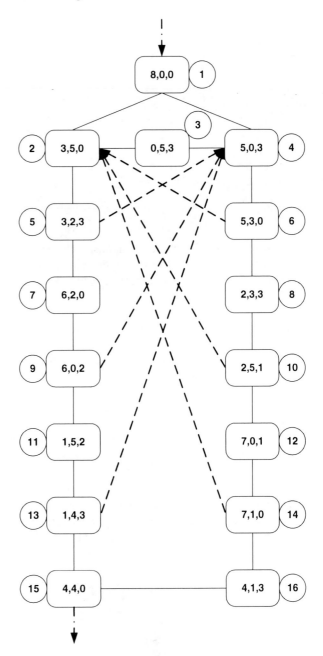

The complete mathematical formulation for the shortest path problem shown in Fig. 6.5 is given below. There are six nodes in the SPP and seven arcs. The corresponding MCNFP has thus seven flow variables and six conservation of flow constraints.

$$
\begin{aligned}
\min \quad & 3x_{s1} + 5x_{s2} + 7x_{s4} + 6x_{13} + 5x_{23} + 3x_{3t} + 6x_{4t} \\
s.t. \quad & 1 - x_{s1} - x_{s2} - x_{s4} = 0 \\
& x_{13} - x_{s1} = 0 \\
& x_{23} - x_{s2} = 0 \\
& x_{3t} - x_{13} - x_{23} = 0 \\
& x_{4t} - x_{s4} = 0 \\
& -x_{3t} - x_{4t} = -1 \\
& x \geq 0
\end{aligned}
$$

Single-commodity MCNFP formulations can be very efficiently solved by a variety of linear programming (LP) solvers, since the basis can be stored very compactly and updating the basis does not require matrix inversion.

6.2.4.1 Solving with Excel Shortest Path Spreadsheet and Solver

The solution of the example problem depicted in Fig. 6.7 with the solver included in Microsoft Excel is illustrated in the following eight figures. The first four figures show the data and status of the solution before the solver has been executed. The two dialog windows for the solver execution are shown next. Finally, the solution is shown in the last two figures.

Figure 6.10 shows the structure of the network through a two-dimensional adjacency matrix. The matrix has a row for every source node and a column for every destination node. If an arc exists in the network from the source to the destination node, the capacity of that arc is given in the corresponding cell. Since in the MCNFP formulation for the SPP only a single-flow unit is transported all capacities in this case can be set equal to one. It should be noted that this adjacency matrix is asymmetrical to correspond to the asymmetrical structure of the network. For

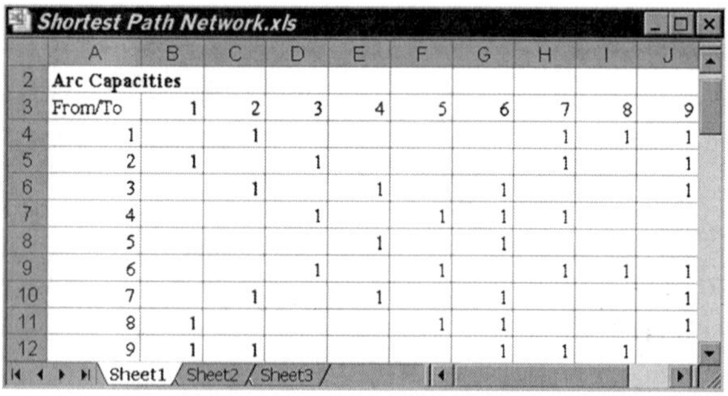
Shortest Path Network.xls

	A	B	C	D	E	F	G	H	I	J
2	**Arc Capacities**									
3	From/To	1	2	3	4	5	6	7	8	9
4	1		1					1	1	1
5	2	1		1				1		1
6	3		1		1		1			1
7	4			1		1	1	1		
8	5				1		1			
9	6			1		1		1	1	1
10	7		1		1		1			1
11	8	1				1	1			1
12	9	1	1				1	1	1	

Sheet1 Sheet2 Sheet3

Fig. 6.10 SPP2 Excel spreadsheet arc capacities

Fig. 6.11 SPP2 Excel spreadsheet arc costs

Arc Cost									
From/To	1	2	3	4	5	6	7	8	9
1		10					3	6	12
2	10		18				2		13
3		18		25		20			7
4			25		5	16	4		
5				5		10			
6			20		10		14	15	9
7		2		4		14			24
8	6				23	15			5
9	12	13				9	24	5	

Fig. 6.12 SPP2 Excel spreadsheet initial flow balance

Arc Flows										
From/To	1	2	3	4	5	6	7	8	9	Out
1										0
2										0
3										0
4										0
5										0
6										0
7										0
8										0
9										0
In	0	0	0	0	0	0	0	0	0	
Balance	0	0	0	0	0	0	0	0	0	
External	1			-1						

example, there is a capacity present from node 4 to node 6, but the corresponding capacity from node 6 to node 4 is not present.

It also should be noted that the adjacency matrix representation of a network is a very simple and intuitive representation method that is highly compatible with spreadsheet software. However, it is highly inefficient with respect to memory storage space and execution time for large problem instances and sparse networks.

Figure 6.11 gives the arc costs in the same two-dimensional adjacency matrix structure.

Figure 6.12 shows the section of the spreadsheet corresponding to the flow variables. It has the same two-dimensional adjacency matrix structure augmented with rows and columns to check for conservation of flow. For each source node the sum of the outgoing flows is computed in column K and for each destination node the sum of all the incoming flows in computed in row 37. The difference between outgoing and incoming flows is computed in row 38. Given the sign convention for incoming and outgoing flows, the difference in row 38 is computed as the sum of the outgoing flows minus the sum of the incoming flows. This difference must equal the external flows for each node, which are shown in row 39.

Figure 6.13 shows the computation of the objective function in the same two-dimensional adjacency structure. Each cell computes the product of the flow quantity times the unit flow cost. Since at this time all flows are still equal to zero, all elements in the matrix are zero. The sum of the flow costs for source nodes and destination nodes is computed in column K and row 52, respectively. The total

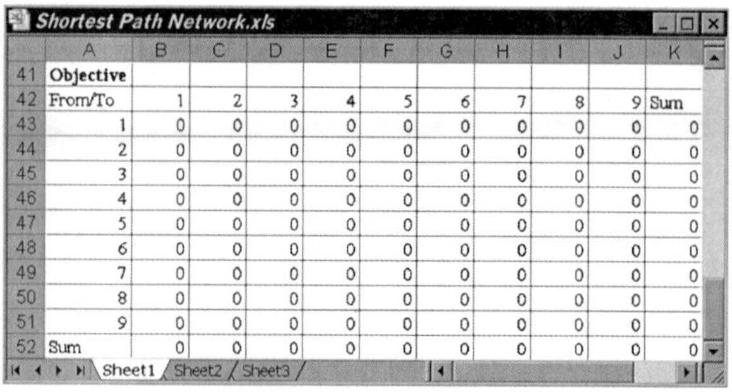

Fig. 6.13 SPP2 Excel
spreadsheet initial objective
function

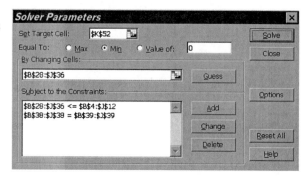

Fig. 6.14 SPP2 Excel
spreadsheet solver parameters

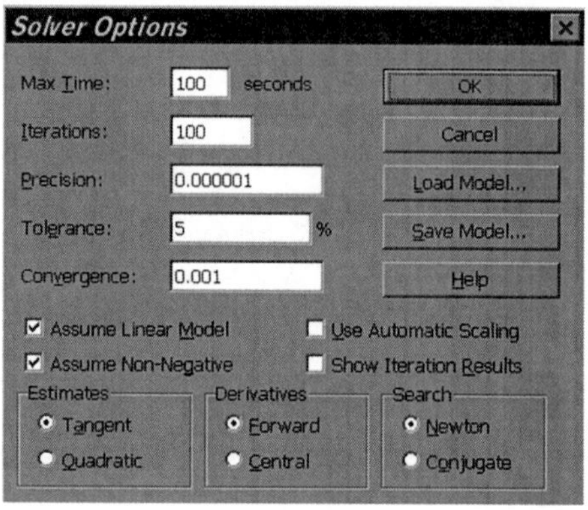

Fig. 6.15 SPP2 Excel
spreadsheet solver options

flow cost is then computed in cell K52. This quantity could have been computed directly with the Excel function SUMPRODUCT but the adjacency matrix structure provides additional information on which individual flows and nodes contribute to the total cost.

Figures 6.14 and 6.15 show the dialog windows that define the problem and specify the solver control parameters for this network flow problem. The objective is to minimize the total flow cost, computed in cell K52 as sum of the products of

Fig. 6.16 SPP2 Excel spreadsheet solution flows

	A	B	C	D	E	F	G	H	I	J	K
26	Arc Flows										
27	From/To	1	2	3	4	5	6	7	8	9	Out
28	1	0	0	0	0	0	0	1	0	0	1
29	2	0	0	0	0	0	0	0	0	0	0
30	3	0	0	0	0	0	0	0	0	0	0
31	4	0	0	0	0	0	0	0	0	0	0
32	5	0	0	0	0	0	0	0	0	0	0
33	6	0	0	0	0	0	0	0	0	0	0
34	7	0	0	0	1	0	0	0	0	0	1
35	8	0	0	0	0	0	0	0	0	0	0
36	9	0	0	0	0	0	0	0	0	0	0
37	In	0	0	0	1	0	0	1	0	0	
38	Balance	1	0	0	-1	0	0	0	0	0	
39	External	1			-1						

Fig. 6.17 SPP2 Excel spreadsheet solution objective function

	A	B	C	D	E	F	G	H	I	J	K
41	Objective										
42	From/To	1	2	3	4	5	6	7	8	9	Sum
43	1	0	0	0	0	0	0	3	0	0	3
44	2	0	0	0	0	0	0	0	0	0	0
45	3	0	0	0	0	0	0	0	0	0	0
46	4	0	0	0	0	0	0	0	0	0	0
47	5	0	0	0	0	0	0	0	0	0	0
48	6	0	0	0	0	0	0	0	0	0	0
49	7	0	0	0	4	0	0	0	0	0	4
50	8	0	0	0	0	0	0	0	0	0	0
51	9	0	0	0	0	0	0	0	0	0	0
52	Sum	0	0	0	4	0	0	3	0	0	7

flow values and unit flow costs. The decision variables are the flow variables stored in the adjacency matrix cells B28:J36. There are two types of constraints present in this formulation. The first set is the upper bound constraints on the individual flow values. Each flow value must be less than or equal to the corresponding arc capacity. This yields the constraint B28:J36 ≤ B4:J12. The second set of constraints model the conservation of flow for each node. The internal flow balance must be equal to the external flow quantities. This yields the constraint B38:J38 = B39:J39.

The MCNFP has only nonnegative variables and linear objective and constraints. It can thus be solved with the linear programming algorithm of the solver. The two major control parameters in the Options dialog window that need to be specified are "Assume Linear Model" and "Assume Nonnegative". The solver finds the optimal solution for this particular example in a fraction of a second.

In Figs. 6.16 and 6.17, the solution flow variables and objective function values are shown. The cells in the spreadsheet have conditional formatting assigned to them, so that they are shaded if there is a nonzero value stored in them. The shortest path from node 1 to node 4 runs through node 7 and the length of the shortest path equals 7. The second figure details the cost contributions of the individual transportation moves.

6.2.4.2   Solving with AMPL Mathematical Programming Language

The solution of the example problem depicted in Fig. 6.7 with the AMPL (*A Math Programming Language*) mathematical programming language is illustrated in the following four listings of text files. The listings correspond to the model, data, execution, and output files, respectively. The first list shows the model, which is a generic single commodity minimum cost network flow (MCNFP) formulation. This model will also be used in the next chapter on multiple flows routing, but since the shortest path problem is subclass of minimum cost network flow problem the model can be used here without any modification. Many alternative AMPL models for the minimum cost network flow problem exist and some of these can be found on the AMPL web site.

The model contains nodes and arcs. The nodes are either sources, sinks, or internal nodes depending on if they have external flow entering as supply, external flow leaving as demand, or no external flow, respectively. AMPL performs a feasi-

```
set SOURCES;
set SINKS;
set INTERNALS;

# MCNFP standard model statements
# set ORIGINS = SOURCES union INTERNALS;
# set DESTINATIONS = INTERNALS union SINKS;

# MCNFP_BD (BiDirectional) model statements
# with sources as destinations and sinks as origin nodes
set ORIGINS = SOURCES union INTERNALS union SINKS;
set DESTINATIONS = INTERNALS union SINKS union SOURCES;

param supply {SOURCES} >= 0;
param demand {SINKS} >= 0;

        check: sum {i in SOURCES} supply[i] >= sum {k in SINKS} demand[k];

set NODES = SOURCES union INTERNALS union SINKS;
set ARCS within {ORIGINS cross DESTINATIONS};

param external_flow {j in NODES} =
        if j in SOURCES then supply[j] else
            if j in SINKS then -demand[j] else 0;

param arc_cost {ARCS} >= 0;
param arc_capacity {ARCS} >= 0;

var arc_flow {(i,j) in ARCS} >= 0, <= arc_capacity[i,j];

minimize total_cost:
        sum {(i,j) in ARCS} arc_cost[i,j] * arc_flow[i,j];

# flow_balance: out - in = external
subject to flow_balance {j in NODES}:
        sum {(j,k) in ARCS} arc_flow[j,k]
        - sum {(i,j) in ARCS} arc_flow[i,j]
        = external_flow[j];
```

Listing 6.1 AMPL MCNFP Model File

```
data;

# NOTE: requires MinCost_Network_BD.mod since sources are also
# destinations and sinks are also origins

set SOURCES := 1;
set SINKS := 4;
set INTERNALS := 2 3 5 6 7 8 9;

set ARCS := (1,2) (1,7) (1,8) (1,9)
            (2,1) (2,3) (2,7) (2,9)
            (3,2) (3,4) (3,6) (3,9)
            (4,3) (4,5) (4,6) (4,7)
            (5,4) (5,6)
            (6,3) (6,5) (6,7) (6,8) (6,9)
            (7,2) (7,4) (7,6) (7,9)
            (8,1) (8,5) (8,6) (8,9)
            (9,1) (9,2) (9,6) (9,7) (9,8);

param supply := 1 1;
param demand := 4 1;

param:              arc_cost     arc_capacity :=
        1     2     10           1
        1     7     3            1
        1     8     6            1
        1     9     12           1
        2     1     10           1
        2     3     18           1
        2     7     2            1
        2     9     13           1
        3     2     18           1
        3     4     25           1
        3     6     20           1
        3     9     7            1
        4     3     25           1
        4     5     5            1
        4     6     16           1
        4     7     4            1
        5     4     5            1
        5     6     10           1
        6     3     20           1
        6     5     10           1
        6     7     14           1
        6     8     15           1
        6     9     9            1
        7     2     2            1
        7     4     4            1
        7     6     14           1
        7     9     24           1
        8     1     6            1
        8     5     23           1
        8     6     15           1
        8     9     5            1
        9     1     12           1
        9     2     13           1
        9     6     9            1
        9     7     24           1
        9     8     5            1;
```

Listing 6.2 AMPL SPP2 Data File

Listing 6.3 AMPL SPP2
Execution File

```
model MinCost_Network_BD.mod;
model ShortestPath_Example.dat;
solve;
display arc_flow;
```

bility check before the solver execution to ensure that the total supply in all of the source nodes is larger than the total demand. The arcs are defined by their origin and destination nodes. Arc origin nodes are either sources or internal nodes. If the sink nodes have also outgoing arcs, then the origin nodes are the union of all three types of nodes. Arc destination nodes are either sink nodes or internal nodes. If the source nodes have also incoming arcs, then the destination nodes are the union of all three types of nodes. Each arc has a cost, capacity, and arc flow, all of which have to be nonnegative. The arc flow has to no larger than the arc capacity. The objective of this formulation is to minimize the total transportation cost which is the sum of the products of the arc flow and arc cost over all the arcs. Finally, for each node a conservation of flow constraints exists, which ensures that the external flow equals the difference between the out flows and the in flows. A supply is modeled with a positive external flow and a demand is modeled as a negative external flow.

The data for the shortest path example is shown in Listing 6.2. There are nine nodes, one source node (1), one sink node (4), and nine internal nodes. Because many of the arcs are bidirectional, the source node 1 and the sink node 4 are at same time internal nodes and source and sink node, respectively. There are 36 one-directional arcs. The arc data is given at the end of the listing with the origin node, destination node, arc cost, and arc capacity listed on a single line for each arc.

Listing 6.3 shows the sequence of the commands in the run file, which controls the execution of the AMPL program. This execution or run file has by convention the extension "run." The name of the run file is the only command line argument for the AMPL program. The first line identifies the model file, which by convention has the extension "mod." For the shortest path problem the model is the standard minimum cost network model. For this particular problem instance the source node is also a destination node and the sink node is also an origin node for several bidirectional arcs, so the extended model file "MinCost_Network_BD.mod" has to be used. The second line identifies the data file, which by convention has the extension "dat." The third line contains the "solve" command, which causes the model to be solved by the default solver. Finally, the fourth line displays the flows in the solution. Further information on the AMPL language can be found in Fourer et al. (2002) and on the website of the AMPL Optimization LLC.

Finally, Listing 6.4 shows the output log generated by the execution of the run file with the AMPL program. The solver used in this case was CPLEX. The optimal solution value found was equal to 7 and there were two nonzero flows on the arc (1,7) and (7,1). This solution is identical to the solution found by the Excel solver and by the manual execution of Dijkstra's algorithm. The listing shows the arc flows in the default output format. The output format can be customized using the AMPL language.

Listing 6.4 AMPL SPP2
Output Log

```
AMPL Version 20080219 (x86_win32)
CPLEX 11.0.1: optimal solution; objective 7
2 dual simplex iterations (0 in phase I)
arc_flow [*,*]
:   1   2   3   4   5   6   7   8   9       :=
1   .   0   .   .   .   .   1   0   0
2   0   .   0   .   .   .   0   .   0
3   .   0   .   0   .   0   .   .   0
4   .   .   0   .   0   0   0   .   .
5   .   .   .   0   .   0   .   .   .
6   .   .   0   .   0   .   0   0   0
7   .   0   .   1   .   0   .   .   0
8   0   .   .   .   0   0   .   .   0
9   0   0   .   .   .   0   0   0   .
;
```

Listing 6.5 SPP1
Example in LP
Format

```
min
3 xs1 + 5 xs2 + 7 xs4 + 6 x13 + 5 x23 + 3 x3t + 6 x4t
s.t.
xs1 + xs2 + xs4 = 1
x13 - xs1 = 0
x23 - xs2 = 0
x3t - x13 - x23 = 0
x4t - xs4 = 0
- x3t - x4t = -1
end
```

The AMPL program uses ASCII text input and output files as its user interface and as consequence does not have the same intuitive graphical user interface as the Excel program. However, the model file size does not change or grow with the size of the instance data and the size of the data file grows proportional to the number of nodes and arcs in the instance. As a consequence the AMPL program can handle much larger problem instances. Typically, AMPL is interfaced with either Excel or a database program such as Access, that contain the arc data and in which the arc flow solution is stored.

Other mathematical programming modeling languages and modeling front-ends for mixed-integer programming solvers exist, both as open source and proprietary applications.

6.2.4.3 Solving the SPP Formulation in LP Format

Finally, a MCNFP problem can be formulated in the LP format and stored in a file. The LP format corresponds to an explicit algebraic formulation of the problem. Many LP solvers have the capability to read a problem formulation in the LP format and then to solve the problem. The LP format is defined in the CPLEX File Formats Manual (ILOG 2003). The SPP1 example formulation in LP format is given in Fig. 6.5. The problem formulation file has by convention the extension "lp" and is an ASCII text file. Note that this file contains both the model and the data in an integrated format. The LP format is nearly identical to the algebraic formulation of the problem.

```
Problem 'ShortestPath_Example.lp' read.
Read time =    0.05 sec.
Tried aggregator 1 time.
LP Presolve eliminated 3 rows and 4 columns.
Aggregator did 3 substitutions.
All rows and columns eliminated.
Presolve time =    0.01 sec.

Dual simplex - Optimal:  Objective =   1.2000000000e+001
Solution time =    0.03 sec.  Iterations = 0 (0)


Variable Name              Solution Value
xs1                             1.000000
x13                             1.000000
x3t                             1.000000
All other variables in the range 1-7 are zero.
```

Listing 6.6 CPLEX Solution Log File of the SPP1 Example

The log file of solving this problem in LP format with the CPLEX solver is shown next in Listing 6.6. The problem is first read from the input file, next is solved, and finally the optimal nonnegative values of the decision variables are written to the log file.

The formulation in LP format uses ASCII text input and output files as its user interface and as consequence does not have the same intuitive graphical user interface as the Excel program. However, the size of the LP file grows proportional to the number of nodes and arcs in the instance. As a consequence the LP formulation file can handle much larger problem instances than Excel. The LP formulation format mixes the model and the data and so if the data changes or another problem has to be solved then a new formulation file has to be generated. The LP formulation also requires additional programming if it is to be interfaced with a database implemented in Excel or Access. In addition, the user is responsible for defining the variable notation and the use of set notation is not allowed. As such the LP formulation is situated in between the very intuitive but less powerful solution methodology using Excel and the powerful and programming oriented solution methodology of mathematical programming languages such as AMPL.

6.3 Exercises

True/False Questions
1. The largest problem instances of the Shortest Path Problem that can be solved in a reasonable amount of computer time contain about 2400 nodes. (T/F) _____.

Shortest Path Exercise Consider the network given in Fig. 6.18. The length of each arcs is shown on the arc, with arrows indicated the arc length in a particular direction. Initial labels are shown above or below the nodes. Find manually

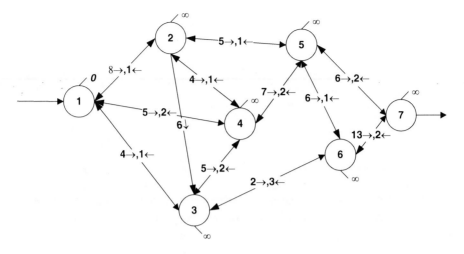

Fig. 6.18 Shortest path exercise

Table 6.2 Troop deployment project data

Symbol	Task	Required time (weeks)	Immediate predecessors
A	Assemble troops and material in home base	3	
B	Transport troops to departure airport	1	A
C	Transport heavy weapons and supplies to departure port	3	A
D	Transport troops to foreign assembly base	3	B,F
E	Transport heavy weapons to foreign port	6	C
F	Transport supplies to foreign port	4	C
G	Transport heavy weapons to foreign base	4	E,F
H	Transport supplies to foreign base	3	F
I	Join troops, supplies, and heavy weapons	3	D,G,H

the shortest path from node 1 to node 7 with Dijkstra's algorithm. Create the files required to solve the shortest path problem given in Fig. 6.18 with AMPL. Give the model, data, execution, and output log file.

Troop Deployment Project You are asked to determine the critical path in the following troop deployment project for which the data are given in Table 6.2 and Fig. 6.19. Immediate predecessor tasks have to be completed before the current task can start.

Complete the project network based on the data given in the table. This includes indicating the length of a task on its arc and drawing any additional precedence arcs if necessary. If you added any arcs, list them next indicating their origin and destination node and length. Give the formula to update the critical path length to a node. Use the notation developed in class and used in the notes. Give a clear legend of the

Fig. 6.19 Troop deployment
project network

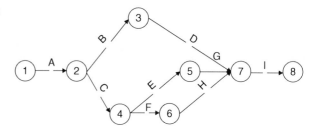

variables, parameters, and other notation you may have used. Determine the critical path to node 8. Show clearly for each node its critical path length next to the node. Finally, clearly show the critical path from node 1 to node 8. Give the length of the critical path and give the sequence of nodes on the critical path.

References

Publications

Ahuja, R., Magnanti, T., & Orlin, J. (1993). *Network flows.* Englewood Cliffs: Prentice-Hall.

AMPL Optimization LLC, www.ampl.com.

Athanasios, P. (2006). Minimum route finder using Dijkstra's algorithm. http://students.ceid.upatras.gr/~papagel/english/java_docs/minDijk.htm. Accessed Jan 2006.

Ball, M. O., Magnanti, T. L., Monma, C. L., & Nemhauser, G. L. (Eds.). (1995). *Network routing.* Amsterdam: Elsevier.

Christofides, N. (1975). *Graph theory: An algorithmic approach.* New York: Academic Press.

Evans, J., & Minieka, E. (1992). *Optimization algorithms for networks and graphs* (2nd ed.). New York: Marcel Dekker.

Fourer, R., Gay, D. M., & Kernighan, B. W. (2002). *AMPL: A modeling language for mathematical programming* (2nd ed.). Belmont: Duxbury Press.

Golden, B., & Assad, A. (Eds.). (1988). *Vehicle routing: Methods and studies.* Amsterdam: North Holland.

ILOG CPLEX File Formats. (2003). ILOG Corporation.

Kennington, J., & Helgason, R. (1980). *Algorithms for network programming.* New York: Wiley.

Chapter 7
Routing Multiple Flows Through a Network

Learning Objectives After you have studied this chapter, you should:

- Know the classification system for vehicle routing problems and algorithms.
- For the class of multiple flows routing through a network you should know:
  - The characteristics of the base problem and various variants.
  - The mathematical formulation.
  - Simple solution algorithms.
  - How to solve problems of modest size with a computer program.

7.1 Introduction

Network flow models are some of the most frequently used tools for the planning of logistics systems because there exists a natural correspondence between the mathematical network flow formulation and the elements of the real-world supply chain network. The supply chain network consists of a number of suppliers that generate products transported over transportation channels through various intermediate facilities to a number of customers. Limiting capacities may exist on the transportation channels, the intermediate facilities, and capacity limitations on available goods at the suppliers may also exist. Demand satisfaction of the customers corresponds to a required outflow of products from the network. The mathematical network consists of nodes and arcs. The nodes can be further classified as sources that generate flow, intermediate nodes that neither generate nor consume flow, and destinations that consume flow. The nodes are connected by directional arcs. The arcs may have capacity limitations for individual flow types or jointly for all flows. A network flow schematic is illustrated in Fig. 7.1.

A supply network for a small single-commodity example is shown in Fig. 7.2. The supply network contains three echelons, consisting of manufacturing plants (M), distribution centers (W), and customers (C). It also contains a common source of raw materials (Sup) and an external supplier of finished products (Ext). The complete network consists of 11 nodes and 24 arcs. All flow enters the network through

M. Goetschalckx, *Supply Chain Engineering,* International Series in Operations Research & Management Science 161, DOI 10.1007/978-1-4419-6512-7_7, © Springer Science+Business Media, LLC 2011

Fig. 7.1 Multiple origin and destination network illustration

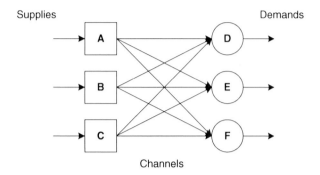

Fig. 7.2 Supply network example

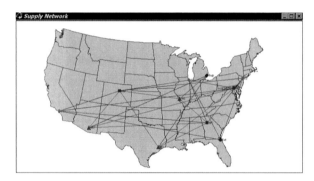

either the Sup or Ext suppliers and leaves the network through the three customer facilities.

If the flow transportations have to be managed and tracked over time, a time-expanded network flow formulation is often used. A time-expanded network consists of a number of parallel network flow structures, one for each time period and each of which has the structure described above. The networks for an individual time period can be thought of as two-dimensional parallel panes or layers in the overall three-dimensional time-expanded network. In addition, there exist a number of arcs that connect the equivalent nodes in the networks for different time periods. An illustration of a time-expanded network is shown in Fig. 7.3, where for simplicity and display reasons, the network for an individual time period is shown in a one-dimensional column and the time-expanded network becomes a two-dimensional network. Diagonal and angled arcs correspond to transportation actions where goods are moved between geographically different nodes and those moves required one or more time units. Those arcs are typically called transportation arcs. Horizontal arcs correspond to goods that move from one time period to the next time period in the same facility. Those arcs correspond to goods held in storage and are often called inventory arcs or holding arcs.

Two types of objectives are common in network flow formulations. The first objective attempts to transport a required or maximum amount of flow from the sources to the sinks. This type of network flow problem is called the "min-cut, max-flow problem" or MCMFP. Some of the early research on this type of network dates back to the early days of the Cold War; see Ford and Fulkerson (1956) and

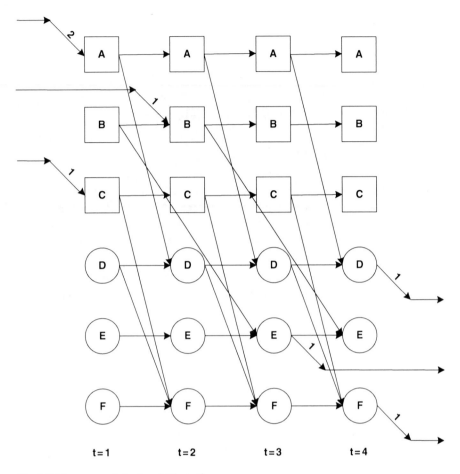

Fig. 7.3 Time-expanded network illustration

Schrijver (1990), where both the United States and Soviet Union were interested in how much flow could be transported over the Soviet rail network to Western Europe (max flow) and in identifying the bottlenecks on the transportation quantities (min cut). MCMFP are often used in flow capacity models and flow models for the public sector. Contemporary examples are emergency evacuation of high-rise buildings and determination of hurricane evacuation routes.

The second type of network flow problem has a cost minimization objective function. Transportation of a unit of flow through a transportation arc incurs a cost. The overall objective is to satisfy all the flow requirements in a feasible manner at a minimal cost. This type of network flow problem is called a "minimum cost network flow problem," or MCNFP. This type of model is very frequently used in the tactical planning for logistics networks.

Because of its prevalence and practical importance, extensive research has been performed on the efficient solution of large-scale network flow problems. At the current time, the most efficient solution method is based on the network simplex algorithm. Single commodity problems with several hundreds of thousands of transportation channels can be solved in acceptable time on contemporary personal computers.

7.2 Network Variants and Applications

7.2.1 Network Variants

Transportation Problem (TP) In addition to the two types of network problems MCMFP and MCNFP as identified above, several other standard network formulations exist. An early type is the transportation problem, or TP. A transportation network consists solely of source and sinks nodes and source nodes can reach sink nodes through a single transportation arc. This is in contrast with a more general transshipment network that also contains intermediate nodes.

Multicommodity Network Flow Problem A network can either have a single type of flow or multiple types. The later is called a multicommodity network. In a multicommodity network, there exists a variable for each arc and commodity combination. There exists a conservation of flow constraint for each node and commodity combination. However, flow capacity constraints are for all commodity flows combined.

Generalized Network A network is a generalized network when coefficients exist in the conservation of flow constraints that are different from zero and one. A network is also a generalized network when there is no conservation of flow for a commodity inside an arc, in other words, there are gains or losses between the entry and the exit flow of an arc. This generalized network is also called a network flow with gains. An example of a generalized network with losses is the municipal water network, where water is lost in the pipes and junctions through leaks. Another example is the distribution network for high-voltage electricity, where the amount of energy entering the transmission line is not equal to the amount leaving the line due to transmission line losses.

7.2.2 Applications

7.2.2.1 Tactical Production-Distribution Planning

The tactical production-distribution planning problem finds the minimal cost production and transportation flows for a set of commodities from a set of production facilities to a set of customers. The demand at the customers for the commodities has to be satisfied and the production facilities have joint-commodity capacity restrictions. Each production or transportation flow has an individual unit cost rate.

The production of commodities at the production facilities have individual resource requirements. The following notation will be used in formulating the problem.

Parameters and Variables

P number of products, indexed by p
F number of production facilities, indexed by i
C number of customers, indexed by j
dem_{jp} demand for product p by customer j
cap_i joint-commodity capacity at production facility i
req_{ip} resources required by the production of one unit of product p at facility i (expressed in the same units as cap_i)
a_{ip} unit production cost for product p at facility i
c_{ijp} unit transportation cost for product p from facility i to customer j
x_{ijp} amount of flow transported of product p from facility i to customer j

The standard network formulation does not allow having capacities or costs on the flow through the nodes, only capacities or costs for flows through the arcs. A standard modeling technique to avoid this limitation is to split the original node with capacity or cost up into two nodes connected by a single arc. On this arc a flow capacity and flow cost can then be specified. This technique is illustrated in Fig. 7.4 for the tactical production-distribution planning problem.

Node Capacity Illustration The formulation of the tactical production–distribution planning problem is given next. If all req_{ip} are equal and can thus be set equal to one, the formulation is a network. If not all req_{ip} are equal, the formulation is a generalized network. The solution times for solving a generalized network are significantly larger than for solving a network of equivalent size. In addition, the integrality property does not longer hold for generalized networks and the optimal solution flows may be fractional.

The formulation has all the production and transportation costs in the objective. The first constraint set assures that the demand for a product at a customer is satisfied with the transportation flows. These constraints are called the demand constraints. The second constraint set ensures that the production at each facility does not consume more resources than are available at this plant. These constraints are called the capacity constraints.

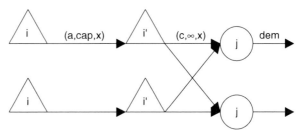

Fig. 7.4 Tactical production–distribution planning network

Model

Formulation 7.1. Tactical Production-Distribution Planning Network

$$Min \quad \sum_{i=1}^{F} \sum_{j=1}^{C} \sum_{p=1}^{P} (a_{ip} + c_{ijp}) x_{ijp}$$

$$s.t. \quad \sum_{i=1}^{F} x_{ijp} = dem_{jp} \qquad \forall jp \qquad (7.1)$$

$$\sum_{j=1}^{C} \sum_{p=1}^{P} req_{ip} x_{ijp} \leq cap_i \quad \forall i$$

$$x_{ijp} \geq 0$$

7.2.2.2 Operator Scheduling

A common labor and resource scheduling task is to determine the number of operators required for each of the periods in a planning horizon so that adequate service can be delivered. Examples are the scheduling of customer service agents in call centers, the scheduling of nurses of different qualification classes in hospital emergency rooms, and the scheduling of cashiers in grocery stores. Each time period requires a number of operators to provide adequate service. The operators or servers are available in a number of candidate patterns, which are called shifts. There is a cost associated with executing a shift and the objective is to minimize the total cost of executed shifts while providing the required service. The following notation will be used in formulating the problem.

Parameters and Variables

M time periods indexed by i
b_i number of operators required during period i
c_j cost for one operator performing shift j
a_j vector for shift j whose elements a_{ij} are equal to one if shift j services time period i, zero otherwise. The shift is assumed to cover consecutive time periods.
x_j number of operators performing shift j

The formulation minimizes the total cost of the operators. The single constraint set ensures that for each time period a sufficient number of operators are on duty.

Model

Formulation 7.2. Operator Scheduling Formulation

$$Min \quad cx$$
$$s.t. \quad Ax \geq b \qquad (7.2)$$
$$x \geq 0$$

The constraints for a small example are shown next. There are five time periods and the required number of workers in each time period is shown in the column b at the right. In this example, there are five possible shifts or work patterns.

$$
\begin{bmatrix}
0 & 1 & 0 & 1 & 1 \\
1 & 1 & 0 & 0 & 1 \\
1 & 1 & 0 & 0 & 1 \\
1 & 1 & 0 & 0 & 0 \\
1 & 1 & 1 & 0 & 0
\end{bmatrix}
x \geq
\begin{bmatrix}
5 \\
12 \\
8 \\
10 \\
4
\end{bmatrix}
$$

This formulation can be transformed into a network flow formulation, provided the work patterns cover consecutive periods. This property is called the *consecutive ones* property. The transformation has three steps.

1. Add the negative identity matrix corresponding to the row surplus variables y.
2. Add a row of zeroes corresponding to the flow balance constraint of node or period $N+1$.
3. Execute iteratively the following linear row operation

$$
row[r+1] = row[r+1] - row[r] \quad for \quad r = N \ down \ to \ 1
$$

The constraint matrix after the transformation is shown below. There are now ten columns, corresponding to five possible work patterns and five time periods. Each column contains a single positive and negative one, indicating this column corresponds to a directed arc. The positive one corresponds to the start node of the arc and the negative one corresponds to the terminal node of the arc. There are six rows, corresponding to the flow conservation constraints for $N+1$ nodes. The first column corresponds to the arc going from node 2 to node 6 and the flow variable x_1. Finally, the right-hand side column now indicates the external flows to the network nodes. Positive external flows indicate flow coming into the node; negative external flows indicated flow leaving the node. The y surplus variables indicate backwards flows.

$$
\begin{bmatrix}
0 & 1 & 0 & 1 & 1 & -1 & 0 & 0 & 0 & 0 \\
1 & 0 & 0 & -1 & 0 & 1 & -1 & 0 & 0 & 0 \\
0 & 0 & 0 & 0 & 0 & 0 & 1 & -1 & 0 & 0 \\
0 & 0 & 0 & 0 & -1 & 0 & 0 & 1 & -1 & 0 \\
0 & 0 & 1 & 0 & 0 & 0 & 0 & 0 & 1 & -1 \\
-1 & -1 & -1 & 0 & 0 & 0 & 0 & 0 & 0 & 1
\end{bmatrix}
\begin{bmatrix} x \\ y \end{bmatrix}
=
\begin{bmatrix}
5 \\
7 \\
-4 \\
2 \\
-6 \\
-4
\end{bmatrix}
$$

Illustration The network corresponding to the constraint matrix above is illustrated in Fig. 7.5. For example, the flow on the arc x_5 denotes the number of operators that start at the beginning of time period 1 and end their shift at the end of time period 4. Note that the requirements for the integrality property are satisfied and the decision variables will automatically take integer values in the optimal solution.

If the cost of executing a shift is equal to the number of periods covered by the shift then the cost coefficients are given by (4, 5, 1, 1, 3). The optimal solution to the example is then (7, 3, 0, 0, 2) with a solution value equal to 49. The network with the optimal solution flows is shown in Fig. 7.6. Arcs with a nonnegative flow are shown in bold. The slack flows corresponding to periods 3 and 5 have positive

Fig. 7.5 Operator scheduling network

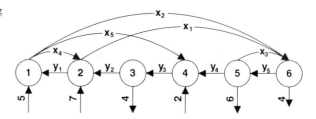

Fig. 7.6 Operator scheduling solution network

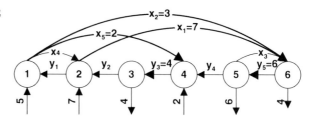

values of 4 and 6, respectively. This implies that there are 4 and 6 extra operators on duty for those periods, respectively.

7.3   Network Solution Algorithms

7.3.1   *Successive Shortest Path Algorithm*

An intuitive greedy solution procedure for the single-commodity minimum cost network flow problem (MCNFP) is to identify the shortest or least cost feasible path from the source node to a sink node and send as much flow as feasibly possible along this path from source to sink. A path is considered feasible if it allows additional flow from source to sink. While this action is optimal by itself, this greedy procedure cannot guarantee optimality for the original problem.

The following algorithm adheres to the same general approach but with two enhancements. The first enhancement is that the arc costs are not only based on the original cost but also on the current length of the shortest paths to its origin and destination node. This allows for the determination of a shortest least cost path based on the current flows in the network. At the start of the algorithm there is no current flow in the network and so the original arc costs are used. The second enhancement is the introduction of backward arcs. A forward arc on the shortest path is oriented following the direction of the arc present in the flow path from the origin node to the destination node for this iteration; a backward arc is oriented the opposite way. Flows on backward arcs correspond to reducing the current forward flow on those arcs. This allows for the current flows to be adjusted or corrected from a greedy solution. The algorithm is denoted as the successive shortest path algorithm and it guarantees convergence to the optimal solution.

While this algorithm can be interpreted in the framework of linear programming, the following exposition does not rely on linear programming, so prior knowledge of linear programming is not required. The algorithm consists of the iterative execution of two steps. While each step is relatively simple, the iterative nature of the algorithm makes manual solutions quite tedious. A solution procedure compatible with Excel spreadsheets and a modeling language solution procedure are presented following this algorithm.

In the following algorithm description, the potential of a node is the equal to the shortest path length to this node based on the current flows and arc capacities in the network. The node potentials are denoted by π and have positive values. The potential of a node will have nondecreasing values during the sequence of iterations of the algorithm. The sign of the node potential depends on if the conservation of flow constraint for a node is written as a greater than or less than or equal constraint. In this text the node potentials have positive values corresponding to a conservation of flow constraint written as a less than or equal constraint.

In the following algorithm two classifications for the arcs will be used. During each iteration a shortest path will be determined. The arcs that are components of that shortest path will be called forward arcs, the arcs that have the opposite direction as the forward arcs will be called backward arcs. Typically there is large number of arcs not involved in the shortest path as either forward or backward arcs. The shortest path and the set of forward and backward arcs changes from iteration to iteration. A second classification identifies arcs as regular arcs if they were present in the original network and as artificial arcs if they were not in the original network. Obviously this classification does not depend on the iteration.

7.3.1.1   Algorithm Description

1. Start all flows $x=0$, all node potentials $\pi=0$.
   If there is more than one source node or more than sink node, add a super source and a super sink node, respectively. Then add arcs from the super source to the sources and from the sinks to the super sink with cost equal to zero and capacity equal to the supply and demand of the source and sink node, respectively. Define the current incremental, residual graph as the original graph. This implies that the cost of all the arcs is equal to their original cost. The latter is equivalent to step 6 for all current flows equal to zero initial flows.
2. Find shortest path from source to sink.
   Find shortest path from the super source node to the super sink node with Dijkstra's algorithm
   If no such path exists, stop, network flow problem is infeasible
3. The arcs on the shortest path are denoted as forward arcs, the arcs in the opposite direction as backflow or backward arcs.
   Compute maximum flow change on the shortest path over the forward arcs
   on artificial arcs, $\delta_{ij} = x_{ij}$
   on regular arcs, $\delta_{ij} = u_{ij} - x_{ij}$

$$\delta = \min \{\delta_{ij}\}$$

4. Augment flow on the forward arcs of the shortest path
   on artificial arcs, $x_{ij} = x_{ij} - \delta$
   on regular arcs, $x_{ij} = x_{ij} + \delta$
   Update remaining supply and demand at the source and sink nodes.
5. If the remaining demand is zero, stop, the current flow solution is optimal.
   Update the node potentials π_i.
   k=shortest path sink node and SPL_i is the shortest path length to node i
   if node i has a permanent label, $\pi_i = \pi_i + SPL_i$
   if node i has a temporary label, $\pi_i = \pi_i + SPL_k$
6. Construct the incremental/residual graph. In the first iteration the residual graph
   is equal to the original graph.
   The residual graph has the same nodes as original graph.
   For the forward arcs on the shortest path, if it does not exist already add the
   backward arc ji
   Update the remaining capacity for the forward arcs along the shortest path
   $u_{ij} = u_{ij} - \delta$ and for the backward arcs $u_{ij} = u_{ij} + \delta$
   If $x_{ij} = u_{ij}$ then eliminate arc ij
   If $x_{ij} < u_{ij}$ then reduced arc cost $rc_{ij} = c_{ij} - \pi_j + \pi_i$
   If $x_{ij} > 0$ then reduced arc cost $rc_{ji} = -c_{ij} + \pi_j - \pi_i = -rc_{ij}$
7. Go to step 2

7.3.1.2 Successive Shortest Path Algorithm Illustration

The five diagrams in Fig. 7.7 illustrate the execution of the iterative steps performed
by the successive shortest path algorithm for a very small network instance. The
first part (a) shows the initial network. The residual or incremental network is equal
to the original network and the arc costs are equal to the initial arc costs. The numbers shown for each arc represent the unit cost and the capacity of the arc, respectively. The number shown for each node is the node potential. Finally, the objective
is to find the minimal cost flows for sending four units of flow from node 1 to node
4. This is illustrated by the external flows into node 1 and out of node 4 with quantities 4 and -4, respectively.

Part (b) shows the solution of the SPP for iteration 1. The shortest path starts at
node 1, traverses node 2 and terminates at node 4 with length equal to 3. Each node
is shown now with two numbers, the first one is the current node potential and the
second one is the length of the optimal shortest path to this node.

In part (c) the residual graph for iteration 1 is shown. First the node potential for
each node is updated. Since the labels of all nodes in the shortest path step have become permanent, for each node the length of its shortest path is added to its original
node potential. The original node potentials were all zero. Next, the maximum flow

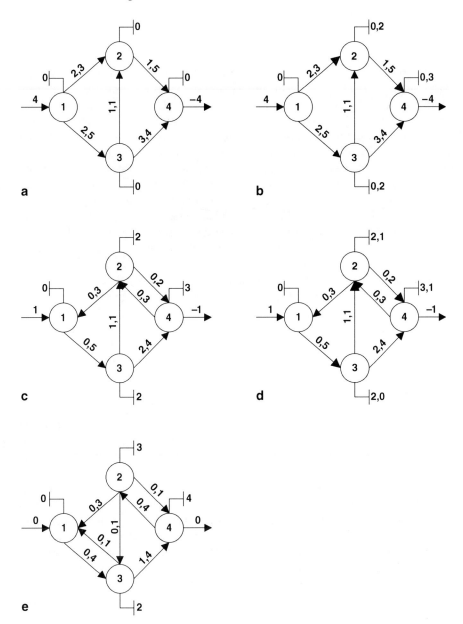

Fig. 7.7 Successive shortest path algorithm illustration

along the new shortest path is determined, new backward arcs are created, the remaining arc capacities are updated, and finally the arc costs are updated. The maximum flow on the shortest path is the minimum of the capacity on the external arcs and internal arcs (1,2) and (2,4), which is equal to min {3, 5} = 3. Arc (1,2) had the limiting capacity. The remaining supply and the remaining demand on the source and sink node of the shortest path are decreased by the flow quantity. This leaves a remaining demand of 1 in node 4, hence the algorithm must execute another iteration after the residual graph is updated. The backward arc for each arc on the shortest path is created, which for this iteration corresponds to the creation of arcs (4,2) and (2,1). The capacity on the forward or original arcs is decreased by the new flow quantity of 3. This reduces the capacity of arcs (1,2) and (2,4) to 0 and 2, respectively. The arc (1,2), which had the limiting capacity, has an updated remaining capacity of zero. No further flow can be sent over this arc and it is eliminated for the shortest path calculations in the next iteration. The capacity on the backward arcs is increased by the new flow quantity of 3. Since they are created in this iteration, the backward arcs had no previous capacity and the both have an updated capacity equal to 3. Finally, the reduced arc costs are updated by subtracting the node potential of the destination node and adding the node potential of the origin node to the original arc cost. Note that forward and backward arcs on the shortest path all must have updated costs equal to zero and no arc can have a negative updated reduced arc cost.

Since remaining demand exists, the algorithm must execute the next iteration on the updated residual graph. In part (d) the shortest path in the updated residual network of part (c) is determined. The second number for each node is the node label or the shortest path length to this node and all node labels are permanent. The shortest path starts at node 1, traverses nodes 3 and 2, and terminates at node 4 with length equal to 1. This path length is the additional length required to reach the destination node above the node potential of the destination node.

In part (e) the residual graph for iteration two is shown. First the potential for every node are updated. Since the labels of all nodes in the shortest path step have become permanent, for each node the length of its optimal shortest path is added to its original node potential. Next, the maximum flow along the new shortest path is determined, new backward arcs are created, the remaining arc capacities are updated, and finally the arc costs are updated. The maximum flow on the shortest path is the minimum of the (remaining) capacity on the external arcs and the internal arcs (1,3), (3,2), and (2,4), which is equal to min $\{1, 5, 1, 2, |-1|\} = 1$. Three arcs have the limiting capacity. When the remaining supply and the remaining demand on the source and sink node of the shortest path are decreased by the flow quantity, the remaining demand is equal to zero and the algorithm will terminate at the end of this step. The backward arc for each arc on the shortest path is created, which for this iteration corresponds to the creation of arcs (2,3) and (3,1). The capacity on the forward or original arcs is decreased by the new flow quantity of 1. This reduces the capacity of arcs (1,3) and (3,2) to 4 and 0, respectively. The arc (3,2), which had the limiting capacity, has an updated remaining capacity of zero. The capacity on the backward arcs is increased by the new flow quantity of 1. The capacity of the backward arcs (4,2), (2,3) and (3, 1) is update to 4, 1, and 1, respectively. Finally, the reduced arc costs are updated by subtracting the node potential of the destination node and adding the node potential of the origin node to the original arc cost. Note that forward and backward arcs on the shortest path all must have updated costs equal to zero and no arc can have a negative updated arc cost.

In each iteration, the first step that finds the shortest path is equivalent to a pricing problem. The pricing problem attempts to find a new feasible flow path to send additional flow. If no such flow path exists, then the problem is infeasible. The second step of each iteration updates the current state of the network and is equivalent to a master problem. The master problem updates the remaining capacities and node potentials and provides new pricing information to the shortest path problem in the form of updates of the reduced arc costs.

7.3.1.3 Successive Shortest Path Algorithm Example

In the following figures the execution of the successive shortest path algorithms for a slightly larger problem instance is illustrated. The algorithm requires five iterations, each consisting out of two steps. The network with the original data is shown in Fig. 7.8. The objective is to find the minimum cost flows to send 30 units of flow from node 1 to node 7. The numbers on the arcs indicated the current cost followed by the remaining capacity on the arc. The numbers on the node in the shortest path step indicated the shortest path length to the node, followed by the index of the predecessor node on the shortest path. An optimal shortest path length or, equivalently, a permanent node label is indicated by an asterisk. In the residual network step, the number on the node indicates the updated node potential.

The first shortest path has a length of 22 and the node labels on all nodes have become permanent. The arcs on the shortest path are shown in bold in Fig. 7.9.

Arc (4,3) has the limiting capacity and twelve flow units can be sent over the shortest path. The four backward arcs are constructed, each with a capacity equal to twelve. The forward arcs on the shortest path have their capacity reduced by twelve. This eliminates are (4,3) which has an updated capacity equal to zero. The

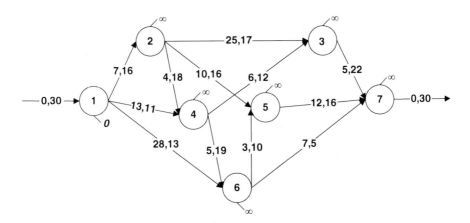

Fig. 7.8 Successive shortest path example data

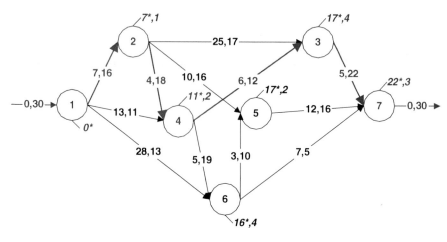

Fig. 7.9 Successive shortest path example first shortest path (Iteration 1A)

updated node potentials are set to the shortest path length to the node. The arc costs
are updated. The costs for the forward and backward arcs on the shortest path are
all equal to zero (Fig. 7.10).

The second shortest path has an incremental length of 1 and the node labels on
all nodes except node 3 have become permanent. The arcs on the shortest path are
shown in bold in Fig. 7.11.

Arc (1,2) has the limiting capacity and four flow units can be sent over the shortest path. Two new backward arcs are constructed. The backward arcs on the path
have their capacity increased by four and the forward arcs on the shortest path have
their capacity reduced by four. This eliminates are (1,2) which has an updated capacity equal to zero. The node potentials for all nodes except node 3 are updated by

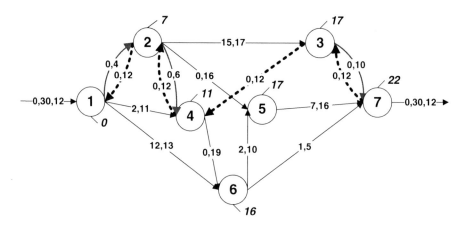

Fig. 7.10 Successive shortest path example first incremental graph (Iteration 1B)

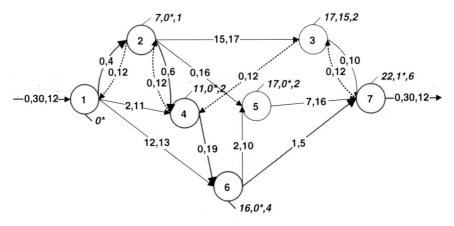

Fig. 7.11 Successive shortest path example second shortest path (Iteration 2A)

adding the shortest path length to this node. The node potential for node 3 is updated by adding the shortest path length of the destination node 7, which is equal to 1. The updated node potential for node 3 is then $17+1=18$. The reduced arc costs are updated. The costs for the forward and backward arcs on the shortest path are all equal to zero. The updated arc cost for the backward arc (3,4) is equal to $-(6-18+11)=1$. The updated arc cost for the corresponding forward arc (4,3) would have been -1 and negative arc costs are not allowed. However, the remaining capacity of arc (4,3) is zero and this arc has been eliminated. See Fig. 7.12.

The third shortest path has a (incremental) length of two and the node labels on all nodes except node 3 have become permanent. The arcs on the shortest path are shown in bold in Fig. 7.13.

Arc (6,7) has the limiting capacity and a single flow unit can be sent over the shortest path. One new backward arc (4,1) is constructed. The backward arcs on the

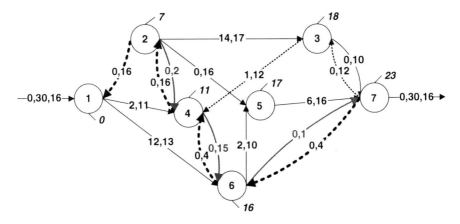

Fig. 7.12 Successive shortest path example second incremental graph (Iteration 2B)

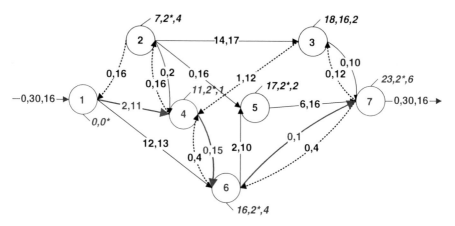

Fig. 7.13 Successive shortest path example third shortest path (Iteration 3A)

path have their capacity increase by 1 and the forward arcs on the shortest path have their capacity reduced by 1. This eliminates are (6,7) which has an updated capacity equal to zero. The node potentials for all nodes except node 3 are updated by adding the shortest path length to the node. The node potential for node 3 is updated by adding the shortest path length of the destination node 7, which is equal to 2. The updated node potential for node 3 is then $18+2=20$. The arc costs are updated. The costs for the forward and backward arcs on the shortest path are all equal to zero. The updated arc cost for the backward arc (3,4) is equal to $(6-20+13)=1$. See Fig. 7.14.

The fourth shortest path has a (incremental) length of six and the node labels on all nodes except node 3 have become permanent. The arcs on the shortest path are shown in bold in Fig. 7.15.

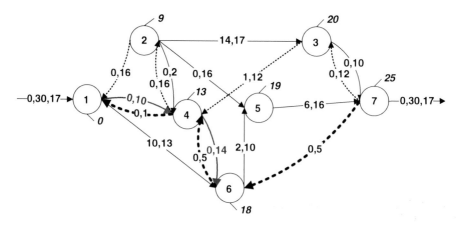

Fig. 7.14 Successive shortest path example third incremental graph (Iteration 3B)

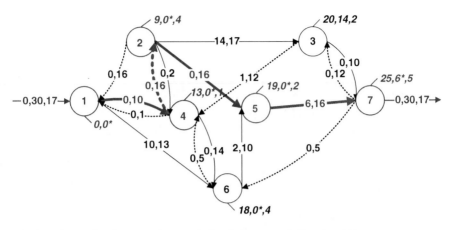

Fig. 7.15 Successive shortest path example fourth shortest path (Iteration 4A)

Arc (1,4) has the limiting capacity and ten units of flow can be sent over the shortest path. Two new backward arcs (7,5) and (5,2) are constructed. The backward arcs on the path have their capacity increased by ten and the forward arcs on the shortest path have their capacity reduced by ten. Observe that artificial arc (4,2) is oriented in the direction of the shortest path, so it is part of the forward arcs and its remaining capacity will be reduced. Regular arc (2,4) is part of the backward arcs in this iteration and its remaining capacity will be increased. This corresponds to the reduction of the flow quantity on arc (2,4) that was found in an earlier iteration. This eliminates arc (1,4) which has an updated capacity equal to zero. The node potentials for all nodes except node 3 are updated by adding the shortest path length to the node. The node potential for node 3 is updated by adding the shortest path length of the destination node 7, which is equal to 6. The updated node potential for node 3 is then $20+6=26$. The reduced arc costs are updated. The costs for the forward and backward arcs on the shortest path are all equal to zero. The updated reduced arc cost for the backward arc (3,4) is equal to $-(6-26+13)=7$. See Fig. 7.16.

The fifth shortest path has a (incremental) length of ten and the node labels on all nodes except node 3 have become permanent. The arcs on the shortest path are shown in bold in Fig. 7.17.

The external arcs into node 1 and out of node 7 have the limiting capacity and three units of flow can be sent over the shortest path. One new backward arc (6,1) is constructed. The backward arcs on the path have their capacity increased by three and the forward arcs on the shortest path have their capacity reduced by three. Observe that arcs (4,2) and (6,4) are oriented in the direction of the shortest path, so they are part of the forward arcs and their remaining capacity will be reduced. Arcs (2,4) and (4,6) are part of the backward arcs in this iteration and their remaining capacity will be increased. This corresponds to the reduction of the flow quantities on arcs (2,4) and (4,6) that were found in an earlier iteration. Since all demands have been satisfied, the algorithm stops at the end of this iteration. The node potentials for all nodes except node 3 are updated by adding the shortest path length to the node. The node potential for node 3 is updated by adding

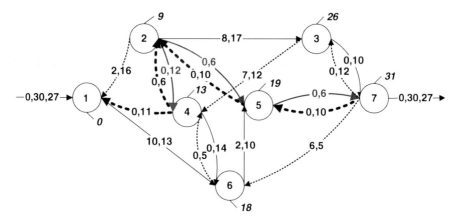

Fig. 7.16 Successive shortest path example fourth incremental graph (Iteration 4B)

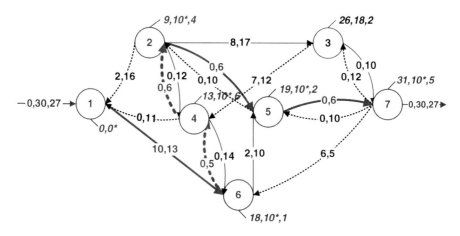

Fig. 7.17 Successive shortest path example fifth shortest path (Iteration 5A)

the shortest path length of the destination node 7, which is equal to 10. The updated node potential for node 3 is then $26+10=36$. The reduced arc costs are updated. The reduced costs for the forward and backward arcs on the shortest path are all equal to zero. The updated reduced arc cost for the backward arc $(3,4)$ is equal to $-(6-36+23)=7$ and for backward arc $(7,6)$ is equal to $-(7-41+28)=6$. See Fig. 7.18.

The optimal solution for the problem is shown in Fig. 7.19. The numbers on the arc indicated the original cost, the original capacity, and the final optimal flow on the arc, respectively. The optimal total cost of sending thirty units of flow from node 1 to node 7 is equal to 814.

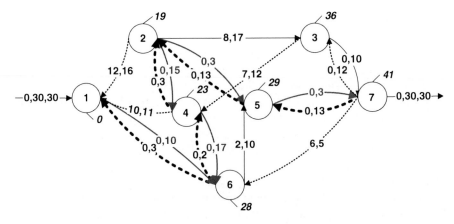

Fig. 7.18 Successive shortest path example fifth incremental graph (Iteration 5B)

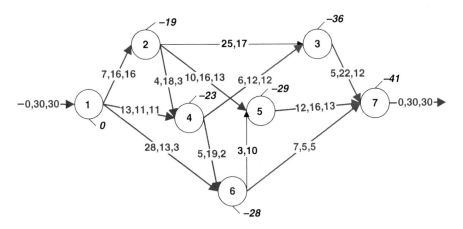

Fig. 7.19 Successive shortest path example final optimal solution

7.3.2 Network Properties

Integrality Property The integrality property, also called the *unimodularity* property, states that for a single-commodity network if all the external flows and the arc capacities of a network formulation are integer numbers, then the optimal solution to this network flow problem will consist of all integer flows. The constraint matrix of such network flow formulations is unimodular. It should be noted that the unimodularity or integrality property does not hold for generalized networks or for multicommodity networks.

7.3.3 Algebraic Formulation

The algebraic formulation for the same example used to illustrate the successive shortest path algorithm is given below. There are three main sections to the formulation: the objective function, the conservation of flow constraints for each node, and the upper bound or capacity constraints for each arc flow. The sign convention for the material flow arcs in the conservation of flow constraints is positive when leaving a node and negative when entering a node. This is also denoted as "*out–in.*" The corresponding sign convention for external flows is that external flows that are supplies and are entering the node from outside the network have a positive sign and that external flows that are demands and are leaving the node to outside the network have a negative sign. The sign in the conservation of flow constraints is then less than or equal. This ensures that the external supply is not exceeded and that the external demand is satisfied.

An alternative sign convention is to indicate internal network entering flow arcs as positive and leaving flow arcs as negative. Either of the two sign convention can be used as long the same sign convention is applied consistently everywhere and sign of the flow balance equation is adjusted. The sign of the node potential also has to be adjusted.

Listing 7.1 Algebraic Formulation of the Network Flow Example

$$
\begin{aligned}
\min\ & 7x_{12} + 13x_{14} + 28x_{16} + 25x_{23} + 4x_{24} + 10x_{25} \\
& + 5x_{37} + 6x_{43} + 5x_{46} + 12x_{57} + 3x_{65} + 7x_{67} \\
s.t.\ & x_{12} + x_{14} + x_{16} \le 30 \\
& x_{23} + x_{24} + x_{25} - x_{12} \le 0 \\
& x_{37} - x_{23} - x_{43} \le 0 \\
& x_{43} + x_{46} - x_{24} - x_{14} \le 0 \\
& x_{57} - x_{25} - x_{65} \le 0 \\
& x_{65} + x_{67} - x_{16} - x_{46} \le 0 \\
& -x_{37} - x_{57} - x_{67} \le -30 \\
& x_{12} \le 16 \\
& x_{14} \le 11 \\
& x_{16} \le 13 \\
& x_{23} \le 17 \\
& x_{24} \le 18 \\
& x_{25} \le 16 \\
& x_{37} \le 22 \\
& x_{43} \le 12 \\
& x_{46} \le 19 \\
& x_{57} \le 16 \\
& x_{65} \le 10 \\
& x_{67} \le 5
\end{aligned}
$$

When creating network flow formulations manually, some consistency checks can be made. Assume there are N nodes and M arcs in the network. There must be M terms in the objective function, $N+M$ constraints, and a total of $2M$ variables in the N conservation of flow constraints. Each flow variable must appear exactly twice in the conservation of flow constraints, once with a positive and once with a negative sign. In the network flow example $N=7$ and $M=12$. Since the total external inflow equals the total external outflow, the network is said to be balanced and the conservation of flow constraints for source and sink nodes can be specified as equalities. If the total available inflow is larger than the total required outflow, not all of the inflow capacity will be used. In that case the conservation of flow constraints for the source and sink nodes must be specified as less than or equal constraints.

In the following discussion the use of two solvers for the network flow problem are illustrated based on the preceding network flow example. The use of those two solvers was also illustrated for the shortest path problem, so the following is an expansion because for the MCNFP multiple flow units are possible. In order to make the following more or less self-contained, some text and content from the SPP exposition is repeated here.

7.3.4 Spreadsheet Formulation and Solution

The following describes the solution of the minimum cost network flow problem example with the Excel spreadsheet software. The steps are similar to the steps for the determination of the solution to the shortest path problem with spreadsheet software. In the case of the MCNFP, the capacities of the arcs may not all be equal to one. The solution of the previous example problem with the solver included in Microsoft Excel is shown in the following figures. The Figs. 7.20–7.23 show the data and status of the solution before the solver has been executed. The two dialog windows for the solver execution are shown next in Figs. 7.24 and 7.25. Finally, the solution is shown in Figs. 7.26 and 7.27.

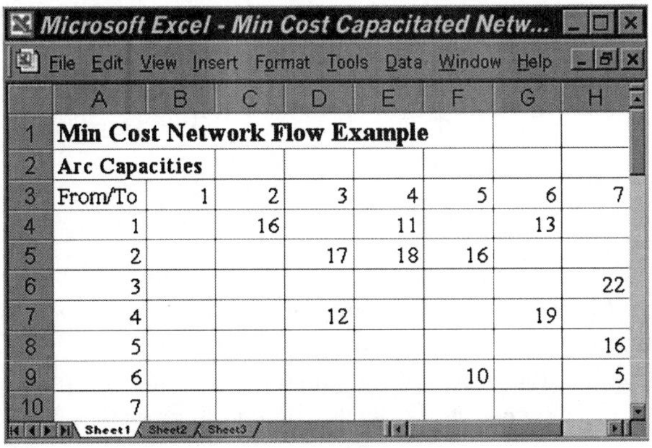

Fig. 7.20 Excel spreadsheet for minimum cost network example arc capacities

From/To	1	2	3	4	5	6	7
1		16		11		13	
2			17	18	16		
3							22
4			12			19	
5							16
6						10	5
7							

Fig. 7.21 Excel spreadsheet for minimum cost network example arc costs

Arc Costs							
From/To	1	2	3	4	5	6	7
1		7		13		28	
2			25	4	10		
3							5
4			6			5	
5							12
6					3		7
7							

Fig. 7.22 Excel spreadsheet for minimum cost network example initial zero flows

Arc Flows								
From/To	1	2	3	4	5	6	7	Out
1								0
2								0
3								0
4								0
5								0
6								0
7								0
In	0	0	0	0	0	0	0	
Balance	0	0	0	0	0	0	0	
External	30						-30	

Fig. 7.23 Excel spreadsheet for minimum cost network example initial zero objective

Objective								
From/To	1	2	3	4	5	6	7	Sum
1	0	0	0	0	0	0	0	0
2	0	0	0	0	0	0	0	0
3	0	0	0	0	0	0	0	0
4	0	0	0	0	0	0	0	0
5	0	0	0	0	0	0	0	0
6	0	0	0	0	0	0	0	0
7	0	0	0	0	0	0	0	0
Sum	0	0	0	0	0	0	0	0

Figure 7.22 shows the area of the spreadsheet corresponding to the flow variables. It has the same two-dimensional adjacency matrix structure augmented with rows and columns to check for conservation of flow. For each source node the sum of the outgoing flows is computed in column I and for each destination node the sum of all the incoming flows in computed in row 31. The difference between outgoing

Fig. 7.24 Excel spreadsheet for minimum cost network example solver

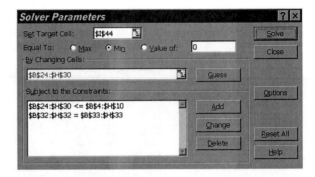

Fig. 7.25 Excel spreadsheet solver options for the network flow problem

	A	B	C	D	E	F	G	H	I
22	**Arc Flows**								
23	From/To	1	2	3	4	5	6	7	Out
24	1	0	16	0	11	0	3	0	30
25	2	0	0	0	3	13	0	0	16
26	3	0	0	0	0	0	0	12	12
27	4	0	0	12	0	0	2	0	14
28	5	0	0	0	0	0	0	13	13
29	6	0	0	0	0	0	0	5	5
30	7	0	0	0	0	0	0	0	0
31	In	0	16	12	14	13	5	30	
32	Balance	30	0	0	0	0	0	-30	
33	External	30						-30	

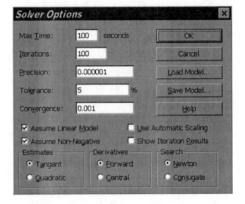

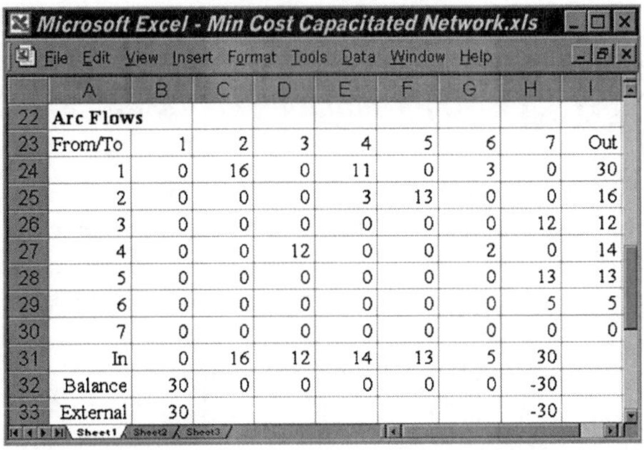

Fig. 7.26 Excel spreadsheet for minimum cost network example solution flows

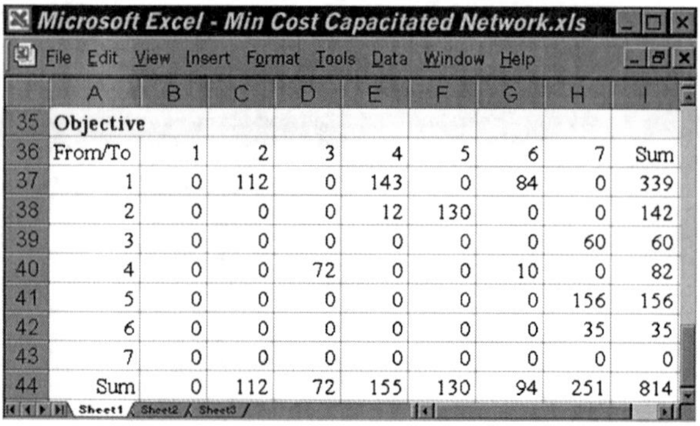

Fig. 7.27 Excel spreadsheet
for minimum cost network
example solution objective

From/To	1	2	3	4	5	6	7	Sum
1	0	112	0	143	0	84	0	339
2	0	0	0	12	130	0	0	142
3	0	0	0	0	0	0	60	60
4	0	0	72	0	0	10	0	82
5	0	0	0	0	0	0	156	156
6	0	0	0	0	0	0	35	35
7	0	0	0	0	0	0	0	0
Sum	0	112	72	155	130	94	251	814

and incoming flows is computed in row 32. Given the sign convention for incoming
and outgoing flows, the difference in row 32 is computed as the sum of the outgoing
flows minus the sum of the incoming flows. This difference must less than or equal
to the external flows, which are shown in row 33. This assumes that external in-flows
(supplies) have a positive sign and external out-flows (demands) have a negative
sign. For this example, the network is balanced so the less than or equal constraints
can be substituted by equality constraints. An alternative method is to introduce an
artificial sink node with as demand the difference between the total supply and the
total demand in the network. All source nodes are then connected to this artificial
sink node with flow arcs with zero cost and infinite capacity. Since the network is
then again balanced, the flow balances can be modeled as equality constraints.

For minimum cost network flow formulations, the model has only linear constraints and objective function and the flow variables cannot be negative. The dialog
window for the solver options in the Excel spreadsheet is shown in Fig. 7.25.

In the two following figures, the solution flow variables and objective function
values are shown. The cells in the spreadsheet in Fig. 7.26 have conditional formatting assigned to them, so that they are shaded if there is a nonzero value stored in
them. The total cost is equal to 814. Figure 7.27 shows the contribution of the flow
on each individual arc to the total cost.

7.3.5 AMPL Formulation and Solution

The solution of the example problem with the AMPL mathematical programming
language is illustrated in the following four listings of text files. The listings correspond to the model, data, execution, and output files, respectively. Listing 7.2
shows the model, which is a generic single-commodity minimum cost network flow
(MCNFP) formulation. This model also has been used in the previous chapter on
single-flow routing, but since the shortest path problem is subclass of minimum cost
network flow problem the model can be used here without any modification. Many
alternative AMPL models for the minimum cost network flow problem exist, and
some of these can be found on the AMPL website.

The model contains nodes and arcs. The nodes are either sources, sinks, or internal nodes depending on if they have external flow entering as supply, external flow leaving as demand, or no external flow, respectively. AMPL performs a feasibility check before the solver execution to ensure that the total supply in all of the source nodes is larger than the total demand. The arcs are defined by their origin and destination nodes. Every node can be the origin node and destination node of an arc. Bidirectional arcs have to be modeled explicitly as two arcs with opposite origin and destination nodes. Each arc has a cost, capacity, and arc flow, all of which have to be nonnegative. The arc flow has to no larger than the arc capacity. The objective of this formulation is to minimize the total transportation cost which is the sum of the product of the arc flow and arc cost over all the arcs. Finally, for each node a conservation of flow constraints exists, which ensures that the difference between the outgoing flows and the incoming flows is less than or equal to the external flow. A supply is modeled with a positive external flow and a demand is modeled as a negative external flow.

Listing 7.2 AMPL MCNFP Model File

```
set SOURCES;
set SINKS;
set INTERNALS;

param supply {SOURCES} >= 0;
param demand {SINKS} >= 0;

        check: sum {i in SOURCES} supply[i] >= sum {k in SINKS} demand[k];

set NODES := SOURCES union INTERNALS union SINKS;
set ARCS within {NODES cross NODES};

param external_flow {j in NODES} :=
        if j in SOURCES then supply[j] else
              if j in SINKS then -demand[j] else 0;

param arc_cost {ARCS} >= 0;
param arc_capacity {ARCS} >= 0;

var arc_flow {(i,j) in ARCS} >= 0, <= arc_capacity[i,j];

minimize total_cost:
        sum {(i,j) in ARCS} arc_cost[i,j] * arc_flow[i,j];

# flow_balance: out - in = external
subject to flow_balance {j in NODES}:
        sum {(j,k) in ARCS} arc_flow[j,k]
        - sum {(i,j) in ARCS} arc_flow[i,j]
        <= external_flow[j];
```

Only the execution and the data files have to be modified for a particular instance. Listing 7.3 shows the sequence of the commands in the run file, which controls the execution of the AMPL program. This execution or run file has by convention the extension "run." The name of the run file is the only command line argument for the AMPL program. The first line identifies the model file, which by convention has the extension "mod." For the MCNFP the model is the standard minimum cost network model. The second line identifies the data file, which by convention has the extension "dat." The third line contains the "solve" command, which causes the model to be solved by the default solver. Finally, the fourth line displays the flows in the solution. Further information on the AMPL language can be found in Fourer et al. (2002) and on the web site of the AMPL Optimization LLC.

Listing 7.3 AMPL MCNFP Example Execution File

```
model MinCost_Network.mod;
model MinCost_Example.dat;
solve;
display arc_flow;
```

The data for the example is shown in Listing 7.4. There are seven nodes, one source node (1), one sink node (7), and five internal nodes. There are 12 one-directional arcs. The arc data is given at the end of the listing with the origin node, destination node, arc cost, and arc capacity listed on a single line for each arc.

Listing 7.4 AMPL MCNFP Example Data File

```
data;

set SOURCES := 1;
set SINKS := 7;
set INTERNALS := 2 3 4 5 6;

set ARCS := (1,2) (1,4) (1,6)
            (2,3) (2,4) (2,5)
            (3,7)
            (4,3) (4,6)
            (5,7)
            (6,5) (6,7);

param supply := 1 30;
param demand := 7 30;

param:            arc_cost    arc_capacity :=
        1    2    7           16
        1    4    13          11
        1    6    28          13
        2    3    25          17
        2    4    4           18
        2    5    10          16
        3    7    5           22
        4    3    6           12
        4    6    5           19
        5    7    12          16
        6    5    3           10
        6    7    7           5;
```

Listing 7.5 shows the output log generated by the execution of the run file with the AMPL program. The solver used in this case was CPLEX. The optimal solution value found was equal to 814. This solution is identical to the solution found by the Excel solver and by the manual execution of the successive shortest paths algorithm. The listing shows the arc flows in the default output format. The output format can be customized using the AMPL language.

Listing 7.5 AMPL MCNFP Example Output Log

```
AMPL Version 20080219 (x86_win32)
CPLEX 11.0.1: optimal solution; objective 814
6 dual simplex iterations (0 in phase I)
arc_flow :=
1 2   16
1 4   11
1 6    3
2 3    0
2 4    3
2 5   13
3 7   12
4 3   12
4 6    2
5 7   13
6 5    0
6 7    5
;
```

The AMPL program uses ASCII text input and output files as its user interface and as consequence does not have the same intuitive graphical user interface as the Excel program. However, the model file size does not change or grow with the size of the instance data and the size of the data file grows proportional to the number of nodes and arcs in the instance. As a consequence the AMPL program can handle much larger problem instances. Typically, AMPL is interfaced with either Excel or a database program such as Access, that contain the node and arc data and in which the arc flow solution is stored.

7.4   Minimum Cost Network Flow Formulation

In the following the solution algorithm of a single commodity minimum cost network flow problem is explained based on the properties of linear programming. This exposition requires prior knowledge of linear programming concepts such as duality, primal and dual formulations, and complementary slackness. Further information on these topics can be found in a textbook on linear programming such as Bazaraa et al. (2005). This material forms the basis of other solution algorithms presented later for other variants of transportation models, but it can be safely skipped if other algorithms based on mathematical programming will also be skipped.

7.4.1   Primal Formulation

The following notation will be used in the primal and dual formulations. The primal notation is identical to notation introduced before but is repeated here to make this section self contained.

7.4.1.1   Parameters and Variables

x_{ij} flow from node i (origin) to node j (destination)

c_{ij} cost of transporting one unit of flow from node i (origin) to node j (destination)

b_i external flow for node i, with the sign convention that external inflows (supply) are positive and external outflows (demand) are negative.

u_{ij} arc capacity or upper bound on the flow from node i (origin) to node j (destination)

r_{ij} remaining arc capacity or upper bound on the flow from node i (origin) to node j (destination)

π_i dual variable corresponding to the conservation of flow constraint for node i (a nonnegative variable when the constraint is written as a larger than or equal constraint)

α_{ij} dual variable corresponding to the capacity upper bound on the flow from node i (origin) to node j (destination)

7.4.1.2   Model

Formulation 7.3. Minimum Cost Network Flow Formulation

$$Min \quad \sum_i^N \sum_j^N c_{ij} x_{ij}$$

$$s.t. \quad -\sum_h^N x_{hi} + \sum_j^N x_{ij} \leq b_i \quad \forall i \quad [-\pi_i] \tag{7.3}$$

$$0 \leq x_{ij} \leq u_{ij} \quad\quad\quad \forall ij \quad [\alpha_{ij}]$$

This formulation has been given previously. The variables inside the square brackets for each constraint are the dual variables for that constraint. The value $-\pi_i$ is the dual variable for the conservation of flow constraint when this constraint is written as a less than or equal constraint.

7.4.2 Residual Network Construction

The residual network is constructed with the same nodes and arcs as the original network. If there exists a flow on arc (i,j), then the artificial arc (j,i) is constructed. rc is the reduced cost of the arc in the original network and the cost of the arc in the residual network.

$$if \quad x_{ij} > 0 \text{ then}$$
$$arc(i,j) \quad rc_{ij} = c_{ij} - \pi_j + \pi_i = c_{ij} - (\pi_j - \pi_i) \quad r_{ij} = u_{ij} - x_{ij}$$
$$arc(j,i) \quad rc_{ji} = -rc_{ij} \qquad\qquad\qquad\qquad r_{ji} = x_{ij} \qquad (7.4)$$

7.4.2.1 Optimality Conditions

For any arc in the network the following optimality condition can be computed based on the optimal flows in the network. If this arc has remaining capacity then the shortest path length to the destination node must be no larger than the shortest path length to the origin node plus the original arc cost, otherwise the total cost could be reduced by sending more flow over this arc.

$$\pi_j \leq \pi_i + c_{ij} \quad \forall(i, j) \qquad (7.5)$$

Equivalently, the reduced cost of an arc rc_{ij} at optimality must be nonnegative, if this arc has remaining capacity. Otherwise the objective function could be reduced by increasing the flow quantity on this arc.

$$rc_{ij} = c_{ij} - \pi_j + \pi_i \geq 0 \quad \forall(i, j) \qquad (7.6)$$

7.4.3 Dual Formulation

In preparation of constructing the dual formulation of the problem, the primal formulation is rewritten in its standard form. The dual variable of the conservation of flow constraint in the standard form is π_i and it has positive values.

7.4.3.1 Standardized Primal Formulation

$$Min \quad \sum_{i}^{N}\sum_{j}^{N} c_{ij}x_{ij}$$
$$s.t. \quad \sum_{h}^{N} x_{hi} - \sum_{j}^{N} x_{ij} \geq -b_i \quad \forall i \quad [\pi_i] \qquad (7.7)$$
$$-x_{ij} \geq -u_{ij} \qquad\qquad \forall ij \quad [\alpha_{ij}]$$

The standard dual formulation can then be written as.

7.4.3.2 Standardized Dual Formulation

$$\max \quad -\sum_i^N b_i \pi_i - \sum_i^N \sum_j^N u_{ij} \alpha_{ij}$$

$$s.t. \quad -\pi_i + \pi_j - \alpha_{ij} \leq c_{ij} \qquad \forall(i,j) \quad [x_{ij}] \qquad (7.8)$$

$$\alpha_{ij} \geq 0$$

$$\pi_i \geq 0$$

Using the definition of the reduced cost given in (7.6), the dual formulation can be condensed to yield the following formulation.

7.4.3.3 Condensed Dual Formulation

$$\min \quad \sum_i^N b_i \pi_i + \sum_i^N \sum_j^N u_{ij} \alpha_{ij}$$

$$s.t. \quad \alpha_{ij} + rc_{ij} \geq 0 \qquad \forall(i,j) \quad [x_{ij}] \qquad (7.9)$$

$$\alpha_{ij} \geq 0$$

$$\pi_i \geq 0$$

7.4.3.4 Complementary Slackness Conditions

The primary and condensed dual formulations yield the following complementary slackness conditions at optimality.

$$(u_{ij} - x_{ij}^*)\alpha_{ij}^* = 0$$

$$(\alpha_{ij}^* + rc_{ij})x_{ij}^* = 0 \qquad (7.10)$$

The complementary slackness conditions together with the sign restrictions on the variables yield the following conditions for optimality.

7.4.3.5 Optimality Conditions

$$if \quad rc_{ij} > 0 \quad then \ (\alpha_{ij}^* + rc_{ij}) > 0 \quad then \ x_{ij}^* = 0$$

$$if \quad 0 < x_{ij}^* < u_{ij} \quad then \ \alpha_{ij}^* = 0 \quad then \ rc_{ij} = 0 \qquad (7.11)$$

$$if \quad rc_{ij} < 0 \quad then \ \alpha_{ij}^* > 0 \quad then \ x_{ij}^* = u_{ij}$$

These optimality conditions correspond to the reduced-cost conditions for the residual graph in the successive shortest path algorithm. Hence, the dual iterations of linear programming and the successive shortest path algorithm execute the same algorithm steps.

7.5   Exercises

True/False Questions
1. Maximum flow networks are primarily used in the design of public sector and government networks. (T/F) _____ .
2. The network simplex algorithm is currently the most efficient method for solving minimum cost network flow problems. (T/F) _____ .
3. The network used to model evacuations of an area forced by an impending hurricane belongs to the class of maximum flow networks. (T/F) _____ .
4. The network used to model the assignment of workers to shifts in a 24-hour service operation belongs to the class of maximum flow networks. (T/F) _____ .
5. The computational complexity of solving network formulations limits the size of the networks that can be solved to optimality to 10,000 arcs. (T/F) _____ .
6. The standard network flow formulation can incorporate capacity restrictions on the nodes without any changes to the network structure. (T/F) _____ .
7. A necessary requirement to convert the operator scheduling problem to a network flow formulation is that any shift or work tour covers an uninterrupted number of time periods. (T/F) _____ .
8. The successive shortest path algorithm belongs to the class of dual algorithms. (T/F) _____ .

Minimum Cost Network Exercise Compute the minimum cost network flows in the following network shown in Fig. 7.28. Show the residual network after each iteration. Interrupt the successive shortest path algorithm after two flow changes have been made. Compute the total cost of the flow solution determined so far. Is the current flow a feasible solution to the original problem? What would you be willing to pay for one extra unit of capacity on arc (1, 7)? Justify your answer in a single sentence. What would you be willing to pay for a reduction of a single unit in the required outgoing flow out of node 6 at this particular stage in the algorithm? Justify your answer in a single sentence.

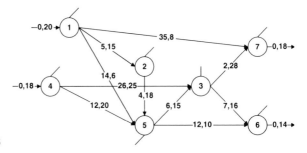

Fig. 7.28 Network exercise 3

References

Ahuja, R., Magnanti, T., & Orlin, J. (1993). *Network flows*. Englewood Cliffs: Prentice-Hall.

AMPL Optimization LLC, www.ampl.com.

Bazaraa, M. S., Jarvis, J. J., & Sherali, H. D. (2005). *Linear programming and network flows* (3rd ed.). Hoboken: Wiley.

Christofides, N. (1975). *Graph theory: An algorithmic approach*. New York: Academic Press.

Evans, J. & Minieka, E. (1992). *Optimization algorithms for networks and graphs* (2nd ed.). New York: Marcel Dekker.

Ford, L. R. Jr., & Fulkerson, D. R. (1956). "Maximal flow through a network". *Canadian Journal of Mathematics,* 99–404.

Fourer, R., Gay, D. M., & Kernighan, B. W. (2002). *AMPL: A modeling language for mathematical programming* (2nd ed.). Duxbury Press/Brooks/Cole Publishing Company.

Kennington, J. & Helgason, R. (1980). *Algorithms for network programming*. New York: Wiley.

Schrijver, A. (1990). "On the history of transportation and maximum flow problems," Unpublished manuscript, Centrum for Wiskunde & Informatica (CWI). Amsterdam, Netherlands, cwi.homepages.nl.

Chapter 8
Single Vehicle Round-trip Routing

Learning Objectives After you have studied this chapter, you should know

- For the class of single vehicle roundtrip routing through a network

  - The characteristics of the base problem and various variants
  - The mathematical formulation
  - Simple solution algorithms
  - How to solve problems of modest size with a computer program

8.1 Introduction

In the single vehicle routing problem a single vehicle is used to serve a set of customers. The vehicle travels on an underlying network consisting of a number of nodes and a number of arcs and edges. If the customers are located in the nodes, the problem is said to be a node routing problem. If the customers are located nearly uniformly along an arc or edge then the problem is said to be an arc routing problem. Node routing is more common in supply chain planning, where the customer correspond to individual customers or facilities in the supply chain. Arc routing is common in public service applications such as mail delivery, garbage collection, and snow removal. The single vehicle roundtrip node routing problem is more commonly known as the Traveling Salesman Problem (TSP). The single vehicle arc routing problem in which the vehicle has to visit a subset of the arcs and edges is also known as the Rural Postman Problem (RPP). If all the edges and arcs have to be visited then the problem is known as the Chinese Postman Problem (CPP). The remainder of this chapter will be focused on the TSP.

The TSP was stated by Lawler et al. (1985) as: "A salesman, starting from its home city, is to visit exactly once each city on a given list and then to return home, so that the total of the distances traveled in his tour is a small as possible." An alternative statement of the TSP is based on graph theory. A cycle in a graph is a sequence of vertices in the graph, so that each vertex in the sequence is visited exactly once and the sequence returns to the vertex where it started. A cycle that

M. Goetschalckx, *Supply Chain Engineering,* International Series in Operations Research & Management Science 161,
DOI 10.1007/978-1-4419-6512-7_8, © Springer Science+Business Media, LLC 2011

visits all vertices is called Hamiltonian. The TSP problem is thus to find the Hamiltonian cycle of shortest length. In transportation planning the vehicle may pass one or more times through the same node of the underlying transportation graph if this node is located on the shortest path between other facilities in the problem. When the vehicle merely passes through the node, it is not considered to be visiting this node. Alternatively, an artificial complete graph can be defined with as nodes the customers in the problem and with as edge lengths the length of the shortest path between the corresponding customers in the problem. The edge lengths of the artificial graph satisfy the triangle inequality.

$$c_{ij} \leq c_{ik} + c_{kj} \quad \forall i, \forall j, \forall k \tag{8.1}$$

The TSP problem can then be solved on this artificial complete graph and each node has to be visited exactly once.

The TSP is one of the most studied problems in several areas of mathematics such as graph theory, mathematical programming, operations research, and combinatorial optimization. Even though the basic problem is easy to define and explain, efficient optimal design algorithms do not exist to this date and may never be found. The problem has been shown to belong to a class of computationally hard problems for which it is difficult to find the exact solution for problems of even modest size. A large number of optimizing algorithms that exploit the fundamental structure of the TSP have been published in the research literature. However, practitioners in logistics and supply chain planning do not have access to or the required resources for such optimizing algorithms. As a result, a large variety of heuristic algorithms has been developed to find a solution of reasonable quality in a reasonable amount of computation time. Some of the TSP applications are described next in further detail. An overview of the TSP problem, its history, fundamental properties and of a large variety of its design algorithms is given in Lawler et al. (1985) and Applegate et al. (2004).

8.1.1 Traveling Salesman Problem Applications

8.1.1.1 Knight's Tour

Knight's Tour is a century old puzzle based on the game of chess. The game of chess is played on a board consisting 64 squares organized in eight rows by eight columns. In chess different pieces are used, but we are only interested in one type, which is called the knight or horse. A knight moves from its current position by moving first two squares in the row or column of its current position and then moving one square perpendicular to the prior direction. From a square in the center of the board, a knight can move to eight different squares. A single knight piece is placed on a random square of the chess board. The objective is to find the sequence of 64 moves so that the knight visits each square exactly once and returns to its original position. If the knight starts in a corner square and only has to visit all the

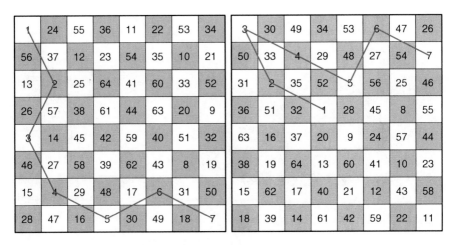

Fig. 8.1 Hamiltonian path and tour solutions to the Knight's tour problem

squares exactly once without returning to its original square, Thomasson (2001) devised a simple solution algorithm "starting from any corner square, move the knight by continuously rotating in the same direction around the board and selecting the square closest to the border of the board." A solution that does not return to its starting point is also called a traveling salesman *path*, as distinguished of a traveling salesman *tour* which returns to its starting position. A traveling salesman path and tour solution to the Knight's Tour problem by Thomasson are shown in the next figures, where the squares are numbered by increasing jump count and the lines illustrate the first few jumps (Fig. 8.1).

8.1.1.2 Person-Aboard Order Picking

In order picking operations for small parts such as service parts, a person-aboard storage and retrieval system may be used. The parts are stored in bins on both sides of a narrow aisle. A crane moves on a top and bottom rail in the aisle. The crane consists of a mast on which a platform or cabin move up and down. Typically the crane is computer controlled and stops in front of the bin from which items have to be picked to satisfy a number of customer orders. The mast and cabin move simultaneously so a first approximation of the travel time can be based on the Chebyshev travel norm.

A graphical schematic of two tours executed by the cabin is shown in the next two figures in Fig. 8.2. The first figure illustrates a random sequence of stops, such as would be created by strictly first-come first-served sequencing of the customer orders and the line items in the orders. The second figure shows a tour that has been created by a heuristic algorithm and then improved with a three-exchange algorithm. The travel distance is reduced by more than 75% from the random sequence tour. The travel time reduction will have a significant impact on the productivity of the order picking system and may even reduce the number of cranes and aisles that

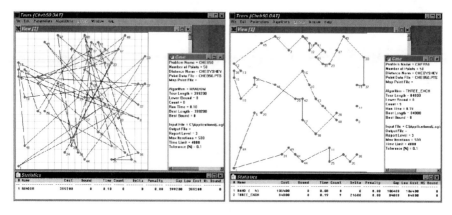

Fig. 8.2 Schematics of random and improved tours in a person-aboard order picking system

is required to achieve a required throughput. The two heuristic algorithms will be
further explained in the following sections (Fig. 8.2).

8.1.1.3 Sequencing Jobs in a Paint Booth

On of the steps in automotive assembly is the painting of the car body. Cars are sequenced for assembly in blocks of cars with identical colors. When a color change
occurs, the paint spray equipment has to be cleaned. The time to clean the equipment depends on the colors between which the change is being made. For example,
it requires much longer time to clean the equipment when the previous color was
black and the next color is white than when the previous color is red and the next
color is black. The assembly line has to produce cars in a variety of colors. The
problem of sequencing the blocks of cars with identical colors so that the cleaning
time for the painting equipment is minimized is an example of an asymmetrical
TSP. The problem is called asymmetrical because the cleaning time is different for
going from color a to color b than from color b to color a. In this application the
"travel time" between the different nodes of the problem has no relationship with
any physical travel.

8.1.1.4 Drilling Mounting Holes in a Printed Circuit Board

Most items currently produced contain one or more sub assemblies of electronic
components. Those electronic components are clustered on one or more printed
circuit boards (PCB). Components may be surface-mounted or soldered. With this
second technology, each component has a number of legs or leads that are inserted
in holes on the circuit board and then the legs are permanently locked in place
and electrical contact is made by a soldering operation on the other side of the
board. High speed assembly of PCBs requires that the holes are exactly positioned.

One technology to create the holes in the exact location uses a laser to melt a hole through the resin board. To minimize the manufacturing time of the board by the laser, the laser has to travel in a cycle of minimum travel time between all the holes required on the particular board. Boards are often transported and positioned under the laser by a horizontal conveyor belt and the laser is mounted on a gantry frame. Since the gantry with the laser typically can move simultaneously in the x and y directions of the board, the travel time can be based on the Chebyshev travel norm.

8.1.1.5 Running Domestic Errands or Sequencing Deliveries

In today's busy life style, it is a common practice to accumulate a number of errands that have to be executed in a single car trip. To minimize the overall time spent on the errands, we sequence the stops so that the travel of a cycle that starts and ends at our residence is minimized. The travel time between two stops is usually only estimated, but the structure of the road network and the traffic patterns yield different travel times for the different directions of travel between two stops. This problem is equivalent to an asymmetrical TSP, where the travel times cannot be estimated based on a travel distance norm. The same principle holds for commercial deliveries. According to Rooney (2007), UPS, which is one of the largest package delivery companies in the world, reported annual savings of more than 3 million gallons of fuel in part by avoiding as much as possible any left turns in the routes for each one of their delivery vehicles. UPS estimated that up 90% of the turns made by their vehicles are right turns. Avoiding left turns, with their associated waits, reduces driving time and improves gas mileage by avoiding idling during the wait.

8.1.1.6 Multiple Vehicle Roundtrip Routing (VRP)

One of the most common tasks in transportation planning is the routing of a number of vehicles in a fleet to perform delivery operations. Many algorithms to route the vehicles have been developed. One class of algorithms, called cluster-first, route-second algorithms, assigns the customers to a vehicle in the first phase of the algorithm. In a second phase the individual vehicles are then routed to deliver to their respective customers. This second problem is a TSP. The use of a TSP as a subroutine in the solution of a VRP is one of the most common applications of the TSP.

8.1.2 Traveling Salesman Problem Definition

Further information on the TSP including its history, early research, and many definitions can be found in Lawler et al. (1985). At the time of its publication, the authors reported that a 318-city problem was the largest problem known to have been solved to optimality. A more recent review of the TSP is provided in Applegate et al. (2004) and in Applegate (2005).

8.1.2.1 Asymmetric Traveling Salesman Problem (ATSP) Formulation

The Asymmetric Traveling Salesman Problem is a variant of the TSP where the two possible travel directions between two nodes are not equivalent. The most common case arise when the travel distance or travel cost from node i to node j is not equal to the travel distance or cost from node j to node i. The ATSP is commonly used in local, intra-city routing, where the distance between two customers may not be symmetrical because of the presence of one-way streets and illegal or more expensive left turns. As reported above, UPS attempts to eliminate inefficient left turns as much as possible and achieves up to 90% right turns in local routing, Rooney (2007). The solution to the ATSP is an oriented tour, consisting of a sequence of (directed) arcs. A directed tour is illustrated in Fig. 8.3.

The following notation will be used in the treatment of the ATSP.

N   set of all the nodes in the problem instance and N is the cardinality of the set, i.e., the number of nodes in the problem.

x_{ij} equals one if the tour travels directly from node i to node j, 0 otherwise. Note that x_{ii} is not defined for any i and these terms are automatically skipped in any summation over i or j.

c_{ij} cost or distance of traveling directly from node i to node j.

S   any sub set of the nodes in the problem instance and $|S|$ is the cardinality of the set, i.e., the number of nodes in the set

Formulation 8.1. Asymmetric Traveling Salesman Problem (Variant 1)

$$Min \quad \sum_{i=1}^{N} \sum_{j=1}^{N} c_{ij} x_{ij} \tag{8.2}$$

$$s.t. \quad \sum_{i=1}^{N} x_{ij} = 1 \quad \forall j \tag{8.3}$$

$$\sum_{j=1}^{N} x_{ij} = 1 \quad \forall i \tag{8.4}$$

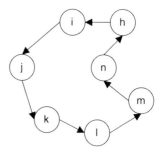

Fig. 8.3 Asymmetric Traveling Salesman Problem illustration

$$\sum_{i \in S} \sum_{j \in S} x_{ij} \leq |S| - 1 \quad \forall S \subset N, |S| \geq 2 \tag{8.5}$$

$$x_{ij} \in \{0,1\} \tag{8.6}$$

The ATSP is basically an Assignment Problem (AP) with the additional constraints (8.5) that eliminate sub tours. Contrary to the case of the AP, for the ATSP the integrality of the decision variables has to be explicitly enforced by the solution algorithm. The solution value of the corresponding AP provides a lower bound on the length of the ATSP solution. This lower bound is weak if the ATSP has many symmetrical or near-symmetrical distances. In this case, the AP solution will tend to consist of many small sub tours, since if the AP solution contains arc (i,j) then it will likely include arc (j,i) as well. Conversely, if the distances in the ATSP are strongly asymmetrical then the AP will tend to provide a strong lower bound.

8.1.2.2 Sub Tour Elimination Constraints

According to Lawler et al. (1985), Dantzig et al. (1954) were the first to propose a TSP formulation with the following type of sub tour elimination constraints. An example of the sub tour elimination constraints is shown in Fig. 8.4 for two subsets. The first subset contains three nodes and the second set contains two nodes. The corresponding sub tour elimination the constraints have to placed after Fig. 8.4 . For the subset that contains three nodes, a sub tour could be formed by a sequence of three arcs. The sub tour elimination constraint allows at maximum two arcs, which have their origin and destination nodes in the subset. This forces at least one incoming arc and one outgoing arc to connect the subset with the rest of the nodes.

$$S = \{i, j, k\}, |S| = 3$$
$$x_{ij} + x_{jk} + x_{ki} + x_{ji} + x_{kj} + x_{ik} \leq 2$$
$$S = \{m, n\}, |S| = 2$$
$$x_{mn} + x_{nm} \leq 1$$

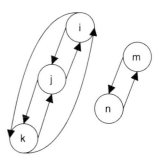

Fig. 8.4 Sub tour elimination illustration

Each of the individual sub tour elimination constraints is rather simple and easy to generate. All the coefficients in the sub tour elimination constraints are equal to one. The difficulty of incorporating sub tour elimination constraints in the ATSP formulation is not caused by an individual constraint but rather by the number of constraints. When we consider all possible sub groups of nodes, each node can be either in a sub group or not. The total number of sub groups is nearly 2^N, where N is the number of nodes. A sub tour elimination constraint is required for each sub group, except for the group containing all the nodes and for the degenerate groups that contain a single node or no node. Hence the total number of sub tour elimination constraints is $2^N - N - 2$. For a problem instance containing five nodes, the number of sub tour elimination constraints is $2^5 - 5 - 2 = 25$. However, for the Knight's Tour problem the number is $2^{64} - 64 - 2$, which is approximately equal to $1.845 \cdot 10^{19}$. No mathematical problem solver can handle problem instances with such a large number of constraints. Sophisticated algorithms have been developed that only generate the very small fraction of the sub tour elimination constraints that are binding the optimal solution. These algorithms are beyond the scope of this book and are not often used in transportation planning.

The sub tour elimination constraints can be rewritten as follows through algebraic substitution, which guarantees that there is at least one arc emanating from every proper subset of S nodes. The number of constraints remains the same.

$$\sum_{i \in S} \sum_{j \notin S} x_{ij} \geq 1 \quad \forall S \subset \mathbf{N}, |S| \geq 2 \tag{8.7}$$

8.1.2.3   Alternative Sub Tour Elimination Constraints

An alternative method for eliminating sub tours generates far fewer sub tour constraints. This formulation is based on the notion of "item inventory" carried by the traveling salesperson on its travels, i.e. on the arcs traversed by the tour. When the salesperson visits a city or node, he "sells" exactly one item. The traveling salesman is assumed to start its travels in node 1, where he obtains an initial inventory of N items from its supplier. At the end of his trip he returns to the starting node to sell one last item to the customer in that node. Node 1 is chosen arbitrarily as the base node from where to start and where to end the tour. The following additional notation is required.

q_{ij} Item inventory carried on the travel arc from node i to node j. Note that q_{jj} is not defined for any j and these terms are automatically skipped in any summation over i or j.

Formulation 8.2. Asymmetric Traveling Salesman Problem (Variant 2)

$$Min \quad \sum_{i=1}^{N} \sum_{j=1}^{N} c_{ij} x_{ij} \tag{8.8}$$

$$s.t. \quad \sum_{i=1}^{N} x_{ij} = 1 \quad \forall j \tag{8.9}$$

$$\sum_{j=1}^{N} x_{ij} = 1 \quad \forall i \tag{8.10}$$

$$\sum_{k} q_{1k} = N \tag{8.11}$$

$$\sum_{k} q_{k1} = 1 \tag{8.12}$$

$$\sum_{i} q_{ij} - \sum_{k} q_{jk} = 1 \quad \forall j > 1 \tag{8.13}$$

$$q_{ij} \leq N x_{ij} \quad \forall i, \forall j, j \neq i \tag{8.14}$$

$$x_{ij} \in \{0,1\}, q_{ij} \geq 0 \tag{8.15}$$

For each node, except node 1, constraint (8.13) assures that the number of items carried by the salesperson when entering a node is equal to one plus the number of items carried when leaving this node. The single item difference is the item "sold" in this particular node. For the first node, the salesperson receives an initial inventory of N items at the start of his tour, which is modeled by constraint (8.11). When he returns to the base node at the end of his tour and "sells" one last item in this node his inventory of items equals zero, which is modeled by constraint (8.12). The maximum inventory carried on any arc between two nodes is thus N. Constraint (8.14) assures that the salesperson can only carry an inventory when he or she follows that particular travel arc. Sub tours that do not include node 1 are eliminated because the traveling salesman has no inventory on such tours and can thus not sell the required single item when he visits a node. As a consequence, all nodes must be visited on the single tour that visits node 1.

The total number of sub tour elimination constraints is equal to $(N-1) + 2 + N(N-1) = O(N^2)$. This number grows only as a quadratic in function of the problem size, rather than the exponential growth exhibited by the previous type of sub tour elimination constraints. This reduced number of sub tour elimination constraints is small enough that the complete model can be generated and submitted to a solver for problems of intermediate size such as 100 nodes. It should be noted that this formulation creates $N(N-1)$ additional continuous variables, since the inventory variables automatically get an integer value at optimality. The integrality of the arc selection variables still has to be enforced explicitly, so this formulation belongs to the class of mixed-integer programming formulations.

This formulation is similar to another variant of the sub tour elimination constraints proposed by Miller et al. (1960).

8.1.2.4   Symmetric Traveling Salesman Problem (STSP) Formulation

The Symmetric Traveling Salesman Problem is a variant of the TSP, where the travel from node i to node j is equivalent to the travel from node j to node i. The total number of edges incident to each node is exactly equal to two. A TSP for which the travel distances are computed with a distance norm is an example of a STSP, since the distance yield by a distance norm are symmetrical by definition. The STSP is commonly used for inter-city routing, since the underlying transportation network consists of the major roads between cities such as interstate and national highways. A symmetric tour is illustrated in Fig. 8.5.

The following different notation will be used in the treatment of the STSP.

x_{ij} equals one if the tour travels directly between node i and node j, where $j > i$.

Formulation 8.3. Symmetric Traveling Salesman Problem

$$Min \quad \sum_{i=1}^{N-1} \sum_{j=i+1}^{N} c_{ij}x_{ij} \tag{8.16}$$

$$s.t. \quad \sum_{i=1}^{j-1} x_{ij} + \sum_{k=j+1}^{N} x_{jk} = 2 \quad \forall j \tag{8.17}$$

$$\sum_{i \in S} \sum_{j \in S, j > i} x_{ij} \leq |S| - 1 \quad \forall S \subset N, |S| \geq 2 \tag{8.18}$$

$$x_{ij} \in \{0,1\} \tag{8.19}$$

The STSP formulation is basically a two-matching formulation with side constraints that eliminate sub tours. You can find further information on the TSP problem and its solution algorithms in Lawler et al. (1985) , Applegate et al. (2004), and Applegate (2005).

The Fig. 8.6 shows an optimal TSP tour of 13509 cities in the continental United States computed by Cook (2004). At the current time, this is one of the largest problem instances solved to optimality. The solution methodology used on some the largest problem instances, including an instance with 89500 points, is described in Applegate et al. (2006).

8.1.3   TSP6 Example

The following example will be used to illustrate the various heuristic and optimization-based algorithms for the TSP. The example problem has six facilities or points

Fig. 8.5 Symmetric traveling
salesman problem illustration

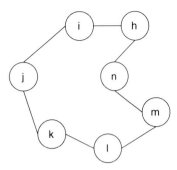

Fig. 8.6 USA 13509 cities
traveling salesman problem
illustration

and is denoted by TSP6. The problem size was chosen as so that the algorithms could be illustrated on a non-trivial case but the same time the amount of tedious calculations is reduced as much as possible. The coordinates of the six points are given in Table 8.1. The distances between the points are based on the Euclidean distance norm and then rounded to the nearest integer. Since the distances are based on a distance norm they are symmetrical and satisfy the triangle inequality. The distances are shown in Table 8.2. Finally, some of the heuristics will use the geometric location of the points. These geometric locations are shown in Fig. 8.7.

Table 8.1 Point locations
for the TSP6 example

#	x	y
1	0	0
2	100	600
3	400	400
4	500	700
5	900	400
6	800	900

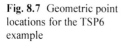

Fig. 8.7 Geometric point locations for the TSP6 example

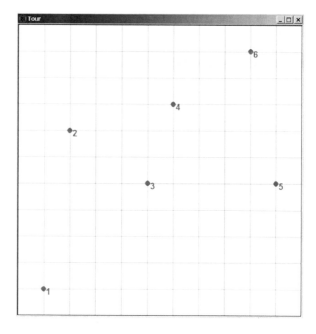

Table 8.2 Euclidean distances for the TSP6 example

	1	2	3	4	5	6
1	0	608	566	860	985	1,204
2	608	0	361	412	825	762
3	566	361	0	316	500	640
4	860	412	316	0	500	361
5	985	825	500	500	0	510
6	1204	762	640	361	510	0

8.2 Simple TSP Heuristics

Since the TSP has so many applications, a large variety of heuristics has been developed. An overall structure for many of the TSP heuristics is given in the following meta-heuristic, which has three phases: construct, insert, and improve. For each of the phases, examples of the corresponding type of heuristic will also be given.

8.2.1 TSP Meta-Heuristic and Heuristic Examples

Create an initial tour using a construction heuristic

- convex hull, sweep, nearest neighbor

Insert remaining free points using an insertion heuristic

- nearest, cheapest, farthest insertion

Improve existing tour using an improvement heuristic

- two, three, or chain-exchanges

8.2.2 Construction Heuristics

Construction heuristics are algorithms that create a TSP tour from the initial data. At minimum the initial data include a complete two-dimensional distance matrix. Some heuristics may also require the location coordinates of the facilities in the problem instance. Since any systematic way to create a TSP tour from the initial data constitutes a construction heuristic, a large variety of such heuristics have been developed. Only a fraction of those heuristics is described next. In general, the description starts from the simplest and chronologically earliest heuristics to more intricate heuristics.

8.2.2.1   Nearest Neighbor

One of the oldest and most intuitive construction heuristics is the Nearest Neighbor. The Nearest Neighbor algorithm starts the tour at an initial point and then appends the nearest unvisited or free point to the tour until all points have been visited. This algorithm was originally described by Rosenkrantz et al. (1977). The initial starting point is an algorithm parameter that you can specify. Different initial starting points may give different tour sequences. Since the Nearest Neighbor algorithm executes very fast, an enhanced algorithm implementation would start a tour at each point and then retain the shortest tour among them. The Nearest neighbor algorithm tends to visit most, but not all, points in a neighborhood and then travels to another neighborhood. The distances to travel to another neighborhood of the problem or to travel to left-over points are typically much longer than the distances of the travel steps inside a neighborhood. The left-over points that are not visited when the tour traverses their neighborhood initially are sometimes also called orphans.

The Nearest Neighbor algorithm is a greedy algorithm. A greedy algorithm will execute the best possible action for the next step in the algorithm in the hope that this will reach the overall optimal solution. In the context of the TSP, the Nearest Neighbor algorithm travels at each step the shortest distance to the next unvisited facility. A greedy algorithm will not change prior decisions. However, a greedy algorithm may not yield the globally optimal solution; in other words, the sequence of optimal single-step actions may not reach the strategic objective of the global optimal solution. Whether a greedy algorithm yields the global optimum is problem specific. In the case of the TSP this is not the case. Dijkstra's algorithm for finding the single origin to destination shortest path is an example of a greedy algorithm that finds the optimal solution. Greedy algorithms are sometimes also called myopic algorithms since they focus exclusively on the next step.

Nearest Neighbor Algorithm for the TSP Example The Nearest Neighbor algorithm is executed for the TSP6 example problem by starting at point 3. The next point to be visited is the point nearest to point 3. The sequence of calculations is shown next, where the number in the parenthesis is the index of the selected node.

$$\text{Min } \{566, 361, 316, 500, 640\} = 316(4)$$

$$\text{Min } \{860, 412, 500, 361\} = 361(6)$$

$$\text{Min } \{1204, 762, 510\} = 510(5)$$

$$\text{Min } \{985, 825\} = 825(2)$$

$$\text{Min } \{608\} = 608(1)$$

Once all points have been visited, the tour returns from the last visited point to the starting point. The sequence of points is thus {3, 4, 6, 5, 2, 1}. The total tour length is the sum of all the distances traversed and is computed to be $(316+361+510+825+608+566)=3,186$. The generated tour is shown in Fig. 8.8.

8.2.2.2 Sweep

The Sweep algorithm creates a tour by appending the points to the tour when they are traversed by a ray rotating around a centrally located rotation point. First, the

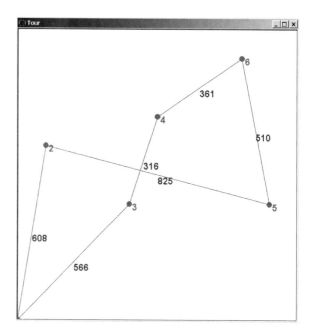

Fig. 8.8 Nearest neightbor tour for the TSP6 example

rotation point has to be determined. Typical candidates are the points with the average coordinates or the center coordinates. The center coordinates are located in the middle of the extreme x and y coordinates. The formulas for the computation of the center coordinates are given next.

$$x_{rot} = \frac{1}{2}\left(\max_i x_i + \min_i x_i\right)$$

$$y_{rot} = \frac{1}{2}\left(\max_i y_i + \min_i y_i\right)$$

(8.20)

The formulas for the computation of the average coordinates, also called the center of gravity coordinates are given next.

$$x_{rot} = \frac{1}{N}\sum_{i=1}^{N} x_i$$

$$y_{rot} = \frac{1}{N}\sum_{i=1}^{N} y_i$$

(8.21)

Then a ray or half line is rotated around this rotation point and the points are added to the tour in the sequence that they are traversed by the ray. The rotation direction and starting angle of the ray have no impact on the final tour. Computationally, the relative polar coordinates of each point with respect to the rotation point are determined and the points are inserted in the tour by increasing polar angle. The algorithm was first described by Gillet and Miller (1974).

Sweep Construction Algorithm for the TSP6 Example The rotation point for the TSP6 example was located at the center of gravity of the points and is indicated by the diamond in Fig. 8.9.

$$x_{rot} = \frac{1}{6}(0 + 100 + 400 + 500 + 900 + 800) = 450$$

$$y_{rot} = \frac{1}{6}(0 + 600 + 400 + 700 + 400 + 900) = 500$$

In this particular example, the starting orientation of the ray is set to be due north and the rotation direction is set to counter-clockwise. A tie exists if two points are traversed by the ray at the same angle. In other words, those two points are collinear with respect to the rotation point. This tie is arbitrarily broken by first selecting the point with the smallest distance to the rotation point. In general, ties are broken by ordering the collinear points by increasing distance to the rotation point. The first encountered facility is facility 2. It becomes the first anchor facility. The next facility traversed by the ray is facility 1 with an append distance equal to 608. The next facility is facility 3 with an append distance of 566. The next facility is facility 5 with an append distance of 500. The next facility is facility 6 with an append distance of

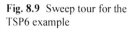

Fig. 8.9 Sweep tour for the
TSP6 example

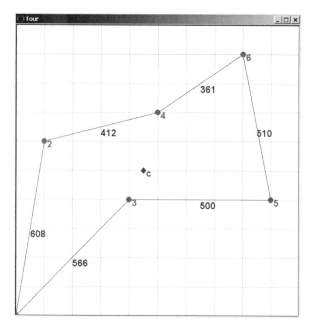

510. The next facility is facility 4 with an append distance equal to 361. Finally, the
next facility traversed by the ray is facility 2, which is the original anchor facility,
with an append distance of 412. The tour is now closed. The tour length is equal to
2,957. The tour created by the Sweep algorithm is shown in Fig. 8.9.

8.2.2.3 Quad

The Quad tour construction algorithm identifies the four points with the extreme
coordinates, i.e., the leftmost, bottom, rightmost, and top point, and visits the points
in that sequence. The tour is thus a quadrilateral or a polygon with four corners and
four sides. The maximum number of points on the generated tour is equal to four.
If the problem contains more than four points, one or more points remain unvisited.
The quad tour is the optimal TSP tour for the four points that are the vertices of the
tour. Because the quad tour only visits a limited set of the points in the problem,
but is the optimal tour for those points, it is also called a skeleton tour. As a consequence, the Quad algorithm belongs to the class of dual algorithms since it finds
the optimal solution or tour for a subset of the problem. The subset consists of the
extreme points.

Quad Tour Algorithm for the TSP Example In the example, the leftmost point is
point 1, the bottom point is also point 1, the rightmost point is point 5, and the top
point is point 6. Because point 1 has two of the extreme coordinates, the quadrilateral degenerates in this case to a triangle. The tour length is 2,699 which is a lower
bound on the optimal tour length. The tour is shown in Fig. 8.10.

Fig. 8.10 Quad tour skeleton for the TSP6 example

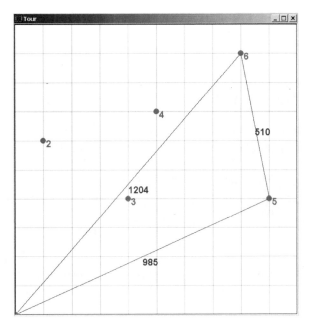

8.2.2.4   Convex Hull

The convex hull, also called the convex envelope, of a set of points is the smallest convex set that contains all the points. This definition is valid for points in vector spaces of any dimension, in other words, with any number of coordinates. In vehicle routing, the facilities are typically located in a plane and the number of coordinates is equal to two. In this case the convex hull is a convex polygon. You can think of the convex hull in the two-dimensional space as the rubber band stretched around the points in the problem. All points in the problem can be described as a convex combination of the vertices of the convex hull. A convex combination is a linear combination of the base points, where all the combination coefficients are nonnegative and sum up to one. Using the following notation, the convex combination is described by the following equations.

X vector of coordinates of any point in the set

V_k vector of coordinates of the kth vertex point of the convex hull of the set, $k = 1 ... K$

λ_k linear combination weights

$$X = \sum_{k=1}^{K} \lambda_k V_k$$

$$\lambda_k \geq 0 \tag{8.22}$$

$$\sum_{k=1}^{K} \lambda_k = 1$$

The convex hull for a set of points can be determined by a number of efficient algorithms. One such algorithm was developed by Akl and Toussaint (1978). However, the convex hull can also be determined graphically by the following algorithm.

Algorithm 8.1 Graphical Algorithm for the Convex Hull

1. Start a point that has an extreme coordinate for the set of points. This point is thus either the leftmost, top, rightmost, or bottom point. The current point is set to this starting point.
2. Select either a clockwise or counter clockwise rotation direction. Select an initial angle equal to east, north, west, or south if the starting point is the rightmost, top, leftmost, or bottom point, respectively. A ray at the current point and with the current angle will point away from all the points in the problem. Set the current angle equal to the starting angle.
3. Move the rotation point to the current point and continue to rotate a ray in the rotation direction around the rotation point starting from its current angle.
4. The first point traversed by the ray is the next point on the convex hull and is selected as the current point. If the current point is the starting point, then stop since the convex hull has been created. Otherwise continue with step 3.

Computationally, the convex hull algorithm by Akl and Toussaint (1978) first constructs a tour through the four extreme points as in the Quad algorithm. It then operates in sequence on the four sides of this quadrilateral, which define four external areas to the current problem. The algorithm first inserts all the points in an area and outside the quadrilateral in the convex hull tour, either by increasing or decreasing x coordinate. It then removes iteratively all points that were inserted but that not lie on the convex hull, i.e. they fall in the interior of the convex hull. It may skip the removal of some of those points during a particular iteration and then remove them during a latter iteration. When only the points on the convex hull in this area remain on the convex hull tour, the algorithm proceeds to the next area.

In general, a number of points will form the sequence of vertices of the convex hull. All the remaining unvisited points will be located in the interior of the convex hull. The tour that follows the edges of the convex hull is the optimal TSP tour for the points that are the vertices of the convex hull. Because the convex hull tour visits only a limited set of the points in the problem, but is the optimal tour for those points, it is also called a skeleton tour. As a consequence, just as the Quad algorithm, the Convex Hull algorithm belongs to the class of dual algorithms since it finds the optimal solution or tour for a subset of the problem. The subset consists of the points that are the vertices of the convex hull. Both the Quad algorithm and the Convex Hull algorithm provide a lower bound on the optimal tour length for all the points. The bound provided by the Convex Hull algorithm is never less than the bound provided by the Quad algorithm and is thus the better bound (Fig. 8.11).

Convex Hull Algorithm for the TSP Example The graphical Convex Hull algorithm is started in the rightmost point, which is point 5. The rotation direction is set to counterclockwise and the initial angle is set do east. The first point traversed by

Fig. 8.11 TSP6 convex hull
tour

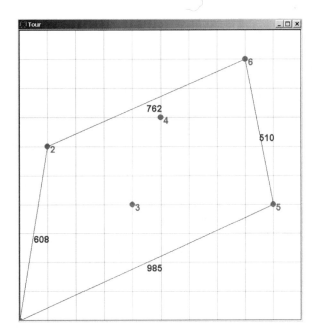

the rotating ray is point 6. The rotation point is moved to point 6 and the rotation of the ray is continued. The sequence of points that are the vertices of the convex hull is {5, 6, 2, 1}. The length of the tour created by the convex hull algorithm is 2,865.

The computational Convex Hull algorithm starts by creating the quadrilateral of the points with extreme coordinates. In this case, the quadrilateral degenerates to a triangle since point 1 has both the bottom-most and left-most extreme coordinate. The triangle tour consists of points {1, 6, 5}. For each side of the triangle, the algorithm then inserts the points outside the side of the triangle into the tour. In this case only the side (1-6) has points located outside it. Points 2 and 4 are inserted in the tour in that sequence, so the tour at this point is {1, 2, 4, 6, 5}. Finally, point 4 is removed from the tour because it falls inside the line connecting its predecessor 2 and successor 6 and is fall thus inside the convex hull thus cannot be part of the convex hull. The final tour is again {1, 2, 6, 5} with length 2,865.

Since the length of the tour generated by the convex hull will never be smaller than the length of the tour created by the quad algorithm, the convex hull tour provides the best bound of the two. In this example, 2,865 is a larger bound than the 2,699 found by the quad algorithm and is the best lower bound of these two and the best bound found so far for this example. No tour for the TSP6 problem, including the optimal tour, can have a length less than 2,865.

8.2.2.5 Savings Heuristic

Clarke and Wright (1964) developed a construction procedure that extends a partial route or route primitive on its two end points. Conceptually the algorithm defines a base point and constructs an Eulerian tour that visits each of the other points and

Fig. 8.12 Tour extension
illustration

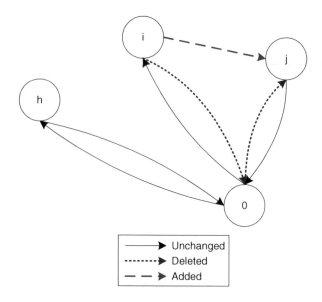

then returns to the base point. The Eulerian tour is then reduced in length by finding
and executing the shortcut with the largest savings. The savings are computed as the
sum of the distances to the base point of the two points minus the distance between
the two points. If the TSP has asymmetrical distances, the savings must be based on
the arcs with their appropriate orientations (Fig. 8.12).

We will use the following notation.

N the set of all points
F the set of points not yet concatenated by the savings procedure. 0 is the index
of the base point. At the start of the algorithm $F = N - \{0\}$.

The first shortcut is found by the pair of nodes that have the largest savings.

$$\max_{i \in F, j \in F} \left\{ s_{ij} = c_{i0} + c_{0j} - c_{ij} \right\} \tag{8.23}$$

Once two points have been joined by a shortcut they are never separated by the savings algorithm. The TSP variant of the algorithm extends the single partial route at
its end points, which are connected to the base point. The next point is then selected
by finding the point with the largest savings shortcut to the current end points of
the partial tour.

Let p and q be the indices of the end points of the partial tour. The next shortcut is
found by the pair of nodes that have the largest savings, where one point is an endpoint of the partial tour and the other point is not on the partial tour or the base point.

$$\max_{h \in F} \left\{ s_{ph} = c_{p0} + c_{0h} - c_{ph}, s_{qh} = c_{q0} + c_{0h} - c_{qh} \right\}$$

$$= \max_{h \in F} \left\{ \max_{j=p,q} \left\{ s_{jh} = c_{j0} + c_{0h} - c_{jh} \right\} \right\} \tag{8.24}$$

Table 8.3 TSP6 initial savings

	3	4	5	6
2	813	1,056	768	1,050
3		1,110	1,051	1,130
4			1,345	1,703
5				1,679

Algorithm 8.2 Savings Algorithm (TSP Variant)

1. Select base point $\{b\}$
2. Construct a tour primitive by finding the two points with the largest savings shortcut
3. While not all points have been added to the partial tour
4. Update the computation of the savings of combining tours
5. Append point with largest savings shortcut to endpoints of the partial tour

Savings Algorithm for the TSP6 Example The variant of the savings algorithm for the TSP requires the identification of a base point, which is typically a point on the perimeter of the point set. In this example point 1 is selected as the base point. The savings of all other pairs of points with respect to this base point are then computed. The sample calculations for four pairs of points are shown next. The savings for all the pairs of points are summarized in the next matrix (Table 8.3).

$$(1\text{-}2\text{-}3\text{-}1)[2, 3] = 608 + 566 - 361 = 813$$
$$(1\text{-}2\text{-}4\text{-}1)[2, 4] = 608 + 860 - 412 = 1056$$
$$(1\text{-}4\text{-}6\text{-}1)[4, 6] = 860 + 1204 - 361 = 1703$$
$$(1\text{-}5\text{-}6\text{-}1)[5, 6] = 985 + 1204 - 510 = 1679$$

The pair with the maximum savings is [4-6] with savings of 1,703 and the partial tour or tour primitive is then (1-6-4-1). This first shortcut is illustrated in Fig. 8.13.

This tour primitive can then be extended at either end node, i.e., at nodes 4 and 6. The point on a singleton route with maximum savings to either end point of the partial tour is selected. The updated savings matrix for this iteration is shown in Fig. 8.14.

The shortcut with the largest possible savings is selected.

$$\text{Max}\{1050(6\text{-}2\text{-}1), 1130(6\text{-}3\text{-}1), 1679(6\text{-}5\text{-}1), 860 + 608 - 412$$
$$= 1056(4\text{-}2\text{-}1), 860 + 566 - 316$$
$$= 1110(4\text{-}3\text{-}1), 860 + 985 - 500$$
$$= 1345(4\text{-}5\text{-}1)\}$$
$$= 1679(1\text{-}5\text{-}6)$$

Fig. 8.13 TSP6 savings tour
after the first shortcut

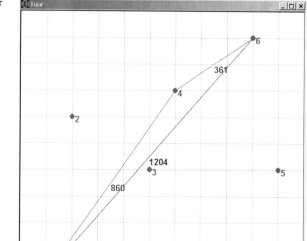

The singleton point appended to the partial route is point 5 inserted between base
point 1 and end point 6 and the tour primitive becomes (1-4-6-5-1). Point 5 now
becomes one of the end points of the partial route. This second shortcut is illustrated
in Fig. 8.14.

Again the point on a singleton route with maximum savings to either end point
of the partial tour is selected. The updated savings matrix for this iteration is shown
in Table 8.5.

The shortcut with the largest possible savings is selected.

$$\text{Max}\{1056(1\text{-}2\text{-}4), 1110(1\text{-}3\text{-}4), 768(1\text{-}2\text{-}5), 1051(1\text{-}3\text{-}5)\}$$
$$= 1110(1\text{-}3\text{-}4)$$

The singleton point appended to the partial route is point 3 inserted between base
point 1 and end point 4 and the tour primitive is then (1-3-4-6-5-1). Point 3 now
becomes one of the end points of the partial route. Again the point on a singleton
route with maximum savings to either end point of the partial tour is selected. At

Table 8.4 TSP6 Clarke
and Wright updated savings
after iteration 1

	4	6
2	1,056	1,050
3	1,110	1,130
5	1,345	1,679

Fig. 8.14 TSP6 savings tour after shortcut 2

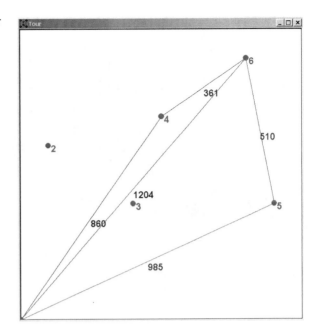

Table 8.5 TSP6 Clarke and Wright updated savings after iteration 2

	4	5
2	1,056	768
3	1,110	1,051

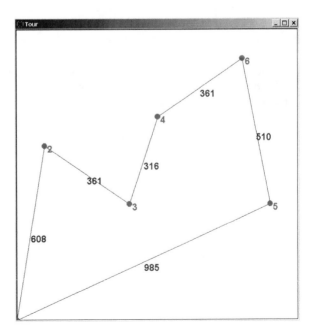

Fig. 8.15 TSP6 savings tour

Fig. 8.16 Space-filling curve
examples (Serpentine or
8-Band and Hilbert 3)

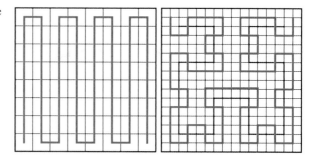

this stage only point 2 remains a free point and the only decision that needs to be
made is on which end of the partial tour it is appended.

$$\text{Max } \{813(1\text{-}2\text{-}3), 768(1\text{-}2\text{-}5)\} = 813(1\text{-}2\text{-}3)$$

The final tour created by the serial savings algorithm is (1-2-3-4-6-5) and its length
is equal to 3,140. The tour is shown in Fig. 8.15.

8.2.2.6 Band

The Band algorithm divides the problem area into a number of horizontal bands of
equal height. The tour will traverse these bands in alternating directions; odd numbered bands are traversed from left to right and even numbered bands are traversed
from right to left. By definition, the number of bands is always an even number. A
larger number of bands will increase the horizontal travel, which is proportional to
the number of bands, but decrease the vertical travel within each band.

The 2-Band algorithm is very commonly used in the control of a person-aboard
order picking crane. The rack is divided into two horizontal bands, items in the bottom band are picked when the crane moves away from the input/output point, items
in the top band are picked when the crane moves back toward the I/O point.

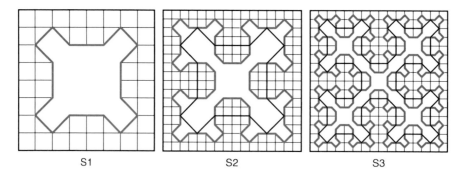

| S1 | S2 | S3 |

Fig. 8.17 Sierpinski curves of order 1, 2, and 3

Fig. 8.18 TSP example
space-filling curve tour

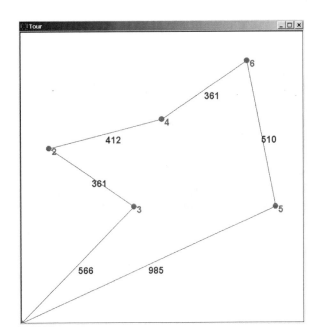

An illustration of the problem area divided into 8 vertically oriented bands is
shown in Fig. 8.16 for the serpentine curve.

8.2.2.7 Space-filling Curve

A space-filling curve is a curve whose ranges contain the entire two-dimensional
problem area. In the limit the curve visits all the points in the problem area or "fills"
the problem area. Space-filling curves were first described by Peano in the second
half of the nineteenth century and are also called Peano curves. Other mathema-
ticians have defined different types of space-filling curves that carry their name.
Examples are the Hilbert and Sierpinski curves. The serpentine curve shown in
Fig. 8.16 is space-filling curve, but it is not a fractal curve. The inverse of a space
filling curve can be used to map the two-dimensional problem area onto the unit
interval. The points in the two-dimensional plane of the TSP problem are mapped
to the unit interval and then sorted by their single coordinate. The TSP tour then
visits those points by increasing (or decreasing) coordinate. Both the mapping and
the sorting can be executed quickly, so the space-filling curve algorithm can be used
on very large problem instances. A second major main advantage of space-filling
curves is that they not leave an area of the problem domain without having visited
all the points in that area, i.e., they do not create orphans like the nearest neighbor
algorithm does.

Fig. 8.19 Node insertion

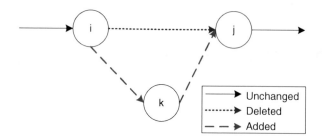

One variant of the space-filling algorithm for the TSP problem uses the Sierpinski curve, which is a closed fractal space filling curve. The Sierpinski curves of order 1, 2, and 3 are illustrated in Fig. 8.17.

Space-filling Curve Algorithm for the TSP6 Example The Space-filling algorithm for the example visits the points in the following sequence {1, 3, 2, 4, 6, 5}. The length of the created tour is equal to 3,194. The tour is shown in Fig. 8.18.

8.2.3 Insertion Heuristics

Insertion algorithms insert the remaining unvisited or free points into a partial tour in the second phase of the TSP meta heuristic. Insertion heuristics must make two types of decisions and also decide which type of decision to make first. The two

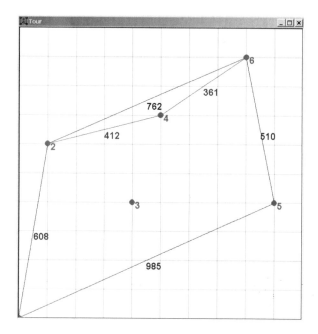

Fig. 8.20 TSP6 cheapest insertion of point 4 on the convex hull tour

decisions are: which point to insert next and on which link to insert this point. In Fig. 8.19, the free point k is inserted on the link from point i to point j, which is currently on the tour. Many variants exist depending on how and in what sequence those two questions are answered.

8.2.3.1 Cheapest Insertion

One of the most intuitive and often used insertion heuristics is cheapest insertion. Cheapest Insertion first determines for every remaining free or unvisited point where the optimal link is to insert this point. This corresponds to the inner minimization in the equation (8.25) over the links (*i-j*) of the tour. The insertion penalty is the sum of the distance to the free point minus the distance of the link that will be removed. Cheapest Insertion then selects the point to insert as the point with the minimum insertion penalty. This corresponds to the outer minimization over the free point k.

$$\min_{k} \left\{ \min_{ij} \left\{ \delta_{kij} = c_{ik} + c_{kj} - c_{ij} \right\} \right\} \tag{8.25}$$

Cheapest Insertion TSP6 Example After the Convex Hull algorithm terminates, the initial tour contains four points and there remain two unvisited points. During each iteration of the cheapest insertion algorithm a single free point is inserted into the tour. First, for each free point the link with the lowest insertion penalty is determined. The unvisited points are points 3 and 4.

$$[3]\, \text{Min}\{566 + 500 - 985 = 81(1\text{-}5), 500 + 640 - 510$$
$$= 630(5\text{-}6), 640 + 361 - 762$$
$$= 239(6\text{-}2), 361 + 566 - 608$$
$$= 319(2\text{-}1)\}$$
$$= 81(1\text{-}5)$$

$$[4]\, \text{Min}\{860 + 500 - 985 = 375(1\text{-}5), 500 + 361 - 510$$
$$= 351(5\text{-}6), 361 + 412 - 762$$
$$= 11(2\text{-}6), 412 + 860 - 608$$
$$= 644(2\text{-}1)\}$$
$$= 11\,(2\text{-}6)^{*}$$

For the cheapest insertion algorithm, the free point with the smallest insertion penalty is selected for insertion. In this example, this is point 4, which is inserted in link (6-2) with an insertion penalty of 11. This first insertion is shown in Fig. 8.20.

Next, the insertion penalties of all the remaining free points are recomputed. For every unvisited point the calculations of the previous iteration can be extended,

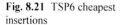

Fig. 8.21 TSP6 cheapest insertions

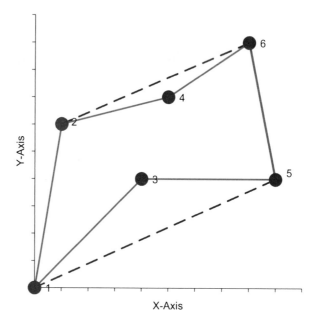

since only two new links have been added to the tour and one link has been re-moved. If the link that was removed, because the inserted point was inserted on this link, is the link with the minimum insertion penalty for a free point, then all the calculations be redone for this free point. In this example, the only remaining free point is point 3. The minimum insertion link for point 3 is link (1-5). Link (1-5) was not removed from the tour when point 4 was inserted, since point 4 was inserted on link (2-6). Updating the savings penalty and identifying the insertion link for point 3 only requires the minimum of three quantities: the old insertion penalty and the insertion penalties on the newly added links (6-4) and (4-2).

$$\text{Min}\,\{81(1\text{-}5), 595(6\text{-}4), 265(4\text{-}2)\} = 81(1\text{-}5)$$

Hence point 3 is inserted on link (1-5) with insertion penalty of 81. The final tour length is then 2,957. The tour created by the cheapest insertion algorithm is shown in Fig. 8.21. The two links removed from the initial partial tour are shown as dashed lines.

8.2.3.2 Priciest Insertion

Priciest Insertion first determines for every remaining free or unvisited point where the optimal link is to insert this point. This corresponds to the inner minimization in the equation (8.26) over the links (*i-j*) of the tour and is identical to the minimization process of the cheapest insertion algorithm. The insertion penalty is the sum of the distance to the free point minus the distance of the link that will be removed.

Priciest Insertion then selects the point to insert as the point with the maximum insertion penalty. This again corresponds to the outer minimization over the free points k.

$$\max_k \left\{ \min_{ij} \left\{ \delta_{kij} = c_{ik} + c_{kj} - c_{ij} \right\} \right\} \qquad (8.26)$$

Priciest Insertion TSP6 Example For the priciest insertion algorithm the calculations during the first step are identical to the calculations of the cheapest insertion algorithm. First, for each free point the link with the lowest insertion penalty is determined. The only remaining free points are points 3 and 4.

$$[3]\,\text{Min}\{566 + 500 - 985 = 81(1\text{-}5), 500 + 640 - 510$$
$$= 630(5\text{-}6), 640 + 361 - 762$$
$$= 239(6\text{-}2), 361 + 566 - 608$$
$$= 319(2\text{-}1)\}$$
$$= 81(1\text{-}5)^*$$

$$[4]\,\text{Min}\{860 + 500 - 985 = 375(1\text{-}5), 500 + 361 - 510$$
$$= 351(5\text{-}6), 361 + 412 - 762$$
$$= 11(6\text{-}2), 412 + 860 - 608$$
$$= 644(2\text{-}1)\}$$
$$= 11(2\text{-}6)$$

For the priciest insertion algorithm, the free point with the largest insertion penalty is selected for insertion. In this example, point 3 is inserted in link (1-5) with an insertion penalty of 81. This first insertion is shown in Fig. 8.22.

$$\text{Max}\,\{81(1\text{-}5), 11(2\text{-}6)\} = 81(1\text{-}5)$$

Next, the insertion penalties of all the remaining free points are recomputed. These calculations are identical to the calculations of the cheapest insertion algorithm and can use the same acceleration techniques. The only remaining unvisited point is point 4, and since it had a different insertion link from point 3, updating its insertion penalties only requires the taking the minimum of three quantities.

$$\text{Min}\,\{11(6\text{-}2), 610(1\text{-}3), 316(3\text{-}5)\} = 11(6\text{-}2)$$

Hence, point 4 is inserted in link (6-2) with insertion penalty of 11. The final tour length is then 2957. The tour created by the priciest insertion algorithm is shown in Fig. 8.21. The two links removed from the initial partial tour are shown as dashed lines. While the final tours created by the cheapest and priciest insertion are identical for this example, this is not the case in general. The sequence of operations is also different. Cheapest insertion first removed link (2-6) and then (1-5), priciest insertion first removed link (1-5) and then (6-2).

Fig. 8.22 TSP6 priciest
insertion of point 3 on the
convex hull tour

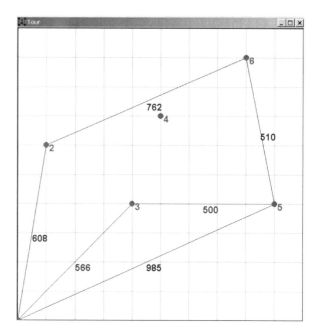

8.2.3.3 Nearest Insertion

Nearest Insertion determines first the free point to insert by finding the free point closest to a point on the tour. The algorithm in essence performs a mini-min operation on the distance from a free point to a point on the tour.

$$\min_{k \notin T, j \in T} \{c_{kj}\} = \min_{k \notin T} \left\{ \min_{j \in T} c_{kj} \right\} \qquad (8.27)$$

Nearest Insertion then determines the best link to insert this point. This process is identical to the minimization process of the cheapest and priciest insertion algorithms.

$$\min_{(i,j) \in T} \{\delta_{ijk} = c_{ik} + c_{kj} - c_{ij}\} \qquad (8.28)$$

Nearest Insertion TSP6 Example Again the only remaining unvisited points are points 3 and 4. First the distance to the closest point on the tour from each of the free points is determined.

[3] Min {566(3-1), 361(3-2), 500(3-5), 640(3-6)} = 361(3-2)*
[4] Min {860(4-1), 412(4-2), 500(4-5), 361(4-6)} = 361(4-6)

Next the free point with the smallest minimum distance to a tour point is selected. In this case there exists a tie. One way to break the tie is to select the point with the lowest index, which is point 3. Only for the selected free point is the link with the minimum insertion penalty is determined. These calculations are identical to the equivalent calculations for the cheapest insertion algorithm.

$$
\begin{aligned}
\text{Min}\{566 + 500 - 985 &= 81(1\text{-}5), 500 + 640 - 510 \\
&= 630(5\text{-}6), 640 + 361 - 762 \\
&= 239(6\text{-}2), 361 + 566 - 608 \\
&= 319(2\text{-}1)\} \\
&= 81(1\text{-}5).
\end{aligned}
$$

As the result, point 3 is inserted on link (1-5). The only remaining point is now point 4. In general, for each free point the minimum distance to a tour point is determined. We can extend the calculations of the previous iteration, since there is only one new tour point, which is the free point inserted in the previous iteration.

$$
[4] \text{ Min } \{361(4\text{-}6), 316(4\text{-}3)\} = 316(4\text{-}3).
$$

The point with the smallest minimum distance to a tour point is selected. Since at this time there is only one free point remaining, the above calculations are solely made to illustrate the algorithm steps rather than to select the only remaining point. For the selected free point, the link with the lowest insertion penalty is then determined. Again these calculations are similar to the ones in the first step of the cheapest insertion algorithm.

$$
\text{Min } \{610(1\text{-}3), 316(3\text{-}5), 351(5\text{-}6), 11(6\text{-}2), 319(2\text{-}1)\} = 11(6\text{-}2)
$$

Hence point 4 is inserted on link (6-2). The tour created by the nearest insertion algorithm is identical to the tour created by cheapest and priciest insertion algorithms and shown in Fig. 8.21.

8.2.3.4   Farthest Insertion

Farthest insertion determines first for every free point the smallest distance to any point already on the tour. Then it inserts the free point with the maximum smallest distance to a point on the tour. The algorithm in essence performs a maxi-min operation on the distance from a free point to a point on the tour.

$$
\max_{k \notin T} \left\{ \min_{j \in T} c_{kj} \right\} \tag{8.29}
$$

Farthest insertion then determines the best link to insert this point. This process is identical to the minimization process of the cheapest, priciest, and nearest insertion algorithms.

$$
\min_{(i,j) \in T} \{\delta_{ijk} = c_{ik} + c_{kj} - c_{ij}\} \tag{8.30}
$$

Farthest Insertion TSP6 Example The calculations for the farthest insertion are analogue to the calculations for the nearest insertion, except that the point with the largest minimum distance to a tour point is selected. The remaining unvisited points are again points 3 and 4. First the distance to the closest point on the tour from each of the free points is determined.

$$[3] \text{ Min } \{566(3\text{-}1), 361(3\text{-}2), 500(3\text{-}5), 640(3\text{-}6)\} = 361(3\text{-}2)^*$$
$$[4] \text{ Min } \{860(4\text{-}1), 412(4\text{-}2), 500(4\text{-}5), 361(4\text{-}6)\} = 361(4\text{-}6)$$

Then the point with the maximum minimum distance is chosen. In this particular example we have a tie. One way to break the tie is to select the point with the lowest index, which is point 3. The rest of the calculations are identical to the equivalent calculations for the nearest Insertion algorithm.

Point 3 is inserted on link (1-5) and then point 4 is inserted on link (6-2).

8.2.3.5   Nearest Addition

Nearest addition determines first the free point to insert by finding the free point closest to a point on the tour. This first step is identical to the first step of the nearest insertion algorithm.

$$\min_{k \notin T, j \in T} \{c_{kj}\} \tag{8.31}$$

Nearest addition then determines the best link to insert this point by examining the two links on the tour incident to the tour point the free point was closest to. This is a more restricted search than the link determination step in the cheapest and farthest insertion algorithms.

$$\min \{\delta_{ijk} = c_{ik} + c_{kj} - c_{ij}, \delta_{jmk} = c_{jk} + c_{km} - c_{jm}\} \tag{8.32}$$

Nearest Addition TSP6 Example Identical to the first step in nearest insertion, nearest addition selects point 3 to be inserted next and its closest point on the tour is point 2. The link to insert it on is selected from the two links on the tour that have point 2 as an endpoint.

Min$\{640 + 361 - 762 = 239(6\text{-}2), 361 + 566 - 608 = 319(2\text{-}1)\} = 239(6\text{-}2)$.

Point 3 is inserted on link (6-2). The only remaining free point is point 4. Its closest point on the tour is updated.

$$[4]\text{Min } \{361(4\text{-}6), 316(4\text{-}3)\} = 316(4\text{-}3).$$

Point 4 is closest to point 3 on the tour. The link to insert point 4 is then selected from the two links on the tour that have point 3 as endpoint.

Min$\{316 + 412 - 361 = 367(3\text{-}2), 566 + 361 - 640 = 287(3\text{-}6)\} = 287(3\text{-}6)$.

Fig. 8.23 TSP6 nearest
addition

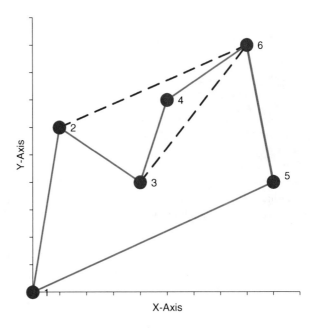

Point 4 is inserted on the link (3-6). The tour created by the nearest addition algorithm is then (1-2-3-4-6-5) and the tour length is equal to 3,140. This tour is shown
in Fig. 8.23. The links removed from the initial and intermediate partial tours are
shown as dashed lines.

8.2.4   Improvement Heuristics

Improvement heuristics attempt to reduce the length of an existing tour by exchanging two or more of the links on the tour by new links so that a new tour of shorter
length is created. Improvement heuristics are executed in the third phase of the TSP
meta heuristic. The main decisions for improvement algorithms are how many and
which links to include in the test for a single removal and what is an acceptable
value for the test result in order to execute the exchange. The possible answers to
the first question are given in the improvement type classification and to the second
question in the improvement framework classification.

8.2.4.1   Improvement Framework Classification

Exchange improvement heuristics can be divided into four classes depending on
which exchange they test for possible improvement and which exchange they select

to execute. For a minimization problem, such as the TSP, where we want to a tour with the lowest possible length, the categories are

1. First Descent
2. Steepest Descent
3. Simulated Annealing
4. Tabu Search

First Descent All possible edge exchanges that can result in a new tour are examined in a structured way until an exchange is found that reduces the tour length. This exchange is executed immediately and the process of examining all possible exchanges starts all over. Hence, during every iteration the first exchange that yields a reduction is executed. The process terminates when no further exchanges can be found that yield a length reduction.

Steepest Descent All possible edge exchanges that can result in a new tour are examined in a structured way and the exchange that yielded the largest reduction in the tour length is retained. If this exchange reduces the tour length then it is executed and the process of examining all possible exchanges starts all over. Hence, during every iteration the exchange that yields the strongest reduction is executed. The process terminates when no further exchanges can be found that yield a length reduction.

Simulated Annealing Both previous improvement algorithms are deterministic, i.e. each algorithm will convert a specific initial tour into specific final tour. Since they are heuristics, this final tour may not be of high quality. To remedy this problem, a probabilistic exchange improvement algorithm was developed. There exists an analogy between the optimization method of simulated annealing and the laws of thermodynamics, specifically with the way in which liquids freeze and crystallize or metals cool and anneal. To create a strong artifact with a casting process, the artifact has to be cooled slowly so that the metal can settle in a stable and strong internal structure. Similarly, the search procedure should not only examine improvements generated by a steepest descent search but widen its search domain by accepting some non-improving exchanges especially early on in the search process. Because of this analogy the search process is called simulated annealing.

The simulated annealing algorithm selects a set of edges for exchange evaluation at random. If the exchange yields a cost reduction, then the exchange is executed immediately as if a first descent algorithm is being executed. If the exchange yields a cost increase, then the exchange is executed with probability P, which is computed in function of the cost increase Δ and the temperature T. T is a search control parameter that is systematically reduced during the algorithm execution.

$$\begin{aligned} if \ \Delta < 0 \quad & P[Exch] = 1 \\ if \ \Delta \geq 0 \quad & P[Exch] = e^{-\Delta/T} \end{aligned} \tag{8.33}$$

This allows early on exchanges with large cost increases. As the temperature is reduced, the number of such exchanges and the size of the allowed cost increases are gradually reduced. The objective of these non-improving exchanges is to avoid a first descent into a local minimum. The process repeats itself until no further improvements can be made. Since the exchanges were selected at random, the improvement algorithm may generate a different final tour if started from the same initial tour if different seeds are used to generate different pseudo-random number streams for sampling the probability function of P. The number of replications of the simulated annealing algorithm is an algorithm parameter. The number of replications also increases the required computation time.

For further information on simulated annealing see Kirkpatrick et al. (1983) and Vechi and Kirkpatrick (1983).

Tabu Search Tabu search is another local search algorithm that enhances the performance of its local search by using memory structures to prohibit certain moves, even if they are improving. The algorithm maintains a list, called the tabu list, of solutions that have been examined recently and that are currently excluded from the local search. Other tabu lists can be based on problem attributes, such as tours that contain a certain arc are placed on the tabu list, or forbidden moves, such as creating a tour that does not contain a certain arc. The tabu tenure is the number of iterations a solution stays in the tabu list and is an algorithm parameter. The original tabu search algorithm was first described by Glover (1989, 1990).

8.2.4.2   Improvement Exchange Classification

Individual improvement exchanges can be classified by the number of links currently on the tour that are removed by the improvement exchange and which links are members of the candidate set for removal. The most commonly used exchange improvements are two-exchange, three-exchange, and chain-exchange.

Two-Exchange A two-exchange attempts to reduce the length of the tour by removing two non-adjacent edges of the current tour and replacing them by two new edges so that again a full tour is formed. In the following illustration the edges *(kn)* and *(li)* are removed and replaced by the edges *(kl)* and *(ni)*. The associated savings are computed with (Fig. 8.24):

$$S_{(kn)(li)} = d_{kn} + d_{li} - d_{kl} - d_{ni} \tag{8.34}$$

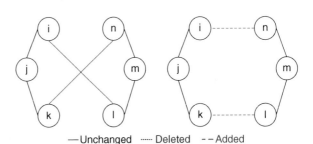

Fig. 8.24 Two-exchange improvement illustration

—Unchanged   ····· Deleted   - - Added

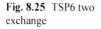

Fig. 8.25 TSP6 two exchange

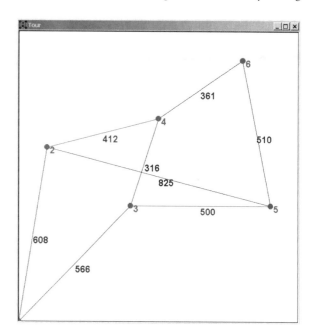

If the savings are positive, the exchange is immediately executed in the first descent procedure and saved in the steepest descent procedure. If the savings are negative, the exchange may still be made with a certain probability in the simulated annealing procedure. After an exchange has been made the evaluation process starts anew. The algorithm stops when no exchanges with positive savings can be found.

Two-Exchange Improvement for the TSP6 Example The nearest neighbor algorithm created an original tour with point sequence (1-2-5-6-4-3) and with a tour length equal to 3,186. This tour has the crossing edges (3-4) and (2-5). For this example, which is a geometric TSP with distances based on the Euclidean distance norm, a tour that has crossing edges cannot be optimal. The savings associated with exchanging the edges (3-4) and (2-5) with the edges (2-4) and (3-5) are $316 + 825 - 412 - 500 = 229$. This two-exchange has positive savings and it will be executed immediately in a first descent framework or compared with the best exchange so far in a steepest descent framework. If the exchange is executed, the reduced tour length is equal to 2,957 (Fig. 8.25).

In this example, the edges for this exchange were identified based on their location. In general, all pairs of non-adjacent edges are evaluated. All possible two-exchanges and their associated savings are shown in Table 8.6. There are only two exchanges with positive savings. If the two exchanges are examined in the sequence as shown in the table, both the steepest descent and the first descent frameworks would select the exchange described above.

Table 8.6 Two-exchange savings computations for the TSP6 example

Edges					
Old 1	Old 2	New 1	New 2	Delta	Savings
1–2	5–6	1–5	2–6	$608 + 510 - 985 - 762$	−629
	6–4	1–6	2–4	$608 + 361 - 1204 - 412$	−647
	4–3	1–4	2–3	$608 + 316 - 860 - 361$	−297
2–5	6–4	2–6	5–4	$825 + 361 - 762 - 500$	−76
	4–3	2–4	5–3	$825 + 316 - 412 - 500$	229
	3–1	2–3	5–1	$825 + 566 - 361 - 985$	45
5–6	4–3	5–4	6–3	$510 + 316 - 500 - 640$	−314
	3–1	5–3	6–1	$510 + 566 - 500 - 1204$	−628
6–4	3–1	6–3	1–4	$361 + 566 - 640 - 860$	−573

Table 8.7 Possible three exchanges

Link 1	Link 2	Link 3	Tour
kh	*ol*	*ni*	Original
ko	*hn*	*li*	
ko	*hl*	*ni*	Two-exchange only
kn	*lh*	*oi*	
kn	*lo*	*hi*	Two-exchange only
kl	*nh*	*oi*	
kl	*no*	*hi*	

8.2.4.3 Three-Exchange

The three-exchange procedure attempts to reduce the tour length by removing three links from the current tour. The three remaining tour segments can be re-combined in four different ways to form a new complete tour. The other feasible re-combinations would either form the original tour again or correspond to a two exchange with one of the original three edges remaining in the new tour (Fig. 8.26 and Table 8.7).

Three-Exchange Improvement for the TSP6 Example The 3-exchange algorithm calls the 2-exchange algorithm as a subprocedure. The 2-exchange algorithm executes the single exchange as described in the 2-exchange algorithm example.

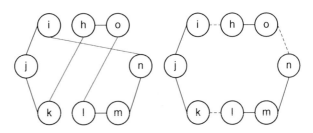

Fig. 8.26 Illustration of a three exchange improvement

— Unchanged ····· Deleted – – Added

Fig. 8.27 2-chain-exchange
improvement illustration

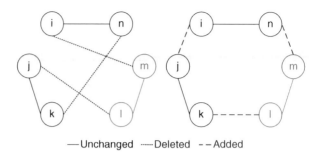

— Unchanged ⋯⋯ Deleted – – Added

After that, no 3-exchange with positive savings can be found and the 3-exchange algorithm terminates. For larger problem instances, typically the 3-exchange algorithm can find improvements after the 2-exchange algorithm has been executed as a subprocedure since it evaluates many more candidate exchanges.

8.2.4.4 Chain-Exchange

The chain-exchange procedure attempts to reduce the tour length by removing a chain of nodes from the current tour and inserting the chain in a new position on the tour so that a new full tour is formed. The length of the chain is an algorithm parameter. If the chain length equals one, this procedure is equivalent to moving a single node to different positions in the tour. Typically, only short chain lengths such as one, two, and three are tested. A chain-exchange removes three links from the tour and replaces them by three new links, so a chain-exchange belongs to the class of the three-exchanges. For a given chain length the number of possible exchanges is a subset of the possible exchanges tested by the three-exchange procedure. The required computational effort of the chain-exchange procedure is thus between that of the two-exchange and the three-exchange procedures. The chain exchange is also called Or-exchange since it was first proposed by Or (1976).

In Fig. 8.27, a two-chain exchange is illustrated. The chain or fixed node sequence consists of nodes m to l and it is relocated from between nodes i and j to between nodes n and k. Observe that this involves removing three old edges and replacing them by three new edges.

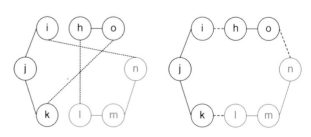

Fig. 8.28 3-chain exchange
improvement illustration

— Unchanged ⋯⋯ Deleted – – Added

In Fig. 8.28, a three-chain exchange is illustrated. The chain consists of nodes n to l and it is relocated from between nodes i to h to between nodes o to k. Again this involves removing three edges and replacing them with three new edges. For further information on two and three exchanges see Goetschalckx (1992). In general, computational processing time increases sharply with the amount of improvement processing.

Chain-Exchange Improvement for the TSP6 Example Recall that the original tour created by the nearest neighbor algorithm had the point sequence (1-2-5-6-4-3) and a tour length equal to 3,186. This tour has the crossing edges (3-4) and (2-5). For this example, which is a geometric TSP with distances based on the Euclidean distance norm, a tour that has crossing edges cannot be optimal.

First, we will execute the 1-chain-exchange algorithm. A 1-chain is a single node, so the 1-chain exchange is equivalent to relocating a single node to a better place in the tour. The first exchange relocates node 2 from the node sequence (1, 2, 5, 6, 4, 3) to the new node sequence (1, 5, 6, 4, 3, 2) with savings of 45. The second exchange relocates node 3 from the node sequence (1, 5, 6, 4, 3, 2) to the node sequence (1, 3, 5, 6, 4, 2) with savings of 184. No further chain-exchanges with positive savings can be found and the 1-chain-exchange algorithm terminates. The total savings are 229. The new tour length is 2,957 and this is the same tour as found by the sweep algorithm.

Next, we will execute the 2-chain-exchange algorithm from the same starting tour as for the 1-chain-exchange. The chain of two nodes (1, 2) is relocated from the node sequence (1, 2, 5, 6, 4, 3) to the new node sequence (1, 3, 5, 6, 4, 2) with savings of 229. No further chain-exchanges with positive savings can be found and the 2-chain-exchange algorithm terminates. The new tour length is 2,957 and this is the same tour as found by the sweep algorithm.

8.3   Optimization Based Heuristics

Heuristic algorithms typically run in a short amount of computation time. Their use is justified because running an exact algorithm for the same problem instance would take an excessive amount of computation time. However, upon completion of the heuristic algorithm a feasible solution has been created but the quality of that solution is unknown. One way to judge the quality of the solution is to compute a lower bound on the solution value. Again it is assumed that the lower bound can be computed in a relatively short amount of time. The lower bound computation typically does not yield a feasible solution. The comparison of the incumbent primal feasible solution value and the lower bound yields a value for the gap, which is the maximum deviation of the feasible solution. Logistics and supply chain practitioners usually are very satisfied if the gap is less than 1 or 2 percent. In order to compute a tight lower bound, optimizing algorithms are typically required. The following section describes a lower bound algorithm for the STSP based on Lagrangean relaxation and the notion of a one-tree. This material can be safely skipped if one is not interested in lower bound on the TSP. Recall that a relatively weak lower bound for the ATSP is provided by the solution of the corresponding AP.

8.3.1 1-Tree Lower Bound

Held and Karp (1970, 1971) developed a solution for the STSP based on the notion of a 1-tree relaxation. A 1-tree is a minimum spanning tree (MST) of a set of points plus one edge not already in the tree connecting a point again to the MST. The node degree of a point is the number of edges in the spanning tree that have this node as one of their end nodes. The number of edges in the 1-tree is equal to $(N - 1) + 1 = N$. The one additional edge is chosen as the maximum over all nodes, which have a node degree equal to 1, of the minimum length new edge of that node to the tree. Each node in the MST with node degree 1 must have a second edge connecting it to the MST in order for it to be on the TSP tour and the best possible second edge for this node is an edge not already in the MST with minimum length. This edge is the second-shortest edge for this node. The length of the 1-tree is a lower bound on the length of the shortest Hamiltonian cycle through all the points. To make the bound as large as possible, the node with the maximum second-shortest edge is selected. Since a 1-tree is a (minimum) spanning tree plus one additional edge from a single point to the tree, a 1-tree contains a single cycle. If the 1-tree is a cycle, then it is a feasible solution and it is the optimal solution to the traveling salesman problem. The 1-tree is a cycle if the node degree of all the nodes is equal to two. The Lagrangean relaxation of this problem relaxes the constraint that the node degree of each node must be equal to two. Since the constraint is an equality constraint, the corresponding Lagrangean multiplier is unrestricted in sign. The master Lagrangean dual problem is solved with subgradient optimization. Further information on Lagrangean relaxation can be found in Bazaraa et al. (2005). The bound provided by the Lagrangean dual was used in a branch-and-bound scheme to solve the TSP. The Lagrangean relaxation is written as

$$Min \quad \sum_{i=1}^{N-1} \sum_{j=i+1}^{N} c_{ij}x_{ij} + \sum_{j=1}^{N} \lambda_j \cdot \left(\sum_{i=1}^{j-1} x_{ij} + \sum_{k=j+1}^{N} x_{jk} - 2 \right) \quad (8.35)$$

$$s.t. \quad x_{ij} \in \{0,1\}, \quad x_{ij} \in 1\text{-}tree$$

After rearranging the terms in the objective function, the Lagrangean relaxation becomes

$$Min \quad \sum_{i=1}^{N-1} \sum_{j=i+1}^{N} (c_{ij} + \lambda_i + \lambda_j)x_{ij} - 2 \sum_{j=1}^{N} \lambda_j \quad (8.36)$$

$$s.t. \quad x_{ij} \in \{0,1\}, \quad x_{ij} \in 1\text{-}tree$$

The subgradient or improvement direction at a particular solution for each Lagrangean multiplier λ_j is given by the following expression, where nd_j denotes the node degree of node j.

$$\sum_{i=1}^{j-1} x_{ij} + \sum_{k=j+1}^{N} x_{jk} - 2 = nd_j - 2 \quad [\lambda_j] \tag{8.37}$$

Held et al. (1974) proposed the following updating procedure for the Lagrangean multipliers in their solution of the symmetrical traveling salesman problem.

$$
\begin{aligned}
t^k &= w^k \frac{\hat{z} - z(\lambda^k)}{\|x^s(\lambda^k)\|^2} \\
\lambda^{k+1} &= \lambda^k + t^k \cdot x^s(\lambda^k) \\
w^0 &= 2 \\
w^{k+m} &= \frac{w^k}{2}
\end{aligned}
\tag{8.38}
$$

Where $\hat{z}$ is the tour length of the best primal feasible solution found so far or, equivalently, the solution value of the incumbent. $x^s(\lambda^k) = nd - 2$ is the signed difference of the node degree of a node minus the desired value of 2 in the current 1-tree and corresponds to the direction of the node penalty update. t is the step size of the node penalty update. The weight parameter w is cut in half after a fixed number of m iterations. This implementation of subgradient optimization is known for its rapid initial convergence, but also for its zigzagging behavior and instability in the neighborhood of the optimal λ^*. The algorithm is terminated when either the current gap is less than the specified allowable gap, when the number of iterations exceeds the maximum number, or when the weight parameter w becomes smaller than a specified limit. Usually the number of allowable iterations grows with the problem size.

Typically, the incumbent solution $\hat{z}$ is computed initially with a primal heuristic and may or may not be updated during the execution of the Lagrangean optimization. Examples of primal heuristics for the TSP are nearest neighbor and sweep, followed by improvement algorithms such as two-exchange and three-exchange.

Algorithm 8.3 1-Tree Relaxation Algorithm for a TSP Bound

1. Initialize all node degree penalties λ to zero, set $w = 2, k = 1$
2. Compute adjusted distances with $c_{ij}^k = c_{ij} + \lambda_i^k + \lambda_j^k$
3. Construct the minimum spanning tree using the adjusted distances c_{ij}^k
4. Using the adjusted distances c_{ij}^k, connect the point with node degree equal to one and the maximum second-shortest edge to the tree
5. If all the node degrees are equal to two, stop.
   Else update node degree penalties with the subgradient method.

$$if \quad nd_j^k = 2 \quad \lambda_j^k \text{ remains unchanged}$$

$$if \quad nd_j^k < 2 \quad \lambda_j^k \text{ is decreased}$$

$$if \quad nd_j^k > 2 \quad \lambda_j^k \text{ is increased}$$

$$t^k = w \frac{\hat{z} - z(\lambda^k)}{\left\|nd_j^k - 2\right\|^2}$$

$$\lambda_j^{k+1} = \lambda_j^k + t^k \cdot \left(nd_j^k - 2\right)$$

6. $k = k + 1$, If $k = k + 1$, If (k modulo m) $= 0$ then $w = w/2$
7. Go to Step 2

The above algorithm requires in step 3 the construction of the minimum spanning tree (MST) of the nodes in the problem. Several efficient algorithms exist to find the MST such as algorithms by Prim (1957) and Kruskal (1956). In the above algorithm, the graph is considered to be complete. The computational effort for Prim's algorithm based on an adjacency matrix implementation of the graph is equal to $O(N^2)$. More efficient implementations are possible using a heap data structure.

Algorithm 8.4 Prim's Algorithm for the MST

1. Select an arbitrary node. Initialize the set of visited nodes (V) to only contain this node. Initialize the MST to empty.
2. Do while V does not contain all the nodes

   a. Find the shortest edge (i,j) for which one endpoint i is in V and one endpoint j is not in V. If required any ties can be broken arbitrarily.
   b. Add j to V and add the edge (i,j) to the MST

Lagrangean Relaxation and 1-Tree Heuristic for the TSP6 Example The determination of the lower bound by the 1-tree algorithm may require many iterations. Only the first three of these iterations are described next for the TSP6 example problem. In Fig. 8.29, the minimum spanning tree of the TSP6 problem using the original distances is shown when point 1 was chosen as the initial point. The calcu-

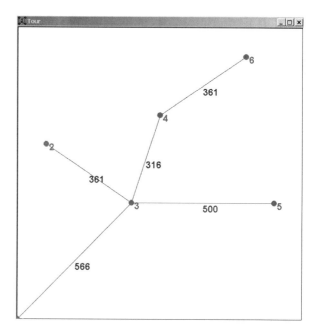

Fig. 8.29 TSP6 example minimum spanning tree

Fig. 8.30 TSP6 example
1-tree for the first iteration

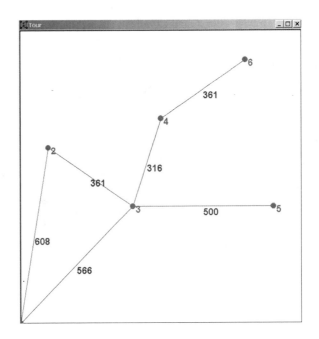

lations to find the first MST are given next, where the number in parentheses is the index of the node that is added to the MST.

$V = \{1\}$ min $\{608(2), 566(3), 860(4), 985(5), 1204(6)\} = 566(3)$
$V = \{1, 3\}$ min $\{361(2), \min \{860, 316\} = 316(4), 500(5), 640(6)\} = 316(4)$
$V = \{1, 3, 4\}$ min $\{\min \{608, 361, 412\} = 361(2), 500(5), 361(6)\} = 361(2)$
$V = \{1, 2, 3, 4\}$ min $\{500(5), \min \{1204, 762, 640, 361\} = 361(6)\} = 361(6)$
$V = \{1, 2, 3, 4, 6\}$ min $\{985, 825, 500, 500, 510\} = 500(5)$

In Fig. 8.30, this spanning tree is extended by the shortest new link from a node with node degree equal to one to the tree. The nodes with node degree equal to one are 1, 2, 5, and 6. The second-shortest edge is found for each these nodes and the node with the maximum second-shortest edge is selected.

$$\max \{608(1\text{-}2), 412(2\text{-}4), 500(5\text{-}4), 510(6\text{-}5)\} = 608(1\text{-}2)$$

In the first iteration of the TSP6 example, the added edge is the edge (1-2) with length 608. This extended tree or 1-tree now contains 6 links and a single cycle. The length of this 1-tree is 2,711, which is a lower bound on the length of the TSP for this problem since at this time all node penalties are still equal to zero.

The node degrees of the points are given by $\{2, 2, 4, 2, 1, 1\}$. The node degree of point 3 is higher than 2 and the node degrees of point 5 and 6 are lower than 2. As a consequence, the node penalty λ for point 3 is decreased, the λ for points 5 and 6 are increased, and all other λ remain unchanged with value equal to zero. The step size at the end of the first iteration is equal to 82. In the next computations the superscripts of variables indicate the iteration.

Table 8.8 TSP6 1-tree node penalties for iteration 2

Node	Degree	Penalty
1	2	0
2	2	0
3	4	164
4	2	0
5	1	−82
6	1	−82

Table 8.9 TSP6 1-tree adjusted distances for iteration 2

	1	2	3	4	5	6
1		608	729	860	903	1,122
2	608		524	412	743	680
3	729	524		480	582	722
4	860	412	480		418	279
5	903	743	582	418		346
6	1,122	680	722	279	346	

$$t^1 = \frac{2 \cdot (2957 - 2711)}{(2^2 + 1^2 + 1^2)} = 82$$

The node penalties to be used in the next iteration are shown in Table 8.8.

In the next iteration, all the pair-wise distances are updated using the new λ values. The updated distances for iteration two are shown in Table 8.9.

$$c_{1,6}^2 = c_{1,6} + \lambda_1^2 + \lambda_6^2 = 1204 + 0 - 82 = 1122$$

The algorithm now executes the same steps with the updated distances. A new minimum spanning tree for all points is determined and this tree is extended with the maximum second-shortest link from any point with node degree equal to one. The calculations to find the second MST are given next.

$V = \{1\}$ $\min\{608(2), 729(3), 860(4), 903(5), 1122(6)\} = 608(2)$

$V = \{1, 2\}$ $\min\{524(3), \min\{860, 412\} = 412(4), 743(5), 680(6)\} = 412(4)$

$V = \{1, 2, 4\}$ $\min\{480(3), 418(5), \min\{1122, 680, 279\} = 279(6)\} = 279(6)$

$V = \{1, 2, 4, 6\}$ $\min\{480(3), \min\{903, 743, 418, 346\} = 346(5)\} = 346(5)$

$V = \{1, 2, 4, 5, 6\}$ $\min\{729, 524, 480, 582, 722\} = 480(3)$

The nodes with node degree equal to one are 1, 3, and 5. The second-shortest edge is found for each these nodes and the node with the maximum second-shortest edge is selected.

$$\max \{729(1\text{-}3), 524(3\text{-}2), 418(5\text{-}4)\} = 729(1\text{-}3)$$

The result is shown in Fig. 8.31. The length of the 1-tree based on the adjusted distances is 2,854. The sum of the node penalties equals zero, so the lower bound

Fig. 8.31 TSP6 example
1-tree for iteration 2

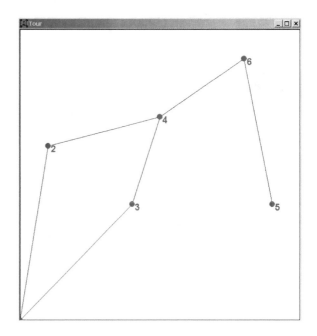

computed with (8.36) is also equal to 2,854. This value becomes the current best bound for the TSP6 problem.

The node degrees of the points are given by {2, 2, 2, 3, 1, 2}. The node degree of point 4 is higher than 2 and the node degree of point 5 is lower than 2. As a con-

Table 8.10 TSP6 1-tree node penalties for iteration 3

Node	Degree	Penalty
1	2	0
2	2	0
3	2	164
4	3	103
5	1	−185
6	2	−82

Table 8.11 TSP6 1-tree adjusted distances for iteration 3

	1	2	3	4	5	6
1	0	608	729	963	800	1,122
2	608	0	524	515	640	680
3	729	524	0	583	479	722
4	963	515	583	0	418	382
5	800	640	479	418	0	243
6	1,122	680	722	382	243	0

Fig. 8.32 TSP6 optimal tour

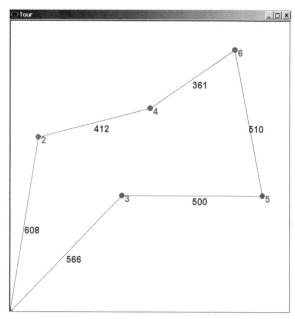

sequence, the node penalty λ for point 4 is decreased, the λ for point 5 is increased, and all other λ remain unchanged. The step size computed at the end of the second iteration is equal to 103.

$$t^2 = \frac{2 \cdot (2957 - 2854)}{(1^2 + 1^2)} = 103$$

The node penalties for the next iteration are shown in Table 8.10. All the pair-wise distances are updated using the new λ values. The updated distances are shown in Table 8.11.

The algorithm now executes the same steps in the next iteration with the updated distances. The algorithm constructs a 1-tree that is a full cycle and with length 2,956. The sum of the node penalties is zero, so the lower bound computed with (8.36) is also equal to the length of the 1-tree. This the same tour as generated by the Cheapest Insertion algorithm with length equal to 2,957. However, the 1-tree algorithm has established that this tour is optimal, since its length is equal to the lower bound. The difference of 1 between the lower bound of 2,956 and the incumbent tour length of 2,957 is created by the rounding process in the sequence of calculations. When the previous calculations are executed with floating point arithmetic, the tour length is equal to the lower bound at the end of the third iteration with a tolerance less than 0.005 (Fig. 8.32).

8.3.2   Christofides' Heuristic

The heuristic algorithm developed by Christofides (1976) uses a sequence of mathematical programming formulations to create a STSP tour. This heuristic is different from the construction heuristics described in this chapter because its implementation is significantly more complex and because its worst case performance bound can be derived to be equal to 1.5. In other words, the tour generated by this heuristic is guaranteed to be at most 50% longer than the optimal tour. Since the performance bound is loose and the implementation is complex, this heuristic is rarely used by practitioners in logistics and supply chain management.

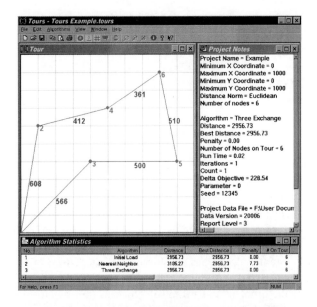

Fig. 8.33 Tours TSP6 example

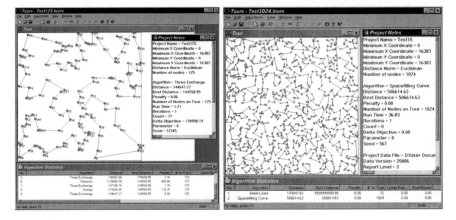

Fig. 8.34 Tours illustrations

8.4   Tours Software Illustration

Many of the algorithms described above for the TSP can be tedious to execute manually. The Tours program by Goetschalckx (2007) provides intuitive and graphical interface to the execution of the various algorithms. Screen captures for the TSP6 example and larger cases with 125 and 1024 facilities, respectively, are shown in Figs. 8.33 and 8.34. The Tours program allows the user to manually construct a tour or to control the sequence of algorithms for finding a tour of acceptable quality. Many data and results can be copied then pasted into other applications such as spreadsheets, optimization solvers, and reports.

8.5   Exercises

True-False Questions

1. The 2-Opt procedure by Lin to improve an existing TSP tour takes a sequence of nodes out of the tour and inserts it into another place in the tour to form a tour of shorter length, (T/F) _____.
2. Consider the classic Traveling Salesman Problem (TSP). The problem is to construct the single shortest cycle that visits all points exactly once, (T/F)_____.
3. If all the points of a TSP fall on the boundary of the convex hull of these points then this boundary of the convex hull is the shortest TSP tour, (T/F)_____.
4. If the two and three exchange improvement procedures by Lin and Kernighan can no longer find any improvements in a traveling salesman tour then this tour is optimal, i.e., has the shortest length, (T/F)_____.
5. The sub tour elimination constraints in the traveling salesman formulations make the problem so hard to solve because of the large coefficients in the right hand side of the constraints, (T/F)_____.

Table 8.12 Point coordinates

Point	x	y
1	5	1
2	8	9
3	3	5
4	7	6
5	1	9
6	2	1
7	4	8
8	8	2

Table 8.13 Delivery points distance table

	1	2	3	4	5	6	7	8
1								
2								
3								
4								
5								
6								
7								
8								

Table 8.14 Clarke and Wright savings

	1	2	3	4	5	6	7	8
1								
2								
3								
4								
5								
6								
7								
8								

TSP Exercise 1

Consider the problem of finding the shortest distance cycle through the following eight delivery points, given that the cycle visits each delivery point exactly once. The coordinates of the eight delivery points are given in Table 8.12.

The travel distances between each pair of points can be approximated with the Euclidean distance norm rounded to two digits behind the decimal point. First show the formula for the distance norm using the notation of Table 8.12 and point indices i and j. Next compute and show the distances in upper triangular format in Table 8.13.

Compute heuristic delivery sequence with the Clarke and Wright (CW) savings algorithm. For the Clarke and Wright savings algorithm assume that the base or anchor point is point 2. First give the formula for the computation of the savings

Table 8.15 Clarke and Wright tours

Route	Shortcut points	Savings	Length	Points
1	2		2	
2				
3				
4				
5				
6				
7				

using the notation of Table 8.12 and observing that point 2 is the base point. For the Clarke and Wright algorithm show the pairwise savings with respect to the anchor or base point in Table 8.14. Show the savings based on points i and j ($j>i$) in matrix element [i,j]. Not all rows and columns in the table have to be computed or filled in!

Write the formula that determines which points first form a shortcut on the tour, observing that point 2 is the base point. Assume that all points that not yet have been part of a shortcut and are not the base point are collected in a set F. Assume that the end points of the tour segment that has been rearranged with the shortcuts have indices p and q, respectively. Further assume that the base point has index b. Write the formula that determines which point will next form a shortcut on the tour.

For the Clarke and Wright savings algorithm, show chronologically the tour that you construct. First, show the length of the tour before any shortcut is made in row 1 of Table 8.15. Then compute and show for each iteration: the point for which you found the shortcut, the savings for the shortcut, the length of the tour after the shortcut, and the sequence of all the points on the tour that have been so far part of a shortcut. In other words, you do not have to list the points that are by themselves on the out and back segments. For row 2, and row 2 only, two points are part of the first shortcut. Give both these points of the first shortcut in the column with "Shortcut Points".

TSP Exercise 2

Consider the problem of finding the shortest distance cycle through the following six delivery points, given that the cycle visits each delivery point exactly once. The coordinates of the six delivery points are given in Table 8.16.

Table 8.16 Delivery point coordinates for exercise 2

#	x	y
1	200	900
2	900	200
3	400	300
4	100	100
5	300	600
6	800	700

Table 8.17 Delivery points distance table for exercise 2

Table 8.18 Insertion penalties on the Convex Hull

Table 8.19 Clarke and Wright savings

	1	2	3	4	5	6
1						
2						
3						
4						
5						
6						

Table 8.20 Heuristics summary statistics

Heuristic	Chronological sequence	Delivery sequence	Length	Ratio
NN				
Sweep				
CH+FI				
CW				

The travel distances between each pair of delivery points can be approximated with the Euclidean distance norm rounded to the nearest integer value. Compute and show the distances in upper triangular format in Table 8.17.

Compute heuristic delivery sequences with the Nearest Neighbor (NN), Sweep, Convex Hull followed by Priciest Insertion (CH+FI), and Clarke and Wright (CW) savings algorithms. For the Nearest Neighbor algorithm the starting point is point 3. For the Sweep algorithm assume that the rotation center is located at coordinates (500, 500), the starting angle for the rotation ray is due east, and the rotation direction is clockwise. For the Clarke and Wright savings algorithm assume that the base or anchor point is point 6.

For the Convex Hull and Priciest Insertion algorithm show the insertion penalties for all points not on the convex hull after the convex hull has been determined in Table 8.18. Each row corresponds to an unvisited point and each column corresponds to an edge on the partial tour. Separate the insertion penalties for each iteration of the Priciest Insertion algorithm by a blank row from the lines for the next iteration. Clearly label your rows and columns. Not all rows and columns in the table have to be used.

Table 8.21 Point
coordinates

Point	x	y
0	0	0
1	9	9
2	3	5
3	4	3
4	1	9
5	2	1
6	5	6
7	9	2

For the Clarke and Wright algorithm show the pairwise savings with respect to the anchor point in Table 8.19. Show the savings based on points i and j ($j>i$) in matrix element $[i,j]$. Not all rows and columns in the table have to be computed.

For each algorithm give the chronological sequence in which you inserted or appended the points (starting with the base point or initial tour if applicable) and the delivery sequence starting with point 1. The chronological sequence is the sequence in which the points are added to the tour, i.e., which point is added first, second, third, etc. The delivery sequence is the sequence in which the points are visited by the tour. For example, is you inserted a point k between points i and j already on the tour, in the chronological sequence point k would be the last point so far in the delivery sequence there would be a segment of points i, then k, and then j. For each heuristic compute the tour length and the ratio of the tour length divided by the length of the best tour you have found. Summarize your answer in the Table 8.20.

Is the tour generated by the Convex Hull followed by Priciest Insertion algorithm guaranteed to be optimal? Base your answer only on the results of executing the Convex Hull and Priciest Insertion (CH+FI) algorithm. Give your answer in a few succinct sentences.

TSP Exercise 3

You are asked to route the crane in a person-aboard order picking system so that the distance traveled by the crane to pick up seven line items for the current customer

Table 8.22 Order picking
bins distance table

	0	1	2	3	4	5	6	7
0								
1								
2								
3								
4								
5								
6								
7								

Table 8.23 Nearest neighbor route construction

Index	Anchor point	Append point	Append distance
1			
2			
3			
4			
5			
6			
7			
8			
Total			

Table 8.24 Sweep route construction

Index	Anchor point	Append point	Append distance
1			
2			
3			
4			
5			
6			
7			
8			
Total			

order is minimized. The cabin with the order picker can move simultaneously up and down the mast of the crane while the crane moves back and forth in the order picking aisle. Therefore, the Chebyshev travel norm is judged an acceptable approximation to compute the travel distance of the crane. The crane starts and ends its picking route at the pickup and deposit (PD) station at lower front corner of the rack. The coordinates of the PD station and the seven bins storing the line items are given in Table 8.21, where the index of the PD station is zero.

Table 8.25 Insertion penalties table structure

Point	Tour edges			
	(a-b)	(b-c)	(c-d)	(d-a)
e				
f				
g				

Point	(a-b)	(b-f)	(f-c)	(c-d)	(d-a)
e					
g					

Table 8.26 Insertion penalties for priciest insertion

Point	Tour edges

Table 8.27 Clarke and Wright savings

	0	1	2	3	4	5	6	7
0								
1								
2								
3								
4								
5								
6								
7								

First show the formula for the distance norm using the notation of Table 8.21 and point indices i and j. Then compute and show the distances in upper triangular format in Table 8.22.

Next, compute heuristic picking sequences with the Nearest Neighbor (NN), Sweep (SW), Convex Hull followed by Priciest Insertion (CH + PI), and Clarke and Wright (CW) savings algorithms. For the Nearest Neighbor algorithm, the starting point is the PD station. For the Sweep algorithm, assume that the rotation center is located at PD station, the starting angle for the rotation ray is due east, and the rotation direction is counter-clockwise. Break any point selection or sequencing ties by selecting the point with the lowest index and any link selection ties by selecting the link first encountered on the tour.

For the Convex Hull, use the point sequence that follows a counter-clockwise direction. For the Convex Hull and Priciest Insertion algorithm show the insertion penalties for all points not on the convex hull after the convex hull has been determined in Table 8.26. Each row corresponds to an unvisited point and each column corresponds to an edge on the partial tour. Separate the insertion penalties for each

Table 8.28 Clarke and Wright tours

	Shortcut		Length	Points
Route	Points	Savings		
1	0		0	
2				
3				
4				
5				
6				
7				

iteration of the Priciest Insertion algorithm by a blank row from the lines for the next iteration. Clearly label your rows and columns. Not all rows and columns in the table have to be used! An example of the table structure is shown in Table 8.25, where the tour consists of points {a, b, c, d}, the remaining free points are {e, f, g} and in the first iteration point {f} is inserted on the link (b-c). This table shows the structure only, is not complete, and you should not modify this table in any way.

Compute heuristic delivery sequence with the Clarke and Wright (CW) savings algorithm. For the Clarke and Wright savings algorithm assume that the base or anchor point is the PD station. First, give the formula for the computation of the savings using the notation of Table 8.21 and observing that the PD station is the base point. For the Clarke and Wright algorithm show the pair-wise savings with respect to the anchor or base point in Table 8.27. Show the savings based on points i and j ($j > i$) in matrix element [i,j]. Not all rows and columns in the table have to be computed or filled in!

Write the formula that determines which points first form a shortcut on the tour, observing that PD station is the base point. Assume that all points that not yet have been part of a shortcut and are not the base point are collected in a set F (indicating Free points). Assume that the end points of the tour segment, that has been rearranged with the shortcuts, have indices p and q, respectively. Further assume that the base point has index b. Write the formula that determines which point will next form a shortcut on the tour. For the Clarke and Wright savings algorithm, show chronologically the tour that you construct. First, show the length of the tour before any shortcut is made in row 1 of Table 8.28. Then compute and show for each iteration the point for which you found the shortcut, the savings for the shortcut, the

Table 8.29 Heuristics summary statistics

Heuristic	Chrono-logical sequence	Delivery sequence	Length	Ratio
NN				
Sweep				
CH + PI				
CW				

length of the tour after the shortcut, and the sequence of all the points on the tour that so far have been part of a shortcut. In other words, you do not have to list the points that are by themselves on the out and back segments. For row 2, and row 2 only, two points are part of the first shortcut. Give both these points of the first shortcut in the column with title "Shortcut Points."

Finally, for each algorithm, give the chronological sequence in which you inserted or appended the points (starting with the base point or initial tour if applicable) and the delivery sequence starting with the PD station. The chronological sequence is the sequence in which the points are added to the tour, i.e., which point is added first, second, third, etc. The delivery sequence is the sequence in which the points are visited by the tour. For example, is you inserted a point k between points i and j already on the tour, in the chronological sequence point k would be the last point so far in the delivery sequence there would be a segment of points i, then k, and then j. For each heuristic compute the tour length and the ratio of the tour length divided by the length of the best tour you have found. Summarize your answer in the Table 8.29.

References

Publications

Akl, S. G., & Toussaint, G. T. (1978). "A fast convex hull algorithm". *Information Processing Letters, 7*(5), 219–222.

Allison, D. C., & Noga, M. T. (1984). "The L_1 traveling salesman problem". *Information Processing Letters, 18*(4), 195–199.

Applegate, D. L., (2005), "The traveling salesman problem," *Chapter 58 in A. Schrijver Combinatorial Optimization: Polyhedra and Efficiency*, Springer Verlag, Berlin.

Applegate, D. L., Bixby, R. E., Chvatal, V., & Cook, W. J. (2006). *The traveling salesman problem: A computational study*. Princeton: Princeton University Press.

Ball, M. O., Magnanti, T. L., Monma, C. L., & Nemhauser, G. L. (Eds.). (1995). *Network routing*. Amsterdam: Elsevier.

Bazaraa, M. S., Jarvis, J. J., & Sherali, H. D. (2005). *Linear programming and network flows* (3rd ed.). Hoboken: Wiley.

Bellmore, M., & Nemhauser, G. L. (1968). "The traveling salesman problem: A survey". *Operations Research, 16*(3), 538–558.

Boyd, S. C., Pulleyblank, W. R., & Cornuejols, G. (1987). "TRAVEL—An interactive traveling salesman problem package for the IBM personal computer". *Operations Research Letters, 6*(3), 141–143.

Christofides, N., & Eilon, S. (1972). "Algorithms for large-scale traveling salesman problems". *Operations Research Quarterly, 23,* 511–518.

Christofides, N. (1975). *Graph theory: An algorithmic approach*. New York: Academic Press.

Cook, W. (2004). "Traveling salesman tour illustrations". www.isye.gatech.edu/faculty-staff.

Clarke, G., & Wright, J. (1964). "Scheduling of vehicles from a Central Depot to a Number of Delivery Points". *Operations Research, 12,* 568–581.

Dantzig, G. B., Fulkerson, D. R., & Johnson, S. M. (1954). "Solution of a large-scale traveling salesman problem". *Operations Research, 2,* 393–410.

Gillett, B., & Miller, L. (1974) "A heuristic algorithm for the vehicle dispatch problem". *Operations Research, 22,* 340–349.

Golden, B. L., Bodin, L., Doyle, T., & Stewart, W. Jr. (1980). "Approximate traveling salesman algorithms". *Operations Research, 28*(3), 694–711.

Glover, F. (1989). "Tabu search—Part I". *ORSA Journal on Computing, 1*(3) 190–206.

Glover, F. (1990). "Tabu search—Part II". *ORSA Journal on Computing, 2*(1), 4–32.

Helbig Hansen, K., & Krarup, J. (1974). "Improvements on the Held-Karp algorithm for the symmetric traveling salesman problem". *Mathematical Programming, 7,* 87–96.

Held, M., & Karp, R. M. (1970). "The traveling-salesman problem and minimum spanning trees". *Operations Research, 18*(6), 1138–1162.

Held, M., & Karp, R. M. (1971). "The traveling-salesman problem and minimum spanning trees: Part II". *Mathematical Programming, 1,* 6–25.

Kirkpatrick, S., Gelat, C., & Vechi, M. (1983). *Science, 220,* 671–680.

Kruskal, J. B. (1956). "On the shortest spanning subtree of a graph and the traveling salesman problem". *Proceedings of the American Mathematical Society, 7*(1), 48–50.

Laporte, G. (1992). "The traveling salesman problem: An overview of exact and approximate algorithms". *European Journal of Operational Research, 59,* 231–247.

Lawler, E. L., Lenstra, J. K., Rinnooy Kan, A. H. G., & Schmoys, D. B. (1985). *The traveling salesman problem.* Chichester: Wiley.

Lin, S., & Kernighan, B. (1973) "An effective heuristic algorithm for the traveling salesman problem". *Operations Research, 21,* 498–516.

Lin, S. (1965). "Computer solutions of the traveling salesman problem". *Bell System Technical Journal, 44,* 2245–2269.

Little, J. D., Murty, K. G., Sweeney, D. W., & Karel, C. (1963). "An algorithm for the traveling salesman problem". *Operations Research, 11*(6), 972–989.

Miller, C. E., Tucker, A. W., & Zemlin, R. A. (1960) "Integer programming formulations and traveling salesman problems". *Journal of the Association of Computing Machinery, 7,* 326–329.

Or, I. (1976). "Traveling salesman-type combinatorial problems and their relation to the logistics of regional blood banking". Unpublished Ph.D. Dissertation, Northwestern University, Evanston.

Parker, R. G., & Rardin, R. L. (1983). "The traveling salesman problem: An update of research". *Naval Research Logistics Quarterly, 30,* 69–99.

Platzman, L. K., & Bartholdi, III, J. J. (1984). "Space-filling curves and the planar traveling salesman problem". PDRC Report Series 83-02, School of Industrial and Systems Engineering, Georgia Institute of Technology.

Prim, R. C. (1957). "Shortest connection networks and some generalizations". *Bell System Technical Journal, 36,* 1389–1401.

Rooney, B. (2007). "UPS figures out the 'Right Way' to save money, Time and Gas". abcnews. com. Accessed 4 April 2007.

Rosenkrantz, D. J., Stearns, R. E., & Lewis, P. M. (1977). "An analysis of several heuristics for the traveling salesman problem". *SIAM Journal of Computing, 6,* 563–581.

Smith T. H., & Thompson, G. L. (1977). "A LIFO implicit enumeration search algorithm for the symmetric traveling salesman problem using Held and Karp's 1-tree relaxation". *Annals of Discrete Mathematics, 1,* 479–493.

Thomasson, D. (2001). http://www.borderschess.org. Accessed 10 Jun 2011.

Vechi, M., & Kirkpatrick, S. (1983). *IEEE Transactions on Computer Aided Design* (Vol. CAD-2, p. 215).

Volgenant, T., & Jonker, R. (1982). "A branch and bound algorithm for the symmetric traveling salesman problem based on the 1-tree relaxation". *European Journal of Operations Research, 9,* 83–89.

Programs

Tours. (1993). Marc Goetschalckx. http://www.isye.gatech.edu/people/faculty/Marc_ Goetschalckx.

Concorde, (2005), William Cook, http://www.tsp.gatech.edu/concorde.html, Accessed 10 Jun 2011.

Chapter 9
Vehicle Routing and Scheduling

Learning Objectives After you have studied this chapter, you should:

- Know the classification system for vehicle routing problems and algorithms.
- Know the following for each of the classes of vehicle routing and scheduling problems:
- The characteristics of the base problem and its variants.
- The mathematical formulation.
- Simple solution algorithms.
- How to solve problems of modest size with a computer program.

9.1 Introduction

9.1.1 Vehicle Routing Problem

One of the most common problems in transportation planning is the management of a fleet of vehicles that are used to provide transportation services. The transportation services either pick up or deliver passengers or goods from or to a number of locations. The transportation operations are subject to a number of constraints such as vehicle capacity, limitations on the trip time and delivery times, precedence constraints, and service constraints. Vehicle capacity can be with respect to weight, or volume, or both. The limitations on delivery times are called time windows and can include or exclude times when deliveries can be made. The total length of time a roundtrip can take may also be limited. Finally, precedence constraints require that certain stops are made before others. Examples are the vehicle routing problem with backhauling where for each individual route all deliveries have to be made before the first pickup, and the dial-a-ride problem where goods have to be picked up before they can be delivered. Service constraints such as percentage of inventory on the shelf in vendor-managed inventory systems or a minimum number of visits per planning horizon in periodic routing systems create the additional decision variables for which customer locations to serve. In addition to the operational routing

M. Goetschalckx, *Supply Chain Engineering,* International Series in Operations Research & Management Science,
DOI 10.1007/978-1-4419-6512-7_9, © Springer Science+Business Media, LLC 2011

and scheduling problem, on the tactical level the size and composition of the fleet of transportation vehicles has to be determined. The algorithms presented here are focusing on the most generic and simple versions of the routing problem.

Vehicle Routing Decisions At the operational level two types of decisions have to be made. The first type of decisions is the assignment of customers or transportation requests are to be serviced by a vehicle. The second type of decision is the determination of the sequence of stops for each vehicle. The number and sizes of vehicles that are available is a constraint at the operational level. At the tactical level the decisions are on how many and what size and type of vehicles to have in the fleet.

9.1.2   Vehicle Routing Variants

The prevalence of transportation operations combined with the large variety of real-world constraints and characteristics have created a multitude of vehicle routing problems. A small fraction of the possible variants is described below.

Traveling Salesman Problem (TSP) The TSP is the simplest of the vehicle routing problems since it involves the routing of a single vehicle without any capacity constraints. This problem has been analyzed extensively in the previous section. The TSP problem arises frequently as the second-stage problem in cluster-first, route-second algorithms for multiple vehicle routing problems, when in the first stage requests have been assigned in a feasible manner to individual vehicles.

Vehicle Routing Problem (VRP) This is the classic variant of the vehicle routing problem. A number of customers with known locations and known demand have to be serviced by a fleet of vehicles of identical capacity and that all start and have to return to a single depot. The objective is to minimize the total length of the routes that are executed.

Vehicle Routing Problem with Backhauling (VRPB) or Linehaul-Backhaul In this variant there are two types of locations that have to be visited. The first type are customers to which goods have to be delivered; the second type are suppliers from which goods have to be picked up. Because of vehicle limitations and the requirement of simple operations at the stops, all customers have to be delivered before any pickups can be made on any route. The most common example is delivery and pickup with rear-loaded long-haul trailers that are used in the United States. The savings of limiting the number of miles that are driven with an empty trailer after all deliveries have been made must be balanced against the additional complexity of having deliveries preceding pickups on every route.

Mixed Pickup and Delivery Problem If there are two type of locations to be visited but deliveries to customers and pickups from suppliers can be intermixed, then the problem is called the mixed pickup and delivery problem. This variant arises when the operations are executed by side-loaded trucks such as soft-drink and beer delivery trucks in the United States and soft-sided trucks used in Europe. It is assumed that all quantities to be delivered are loaded on the vehicle at the depot before its route is started. If the vehicle picks up goods or passengers and delivers them on the same trip, the variant is often called the dial-a-ride problem. This name originates from a common example, where patients call a local transportation service that picks them up and drops them off so that they can attend medical appointments. In this case, each service request has a pickup location that must be visited before its drop off location. At the same time, vehicle capacity constraints must be observed during the entire trip.

Vehicle Routing with Time Windows (VRPTW) In this variant the classic VRP is extended by the additional specification of the allowable time interval for the start of service for each customer. The time windows can be hard or soft. In the case of a hard time window, a vehicle can arrive at the customer location early and is permitted to wait until the start of the service time window. However, a vehicle is not allowed to arrive after the closure of the service time window. In the case of a soft time window, the service interval can be violated with a certain penalty.

Inventory Vehicle Routing (IRP) In this variant the objective is to minimize the sum of the transportation cost by the vehicles and the holding inventory cost while avoiding stock-outs and observing the storage capacity limitations. An example of a multicommodity IRP is the dispatching and routing of tanker trucks to resupply gasoline sales stations from a local fuel farm. In the United States, typically three grades of fuel are sold by the gas stations and resupplied by the tanker trucks. Under normal situations, running out of a grade of gasoline at a station has to be avoided because of the loss of revenue and goodwill. Both the stations and the tanker trucks have a limited capacity for each of the grades of fuel.

9.1.3   *Vehicle Routing Algorithms Classification*

The algorithms for solving a vehicle routing problem can be classified depending on their most important resource requirements. For VRP algorithm the two primary resource requirements are the amount of input data and the amount of computational resources, i.e., computation time.

Algorithm Classification by Required Input Data In general, an *alternative-generating* algorithm creates feasible solutions from the basic problem data. For the VRP, the basic problem data consist of the number and demand quantities of the customers, the number and capacity of the vehicles, and the location of all the facilities or alternatively the pairwise distances between the facilities. An *alternative-selecting* algorithm assembles the solution of the highest quality from a set of feasible candidate solutions provided to it as input data. In the context of vehicle routing, the feasible solutions or candidate solutions are feasible vehicle routes.

Because the VRP is a common and significant problem in the planning of vehicle operations, a large variety of route-generating algorithms have been developed. These algorithms can be specific for the VRP or optimization based such as solution algorithms for the Generalized Assignment Problem (GAP). In general, route-generating algorithms have been most successful when the VRP is tightly capacitated and the routing cost can be computed with sufficient accuracy from the distances between the facilities. The solution algorithms for the Set Partitioning Problem (SPP) are the prime example of route-selecting algorithms. These solution algorithms have been implemented with success when the cost or constraint structures of the problem are complex. Feasible candidate routes are either generated based on the experience of the dispatcher or drivers or by an automated column generation procedure. Each column represents a feasible candidate alternative in the SPP and a feasible route in the VRP.

Algorithm Classification by Their Basic Methodology Specific solution algorithms for the VRP have been developed by practitioners, routing software designers, and academic researchers. These algorithms can be either ad hoc heuristics or optimization-based. The use of optimal algorithms has been restricted to small problems or very specialized applications. The difference in solution quality between comprehensive heuristic algorithms and optimal algorithms has not been sufficient to warrant the vastly longer execution times of the optimal algorithms. The use of artificial intelligence-based heuristics in vehicle routing software has been very rare.

9.2 Classic Vehicle Routing (VRP)

VRP Definition The classic vehicle routing problem is the simplest variant of routing problems for multiple vehicles. The problem has a single depot and N customer facilities with known locations. The amount of goods to be delivered to each customer, also called the demand, is known with certainty. There are K identical vehicles available with a known vehicle carrying capacity. Each vehicle starts at the depot, can execute a single route, and returns to the depot. Each customer can only be visited by a single vehicle, in other words the single sourcing service constraint applies. The objective is to deliver the required demand to each customer at the minimal cost. The cost is proportional to the total distance traveled by all the vehicles. Finally, the distance between facilities is based on the Euclidean distance norm and is thus symmetrical and satisfies the triangle inequality. The triangle inequality assures that the direct travel between two points has the shortest travel distance between those two points.

Vehicle Routing Example (VRP8) The following example will be used to illustrate all the algorithms for the VRP. This example has eight delivery facilities or customers and it will be denoted in all following tables and figures as VRP8. The distances are based on the Euclidean distance norm without any adjustment factor and then rounded to the nearest integer value. The facility data and distance data are shown in Tables 9.1 and 9.2 and the facility locations are shown in Fig. 9.1. In the figure, the top index for each facility is the facility label and the bottom index

Table 9.1 VRP8 facility data

Label	X-Coord.	Y-Coord.	Quant.
c1	2,440	1,794	23
c2	2,844	2,820	28
c3	1,434	3,669	32
c4	372	1,745	37
c5	1,592	2,077	31
c6	3,257	873	57
c7	663	2,877	46
c8	929	453	41
d1	1,164	1,083	0

Table 9.2 VRP8 facility distances

	c1	c2	c3	c4	c5	c6	c7	c8	d1
c1	0	1,103	2,128	2,069	894	1,231	2,081	2,020	1,461
c2	1,103	0	1,646	2,696	1,456	1,990	2,182	3,045	2,417
c3	2,128	1,646	0	2,198	1,600	3,338	1,105	3,255	2,600
c4	2,069	2,696	2,198	0	1,264	3,014	1,169	1,407	1,032
c5	894	1,456	1,600	1,264	0	2,055	1,226	1,754	1,082
c6	1,231	1,990	3,338	3,014	2,055	0	3,278	2,366	2,104
c7	2,081	2,182	1,105	1,169	1,226	3,278	0	2,439	1,863
c8	2,020	3,045	3,255	1,407	1,754	2,366	2,439	0	672
d1	1,461	2,417	2,600	1,032	1,082	2,104	1,863	672	0

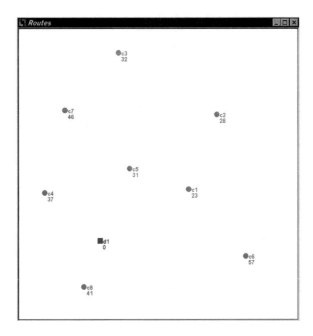

Fig. 9.1 VRP8 facility locations and demand

indicates the demand. The depot facility is indicated by $d1$. There are three vehicles available, each with a capacity of 120, and it is assumed that each vehicle can only execute a single route.

Number of Vehicles The maximum number of vehicles is typically an input parameter specified by the user. If each vehicle can only a single route, the maximum number of routes is equal to the maximum number of vehicles. The constraint that a vehicle can only execute a single route is often caused by the loading operations. The following example describes typical operations at a distribution center in the United States when deliveries are made by rear-loaded vehicles. Customer orders may be accepted until 8:00 PM of the preceding day. The dispatchers or vehicle routing software determines a set of routes by 10:00 PM and the a warehouse management system determines a set or order picking routes inside the warehouse. From 10:00 PM to 6:00 AM of the delivery day, order pickers collect the products of the warehouse and load the trucks in the reserve order of the vehicle stops for each vehicle. Even if a vehicle returns early in the day to the distribution center, the infrastructure to load this vehicle for another route is not available.

The first quantity to be determined in solving the routing problem is the minimum number of routes required to service all customer demands. This minimum number must be less than or equal to the maximum number of routes for the problem to have a feasible solution.

The following notation will be used throughout the discussion on vehicle routing.

dem_i quantity to be delivered to customer facility i, $i = 1,...,N$

cap_k capacity of vehicle k, $k = 1,...,K$. The subscript is omitted if all vehicles have equal capacity

c_{ijk} cost for vehicle k to travel from customer i to customer j. If the cost is used with only two subscripts, it is assumed that costs are identical for all vehicles and only depend on the facilities.

vc_k cost of using vehicle k in the solution

x_i, y_i location coordinates of facility i

z_{ik} is equal to 1 if customer i is assigned to vehicle k, zero otherwise

z_{0k}, z_k is equal to 1 if vehicle k is used, zero otherwise. The notation with a single subscript is used if there is no confusion possible with the customer assignment variables.

If all the vehicles have the same capacity, the fleet is said to be homogeneous. A lower bound on the required number of routes for a homogeneous fleet is given by

$$\text{min } \# \; routes = \left\lceil \frac{\sum\limits_{i=1}^{N} dem_i}{cap} \right\rceil \tag{9.1}$$

where $\lceil x \rceil$ indicates the smallest integer greater than or equal to x and which is called the ceiling function.

The maximum number of routes in the VRP8 example is equal to 3, since there are three vehicles that each can execute a single route. The minimum number of routes in this example is equal to

$$\text{min \# } routes = \left\lceil \frac{\sum_{i=1}^{N} dem_i}{cap} \right\rceil = \left\lceil \frac{295}{120} \right\rceil = \lceil 2.46 \rceil = 3$$

In the example all the vehicles will be used by a feasible set of routes. The average vehicle utilization is $2.46/3 = 82\%$.

The above formula is valid if all the vehicles have an identical capacity. If the fleet has vehicles of different types, a GAP formulation can be used to determine the number of vehicles of each type. In the following formulation vehicles of different types have a different cost and capacity. If we are only interested in determining the minimum number of vehicles then all costs coefficients c_k can be set equal to 1. This formulation is a variant of the Assignment Problem (AP) called the generalized assignment, since the coefficients dem_i of the assignment variables z_{ik} in the capacity constraints are different from one. The objective of the formulation is to determine which vehicles have to be used in order to minimize the total cost of using delivery vehicles while observing the single sourcing constraints.

Formulation 9.1. Fleet Sizing GAP Formulation

$$\min \quad \sum_{k} vc_k \cdot z_{0k}$$

$$s.t. \quad \sum_{i=1}^{N} dem_i \cdot z_{ik} \leq cap_k \cdot z_{0k} \quad \forall k$$

$$\sum_{k=1}^{K} z_{ik} = 1 \quad \forall i \tag{9.2}$$

$$z_{0k} \in \{0, 1\}, z_{ik} \in \{0, 1\}$$

This formulation illustrates that the GAP is focused on the capacity and the number of vehicles, rather than focused on finding the minimum distance traveled.

For the VRP8 example, the detailed GAP formulation is given by

Listing 9.1 Algebraic Formulation of the Heterogeneous Fleet Size Problem for the VRP8 Example

$Min \quad z_{01} + z_{02} + z_{03}$

$s.t. \quad 23z_{11} + 28z_{21} + 32z_{31} + 37z_{41} + 31z_{51} + 57z_{61} + 46z_{71} + 41z_{81} \leq 120z_{01}$

$\qquad 23z_{12} + 28z_{22} + 32z_{32} + 37z_{42} + 31z_{52} + 57z_{62} + 46z_{72} + 41z_{82} \leq 120z_{02}$

$\qquad 23z_{13} + 28z_{23} + 32z_{33} + 37z_{43} + 31z_{53} + 57z_{63} + 46z_{73} + 41z_{83} \leq 120z_{03}$

$\qquad z_{11} + z_{12} + z_{13} = 1$

$\qquad z_{21} + z_{22} + z_{23} = 1$

$\qquad z_{31} + z_{32} + z_{33} = 1$

$\qquad z_{41} + z_{42} + z_{43} = 1$

$\qquad z_{51} + z_{52} + z_{53} = 1$

$\qquad z_{61} + z_{62} + z_{63} = 1$

$\qquad z_{71} + z_{72} + z_{73} = 1$

$\qquad z_{81} + z_{82} + z_{83} = 1$

$\qquad \forall z \in \{0, 1\}$

When this formulation is solved, many alternative optimal solutions are possible, but all have an objective function value equal to three routes. If the explicit integrality requirement is removed from the variables, which implies that single sourcing is no longer required, then the optimal linear solution value is 2.458. The integrality gap is thus 0.542 or 18.07% and a mixed-integer solver is required to obtain an integer solution. The linear programming solution is exactly the fractional solution found by the ratio method for the homogeneous fleet. The z variables at optimality are $\{1.000, 0.758, 0.700\}$ and one possible set of customer assignments at optimality is $\{2 + 3 + 7(40\%) + 8, 1 + 4 + 5, 6 + 7(60\%)\}$ which results in vehicle loads of $\{120, 91, 84\}$, respectively. Note that the delivery of the demand of customer 7 is split over two routes. Clearly using a GAP formulation to solve a fleet sizing question where all the vehicles have equal capacity and equal cost is only warranted when each customer has to be assigned completely to a single route. In other words, the *single sourcing* service level constraint must be satisfied and this makes the solution of the VRP significantly harder since it requires that the z variables take only binary values. This in turn requires the use of a mixed-integer programming solver.

One indication of the difficulty of finding a set of routes for a particular problem instance is the average utilization of the vehicles, which is computed as the ratio of the total demand divided by the total capacity and is denoted by $\bar{\rho}$. A similar indicator of the difficulty of finding a set of routes is the average slack capacity on the vehicles. The average slack capacity, denoted by $\bar{s}$, is computed as the difference between the vehicle capacity and the average vehicle load, which is denoted by $\bar{q}$. For the case of vehicles of equal size, these characteristics can be computed with the following formulas. For the case of a heterogeneous fleet the expected vehicle load and expected slack capacity have different values for each individual vehicle. The average slack capacity can be compared with the average customer demand to determine if it will be easy to add an additional customer to an average route. The statistics for the case of the homogeneous fleet can be computed with the following formulas.

$$\bar{\rho} = \frac{\sum_i dem_i}{K \cdot cap} \tag{9.3}$$

$$\bar{q} = \rho \cdot cap = \frac{\sum_i dem_i}{K} \tag{9.4}$$

$$\bar{s} = cap - \bar{q} \tag{9.5}$$

The statistics for the case of an heterogeneous fleet can be computed with the following formulas.

$$\bar{\rho} = \frac{\sum_i dem_i}{\sum_k cap_k} \tag{9.6}$$

$$\bar{q_k} = \rho \cdot cap_k = \frac{\sum_i dem_i}{\sum_k cap_k} cap_k \tag{9.7}$$

$$\bar{s_k} = cap_k - \bar{q_k} \tag{9.8}$$

The values of the VRP8 example are computed next.

$$\bar{\rho} = \frac{\sum_i dem_i}{K \cdot cap} = \frac{295}{3 \cdot 120} = 0.82$$

$$\bar{q} = \rho \cdot cap = \frac{\sum_i dem_i}{K} = \frac{295}{3} = 98.3$$

$$\bar{s} = cap - \bar{q} = 120 - 98.3 = 21.7$$

$$\overline{dem_i} = \frac{\sum_{i=1}^{N} dem_i}{N} = \frac{295}{8} = 36.9$$

Since the average demand of 36.9 is larger than the average slack capacity on a vehicle of 21.7, it will be difficult to improve the routes by just moving a customer to a different route. Route improvement algorithms that attempt to reduce the total route length by swapping two customers between two routes will have a better change for route improvement than improvement algorithms that rely on moving a customer to another route. The above calculations and algorithm selection are another illustration of the progression in a project from data, to information and finally to knowledge. The data on the customer and vehicle characteristics constitute the data, the different average statistics represent the problem information, and the choice of improvement algorithm corresponds to the knowledge about this particular VRP instance.

9.2.1 Route-Generation Algorithms for the Classic VRP

In this section, a number of route-generation algorithms are presented. These algorithms create a solution composed of feasible routes. They require the problem data and may also require a partial or full initial set of routes. Route-selection algorithms will be discussed in the next section. The prominent example of route-selection algorithms is set partitioning. Route-selection algorithms require a list of feasible candidate routes and assemble a solution from the candidates.

Similar to the case of the TSP, the route-generation algorithms for the VRP can be further divided into route-construction and route-improvement algorithms. Route-construction algorithms that will be described are nearest neighbor and the savings algorithm by Clarke and Wright. Route-improvement algorithm that will be discussed are 2-opt, 3-opt, and chain-opt intraroute improvement algorithms and move and swap interroute improvement algorithms. Several construction algorithms have two distinct steps. In one phase the customer facilities are assigned to vehicles based on their demands and the vehicle capacity. This phase is called the clustering or assignment phase. In another phase, the facilities are routed based on their interfacility distances, but their demand and vehicle capacity are ignored. This phase is called the routing or sequencing phase. Based on which phase is executed first and on the algorithms used for each phase, many different algorithms have been developed. Algorithms that have this two-phase structure are the two variants of the sweep algorithm, giant tour algorithm, and the generalized assignment algorithm.

Nearest Neighbor Algorithm The nearest neighbor algorithm starts a new route at the depot and travels next to the closest unvisited customer. If the vehicle capacity is sufficient, then this customer is added to the route and the vehicle continues to travel to the next closest unvisited customer. If adding that customer to the route would violate the truck capacity, the route is terminated and the vehicle returns to the depot. The vehicle then starts a new route at the depot if the maximum number of routes has not been reached.

VPP8 Nearest Neighbor Example The closest customer to the depot is customer $c8$, which has a distance of 672 units. The vehicle load after visiting customer $c8$ is equal to 41. The closest unvisited customer to customer $c8$ is customer $c4$ with a distance of 1,407. The demand of customer $c4$ is 37 units so the total demand would be 78 units and not violate the truck capacity of 120. Customer $c4$ is added to the route. The closest unvisited customer to customer $c4$ is customer $c7$ with a distance of 1,169. However, the demand of customer $c7$ is 46 units and the total demand would be 124, which would violate the truck capacity of 120. Hence, customer $c7$ is not added to the route. The vehicle returns to the depot after customer $c4$ and the

Table 9.3 VRP8 nearest neighbor algorithm steps

Index	Anchor point	Append point	Append distance	Vehicle quantity
1	$d1$	$c8$	672	41
2	$c8$	$c4$	1,407	78
3	$d1$	$c5$	1,082	31
4	$c5$	$c1$	894	54
5	$c1$	$c2$	1,103	82
6	$c2$	$c3$	1,646	114
7	$d1$	$c7$	1,863	46
8	$c7$	$c6$	3,278	103

Table 9.4 VRP8 nearest neighbor routes summary

Route	Facility							Quantity	Length
	0	1	2	3	4	5	6		
1	$d1$	$c8$	$c4$	$d1$				78	3,111
2	$d1$	$c5$	$c1$	$c2$	$c3$	$d1$		114	7,325
3	$d1$	$c7$	$c6$	$d1$				103	7,245
Total								295	17,681

length of this route equals 3,112. Observe that customer $c5$ is the next closest customer to customer $c4$ with a distance of 1,264 and a demand of 31, so customer $c5$ could have been added to the partial route after customer $c4$, but this action is not considered since the nearest neighbor is a greedy algorithm. Since there is currently only one route out of a maximum of three possible routes a new route is started. The algorithm continues until all customers have been routed. The algorithm steps are summarized in Table 9.3. Notice again the large travel distance 3,278 for the step to append the last customer $c6$. This behavior is typical for the myopic or greedy nearest neighbor algorithm. The routes created by the nearest neighbor algorithm are shown in Table 9.4 and Fig. 9.2.

Clarke and Wright Savings The savings algorithm was originally introduced by Clarke and Wright (1964) and is known both as the savings and the Clarke and Wright algorithm. The savings algorithm is a construction procedure that extends a partial route or route primitive at its two endpoints. Conceptually the algorithm defines the depot as the base facility and constructs an Eulerian tour that visits each of the customer facilities and the returns to the depot. The Eulerian tour is then reduced in length by finding and executing the feasible shortcut with the largest savings. The savings are computed as the sum of the distances to depot of the two customers minus the distance between the two customers, provided the two customers can be combined to form a feasible route. Routes become infeasible when the total quantity exceeds the vehicle capacity. If the resulting route would not be feasible, the savings are set to negative infinity. The binary or pair wise savings for a feasible combination are computed as follows and a shortcut is illustrated Fig. 9.3.

Fig. 9.2 VRP8 nearest neighbor routes

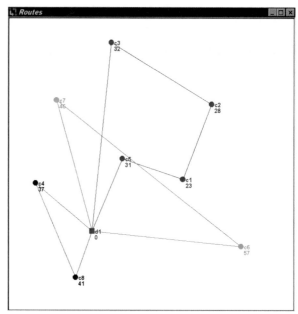

Fig. 9.3 Clarke and Wright shortcut illustration

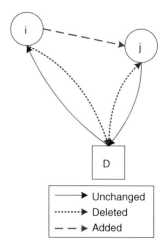

$$s_{ij} = c_{i0} + c_{0j} - c_{ij} \qquad (9.9)$$

The maximum number of routes, denoted by K, is an algorithm input parameter. The savings algorithm has been widely used for an extended period of time and a multitude of variants and derivative algorithms exist. The algorithm has both a serial and a parallel variant. The serial variant constructs one route at a time. In each step, either the current partial route is extended at its endpoints or a new partial route is

Fig. 9.4 Clarke and Wright
serial route extension
illustration

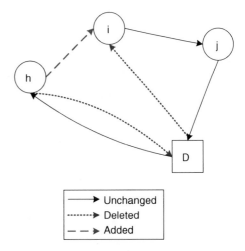

started. The parallel variant constructs up to K routes simultaneously. In each step, any of the current partial routes is extended at its endpoints, a new partial route is started, or two partial routes are combined. The parallel variant has more flexibility in constructing the routes but this flexibility comes at a significantly more complex implementation. This has resulted in more widely adaptation of the serial variant.

The savings algorithm is a greedy algorithm, so once two points have been joined by a shortcut they are never separated by the savings algorithm. Equivalently, once a partial route has been created, the sequence of the nodes on this route is not changed by the savings algorithm. The partial route can only be extended at its end facilities, which in turn are connected to the base point. In the serial variant, the next point h is then selected by finding the point with the largest savings shortcut to the current end points $\{i, j\}$ of the partial tour. See Fig. 9.4.

$$\max_{i,j} \left\{ \max_h \{s_{ih} = c_{i0} + c_{h0} - c_{ih}\} \right\} \tag{9.10}$$

The computations of the savings in the parallel variant of the savings algorithm are shown in the next figure. Note that only the savings associated with feasible short-cuts are computed. A route becomes infeasible when appending either a singleton facility or another partial route to it causes the combined demand to exceed the vehicle capacity. In Fig. 9.5, all the facilities starting with node j and ending with node k will always have the same sequence.

$$s_{ij} = (c_{i0} + c_{0j}) - c_{ij}$$
$$s_{km} = (c_{k0} + c_{0m}) - c_{km}$$

VRP8 Serial Savings Example The first step in the savings algorithm is to compute the savings for every feasible combination of two points. The computations for two of the pairs are shown next as an example.

Fig. 9.5 Parallel savings illustration

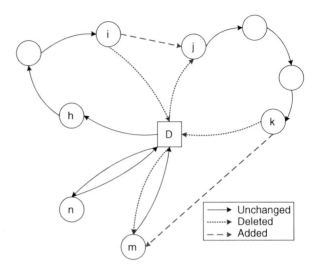

$$dem_1 + dem_2 = 23 + 28 = 51 \leq 120$$
$$s_{12} = d_{10} + d_{02} - d_{12} = 1461 + 2417 - 1103 = 2775$$
$$dem_5 + dem_8 = 31 + 41 = 72 \leq 120$$
$$s_{58} = d_{50} + d_{08} - d_{58} = 1082 + 672 - 1754 = 0$$

The savings can be organized into a two-dimensional table (Table 9.5). The rows of the matrix correspond to the origin node of the savings shortcut and the columns correspond to the destination node. In all the following calculations, these savings do not need to be recomputed but can be copied from this initial savings table. The matrix has one additional row and column. The values in the row and column with label Q indicate the quantity included on this route. In the initial savings table, all facilities are considered to be on singleton routes, so these quantities are equal to the customer demands.

The pair with the largest savings that forms a feasible partial tour is selected. In this example, pair $c2$–$c3$ is selected with maximum savings of 3,371. If ties exist for the maximum savings, then selecting the pair with maximum savings by increasing indices arbitrarily breaks the ties. The partial tour ($c2$–$c3$) of nodes $c2$ followed by

Table 9.5 Pair-wise savings for the VRP8 example

	$c1$	$c2$	$c3$	$c4$	$c5$	$c6$	$c7$	$c8$	Q
$c1$		2,775	1,933	424	1,649	2,334	1,243	113	23
$c2$	2,775		3,371	753	2,043	2,531	2,098	44	28
$c3$	1,933	3,371		1,434	2,082	1,366	3,358	17	32
$c4$	424	753	1,434		850	122	1,726	297	37
$c5$	1,649	2,043	2,082	850		1,131	1,719	0	31
$c6$	2,334	2,531	1,366	122	1,131		689	410	57
$c7$	1,243	2,098	3,358	1,726	1,719	689		96	46
$c8$	113	44	17	297	0	410	96		41
Q	23	28	32	37	31	57	46	41	

Table 9.6 Pair-wise serial savings for the VRP8 example (Iteration 2)

	c1	c2:c3	c4	c5	c6	c7	c8	Q
c1		2,775	424	1,649	2,334	1,243	113	23
c2:c3	1,933		1,434	2,082	1,366	3,358	17	60
c4	424	753		850	122	1,726	297	37
c5	1,649	2,043	850		1,131	1,719	0	31
c6	2,334	2,531	122	1,131		689	410	57
c7	1,243	2,098	1,726	1,719	689		96	46
c8	113	44	297	0	410	96		41
Q	23	60	37	31	57	46	41	

$c3$ is created. To compute the reduced savings matrix, the following operations are executed: (1) eliminate the origin row, which in this case is the row of customer $c2$, because the origin node can no longer be the origin node for another shortcut; (2) eliminate the destination column, which in this case is the column of customer $c3$, because the destination node can no longer be the destination for another shortcut; (3) change the label of the destination row by preceding it with the origin label, which in this case yields $c2:c3$; (4) change the label of the origin column by appending it with the destination label, which in this case yields $c2:c3$; (5) clear the element on the intersection of the row and column corresponding to this shortcut; (6) change the quantities in the row and column for the partial route of the current shortcut to reflect the combined quantities, which in this case yields $28 + 32 = 60$. The updated matrix is shown in Table 9.6.

In the serial variant of the savings algorithm only one tour at the time is constructed, so only savings of combining other points with the endpoints of the current partial tour are relevant. These savings are shown as shaded in green in Table 9.6. If adding a point to the current partial tour would violate the vehicle capacity, those savings would be shown as shaded in purple. There are no such points after the first iteration. The updated savings matrix for the second iteration is shown in Table 9.6.

The shortcut with the largest savings corresponds to connecting the endpoint $c3$ to singleton customer $c7$. The same update operations are executed which results in the following updated savings matrix for iteration 3 (Table 9.7).

There are no remaining points that can be combined with the partial route $c2:c7$ without violating the vehicle capacity, hence the current route is archived. The number of routes is less than the number of vehicles and thus a new route can be started.

Table 9.7 Pair-wise serial savings for the VRP8 example (Iteration 3)

	c1	c2:c7	c4	c5	c6	c8	Q
c1		2,775	424	1,649	2,334	113	23
c4	424	753		850	122	297	37
c5	1,649	2,043	850		1,131	0	31
c6	2,334	2,531	122	1,131		410	57
c2:c7	1,243		1,726	1,719	689	96	106
c8	113	44	297	0	410		41
Q	23	106	37	31	57	41	

Table 9.8 Pair-wise serial savings for the VRP example (Iteration 3)

	c1	c4	c5	c6	c8	Q
c1		424	1,649	2,334	113	23
c4	424		850	122	297	37
c5	1,649	850		1,131	0	31
c6	2,334	122	1,131		410	57
c8	113	297	0	410		41
Q	23	37	31	57	41	

Table 9.9 Pair-wise serial savings for the VRP example (Iteration 4)

	c1:c6	c4	c5	c8	Q
c4	424		850	297	37
c5	1,649	850		0	31
c1:c6		122	1,131	410	80
c8	113	297	0		41
Q	80	37	31	41	

The row and column corresponding to the current route are eliminated from the savings matrix (Table 9.8).

The largest savings correspond to shortcut of customers $c1$ and $c6$. The savings matrix is updated using the same sequence of operations (Table 9.9).

Only the savings in the row and column $c1:c6$ are eligible in the serial variant. Combining customer $c8$ with the current partial route would yield a vehicle load of $80+41=121$, which is larger than the vehicle capacity. So the savings in cells at the intersection of $c8$ and $c1:c6$ are ineligible. The largest savings corresponds to the feasible shortcut from customer $c5$ to the customer $c1$ on the partial route. The savings matrix is updated (Table 9.10).

There are no remaining points that can be combined with the partial tour $c5:c6$ without violating the vehicle capacity, hence the current route is archived. The number of routes is less than the number of vehicles and thus a new route can be started. The row and column corresponding to the current route are eliminated from the savings matrix (Table 9.11).

The last two customers $c4$ and $c8$ are combined. At this time all points have been included on a route and the algorithm terminates. The operations of the serial vari-

Table 9.10 Pair-wise serial savings for the VRP example (Iteration 5)

	c4	c5:c6	c8	Q
c4		850	297	37
c5:c6	122		410	111
c8	297	0		41
Q	37	111	41	

Table 9.11 Pair-wise serial savings for the VRP example (Iteration 6)

	c4	c8	Q
c4		297	37
c8	297		41
Q	37	41	

Table 9.12 Serial savings steps for the VRP8 example

Step	Shortcut Points	Savings	Length	26,462	Facilities 1	2	3	4	5	6	7	8
1	c2:c3	3,371	6,663	23,091	d1	c2	c3	d1				
2	c3:c7	3,358	7,031	19,733	d1	c2	c3	c7	d1			
3	c1:c6	2,334	4,796	17,399	d1	c1	c6	d1				
4	c5:c1	1,649	5,311	15,750	d1	c5	c10	c6	d1			
5	c4:c8	297	3,111	15,453	d1	c4	c8	d1				

Table 9.13 Serial savings routes summary

Route	Facility 0	1	2	3	4	5	6	Quantity	Length
1	d1	c2	c3	c7	d1			106	7,031
2	d1	c5	c1	c6	d1			111	5,311
3	d1	c4	c8	d1				78	3,111
Total								295	15,453

ant are summarized in Table 9.12. The length in the fourth column of the table is the length of the partial route after it has been extended through the shortcut. This length will increase when points are added to the partial route. The length in the fifth column is the total route length after the shortcut. It includes the length of the out-and-back routes to points that have not yet been included on a partial route. The value in the header row of the fifth column is the total length of all the out-and-back routes and equal to twice the sum of the distances from the depot to every facility. The length value in the fifth column will decrease by the savings of the shortcuts when points are added to the partial routes. The value in the fifth column and the last row is the total length of the routes upon completion of the algorithm and should be equal to the total length of the routes in the summary table (Table 9.13 and Fig. 9.6).

Parallel Savings The parallel variant starts off with the same binary savings table and first shortcut as the serial variant. However, after the first shortcut and update of the savings table, all savings elements remain eligible, not just the savings in the row and column of the current partial route. In this small example, the second short-cut selected, the closure of the first partial route, the third shortcut, the fourth short-cut, the closure of the second partial route, and the fifth shortcut are all the same for the serial and parallel variant. For this VRP8 example, the serial and partial variants yield the same routes. This is not true in general. An example of this is shown in the appendix where the algorithms are applied to the larger example VRP16, which has 16 customer facilities.

So far the algorithm have considered simultaneously the distance between two facilities and the demand of the customer, the load already allocated to the route, and the vehicle capacity. The following algorithms separate the decisions that are based on the interfacility distances and on the load and capacity quantities.

Sweep: Cluster-First, Route-Second Variant The sweep algorithm creates a route by appending the points to the route when they are conceptually traversed by a ray

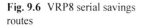

Fig. 9.6 VRP8 serial savings routes

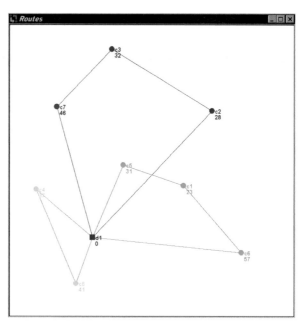

rotating around the depot. Computationally, the relative polar coordinates of each point with respect to the depot are determined and the points are inserted in the route by increasing polar angle. The algorithm was first described by Gillet and Miller (1974) for the vehicle routing problem. The starting angle of the rotation ray is an algorithm input parameter. The polar angle of a facility with respect to the depot and with a starting angle is computed with the following formula, where the angles are expressed in radians and arctan2 is the inverse tangent function with the sign of the result determined by the values and the sign of its arguments y and x. The function arctan2 itself or the subtraction of the starting angle may yield a negative value for θ. To normalize the θ angle in the interval $[0, 2\pi]$, 2π is repeatedly added until the value of θ is positive.

$$\theta_i = \arctan2(y_i - y_{depot}, x_i - x_{depot}) - starting\_angle$$
$$while\,(\theta_i < 0)$$
$$\theta_i = \theta_i + 2\pi$$

(9.11)

It should be noted that the arctan2 function in the C standard type library has the function arguments in the sequence y-first, x-second, but the ARCTAN2 function in the Excel spreadsheet has the function arguments in the sequence x-first, y-second.

The cluster-first variant of the sweep algorithm assigns the customer facilities to routes in the first phase based on the customer demand. It routes the facilities for each cluster in the second phase. The sweep algorithm rotates a ray with origin at the distribution center and the facilities are assigned to the current group or cluster when they are traversed by the ray. The current cluster is closed if the next facility would violate the truck capacity. Note that the groupings are only clusters without any facility sequencing information. After all the clusters have been determined,

TSP algorithms must be used to construct the actual route for each cluster. For each cluster the depot is added to the customer facilities in the cluster to determine the tour by the TSP algorithms.

VRP8 Cluster-First Sweep (Variant A) Example The starting direction of the ray is a user-specified algorithm parameter. In this example, the starting position of the ray is due east and rotation direction is counterclockwise. The first customer traversed by the sweep ray is $c1$ and the cluster quantity is 23. The next facility traversed is customer $c2$ with demand 28. The combined cluster load would $23 + 28 = 51$, which is less than the vehicle capacity so customer $c2$ is added to the cluster. The next facility traversed is customer $c5$ with demand 31. The combined cluster load would be $51 + 31 = 82$, which is less than the vehicle capacity so customer $c5$ is added. The next facility traversed is customer $c3$ with demand 32. The combined cluster load would be $82 + 32 = 114$ and customer $c3$ is added. The next facility traversed is customer $c7$ with demand 46. This facility does not fit in the first cluster since $114 + 46 = 160$ is larger than the vehicle capacity of 120. Customer $c7$ starts cluster two, which has an initial load of 46. Continuing this process yields the following clusters $\{c1, c2, c5, c3\}$, $\{c7, c4\}$, $\{c8, c6\}$ with loads equal to 114, 83, and 98 respectively. These steps are summarized in Table 9.14.

A TSP algorithm then needs to be used to sequence the points in each cluster. For this particular example, there are only two customers in clusters two and three and the distances are symmetrical, so the problem of determining the optimal facility routing sequence is trivial. The first cluster contains four facilities plus the depot facility and a TSP algorithm must be used. The convex hull algorithm is used to construct an initial tour, with the following facility sequence ($c1, c2, c3, d1$). The single facility that is not yet sequenced is customer $c5$. Cheapest insertion is used to insert it on the link from $c3$ to $d1$. Other TSP algorithms could have been used to route the customers in the first cluster. The routes created by this variant are summarized in Table 9.15 and are shown in Fig. 9.7. Note that the routes created are the optimal TSP routes for each cluster, but this does not assure that the created routes form the optimal solution for the VRP instance.

Sweep: Route-First, Cluster-Second Variant The route-first variant of the sweep algorithm first sequences all the customers based on their locations into a single route. It ignores the customer demand requirements during the routing phase. The

Table 9.14 Cluster-First sweep routes steps	Index	Cluster Point	Cluster	Vehicle Quantity
	1	$c1$	1	23
	2	$c2$	1	51
	3	$c5$	1	82
	4	$c3$	1	114
	5	$c7$	2	46
	6	$c4$	2	83
	7	$c8$	3	41
	8	$c6$	3	98
	Total			295

Table 9.15 Cluster-First sweep routes summary

Route	Facility							Quantity	Length
	0	1	2	3	4	5	6		
1	d1	c1	c2	c3	c5	d1		114	6,892
2	d1	c7	c4	d1				83	4,064
3	d1	c8	c6	d1				98	5,142
Total								295	16,098

algorithm then creates routes that observe customer demand and satisfy truck capacity during the clustering phase.

This variant of the sweep algorithm sequences all customers to be visited on a single route by rotating a line segment or ray around the distribution center. Customers are added to the sequence when they are traversed by the rotating line. The starting angle and the rotational direction of the line have no impact on the tour that is created in this routing phase. At the end of the first phase, a single tour consisting of all the customers has been created. After all customers have been sequenced, a customer is selected to start the first route. The route visits each customer according to the sequence determined above until appending the next customer would violate the truck capacity. That next customer starts a new route. The starting customer and the direction in which the sequence is traversed are algorithm parameters. The customers are sequenced on the routes following their sequence on the initial single tour. After the routes have been determined, they can be improved by TSP improvement routines such as steepest descent improvement exchanges. However, these improvements are not part of the sweep algorithm.

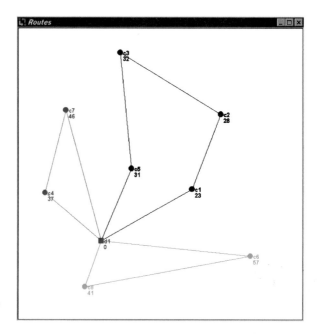

Fig. 9.7 Cluster-First sweep routes for VRP8

Table 9.16 Route-First sweep routes summary

Route	Facility							Quantity	Length
	0	1	2	3	4	5	6		
1	*dl*	*c1*	*c2*	*c5*	*c3*	*dl*		114	8,220
2	*dl*	*c7*	*c4*	*dl*				83	4,064
3	*dl*	*c8*	*c6*	*dl*				98	5,142
Total								295	17,426

VRP8 Route-First Sweep (Variant B) Example The starting angle of the ray is again set to due east. The sequence of customers as traversed by the ray is equal to (*c1, c2, c5, c3, c7, c4, c8, c6*). This sequence is then divided into segments so that the demand on each segment does not violate the truck capacity. The break points are the same as for the cluster-first variant. The first route is then (*c1, c2, c5, c3*), which is different from the first route for the cluster-first variant. Is this particular example the second and third route are identical in the two variants. See Table 9.16 and Fig. 9.8.

Giant Tour The giant tour algorithm creates the shortest-length traveling salesman tour of all the customers plus the depot facility, while ignoring their demand requirements, during the routing phase. The route starts with the depot and visits each customer according to the TSP sequence until the next customer would violate the truck capacity. That next customer starts a new route. The direction in which the sequence is traversed is an algorithm input parameter.

An alternative giant tour algorithm creates the shortest-length TSP tour of all the customers, but excluding the depot. Again the demand requirements are ignored

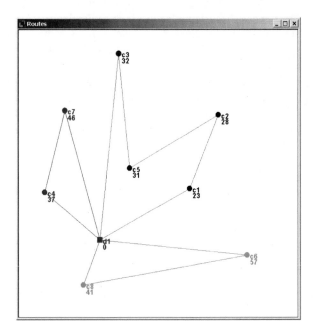

Fig. 9.8 Route-First Sweep routes for VRP8

Fig. 9.9 Giant tour for VRP8

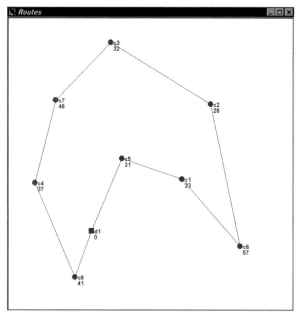

during this phase. The route starts at a customer in the sequence and visits each customer according to the TSP sequence until the next customer would violate the truck capacity. The starting customer and the sequence direction are input parameters for this variant.

VRP8 Giant Tour Example The tour shown in Fig. 9.9 was determined for the eight customers and the depot by the convex hull algorithm followed by the priciest insertion, i.e, the first variant of the giant tour algorithm is executed. The length of this tour is not relevant, only the sequence of the customers on the tour. The sequence of facilities is (*d1, c5, c1, c6, c2, c3, c7, c4, c8*).

The routes start at the depot, and the direction of progress through the sequence is specified by selecting customer *c5* as the next customer. This sequence is divided into segments so that the demand on a segment does not violate the truck capacity. After customer *c6* has been added to the first route, the vehicle load is $31 + 23 + 57 = 111$. Adding the next customer *c2* would violate the capacity, so the first route is closed and customer *c2* starts a new route. The routes created by the giant tour algorithm are summarized in Table 9.17.

Table 9.17 Giant tour routes summary

Route	Facility							Quantity	Length
	0	1	2	3	4	5	6		
1	d1	c5	c1	c6	d1			111	5,311
2	d1	c2	c3	c7	d1			106	7,031
3	d1	c4	c8	d1				78	3,111
Total								295	15,453

Fig. 9.10 Giant tour routes for VRP8

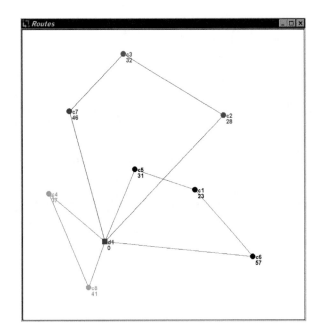

Generalized Assignment Problem Formulation (GAP) The classic vehicle routing problem can be seen as a clustering or assignment problem, where the cost of assigning a facility to a route is a function of customer facilities assigned to the route and the vehicle. However, this cost function cannot be written in a closed algebraic form, but is written as the optimal solution value of a set of independent secondary optimization problems. Each of these secondary problems is a traveling salesman problem over the facilities assigned to that vehicle plus the depot facility.

The GAP formulation is shown next using the notation developed before for the vehicle routing problem. The clustering formulation is given first, followed by the secondary sequencing formulation.

Formulation 9.2. Clustering Master Problem of the Bilevel GAP Formulation

$$\min \quad \sum_k f(z_{ik})$$

$$s.t. \quad \sum_{i=1}^{N} dem_i z_{ik} \leq cap_k \cdot z_{0k} \qquad \forall k$$

$$\sum_k z_{0k} \leq K \tag{9.12}$$

$$\sum_k z_{ik} = 1 \qquad\qquad i = 1, ..., N$$

$$z_{ik} \in \{0, 1\}$$

The following decision variable and set need to be defined in addition to the standard notation for the VRP.

x_{ijk} equals 1 if vehicle k travels directly from customer i to customer j, zero otherwise

$N(z_{ik})$ set of customers visited by vehicle k and the depot, i.e., $N(z_{ik}) = \{i \in N \cup 0 \mid z_{ik} = 1\}$, where 0 is the index corresponding to the depot

Formulation 9.3. Sequencing Subproblem of the Bilevel GAP Formulation

$$f(z_{ik}) = \min \quad \sum_i \sum_j c_{ijk} x_{ijk}$$

$$s.t. \quad \sum_i x_{ijk} = z_{jk} \qquad \forall jk$$

$$\sum_j x_{ijk} = z_{ik} \qquad \forall i \qquad\qquad (9.13)$$

$$\sum_{i \in S} \sum_{j \in S} x_{ijk} \le |S| - 1 \quad S \subseteq N(z_{ik})$$

$$x_{ijk} \in \{0, 1\}$$

In this routing formulation the indices i and j range from 0 to N. In the clustering formulation, z_{0k} indicates if vehicle k is used or not. This formulation is a bilevel programming problem which has its master problem the assignment problem and as its subproblems the individual traveling salesman problems. While the above formulation clearly demonstrates the structure of the vehicle routing problem, it is not particularly useful for its solution. Bilevel programming problems are very difficult to solve to optimality. The secondary routing formulation is itself known to be a hard problem that cannot be solved to optimal ity for large problem instances in a reasonable amount of computer time. To reduce the computational effort, the secondary optimization problem can be replaced by a linear expression that approximates the optimal clustering costs.

$$f(y_{ik}) \approx \sum_i d_{ik} y_{ik} \qquad\qquad (9.14)$$

It is desirable that this approximation is as accurate as possible, i.e., as close as possible to the optimal solution of the secondary optimization problem, but also that the linearized costs can be computed efficiently. Many different approximations have been developed. They can be divided into single-pass or iterative approximations. In single-pass approximations, the cost are computed once and based on these costs the VRP is solved. In iterative approximations, the solution of the VRP is used to further refine the linear clustering costs and the problems are solved again until the solution converges.

One heuristic single-pass approximation was proposed by Fisher and Jaikumar (1981). It relies on the determination of a seed point as a surrogate for the center of each route. The assignment cost for a customer to a route is then approximated by the insertion penalty of this customer on the route to the seed point and back.

$$d_{ik} = c_{0i} + c_{is_k} - c_{0s_k} \tag{9.15}$$

If the VRP is using a distance table rather than a distance norm calculation, distances to the original continuous location of the seed point may not be available. In this case the seed point is moved to the closest point to the seed point that is located inside the current route sector and that is included in the distance table. Typically this is the closest customer to the seed point inside the route sector. Clearly many alternative rules for determining the seed point location and the assignment cost are possible and have been used. The linearized clustering formulation for the case where all K vehicles are used is given next.

Formulation 9.4. Approximate Master Clustering Problem of the GAP Formulation

$$\min \sum_k \sum_i d_{ik} z_{ik}$$

$$s.t. \quad \sum_{i=1}^{N} dem_i z_{ik} \leq cap_k \quad \forall k \tag{9.16}$$

$$\sum_k z_{ik} = 1 \qquad i = 1, ..., N$$

$$z_{ik} \in \{0, 1\}$$

It should be observed that the GAP heuristic approximates the routing costs but accurately models the capacity constraints. This method is thus most suitable for problems where the capacity constraints are strongly limiting the solution and where the routing costs are less important. The solution of the approximation GAP belongs to the class of the two-phase construction algorithms, where the first phase focuses on clustering and the second phase focuses on sequencing the customers.

Fisher and Jaikumar (1981) determined the location of the seed points in the following manner. The goal is to locate the seed points in such way that they represent the center of the routes. For the seed point determination, each route is assumed to be located in a cone with the tip of the cone located at the depot. For a given number of vehicles, each route will deliver on the average the quantity $\overline{q_k}$, where

$$\overline{q_k} = \frac{\sum_{i=1}^{N} dem_i}{K} \tag{9.17}$$

If the trucks have different capacities, the expected quantity delivered by a truck is computed such that the expected utilizations of all the trucks are identical.

$$\overline{q_k} = \frac{\sum\limits_{i=1}^{N} dem_i}{\sum\limits_{k=1}^{K} cap_k} \cdot cap_k = \overline{p} \cdot cap_k \qquad (9.18)$$

The route cones are determined by a sweep algorithm. The starting orientation and rotation direction are algorithm input parameters. If the trucks have different capacities, the sequence of trucks is also an algorithm parameter. The sweep procedure determines a sequence for the customers. Each customer also has a cone with its tip located at the depot. The boundaries of this cone are the bisectors of the angles to the preceding and succeeding customers. The starting boundary line of the first sector is the starting boundary line of the customer cone of the first customer traversed by the rotating ray. The rotating ray adds customers to the sector, until the next customer would violate the average quantity on a route, given by $\overline{q_k}$. The cone of the customer that would violate the average load is split proportional to the quantities that fit and do not fit on the current route. The ray corresponding to this split forms the end ray of the sector, which is also the start ray of the next sector. The continuous location of the seed point is then determined by its polar coordinates. The angle of the seed point is equal to the bisector line of the current sector. The radius of the seed point is equal to the radius so that at exactly 75% of the total demand in this sector, given by $\overline{q_k}$, falls inside the radius.

The continuous location of the seed point is illustrated in Fig. 9.11. Customers m and r determine the boundary lines of the current sector, which in turn determines

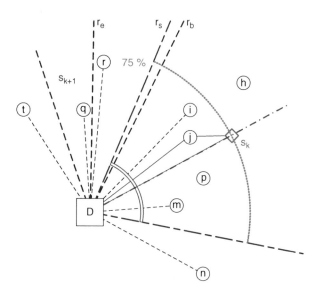

Fig. 9.11 Continuous location of the seed points in the GAP heuristic

the bisector. The boundary rays of the cone of customer r are indicated by r_b and r_e. They are determined as the bisectors of the rays through customers i and r and customers r and q, respectively. The ray r_s splits the cone of customer r proportional to the fraction of the load of customer r that fits on route k and $k + 1$ when the truck capacity is equal to $\overline{q}$. Assume that α percent of the load of customer r fits on route k. The angles expressed in radians are then computed by the following formulas.

$$\theta_k^{start} = \frac{1}{2}(\theta_n + \theta_m) \tag{9.19}$$

$$\theta_{r_b} = \frac{1}{2}(\theta_i + \theta_r), \ \theta_{r_e} = \frac{1}{2}(\theta_r + \theta_q) \tag{9.20}$$

$$\theta_k^{end} \equiv \theta_{k+1}^{start} = \theta_{r_s} = \theta_{r_b} + \alpha(\theta_{r_e} - \theta_{r_b}) = \frac{1}{2}(\theta_i + \theta_r) + \frac{\alpha}{2}(\theta_q - \theta_i) \tag{9.21}$$

If the ray with zero angle is located between the rays of two customers in the above formulas, then 2π must be subtracted from the sum and added to the difference of those two angles.

In sector k, customers i and h determine the 75% radius. Assume that β percent of the load of customer h fits inside 75% of the average vehicle load $\overline{q}_k$. The radial coordinate of the seed point is then calculated with the following formula.

$$r_s = r_i + \beta(r_h - r_i) \tag{9.22}$$

The seed point is located at the intersection of the bisector and radial curve. The 75% boundary value is an estimated value for the radius of the center of the route. An alternative method is to determine the radius of the seed point as the weighted average of the radii of the customers on the route, where the weights are the customer quantities. The radius of the seed point is then located at the center of gravity of the radii of the customers on the route. The remaining steps in the algorithm are identical to the algorithm variant proposed by Fisher and Jaikumar that has been described above.

$$\rho_k = \frac{\sum\limits_{j \in route\ k} r_j \cdot dem_j}{\sum\limits_{j \in route\ k} dem_j} \tag{9.23}$$

Algorithm 9.1. GAP Heuristic for the VRP

1. For each customer, convert Cartesian coordinates to polar coordinates relative to the depot $\forall i \quad (x_i, y_i) \to (r_i, \theta_i)$
2. Sort customers by increasing (counterclockwise rotation) or decreasing (clockwise rotation) angle θ starting from an initial angle and index the customers by this sorting order. Note that starting angle and rotation direction are algorithm parameters.

3. Determine boundary angles of customer cones $\left(\varphi_i^{start}, \varphi_i^{end}\right)$ as bisectors of angles of subsequent customers $\varphi_i^{start} = (\theta_{i-1} + \theta_i)/2$, $\varphi_i^{end} = (\theta_i + \theta_{i+1})/2$.
4. Determine average load for every route $\overline{q_k} = \sum_{i=1}^{N} dem_i/K$, which becomes the route capacity
5. Determine boundary angles of vehicle cones by sweep algorithm. A customer that fits only partially in a vehicle cone is split into two according to (9.21). At completion ϕ_k^{start} and ϕ_k^{end} have been determined.
6. Determine bisector angles of the vehicle cones $\psi_k = (\phi_k^{start} + \phi_k^{end})/2$.
7. Determine the radius of the seed point of the vehicle route as the average radius in the vehicle cone with (9.23) or with a similar equation.
8. For each vehicle determine Cartesian coordinates of the seed point from polar coordinates with respect to the depot, $\forall k \quad (\rho_k, \psi_k) \rightarrow (x_k, y_k)$
9. For each combination of customer and route seed point, determine the distance between them c_{is_k}.
10. For each combination of customer and route determine the assignment cost of this customer to this route $d_{ik} = c_{0i} + c_{is_k} - c_{0s_k}$.
11. Solve the GAP. At the completion the z_{ik} have been determined.
12. For each vehicle, solve the sequencing problem, which is a TSP, for the depot and the customers assigned to that route, i.e., $\{i \,|z_{ik} = 1\} \cup \{0\}$.

Heuristic Generalized Assignment Problem (GAP) Example The computations for the heuristic approximation to the VRP formulation based on the GAP are given next. The assignment cost of a customer to a route is approximated by the insertion cost of the customer on the route from the depot to the route seed point. The seed points are located in route sectors. Since all truck capacities are equal, the route sectors divide the problem area into sectors with equal demand. The starting angle of the route sectors is an algorithm input parameter.

In the VRP8 example, three vehicles with a capacity equal to 120 are available. The total demand equals 295. If all routes serve the same demand, each route should serve approximately a demand of $295/3 = 98.3$. The starting angle of the route sector is due east and the rotation is counterclockwise. For the Fisher and Jaikumar variant of the heuristic, the rotation direction does not have an impact, but this may not be true for the sector determination methods used in other variants. The Cartesian and relative polar coordinates of the customer facilities with respect to the depot facility are shown in Tables 9.18 and 9.19. The second table shows the facilities sorted by increasing polar angle.

The starting angle of the ray is 0.000 for a due east direction. The first sector starts with customer $c1$ with polar angle equal to 0.508. The start angle of the first sector is then the bisector between customer $c1$ and customer $c6$, which is the customer with the largest polar angle. The angle of the bisector in radians is then computed with the following calculations.

$$\theta_1^{begin} = \frac{\theta_{c1} + \theta_{c6} - 2\pi}{2} = \frac{0.508 + 6.183 - 2 \cdot 3.14}{2} = 0.204$$

Table 9.18 VRP8 facilities with cartesian and polar coordinates

Label	Cartesian		Polar		Quantity
	X-Coord	Y-Coord	Angle	Radius	
d1	1,164	1,083			
c1	2,440	1,794	0.508	1,461	23
c2	2,844	2,820	0.802	2,417	28
c3	1,434	3,669	1.467	2,600	32
c4	372	1,745	2.445	1,032	37
c5	1,592	2,077	1.164	1,082	31
c6	3,257	873	6.183	2,104	57
c7	663	2,877	1.843	1,863	46
c8	929	453	4.355	672	41

Table 9.19 VRP8 facilities sorted by polar coordinates

Label	Cartesian		Polar		Quantity
	X-Coord	Y-Coord	Angle	Radius	
c1	2,440	1,794	0.508	1,461	23
c2	2,844	2,820	0.802	2,417	28
c5	1,592	2,077	1.164	1,082	31
c3	1,434	3,669	1.467	2,600	32
c7	663	2,877	1.843	1,863	46
c4	372	1,745	2.445	1,032	37
c8	929	453	4.355	672	41
c6	3,257	873	6.183	2,104	57

The starting angle for the first sector is equal to the end angle for the last sector. 2π, equivalent to one full circle, needs to be subtracted from the sum of the customer angles if the ray with an angle of zero radians is located in between the two customer rays.

Adding customers systematically by increasing polar angle, the sector quantity for customer $c2$ is 51 and $c5$ is 82 and the sector quantity for further adding customer $c3$ would be 114. This violates the route or sector capicity constraint of 98.3 and customer $c3$ will be split between sector 1 and sector 2. The fraction of customer $c3$ that is located in sector 1 and the boundary angle of sector 1 are computed with the following calculations.

$$\alpha_{c3} = \frac{98.3 - 82}{32} = \frac{16.3}{32} = 51.0\%$$

$$\theta_1^{end} = \frac{\theta_{c3} + \theta_{c5}}{2} + \alpha_{c3}\frac{\theta_{c7} - \theta_{c5}}{2} = \frac{1.467 + 1.164}{2} + 0.510\frac{1.843 - 1.164}{2} = 1.489$$

Sector 2 starts with customer $c3$, but only with its remainder load of $32 - 16.3 = 15.7$ and at the end angle of sector 1, i.e., 1.489. Adding customers systematically by increasing the polar angle, the sector quantity for customer $c7$ is 61.7 and the sector quantity for adding customer $c4$ would be 98.7. This violates the sector load

Table 9.20 VRP8 sector angles

Sector	Angles		
	Start	End	Center
S1	0.204	1.489	0.846
S2	1.489	3.389	2.439
S3	3.389	6.487	4.938

constraint and customer $c4$ will be split between sector 2 and 3. The fraction of customer $c4$ that is located in sector 2 and the boundary angle of sector 2 are computed with the following calculations.

$$\alpha_{c4} = \frac{98.3 - 61.7}{37} = \frac{36.6}{37} = 99.1\%$$

$$\theta_2^{end} = \frac{\theta_{c4} + \theta_{c7}}{2} + \alpha_{c4} \frac{\theta_{c8} - \theta_{c7}}{2} = \frac{2.445 + 1.843}{2} + 0.991 \frac{4.355 - 1.843}{2} = 3.389$$

This process is repeated to determine all the remaining sectors. The end angle for the last sector is equal to the starting angle for the first sector. 2π, equivalent to one full circle, needs to be added to the sum of the customer angles if the ray with an angle of zero radians is located in between the two customer rays.

$$\theta_3^{end} = \theta_1^{start} + 2\pi = 0.204 + 6.283 = 6.487$$

The angular polar coordinate for each seed point is on the center ray for each sector. The bisector or center angle for each of the sectors is then computed as the average of the two boundary angles. The angles for the three sectors are summarized in Table 9.20.

The second polar coordinate of each seed point is its radius. In the Fisher and Jaikumar variant of the GAP heuristic algorithm, the seed radius in a cluster is the boundary radius where exactly 75% of the average vehicle load is contained inside the radius. This radius is computed next for each sector. To satisfy the 75% boundary, at most one customer per sector may have to split between inside and outside the radius. In this example, 75% of the average vehicle load is $0.75 \cdot 98.3 = 73.8$. The customers in each cluster, sorted by increasing radius per cluster, are shown in Table 9.21. Observe that the split customers from the previous calculations each appear in two sectors, indicated by the postscript a or b, respectively. They have identical radius in each sector but different quantities, equal to the split delivery quantities computed in the previous step.

The calculations are for sector 1 are given next. When adding customers by increasing radius, the cumulative quantity is 54 for customer $c1$ and would be 82 for customer $c2$. This is larger than 73.8, so customer $c2$ will be split between inside and outside the boundary radius. The fraction of customer $c2$ inside the radius and the boundary radius are computed in the next calculations.

Table 9.21 VRP8 facilities by cluster sorted by increasing radius

Label	Cartesian		Polar		Quantity
	X-Coord	Y-Coord	Angle	Radius	
c5	1,592	2,077	1.164	1,082	31
c1	2,440	1,794	0.508	1,461	23
c2	2,844	2,820	0.802	2,417	28
c3_a	1,434	3,669	1.467	2,600	16.3
c4_a	372	1,745	2.445	1,032	36.7
c7	663	2,877	1.843	1,863	46
c3_b	1,434	3,669	1.467	2,600	15.7
c8	929	453	4.355	672	41.0
c4_b	372	1,745	2.445	1,032	0.3
c6	3,257	873	6.183	2,104	57

$$\beta_{c2} = \frac{73.8 - 54}{28} = \frac{19.8}{28} = 70.5\%$$
$$r_{s1} = r_{c1} + \beta_{c2} \cdot (r_{c2} - r_{c1}) = 1,461 + 0.705 \cdot (2,417 - 1,461) = 2,134.9$$

These calculations are then repeated for each of the remaining sectors. For sector 2, when adding the customers by increasing radius, the cumulative quantity is 36.7 for customer $c4$ and 82.7 for customer $c7$. This is larger than the 75% percentage of the average load, so customer $c7$ will be split between inside and outside the boundary radius. The seed point radius is computed with the following calculations.

$$\beta_{c7} = \frac{73.8 - 36.7}{46} = \frac{37.1}{46} = 80.6\%$$
$$r_{s2} = r_{c4} + \beta_{c7} \cdot (r_{c7} - r_{c4}) = 1,032 + 0.806 \cdot (1,863 - 1,032) = 1,701.7$$

These calculations are repeated for the remaining sectors. The polar coordinates of each seed point are then transformed to Cartesian coordinates. Note that the polar coordinates are with respect to the depot. In order to compute the Cartesian coordinates of the seed points in the original problem domain the depot coordinates have to be added.

$$\begin{aligned} x_s &= r_s \cdot \cos(\theta_s) + x_{depot} \\ y_s &= r_s \cdot \sin(\theta_s) + y_{depot} \end{aligned} \tag{9.24}$$

The Cartesian coordinates for the seed point of route 1 are then computed as follows.

$$x_{s1} = r_{s1} \cdot \cos(\theta_{s1}) + x_{depot} = 2,134.9 \cdot \cos(0.846) + 1,164 = 2,579$$
$$y_{s1} = r_{s1} \cdot \sin(\theta_{s1}) + y_{depot} = 2,134.9 \cdot \sin(0.846) + 1,083 = 2,682$$

The coordinates of the three seed points for this example are shown in Table 9.22. The location of the seed points is illustrated in Fig. 9.12. Note that the scale of the

Table 9.22 VRP8 polar and cartesian coordinates for the seed points

Sector	Radius	Angle	X-Coord	Y-Coord
S1	2,134.9	0.846	2,579	2,682
S2	1,701.7	2.439	−135	2,183
S3	1,641.5	4.938	1,532	−517

figures that display the seed points is different from the scale of all other figures illustrating VRP8 since some of the seed point locations fall outside the original problem domain.

The cost of assigning a customer to a route is computed as the insertion penalty of the customer for the out-and-back route from the depot to the seed point. In order to compute those insertion penalties, we need first to compute the distances from every customer to every seed point. For the VRP8 example the distances are computed with the Euclidean distance norm without adjustment factor. The computed distances are shown in Table 9.23, rounded to the nearest integer.

The assignment cost for customer $c1$ to seed point $S1$ is computed as the insertion penalty of customer $c1$ into route ($d1$, $S1$, $d1$) as shown in the following calculations.

$$c_{c1,S1} = c_{d1,c1} + c_{c1,S1} - c_{d1,S1} = 1{,}461 + 899 - 2{,}135 = 225$$

The other assignment costs are computed in a similar way. The assignment costs are shown in Table 9.24.

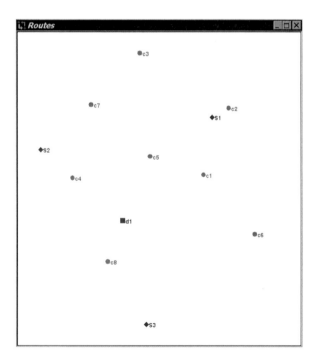

Fig. 9.12 VRP8 facility and seed point locations

Table 9.23 VRP8 customer to seed point distances

Distance	S1	S2	S3	d1
c1	899	2,604	2,683	1,461
c2	299	3,046	3,785	2,417
c3	1,512	2,161	4,421	2,600
c4	2,398	670	2,773	1,032
c5	1,158	1,730	2,826	1,082
c6	1,932	3,636	2,329	2,104
c7	1,926	1,058	3,741	1,863
c8	2,773	2,031	1,369	672
d1	2,135	1,702	1,880	

Table 9.24 VRP8 customer to seed point assignment costs

Cost	S1	S2	S3
c1	225	2,363	2,264
c2	581	3,761	4,322
c3	1,977	3,059	5,141
c4	1,295	0	1,925
c5	105	1,110	2,028
c6	1,901	4,038	2,553
c7	1,654	1,219	3,724
c8	1,310	1,001	161

The GAP now can be solved using an integer programming (IP) solver. The GAP formulation can and will tend to yield fractional solutions if solved with a linear programming solver. The solver included in Excel will be used here, but other solvers can be used. The problem setup in Excel is shown in Fig. 9.13.

On the left, the two-dimensional matrix with the assignment costs is given in cells O63:Q70. On the right, the two-dimensional matrix in cells U63:W70 contains the assignment variables. Column X contains the sum of the assignment variables for each customer, which must sum up to 1. Row 71 contains the sum of the quantities assigned to the respective routes. The cumulative quantity for seed S1 is computed in cell U71 and is computed with the Excel function

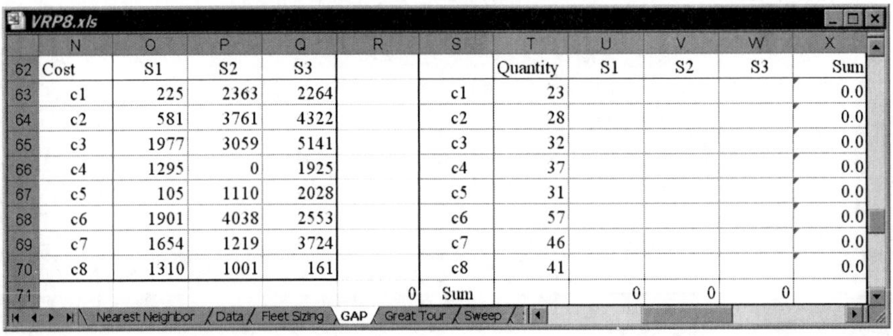

Fig. 9.13 VRP8 excel GAP problem

Fig. 9.14 VRP8 excel GAP
solver parameters

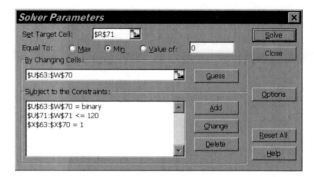

SUMPRODUCT($T63:$T70,U63:U70). The vehicle capacity in this example is 120, so the cumulative quantities have to less than or equal to 120. Finally, the total assignment cost is stored in cell R71 and is computed with the Excel function SUMPRODUCT(O63:Q70,U63:W70). Initially, all the assignment variables, sums, and assignment costs are zero. The solver problem setup for this example is shown in Fig. 9.14.

The solver will minimize the contents of cell R71, which contains the sum of the assignment costs. The decision variables are stored in the rectangular matrix of cells U63:W70. There are only three types of constraints for the problem. To avoid splitting customers among routes, in the first constraint the assignment variables in cells U63:W70 are forced to be either zero or one, i.e., they must be binary. The second constraint is the capacity constraint, which ensures that the cumulative quantity on each route is less than the vehicle capacity. The cumulative quantities are stored in cells U71:W71, and the vehicle capacity is 120. Finally, the third constraint is the assignment constraint, which ensures that the sum of the assignment variables for each customer is equal to 1. The sums are stored in cells X63:X70 (Fig. 9.15).

The optimal solution value returned by the solver is 6,821 but is not relevant. The assignment of customers to routes is shown in Table 9.25. It should be noted that at this time, this assignment only provides route clusters and that the customers have

VRP8.xls										_ □ ×
	N	O	P	Q	R	S	T	U	V	W	X
62	Cost	S1	S2	S3			Quantity	S1	S2	S3	Sum
63	c1	225	2363	2264		c1	23	1.0	0.0	0.0	1.0
64	c2	581	3761	4322		c2	28	1.0	0.0	0.0	1.0
65	c3	1977	3059	5141		c3	32	1.0	0.0	0.0	1.0
66	c4	1295	0	1925		c4	37	0.0	1.0	0.0	1.0
67	c5	105	1110	2028		c5	31	1.0	0.0	0.0	1.0
68	c6	1901	4038	2553		c6	57	0.0	0.0	1.0	1.0
69	c7	1654	1219	3724		c7	46	0.0	1.0	0.0	1.0
70	c8	1310	1001	161		c8	41	0.0	0.0	1.0	1.0
71					6821	Sum		114	83	98	

Nearest Neighbor / Data / Fleet Sizing \ GAP / Great Tour / Sweep /

Fig. 9.15 VRP8 excel GAP solution

Table 9.25 VRP8 GAP
route clusters

Route	Customers	Quantity
S1	c1,c2,c3,c5	114
S2	c4,c7	83
S3	c6,c8	98

not been routed yet. In this particular case, route 1 contains four customers and the depot and routes 2 and 3 contain each two customers and the depot.

Routes 2 and 3 are solved trivially by the convex hull algorithm for the TSP. Route 1 is created by the convex hull algorithm followed by cheapest insertion algorithm if necessary. The convex hull provides the optimal tour for the facilities on the convex hull and the optimal sequence of the facilities on any optimal route with additional facilities. Since route 1 has only one facility not on the convex hull, the cheapest insertion creates a route with minimal length. The three vehicle routes created with the sequence of these two algorithms are guaranteed to be optimal for the given route clusters. This property is only valid for this case and not likely to be satisfied for larger problem instances. The resulting routes are shown in Tables 9.26 and 9.27. The total length of all the routes is 16,098. This solution is not guaranteed to be optimal. The resulting routes are shown Fig. 9.16.

If the radii of the seed points are computed with the center of gravity method, then the coordinates for the seed points are computed as shown in Table 9.28. It should be noted that the angular coordinates are identical to polar angles determined by the Fisher and Jaikumar heuristic, only the radii are different. But the different radii yield different Cartesian coordinates.

Since the optimal assignment solution generated by the center-of-gravity variant is the same as the solution generated by the Fisher and Jaikumar variant, the route clusters and the routes will also be the same. This property is not true in general, especially for larger problem instances.

Table 9.26 VRP8 GAP facility routing

Route	Convex hull	Insertion	Final route	Length
S1	c1,c2,c3	c5	c1,c2,c3,c5	6,892
S2	c4,c7		c4,c7	4,064
S3	c6,c8		c6,c8	5,142
				16,098

Table 9.27 VRP8 GAP route statistics

Route	Facility						Quantity	Length
	0	1	2	3	4	5		
1	d1	c1	c2	c3	c5	d1	114	6,892
2	d1	c4	c7	d1			83	4,064
3	d1	c6	c8	d1			98	5,142
Total							295	16,098

Fig. 9.16 VRP8 GAP routes with seed locations

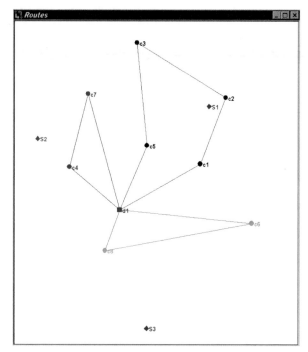

At the end of the construction or the insertion phase, a set of routes has been created that do not violate vehicle capacities. In the following improvement algorithms, the routes are changed if this decreases the total travel length.

Table 9.28 VRP8 polar and cartesian coordinates for the seed points (center-of-gravity variant)

Vehicle	Angle	Radius	X Coord	Y Coord
v 1	0.847	1,803	2,359	2,433
v 2	2.439	1,671	−111	2,163
v 3	4.938	1,503	1,501	−382

Table 9.29 VRP8 customer to seed point distances (center-of-gravity variant)

	v1	v2	v3	d1
c1	644	2,577	2,370	1,461
c2	621	3,027	3,472	2,417
c3	1,543	2,158	4,052	2,600
c4	2,102	638	2,408	1,032
c5	845	1,705	2,461	1,082
c6	1,800	3,606	2,159	2,104
c7	1,753	1,053	3,365	1,863
c8	2,442	2,001	1,012	672
d1	1,803	1,670	1,503	

Table 9.30 VRP8 customer to seed point assignment costs (center-of-gravity variant)

	$v1$	$v2$	$v3$
$c1$	302	2,367	2,328
$c2$	1,234	3,773	4,386
$c3$	2,341	3,087	5,148
$c4$	1,332	0	1,937
$c5$	125	1,117	2,040
$c6$	2,101	4,039	2,759
$c7$	1,813	1,245	3,724
$c8$	1,312	1,003	181

Table 9.31 VRP8 GAP route clusters solution (center-of-gravity variant)

	$v1$	$v2$	$v3$
$c1$	1	0	0
$c2$	1	0	0
$c3$	1	0	0
$c4$	0	1	0
$c5$	1	0	0
$c6$	0	0	1
$c7$	0	1	0
$c8$	0	0	1

9.2.1.1 Improvement Algorithms

Intra-route Improvements Algorithms (TSP) All intra-route improvement algorithms attempt to reduce the length of a single route by link exchanges on this route. They operate on each route sequentially to reduce the total route length. Since the route is feasible at the start of the algorithm, it will remain feasible throughout the algorithm execution. These procedures are identical to the improvement procedures for the TSP. The most often executed procedures are 2-opt, 3-opt, and chain-opt. Further information on these intra-route improvement algorithms can be found in the section on the improvement procedures for the TSP.

Two-Opt Improvement for Example VRP8 The 2-opt intra-route improvement procedure will be executed on the routes created by the nearest neighbor algorithm. The nearest neighbor route statistics are given in Table 9.4 and the routes are shown in Fig. 9.2. Only route 2 with four customers is eligible for improvement by a two-exchange improvement since the route has to have at least four edges. The exchange of edges $(c5–c1)$ and $(c3–d1)$ with edges $(c5–c3)$ and $(c1–d1)$ yields the largest savings of $894 + 2,600 - 1,461 - 1,600 = 433$. The total route length is decreased from 17,681 to 17,248. The improved routes are shown in Fig. 9.17.

Inter-route Improvements Algorithms All inter-route improvement algorithms attempt to reduce the total route length by moving one or more facilities to a differ-

Fig. 9.17 VRP8 nearest
neighbor plus two-opt routes

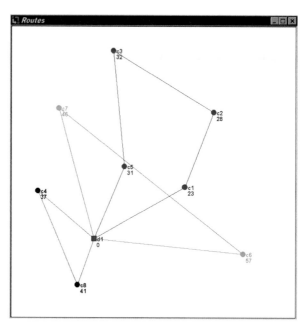

ent route. A move is feasible if the demand of the moved facility does not violate the vehicle capacity on the route it is moved to. Only feasible moves are tested. So the inter-route improvement routines will always maintain feasibility of the routes. The most common improvement algorithms are move and swap, while cyclic exchange is a much more complex improvement algorithm.

The move improvement algorithm attempts to reduce the total route length by moving a single facility to a new route. The facility is inserted in its best position on any route, while maintaining feasibility. If the routes are highly capacitated, i.e., the vehicle servicing that route is nearly full, then few feasible moves exist. In that case the move algorithm may find few or no feasible moves. All moves are tested and the move with the largest positive savings is executed. The algorithm thus belongs to the class of steepest descent improvement algorithms. For example, in Fig. 9.18 facility i is moved from route 1 to route 2. The simultaneous insertion and removal of a facility eliminates a total of three links and adds a total of three new links on the origin and destination routes combined. The move improvement algorithm can also be executed in the framework of first descent or simulated annealing.

Move Improvement for the VRP8 Example The 2-opt intra-route improvement procedure is first executed on all the routes created by the above construction procedures. After 2-opt has run, no further improvements on any of the routes can be made by the move improvement procedure.

The swap improvement procedure attempts to reduce the total route length by moving two facilities that are located on different routes to the other route. Swapping facilities tests more feasible exchanges than moving a facility, since removing one facility creates additional capacity on the vehicle to add the other facility. All

Fig. 9.18 Move exchange
illustration

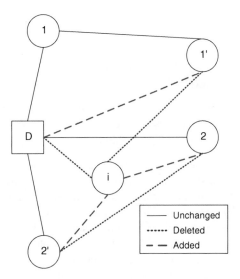

swaps are tested and the swap with the largest positive savings is executed. The algorithm thus belongs to the class of steepest descent improvement algorithms. The swap improvement algorithm can also be executed in the framework of first descent or simulated annealing. For example, in Fig. 9.19 facility *i* on route *1* is moved to its best position on route *2* without facility *j*, and facility *j* on route *2* is moved to its best position on route *1* without facility *i*. The simultaneous insertion and removal of a facility eliminates three links and adds three new links for each route.

Swap Improvement for the VRP8 Example The swap inter-route improvement procedure will be executed on the routes created by the serial savings algorithm. The

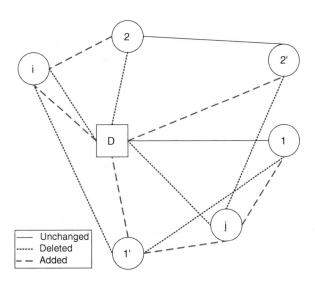

Fig. 9.19 Swap exchange
illustration

serial savings route statistics are given in Table 9.13 and the routes are shown in Fig. 9.6. The swap, which moves customer c_2 from between (d_1-c_3) on route 1 to between (c_1-c_6) on route 2 and customer c_5 from between (d_1-c_1) on route 2 to between (d_1-c_3) on route 1, has the largest savings. The savings are computed as follows.

remove $(d_1-c_2-c_3)$ + remove $(d_1-c_5-c_1)$ − add $(c_1-c_2-c_6)$ − add $(d_1-c_5-c_3)$ = $(2{,}417 + 1{,}646 − 2{,}600) + (1{,}082 + 894 − 1{,}461) − (1{,}103 + 1{,}990 − 1{,}231) − (1{,}082 + 1{,}600 − 2{,}600) = 1{,}463 + 515 − 1{,}862 − 82 = 34$

The total route length is decreased from 15,453 to 15,419. The improved routes statistics are summarized in Table 9.32 and shown in Fig. 9.20.

The cycle exchange improvement algorithm attempts to improve the combined length of the current routes by moving facilities in a cyclical fashion, provided the resulting routes remain feasible. A route can become infeasible if the quantity exceeds the truck capacity. For example, for a cycle consisting of three routes, facility i on route 1 is moved to its best position on route 2 without facility j, facility j on route 2 is moved to its best position on route 3 without facility k, and facility k on route 3 is move to its best position on route 1 without facility i. All cycle exchanges are tested and the cycle exchange with the largest positive savings is executed. The algorithm thus belongs to the class of steepest descent improvement algorithms. The cycle exchange improvement algorithm can also be executed in the framework of first descent or simulated annealing. The cycle length C is an algorithm parameter. C routes are examined in sequence, i.e., first routes 1 through C, then routes 2 through C + 1, ... and last routes C through C − 1. A 3-cycle exchange for three routes is illustrated in Fig. 9.21. The simultaneous insertion and removal of a facility eliminates three links and adds three new links for each route, unless the inserted facility is inserted between the same nodes as the removed facility. In this case only two links are added and deleted on that route, as shown in route 1 in the figure below. A 2-cycle exchange attempts to swap two facilities between two successively numbered routes, while the swap exchange algorithm attempts to swap two facilities between any two routes. A 2-cycle exchange will not find any improving exchanges after the swap algorithm has been executed.

Table 9.32 VRP8 serial savings followed by swap route statistics

Route	Facility							Quantity	Length
	0	1	2	3	4	5	6		
1	d_1	c_5	c_3	c_7	d_1			109	5,650
2	d_1	c_1	c_2	c_6	d_1			108	6,658
3	d_1	c_4	c_8	d_1				78	3,111
Total								295	15,419

Fig. 9.20 VRP8 serial savings plus swap routes

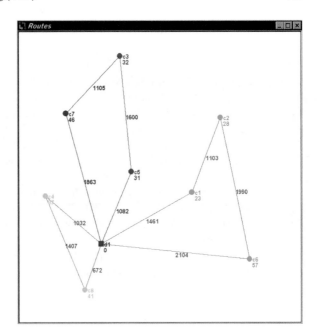

Fig. 9.21 3-Cycle exchange illustration

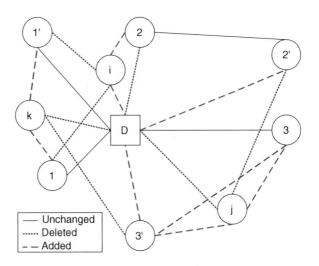

All the algorithms discussed so far belong to the class or route-generating algorithms, since the algorithm itself generates the routes. The formulation and solution algorithm for the set partitioning problem are the most prominent example of the class of route-selecting algorithms.

9.2.2 Set Partitioning Problem Formulation for the Classic VRP

The set partitioning problem (SPP) formulation belongs to the class of alternative selecting algorithms. The SPP selects and combines provided feasible service alternatives to satisfy service requirements at the lowest possible cost. The alternatives can be provided to the SPP by an external source or an auxiliary problem has to be solved to generate promising new alternatives. In the context of the classic vehicle routing problem, the service alternatives are feasible routes and the service requests are deliveries to customers. The cost of the alternative is typically either the route length or the route cost.

The SPP solution paradigm is very powerful in the sense that many realistic route constraints and route cost functions can be incorporated during the route generation process. The generation of service alternatives should be able to generate all possible feasible alternatives. The most obvious disadvantage of this approach is extremely large number of routes that may be generated. Since the service alternatives are either executed or not, the solution of the SPP requires the use of an integer programming solver. Efficient solution procedures must keep the number of service alternatives that are explicitly considered as small as possible. Solution procedures that are efficient and effective cannot simply rely on the "brute force" generation of alternatives, but must rather generate only a few highly promising alternatives. As such, set partitioning is more of solution approach rather than a fully specified solution algorithm, since many algorithm details have to be specialized for the problem that is being solved.

Formulation The problem is formulated based on the notion of a cover matrix A. The columns of the matrix correspond to feasible service alternatives and actions. There are N columns, which are indexed by j. The terms service alternative, column, feasible alternative, cover, and route are used interchangeably. The rows of the matrix correspond to the service requests. There are M rows, which are indexed by i. The terms service requests, rows, and customers will be used interchangeable. The objective is to minimize the overall cost for servicing all the requests with a subset of the feasible alternatives. The cost of executing a particular alternative is denoted by c_j. The elements a_{ij} of the cover matrix A are equal to 1 if the service alternative j covers or serves service request i, and are equal to zero otherwise. The variables x_j correspond to the binary decision to execute a feasible service alternative or not. The decision variables can only assume the values zero or one. Finally, the estimated cost of servicing request i with the best combination of alternatives found so far is denoted by p_i. If this cost based on the dual variable of the service constraint in the linear programming relaxation then it is denoted by π_i. The cost of servicing a request is also called the *row price*. The set partitioning formulation is given next.

Formulation 9.5. Set Partitioning Problem (SPP)

$$\min \quad \sum_{j=1}^{N} c_j x_j$$

$$s.t. \quad \sum_{j=1}^{N} a_{ij} x_j = 1 \qquad \forall i \quad [\pi_i] \tag{9.25}$$

$$x_{ij} \in \{0, 1\}$$

The set partitioning problem belongs to the class of binary integer programming problems and, as such, is difficult to solve to optimality for large problems.

In the above generic SPP formulation, the number of feasible alternatives that is executed is not restricted. In the VRP the number of routes is typically bounded. If the constraint that bounds the number of partitions is added, the following formulation is generated, which will be denoted by K-SPP. In the original SPP the value of K can thought off as being infinite. π_0 is the dual variable of the upper bound constraint on the number of routes. It can be interpreted as the opportunity cost of using one of the K possible routes.

Formulation 9.6. Set Partitioning Problem with Partition Count Constraint (K-SPP)

$$\min \quad \sum_{k=1}^{N} c_k x_k$$

$$s.t. \quad \sum_{k=1}^{N} a_{ik} x_k = 1 \qquad \forall i \quad [\pi_i]$$

$$\sum_{k=1}^{N} x_k \leq K \qquad\qquad [\pi_0] \tag{9.26}$$

$$x_k \in \{0, 1\}$$

A feasible partition, denoted by J^+, is a set of no more than K feasible alternatives that service all requests and is thus a feasible solution to (9.25) or (9.26). The decision variables x_j of all the alternatives in a feasible partition are equal to 1.

$$J^+ = \{j = 1.. N \,|\, x_j = 1\} \tag{9.27}$$

Based on a feasible partition, the nonnegative row prices can be determined. The prices must satisfy the condition that the cost of the alternative in the feasible partition is exactly equal to the sum of the prices of the service requests it covers, i.e.,

$$c_j^+ = \sum_{i=1}^{M} a_{ij} p_i \qquad \forall j \in J^+ \tag{9.28}$$

An alternative way of interpreting (9.28) is to state that the cost of the route is split or allocated among all the customers that are serviced by this route. The set of customers included on or serviced by route j is indicated by I_j. The row prices p_i can be determined either by heuristic allocation schemes or based on the linear programming relaxation of the SPP. The general expression of the computation of the row prices is given next, where w_i is the "weight" or difficulty measure of customer i used in the allocation of the route cost among the customers serviced by this route.

$$I_j = \left\{ i = 1.. \, M \,|\, a_{ij} = 1 \right\} \tag{9.29}$$

$$p_i = \frac{w_i}{\sum\limits_{i \in I_j} w_i} c_j^+ \tag{9.30}$$

The performance of solution algorithms for the SPP is improved if the row prices are based on an "equitable" or realistic allocation, i.e., they reflect the true cost of satisfying the service requests. In the vehicle routing framework, two important factors in the cost of servicing a customer are its distance to the distribution center, denoted by d_{0i}, and its demand, denoted by dem_i.

Intuitive price allocation schemes are be based solely on distance to the depot or the demand.

$$p_i = \frac{d_{0i}}{\sum\limits_{i \in I_j} d_{0i}} c_j^+ \tag{9.31}$$

$$p_i = \frac{dem_i}{\sum\limits_{i \in I_j} dem_i} c_j^+ \tag{9.32}$$

Another price allocation scheme is to allocate them based on a customer difficulty measure which is the product of distance to the depot and the demand, i.e.,

$$p_i = \frac{dem_i \cdot d_{0i}}{\sum\limits_{k \in I_j} dem_k \cdot d_{0k}} c_j^+ = \frac{dem_i \cdot d_{0i}}{\sum\limits_{k} a_{kj} \cdot dem_k \cdot d_{0k}} c_j^+ \tag{9.33}$$

A new feasible alternative or column can never be economically desirable if its total cost is more than the current cost for the rows it covers. In other words, a new column needs only to be considered if its savings s_j are positive, where the savings are computed as

$$s_j = \sum_{i=1}^{M} a_{ij} p_i - c_j \tag{9.34}$$

Instead of the savings, often the negative savings or the reduced cost rc_j are used to compute the desirability of a column. A candidate service request is desirable if it has a negative reduced cost in the corresponding SPP. The expression for the reduced cost of a route in the K-SPP is derived later on in the section on the auxiliary pricing problem.

$$rc_j = -s_j = c_j - z_j = c_j - \sum_{i=1}^{M} a_{ij} p_i \qquad (9.35)$$

Solution Approaches for the SPP As indicated before, the SPP formulation can be solved in many different ways. Most of these solution approaches are heuristics. In addition, a solution approach may have to be adapted to a particular problem to create a solution algorithm. The following discussion of various solution approaches will use the classic VRP as its target problem. In all of the solution approaches a tradeoff has to be made between, on the one hand, the size of the SPP problem and thus the solution effort require to solve the SPP problem and, on the other hand, the algorithmic complexities and work required to keep the size of SPP small. The SPP problem is also denoted as the master problem in the following approaches.

(1) Complete Generation All the possible feasible service alternatives or columns are generated and added to the master problem. The SPP problem is then solved with an integer programming solver. Since the number of feasible service alternatives grows exponentially with the problem size and each has an associated binary decision variable, this approach is only feasible for the smallest of problem instances.

(2) Row Price Heuristic A current feasible partition is generated by a heuristic. Based on the current feasible solution or partition, the cost of service is allocated to the customers or rows using a pricing scheme. New service alternatives are evaluated using these row prices and a service alternative is only added to the master problem if it has positive savings. Periodically the master problem is resolved, which may yield a new lowest-cost feasible partition and a new set of row prices. All the feasible service alternatives are evaluated in a systematic process, but typically only a very small fraction of service alternatives has positive savings and thus the master problem remains small.

(3) Auxiliary Pricing Problem A small number of desirable service alternatives are added initially to the master problem. The linear programming relaxation of the master problem is solved which yields a set of dual variables for the rows. An auxiliary pricing problem is solved using the dual variables to identify improving service alternatives. Those alternatives are added to the master problem and the algorithm iterates until no further improving alternatives can be found. Only a small fraction of the feasible alternatives is generated. When the algorithm stops, the linear programming solution provides a lower bound on the solution value. The linear programming solution is typically fractional. Most of the computational work is performed by the pricing problem.

If the linear programming solution is integer then it is the optimal solution. Otherwise, the final SPP can be solved as an integer problem for the current set of alternatives but this only yields a heuristic solution for the original VRP. The SPP can also be solved in a branch-and-price scheme to find the optimal solution, but this requires solving the pricing problem at every node of the search tree.

The solution approaches based on the row prices heuristic and the auxiliary pricing problem are more efficient if they are started from a high-quality feasible partition. This initial partition is typically generated with heuristics.

It should be noted that the heuristics used in the initialization phase, the cost allocation scheme of the row price heuristic, and the auxiliary pricing problem are all problem specific and should exploit the structural properties of the problem in order to make the solution approach efficient.

Row Price Heuristic This heuristic was originally proposed in Cullen et al. (1981). The heuristic is based on the principle that only feasible alternatives that can improve the current best solution are added to the SPP. This possible improvement is based on the computation of the estimated savings for each feasible alternative. The SPP is also called the master problem and the function to generate additional feasible alternatives is called the sub problem or generation problem.

Algorithm 9.2. Row Price Heuristic for the Set Partitioning Problem

1. Start with a feasible partition J^+ and construct a master SPP that contains just this feasible partition.
2. Determine the new row prices by allocating the column prices "equitable" among the service requests covered by it using (9.30) or a similar allocation scheme.
3. Generate the next feasible alternative and compute its estimated savings s_j with (9.31).
4. If the savings are positive add this alternative to the master SPP, otherwise discard this alternative
5. If enough new alternatives have been added to the master SPP formulation or if all possible alternatives have been evaluated, stop the generation process and solve the current master SPP and continue with step 6. Otherwise return to step 3.
6. If the solution of the master SPP is within the desired tolerance or if all possible alternatives have been evaluated, then stop, else go to step 2.

This algorithm is a heuristic because the row prices have been determined in a heuristic manner, i.e., Eq. (9.30) was used to allocate the row prices. The row prices in turn determined if a feasible alternative entered the master SPP or not. If for any set of row prices satisfying Eq. (9.27), no feasible alternatives existed with negative reduced cost, then the current feasible partition would be an optimal solution. In the next section, the row prices at each iteration are determined with linear programming as the dual variables of the service constraints.

Row Price Heuristic for the SPP for the VRP8 Example In this problem all routes will be systematically generated by the number of customers on the route, i.e., in route set h all routes that visit exactly h customers will be generated. Recall that the capacity for all vehicles was equal to 120. The sum of the four smallest demands equals 114, so routes of four customers are possible, but many of the routes with four customers will have an infeasible quantity that exceeds the vehicle capacity.

Table 9.33 VRP8 customer relative weights

Facility	Distance	Quantity	Weight
c1	1,461	23	33,603
c2	2,417	28	67,676
c3	2,600	32	83,200
c4	1,032	37	38,184
c5	1,082	31	33,542
c6	2,104	57	119,928
c7	1,863	46	85,698
c8	672	41	27,552

The sum of the five smallest demands equals 151, so no routes of five customers are possible. All routes that contain the same customers will be treated and counted as a single route. This implies that if a route has a feasible quantity, then a TSP is solved for the customer facilities plus the depot facility on the route, so that the shortest route length for that set of customers is determined. The sequence of customers that yielded the shortest route length must be saved. If the route quantity exceeds the vehicle capacity then the shortest route length can be considered to be infinite. The number of route candidates is then computed as the sum of combinations of N customers in groups of 1, 2, 3, and 4. This is an upper bound on the number of feasible route candidates since some routes containing three and four customers may exceed the vehicle capacity.

$$\# \ route \ candidates = C_1^8 + C_2^8 + C_3^8 + C_4^8 = 8 + 28 + 56 + 70 = 162$$

The potential savings of the feasible route candidates are evaluated based on the best-known feasible partition. The lowest total route length known at this time is 15,419 and the route summary statistics are shown in Table 9.32 and the routes are shown in Fig. 9.20. The weight of each customer is computed as the product of its demand and distance to the depot. The weight for each customer can be interpreted as a relative difficulty index of servicing that customer, where higher indices indicate customers that are more difficult to serve (Table 9.33).

The row prices based on these routes and customer weights are shown in Table 9.34. Each route cost is allocated to the customers served by this route proportional to the customer weights.

Table 9.34 VRP8 customer initial row prices based on best known partition

Facility	Route	Total route		Individual facility	
		Cost	Weight	Weight	Cost
c1	2	6,658	221,207	33,603	1,011
c2	2	6,658	221,207	67,676	2,037
c3	1	5,650	202,440	83,200	2,322
c4	3	3,111	65,736	38,184	1,807
c5	1	5,650	202,440	33,542	936
c6	2	6,658	221,207	119,928	3,610
c7	1	5,650	202,440	85,698	2,392
c8	3	3,111	65,736	27,552	1,304

Fig. 9.22 VRP8 SPP row price master problem

	X	Y	Z	AA	AB	AC	AD	AE	AF	AG	AH	AI
					Route	1	2	3	4	5	6	7	Sum
44					Route	1	2	3	4	5	6	7	Sum
45	Facility	Quant.		Cost	Cost	5650	6658	3111	4064	5311	5906	4509	0
46	c1	23	1011				1			1			0
47	c2	28	2037				1						0
48	c3	32	2322			1					1		0
49	c4	37	1807					1	1		1	1	0
50	c5	31	936			1				1		1	0
51	c6	57	3610				1			1			0
52	c7	46	2392			1			1		1	1	0
53	c8	41	1304					1					0
54					Exec.								0
55					Load	109	108	78	83	111	115	114	
56					Red.C.	0	0	0	-135	-246	-615	-626	

$$p_1 = L_2\left(\frac{w_1}{w_1 + w_2 + w_6}\right) = 6{,}658\left(\frac{33{,}603}{221{,}207}\right) = 1{,}011$$

All possible 162 candidate routes are now evaluated. Routes that are infeasible because of customer quantities are considered to have savings equal to negative infinity. Consider for example the route $\{c1, c2, c3, c5\}$ created by the sweep cluster-first algorithm and which has a length of 6,892, and the route $\{c5, c1, c6\}$ created by the serial savings algorithm, which has a length equal to 5,311. Their respective savings are computed next.

$$s_{5321} = (1{,}011 + 2{,}037 + 2{,}322 + 936) - 6{,}892 = -586$$
$$s_{516} = (1{,}011 + 936 + 3{,}610) - 5{,}311 = 246$$

The route $\{c5, c1, c6\}$ has positive savings. Out of the 162 possible candidate routes, only four feasible routes have positive savings. Those four routes are added to the initial feasible partition routes in the SPP master model. The route $\{c5, c1, c6\}$ has index 5 in the master problem. The SPP master problem is then solved with an IP solver. The IP solver in Excel is used. The master problem is shown in Fig. 9.22. The eight customer facilities, with their demand and cost allocation are shown in rows 46–53. The problem contains seven candidate routes, routes 1–3 are the initial feasible partition, and routes 4–7 are added because they have a negative reduced cost. The shortest route length, the total quantity on the route, and the reduced costs are shown in rows 45, 55, and 56, respectively.

The reduced costs for the routes in the feasible partition that generated the row prices are equal to zero as required. The reduced costs for the additional routes are negative. The elements in column AI are computed with the SUMPRODUCT function. For example, element AI45 contains the total cost of the executed routes and is given by SUMPRODUCT(AB$54:AH$54,AB45:AH45), and element AI46 contains the number of executed routes customer $c1$ is included on and is given by SUMPRODUCT(AB$54:AH$54,AB46:AH46). It should be noted that rows 55 and 56 are not part of the master problem and are only shown to indicate that the corresponding routes have feasible quantities and zero or negative reduced costs. While routes 4–7 have negative reduced costs, they have not been selected to be executed in the optimal solution of the integer (binary) programming formulation. This is not

Fig. 9.23 VRP8 SPP
row price master solver
parameters

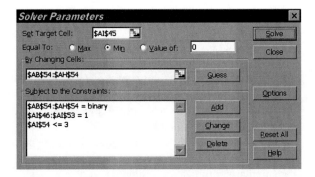

Fig. 9.24 VRP8 SPP row
price master problem solution

	X	Y	Z	AA	AB	AC	AD	AE	AF	AG	AH	AI	
44				Route	1	2	3	4	5	6	7	Sum	
45	Facility	Quant.	Cost	Cost	5650	6658	3111	4064	5311	5906	4509	15419	
46	c1	23	1011			1			1			1	
47	c2	28	2037			1						1	
48	c3	32	2322		1					1		1	
49	c4	37	1807				1	1		1	1	1	
50	c5	31	936		1				1		1	1	
51	c6	57	3610			1			1			1	
52	c7	46	2392		1			1		1	1	1	
53	c8	41	1304				1					1	
54				Exec.	1	1	1	0	0	0	0	3	
55				Load	109	108	78	83	111	115	114		
56				Red.C.	0	0	0	-135	-246	-615	-626		

an error or contradiction since an integer programming and not a linear programming
formulation is solved.

The solver parameters for the master problem are shown in Fig. 9.23. The objective is the total cost in cell AI45. The decision variables are the route execution
variables in cells AB54:AH54. There are only three constraints. The first constraint
forces the decision variables to be either zero or one. The second constraint forces
each customer to be exactly on one route. The third constraint forces the number of
routes to be less than or equal to 3.

The optimal solution is shown in Fig. 9.24. The selected routes are identical to the
initial feasible partition and none of the new routes is selected. The total route length
remains 15,419. Since the same routes have been selected, the row prices also remain
unchanged and the algorithm terminates. The obtained solution is not guaranteed to be
optimal. Only solving a SPP problem with the 162 possible routes would have guaranteed to yield the optimal solution. The tradeoff is the small size and solvability of the
master problem versus the optimality of the routes that are selected. For larger problem instances, generating all feasible route candidates is computationally not possible.

In the VRP16 example which is given at the end of this chapter, the route alternatives are generated in stages. Each stage evaluates the routes with exactly h customers on a route. At the end of each stage the SPP is solved which may yield new row
prices. This is often called the bootstrap method for route generation. Because this
latter approach starts from an initial partition of lower quality than the one shown
above, many more alternatives will be added to the SPP.

Optimal Solution based on an Auxiliary Pricing Problem The following exposition requires prior knowledge of linear programming concepts such as duality, primal and dual formulations, and dynamic programming. Further information on these topics can be found in a textbook on linear programming such as Bazaraa et al. (2005). This material forms the basis of solution algorithms for more complicated variants of the vehicle routing problem such as vehicle routing with backhauling or vehicle routing with time windows, but it can be safely skipped if those variants will also be skipped.

One way to avoid the problems of selecting the proper row pricing scheme and the generation of all feasible routes is to use a pricing problem. A pricing problem is an auxiliary optimization problem that determines one or more desirable service covers based on a current feasible solution or it establishes that no new desirable service cover exists. The current feasible solution typically corresponds to optimal solution of the master problem and its linearization yields the current values of the prices. Since desirable service covers are added to the master problem, this approach is also called *column generation*. The three terms *route*, *column*, and *cover* all refer to the same type of service provided.

Recall that the following notation is used when using a pricing problem

z_{ik}	decision indicating if service request or customer i is assigned to service cover or route k or not
$C_k(z_{ik})$	service cover or route k, based on decision variables z_{ik}
c_k	cost (or length) of service cover k
π_i	dual variable associated with cost of servicing customer i based on the linear relaxation of the current master problem
π_0	dual variable associated with the constraint that limits the maximum number of covers (routes) that can be executed

The linear programming relaxation of the SPP can be written in the following canonical form, i.e., for a minimization objective all constraints are either equality or greater-than constraints.

Formulation 9.7. Primal Linear Relaxation of the K-SPP

$$\min \quad \sum_{k=1}^{N} c_k x_k$$

$$s.t. \quad \sum_{k=1}^{N} a_{ik} x_k = 1 \qquad \forall i \quad [\pi_i] \tag{9.36}$$

$$-\sum_{k=1}^{N} x_k \geq -K \qquad [\pi_0]$$

$$0 \leq x_k \leq 1$$

The corresponding dual formulation is then given by.

Formulation 9.8. Dual Linear Relaxation of the K-SPP

$$\max \quad \sum_{i=1}^{M} \pi_i - K\pi_0$$

$$s.t. \quad \sum_{i=1}^{M} a_{ik}\pi_i - \pi_0 \leq c_k \quad \forall k[x_k] \tag{9.37}$$

$$\pi_0 \geq 0, \; \pi_i \text{ unrestricted}$$

The primal K-SPP formulation above uses the equality sign for the assignment constraints and the corresponding dual variables are unrestricted in sign. If the cost or length of a tour satisfies the triangle inequality for all triplets of facilities on the tour, then the assignment constraint can be written as a greater-than-or-equal constraint and the two formulations, with the equality constraint and the greater-than-or-equal constraint, respectively, will yield the same solution. In the later case of the greater-than-or-equal constraint, the dual variable corresponding to the assignment constraint can only have nonnegative values. For the classic vehicle routing problem, the distances are based on the Euclidean distance norm and satisfy the triangle inequality, so an optimal solution for which all the dual variables are nonnegative exists.

An additional desirable service cover will have a negative reduced cost rc.

$$rc_k = c_k - \sum_i a_{ik}\pi_i + \pi_0 \tag{9.38}$$

This can be interpreted as follows. The cost of an additional route plus the opportunity cost of consuming one of the possible K routes ($c_k + \pi_0$) must be less than the sum of the current costs servicing the customers on the route ($\sum_i a_{ik}\pi_i$) for this additional route to be desirable. Alternatively, assume that the optimal solution for the primal and dual formulation has been found. If a new cover or column is generated and its reduced cost rc computed based on the current optimal values of the dual variables is negative, then the dual problem becomes infeasible and the primal problem is no longer optimal and this new column must be added to the problem. Conversely, if no new service cover with a negative reduced cost exists then the current solution is the optimal. It should be noted that optimality is only assured if all possible feasible service covers are examined. If one or more service covers with a negative reduced cost are found, then they are added to the master problem. Finding a service cover with negative reduced cost or proving that such service cover does not exist is called the pricing problem PP_j.

Formulation 9.9. Generative Variant of Pricing Problem for the K-SPP

$$\min \quad c_j - \sum_i \pi_i \cdot z_{ij} + \pi_0$$

$$s.t. \quad C_j(z_{ij}) = feasible \tag{9.39}$$

$$z_{ij} \in \{0, 1\}$$

If $\overline{PP_j}$, the linear programming relaxation of PP_j, has a positive solution value, then PP_j also has a positive solution value. This indicates that the current solution to the master problem is optimal since no new cover with a negative reduced cost can be found.

For the pricing problem to be part of an efficient solution algorithm it has to have three structural properties. First, the objective function can be written as a mathematical expression of the decision variables. Second, the description of a feasible service cover can be written as a set of constraints in the decision variables. Third, the pricing problem can solved efficiently to optimality.

For the case of the classic vehicle routing, a service cover is feasible if the total customer demand on the route does not violate the truck capacity. Since in the classic vehicle routing problem the costs and capacities are independent of the vehicle, we can eliminate in this case the subscript j from the pricing problem. For the classic vehicle routing problem, the pricing problem is given below. x_{ij} indicates if the vehicle travels directly from node i to node j at a cost of d_{ij}. The number of customer nodes is equal to M, customer nodes are indicated by the index i and the depot is indicated by the index 0. The cost of a column or route is given by the following expression in function of the x_{ij}.

$$c_k = \sum_{i=0}^{M} \sum_{j=1}^{M} d_{ij} x_{ij} + \sum_{i=1}^{M} d_{i0} x_{i0} \qquad (9.40)$$

Using

$$z_{jk} = \sum_{i=0}^{M} x_{ij}$$
$$\sum_{i=1}^{M} x_{i0} = 1 \qquad (9.41)$$

the objective function of the pricing problem is then.

$$c_k - \sum_{j=1}^{M} \pi_j z_{jk} + \pi_0 = \sum_{i=0}^{M} \sum_{j=1}^{M} d_{ij} x_{ij} + \sum_{i=1}^{M} d_{i0} x_{i0}$$
$$- \sum_{j=1}^{M} \pi_j \left(\sum_{i=0}^{M} x_{ij} \right) + \pi_0 \left(\sum_{i=1}^{M} x_{i0} \right) \qquad (9.42)$$

The pricing problem formulation can thus also be written as follows.

Formulation 9.10. Pricing Problem Shortest Path Formulation for the K-SPP

$$Min \sum_{i=0}^{M}\sum_{j=1}^{M}(d_{ij} - \pi_j)x_{ij} + \sum_{i=1}^{M}(d_{i0} + \pi_0)x_{i0}$$

$$s.t. \sum_{j=1}^{M}x_{0j} = 1$$

$$\sum_{j=0,j\neq i}^{M} x_{ij} - \sum_{j=0,j\neq i}^{M} x_{ji} = 0 \qquad \forall i = 1...M$$

$$-\sum_{j=1}^{M}x_{j0} = -1$$

$$\sum_{i=0}^{M}\sum_{j=1}^{M}dem_j x_{ij} \leq cap$$

$$x_{ij} \in \{0, 1\}$$

(9.43)

This is also called the generative variant of the pricing problem, since the pricing problem constructs the new route with the best reduced cost. It is not necessary to always find the optimal solution to the pricing problem. As soon as any feasible cover with negative reduced cost has been found, it can be added to the master problem to generate a new set of row prices. Clearly, it is essential to the overall algorithm convergence that the pricing problem only generates feasible covers and that it can be solved quickly. It should also be observed that the dual variable π_0 has no impact on the decision values or the optimization problem, but it must be incorporated when determining if the objective function value is negative or not.

In the preceding derivations the constraint corresponding to the maximum number of routes was written as a greater-than constraint in the canonical form, which has its corresponding dual variable π_0 nonnegative. If the constraint is written as a less-than constraint, the corresponding dual variable π_0 is then negative or zero. The sign of π_0 in the pricing problem becomes then negative everywhere. Since the sign of π_0 is now identical to the sign of the other dual variables π_i the notation can be simplified. In the dual objective, $K\pi_0$ is now added to the sum of the π_i dual variables, but π_0 itself is negative. Either sign convention can be used, provided the convention is applied consistently.

For this small example, an alternative pricing problem is to enumerate all possible feasible service covers, computing the optimal TSP tour length for each service cover, and then to compute the reduced cost for each cover. This is also called the selective variant of the pricing problem, since the pricing problem selects the best new route from a list of feasible routes. For a known service cover k, the decision variables z_{ik} then reduce to parameters a_{ik}.

Formulation 9.11. Selective Variant of Pricing Problem for the K-SPP

$$\min \quad \left(c_k - \sum_i a_{ik}\pi_i + \pi_0\right)x_k \tag{9.44}$$
$$s.t. \quad x_k \in \{0, 1\}$$

In this case the linear relaxation of the pricing problem will automatically yield integer answers, so we can use a linear programming solver for the relaxed pricing problem and still get integer answers.

Formulation 9.12. Linear Selective Variant of Pricing Problem for the K-SPP

$$\min \quad \left(c_k - \sum_i a_{ik}\pi_i + \pi_0\right)x_k \tag{9.45}$$
$$s.t. \quad 0 \le x_k \le 1$$

Consider again the generative variant of the pricing problem variant, which has to generate the route with lowest possible reduced cost. The generative variant of the generative pricing problem can be written in a more general format so that it can later on be extended for more complicated vehicle routing problems such as the Vehicle Routing Problem with Backhauling (VRPB) or the Vehicle Routing Problem with Time Windows (VRPTW).

Formulation 9.13. Generalized Generative Variant of Pricing Problem for the K-SPP

$$Min \quad \sum_{i=0}^{M}\sum_{j=1}^{M}(d_{ij} - \pi_j)x_{ij} + \sum_{i=1}^{M}(d_{i0} + \pi_0)x_{i0}$$

$$s.t. \quad \sum_{j=1}^{M} x_{0j} = 1$$

$$\sum_{j=0,j\neq i}^{M} x_{ij} - \sum_{j=0,j\neq i}^{M} x_{ji} = 0 \quad \forall i \tag{9.46}$$

$$-\sum_{k=1}^{M} x_{j0} = -1$$

$$x_{ij}(q_i + dem_j - q_j) \le 0 \quad \forall i \forall j$$
$$LB_i \le q_i \le UB_i \quad \forall i$$
$$x_{ij} \in \{0, 1\}$$

This pricing problem has two types of variables x and q. The x variables indicate if the arc in the network is taken, the q variables indicate the load initially on the vehicle required to service the nodes on the route up to and including the current node. For the classic vehicle routing problem the following boundary conditions apply.

$$q_0 = 0$$
$$LB_i = 0 \quad \forall i \qquad\qquad (9.47)$$
$$UB_i = cap \quad \forall i$$

If the arc selection variables x_{ij} are binary, then the capacity constraints can be linearized and rewritten as

$$q_i + dem_j - q_j \leq \left(1 - x_{ij}\right) \cdot cap \qquad\qquad (9.48)$$

This pricing problem is a shortest-path formulation with additional constraints that limits the total demand of the nodes visited on the path to the vehicle capacity. This formulation can be extended to multiple resource constraints, such as load weight and load volume, and even to time window constraints. Hence its name is the Shortest Path Problem with Resource Constraints (SPPRC). The first three constraints are the conservation of flow constraints for the origin (depot), for the intermediate nodes (customers), and for the destination (depot), respectively. Because of the additional knapsack constraint, solutions are not automatically integer and the use of integer programming solution algorithm and solver is required. If this problem is solved with dynamic programming, the solution has the integrality property. If the underlying graph is acyclic, the dynamic programming solution is optimal. If the underlying graph is not acyclic, as is usual the case in vehicle routing problems, the solution may include paths with finite cycles. Even though the cycle may have a net negative cost, and so it would be beneficial to traverse the cycle infinitely many times, the number of cycles is kept finite because of the load constraints. If negative cycles are allowed and thus a node can be visited more than once, then the problem includes the knapsack problem as a special case and is still hard to solve to optimality for very large problem instances. Its complexity is said to be pseudo-polynomial because it is polynomial for a given set of parameter values but large parameter values may require excessive computation times. However, in this case several algorithms for the solution of the SPPRC are given in Ball et al. (1995) that can solve realistic problem sizes in acceptable time, but they require complicated algorithm steps and data structures.

When a route k containing negative cycles is added to the master problem, the definition of a_{ik} is changed to be the number of times customer i is visited by route k. The covering constraints in the master problem ensure that each customer is visited exactly once; hence routes with negative cycles can never be elements of the integer solution of the vehicle routing problem. Alternatively, the algorithm itself can be prevented from generating any cycles, i.e., a route cannot visit a customer more than once. This requires a data structure that captures which customers are already visited by a route and a step to check that the additional customer is not already on the route. This alternative of the pricing problem will generate fewer additional routes. Observe that while the original arc costs in the example are symmetric and all positive, the reduced arc costs are asymmetric and negative reduced costs occur frequently.

The pricing problem is a classic example of forward dynamic programming. Dynamic programming is characterized by states, stages, feasible transitions, and an evaluation function for a state. The dynamic programming algorithm proceeds systematically from state to state through feasible transitions to reach the final state with the best evaluation function. At each state the decision has to be made which transition to execute to reach the next state. Each executed transition corresponds to a stage of the algorithm. In the pricing problem each node i has a set of states indicated by the tuple (i, q_k) and each state has a label or evaluation function $PL(i, q_k)$. q_k indicates the initial load required on the route to service all the nodes on the route including the current node i. PL indicates the current lowest travel distance to reach this state from the origin node. A node can have multiple states because several routes, that have visited different combinations of customers, can reach that node and each route may have a different initial load on the vehicle. In each stage of the algorithm, one label is converted from temporary to permanent. Recall that a temporary label corresponds to the upper bound on the shortest path length and that a permanent label indicates the actual shortest path length. Since the load that has to be placed on the vehicle always increases when another customer is added to the route, this load becomes the state selector used by the dynamic programming algorithm. Initially, all labels on the nodes are temporary. The dynamic programming algorithm selects the state with the lowest load, updates the labels of its feasible successor states, and then makes this label permanent. The algorithm terminates when all the temporary labels of all the facilities have become permanent. The labels of the destination node, i.e., the depot to which the vehicle returns, are excluded of this test. If there is a state for the destination (depot) node which has a label with negative cost, this corresponds to a route with negative reduced cost that is added to the master problem. The route is constructed by tracing backwards from the state with the negative cost label of the destination node.

For the SPPRC problem, the number of states and stages is not known in advance. For the case of the SPP with positive arc lengths, which was previously solved with Dijkstra's algorithm, each node has only one state and thus one label and the number of stages is equal to the number of nodes. For the SPPRC, when a vehicle travels from state to state, the load on the vehicle monotonically increases so the dynamic programming algorithm completes in a final number of steps since the vehicle has a finite capacity. The values of the label that are converted from temporary to permanent in the sequence of stages may increase or decrease. In fact, the goal of the pricing problem is to find routes with a negative reduced path length. An upper bound on the number of possible states is the product of the number of nodes times the vehicle capacity, when this capacity expressed as an integer number. The

Table 9.35 VRP8 linear programming relaxation solution of the master problem (Iteration 0)

Facility	Route	1	2	3	Sum	Dual
	Cost	7,031	5,311	3,111	15,453	15,453
c1			1		1	954
c2		1			1	2,011
c3		1			1	2,473
c4				1	1	1,807
c5					1	953
c6			1		1	3,404
c7		1	1		1	2,547
c8				1	1	1,304
	Exec.	1	1	1	3	0

Table 9.36 VRP8 reduced arc costs for the shortest path pricing problem (Iteration 1)

	c1	c2	c3	c4	c5	c6	c7	c8	d1
c1		−908	−345	262	−59	−2,173	−466	716	1,461
c2	149		−827	889	503	−1,414	−365	1,741	2,417
c3	1,174	−365		391	647	−66	−1,442	1,951	2,600
c4	1,115	685	−275		311	−390	−1,378	103	1,032
c5	−60	−555	−873	−543		−1,349	−1,321	450	1,082
c6	277	−21	865	1,207	1,102		731	1,062	2,104
c7	1,127	171	−1,368	−638	273	−126		1,135	1,863
c8	1,066	1,034	782	−400	801	−1,038	−108		672
d1	507	406	127	−775	129	−1,300	−684	−632	

running time of the algorithm is said to be pseudo-polynomial since it is polynomial in the problem size, i.e., the number of nodes, but the running time increases with value of a parameter, i.e. the vehicle capacity. The dynamic programming algorithm can thus handle negative costs and even cost structures that are more complicated than a linear expression.

SPP with Linear Programming Pricing for the VRP8 Example The performance characteristics of the iterations of the linear programming based pricing problem depend on the initial partition. This example starts with the routes generated by the parallel savings algorithm. Recall that the total length of those four routes is 15,453. The linear programming master problem starts off with those three routes only, and the value of the primal feasible solution and the objective function of the master problem are both equal to 15,453.

The reduced costs are based on the interfacility distance and the dual variables in the solution of the linear relaxation of the first master problem (Table 9.35). The first master problem is highly dual degenerate, and the dual variables used are equal to the heuristic allocation of the row prices and π_0 is set equal to zero.

Table 9.37 VRP8 shortest path pricing problem (Iteration 1, Step 1)

Node 1				Node 2				Node 3			
q	C	pred	ip	q	C	pred	ip	q	C	pred	ip
23	507	0 (0,0)		28	406	0 (0,0)		32	127	0 (0,0)	
Node 4				**Node 5**				**Node 6**			
q	C	pred	ip	q	C	pred	ip	q	C	pred	ip
37	-775	0 (0,0)		31	129	0 (0,0)		57	-1300	0 (0,0)	
Node 7				**Node 8**				**Node t**			
q	C	pred	ip	q	C	pred	ip	q	C	pred	ip
46	-684	0 (0,0)		41	-632	0 (0,0)					

Table 9.38 VRP8 shortest path pricing problem (Iteration 1, Step 2)

Node 1				Node 2				Node 3			
q	C	pred	ip	q	C	pred	ip	q	C	pred	ip
23	507	0 (0,0)	2	28	406	0 (0,0)		32	127	0 (0,0)	
				51	-401	1 (23, 507)		55	162	1 (23, 507)	
Node 4				**Node 5**				**Node 6**			
q	C	pred	ip	q	C	pred	ip	q	C	pred	ip
37	-775	0 (0,0)		31	129	0 (0,0)		57	-1300	0 (0,0)	
60	769	1 (23, 507)		54	449	1 (23, 507)		80	-1666	1 (23, 507)	
Node 7				**Node 8**				**Node t**			
q	C	pred	ip	q	C	pred	ip	q	C	pred	ip
46	-684	0 (0,0)		41	-632	0 (0,0)		23	1968	1 (23, 507)	
69	42	1 (23, 507)		64	1223	1 (23, 507)					

The reduced arc costs are computed with the following formulas.

$$rc_{ik} = d_{ik} - \pi_k$$
$$rc_{ki} = d_{ki} - \pi_i \qquad\qquad (9.49)$$
$$rc_{i0} = d_{i0} + \pi_0$$

The reduced costs on the arcs of the shortest path network are given in Table 9.36. Observe that these reduced arc costs are no longer symmetrical and that many of them are negative.

The first three steps of the algorithm to find the shortest paths with negative reduced length are shown in the next three tables. Table 9.37 shows the shortest labels when the artificial source node is made permanent. The node-and-label combination with the lowest load is node 1 with load 23. For each node, the table shows the list of labels with the label information. This includes the load q, the shortest known length of the path to this node with this load and the predecessor label on this shortest path, and finally ip which is empty for a temporary label and equal to the step index when this label became permanent.

The node 1 with load 23 combination will be made permanent in step 2, as indicated by the shaded area in Table 9.38. The node-and-label combinations that can be reached from node 1 with load 23 are updated or added to the table if they did not already exist. Since the load 23 of node 1 can be followed by each of the

Table 9.39 VRP8 shortest path pricing problem (Iteration 1, Step 3)

Node 1				Node 2				Node 3			
q	C	pred	ip	q	C	pred	ip	q	C	pred	ip
23	507	0 (0,0)	2	28	406	0 (0,0)	3	32	127	0 (0,0)	
51	555	2 (28, 406)		51	-401	1 (23, 507)		55	162	1 (23, 507)	
								60	-421	2 (28, 406)	

Node 4				Node 5				Node 6			
q	C	pred	ip	q	C	pred	ip	q	C	pred	ip
37	-775	0 (0,0)		31	129	0 (0,0)		57	-1300	0 (0,0)	
60	769	1 (23, 507)		54	449	1 (23, 507)		80	-1666	1 (23, 507)	
65	1295	2 (28, 406)		59	909	2 (28, 406)		85	-1008	2 (28, 406)	

Node 7				Node 8				Node t			
q	C	pred	ip	q	C	pred	ip	q	C	pred	ip
46	-684	0 (0,0)		41	-632	0 (0,0)		23	1968	1 (23, 507)	
69	42	1 (23, 507)		64	1223	1 (23, 507)		28	406	2 (28, 406)	
74	41	2 (28, 406)		69	2147	2 (28, 406)					

other nodes on feasible routes, a new row corresponding to a new load will be added to all the nodes. For instance, traveling from node 1 with load 23 to node 2 with load 28 generates a new node and load combination of node 2 with load 51. The shortest length to this node and load combination is the path length to node 1 plus the adjusted distance between node 1 and node 2, i.e. $507+(-908)=-401$. Similarly for node 3, a new node-and-load combination is added with load equal to $23+32=55$ and path length $507+(-345)=162$. Finally, for node t which corresponds to the destination depot, the new node-and-load combination has a load of 23 and a path length of $507+1461=1968$. This combination corresponds to a route starting at the depot, visiting node 1 only, and then returning to the depot. This route is not a route candidate that has the possibility of improving the current route set as indicated by its large positive reduced cost. The algorithm now progresses to the next iteration by making the node-and-load combination with the smallest load permanent. At step 1, the node-and-load combination with the smallest load is node 2 with load 28.

This node-and-label combination will be made permanent in step 3, as indicated by the shaded area in Table 9.39. The node-and-label combinations that can be reached from node 2 with load 28 are added to the table. From node 2 with load 28 the route can still visit all other nodes and remain feasible with respect to vehicle capacity. In this variant visiting the same node more than once is also not allowed. So for every node except the current origin node 2 a new node and load combination is added. For node 1, the new combination has load $28+23=51$ and has shortest path distance of $406+149=555$. For node 3, the new combination has load $28+32=60$ and has a shortest path distance of $406+(-827)=-421$. For node 8, the new combination has load $28+41=69$ and has shortest path distance of $406+1741=2147$. The node-and-label combination with the smallest load is node 5 with load 31 and this combination is converted from temporary to permanent in the next step.

Table 9.40 VRP8 negative reduced cost routes for iteration 1

Route	Red.Cost	Length	Quantity	Facilities				
4	−290	4,064	83	d1	c7	c4	d1	
5	−322	5,650	109	d1	c7	c3	c5	d1
6	−797	4,509	114	d1	c5	c7	c4	d1
7	−920	5,906	115	d1	c3	c7	c4	d1

Table 9.41 VRP8 iteration characteristics for the linear programming relaxation

Routes			Primal	LP-Master
Iteration	# New	# Total		
0	3	3	15,453	15,453
1	4	7		15,453
2	33	40	15,419	15,419
3	4	44		15,225

This process continues until all the node-and-load combinations have become permanent. For this example, it takes 182 steps to make all labels, which consist out of a node-and-load combination, permanent. At that time the paths that have a negative length in node t, which corresponds to the sink depot node for each route, are added to the master problem. In this particular example there are four paths with negative reduced cost, which are added to the master problem. The master problem is solved and the dual variables updated and then the arc lengths are updated. The second iteration can then start. The routes with negative reduced length for iteration 1 are shown in Table 9.40.

After three iterations, the pricing problem terminates because it can no longer generate routes with a negative reduced cost. The pricing problem generated 44 columns corresponding to desirable routes in the two iterations. The lower bound, generated by the linear programming relaxation is equal to 15,225.25 (Table 9.41).

The optimal linear solution contained six routes, all of which had a fractional value equal to 0.500. The routes and their execution value in the linear programming relaxation are shown in Table 9.42. Recall that the total number of routes possible with either one, two, three, or four customers was equal to 162. Not all of these routes are feasible with respect to the vehicle capacity. So, the total number of possible routes for the pricing problem cannot be computed easily in advance, but is

Table 9.42 VRP8 optimal routes for the linear programming relaxation

Route	Value	Length	Quantity	Facilities				
6	0.500	4,509	114	d1	c5	c7	c4	d1
7	0.500	5,906	115	d1	c3	c7	c4	d1
10	0.500	1,344	41	d1	c8	d1		
33	0.500	6,658	108	d1	c6	c2	c1	d1
36	0.500	6,892	114	d1	c5	c3	c2	c1	d1
41	0.500	5,142	98	d1	c6	c8	d1	
Total	3.000	15,226	295					

Table 9.43 VRP8 optimal prices for the linear programming relaxation

Facility	Dual price
c1	1,342
c2	2,663
c3	2,714
c4	1,764
c5	1,317
c6	3,797
c7	2,573
c8	2,490
# routes	1,145
Dual Obj.	15,225

no more than 162. The pricing problem generated thus 44 desirable routes out 162 routes, or 27.2% of possible routes.

The optimal dual variables of the master problem for iteration 3 are shown in Table 9.43. The dual variables for the customers represent the best estimate of the cost to serve each customer. The dual variable for the route count represents the best estimate of the savings for allowing one more vehicle and route. The linear programming relaxation is highly dual degenerate; so many alternative sets of values for the dual variables exist.

The binary solution based on these 44 routes generated the same three routes with a solution value of 15,419. The gap for this solution is 194, or 1.25%. In other words, the length of these routes can never be more than 1.25% longer than the length of the optimal routes. In general, the lower bound can be further improved by a complete branch-and-price solution algorithm. However, implementing a full branch-and-price algorithm is a complex and extensive task. This programming effort is most likely not justified unless the routing decisions are very expensive or executed repeatedly. In this particular example, the gap is 1.25%, which is more than close enough to optimality for typical vehicle routing applications. The routes are identical to the routes found by applying the swap improvement algorithm to routes generated by the serial savings algorithm. The summary statistics of these routes are shown in Table 9.32 and the routes are shown in Fig. 9.20.

The execution of the pricing problem in general depends on the starting feasible partition. The execution statistics for different starting partitions are shown in Table 9.44. The routes of the starting partition are generated by the indicated algorithm. For each starting point, the pricing algorithm was run with candidates that do not and do allow multiple visits to the same customer facility. The primal length is the length found either by the linear relaxation of the master problem during the iterations or by the integer master problem at the end of the final iteration.

It can be observed that the two types of candidate routes with or without revisits consistently yield the same lower bound regardless of their starting points. In this small example, the identical best primal solution is found by either lower bound type and from all starting points. Furthermore, for this example the number of iterations and the number of candidate routes generated also does not depend on the

Table 9.44 Characteristics of the SPP algorithm with auxiliary pricing depending on the starting point

Algorithm	Initial length	Revisits allowed	Primal length	Bound length	# Iterat.	# Cand.
GAP	16,096	No	15,419	15,225	2	45
	16,096	Yes	15,419	14,892	2	49
Savings	15,453	No	15,419	15,225	3	44
serial	15,453	Yes	15,419	14,892	4	66
Sweep	17,424	No	15,419	15,225	2	50
	17,424	Yes	15,419	14,892	2	57
Nearest	17,680	No	15,419	15,225	2	25
neighbor	17,680	Yes	15,419	14,892	2	33
Best	15,419	No	15,419	15,225	3	41
	15,419	Yes	15,419	14,892	3	56

quality of the starting feasible partition. Neither of these characteristics is however true in general. An example of this is shown in the VRP16 example which is included as an appendix to this chapter.

9.3 Vehicle Routing with Backhauling (VRPB)

Introduction Consider one route in the solution to the classic vehicle routing problem. The vehicle is delivering to one or more customers. After the last customer has been visited the vehicle is empty and travels back empty to the distribution center. Empty vehicle traveling is also called *deadheading* and the corresponding distance is denoted as deadhead miles. The empty vehicle travel only generates costs and thus is avoided by vehicle dispatchers. One way to reduce the empty travel distance is to visit one or more of suppliers and pick up inbound products from the suppliers and carry them back to the depot. This activity is called *backhauling* and it avoids either the cost or the separate vehicle trip of transporting those goods to the depot. The vehicle routing variant that includes backhauling is called the Vehicle Routing Problem with Backhauling (VRPB) or also linehaul–backhaul. It has been one of the most widespread cost reduction techniques for over-the-road private fleet operations, A.T. Kearney (1984, pp. 80–81).

There are two major subclasses of the VRPB depending on the configuration of the transportation vehicle used. In the United States the vast majority of long-haul trailers are rear-loaded, i.e., they have a single door at the end of the trailer. With this configuration, picking up goods from a supplier before all the customers on the route have been delivered requires that the loads are rearranged at any customer visited after goods have been picked up. This entails additional handling time and costs and the possibility of additional damage. To avoid this, the linehaul–backhaul vehicle routing problem requires that all customers on a single route are visited before any supplier can be visited. On the other hand, if the transportation vehicle

Fig. 9.25 Vehicle routing with backhauling route illustration

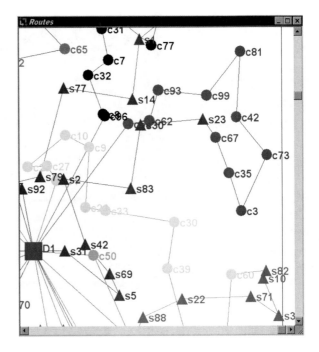

used has either side access with soft tarp sides or roll closures, or an internal central access aisle, then random access to all the goods on the vehicle is possible. With this configuration, the visits to the customers and the suppliers can be intermixed. This problem is called the mixed pickup and delivery problem. Trucks with soft sides are commonly used in Europe; local delivery trucks with side access are often used by brewery and soft-drink industry; finally, vehicles with a central travel aisle are used in the delivery to retailers were the goods are transported in rolling wire cages.

VRPB Problem Definition The VRPB is one of the simplest extensions to the classic VRP. A number of customers with known location and demand and a number of suppliers with known location and supply have to be serviced by a homogeneous fleet of vehicles from a single depot. All vehicles have the same capacity. All vehicles are considered rear-loaded so that on each route all customers have to be visited before any supplier can be visited. The objective is to minimize the total travel distance of the routes. The travel between two facilities is computed with a travel distance norm.

The following notation will be used. There are NL linehaul customers with location and demand (x_i, y_i, dem_i) and there are NB backhaul suppliers with location and supply (x_i, y_i, sup_i). There are K vehicles with capacity cap_k. A linehaul–backhaul route is illustrated in Fig. 9.25. The vehicle leaves the depot and visits first customers $c55$–$c67$, then it deadheads to supplier $s23$, continues to visit suppliers $s30$–$s31$, and then returns to the depot. A larger example of linehaul–backhaul routes is shown in Fig. 9.26.

Fig. 9.26 Lineback linehaul–backhaul routes for case01

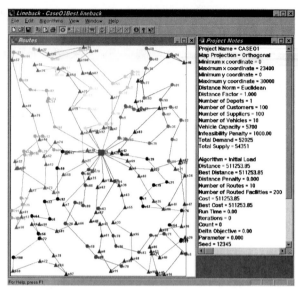

Table 9.45 Facility data for the VRPB8 example

Facility	X-Coord.	Y-Coord.	Quantity	Shape	Color	Type
c1	190	701	12	Circle	Red	Customer
c2	808	585	29	Circle	Red	Customer
c3	350	895	49	Circle	Red	Customer
c4	746	174	51	Circle	Red	Customer
c5	327	305	18	Circle	Red	Customer
s1	137	119	23	Triangle	Green	Supplier
s2	661	840	66	Triangle	Green	Supplier
s3	445	119	46	Triangle	Green	Supplier
d1	362	465	0	Square	Blue	Depot

Vehicle Routing with Backhauling Example (VRPB8) All algorithms for the VRPB will be illustrated using the same example. This example has five customer facilities and three supplier facilities and will be denoted as VRPB8. The facility data are given in Table 9.45 and the locations of the facilities and their demands or supplies illustrated in Fig. 9.27. All routes start and terminate at the single depot. The depot is indicated by a square. All suppliers are indicated by triangles and all customers are indicated by circles. The distances between the various facilities are shown in Table 9.46. The distances were computed with the Euclidean distance norm without any adjustment factor and rounded to two significant digits after the decimal point. There are four trucks available and all trucks have identical capacities equal to 75. Due to loading constraints at the depot a truck can only execute a single route.

Fig. 9.27 Facility locations
and requirements for the
VRPB8 example

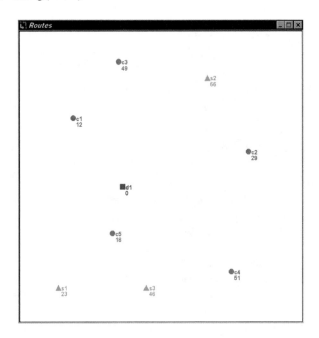

Table 9.46 Distance data for the VRPB8 example

	c1	c2	c3	c4	c5	s1	s2	s3	d1
c1		628.79	251.47	766.07	419.03	584.41	491.08	635.41	292.03
c2	628.79		553.05	415.65	556.56	816.94	294.34	590.70	461.86
c3	251.47	553.05		822.59	590.45	804.70	315.83	781.79	430.17
c4	766.07	415.65	822.59		439.00	611.48	671.40	305.98	481.81
c5	419.03	556.56	590.45	439.00		265.89	630.70	220.27	163.78
s1	584.41	816.94	804.70	611.48	265.89		891.30	308.00	412.72
s2	491.08	294.34	315.83	671.40	630.70	891.30		752.66	479.61
s3	635.41	590.70	781.79	305.98	220.27	308.00	752.66		355.82
d1	292.03	461.86	430.17	481.81	163.78	412.72	479.61	355.82	

9.3.1 Vehicle Routing with Backhauling Algorithms

The algorithms for the VRPB are extensions and modifications of the algorithms for
the classic VRP. In general, the algorithms have to observe two independent capacity constraints, one for the linehaul segment of the route and one for the backhaul
segment, one service constraint per customer and supplier facility, and one precedence constraint prohibiting visiting any supplier before any customer on a route.
The supplier capacity and the precedence constraints are additional compared to the
classic vehicle routing problem and its algorithms.

Table 9.47 Nearest neighbor algorithm steps for VRPB8

Index	Anchor facility	Append facility	Append distance	Linehaul quantity	Backhaul quantity
1	$d1$	$c5$	164	18	0
2	$c5$	$c1$	419	30	0
3	$c1$	$s2$	491	30	66
4	$d1$	$c3$	430	49	0
5	$c3$	$s3$	782	49	46
6	$s3$	$s1$	308	49	69
7	$d1$	$c2$	462	29	0
8	$d1$	$c4$	482	51	0

9.3.1.1 Nearest Neighbor

The nearest neighbor algorithm starts each route at the depot facility and then iteratively appends the nearest unvisited customer to the route. When appending the next customer would violate the truck capacity, the algorithm switches to iteratively appending the nearest unvisited supplier to the route. When appending the next supplier would violate truck capacity, then the route returns to the depot. If unvisited customers or suppliers remain and the maximum number of routes has not been reached, then a new route is started. This algorithm was originally described by Rosenkrantz et al. (1977) for the traveling salesman problem and is extended in a straightforward manner to the case of linehaul–backhaul vehicle routing.

9.3.1.2 Nearest Neighbor for VRPB8

The nearest neighbor algorithm is used first to construct the routes. Every time a facility is added to a route, the append facility and the anchor facility are given in Table 9.47. The anchor facility is the facility already on the route to which this newly added facility is connected. In addition, the append distance to the new facility, and the linehaul and backhaul quantity on the truck on this partial route, are also given. When a new route is started, the anchor facility is the depot. Since the algorithm repeatedly performs the same test and actions, several sentences are repeated in each step to give a complete description of the algorithm execution.

The closest unvisited customer to the depot $d1$ is customer $c5$ with a distance equal to 163.8. Since this is the first customer on the route its demand will never exceed the truck capacity, so customer $c5$ is added to the route and the total demand or linehaul quantity on the route so far is equal to 18 units and the remaining linehaul capacity is also 57 units.

The unvisited customer closest to customer $c5$ is customer $c1$ with a distance equal to 419. The demand of customer $c1$ is 12 units and the remaining linehaul capacity on this route is 57 units, so customer $c1$ is appended to this route. The total demand or linehaul quantity on the route so far is equal to 30 units and the remaining linehaul capacity is also 45 units.

The unvisited customer closest to customer $c1$ is customer $c3$ with a distance equal to 251. The demand of customer $c3$ is 49 units. The remaining linehaul capacity on the route is 45 units, so customer $c3$ cannot be appended to this route. The route now switches from delivery to pickup operations.

The unvisited supplier closest to customer $c1$ is supplier $s2$ with a distance equal to 491. Since this is the first supplier on the route its supply will never exceed the truck capacity, so supplier $s2$ is appended to the route. The backhaul quantity so far is equal to 66 units and the remaining backhaul capacity is 9 units.

The unvisited supplier closest to supplier $s2$ is supplier $s3$ with a distance equal to 753. The supply quantity of supplier $s3$ is 46 units and the remaining backhaul capacity on the route is equal to 9 units, so supplier $s3$ cannot be appended to this route. The route is closed and since the number of routes is less than the maximum number of routes a new route is started.

The unvisited customer closest to the depot $d1$ is customer $c3$ with a distance equal to 430. Since this is the first customer on the route its demand will never exceed the truck capacity, so customer $c3$ is appended to the route and the linehaul quantity on the route so far is equal to 49 units and the remaining linehaul capacity on the route is 26 units.

The unvisited customer closest to customer $c3$ is customer $c2$ with a distance equal to 553. The demand of customer $c2$ is 29 units and the remaining linehaul capacity on this route is 26 units, so customer $c2$ cannot be appended to this route. The route now switches from delivery to pickup operations.

The unvisited supplier closest to customer $c3$ is supplier $s3$ with a distance equal to 782. Since this is the first supplier on the route its supply will never exceed the truck capacity, so supplier $s3$ is appended to the route. The backhaul quantity so far is equal to 46 units and the remaining backhaul capacity is 29 units.

The unvisited supplier closest to supplier $s3$ is supplier $s1$ with a distance equal to 308. The supply quantity of supplier $s1$ is 23 units and the remaining backhaul capacity on the route is equal to 29 units, so supplier $s1$ is appended to this route. The total backhaul quantity on the route is now 69 units and the remaining backhaul capacity is 6 units. Since there are no remaining unvisited suppliers, this route is closed and since the number of routes is less than the maximum number of routes a new route is started.

The unvisited customer closest to the depot $d1$ is customer $c2$ with a distance equal to 462. Since this is the first customer on the route its demand will never exceed the truck capacity, so customer $c2$ is appended to the route and the linehaul quantity on the route so far is equal to 29 units and the remaining linehaul capacity is 46 units.

The unvisited customer closest to customer $c2$ is customer $c4$ with a distance equal to 416. The demand of customer $c4$ is 51 units and the remaining linehaul capacity on this route is 51 units, so customer $c4$ cannot be appended to this route. The route now switches from delivery to pickup operations. Since there are no remaining unvisited suppliers, this route is closed and since the number of routes is less than the maximum number of routes a new route is started.

The unvisited customer closest to the depot $d1$ is customer $c4$ with a distance equal to 482. Since this is the first customer on the route its demand will never

Table 9.48 Nearest neighbor routes for VRPB8

Route	Facility								Length
	1	2	3	4	5	6	7	8	
1	*d1*	*c5*	*c1*	*s2*	*d1*				1,553.50
2	*d1*	*c3*	*s3*	*s1*	*d1*				1,932.68
3	*d1*	*c2*	*d1*						923.72
4	*d1*	*c4*	*d1*						963.61
Total									5,373.51

exceed the truck capacity, so customer *c4* is appended to the route and the linehaul quantity on the route so far is equal to 51 units and the remaining linehaul capacity is 24 units. Since there are no remaining unvisited customers or suppliers, this route is closed and Nearest Neighbor algorithm terminates after having created four routes.

In Table 9.48 the route data are summarized, with one route per line or row. Each route starts and ends with the depot. The route length of each individual route and the total route length of all the routes created by this algorithm are also shown.

9.3.1.3 Sweep (Variant B)

There exist many variants of the basic sweep algorithm, but they can be grouped into two basic categories: (A) cluster-first, route-second, and (B) route-first, cluster-

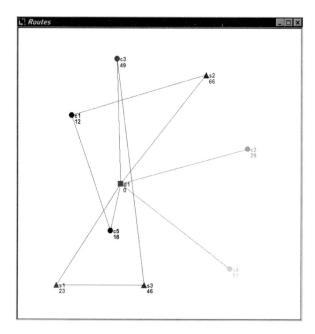

Fig. 9.28 Nearest neighbor routes for the VRPB8 example

second. The difference between the types is based on when the delivery or pickup quantity of the facilities is considered and when the facilities are sequenced on a route. In all variants the facilities are sequenced in an ordered list by rotating a half-line or ray around a rotation point and facilities are added to list when the ray traverses them.

The algorithm was first described by Gillet and Miller (1974) for the vehicle routing problem. It is extended to the vehicle routing problem with backhauling in the following way. The algorithm creates two lists, one for linehaul customer and one for backhaul suppliers. Both lists are partitioned into individual routes at the same rotational angles. When starting a new route, the first customer traversed by the ray becomes the first customer on the route, and the first supplier traversed by the ray becomes the last supplier on this route. When adding a facility to the route, it is inserted at one of the two endpoints of the empty vehicle travel link of the current tour and thus one of the two interface points of the empty vehicle travel link will change. When either a customer or supplier facility is traversed by the rotating ray, it is inserted between the most recently appended customer and supplier facility on that route. When the inserting either the next customer of supplier would violate truck capacity, then the route is terminated. If unvisited customers or suppliers remain and the maximum number of routes has not been reached, then a new route is started. Computationally, the relative polar coordinates of each point with respect to the depot are determined and the points are inserted in the route by increasing polar angle.

In vehicle routing problems the rotation point is typically the distribution center. The starting angle of the rotation ray and the rotation direction are algorithm parameters. Different parameter values may generate different routes. Note that the sweep algorithm in the Lineback program (Goetschalckx 1990) is of the second type.

9.3.1.4 Sweep Variant B for VRPB8 Example

We will start the rotating ray in the due east direction and turn the ray counterclockwise. Each time we add a facility to a route, we will show the added or append facility, the anchor facility on the route to which this newly added facility is connected, the append distance to the new facility, and the linehaul and backhaul quantity on the truck on that route so far. When we start a new route, the anchor facility is the depot for both the linehaul and the backhaul section of the route. Since the algorithm repeatedly performs the same test and actions, several sentences are repeated in each step to give a complete description of the algorithm execution.

The next facility traversed by the ray is customer $c2$. Since this is the first customer on the route its demand will never exceed the truck capacity, so customer $c2$ is included in the route and the linehaul quantity on the route so far is equal to 29 units and the remaining linehaul capacity is 46 units.

The first encountered facility is supplier $s2$. Since this is the first supplier on the route its supply will never exceed the truck capacity, so supplier $s2$ is included in the route. The total backhaul quantity on this route is now 66 units and the remaining backhaul capacity is 9 units.

Table 9.49 Sweep algorithm steps for VRPB8

Index	Anchor facility	Append facility	Append distance	Linehaul quantity	Backhaul quantity
1	$d1$	$c2$	462	29	0
2	$d1$	$s2$	480	29	66
3	$d1$	$c3$	430	49	0
4	$c3$	$c1$	251	61	0
5	$d1$	$s1$	413	61	23
6	$d1$	$c5$	164	18	0
7	$d1$	$s3$	356	18	46
8	$c5$	$c4$	439	69	46

The next facility traversed by the ray is customer $c3$. The demand of customer $c3$ is 49 units and the remaining linehaul capacity on the route is 46 units, so customer $c3$ cannot be inserted in the route. So this route is closed by connecting customer $c2$ to supplier $s2$. Since the number of routes is less than the maximum number of routes a new route is started.

The next facility traversed by the ray is customer $c3$. Since this is the first customer on the route its demand will never exceed the truck capacity, so customer $c3$ is included in the route and the linehaul quantity on the route so far is equal to 49 units and the remaining linehaul capacity is 26 units.

The next facility traversed by the ray is customer $c1$. The demand of customer $c1$ is 12 units and the remaining linehaul capacity on the route is 26 units, so customer $c1$ is inserted after customer $c3$. The linehaul quantity on the route so far is equal to 61 units and the remaining linehaul capacity is 14 units.

The first encountered facility is supplier $s1$. Since this is the first supplier on the route its supply will never exceed the truck capacity, so supplier $s1$ is included in the route. The total backhaul quantity on this route is now 23 units and the remaining backhaul capacity is 52 units.

The next facility traversed by the ray is customer $c5$. The demand of customer $c5$ is 18 units and the remaining linehaul capacity on the route is 14 units, so customer $c5$ cannot be inserted in the route. So this route is closed by connecting customer $c1$ to supplier $s1$. Since the number of routes is less than the maximum number of routes a new route is started.

The next facility traversed by the ray is customer $c5$. Since this is the first customer on the route its demand will never exceed the truck capacity, so customer $c5$ is included in the route and the linehaul quantity on the route so far is equal to 18 units and the remaining linehaul capacity is 57 units.

The first encountered facility is supplier $s3$. Since this is the first supplier on the route its supply will never exceed the truck capacity, so supplier $s3$ is included in the route. The total backhaul quantity on this route is now 46 units and the remaining backhaul capacity is 29 units.

The next facility traversed by the ray is customer $c4$. The demand of customer $c4$ is 51 units and the remaining linehaul capacity on the route is 57 units, so customer $c1$ is inserted after customer $c5$. The linehaul quantity on the route so far is equal to 69 units and the remaining linehaul capacity is 6 units. All the customers and suppliers have been visited, so the sweep algorithm terminates with three routes.

Table 9.50 Sweep routes for VRPB8

Route	Facility								Length
	1	2	3	4	5	6	7	8	
1	d1	c2	s2	d1					1,235.81
2	d1	c3	c1	s1	d1				1,678.77
3	d1	c5	c4	s3	d1				1,264.58
4									
Total									4,179.16

Fig. 9.29 Sweep routes for the VRPB8 example

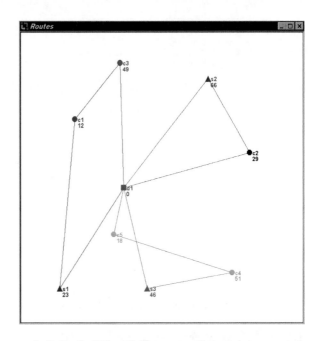

We will list the sequence of all the facilities on the routes that we have created, with one route per row in the following matrix. Each route starts and ends with the depot. We compute the route length of each individual route and compute the total route length of all the routes created by this sweep algorithm. Since the sweep algorithm created three routes, the last row in the matrix is not used. See Table 9.50 and Fig. 9.29.

9.3.1.5 Savings

Deif and Bodin (1984) adapted the original savings algorithm of Clarke and Wright (1964) to the case of the linehaul–backhaul vehicle routing. They observed that once the crossover link corresponding to the empty vehicle travel is added to a tour, the tour becomes asymmetric and the possibilities for adding further facilities are cut in half. To avoid this phenomenon, they reduced the savings of the crossover link to delay the creation of this crossover link. They computed the savings as follows using a crossover savings penalty factor α:

Table 9.51 Binary savings for VRPB8

	c1	c2	c3	c4	c5	s1	s2	s3	Line-Q	Back-Q
c1		125.10	470.73	7.76	36.78	90.26	210.42	9.32	12	
c2	125.10				69.08	43.23	485.35	170.23	29	
c3	470.73				3.50	28.64	445.46	3.14	49	
c4	7.76				206.59	212.29	217.51	398.73	51	
c5	36.78	69.08	3.50	206.59		232.97	9.52	224.50	18	
s1								460.54		23
s2										66
s3						460.54				46

$$S = \max_{i,j} \left\{ d_{0j} + d_{i0} - d_{ij} \right\}$$

$$s_{ij} = \begin{cases} d_{0j} + d_{i0} - d_{ij} - \alpha S & \text{if } i \in \mathbf{C}, j \in \mathbf{S} \\ d_{0j} + d_{i0} - d_{ij} & \text{if } i,j \in \mathbf{C} \text{ or } i,j \in \mathbf{S} \end{cases} \qquad (9.50)$$

They found that a good value for α is around 0.2. This savings adjustment method has the disadvantage that it can create negative savings for the crossover links, even though using these links may still yield positive savings.

A more consistent method for adjusting the savings of the crossover link reduces the savings by percentage of the savings for that link. With this adjustment the savings for the crossover links are reduced but remain desirable if the original savings for that link were desirable.

$$s_{ij} = \begin{cases} (1 - \alpha) \cdot (d_{0j} + d_{i0} - d_{ij}) & \text{if } i \in \mathbf{C}, j \in \mathbf{S} \\ d_{0j} + d_{i0} - d_{ij} & \text{if } i,j \in \mathbf{C} \text{ or } i,j \in \mathbf{S} \end{cases} \qquad (9.51)$$

9.3.1.6 Savings Algorithm for the VRPB8 Example

The parallel variant followed by the serial variant of the savings algorithm will be executed for this example. The savings for the crossover links between the linehaul and the backhaul section of a route will be adjusted by a 25% penalty. In other words

$$s_{ij}^{adj} = s_{ij}^{orig} \cdot (1 - 0.25)$$

The pairwise savings for this example are shown in Table 9.51. Savings for infeasible combinations of facilities are not shown. The largest feasible savings are 485.35 when customer $c2$ and supplier $s2$ are combined. The cell of the largest feasible savings is shown as shaded.

In the reduced savings matrix for the serial variant, only savings with facilities that can be inserted before customer $c2$ or after supplier $s2$ are considered since only one partial tour can be active at the time. Hence, only savings in the column $\{c2{-}s2\}$ and in the row $\{c2{-}s2\}$ have to be considered. In this case there are only two candidate savings—125.1 and 69.08. The largest feasible savings are 125.10 when customer $c1$ is inserted before customer $c2$ in the partial tour. The cell of the largest feasible savings is shown as shaded in Table 9.52.

Table 9.52 Second iteration savings matrix for the serial variant for VRPB8

	c1	c2–s2	c3	c4	c5	s1	s3	Line-Q	Back-Q
c1		125.10	470.73	7.76	36.78	90.26	9.32	12	
c3	470.73				3.50	28.64	3.14	49	
c4	7.76				206.59	212.29	398.73	51	
c5	36.78	69.08	3.50	206.59		232.97	224.50	18	
s1							460.54		23
c2–s2								29	66
s3						460.54			46

Table 9.53 Third iteration savings matrix for the serial variant for VRPB8

	c1–s2	c3	c4	c5	s1	s3	Line-Q	Back-Q
c3	470.73			3.50	28.64	3.14	49	
c4	7.76			206.59	212.29	398.73	51	
c5	36.78	3.50	206.59		232.97	224.50	18	
s1						460.54		23
c1–s2							41	66
s3					460.54			46

After the combination of customer $c1$ with the partial tour $c2{:}s2$ the savings matrix is reduced to the following matrix in Table 9.53. In the reduced savings matrix, only savings with facilities that can be inserted before customer $c1$ or after supplier $s2$ are considered since only one partial tour can be active at the time. Hence, only savings in the column $\{c1{-}s2\}$ and in the row $\{c1{-}s2\}$ have to be considered. Savings that would create infeasible tours also do not have to be considered. In this case there is only one candidate savings 36.78, since the other two savings in the first column would create infeasible routes that violate the truck capacity.

After the combination of customer $c5$ and the partial tour $c1{:}s2$ the savings matrix is reduced to the matrix in Table 9.54. In the reduced savings matrix, only savings with facilities that can be inserted before customer $c5$ or after supplier $s2$ are considered since only one partial tour can be active at the time. Hence, only savings in the column $\{c5{-}s2\}$ and in the row $\{c5{-}s2\}$ have to be considered. Savings that would create infeasible tours also do not have to be considered. In this case there is no feasible savings candidate, since the two savings in the column would create infeasible routes that violate the truck capacity.

The current partial route is saved and a new partial route is started based on the remaining rows and columns of the savings matrix. The largest feasible savings are 460.54 when suppliers $s1$ and $s3$ are combined. The cell of the largest feasible savings is shown as shaded in Table 9.55.

Table 9.54 Fourth iteration savings matrix for the serial variant for VRPB8

	c3	c4	c5–s2	s1	s3	Line-Q	Back-Q
c3			3.50	28.64	3.14	49	
c4			206.59	212.29	398.73	51	
s1					460.54		23
c5–s2						59	66
s3				460.54			46

Table 9.55 Fifth iteration savings matrix for the serial variant for VRPB8

	c3	c4	s1	s3	Line-Q	Back-Q
c3			28.64	3.14	49	
c4			212.29	398.73	51	
s1				460.54		23
s3			460.54			46

Table 9.56 Sixth iteration savings matrix for the serial variant for VRPB8

	c3	c4	s1–s3	Line-Q	Back-Q
c3			28.64	49	
c4			212.29	51	
s1–s3					69

Table 9.57 Seventh iteration savings matrix for the serial variant for VRPB8

	c3	c4–s3	Line-Q	Back-Q
c3			49	
c4–s3			51	69

After the combination of suppliers $s1$ and $s3$ the savings matrix is reduced to the matrix in Table 9.56. The largest feasible savings are 212.29 when customer $c4$ is inserted before supplier $s1$. The cell of the largest feasible savings is shown as shaded.

After the combination of customer $c4$ and supplier $s1$ the savings matrix is reduced to the matrix in Table 9.57. There is no feasible savings, so the current partial route is saved. A new partial route is started. Since the only facility not yet placed on a route is facility customer $c3$, this facility will form a singleton route and the algorithm terminates. The savings matrix for this last iteration would only contain a row and column for $c3$ and is not shown.

The routes for the serial version of the savings algorithm are summarized in Table 9.58 and Fig. 9.30.

The parallel variant of the savings algorithm is executed next. The first iteration is identical to the serial variant. After the combination of customer $c2$ and supplier $s2$ the savings matrix is reduced to the matrix in Table 9.59. The largest feasible savings are 470.73 when customers $c1$ and $c3$ are combined. The cell of the largest feasible savings is shown as shaded.

After the combination of customers $c1$ and $c3$ two partial routes are active and the savings matrix is reduced to the matrix in Table 9.60. The largest feasible sav-

Table 9.58 Serial savings routes for VRPB8

Route	Facility								Length
	1	2	3	4	5	6	7	8	
1	d1	c5	c1	c2	s2	d1			1,985.55
2	d1	c4	s1	s3	d1				1,757.10
3	d1	c3	d1						860.33
4									
Total									4,602.98

Fig. 9.30 Serial savings routes for the VRPB8 example

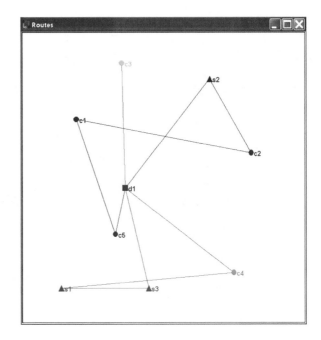

Table 9.59 Second iteration savings matrix for the parallel variant for VRPB8

	c1	c2–s2	c3	c4	c5	s1	s3	Line-Q	Back-Q
c1		125.1	470.73	7.76	36.78	90.26	9.32	12	
c3	470.73				3.5	28.64	3.14	49	
c4	7.76				206.59	212.29	398.73	51	
c5	36.78	69.08	3.5	206.59		232.97	224.50	18	
s1							460.54		23
c2–s2								29	66
s3						460.54			46

Table 9.60 Third iteration savings matrix for the parallel variant for VRPB8

	c1–c3	c2–s2	c4	c5	s1	s3	Line-Q	Back-Q
c1–c3				3.5	28.64	3.14	61	
c4	7.76			206.59	212.29	398.73	51	
c5	36.78	69.08	206.59		232.97	224.50	18	
s1						460.54		23
c2–s2							29	66
s3					460.54			46

ings are 460.54 when suppliers *s1* and *s3* are combined. The cell of the largest feasible savings is shown as shaded.

After the combination of suppliers *s1* and *s3* three partial routes are active and the savings matrix is reduced to the matrix in Table 9.61. Since there are four trucks, it is still possible to create one new partial route. For example, the additional partial

Table 9.61 Fourth iteration savings matrix for the parallel variant for VRPB8

	c1–c3	c2–s2	c3	c5	s1–s3	Line-Q	Back-Q
c1–c3				3.5	28.64	61	
c4	7.76			206.59	212.29	51	
c5	36.78	69.08	206.59		232.97	18	
c2–s2						29	66
s1–s3							69

Table 9.62 Fifth iteration savings matrix for the parallel variant for VRPB8

	c1–c3	c2–s2	c4	c5–s3	Line-Q	Back-Q
c1–c3				3.5	61	
c4	7.76			206.59	51	
c2–s2					29	66
c5–s3					18	69

route from customer $c4$ to customer $c5$ is still a feasible possibility with corresponding savings of 206.59. However, the largest feasible savings are 232.97 when customer $c5$ is inserted at the head of the partial route with suppliers $s1$ and $s3$. The cell of the largest feasible savings is shown as shaded.

After the insertion of customer $c5$ in the partial tour $\{s1–s3\}$ the savings matrix is reduced to the matrix in Table 9.62. The largest feasible savings are 206.59 when customer $c4$ is inserted at the head of the partial tour with facilities $\{c5–s3\}$. The cell of the largest feasible savings is shown as shaded.

After the insertion of customer $c4$ in the partial tour $\{c5–s3\}$ all the facilities have been inserted on a partial tour and no partial tours can be combined, so the algorithm terminates. The routes for the parallel version of the savings algorithm are summarized in Table 9.63 and Fig. 9.31.

9.3.1.7 Extreme Crossovers

The extreme crossovers algorithm creates a number of partial routes with on each route a single customer and a single supplier. It matches the customer and supplier that have the largest savings if they were visited on single route instead of on separate routes. This is the same savings definition as used in the savings algorithm with a crossover penalty factor equal to zero. The number of routes is equal to the

Table 9.63 Parallel savings routes for VRPB8

Route	Facility								Length
	1	2	3	4	5	6	7	8	
1	d1	c2	s2	d1					1,235.81
2	d1	c1	c3	d1					973.66
3	d1	c4	c5	s1	s3	d1			1,850.51
4									
Total									4,059.98

Fig. 9.31 Parallel savings routes for the VRPB8 Example

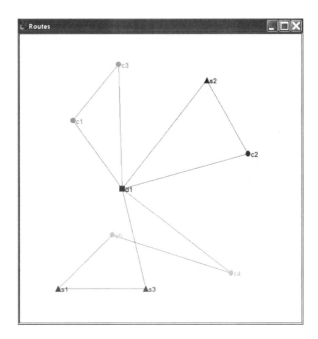

minimum of the number of vehicles, the number of customers, and the number of suppliers.

$$s_{ij} = d_{i0} + d_{0j} - d_{ij} \qquad i \in \mathbf{C}, j \in \mathbf{S} \qquad (9.52)$$

The typical result of this algorithm is a number of routes with very acute aperture of the covering sector and with short crossover link far away from the depot.

If not all the facilities are visited by the crossover routes, then the total route length of the crossover routes is a lower bound on the optimal total route length. If all the facilities are included on the crossover routes, then these routes constitute the optimal solution.

The number of crossovers is the minimum of the number linehaul customer, the number of backhaul suppliers, and the number of vehicles. In the case of the example, the number is equal to $\min \{5, 3, 4\} = 3$. The savings for the crossover route between the first customer and supplier are computed next.

$$
\begin{aligned}
s_{c1,s1} &= d_{c1,d1} + d_{d1,s1} - d_{c1,s1} \\
&= 292.03 + 412.72 - 584.41 = 120.34
\end{aligned}
$$

All the crossover assignment savings for the VRPB8 example are shown in Table 9.64, where the customers are listed in the rows and the suppliers in the columns.

In general, finding the optimal solution for this Assignment Problem (AP) requires a linear programming formulation and solution. However, for this small example, when for each supplier the customer with the maximum savings is selected, there are no conflicts in the customer selection, so this greedy solution is also the optimal solution. The maximum savings are achieved by pairing customer $c2$ with supplier $s2$, customer $c4$ with supplier $s3$, and customer $c5$ with supplier $s1$. The

Table 9.64 VRPB6
example crossover savings

	s1	s2	s3
c1	120.34	280.56	12.43
c2	57.64	647.14	226.98
c3	38.19	593.95	4.19
c4	283.05	290.01	531.64
c5	310.62	12.69	299.33

Table 9.65 VRPB6 example crossover routes

Route	Facility								Length
	1	2	3	4	5	6	7	8	
1	d1	c2	s2	d1					1,235.81
2	d1	c4	s3	d1					1,143.61
3	d1	c5	s1	d1					842.39
4									
Total									3,221.81

resulting crossover routes are shown in Table 9.65 and Fig. 9.32. This set of routes does not include all facilities, so the current solution value is a lower bound on the optimal total route length.

9.3.1.8 Cheapest Insertion

To illustrate the insertion algorithms, the routes created by the extreme crossover algorithm will be used as initial routes. The two customer $c1$ and $c3$ facilities are

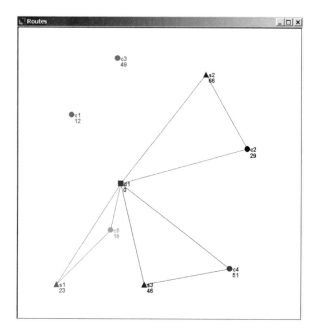

Fig. 9.32 Extreme crossover routes for the VRPB8
example

Table 9.66 Insertion penalties for VRPB8

	r1		r2		r3		min
	dl–c2	c2–s2	dl–c4	c4–s3	dl–c5	c5–s1	
c1	458.93	825.53	576.29	1,095.50	547.28	737.55	458.93
c3			-		856.84	1,129.26	856.84

not yet included on a route and they have delivery quantities of 12 and 49, respectively. The linehaul quantities of the initial routes are 29, 51, and 18, respectively. It is computationally the most efficient to check first if a facility can be inserted on a route based on the facility and route quantities. Customer $c1$ can be inserted on all three routes, while customer $c3$ can only be inserted on route 3. Customer facilities can only be inserted on links before the first supplier on that route.

The insertion penalty for customer $c1$ on link $(dl, c2)$ is computed as

$$[c1]\,(dl, c2)\ 292.03 + 628.79 - 461.89 = 458.93.$$

The insertion penalties for all feasible insertions are computed next and shown in Table 9.66. The last column indicates the minimum insertion penalty for each free facility.

The cheapest insertion algorithm selects the free facility with the minimum insertion penalty. In this example this is customer $c1$ with insertion penalty 458.93 on link $(dl, c2)$ of route 1. The insertion penalties for the remaining free facilities are now updated. However, in this example customer $c3$ can only be inserted on route 3 and customer $c1$ was inserted on route 1, so no insertion penalties for customer $c3$ change. Customer $c3$ is inserted next with insertion penalty 856.84 on link $(dl, c5)$. All facilities have been routed and the algorithm terminates. The routes statistics are given in Table 9.67 and the routes are shown in Fig. 9.33.

9.3.1.9 Priciest Insertion

The priciest insertion algorithm starts of identically to the cheapest insertion algorithm. However, it selects the facility to insert as the facility with the largest insertion penalty. In this example, this is customer $c3$ with insertion penalty 856.84 on link $(dl, c5)$ of route 3. The insertion penalties for the remaining free facilities are

Table 9.67 Cheapest insertion routes for VRPB8

Route	Facility								Length
	1	2	3	4	5	6	7	8	
1	dl	c1	c2	s2					1,694.77
2	dl	c4	s3	dl					1,143.61
3	dl	c3	c5	s1	dl				1,699.23
4									
Total									4,537.61

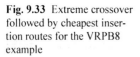

Fig. 9.33 Extreme crossover followed by cheapest insertion routes for the VRPB8 example

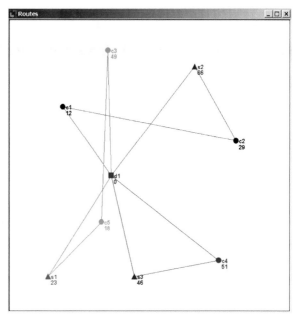

now updated. The linehaul quantity on route 3 is now $49+18=67$ and customer $c1$ can no longer be inserted on route 3. The insertion penalties for customer $c1$ on all links of route 3 are eliminated, or equivalently set to infinity, and no insertion penalties for customer $c1$ change. Customer $c1$ is inserted with insertion penalty 458.93 on link $(d1, c2)$ of route 1. All facilities have been routed and the algorithm terminates. The routes are identical to those generated by the cheapest insertion algorithm and are shown in Fig. 9.33 and their statistics are given in the previous table. In general, the cheapest and priciest insertion algorithms may generate different routes.

9.3.1.10 Two Exchange, Chain Exchange, Three Exchange

To illustrate the exchange algorithms, the routes created by the cheapest insertion algorithm will be used as initial routes. The number of facilities on each route for this small example is so small that very few intra-route exchanges can be executed. Route 2 has a single customer and supplier, so no intra-route exchanges are possible. Routes 1 and 3 each have two customers and one supplier, so the two exchange, the chain exchange with chain length equal to one, and the three exchange algorithm all will test the exchanges that corresponds to swapping the sequence of the two customers on each route. These routes are equivalent to inserting the free customers on different links for the insertion algorithms. The insertion algorithms selected the link with the minimum insertion penalty for each facility, so no improving exchanges can be found.

Table 9.68 Move algorithm iteration 1 for VRPB8

				r1			r2			r3		Max
			L	B		L	B		L	B		
			41	66		51	46		67	23		
	Route	L	B	d1–c1	c1–c2	c2–s2	d1–c4	c4–s3	s3–d1	c5–s1	s1–d1	
c1	r1	12					-117.33	-636.54				-117.33
c2	r1	29										
c3	r3	49										
c4	r2	51										
c5	r3	18		-239.14	-295.16	-841.28	-69.33	-301.65				-69.33
s1	r3		23					-98.97	149.93			149.93
s2	r1		66									
s3	r2		46							-82.39	-71.11	-71.11

9.3.1.11 Move

Again, the routes created by the cheapest insertion algorithm will be used as the initial routes. The move algorithm attempts to improve the current routes by moving a single facility to another route. The best possible insertion place is determined for this facility on the destination route. Eliminating possible moves first because of the facility quantity and current route quantities is the most efficient. For example, customer $c4$ with quantity 51 and currently on route 2 cannot be moved to another route because routes 1 and 3 have current linehaul quantities of 41 and 67 or, equivalently, remaining linehaul capacity of 34 and 8, respectively. A facility can also not be moved to a different location on the same route, since the move algorithm is an inter-route improvement algorithm. In the next table, infeasible moves are indicated by shaded cells. For this example, only five facilities can be moved to another route without violating capacity constraints.

Each move involves removing one facility from the origin route and inserting it in the destination route. A move changes a total of six links, three in the origin and destination routes each. The savings of moving customer $c1$ from route 1 and inserting it in link ($c4$–$s3$) are computed as follows

$$(-d_{d1,c1} - d_{c1,c2} + d_{d1,c2}) + (d_{c4,c1} + d_{c1,s3} - d_{c4,s3})$$
$$= (-292.03 - 628.79 + 461.86) + (766.07 + 635.41 - 305.98) = -636.54$$

This is not an improving move and would not be selected. The savings of moving supplier $s1$ from route 3 and inserting it in link ($s3$–$d1$) are computed as follows.

$$(-d_{c5,s1} - d_{s1,d1} + d_{c5,d1}) + (d_{s3,s1} + d_{s1,d1} - d_{s3,d1})$$
$$= (-265.89 - 412.72 + 163.78) + (308.00 + 412.72 - 355.82) = 149.93$$

The last column in Table 9.68 shows the maximum savings achieved by moving each facility. The algorithm selects the move with the largest positive savings, which is in this iteration the move of supplier $s1$ from route 3 and inserting it in link ($s3$–$d1$) or route 2 with a savings of 149.93. The backhaul quantity of route 2 increases to 69 and of route 3 decreases to zero, while all other quantities remain unchanged.

The move algorithm now repeats the same steps in its next iteration. The savings are shown in Table 9.69. The algorithm selects the move with the largest positive savings, which is the move of customer $c5$ from route 3 and inserting it in link ($d1$–

Table 9.69 Move algorithm iteration 2 for VRPB8

				r1			r2		r3		Max
				L	B		L	B	L	B	
				41	66		51	69	67	0	
	Route	L	B	dl-c1	c1-c2	c2-s2	dl-c4	c4-s3	c5-d1		
c1	r1	12					-117.33	-636.54			-117.33
c2	r1	29									
c3	r3	49									
c4	r2	51									
c5	r3	18		33.28	-22.74	-568.86	203.09	-29.23			203.09
s1	r2		23						-149.92		-149.92
s2	r1		66						-634.44		-634.44
s3	r2		46						-409.80		-409.80

Table 9.70 Move algorithm iteration 3 for VRPB8

				r1			r2		r3		Max
				L	B		L	B	L	B	
				41	66		69	69	49	0	
	Route	L	B	dl-c1	c1-c2	c2-s2	dl-c5	c5-c4	dl-c3	c3-d1	
c1	r1	12							345.63	345.63	345.63
c2	r1	29									
c3	r3	49									
c4	r2	51									
c5	r2	18		-169.81	-225.82	-771.95			-203.09	-203.09	-169.81
s1	r2		23							-422.35	-422.35
s2	r1		66							-53.18	-53.18
s3	r2		46							-704.94	-704.94

c4) or route 2 with a savings of 203.09. The linehaul quantity of route 2 increases to 69 and of route 3 decreases to 49, while all other quantities remain unchanged.

Clearly, determining and evaluating all feasible moves is a tedious process best left to a computer implementation. The savings for iteration 3 are shown in Table 9.70.

The move with the largest positive savings is the move of customer c1 from route 1 and inserting it in link (dl-c3) or route 3 with a savings of 345.63. The linehaul quantity of route 1 decreases to 29 and of route 3 increases to 61, while all other quantities remain unchanged. The savings for iteration four are shown in Table 9.71.

Table 9.71 Move algorithm iteration 4 for VRPB8

				r1			r2		r3		Max
				L	B		L	B	L	B	
				29	66		69	69	61	0	
	Route	L	B	dl-c2	c2-s2		dl-c5	c5-c4	c1-c3	c3-d1	
c1	r3	12		-345.63	-712.21						-345.63
c2	r1	29									
c3	r3	49									
c4	r2	51									
c5	r2	18		-137.51	-771.95						-137.51
s1	r2		23							-422.35	-422.35
s2	r1		66							-53.18	-53.18
s3	r2		46							-704.94	-704.94

Table 9.72 Move improvement routes for VRPB8

Route	Facility								Length
	1	2	3	4	5	6	7	8	
1	*d1*	*c1*	*c3*	*d1*					973.66
2	*d1*	*c2*	*s2*	*d1*					1,235.81
3	*d1*	*c5*	*c4*	*s3*	*s1*	*d1*			1,629.49
4									
Total									3,838.96

Fig. 9.34 Move improvement routes for the VRPB8
example

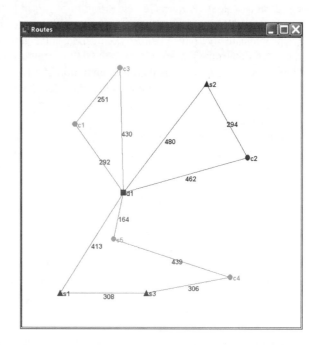

No moves with positive savings can be determined, so the move algorithm terminates. The total savings of all the moves equal 698.64. The total route length
after the move improvements equals 3,838.96. The route statistics are shown in
Table 9.72 and the routes in Fig. 9.34.

9.3.1.12 Swap

Again the routes created by the cheapest insertion algorithm will be used as the
initial routes. The swap algorithm attempts to improve the current routes by first
removing a single facility from two different routes and then inserting the two facilities in the best place in the opposite route if this is feasible. Because both swap
facilities are first removed, the routes will have more remaining capacity and so
more improvement swaps are feasible as compared to the move algorithm. The
feasible improvement swaps and their associated savings are shown in the next

table. Because more feasible improvement swaps exists, the manual execution of this improvement algorithm is even more tedious.

9.3.1.13 Set Partitioning Algorithm

For this small example, four alternative solution algorithms exist that are based on set partitioning. The first algorithm enumerates all feasible routes and includes them in a single monolithic MIP. The second algorithm evaluates all possible routes based on a systematic iterative generation of all feasible routes. It determines the row prices with a heuristic allocation scheme and includes routes in the master integer problem if they have positive savings. An integer solution to master problem has to be determined at each iteration. The third algorithm evaluates all possible routes based on a systematic iterative generation of all feasible routes. It determines the row prices with linear programming and includes routes in the master linear programming problem if they have positive savings or a negative reduced cost. The fourth algorithm uses an auxiliary pricing problem, which is an SPPRC solved with dynamic programming, to add routes to a linear master model until no new routes with a negative reduced cost can be found. The algorithm and programming complexity increases sharply from alternative algorithm one to four. At the same time, the required computation time increases exponentially going from alternative algorithm one to four. In algorithm one a single very large integer program has to be solved, in algorithm two a sequence of smaller integer programs have to be solved. In algorithm three a sequence of linear programs has to be solved but the final solution may not consist of integer routes. Finally, in the fourth algorithm a larger sequence of smaller linear programs has to be solved in addition to a dynamic program for every linear program. Again the final solution may not consist of integer routes and an extra computational step may be required to construct an integer and executable set of routes. For logistic practitioners, the selection of the appropriate solution algorithm depends on the cost of executing the routes and on the frequency with which this type of problem has to be solved. All four algorithms will be shown here in detail to illustrate their characteristics.

9.3.1.14 Set Partitioning Based on Complete Enumeration of All Feasible Routes

Table 9.73 with all the feasible routes and their characteristics. For the VRPB8 example, 68 feasible routes exist. The facilities on the routes are indexed from 1–8, corresponding to customers $c1–c5$ followed by suppliers $s1–s3$. The route listed in the table is the shortest feasible route containing the indicated facilities. In other words, the route is the solution of a single-vehicle VRPB for the indicated facilities. In general, the number of feasible routes is extremely large and the routes cannot be generated explicitly for problem instances of realistic size. So this algorithm is only applicable for very small example problems.

Table 9.73 Complete set of feasible routes for VRPB8

Index	Length	Sequence					LineL	BackL
1	584.06	1					12	0
2	923.72	2					29	0
3	860.34	3					49	0
4	963.62	4					51	0
5	327.56	5					18	0
6	825.44	6					0	23
7	959.22	7					0	66
8	711.64	8					0	46
9	1382.68	1	2				41	0
10	973.67	1	3				61	0
11	1539.91	1	4				63	0
12	874.84	1	5				30	0
13	1289.16	1	6				12	23
14	1262.72	1	7				12	66
15	1283.26	1	8				12	46
16	1182.20	2	5				47	0
17	1691.52	2	6				29	23
18	1235.81	2	7				29	66
19	1408.38	2	8				29	46
20	1184.40	3	5				67	0
21	1647.59	3	6				49	23
22	1225.61	3	7				49	66
23	1567.78	3	8				49	46
24	1084.59	4	5				69	0
25	1506.01	4	6				51	23
26	1632.82	4	7				51	66
27	1143.61	4	8				51	46
28	842.39	5	6				18	23
29	1274.09	5	7				18	66
30	739.87	5	8				18	46
31	1076.54	6	8				0	69
32	2087.78	2	1	6			41	23
33	1678.77	3	1	6			61	23
34	2082.30	1	4	6			63	23
35	1389.67	1	5	6			30	23
36	1694.77	1	2	7			41	66
37	1338.94	1	3	7			61	66
38	2209.11	1	4	7			63	66
39	1553.50	5	1	7			30	66
40	1867.34	1	2	8			41	46
41	1672.87	3	1	8			61	46
42	1719.90	1	4	8			63	46
43	1287.15	1	5	8			30	46
44	1697.03	2	5	6			47	23
45	1494.29	5	2	7			47	66
46	1594.51	2	5	8			47	46
47	1699.23	3	5	6			67	23
48	1549.67	5	3	7			67	66
49	1596.71	3	5	8			67	46
50	1599.42	4	5	6			69	23
51	1753.79	5	4	7			69	66
52	1264.58	5	4	8			69	46
53	1540.26	1	6	8			12	69
54	1773.28	2	8	6			29	69
55	1898.69	3	6	8			49	69
56	1508.51	4	8	6			51	69
57	1093.49	5	6	8			18	69
58	2155.99	1	2	5	6		59	23
59	1985.55	5	1	2	7		59	66
60	2053.47	1	2	5	8		59	46
61	2232.24	1	2	8	6		41	69
62	1929.87	3	1	6	8		61	69
63	2084.80	1	4	8	6		63	69
64	1640.77	1	5	6	8		30	69
65	1948.13	2	5	6	8		47	69
66	1950.33	3	5	6	8		67	69
67	1629.48	5	4	8	6		69	69
68	2407.09	1	2	5	6	8	59	69

Table 9.74 Optimal routes for VRPB8

Route	Facility								Length
	1	2	3	4	5	6	7	8	
1	d1	c1	c3	d1					973.66
2	d1	c2	s2	d1					1,235.81
3	d1	c5	c4	s3	s1	d1			1,629.49
4									
Total									3,838.96

The solution of the linear relaxation of this SPP yields an integer solution consisting of three routes, with indices 10, 18, and 67. Equivalently, the branch-and-bound algorithm finds an integer solution at the root node of the search tree. In general, the linear relaxation of the SPP does not yield an integer solution, and finding the integer solution is the most time-consuming phase of the solution algorithm. The optimal routes are given in Table 9.74 and shown in Fig. 9.35. These routes are identical to the ones determined by the move improvement algorithm before, but now it has been established that these are the optimal routes.

Fig. 9.35 Optimal routes for
the VRPB8 example

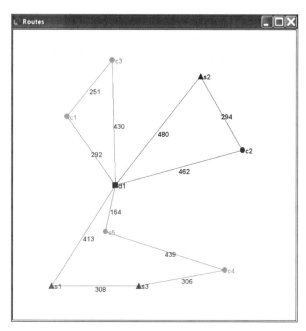

9.3.1.15 Set Partitioning Using Heuristic Row Prices and Bootstrapping the Route Generation

If access to a linear programming solver is not available, the row prices can be determined with a heuristic cost allocation scheme rather than using the values of the dual variables of the linear relaxation of the SPP. The cost allocation schemes developed for the classic VRP can be used without change for the VRPB since the principle that the total route cost has to be allocated to all the facilities serviced by that route remains unchanged. The VRP and VRPB differ in the generation of the feasible routes. For the VRP only one capacity constraint needs to be observed, while for the VRPB two separate capacity constraints have to be observed, one for the linehaul section and one for the backhaul section of the route, respectively. All feasible routes can be generated and evaluated in every iteration as was illustrated above. The algorithm can be started from any feasible solution and with row prices computed from that feasible solution.

To further reduce the computational burden, the routes can be generated in a bootstrap fashion. In the first iteration, only routes with a single facility one each route are generated. In the following iterations, the number of facilities on each route is increased each iteration by one. So in iteration k only routes with exactly a combined total of k linehaul and backhaul facilities are evaluated based on the row prices determined heuristically from the solution based on routes that have between 1 and $k-1$ facilities on each route. This bootstrap algorithm is purely heuristic and no statement can be made with respect to the quality of the routes generated or a lower bound on the total route length.

Table 9.75 Stage one set partitioning formulation for VRPB8

Route	1	2	3	4	5	6	7	8		Row P.
Cost	584.06	923.72	860.34	963.62	327.56	825.44	959.22	711.64	RHS	6,155.60
LineLoad	12	29	49	51	18	0	0	0		
Backload	0	0	0	0	0	23	66	46		
1	1								1	584.06
2		1							1	923.72
3			1						1	860.34
4				1					1	963.62
5					1				1	327.56
6						1			1	825.44
7							1		1	959.22
8								1	1	711.64
x	1	1	1	1	1	1	1	1		

In the first stage, all singleton routes are generated (Table 9.75). Solving the master problem for these routes yields the optimal solution in which all routes are selected. This set of routes is not feasible because it requires eight vehicles, but is used here to start the algorithm. This implies that the constraint on the maximum number of routes was temporarily ignored. The objective function value is 6,155.60. The row prices for each route are equal to the route length. The row prices are used to evaluate feasible routes with two facilities in stage two.

In stage two, 23 new feasible routes with two facilities are generated with route indices 9 through 31. Based on the row prices of stage one, all of these two-facility routes have positive savings or negative reduced costs. All these routes are thus added to the master problem, which now contains 31 columns. The integer master problem is solved. The optimal solution contains four routes each with two facilities, namely routes 10, 18, 27, and 28. The objective function value is 4,195.48. The new row prices are computed with the allocation scheme based on facility weights equal to the product of their load and distance to the depot and divided by 100. For example, the calculation of the row prices of facilities 2 and 7 visited by route 18 with length 1,235.81 are shown next. The results of all the calculations are summarized in Table 9.76.

Table 9.76 Stage two heuristic row prices for VRPB8

Facility	Origin distance	Load	Cost weight	Heuristic row price
1	292.03	12.00	35.04	138.80
2	461.86	29.00	133.94	367.44
3	430.17	49.00	210.78	834.87
4	481.81	51.00	245.72	686.40
5	163.78	18.00	29.48	199.62
6	412.72	23.00	94.93	642.77
7	479.61	66.00	316.54	868.37
8	355.82	46.00	163.68	457.21
Sum				4,195.48

Table 9.77 Stage three route evaluations for VRPB8

Index	Length	Facilities sequence			Line. Q.	Back. Q.	Savings
32	2,087.78	2	1	6	41	23	−938.77
33	1,678.77	3	1	6	61	23	−62.33
34	2,082.3	1	4	6	63	23	−614.33
35	1,389.67	1	5	6	30	23	−408.48
36	1,694.77	1	2	7	41	66	−320.16
37	1,338.94	1	3	7	61	66	503.10
38	2,209.11	1	4	7	63	66	−515.54
39	1,553.5	5	1	7	30	66	−346.71
40	1,867.34	1	2	8	41	46	−903.89
41	1,672.87	3	1	8	61	46	−241.99
42	1,719.9	1	4	8	63	46	−437.49
43	1,287.15	1	5	8	30	46	−491.52
44	1,697.03	2	5	6	47	23	−487.20
45	1,494.29	5	2	7	47	66	−58.86
46	1,594.51	2	5	8	47	46	−570.24
47	1,699.23	3	5	6	67	23	−21.97
48	1,549.67	5	3	7	67	66	353.19
49	1,596.71	3	5	8	67	46	−105.01
50	1,599.42	4	5	6	69	23	−70.63
51	1,753.79	5	4	7	69	66	0.60
52	1,264.58	5	4	8	69	46	78.65
53	1,540.26	1	6	8	12	69	−301.48
54	1,773.28	2	8	6	29	69	−305.86
55	1,898.69	3	6	8	49	69	36.16
56	1,508.51	4	8	6	51	69	277.87
57	1,093.49	5	6	8	18	69	206.11

$$w_2 = (d_{02} \cdot q_2)/100 = (461.86 \cdot 29)/100 = 133.94$$

$$w_7 = (d_{07} \cdot q_7)/100 = (479.61 \cdot 66)/100 = 316.54$$

$$p_2 = \frac{133.94}{133.94 + 316.52} \cdot 1{,}235.81 = 367.44$$

$$p_7 = \frac{316.52}{133.94 + 316.51} \cdot 1{,}235.61 = 868.37$$

In stage three, all routes with exactly three facilities are evaluated with the row prices in Table 9.78. The feasible routes with three facilities are routes 32–57. The savings for the 26 routes with three facilities are shown in Table 9.77. Seven routes have positive savings and are added to the master problem; 19 routes have negative savings and are discarded. The master problem now contains 38 routes.

The integer master problem is solved. The optimal solution contains four routes, namely routes 5, 10, 18, and 56. The total route length is 4,045.55. The new row prices are computed with the allocation scheme based on facility weights equal to the product of their load and distance to the depot and divided by 100. Only the

Table 9.78 Stage three row price calculations for VRPB8

Facility	Weight	Fraction	New price	Row price
1				138.80
2				367.44
3				834.87
4	245.72	0.49	734.99	734.99
5				327.56
6	94.93	0.19	283.94	283.94
7				868.37
8	163.68	0.32	489.58	489.58
Sum	504.33	1.00	1,508.51	4,045.55

calculations of the row prices of facilities 4, 8, and 6 visited by route 56 with length 1,508.51 have to be updated and are shown next. The row prices for all other facilities are based on routes that were determined earlier. The results of all the calculations are summarized in Table 9.78.

$$p_4 = \frac{245.72}{245.72 + 94.93 + 163.68} \cdot 1,508.81$$

$$= \frac{245.72}{504.33} \cdot 1508.81 = 0.49 \cdot 1,508.81 = 734.99$$

$$p_6 = \frac{94.93}{504.33} \cdot 1508.81 = 0.19 \cdot 1,508.81 = 283.94$$

$$p_8 = \frac{163.68}{504.33} \cdot 1508.81 = 0.32 \cdot 1,508.81 = 589.58$$

In stage four, all routes with exactly four facilities are evaluated with the row prices in Table 9.78. The feasible routes with three facilities are routes 58–67. The savings for the ten routes with four facilities are shown in Table 9.79. One route has positive savings and is added to the master problem, nine routes have negative savings and are discarded. The master problem now contains 39 routes.

The integer master problem is solved. The optimal solution contains three routes, namely routes 10, 18, and 67. The total route length is 3,838.96. Note that this is the

Table 9.79 Stage four route evaluations for VRPB8

Index	Length	Facilities sequence				Line. Q.	Back. Q.	Savings
58	2,155.99	1	2	5	6	59	23	−1,038.26
59	1,985.55	5	1	2	7	59	66	−283.38
60	2,053.47	1	2	5	8	59	46	−730.09
61	2,232.24	1	2	8	6	41	69	−952.49
62	1,929.87	3	1	6	8	61	69	−182.68
63	2,084.8	1	4	8	6	63	69	−437.49
64	1,640.77	1	5	6	8	30	69	−400.89
65	1,948.13	2	5	6	8	47	69	−479.62
66	1,950.33	3	5	6	8	67	69	−14.38
67	1,629.48	5	4	8	6	69	69	206.59

Table 9.80 Stage four row price calculations for VRPB8

Facility	Weight	Fraction	New price	Row price
1				138.80
2				367.44
3				834.87
4	245.72	0.46	750.09	750.09
5	29.48	0.06	89.99	89.99
6	94.93	0.18	289.77	289.77
7				868.37
8	163.68	0.31	499.64	499.64
Sum	533.81	1.00	1,629.48	3,838.96

optimal solution, but the optimality of this solution is not known solely based on the current algorithm. Only the calculation of the row prices of facilities 4, 5, 6, and 8 visited by route 67 with length 1,629.48 have to updated and are shown next. The row prices for all other facilities are based on routes that were determined earlier. The results of the calculations are summarized in Table 9.80.

In stage five, all routes with exactly five facilities are evaluated with the above row prices. There is only one feasible route with five facilities which is route 68. The savings for route 68 with five facilities are shown in Table 9.81. The route has negative savings and is discarded. The master problem was not extended and does not have to be resolved. No route can contain six facilities so the algorithm terminates.

9.3.1.16 Set Partitioning Using Iterative Linear Programming

The set partitioning algorithm will be started from scratch, without using the best primal feasible solution found so far. This is not the most efficient approach, but is used in this example to detail the steps of the set partitioning algorithm. In order to limit the number of columns to the master problem, the feasible routes will be generated in five stages in a bootstrapping fashion. In each stage k, new feasible routes with exactly k facilities will be generated. The row prices will be based on the dual variables of the linear relaxation of the master problem of the previous stage. After the last stage, all feasible routes that were not added to the master problem are evaluated and added if they have a negative reduced cost. It would be more efficient to jump start the set partitioning algorithm with the best routes found so far. These steps are left to the interested reader.

The first iteration is identical to the first iteration of the algorithm that uses the heuristic row prices since each route only contains one facility. The solution to the linear relaxation of the master problem will be automatically integer and the row prices based on the dual variables are equal to the route lengths. The same routes

Table 9.81 Stage five route evaluations for VRPB8

Index	Length	Facilities sequence					Line. Q.	Back. Q.	Savings
68	2,407.09	1	2	5	6	8	59	69	−1,021.46

are generated and added to the master problem for the second iteration in both algorithms. However, in the following steps the algorithms may and most likely will generate different route sets. In this algorithm the linear relaxation of the master problem is solved and its solution is shown in Table 9.35. The table contains all the columns and is split into three segments to fit the page limitations. The optimal solution contains four routes each with two facilities, namely routes 10, 18, 27, and 28. The objective function value is 4,195.48. The continuous decision variables at optimality are automatically an integer. This implies that for this iteration, this algorithm and the previous algorithm will use the same feasible set of routes to determine the row prices. The prior algorithm uses a heuristic allocation scheme and this algorithm uses the dual variables of each row to evaluate feasible routes with three facilities in stage three. Most linear programming solvers will output the dual variables at optimality upon request. The dual variables are requested with the sensitivity report of the Excel solver (Fig. 9.36). A sample output of the Excel solver is shown for iteration two in Fig. 9.37.

In stage three, 26 new feasible routes are generated, each with exactly three facilities. Based on the row prices of stage two, eight routes have positive savings or equivalently have a negative reduced cost. These eight routes are added to the master problem. The master problem now contains 39 routes. The linear programming relaxation of the master problem is solved. Some of the continuous decision variables are equal to 0.5. The objective function value is equal to 4,017.22. The integer solution of this problem is not used in this algorithm, but if the variables are forced to be binary, the optimal objective function value increases to 4,045.55 as computed in the previous algorithm. The selected routes are then 5, 10, 18, and 56.

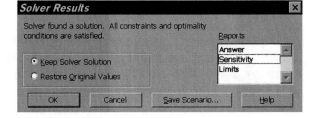

Fig. 9.36 Excel sensitivity report request for example VRPB8

Fig. 9.37 Excel sensitivity report for iteration 2 of the VRPB8 example

Cell	Name	Final Value	Shadow Price	Constraint R.H. Side	Allowable Increase	Allowable Decrease
$AJ$6	RHS	1	458.96	1	0	0
$AJ$7	RHS	1	923.72	1	0	0
$AJ$8	RHS	1	514.71	1	0	0
$AJ$9	RHS	1	786.54	1	0	0
$AJ$10	RHS	1	122.92	1	0	1
$AJ$11	RHS	1	719.47	1	0	0
$AJ$12	RHS	1	312.09	1	0	1
$AJ$13	RHS	1	357.07	1	0	0
$AJ$14	x RHS	4	0	4	1E+30	0

In stage four, ten new feasible routes are generated, each with exactly four facilities. Based on the row prices of stage three, only one route has positive savings. So, in stage four one column is added to the master problem. The master problem now contains 40 columns. The linear programming relaxation of the master problem is solved. The continuous decision variables at optimality are automatically integer. The objective function value at optimality is 3,838.96. The three routes selected are 10, 18, and 67.

In stage five, one new feasible route is generated with five facilities. Based on the row prices of stage four, this route does not have positive savings and is not added to the master problem. The optimal solution of the master problem or the current values of the row prices do not change.

Since no route can include more than five facilities, all feasible routes have been generated during stages one through five. A lower bound is assured when all the routes not currently in the master problem have nonpositive savings. When all the routes that are not currently included in the master problem are evaluated with the row prices of stage five, seven of them have positive savings. These routes are added to the master problem in stage six. The master problem now contains 47 columns. The linear programming relaxation of the master problem is solved. The objective function remains unchanged from stage four at 3,838.96. This objective function value is a lower bound on the optimal solution since it is the solution of the linear programming relaxation. All continuous decision variables are automatically integer. All routes currently not in the master problem are evaluated with the new row prices and none of them has positive savings, so the current solution is optimal. The final master problem formulation is shown in the next table. The three optimal routes are shown in the Fig. 9.34.

It should be noted that this optimal solution was obtained by solving a sequence of linear programming formulations, which can be done very efficiently. In addition, for this example the final solution of the linear relaxation was automatically integer. So no integer programming formulation had to be solved to find an integer primal feasible solution. The proof of the optimality of this solution requires that (1) all feasible routes can be generated and when evaluated with current the row prices have nonnegative reduced cost and (2) that the solution of the linear programming formulation has integer decision variables. In real-life problems, it is virtually impossible to enumerate all possible feasible routes and one or more decision variables have fractional values.

9.3.1.17 Set Partitioning Using an Auxiliary Pricing Problem

The need to generate all feasible routes can be eliminated and a lower bound on the total route length is determined if an auxiliary pricing problem is used. Using an auxiliary pricing problem is the only computationally reasonable alternative for larger problem instances. However, there is a significant software implementation cost associated with this mathematical programming solution approach, so it should only be undertaken when it is warranted by the cost difference between an optimal

Table 9.82 Original heuristic row prices for VRPB8 (Iteration 0)

Facility	$c1$	$c2$	$c3$	$c4$	$c5$	$s1$	$s2$	$s3$	vc
Row price	138.8	367.4	834.9	851.8	102.2	329.1	868.4	567.4	0.0

Table 9.83 Additional route candidates for iteration 1 for VRPB8

Index	Facilities					Cost	Red. Cost
4	$d1$	$c4$	$s3$	$d1$		1,143.61	−275.63
5	$d1$	$c1$	$c3$	$s2$	$d1$	1,338.93	−503.10
6	$d1$	$c4$	$s3$	$s1$	$d1$	1,508.51	−239.80

Table 9.84 Row prices after iteration 1 for VRPB8

Facility	$c1$	$c2$	$c3$	$c4$	$c5$	$s1$	$s2$	$s3$	vc
Row price	973.7	1,235.8	0.0	1,143.6	706.9	0.0	0.0	0.0	0.0

and heuristic solution. If the solution based on the auxiliary pricing problem is integer, then it is the optimal solution. If the solution based on the auxiliary pricing problem is not integer, then this solution provides only a lower bound. The optimal primal feasible solution then must be determined with additional computations.

The algorithm starts with the solution generated by the parallel savings algorithm. The total route length is equal to 4,059.98. The heuristic row prices are based on the product of distance to the depot and facility load. They are shown in Table 9.82, where vc indicates the price or dual variable associated with the constraint on the number of routes.

The SPPRC generates three additional route candidates with negative reduced cost for iteration 1. These candidates are shown in Table 9.83.

The linear master problem is solved with a total of six route candidates, the three original routes, and the three additional routes. The optimal solution is 4,059.98. The solution variables have integer values, the first three routes have a value of 1, and the last three have a value of zero. The new row prices are shown in Table 9.84.

The SPPRC generates 14 additional route candidates with negative reduced cost for iteration two. These candidates are shown in Table 9.85.

The linear master problem is solved with a total of 20 route candidates. The optimal solution is 4,029.65. The solution variables have integer values, routes 5, 6, and 12 have a value of 1 and the remaining variables have a value of zero. The new row prices are shown in Table 9.86.

The SPPRC generates three additional route candidates with negative reduced cost for iteration 3. These candidates are shown in Table 9.87. The total number of route candidates in the master problem is now 23.

The linear master problem is solved with a total of 23 route candidates. The optimal solution is 3,838.96. The solution variables have integer values, routes 1, 2, and 23 have a value of 1 and the remaining variables have a value of zero. The new row prices are shown in Table 9.88.

Table 9.85 Additional route candidates for iteration 2 for VRPB8

Index	Facilities						Cost	Red. Cost
7	d1	c1	d1				584.06	−389.61
8	d1	c5	d1				327.57	−379.34
9	d1	c2	d1				923.72	−312.09
10	d1	c5	c1	d1			874.84	−805.73
11	d1	c1	c2	d1			1,382.68	−826.79
12	d1	c2	c5	d1			1,182.21	−760.51
13	d1	c4	d1				963.61	−179.99
14	d1	c1	c2	c5	d1		1,641.17	−1,275.21
15	d1	c4	c1	d1			1,539.91	−577.36
16	d1	c5	c4	d1			1,084.59	−765.92
17	d1	c1	c2	c5	s1	d1	2,155.99	−760.38
18	d1	c1	c2	c5	s3	d1	2,053.47	−862.91
19	d1	c5	c1	c2	s2	d1	1,985.55	−930.82
20	d1	c1	c2	c5	s1	s3	d1	2,407.09	−509.29

Table 9.86 Row prices after iteration 2 for VRPB8

Facility	c1	c2	c3	c4	c5	s1	s2	s3	vc
Row Price	222.3	854.6	735.5	757.0	327.6	751.5	381.2	0.0	0.0

Table 9.87 Additional route candidates for iteration 3 for VRPB8

Index	Facilities						Cost	Red. Cost
21	d1	c5	s1	d1			842.39	−236.66
22	d1	c5	c2	s2	d1		1,494.29	−69.08
23	d1	c5	c4	s3	s1	d1	1,629.49	−206.59

Table 9.88 Row prices after iteration 3 for VRPB8

Facility	c1	c2	c3	c4	c5	s1	s2	s3	vc
Row price	389.9	923.7	583.8	826.1	258.5	583.9	312.1	−39.0	0.0

Table 9.89 Additional route candidates for iteration 4 for VRPB8

Index	Facilities					Cost	Red. Cost
24	d1	c2	c5	s1	d1	1,697.03	−69.08

The SPPRC generates one additional route candidate with negative reduced cost for iteration four. This candidate is shown in Table 9.89. The total number of route candidates in the master problem is now 24.

The linear master problem is solved with a total of 24 route candidates. The optimal solution does not change from the previous iteration and is 3,838.96. The solution variables have integer values, routes 1, 2, and 23 have a value of 1 and the remaining variables have a value of zero. The new row prices are shown in Table 9.90.

Table 9.90 Row prices after iteration 4 for VRPB8

Facility	$c1$	$c2$	$c3$	$c4$	$c5$	$s1$	$s2$	$s3$	vc
Row price	459.0	923.7	514.7	826.1	258.5	514.8	312.1	30.1	0.0

No new route candidates are found for the current values of the row prices. The current solution value of 3,838.96 is a lower bound on the total route length. Because, the solution to the master problem is also integer, it is the optimal primal feasible solution.

Recall that the complete enumeration required 68 route candidates, the algorithm using heuristic row prices required 39 route candidates; the iterative evaluation method using linear programming generated 47 route candidates; and the last algorithm using an auxiliary pricing problem generated only 24 route candidates. The difference between the numbers of route candidates that are generated increases significantly when the problem size increases. Even for small to medium problem sizes, the first two algorithms no longer run to completion. The algorithm using the auxiliary pricing problem can find a lower bound for problem instances up to 50 facilities. But the solution is nearly always fractional, so the SPP solution only provides a lower bound and not the optimal solution to the VRPB. Solving the auxiliary pricing problem requires the implementation of a dynamic programming algorithm to find the shortest path under resource constraints that does not have any sub tours. In general, the lower bound could be further improved by a complete branch-and-price solution algorithm. However, implementing a full branch-and-price algorithm is a complex and extensive task. This programming effort is most likely not justified unless the routing decisions are very expensive or executed repeatedly.

9.4 Vehicle Routing Problem with Time Windows (VRPTW)

The vehicle routing problem with time windows consists of determining a set of routes with minimum cost that originate and terminate at a central depot. The location of the depot and the customers, the demand of the customers, and the allowable time interval for the start of service for each customer are assumed to be known. The service at each customer must begin within the time window specified for that customer.

The time windows can be hard or soft. In the case of a hard time window, a vehicle can arrive at the customer location early and is permitted to wait until the start of the service time window. However, a vehicle is not allowed to arrive after the closure of the service time window. In the case of a soft time window, the service interval can be violated with a certain penalty. The VRPTW is a generalization of the classic vehicle routing problem through the addition of an allowable time interval for the start of service. It has been studied extensively in literature. A recent comprehensive review is provided in Ball et al. (1995).

Just as in case of the vehicle routing problem with backhauling, the optimal routes for the VPRTW no longer exhibit the geographical separation, but significant overlap of the routes and crossing of the arcs of a single route may occur.

Because of the inherent difficulty of finding optimal or even a feasible set of routes, the early algorithms were heuristics. The same types of algorithms were adapted to the case of the VRPTW. A number of route construction and route improvement algorithms has been developed. Route insertion algorithms build a feasible set of routes by inserting at every iteration 1 unvisited customer into a partial route. Sequential algorithms build one route at the time, while parallel algorithms build several routes simultaneously. Improvement algorithms start from a feasible set of routes and attempt to reduce the total route length through a set of exchanges. Exchanges can be within a single route or between routes. The procedures terminate is no other favorable exchanges can be found. During every iteration either the first exchange that generates savings can be selected (first descent), the exchange with the largest savings can be selected (steepest descent), or exchanges that increase the route length may also be selected initially (simulated annealing).

The GAP formulation of Fisher and Jaikumar (1981) has been extended to construct a problem with an assignment and clustering phase, followed by the solution of independent TSP problems with time windows. However, most of the optimization-based algorithms use the following general vehicle routing formulation which incorporates time windows and resources.

The following additional notation is used:

N	set containing the customers, indexed by i and j
K	set containing the different vehicles, indexed by k
$O_k = \{o_k\}$	set containing the origin depot for vehicle k
$D_k = \{d_k\}$	set containing the destination depot for vehicle k
$V_k = N \cup O_k \cup D_k$	set of nodes that can be visited by vehicle k
A_k	set or arcs (i,j) than can be used by vehicle k
dem_i	demand to be delivered to customer i
cap_k	capacity of vehicle k
V	maximum number of vehicles, $V \leq K$
$[a_i, b_i]$	time window during which service for customer i is allowed to start
$[a_{o_k}, b_{o_k}]$	time window during which vehicle k can depart from its origin depot
$[a_{d_k}, b_{d_k}]$	time window during which vehicle k can arrive at its destination depot
t_{ijk}	transit time from the beginning of service to customer i to arrival at customer j when the vehicle k travels from directly customer i to customer j, which includes unloading (service) time at customer i and travel time from customer i to customer j

$q_{o_k k}$	initial load on vehicle k when departs from its origin depot
x_{ijk}	flow variable indicating if vehicle k travels directly from node i to node j
q_{ik}	load variable indicating the load on vehicle k just after servicing customer i
h_{ik}	time variable indicating the time when vehicle k starts servicing customer i

Formulation 9.14. General Vehicle Routing Formulation

$$Min \quad \sum_{k \in K} \sum_{(i,j) \in A_k} c_{ijk} x_{ijk}$$

$$s.t. \quad \sum_{k \in K} \sum_{j \in N \cup D_k} x_{ijk} = 1$$

$$\sum_{k \in K} \sum_{j \in N} x_{o_k jk} \leq V$$

$$\sum_{j \in N \cup D_k} x_{o_k jk} = 1$$

$$\sum_{i \in N \cup O_k} x_{ijk} - \sum_{i \in N \cup D_k} x_{jik} = 0 \qquad (9.53)$$

$$\sum_{i \in N \cup O_k} x_{id_k k} = 1$$

$$x_{ijk} \left(h_{ik} + t_{ijk} - h_{jk} \right) \leq 0$$

$$a_i \leq h_{ik} \leq b_i$$

$$x_{ijk} \left(q_{ik} + dem_j - q_{jk} \right) \leq 0$$

$$dem_i \leq q_{ik} \leq cap_k$$

$$x_{ijk} \in B$$

$$x_{ijk} \geq 0$$

This is a nonlinear formulation. If the arc selection variables are binary, the time window and capacity constraints can be linearized and rewritten as

$$h_{ik} + t_{ijk} - h_{jk} \leq \left(1 - x_{ijk} \right) \cdot M_{ijk}$$
$$q_{ik} + dem_j - q_{jk} \leq \left(1 - x_{ijk} \right) \cdot cap_k \qquad (9.54)$$

The large positive constant M_{ijk} can be reduced based on the following

$$M_{ijk} = \max_{(i,j) \in A_k} \left\{ b_i + t_{ijk} - a_j, 0 \right\} \qquad (9.55)$$

The arc costs can be extended to incorporate the fixed vehicle costs by adding this vehicle cost to the transportation cost of all the arcs emanating out of the origin location of the vehicle.

$$c_{o_k jk} = tc_{o_k jk} + vc_k \tag{9.56}$$

To minimize the number of vehicles, all transportation costs tc_{ijk} can be set equal to zero. To ignore vehicle costs, all vehicle costs vc_k can be set equal to zero. Finally, the number of routes can be forced to be exactly equal to V by changing the inequality constraint to an equality constraint. This formulation accommodates a homogeneous as well as heterogeneous fleet of vehicles, single and multiple depots. It can be easily extended to multiple resources such as demand and vehicle capacities expressed in both weight and volume.

The richness and power of the above formulation has led to an extensive body of research on solving this formulation and several of its derivatives or variants, such as the TSP with time windows (TSPTW). Many solution approaches rely on column generation and the use of the corresponding pricing problem. An overview can be found in Ball et al. (1995).

9.5   Fleet Sizing and Fleet Mix

The previous problems all belong to the class of operational planning problems. A typical situation is when a delivery vehicle is making customer stops to satisfy orders that have been placed the previous day. The goods have been placed on the vehicle in the reverse order of the customer stops. The data for the operational planning problems can be assumed to be known with certainty. The problem described next belongs to the class of tactical planning problems. The decision to buy or lease a vehicle has to be made at the current time, but the vehicle will be used to satisfy customer service requests occurring in the future. Those individual service requests are not known at the time the acquisition decision has to be made. However, certain information about the service requests is known such as their estimated mean and distribution. This information is typically based on forecasts.

The fleet sizing problem finds the size of the privately owned fleet that minimizes the long range expected cost with respect to a stochastic demand for vehicles. The demand for vehicles is assumed to be a random variable with a known distribution. The decision variable is the number of vehicles in the privately owned fleet. For each of the owned vehicles a fixed cost per period must be paid every period regardless if the vehicle is used or not. If the vehicle is used, an additional variable cost per period must be paid. If the demand for vehicles exceeds the number of privately owned vehicles, additional vehicles can be rented on a short-term basis in the spot market. A rental fee per period must be paid for each rented vehicle. The solution to the fleet sizing problem is analogous to the solution of the newsvendor problem.

9.5.1 Definitions

N	number of periods in the planning horizon
c_F, c_V	fixed and variable cost per period for privately owned vehicles
c_H	rental fee per period for rented vehicles
d_t	demand for vehicles during period t, and d_{MAX} is the maximum possible demand
v	number of privately owned vehicles (fleet size)
$\Delta f_n, \Delta^2 f_n$	first-and second-order forward difference of the sequence f_n (which themselves are sequences)

$$\Delta f_n = f_{n+1} - f_n$$
$$\Delta^2 f_n = \Delta f_{n+1} - \Delta f_n = f_{n+2} - 2 f_{n+1} + f_n \qquad (9.57)$$

The total annual cost in function of the fleet size is equal to the sum of the fixed and variable costs for the private vehicles and the variable cost of the rental vehicles as expressed in the following equation.

$$C(v) = N \cdot v \cdot c_F + c_V \sum_{t=1}^{N} \min(d_t, v) + c_H \sum_{t=1}^{N} \max(d_t - v, 0) \qquad (9.58)$$

In order to have meaningful answers, it is also assumed that

$$0 < c_F < c_H - c_V \qquad (9.59)$$

We define a new variable $m(v)$ as the number of periods during which the demand for vehicles is larger than the fleet size.

$$m(v) = \sum_{t \mid d_t > v} 1 \qquad (9.60)$$

The sequence of values of $m(v)$ ordered by increasing values of the index $v = 1, 2, \ldots$ defines the sequence m_v. Observe that the sequence contains zero values for index values starting with $v = d_{MAX}$. $m(v)$ is monotonically nonincreasing in function of v and has the following boundary values

$$m(0) = N$$
$$m(d_{MAX}) = 0 \qquad (9.61)$$

Equivalently, if the fleet size increases, then the number of time periods that the demand is larger than the fleet size either decreases or remains the same.

$$\Delta m_v \leq 0 \qquad (9.62)$$

The sequence of values of $C(v)$ ordered by increasing values of the index $v = 1, 2, \ldots$ defines the sequence C_v. The first forward difference can be computed as follows

$$\Delta C_v = N \cdot c_F \cdot (v + 1 - v) + c_V \left[\sum_{t=1}^{N} \min(d_t, v+1) - \sum_{t=1}^{N} \min(d_t, v) \right]$$

$$+ c_H \left[\sum_{t=1}^{N} \max(d_t - v - 1, 0) - \sum_{t=1}^{N} \max(d_t - v, 0) \right]$$

$$= N \cdot c_F + c_V \left[\sum_{t|d_t > v} \min(d_t, v+1) - \sum_{t|d_t > v} \min(d_t, v) \right.$$

$$\left. + \sum_{t|d_t \leq v} \min(d_t, v+1) - \sum_{t|d_t \leq v} \min(d_t, v) \right]$$

$$+ c_H \left[\sum_{t|d_t > v} \max(d_t - v - 1, 0) - \sum_{t|d_t > v} \max(d_t - v, 0) \right.$$

$$\left. + \sum_{t|d_t \leq v} \max(d_t - v - 1, 0) - \sum_{t|d_t \leq v} \max(d_t - v, 0) \right]$$

$$N \cdot c_F + c_V \left[\sum_{t|d_t > v} (v + 1) - \sum_{t|d_t > v} v + \sum_{t|d_t \leq v} d_t - \sum_{t|d_t \leq v} d_t \right]$$

$$+ c_H \left[\sum_{t|d_t > v} (d_t - v - 1) - \sum_{t|d_t > v} (d_t - v) + \sum_{t|d_t \leq v} 0 - \sum_{t|d_t \leq v} 0 \right]$$

$$= N \cdot c_F + c_V \left[\sum_{t|d_t > v} 1 \right] - c_H \left[\sum_{t|d_t > v} 1 \right]$$

The first-and second-order forward differences of the cost are thus given by

$$\Delta C_v = N \cdot c_F - m_v(c_H - c_V) \tag{9.63}$$

$$\Delta^2 C_v = -\Delta m_v(c_H - c_V) \tag{9.64}$$

This first difference is negative at index $v=0$ and is positive at index $v = d_{MAX}$. Since the second forward difference is nonnegative everywhere, the objective function has a globally optimal fleet size. This optimal value can be found when the first-order difference becomes nonnegative, or equivalently, it is the smallest value of v for which the following holds.

$$v^* = \min \left\{ v \,\middle|\, m_v \leq \frac{c_F}{c_H - c_V} \cdot N \right\} \tag{9.65}$$

If the demand data is not given as a historical time series but rather as a forecasted demand distribution, then optimality condition can be computed with the following calculations, where $F(x)$ is the cumulative probability distribution function of the demand.

$$m(v) = N \cdot (1 - F(v)) \tag{9.66}$$

$$v^* = \min \left\{ v \,\middle|\, F(v) \geq 1 - \frac{c_F}{c_H - c_V} \right\} \tag{9.67}$$

If the number of vehicles is a continuous decision variable, the optimal number of vehicles can also be determined based on equilibrium theory. In the following equation, the quantity on the left is the marginal cost increase if v is decreased and the quantity on the right is the marginal cost increase if v is increased. When increasing the fleet size from $v-1$ to v, for exactly $m(v)$ periods during the planning horizon one has to pay only the variable cost for an owned vehicle rather than the variable cost for a rented vehicle, but during all the periods in the planning horizon on has to pay the fixed cost for one additional owned vehicle. At equilibrium, those two quantities have to be equal.

$$m\left(v^*\right) \cdot (c_H - c_V) = N \cdot (1 - F\left(v\right)) \cdot (c_H - c_V) = N \cdot c_F \tag{9.68}$$

or

$$m\left(v^*\right) = \frac{N \cdot c_F}{c_H - c_V} \tag{9.69}$$

or

$$F(v^*) = 1 - \frac{c_F}{c_H - c_V} \tag{9.70}$$

The above equation assumes that the number of vehicles can be fractional. This assumption is invalid for most realistic fleet sizes and so the equation is only a very rough approximation. Its primary use is as a sanity check for the more accurate calculations that use discrete values of v.

Fleet Composition Example Executive Travel, Inc., provides full service travel services by corporate jets to corporations and wealthy individuals on a worldwide basis. They charge their customers a comprehensive fee based on the origin, intermediate stops, and destination of the travel and on the start date and stop date of the service. To provide this service they are using a fleet of corporate jets that they lease on a long-term basis. The long-term lease cost for a Gulf Jet VII is $40,000 per week. If a jet of this model is used it costs an additional $8,000 per week for maintenance and regulatory requirements. Executive Travel can also lease a Gulf Jet VII on a short-term weekly basis for $95,000 per week. This fee includes the charges

Table 9.91 Demand data for the fleet composition example

t	$d(t)$	t	$d(t)$	t	$d(t)$	t	$d(t)$
1	12	7	4	13	9	19	7
2	8	8	8	14	6	20	4
3	3	9	9	15	5	21	9
4	9	10	7	16	2	22	6
5	6	11	12	17	7	23	3
6	7	12	8	18	8	24	1

for maintenance and regulatory requirements. Executive travel has recorded the demand for the Gulf Jet VII on a weekly basis during the last six months (24 weeks). The demand is shown in Table 9.91 and Fig. 9.38.

Based on the data in Table 9.92 which shows the sequence of m_v, the optimal number of aircraft is equal to 7.

The same optimal fleet size can also be determined with (9.62).

$$m_v \leq \frac{c_F}{c_H - c_V} \cdot N \Rightarrow \quad m_v \leq \frac{40000}{95000 - 8000} \cdot 24 = 11.03$$

$$m_6 = 14 > 11.03$$

$$m_7 = 10 \leq 11.03$$

$$v^* = 7$$

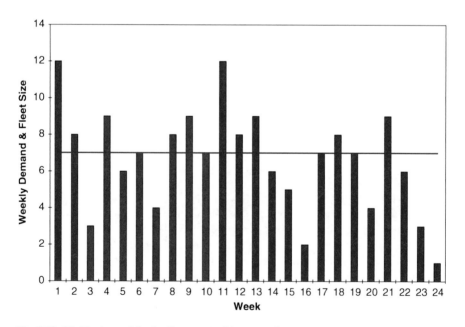

Fig. 9.38 Weekly demand for the fleet composition example

Table 9.92 Solution for the fleet composition example

v	Frequency	Cumulative	$m(v)$	$\Delta C(v)$	$C(v)$
0	0	0	24	−1,128,000	15,200,000
1	1	1	23	−1,041,000	14,072,000
2	1	2	22	−954,000	13,031,000
3	2	4	20	−780,000	12,077,000
4	2	6	18	−606,000	11,297,000
5	1	7	17	−519,000	10,691,000
6	3	10	14	−258,000	10,172,000
7	4	14	10	90,000	9,914,000
8	4	18	6	438,000	10,004,000
9	4	22	2	786,000	10,442,000
10	0	22	2	786,000	11,228,000
11	0	22	2	786,000	12,014,000
12	2	24	0	960,000	12,800,000

9.6 Exercises

True/False Questions

1. The use of computerized methods becomes more important in single vehicle roundtrip routing if the spatial relationships between the delivery points does not represent their true travel time, travel distance, or travel cost. (T/F)_____
2. If all possible columns, when evaluated with the current row prices, yield non-positive savings or equivalently non-negative reduced cost, then the current feasible partition on which the row prices are based is optimal. (T/F)_____
3. One of the main advantage of set partitioning–based solution methods is the fact that they can incorporate many complex feasibility constraints. (T/F)_____
4. The vehicle routing problem attempts to minimize the cost of vehicles and distance traveled necessary to deliver goods to a number of customers with a fleet of vehicles. (T/F)_____
5. The row price determination in the set partitioning algorithm can assign prices to the customers served on a particular route without any other conditions. (T/F)_____
6. Consider the set partitioning problem solved with the row pricing algorithm as presented in class. If the master problem in the set partitioning algorithm is solved to optimality, then the routes selected by the master problem are optimal. (T/F)_____

Vehicle Routing with Backhauling (VRPB7) The vehicle routing problem contains four customers and three suppliers. The location of the facilities is given by their Cartesian coordinates (Table 9.93). The facility data are given in Fig. 9.39. The distance between the facilities is computed with the Euclidean distance norm (and without any over-the-road adjustment) (Table 9.94). Compute and use the integer distances (with

Table 9.93 VRPB7 point data

Label	X-Coord.	Y-Coord.	Quantity
0	261	745	0
1	73	497	50
2	808	585	54
3	350	895	41
4	746	174	43
5	710	513	58
6	592	182	49
7	147	165	88

Fig. 9.39 VRPB7 point locations

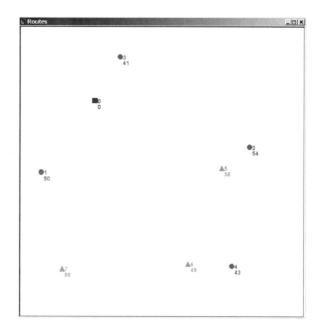

Table 9.94 VRPB7 distances

	1	2	3	4	5	6	7	0
1		740	485	747	637	607	340	311
2	740		553	416	122	457	783	570
3	485	553		823	525	753	758	174
4	747	416	823		341	154	599	749
5	637	122	525	341		351	662	505
6	607	457	753	154	351		445	653
7	340	783	758	599	662	445		591
0	311	570	174	749	505	653	591	

zero significant digits after the decimal point). There are three identical vehicles, each having a capacity of 100 units. Each vehicle can only execute one route.

Nearest Neighbor First construct the routes with the nearest neighbor algorithm (Table 9.95). Each time that you add a facility to a route, show the added or append

Table 9.95 VRPB7 nearest neighbor algorithm steps

Index	Append facility	Anchor facility	Append distance	Linehaul quantity	Backhaul quantity
1					
2					
3					
4					
5					
6					
7					

Table 9.96 VRPB7 nearest neighbor routes

Route	Facility								Length
	1	2	3	4	5	6	7	8	
1	D								
2	D								
3	D								
4	D								
5	D								
6	D								
7	D								
Total									

facility, the anchor facility on the route that this newly added facility is connected to, the append distance to the new facility, and the linehaul and backhaul quantity on the truck on that route so far. When a new route is started, the anchor facility is the depot.

List the sequence of all the facilities on the routes that you have created, with one route per line or row. Each route must start and end with the depot. Compute the route length of each individual route and the total route length of all the routes created by this algorithm. Not all rows or columns in the table have to be used. Use Table 9.96 to report your answer.

Sweep Execute the sweep algorithm for the VRPB problem where a route is terminated or closed as soon as adding either the next customer or supplier facility would violate the truck capacity and where the facilities are sequenced on the route by the rotating ray (Table 9.97). Start the rotating ray in the due east direction and turn the ray counterclockwise. For each time you add a facility to a route, show the added or append facility, the anchor facility on the route this newly added facility is connected to, the append distance to the new facility, and the linehaul and backhaul quantity on the truck on that route so far. When you start a new route, the anchor facility is the depot.

List the sequence of all the facilities on the routes that you have created, with one route per line. Each route must start and end with the depot. Compute the route length

Table 9.97 VRPB7 sweep algorithm steps

Index	Append facility	Anchor facility	Append distance	Linehaul quantity	Backhaul quantity
1					
2					
3					
4					
5					
6					
7					

Table 9.98 VRBP7 sweep routes

Route	Facility								Length
	1	2	3	4	5	6	7	8	
1	D								
2	D								
3	D								
4	D								
5	D								
6	D								
7	D								
Total									

of each individual route and compute the total route length of all the routes created by this algorithm (Table 9.98). Not all rows or columns in the table have to be used.

Parallel Savings Construct the routes with the parallel version of the Clarke and Wright algorithm. The savings penalty for the crossover link between linehaul and backhaul is zero, in other words there is no penalty on the savings for crossing from the linehaul segment to the backhaul segment. A matrix of partial initial feasible savings is shown in Table 9.99. Complete and show the initial feasible savings matrix.

In Table 9.100, compute and show for every iteration the two points for which you found the shortcut, the savings for the shortcut, the length of the partial route that was constructed using this shortcut, and the sequence of all the points on this partial route.

Table 9.99 VRPB7 savings matrix

	1	2	3	4	5	6	7
1			1	314	179	357	562
2			191	903	954	766	378
3	1	191		101	155	75	8
4	314	903	101		914	1,248	741
5							
6							
7							

Table 9.100 VRPB7 parallel savings routes

Step	Shortcut points	Savings	Length	Points
1				
2				
3				
4				
5				
6				
7				
8				
9				

Table 9.101 VRPB7 updated savings matrix

Table 9.102 VRPB7 parallel savings routes summary

Route	Facility 1	2	3	4	5	6	7	8	Length
1	D								
2	D								
3	D								
4	D								
5	D								
6	D								
7	D								
Total									

Show the updated savings matrix after you have executed the first *two* shortcuts. See Tables 9.101 and 9.102.

Vehicle Routing with Backhauls (VRPB6) Consider the single-origin Vehicle Routing Problem with Backhauls (VRPB6) illustrated in Fig. 9.40. All routes start and terminate at the single depot. The depot is indicated by a square. All suppliers are indicated by triangles and all customers are indicated by circles. The distances between the various facilities are also shown. All travel occurs over the network links. The supplies and demands are expressed in fractions of truck capacity and are shown in Table 9.103. Due to the long load and unload times, there is only enough time to visit three facilities on a single truck route. Hence, an additional constraint requires that there are at most three facilities on a route, aside from the origin and destination depot.

Fig. 9.40 VRPB6 transportation network

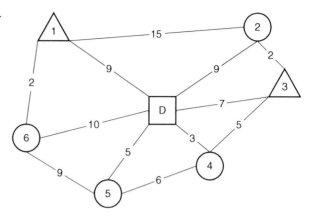

Table 9.103 VRPB6 facility
data

Customer or supplier	Demand or supply	Distance to depot
1	0.10	9
2	0.20	9
3	0.30	7
4	0.40	3
5	0.50	5
6	0.45	10

Table 9.104 VRPB6 interfacility distances

	D	1	2	3	4	5	6
D							
1							
2							
3							
4							
5							
6							

Nearest Neighbor First, construct the routes with the nearest neighbor algorithm
(Table 9.105). Each time you add a facility to a route, show the added or append
facility, the anchor facility on the route this newly added facility is connected to,
the append distance to the new facility, and the linehaul and backhaul quantity on
the truck on that route so far. When a new route is started, the anchor facility is the
depot.

List the sequence of all the facilities on the routes that you have created, with one
route per line or row (Table 9.106). Each route must start and end with the depot.
Compute the route length of each individual route and the total route length of all
the routes created by this algorithm. Not all rows or columns in the table have to
be used.

Table 9.105 VRPB6 nearest neighbor algorithm steps

Index	Append facility	Anchor facility	Append distance	Linehaul quantity	Backhaul quantity
1					
2					
3					
4					
5					
6					

Table 9.106 VRPB6 nearest neighbor routes

Route	Facility								Length
	1	2	3	4	5	6	7	8	
1	D								
2	D								
3	D								
4	D								
5	D								
6	D								
Total									

Table 9.107 VRPB6 sweep algorithm steps

Index	Append facility	Anchor facility	Append distance	Linehaul quantity	Backhaul quantity
1					
2					
3					
4					
5					
6					

Sweep There exist many variants of the sweep algorithm (Table 9.107). Execute the sweep algorithm for the VRPB problem where a route is terminated or closed as soon as adding either the next customer or supplier facility would violate the truck capacity and where the facilities are sequenced on the route by the rotating ray. Start the rotating ray in the due east direction and turn the ray clockwise. For every time you add a facility to a route, show the added or append facility, the anchor facility on the route this newly added facility is connected to, the append distance to the new facility, and the linehaul and backhaul quantity on the truck on that route so far. When you start a new route, the anchor facility is the depot.

List the sequence of all the facilities on the routes that you have created, with one route per line (Table 9.108). Each route must start and end with the depot. Compute the route length of each individual route and compute the total route length of all the routes created by this algorithm. Not all rows or columns in the table have to be used.

Table 9.108 VRPB6 sweep routes

Route	Facility								Length
	1	2	3	4	5	6	7	8	
1	D								
2	D								
3	D								
4	D								
5	D								
6	D								
Total									

Set Partitioning Algorithm In the next column generation step, we consider only routes that have at most two facilities on each route (besides the depot). Observe that these routes have to satisfy the standard vehicle routing with backhauls condition that all customers on a route are visited before any supplier can be visited. We use the standard formula to compute the savings for each route candidate. See Tables 9.109–9.113.

Vehicle Routing Problem with Backhauling (VRPB50) Find the routes that minimize the total distance traveled to supply a number of customers from a single depot and to pick up from a number of suppliers and return to the depot. The trailers are assumed to be rear-loaded, and therefore on every trip all deliveries have to be made

Table 9.109 VRPB6 one-facility routes

Route	Facility								Length
	1	2	3	4	5	6	7	8	
1	D								
2	D								
3	D								
4	D								
5	D								
6	D								
Total									

Table 9.110 VRPB6 two-facility route evaluations

Index	Facility sequence	Length	Savings	Added (Y/N)

Table 9.111 VRPB6 two-facility routes

Route	Facility								Length
	1	2	3	4	5	6	7	8	
1	D								
2	D								
3	D								
4	D								
5	D								
6	D								
Total									

Table 9.112 VRPB6 three-facility route evaluations

Index	Facility sequence	Length	Savings	Added (Y/N)

Table 9.113 VRPB6 three-facility routes

Route	Facility								Length
	1	2	3	4	5	6	7	8	
1	D								
2	D								
3	D								
4	D								
5	D								
6	D								
Total									

before any pickup can be made. All trucks are assumed to be the same size. There are four vehicles, each with a capacity of 160. Due to loading and time constraints, each vehicle can only execute a single route. There are a total of 34 linehaul customers and 16 backhaul suppliers. The location of the customers and suppliers and their respective demand and supply are given in Fig. 9.41 and Table 9.114 below. Use the Euclidean distance norm without any adjustment factor to determine the interfacility distances.

You can use any computer algorithm and program that you desire to determine the routes. You need to show the routes on a graph and provide the following summary statistics for each route and for the total problem: route distance, number

Fig. 9.41 VRPB50 facility
locations

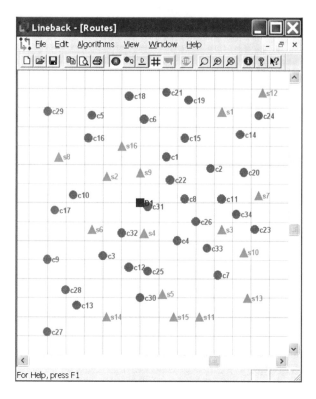

of linehaul customers, total linehaul demand, number of backhaul suppliers, total backhaul supply. Report which computer program and what computer hardware you used. If you use a commercial software package, you are encouraged to report the purchase price of the software. Describe clearly and succinctly the algorithmic steps you or the computer program used to generate the routes. Record and the report the time it took to enter the data, to find the shortest distance routes, and to decode the solution of the computer program and to copy it to the solution graph. So, you need to report three different times. Part of the grade will be based on the total length of the routes you generated, i.e., shorter routes will get you a better grade.

Appendix A. Extended VRP Example (VRP16)

Some of the more intricate algorithms for solving the standard VRP are illustrated in this appendix for a problem with 16 customers. This problem size is a compromise that allows for the meaningful demonstration of the detailed working of the algorithms, while at the same time limiting the amount of tedious detail of the example.

The location of the depot and customers and their demand is shown in Fig. 9.42 and given in Table 9.115. For each facility, the facility label is displayed to the right of the facility symbol and the required delivery quantity is displayed under the

Table 9.114 VRPB50 facility locations

Label	X	Y	Demand/Supply
Depot			
D1	10000	10000	0
Linehaul Customers			
1	10070	10120	7
2	10190	10090	30
3	9900	9860	9
4	10100	9900	21
5	9870	10230	19
6	10010	10220	23
7	10210	9810	5
8	10120	10010	19
9	9750	9850	23
10	9820	10020	21
11	10220	10010	15
12	9970	9830	3
13	9830	9730	9
14	10270	10180	28
15	10120	10170	8
16	9860	10170	16
17	9770	9980	28
18	9970	10280	7
19	10130	10270	14
20	10280	10080	6
21	10070	10290	11
22	10080	10060	12
23	10310	9930	26
24	10320	10230	17
25	10020	9820	9
26	10150	9950	15
27	9750	9660	7
28	9800	9770	27
29	9750	10240	11
30	10000	9750	16
31	10020	9990	5
32	9950	9920	25
33	10180	9880	18
34	10260	9970	10
Backhaul Suppliers			
1	10220	10240	16
2	9910	10070	15
3	10220	9930	11
4	10010	9920	29
5	10060	9760	10
6	9870	9930	41
7	10320	10020	8
8	9780	10120	10
9	10000	10080	15
10	10280	9870	19
11	10160	9700	23
12	10330	10290	6
13	10290	9750	14
14	9910	9700	13
15	10090	9700	10
16	9950	10150	17

Note: Use euclidean distance norm (no adjustments).

Fig. 9.42 VRP16 facility
locations

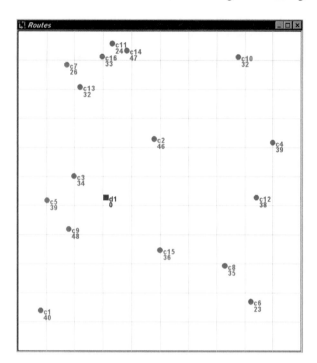

Table 9.115 VRP16 facility coordinates and demand

Label	X-Coord	Y-Coord	Quantity
c1	79	39	40
c2	480	629	46
c3	198	501	34
c4	899	617	39
c5	102	417	39
c6	822	69	23
c7	172	884	26
c8	729	193	35
c9	179	318	48
c10	776	911	32
c11	332	957	24
c12	842	427	38
c13	219	807	32
c14	383	933	47
c15	500	246	36
c16	297	912	33
d1	311	427	0

label. The depot has a dummy quantity equal to zero. The distances between the facilities are computed with the Euclidean distance norm without any adjustment factor (Table 9.116). They will be displayed with one significant digit after the decimal point, but are used in the algorithms as floating point numbers.

The total customer demand is equal to 572. There are four vehicles available, each with a capacity of 160. It is assumed that each vehicle can only execute a single route during the planning horizon. The total vehicle capacity is then 640.

The calculations for the average vehicle utilization, the average vehicle load, and the average slack capacity for this example are shown below. The average utilization is approximately 90%, the average vehicle load is 143, and the average slack is 17, which is smaller than the smallest customer delivery quantity. This indicates that this case is significantly capacity constrained.

$$\overline{\rho} = \frac{\sum\limits_{i} dem_i}{N \cdot cap} = \frac{572}{4 \cdot 160} = 89.4\%$$

$$\overline{q} = \rho \cdot cap = \frac{\sum\limits_{i} dem_i}{N} = \frac{572}{4} = 143$$

$$\overline{s} = cap - \overline{q} = 160 - 143 = 17$$

Nearest Neighbor The nearest neighbor heuristic travels from the last point added to the route to its nearest neighbor, unless this would violate the truck capacity. In that case, the heuristic closes the current route and starts a new route if the maximum number of routes has not been reached. The facility previously added is called the anchor facility. For the start of a new route, the depot is the anchor facility. The sequence of additions is shown in Table 9.117.

When the fourth route is started, the unvisited facility closest to the depot is $c1$. However, the unvisited facility closest to $c1$ is customer $c14$, which is located far away from customer $c1$. This route edge with a long distance is a typical characteristic of routes created with the nearest neighbor heuristic. The algorithm continues by adding facilities $c11$ and $c10$. At that time the load on the vehicle is 143. The closest unvisited facility is customer $c4$ with a quantity of 39. This customer does not fit on the current route and the maximum number of routes has been reached, so customer $c4$ remains unrouted. The route statistics are shown in Table 9.118. Observe that the total length of 5,953.6 is only for visiting 15 customers and is thus not the length of a feasible route set for the full problem. The routes are illustrated in Fig. 9.43.

Cheapest Insertion After the initial routes have been created, an attempt is made to insert the remaining unvisited facilities in the initial routes. For this particular example, only one unvisited facility remains and its quantity of 39 can only be added to route 1 without violating the truck capacity. The nearest insertion, farthest insertion, cheapest insertion, and priciest insertion algorithms all will insert the single unvisited facility in the same place in route 1. The insertion penalties for inserting facility $c4$ on the four edges of tour 1 are shown in Table 9.119.

Table 9.116 VRP16 distances between facility pairs

dis-tance	c1	c2	c3	c4	c5	c6	c7	c8	c9	c10	c11	c12	c13	c14	c15	c16	d1
c1		713.4	477.1	1,003.2	378.7	743.6	850.1	668.0	296.4	1,116.3	952.2	856.0	780.7	944.3	469.1	899.8	452.1
c2	713.4		309.7	419.2	433.4	656.2	399.9	502.1	432.8	408.8	359.8	414.6	315.9	319.1	383.5	337.0	263.4
c3	477.1	309.7		710.5	127.6	759.0	383.9	613.9	184.0	708.7	475.3	648.2	306.7	470.0	395.3	422.8	135.1
c4	1,003.2	419.2	710.5		821.7	553.4	774.5	456.8	779.6	318.7	661.1	198.4	706.1	605.1	544.8	670.4	617.9
c5	378.7	433.4	127.6	821.7		799.7	472.2	665.8	125.4	835.7	586.9	740.1	407.2	587.6	433.2	532.0	209.2
c6	743.6	656.2	759.0	553.4	799.7		1,042.5	155.0	689.5	843.3	1,014.2	358.6	953.0	969.1	367.4	993.1	623.9
c7	850.1	399.9	383.9	774.5	472.2	1,042.5		887.5	566.0	604.6	175.9	811.0	90.2	216.6	717.4	128.1	477.7
c8	668.0	502.1	613.9	456.8	665.8	155.0	887.5		564.0	719.5	861.0	259.9	798.2	816.9	235.1	838.8	479.0
c9	296.4	432.8	184.0	779.6	125.4	689.5	566.0	564.0		841.5	657.1	671.9	490.6	648.0	329.0	605.6	171.2
c10	1,116.3	408.8	708.7	318.7	835.7	843.3	604.6	719.5	841.5		446.4	488.5	566.6	393.6	720.0	479.0	671.2
c11	952.2	359.8	475.3	661.1	586.9	1,014.2	175.9	861.0	657.1	446.4		735.5	187.8	56.4	730.6	57.0	530.4
c12	856.0	414.6	648.2	198.4	740.1	358.6	811.0	259.9	671.9	488.5	735.5		729.8	683.2	386.9	729.6	531.0
c13	780.7	315.9	306.7	706.1	407.2	953.0	90.2	798.2	490.6	566.6	187.8	729.8		206.8	627.4	130.8	391.0
c14	944.3	319.1	470.0	605.1	587.6	969.1	216.6	816.9	648.0	393.6	56.4	683.2	206.8		696.9	88.5	511.1
c15	469.1	383.5	395.3	544.8	433.2	367.4	717.4	235.1	329.0	720.0	730.6	386.9	627.4	696.9		696.3	261.7
c16	899.8	337.0	422.8	670.4	532.0	993.1	128.1	838.8	605.6	479.0	57.0	729.6	130.8	88.5	696.3		485.2
d1	452.1	263.4	135.1	617.9	209.2	623.9	477.7	479.0	171.2	671.2	530.4	531.0	391.0	511.1	261.7	485.2	

Table 9.117 VRP16 nearest neighbor additions

Index	Anchor facility	Append facility	Append distance	Linehaul quantity
1	*d1*	*c3*	135.1	34
2	*c3*	*c5*	127.6	73
3	*c5*	*c9*	125.4	121
4	*d1*	*c15*	261.7	36
5	*c15*	*c8*	235.1	71
6	*c8*	*c6*	155.0	94
7	*c6*	*c12*	358.6	132
8	*d1*	*c2*	263.4	46
9	*c2*	*c13*	315.9	78
10	*c13*	*c7*	90.2	104
11	*c7*	*c16*	128.1	137
12	*d1*	*c1*	452.1	40
13	*c1*	*c14*	944.3	87
14	*c14*	*c11*	56.4	111
15	*c11*	*c10*	446.4	143
16				

Table 9.118 VRP16 nearest neighbor route statistics

Route	Facility						Quantity	Length
	0	1	2	3	4	5		
1	*d1*	*c3*	*c5*	*c9*	*d1*		121	559.2
2	*d1*	*c15*	*c8*	*c6*	*c12*	*d1*	132	1,541.3
3	*d1*	*c2*	*c13*	*c7*	*c16*	*d1*	137	1,282.8
4	*d1*	*c1*	*c14*	*c11*	*c10*	*d1*	143	2,570.3
Total							533	5,953.6

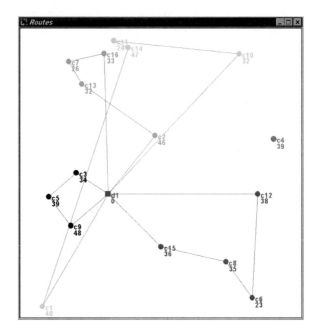

Fig. 9.43 VRP16 nearest neighbor routes

Table 9.119 VRP16 insertion penalties on nearest neighbor routes

Penalty	dl–c3	c3–c5	c5–c9	c9–dl
c4	1,193.4	1,404.7	1,475.9	1,226.4

Table 9.120 VRP16 nearest neighbor plus cheapest insertion routes

Route	Facility						Quantity	Length
	0	1	2	3	4	5		
1	dl	c4	c3	c5	c9	dl	160	1,752.6
2	dl	c15	c8	c6	c12	dl	132	1,541.3
3	dl	c2	c13	c7	c16	dl	137	1,282.8
4	dl	c1	c14	c11	c10	dl	143	2,570.3
Total							572	7,147.0

The edge with the smallest insertion penalty is $dl{:}c3$ and facility will be inserted on that edge. The total length of the routes increases to 7,147.0. The route statistics and routes are shown in Table 9.120 and Fig. 9.44.

Sweep The route-first variant of the sweep algorithm will be executed. The starting angle of the rotating ray is an algorithm parameter and is set to zero in this example. This corresponds to a starting direction that is due east. The relative polar coordinates of the customers with respect to the starting angle are computed and shown in Table 9.121 and the customers sorted by increasing polar angle are shown in Table 9.122.

The first sector starts with customer $c12$ with polar angle equal to 0.000 and route load of 38. Adding customers systematically by increasing polar angle, the

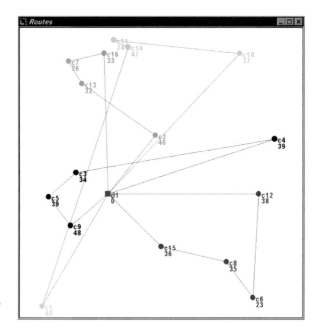

Fig. 9.44 VRP16 nearest neighbor followed by cheapest insertion routes

Table 9.121 VRP16 facility cartesian and polar coordinates

Facility		Cartesian		Polar		Quantity
Type	Label	X-Coord	Y-Coord	Angle	Radius	
Depot	d1	311	427			
Customer	c1	79	39	4.17349	452.1	40
Customer	c2	480	629	0.87411	263.4	46
Customer	c3	198	501	2.56180	135.1	34
Customer	c4	899	617	0.31254	617.9	39
Customer	c5	102	417	3.18940	209.2	39
Customer	c6	822	69	5.67207	623.9	23
Customer	c7	172	884	1.86606	477.7	26
Customer	c8	729	193	5.77284	479.0	35
Customer	c9	179	318	3.83184	171.2	48
Customer	c10	776	911	0.80542	671.2	32
Customer	c11	332	957	1.53119	530.4	24
Customer	c12	842	427	0.00000	531.0	38
Customer	c13	219	807	1.80833	391.0	32
Customer	c14	383	933	1.42945	511.1	47
Customer	c15	500	246	5.51941	261.7	36
Customer	c16	297	912	1.59965	485.2	33

Table 9.122 VRP16 customers sorted by polar angle

Facility		Cartesian		Polar		Quantity
Type	Label	X-Coord	Y-Coord	Angle	Radius	
Customer	c12	842	427	0.00000	531.0	38
Customer	c4	899	617	0.31254	617.9	39
Customer	c10	776	911	0.80542	671.2	32
Customer	c2	480	629	0.87411	263.4	46
Customer	c14	383	933	1.42945	511.1	47
Customer	c11	332	957	1.53119	530.4	24
Customer	c16	297	912	1.59965	485.2	33
Customer	c13	219	807	1.80833	391.0	32
Customer	c7	172	884	1.86606	477.7	26
Customer	c3	198	501	2.56180	135.1	34
Customer	c5	102	417	3.18940	209.2	39
Customer	c9	179	318	3.83184	171.2	48
Customer	c1	79	39	4.17349	452.1	40
Customer	c15	500	246	5.51941	261.7	36
Customer	c6	822	69	5.67207	623.9	23
Customer	c8	729	193	5.77284	479.0	35

route quantity for customer $c4$ is 77, for customer $c10$ is 109, for customer $c2$ is 155, and for customer $c14$ would be 202. This violates the vehicle capacity constraint of 160 and the route will be terminated after customer $c2$. The depot is connected to the first customer facility of the route and the last customer facility of the route is also connected back to the depot. The total route length is 1,720.3. The maximum

Table 9.123 VRP16 Route-First Sweep route (from Starting Angle 0)

Route	Facility						Quantity	Length
	0	1	2	3	4	5		
1	*d1*	*c12*	*c4*	*c10*	*c2*	*d1*	155	1,720.3
2	*d1*	*c14*	*c11*	*c16*	*c13*	*d1*	136	1,146.2
3	*d1*	*c7*	*c3*	*c5*	*c9*	*d1*	147	1,285.7
4	*d1*	*c1*	*c15*	*c6*	*c8*	*d1*	134	1,922.7
Total							572	6,074.9

number of routes has not been reached, so the process repeats itself. The route summary is shown in Table 9.123. The Sweep algorithm routes all the customers and the total length of the routes is 6,074.9.

The individual routes are not guaranteed to be optimal for the customers on the route. In fact, route 4 can be improved with two-exchanges. The cluster-first variant of the sweep algorithm will create route clusters with the same customers in a cluster as are assigned by the route-first algorithm to a route. However, the cluster-first algorithm then solves a TSP problem either optimally or heuristically for every cluster. Inter-route exchanges may also be able to further improve the routes. For this example, after improving route 4 individually, the overall route length can be further improved by swapping customers $c13$ and $c7$ between routes 2 and 3.

Starting from a different starting angle, may generate different routes and may leave some of the customers unrouted. For this example, starting with an initial angle of 90 degrees or 1.57080 radians or due north leaves customers $c14$ and $c11$ un-routed.

Serial Savings The initial savings are computed for every possible shortcut between a pair of customers. Since any combination of two customers has a combined load less than the truck capacity and the distances are based on the Euclidean distance norm, all initial shortcuts are feasible and the initial savings matrix has positive elements everywhere except on the main diagonal. Any distance norm satisfies the triangle inequality, so negative shortcut savings are impossible if distances are based on a distance norm. For the Euclidean distance norm, zero shortcut savings are theoretically possible, but it would require that the two customers and the depot are all three collinear, which is extremely rare. On the other hand, when the distances are computed by over-the-transportation network shortest path distances, shortcut savings with zero value are very common. Executing a shortcut with zero value, typically occurs in the later stages of the algorithm and may be required to reduce the number of partial routes to be less than or equal to the number of vehicles. The savings for this example are shown in Table 9.124.

The shortcut selected first is identical for the serial and parallel versions of the savings algorithm. The largest savings in the matrix corresponds to the shortcut from customer $c11$ to customer $c14$ with savings equal to 985.2. This cell is highlighted in Table 9.124. At this time, the symmetric shortcut has the same savings value, since the distance in this problem are computed with the Euclidean distance norm and are thus symmetric. Ties in the selection of the maximum savings will be

Table 9.124 VRP16 binary savings

Savings	c1	c2	c3	c4	c5	c6	c7	c8	c9	c10	c11	c12	c13	c14	c15	c16	Quantity
c1		2.1	110.1	66.8	282.6	332.4	79.6	263.1	326.9	6.9	30.3	127.1	62.4	18.9	244.6	37.5	40
c2	2.1		88.8	462.1	39.2	231.1	341.2	240.3	1.8	525.7	433.9	379.8	338.4	455.4	141.5	411.6	46
c3	110.1	88.8		42.5	216.8	0.1	228.9	0.3	122.3	97.6	190.2	17.8	219.3	176.2	1.5	197.5	34
c4	66.8	462.1	42.5		5.5	688.5	321.1	640.2	9.5	970.4	487.2	950.6	302.9	524.0	334.8	432.7	39
c5	282.6	39.2	216.8	5.5		33.5	214.7	22.5	255.0	44.8	152.7	0.2	193.1	132.8	37.8	162.4	39
c6	332.4	231.1	0.1	688.5	33.5		59.1	948.0	105.6	451.9	140.1	796.4	61.9	165.9	518.2	116.0	23
c7	79.6	341.2	228.9	321.1	214.7	59.1		69.2	82.8	544.3	832.2	197.7	778.4	772.2	22.0	834.8	26
c8	263.1	240.3	0.3	640.2	22.5	948.0	69.2		86.2	430.7	148.5	750.2	71.8	173.2	505.7	125.4	35
c9	326.9	1.8	122.3	9.5	255.0	105.6	82.8	86.2		0.9	44.5	30.3	71.5	34.3	103.9	50.8	48
c10	6.9	525.7	97.6	970.4	44.8	451.9	544.3	430.7	0.9		755.2	713.7	495.5	788.7	212.9	677.4	32
c11	30.3	433.9	190.2	487.2	152.7	140.1	832.2	148.5	44.5	755.2		325.9	733.6	985.2	61.5	958.6	24
c12	127.1	379.8	17.8	950.6	0.2	796.4	197.7	750.2	30.3	713.7	325.9		192.2	358.9	405.8	286.7	38
c13	62.4	338.4	219.3	302.9	193.1	61.9	778.4	71.8	71.5	495.5	733.6	192.2		695.3	25.2	745.4	32
c14	18.9	455.4	176.2	524.0	132.8	165.9	772.2	173.2	34.3	788.7	985.2	358.9	695.3		75.9	907.8	47
c15	244.6	141.5	1.5	334.8	37.8	518.2	22.0	505.7	103.9	212.9	61.5	405.8	25.2	75.9		50.6	36
c16	37.5	411.6	197.5	432.7	162.4	116.0	834.8	125.4	50.8	677.4	958.6	286.7	745.4	907.8	50.6		33
Quantity	40	46	34	39	39	23	26	35	48	32	24	38	32	47	36	33	

broken by selecting the maximum savings when traversing the matrix by row and then by column order. The first shortcut selected is thus from customer $c11$ to customer $c14$. The savings matrix needs to be updated to reflect the impact of possible future shortcuts given the existence of the partial route $\{d_1, c_{11}, c_{14}, d_1\}$.

To compute the reduced savings matrix, the following operations are executed: (1) eliminate the origin row, which in this case is the row of customer $c11$; (2) eliminate the destination column, which in this case is the column of customer $c14$; (3) change the label of the destination row by preceding it with the origin label, which in this case yields $c11{:}c14$; (4) change the label of the origin column by appending it with the destination label, which in this case yields $c11{:}c14$; (5) clear the element on the intersection of the row and column corresponding to this shortcut; (6) change the quantities in the row and column for the partial route with the current shortcut to reflect the combined quantities, which in this case yields $24+47=71$.

The next shortcut must involve one of the two endpoints of the current partial route $c11{:}c14$. These eligible savings are members of the column and row corresponding to the partial route and are shown shaded in the next savings matrix (Table 9.125).

The largest savings in the row and column corresponding to the partial route corresponds to the shortcut from customer $c16$ to partial route $c11{:}c14$ with savings equal to 958.6. This cell is highlighted in the Table 9.125. The same seven update operations are executed. The eliminated row corresponds to customer $c16$, the eliminated column corresponds to partial route $c11{:}c14$, the label of row $c11{:}c14$ is changed to $c16{:}c14$, the label of column $c16$ is changed to $c16{:}c14$, the element on the intersection of row and column $c16{:}c14$ is cleared, and the quantities for row and column $c16{:}c14$ are changed to $71+33=104$. Since the current partial routes can still be combined with any singleton customer, all savings remain feasible and no further actions have to be taken. The updated savings matrix after iteration 2 is shown in Table 9.126.

The largest savings in the row and column corresponding to the partial route corresponds to the shortcut from customer $c7$ to partial route $c16{:}c14$ with savings equal to 834.8. This cell is highlighted in the table shown above. The same seven update operations are executed. The eliminated row corresponds to customer $c7$, the eliminated column corresponds to partial route $c16{:}c14$, the label of row $c16{:}c14$ is changed to $c7{:}c14$, the label of column $c7$ is changed to $c7{:}c14$, the element on the intersection of row and column $c7{:}c14$ is cleared, and the quantities for row and column $c7{:}c14$ are changed to $104+26=130$. Since the current partial route can only be combined with customer $c6$, the elements in the row and column corresponding to partial route $c7{:}c14$ are cleared and also shaded as infeasible, except the elements corresponding to customer $c6$. This implies that only two feasible shortcuts exist, corresponding to extending the partial route either at the front or at the end with customer $c6$. The updated savings matrix after iteration 3 is shown in Table 9.127.

The largest feasible savings in the row and column corresponding to the partial route corresponds to the shortcut from partial route $c7{:}c14$ to customer $c6$ with savings equal to 165.9. This cell is highlighted in Table 9.127. The same seven update

Table 9.125 VRP16 updated serial savings after iteration 1

Savings	c1	c2	c3	c4	c5	c6	c7	c8	c9	c10	c11:c14	c12	c13	c15	c16	Quantity
c1		2.1	110.1	66.8	282.6	332.4	79.6	263.1	326.9	6.9	30.3	127.1	62.4	244.6	37.5	40
c2	2.1		88.8	462.1	39.2	231.1	341.2	240.3	1.8	525.7	433.9	379.8	338.4	141.5	411.6	46
c3	110.1	88.8		42.5	216.8	0.1	228.9	0.3	122.3	97.6	190.2	17.8	219.3	1.5	197.5	34
c4	66.8	462.1	42.5		5.5	688.5	321.1	640.2	9.5	970.4	487.2	950.6	302.9	334.8	432.7	39
c5	282.6	39.2	216.8	5.5		33.5	214.7	22.5	255.0	44.8	152.7	0.2	193.1	37.8	162.4	39
c6	332.4	231.1	0.1	688.5	33.5		59.1	948.0	105.6	451.9	140.1	796.4	61.9	518.2	116.0	23
c7	79.6	341.2	228.9	321.1	214.7	59.1		69.2	82.8	544.3	832.2	197.7	778.4	22.0	834.8	26
c8	263.1	240.3	0.3	640.2	22.5	948.0	69.2		86.2	430.7	148.5	750.2	71.8	505.7	125.4	35
c9	326.9	1.8	122.3	9.5	255.0	105.6	82.8	86.2		0.9	44.5	30.3	71.5	103.9	50.8	48
c10	6.9	525.7	97.6	970.4	44.8	451.9	544.3	430.7	0.9		755.2	713.7	495.5	212.9	677.4	32
c12	127.1	379.8	17.8	950.6	0.2	796.4	197.7	750.2	30.3	713.7	325.9		192.2	405.8	286.7	38
c13	62.4	338.4	219.3	302.9	193.1	61.9	778.4	71.8	71.5	495.5	733.6	192.2		25.2	745.4	32
c11:c14	18.9	455.4	176.2	524.0	132.8	165.9	772.2	173.2	34.3	788.7		358.9	695.3	75.9	907.8	71
c15	244.6	141.5	1.5	334.8	37.8	518.2	22.0	505.7	103.9	212.9	61.5	405.8	25.2		50.6	36
c16	37.5	411.6	197.5	432.7	162.4	116.0	834.8	125.4	50.8	677.4	958.6	286.7	745.4	50.6		33
Quantity	40	46	34	39	39	23	26	35	48	32	71	38	32	36	33	

Table 9.126 VRP16 updated serial savings after iteration 2

Savings	c1	c2	c3	c4	c5	c6	c7	c8	c9	c10	c12	c13	c15	c16:c14	Quantity
c1		2.1	110.1	66.8	282.6	332.4	79.6	263.1	326.9	6.9	127.1	62.4	244.6	37.5	40
c2	2.1		88.8	462.1	39.2	231.1	341.2	240.3	1.8	525.7	379.8	338.4	141.5	411.6	46
c3	110.1	88.8		42.5	216.8	0.1	228.9	0.3	122.3	97.6	17.8	219.3	1.5	197.5	34
c4	66.8	462.1	42.5		5.5	688.5	321.1	640.2	9.5	970.4	950.6	302.9	334.8	432.7	39
c5	282.6	39.2	216.8	5.5		33.5	214.7	22.5	255.0	44.8	0.2	193.1	37.8	162.4	39
c6	332.4	231.1	0.1	688.5	33.5		59.1	948.0	105.6	451.9	796.4	61.9	518.2	116.0	23
c7	79.6	341.2	228.9	321.1	214.7	59.1		69.2	82.8	544.3	197.7	778.4	22.0	834.8	26
c8	263.1	240.3	0.3	640.2	22.5	948.0	69.2		86.2	430.7	750.2	71.8	505.7	125.4	35
c9	326.9	1.8	122.3	9.5	255.0	105.6	82.8	86.2		0.9	30.3	71.5	103.9	50.8	48
c10	6.9	525.7	97.6	970.4	44.8	451.9	544.3	430.7	0.9		713.7	495.5	212.9	677.4	32
c12	127.1	379.8	17.8	950.6	0.2	796.4	197.7	750.2	30.3	713.7		192.2	405.8	286.7	38
c13	62.4	338.4	219.3	302.9	193.1	61.9	778.4	71.8	71.5	495.5	192.2		25.2	745.4	32
c16:c14	18.9	455.4	176.2	524.0	132.8	165.9	772.2	173.2	34.3	788.7	358.9	695.3	75.9		104
c15	244.6	141.5	1.5	334.8	37.8	518.2	22.0	505.7	103.9	212.9	405.8	25.2		50.6	36
Quantity	40	46	34	39	39	23	26	35	48	32	38	32	36	104	

Table 9.127 VRP16 updated serial savings after iteration 3

Savings	c1	c2	c3	c4	c5	c6	c7:c14	c8	c9	c10	c12	c13	c15	Quantity
c1		2.1	110.1	66.8	282.6	332.4		263.1	326.9	6.9	127.1	62.4	244.6	40
c2	2.1		88.8	462.1	39.2	231.1		240.3	1.8	525.7	379.8	338.4	141.5	46
c3	110.1	88.8		42.5	216.8	0.1		0.3	122.3	97.6	17.8	219.3	1.5	34
c4	66.8	462.1	42.5		5.5	688.5		640.2	9.5	970.4	950.6	302.9	334.8	39
c5	282.6	39.2	216.8	5.5		33.5		22.5	255.0	44.8	0.2	193.1	37.8	39
c6	332.4	231.1	0.1	688.5	33.5		59.1	948.0	105.6	451.9	796.4	61.9	518.2	23
c8	263.1	240.3	0.3	640.2	22.5	948.0			86.2	430.7	750.2	71.8	505.7	35
c9	326.9	1.8	122.3	9.5	255.0	105.6		86.2		0.9	30.3	71.5	103.9	48
c10	6.9	525.7	97.6	970.4	44.8	451.9		430.7	0.9		713.7	495.5	212.9	32
c12	127.1	379.8	17.8	950.6	0.2	796.4		750.2	30.3	713.7		192.2	405.8	38
c13	62.4	338.4	219.3	302.9	193.1	61.9		71.8	71.5	495.5	192.2		25.2	32
c7:c14						165.9								130
c15	244.6	141.5	1.5	334.8	37.8	518.2		505.7	103.9	212.9	405.8	25.2		36
Quantity	40	46	34	39	39	23	130	35	48	32	38	32	36	

operations are executed. The eliminated row corresponds to partial route $c7:c14$, the eliminated column corresponds to customer $c6$, the label of row $c6$ is changed to $c7:c6$, the label of column $c7:c14$ is changed to $c7:c6$, the element on the intersection of row and column $c7:c6$ is cleared, and the quantities for row and column $c7:c6$ are changed to $130+23=153$. Since the current partial route cannot be combined any customer, the elements in the row and column corresponding to partial route $c7:c6$ are cleared and shown shaded to indicate infeasibility. The updated savings matrix after iteration 3 is shown in Table 9.128.

Since there are no feasible savings to extend the current partial route, this partial route is closed and a new partial route is started. The closed partial route is eliminated from the savings matrix, which is shown in Table 9.129.

The largest savings corresponds to the shortcut from customer $c4$ to customer $c10$ with savings equal to 970.4. This cell is highlighted in Table 9.129. The same seven update operations are executed. The eliminated row corresponds to customer $c4$, the eliminated column corresponds to customer $c10$, the label of row c10 is changed to $c4:c10$, the label of column c4 is changed to $c4:c10$, the element on the intersection of row and column $c4:c10$ is cleared, and the quantities for row and column $c4:c10$ are changed to $39+32=71$. Since the current partial route can still be combined with any singleton customer, all savings remain feasible and no further actions have to be taken. The updated savings matrix after iteration 5 is shown in Table 9.130.

The largest feasible savings in the row and column corresponding to the partial route corresponds to the shortcut from customer $c12$ to partial route $c4:c10$ with savings equal to 950.6. This cell is highlighted in Table 9.130 shown above. The same seven update operations are executed. The eliminated row corresponds to customer $c12$, the eliminated column corresponds to partial route $c4:c10$, the label of row $c4:c10$ is changed to $c12:c10$, the label of column $c12$ is changed to $c12:c10$, the element on the intersection of row and column $c12:c10$ is cleared, and the quantities for row and column $c12:c102$ are changed to $71+38=109$. Since the current partial route can still be combined with any singleton customer, all savings remain feasible and no further actions have to be taken. The updated savings matrix after iteration 6 is shown in Table 9.131.

The largest feasible savings in the row and column corresponding to the partial route corresponds to the shortcut from customer c8 to partial route $c12:c10$ with savings equal to 750.2. This cell is highlighted in Table 9.131. The same seven update operations are executed. The eliminated row corresponds to customer $c8$, the eliminated column corresponds to partial route $c12:c10$, the label of row $c12:c10$ is changed to $c8:c10$, the label of column $c8$ is changed to $c8:c10$, the element on the intersection of row and column $c8:c10$ is cleared, and the quantities for row and column $c8:c10$ are changed to $109+35=144$. Since the current partial route cannot be combined any customer, the elements in the row and column corresponding to partial route $c8:c10$ are cleared and shown shaded to indicate infeasibility. The updated savings matrix after iteration 7 is shown in Table 9.132.

Since there are no feasible savings to extend the current partial route, this partial route is closed and a new partial route is started. The closed partial route is eliminated from the savings matrix, which is shown in Table 9.133.

Table 9.128 VRP16 updated serial savings after iteration 4 before route closing

Savings	c1	c2	c3	c4	c5	c7:c6	c8	c9	c10	c12	c13	c15	Quantity
c1		2.1	110.1	66.8	282.6		263.1	326.9	6.9	127.1	62.4	244.6	40
c2	2.1		88.8	462.1	39.2		240.3	1.8	525.7	379.8	338.4	141.5	46
c3	110.1	88.8		42.5	216.8		0.3	122.3	97.6	17.8	219.3	1.5	34
c4	66.8	462.1	42.5		5.5		640.2	9.5	970.4	950.6	302.9	334.8	39
c5	282.6	39.2	216.8	5.5			22.5	255.0	44.8	0.2	193.1	37.8	39
c7:c6													153
c8	263.1	240.3	0.3	640.2	22.5			86.2	430.7	750.2	71.8	505.7	35
c9	326.9	1.8	122.3	9.5	255.0		86.2		0.9	30.3	71.5	103.9	48
c10	6.9	525.7	97.6	970.4	44.8		430.7	0.9		713.7	495.5	212.9	32
c12	127.1	379.8	17.8	950.6	0.2		750.2	30.3	713.7		192.2	405.8	38
c13	62.4	338.4	219.3	302.9	193.1		71.8	71.5	495.5	192.2		25.2	32
c15	244.6	141.5	1.5	334.8	37.8		505.7	103.9	212.9	405.8	25.2		36
Quantity	40	46	34	39	39	153	35	48	32	38	32	36	

Table 9.129 VRP16 updated serial savings after iteration 4

Savings	c1	c2	c3	c4	c5	c8	c9	c10	c12	c13	c15	Quantity
c1		2.1	110.1	66.8	282.6	263.1	326.9	6.9	127.1	62.4	244.6	40
c2	2.1		88.8	462.1	39.2	240.3	1.8	525.7	379.8	338.4	141.5	46
c3	110.1	88.8		42.5	216.8	0.3	122.3	97.6	17.8	219.3	1.5	34
c4	66.8	462.1	42.5		5.5	640.2	9.5	970.4	950.6	302.9	334.8	39
c5	282.6	39.2	216.8	5.5		22.5	255.0	44.8	0.2	193.1	37.8	39
c8	263.1	240.3	0.3	640.2	22.5		86.2	430.7	750.2	71.8	505.7	35
c9	326.9	1.8	122.3	9.5	255.0	86.2		0.9	30.3	71.5	103.9	48
c10	6.9	525.7	97.6	970.4	44.8	430.7	0.9		713.7	495.5	212.9	32
c12	127.1	379.8	17.8	950.6	0.2	750.2	30.3	713.7		192.2	405.8	38
c13	62.4	338.4	219.3	302.9	193.1	71.8	71.5	495.5	192.2		25.2	32
c15	244.6	141.5	1.5	334.8	37.8	505.7	103.9	212.9	405.8	25.2		36
Quantity	40	46	34	39	39	35	48	32	38	32	36	

Table 9.130 VRP16 updated serial savings after iteration 5

Savings	c1	c2	c3	c4:c10	c5	c8	c9	c12	c13	c15	Quantity
c1		2.1	110.1	66.8	282.6	263.1	326.9	127.1	62.4	244.6	40
c2	2.1		88.8	462.1	39.2	240.3	1.8	379.8	338.4	141.5	46
c3	110.1	88.8		42.5	216.8	0.3	122.3	17.8	219.3	1.5	34
c5	282.6	39.2	216.8	5.5		22.5	255.0	0.2	193.1	37.8	39
c8	263.1	240.3	0.3	640.2	22.5		86.2	750.2	71.8	505.7	35
c9	326.9	1.8	122.3	9.5	255.0	86.2		30.3	71.5	103.9	48
c4:c10	6.9	525.7	97.6		44.8	430.7	0.9	713.7	495.5	212.9	71
c12	127.1	379.8	17.8	950.6	0.2	750.2	30.3		192.2	405.8	38
c13	62.4	338.4	219.3	302.9	193.1	71.8	71.5	192.2		25.2	32
c15	244.6	141.5	1.5	334.8	37.8	505.7	103.9	405.8	25.2		36
Quantity	40	46	34	71	39	35	48	38	32	36	

Table 9.131 VRP16 updated serial savings after iteration 6

Savings	c1	c2	c3	c5	c8	c9	c12:c10	c13	c15	Quantity
c1		2.1	110.1	282.6	263.1	326.9	127.1	62.4	244.6	40
c2	2.1		88.8	39.2	240.3	1.8	379.8	338.4	141.5	46
c3	110.1	88.8		216.8	0.3	122.3	17.8	219.3	1.5	34
c5	282.6	39.2	216.8		22.5	255.0	0.2	193.1	37.8	39
c8	263.1	240.3	0.3	22.5		86.2	750.2	71.8	505.7	35
c9	326.9	1.8	122.3	255.0	86.2		30.3	71.5	103.9	48
c12:c10	6.9	525.7	97.6	44.8	430.7	0.9		495.5	212.9	109
c13	62.4	338.4	219.3	193.1	71.8	71.5	192.2		25.2	32
c15	244.6	141.5	1.5	37.8	505.7	103.9	405.8	25.2		36
Quantity	40	46	34	39	35	48	109	32	36	

Table 9.132 VRP16 updated serial savings after iteration 7 before route closing

savings	c1	c2	c3	c5	c8:c10	c9	c13	c15	Quantity
c1		2.1	110.1	282.6		326.9	62.4	244.6	40
c2	2.1		88.8	39.2		1.8	338.4	141.5	46
c3	110.1	88.8		216.8		122.3	219.3	1.5	34
c5	282.6	39.2	216.8			255.0	193.1	37.8	39
c9	326.9	1.8	122.3	255.0			71.5	103.9	48
c8:c10									144
c13	62.4	338.4	219.3	193.1		71.5		25.2	32
c15	244.6	141.5	1.5	37.8		103.9	25.2		36
Quantity	40	46	34	39	144	48	32	36	

Table 9.133 VRP16 updated serial savings after iteration 7

savings	c1	c2	c3	c5	c9	c13	c15	Quantity
c1		2.1	110.1	282.6	326.9	62.4	244.6	40
c2	2.1		88.8	39.2	1.8	338.4	141.5	46
c3	110.1	88.8		216.8	122.3	219.3	1.5	34
c5	282.6	39.2	216.8		255.0	193.1	37.8	39
c9	326.9	1.8	122.3	255.0		71.5	103.9	48
c13	62.4	338.4	219.3	193.1	71.5		25.2	32
c15	244.6	141.5	1.5	37.8	103.9	25.2		36
Quantity	40	46	34	39	48	32	36	

The largest savings corresponds to the shortcut from customer $c2$ to customer $c13$ with savings equal to 338.4. This cell is highlighted in Table 9.133. The same seven update operations are executed. The eliminated row corresponds to customer $c2$, the eliminated column corresponds to customer $c13$, the label of row $c13$ is changed to $c2{:}c13$, the label of column $c2$ is changed to $c2{:}c13$, the element on the intersection of row and column $c2{:}c13$ is cleared, and the quantities for row and column $c2{:}c13$ are changed to $46+32=78$. Since the current partial route can still be combined with any singleton customer, all savings remain feasible and no further actions have to be taken. The updated savings matrix after iteration 8 is shown in Table 9.134.

The largest savings corresponds to the shortcut from partial route $c2{:}c13$ to customer $c3$ with savings equal to 219.3. This cell is highlighted in Table 9.134. The

Table 9.134 VRP16 updated serial savings after iteration 8

Savings	c1	c2:c13	c3	c5	c9	c15	Quantity
c1		2.1	110.1	282.6	326.9	244.6	40
c3	110.1	88.8		216.8	122.3	1.5	34
c5	282.6	39.2	216.8		255.0	37.8	39
c9	326.9	1.8	122.3	255.0		103.9	48
c2:c13	62.4		219.3	193.1	71.5	25.2	78
c15	244.6	141.5	1.5	37.8	103.9		36
Quantity	40	78	34	39	48	36	

Table 9.135 VRP16 updated serial savings after iteration 9

Savings	$c1$	$c2{:}c3$	$c5$	$c9$	$c15$	Quantity
$c1$		2.1	282.6	326.9	244.6	40
$c2{:}c3$	110.1		216.8	122.3	1.5	112
$c5$	282.6	39.2		255.0	37.8	39
$c9$	326.9	1.8	255.0		103.9	48
$c15$	244.6	141.5	37.8	103.9		36
Quantity	40	112	39	48	36	

same seven update operations are executed. The eliminated row corresponds to partial route $c2{:}c13$, the eliminated column corresponds to customer $c3$, the label of row $c3$ is changed to $c2{:}c3$, the label of column $c2{:}c13$ is changed to $c2{:}c3$, the element on the intersection of row and column $c2{:}c3$ is cleared, and the quantities for row and column $c2{:}c3$ are changed to $78+34=112$. Since the current partial route can still be combined with any singleton customer, all savings remain feasible and no further actions have to be taken. The updated savings matrix after iteration 9 is shown in Table 9.135.

The largest savings corresponds to the shortcut from partial route $c2{:}c3$ to customer $c5$ with savings equal to 216.8. This cell is highlighted in Table 9.134 shown above. The same seven update operations are executed. The eliminated row corresponds to partial route $c2{:}c3$, the eliminated column corresponds to customer $c5$, the label of row $c5$ is changed to $c2{:}c5$, the label of column $c2{:}c3$ is changed to $c2{:}c5$, the element on the intersection of row and column $c2{:}c5$ is cleared, and the quantities for row and column $c2{:}c5$ are changed to $112+39=151$. Since the current partial route cannot be combined any customer, the elements in the row and column corresponding to partial route $c2{:}c5$ are cleared and shown shaded to indicate infeasibility. The updated savings matrix after iteration ten is shown in Table 9.136.

Since there are no feasible savings to extend the current partial route, this partial route is closed and a new partial route is started. The number of routes and partial routes is now equal to the number of vehicles, so new partial routes can be started after the current partial route. The closed partial route is eliminated from the savings matrix, which is shown in Table 9.137.

The largest savings corresponds to the shortcut from customer $c1$ to customer $c9$ with savings equal to 326.9. This cell is highlighted in Table 9.137. The same seven update operations are executed. The eliminated row corresponds to customer $c1$, the eliminated column corresponds to customer $c9$, the label of row $c9$ is changed to

Table 9.136 VRP16 updated serial savings after iteration 10 before route closure

Savings	$c1$	$c2{:}c5$	$c9$	$c15$	Quantity
$c1$			326.9	244.6	40
$c2{:}c5$					151
$c9$	326.9			103.9	48
$c15$	244.6		103.9		36
Quantity	40	151	48	36	

Table 9.137 VRP16 updated serial savings after iteration 10

Savings	c1	c9	c15	Quantity
c1		326.9	244.6	40
c9	326.9		103.9	48
c15	244.6	103.9		36
Quantity	40	48	36	

Table 9.138 VRP16 updated serial savings after iteration 11

Savings	c1:c9	c15	Quantity
c1:c9		103.9	88
c15	244.6		36
Quantity	88	36	

Table 9.139 VRP16 updated serial savings after iteration 12

Savings	c15:c9	Quantity
c15:c9		124
Quantity	124	

$c1:c9$, the label of column $c1$ is changed to $c1:c9$, the element on the intersection of row and column $c1:c9$ is cleared, and the quantities for row and column $c1:c9$ are changed to $40+48=88$. Since the current partial route can still be combined with any singleton customer, all savings remain feasible and no further actions have to be taken. The updated savings matrix after iteration 11 is shown in Table 9.138.

The largest savings corresponds to the shortcut from customer $c15$ to partial route $c1:c9$ with savings equal to 244.6. This cell is highlighted in Table 9.138. The same seven update operations are executed. The eliminated row corresponds to customer $c15$, the eliminated column corresponds to partial route $c1:c9$, the label of row $c1:c9$ is changed to $c15:c9$, the label of column $c15$ is changed to $c15:c9$, the element on the intersection of row and column $c15:c9$ is cleared, and the quantities for row and column $c15:c9$ are changed to $88+36=124$. The updated savings matrix after iteration 12 is shown in Table 9.139.

There are no more feasible shortcuts in the savings matrix and the savings algorithm terminates. All the customers have been routed and four routes have been created, so the savings algorithm created a complete feasible solution. The statistics of the executed shortcuts and the partial routes are summarized in Table 9.140.

The route statistics are summarized in Table 9.141 and shown in Fig. 9.45. The total route length is 6,660.5.

Note the route that includes a number of customers in the northwest corner of the area and also a single customer in the southeast corner. This shortcut was made because it was feasible and it had positive, albeit small, savings. This is typical behavior for a savings algorithm. An improvement algorithm may relocate this customer to another route, to create routes with a shorter total route length and that also would be more acceptable to the vehicle drivers.

Table 9.140 VRP16 serial savings shortcut statistics

Step	Shortcut			Facilities							
	Points	Savings	Length	1	2	3	4	5	6	7	8
1	c11:c14	985.2	1,097.9	d1	c11	c14	d1				
2	c16:c11	958.6	1,109.7	d1	c16	c11	c14	d1			
3	c7:c16	834.8	1,230.2	d1	c7	c16	c11	c14	d1		
4	c14:c6	165.9	2,312.2	d1	c7	c16	c11	c14	c6	d1	
5	c4:c10	970.4	1,607.8	d1	c4	c10	d1				
6	c12:c4	950.6	1,719.2	d1	c12	c4	c10	d1			
7	c8:c12	750.2	1,927.1	d1	c8	c12	c4	c10	s1		
8	c2:c13	338.4	920.3	d1	c2	c13	d1				
9	c13:c3	219.3	1,021.1	d1	c2	c13	c3	d1			
10	c3:c5	193.1	1,222.8	d1	c2	c13	c3	c5	d1		
11	c1:c9	326.9	319.64	d1	c1	c9	d1				
12	c15-c1	244.6	1,198.4	d1	c15	c1	c9	d1			

Table 9.141 VRP16 serial savings routes

Route	Facility							Quantity	Length
	0	1	2	3	4	5	6		
1	d1	c7	c16	c11	c14	c6	d1	153	2,312.2
2	d1	c8	c12	c4	c10	d1		144	1,927.1
3	d1	c2	c13	c3	c5	d1		151	1,222.8
4	d1	c15	c1	c9	d1			124	1,198.4
Total								572	6,660.5

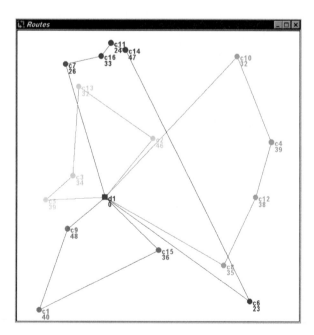

Fig. 9.45 VRP16 serial savings routes

Parallel Savings The parallel savings algorithm starts with the same initial short-cut as the serial variant. It also executes the same seven update operations on the savings matrix. Since the current partial route can still be combined with any single-ton customer, all savings remain feasible and no further actions have to be taken. The updated savings matrix after iteration 1 is shown in Table 9.142.

The largest savings in the matrix corresponds to the shortcut from customer $c4$ to customer $c10$ with savings equal to 970.4. This cell is highlighted in Table 9.142. The same seven update operations are executed. The eliminated row corresponds to customer $c4$, the eliminated column corresponds to customer $c10$, the label of row $c10$ is changed to $c4$:$c10$, the label of column $c4$ is changed to $c4$:$c10$, element on the intersection of row and column $c4$:$c10$ is cleared, and the quantities for row and column $c4$:$c10$ are changed to $32+39=71$. Since the current partial routes can still be combined with each other and with any singleton customer, all savings remain feasible and no further actions have to be taken. The updated savings matrix after iteration 2 is shown in Table 9.143.

The largest savings in the matrix corresponds to the shortcut from customer $c16$ to partial route $c11$:$c14$ with savings equal to 958.6. This cell is highlighted in Table 9.143. The same seven update operations are executed. The eliminated row corresponds to customer $c16$, the eliminated column corresponds to route $c11$:$c14$, the label of row $c11$:$c14$ is changed to $c16$:$c14$, the label of column $c11$:$c14$ is changed to $c16$:$c14$, element on the intersection of row and column $c16$:$c14$ is cleared, and the quantities for row and column c16:c14 are changed to $71+33=104$. The quantity of the combined partial routes $c4$:$c10$ and $c16$:$c14$ would be $71+104=175$, which would violate the truck capacity. Hence the cells on the intersection of the corresponding rows and columns are cleared and shown as shaded to indicate that this savings belongs to an infeasible shortcut and these savings will never be feasible again during the execution of this algorithm. The updated savings matrix after iteration 3 is shown in Table 9.144.

The largest savings in the matrix corresponds to the shortcut from customer $c12$ to partial route $c4$:$c10$ with savings equal to 950.6. This cell is highlighted in Table 9.144. The same seven update operations are executed. The eliminated row corresponds to customer $c12$, the eliminated column corresponds to route $c4$:$c10$, the label of row $c4$:$c10$ is changed to $c12$:$c10$, the label of column $c12$ is changed to $c12$:$c10$, element on the intersection of row and column $c12$:$c10$ is cleared, and the quantities for row and column $c12$:$c10$ are changed to $71+38=109$. The quantity of the combined partial routes $c12$:$c10$ and $c16$:$c14$ would be $109+104=213$, which would violate the truck capacity and the corresponding cells are cleared and shown as shaded to indicate an infeasible shortcut. The updated savings matrix after itera-tion four is shown in Table 9.145.

The largest savings in the matrix corresponds to the shortcut from customer $c6$ to customer $c8$ with savings equal to 948.0. This cell is highlighted in Table 9.145. The same seven update operations are executed. The eliminated row corresponds to customer $c6$, the eliminated column corresponds to customer $c8$, the label of row c8 is changed to $c6$:$c8$, the label of column $c6$ is changed to $c6$:$c8$, element on the intersection of row and column $c6$:$c8$ is cleared, and the quantities for row and col-

Table 9.142 VRP16 updated parallel savings after iteration 1

Savings	c1	c2	c3	c4	c5	c6	c7	c8	c9	c10	c11:c14	c12	c13	c15	c16	Quantity
c1		2.1	110.1	66.8	282.6	332.4	79.6	263.1	326.9	6.9	30.3	127.1	62.4	244.6	37.5	40
c2	2.1		88.8	462.1	39.2	231.1	341.2	240.3	1.8	525.7	433.9	379.8	338.4	141.5	411.6	46
c3	110.1	88.8		42.5	216.8	0.1	228.9	0.3	122.3	97.6	190.2	17.8	219.3	1.5	197.5	34
c4	66.8	462.1	42.5		5.5	688.5	321.1	640.2	9.5	970.4	487.2	950.6	302.9	334.8	432.7	39
c5	282.6	39.2	216.8	5.5		33.5	214.7	22.5	255.0	44.8	152.7	0.2	193.1	37.8	162.4	39
c6	332.4	231.1	0.1	688.5	33.5		59.1	948.0	105.6	451.9	140.1	796.4	61.9	518.2	116.0	23
c7	79.6	341.2	228.9	321.1	214.7	59.1		69.2	82.8	544.3	832.2	197.7	778.4	22.0	834.8	26
c8	263.1	240.3	0.3	640.2	22.5	948.0	69.2		86.2	430.7	148.5	750.2	71.8	505.7	125.4	35
c9	326.9	1.8	122.3	9.5	255.0	105.6	82.8	86.2		0.9	44.5	30.3	71.5	103.9	50.8	48
c10	6.9	525.7	97.6	970.4	44.8	451.9	544.3	430.7	0.9		755.2	713.7	495.5	212.9	677.4	32
c12	127.1	379.8	17.8	950.6	0.2	796.4	197.7	750.2	30.3	713.7	325.9		192.2	405.8	286.7	38
c13	62.4	338.4	219.3	302.9	193.1	61.9	778.4	71.8	71.5	495.5	733.6	192.2		25.2	745.4	32
c11:c14	18.9	455.4	176.2	524.0	132.8	165.9	772.2	173.2	34.3	788.7		358.9	695.3	75.9	907.8	71
c15	244.6	141.5	1.5	334.8	37.8	518.2	22.0	505.7	103.9	212.9	61.5	405.8	25.2		50.6	36
c16	37.5	411.6	197.5	432.7	162.4	116.0	834.8	125.4	50.8	677.4	958.6	286.7	745.4	50.6		33
Quantity	40	46	34	39	39	23	26	35	48	32	71	38	32	36	33	

Table 9.143 VRP16 updated savings after iteration 2

Savings	c1	c2	c3	c4:c10	c5	c6	c7	c8	c9	c11:c14	c12	c13	c15	c16	Quantity
c1		2.1	110.1	66.8	282.6	332.4	79.6	263.1	326.9	30.3	127.1	62.4	244.6	37.5	40
c2	2.1		88.8	462.1	39.2	231.1	341.2	240.3	1.8	433.9	379.8	338.4	141.5	411.6	46
c3	110.1	88.8		42.5	216.8	0.1	228.9	0.3	122.3	190.2	17.8	219.3	1.5	197.5	34
c5	282.6	39.2	216.8	5.5		33.5	214.7	22.5	255.0	152.7	0.2	193.1	37.8	162.4	39
c6	332.4	231.1	0.1	688.5	33.5		59.1	948.0	105.6	140.1	796.4	61.9	518.2	116.0	23
c7	79.6	341.2	228.9	321.1	214.7	59.1		69.2	82.8	832.2	197.7	778.4	22.0	834.8	26
c8	263.1	240.3	0.3	640.2	22.5	948.0	69.2		86.2	148.5	750.2	71.8	505.7	125.4	35
c9	326.9	1.8	122.3	9.5	255.0	105.6	82.8	86.2		44.5	30.3	71.5	103.9	50.8	48
c4:c10	6.9	525.7	97.6		44.8	451.9	544.3	430.7	0.9	755.2	713.7	495.5	212.9	677.4	71
c12	127.1	379.8	17.8	950.6	0.2	796.4	197.7	750.2	30.3	325.9		192.2	405.8	286.7	38
c13	62.4	338.4	219.3	302.9	193.1	61.9	778.4	71.8	71.5	733.6	192.2		25.2	745.4	32
c11:c14	18.9	455.4	176.2	524.0	132.8	165.9	772.2	173.2	34.3		358.9	695.3	75.9	907.8	71
c15	244.6	141.5	1.5	334.8	37.8	518.2	22.0	505.7	103.9	61.5	405.8	25.2		50.6	36
c16	37.5	411.6	197.5	432.7	162.4	116.0	834.8	125.4	50.8	958.6	286.7	745.4	50.6		33
Quantity	40	46	34	71	39	23	26	35	48	71	38	32	36	33	

Table 9.144 VRP16 updated savings after iteration 3

Savings	c1	c2	c3	c4:c10	c5	c6	c7	c8	c9	c12	c13	c15	c16:c14	Quantity
c1		2.1	110.1	66.8	282.6	332.4	79.6	263.1	326.9	127.1	62.4	244.6	37.5	40
c2	2.1		88.8	462.1	39.2	231.1	341.2	240.3	1.8	379.8	338.4	141.5	411.6	46
c3	110.1	88.8		42.5	216.8	0.1	228.9	0.3	122.3	17.8	219.3	1.5	197.5	34
c5	282.6	39.2	216.8	5.5		33.5	214.7	22.5	255.0	0.2	193.1	37.8	162.4	39
c6	332.4	231.1	0.1	688.5	33.5		59.1	948.0	105.6	796.4	61.9	518.2	116.0	23
c7	79.6	341.2	228.9	321.1	214.7	59.1		69.2	82.8	197.7	778.4	22.0	834.8	26
c8	263.1	240.3	0.3	640.2	22.5	948.0	69.2		86.2	750.2	71.8	505.7	125.4	35
c9	326.9	1.8	122.3	9.5	255.0	105.6	82.8	86.2		30.3	71.5	103.9	50.8	48
c4:c10	6.9	525.7	97.6		44.8	451.9	544.3	430.7	0.9	713.7	495.5	212.9	71	71
c12	127.1	379.8	17.8	950.6	0.2	796.4	197.7	750.2	30.3		192.2	405.8	286.7	38
c13	62.4	338.4	219.3	302.9	193.1	61.9	778.4	71.8	71.5	192.2		25.2	745.4	32
c16:c14	18.9	455.4	176.2		132.8	165.9	772.2	173.2	34.3	358.9	695.3	75.9		104
c15	244.6	141.5	1.5	334.8	37.8	518.2	22.0	505.7	103.9	405.8	25.2		50.6	36
Quantity	40	46	34	71	39	23	26	35	48	38	32	36	104	

Table 9.145 VRP16 updated savings after iteration 4

Savings	c1	c2	c3	c5	c6	c7	c8	c9	c12:c10	c13	c15	c16:c14	Quantity
c1		2.1	110.1	282.6	332.4	79.6	263.1	326.9	127.1	62.4	244.6	37.5	40
c2	2.1		88.8	39.2	231.1	341.2	240.3	1.8	379.8	338.4	141.5	411.6	46
c3	110.1	88.8		216.8	0.1	228.9	0.3	122.3	17.8	219.3	1.5	197.5	34
c5	282.6	39.2	216.8		33.5	214.7	22.5	255.0	0.2	193.1	37.8	162.4	39
c6	332.4	231.1	0.1	33.5		59.1	948.0	105.6	796.4	61.9	518.2	116.0	23
c7	79.6	341.2	228.9	214.7	59.1		69.2	82.8	197.7	778.4	22.0	834.8	26
c8	263.1	240.3	0.3	22.5	948.0	69.2		86.2	750.2	71.8	505.7	125.4	35
c9	326.9	1.8	122.3	255.0	105.6	82.8	86.2		30.3	71.5	103.9	50.8	48
c12:c10	6.9	525.7	97.6	44.8	451.9	544.3	430.7	0.9		495.5	212.9	109	109
c13	62.4	338.4	219.3	193.1	61.9	778.4	71.8	71.5	495.5		25.2	745.4	32
c16:c14	18.9	455.4	176.2	132.8	165.9	772.2	173.2	34.3	192.2	695.3	75.9		104
c15	244.6	141.5	1.5	37.8	518.2	22.0	505.7	103.9	405.8	25.2		50.6	36
Quantity	40	46	34	39	23	26	35	48	109	32	36	104	

umn $c6{:}c8$ are changed to $23+35=58$. The quantity of the combined partial routes $c6{:}c8$ and $c16{:}c14$ would be $58+104=162$ and the quantity of the combined partial routes $c6{:}c8$ and $c12{:}c10$ would be $58+109=167$. Both would violate the truck capacity, so the savings in the corresponding cells are cleared and the cells are shown as shaded. The updated savings matrix after iteration 5 is shown in Table 9.146.

The largest savings in the matrix corresponds to the shortcut from customer $c7$ to partial route $c16{:}c14$ with savings equal to 834.8. This cell is highlighted in Table 9.146. The same seven update operations are executed. The eliminated row corresponds to customer $c7$, the eliminated column corresponds to route $c16{:}c14$, the label of row c16:c14 is changed to $c7{:}c14$, the label of column $c7$ is changed to $c7{:}c14$, element on the intersection of row and column $c7{:}c14$ is cleared, and the quantities for row and column $c7{:}c14$ are changed to $104+26=130$. The combination of any singleton customer or partial route with route $c7{:}c14$ would violate the truck capacity of 160. All the savings in row and column $c7{:}c14$ are cleared and the cells are shown as shaded. The updated savings matrix after iteration six is shown in Table 9.147.

The largest savings in the matrix corresponds to the shortcut from partial route $c12{:}c10$ to customer $c2$ with savings equal to 525.7. This cell is highlighted in Table 9.147. The same seven update operations are executed. The eliminated row corresponds to partial route $c12{:}c10$, the eliminated column corresponds to customer $c2$, the label of row $c2$ is changed to $c12{:}c2$, the label of column $c12{:}c10$ is changed to $c12{:}c2$, element on the intersection of row and column $c12{:}c2$ is cleared, and the quantities for row and column $c12{:}c2$ are changed to $109+46=155$. The combination of any singleton customer or partial route with route $c12{:}c2$ would violate the truck capacity of 160. All the savings in row and column $c12{:}c2$ are cleared and the cells are shown as shaded. The updated savings matrix after iteration 7 is shown in Table 9.148.

The largest savings in the matrix corresponds to the shortcut from customer $c15$ to partial route $c6{:}c8$ with savings equal to 518.2. This cell is highlighted in Table 9.148. The same seven update operations are executed. The eliminated row corresponds to customer $c15$, the eliminated column corresponds to partial route $c6{:}c8$, the label of row c6:c8 is changed to $c15{:}c8$, the label of column $c15$ is changed to $c15{:}c8$, element on the intersection of row and column $c15{:}c8$ is cleared, and the quantities for row and column $c15{:}c8$ are changed to $58+36=94$. The combination of the other partial routes with route $c15{:}c8$ would violate the truck capacity of 160 and the savings in the cells corresponding to the other partial routes in row and column $c15{:}c8$ are cleared and the cells are shown as shaded. The updated savings matrix after iteration 8 is shown in Table 9.149.

The largest savings in the matrix corresponds to the shortcut from customer $c1$ to customer $c9$ with savings equal to 326.9. This cell is highlighted in Table 9.149. The same seven update operations are executed. The eliminated row corresponds to customer $c1$, the eliminated column corresponds to customer $c9$, the label of row $c9$ is changed to $c1{:}c9$, the label of column $c1$ is changed to $c1{:}c9$, element on the intersection of row and column $c1{:}c9$ is cleared, and the quantities for row and column $c1{:}c9$ are changed to $40+48=88$. The combination of the other partial routes with route $c1{:}c9$ would violate the truck capacity of 160 and the savings in the cells corresponding to the other partial routes in row and column $c1{:}c9$ are cleared and

Table 9.146 VRP16 updated savings after iteration 5

Savings	c1	c2	c3	c5	c6:c8	c7	c9	c12:c10	c13	c15	c16:c14	Quantity
c1		2.1	110.1	282.6	332.4	79.6	326.9	127.1	62.4	244.6	37.5	40
c2	2.1		88.8	39.2	231.1	341.2	1.8	379.8	338.4	141.5	411.6	46
c3	110.1	88.8		216.8	0.1	228.9	122.3	17.8	219.3	1.5	197.5	34
c5	282.6	39.2	216.8		33.5	214.7	255.0	0.2	193.1	37.8	162.4	39
c7	79.6	341.2	228.9	214.7	59.1		82.8	197.7	778.4	22.0	834.8	26
c6:c8	263.1	240.3	0.3	22.5		69.2	86.2		71.8	505.7		58
c9	326.9	1.8	122.3	255.0	105.6	82.8		30.3	71.5	103.9	50.8	48
c12:c10	6.9	525.7	97.6	44.8		544.3	0.9		495.5	212.9		109
c13	62.4	338.4	219.3	193.1	61.9	778.4	71.5	192.2		25.2	745.4	32
c16:c14	18.9	455.4	176.2	132.8		772.2	34.3	405.8	695.3	75.9		104
c15	244.6	141.5	1.5	37.8	518.2	22.0	103.9	405.8	25.2		50.6	36
Quantity	40	46	34	39	58	26	48	109	32	36	104	

Table 9.147 VRP16 updated savings after iteration 6

Savings	c1	c2	c3	c5	c6:c8	c7:c14	c9	c12:c10	c13	c15	Quantity
c1		2.1	110.1	282.6	332.4		326.9	127.1	62.4	244.6	40
c2	2.1		88.8	39.2	231.1		1.8	379.8	338.4	141.5	46
c3	110.1	88.8		216.8	0.1		122.3	17.8	219.3	1.5	34
c5	282.6	39.2	216.8		33.5		255.0	0.2	193.1	37.8	39
c6:c8	263.1	240.3	0.3	22.5			86.2		71.8	505.7	58
c9	326.9	1.8	122.3	255.0	105.6			30.3	71.5	103.9	48
c12:c10	6.9	525.7	97.6	44.8			0.9		495.5	212.9	109
c13	62.4	338.4	219.3	193.1	61.9		71.5	192.2		25.2	32
c7:c14											130
c15	244.6	141.5	1.5	37.8	518.2		103.9	405.8	25.2		36
Quantity	40	46	34	39	58	130	48	109	32	36	

Table 9.148 VRP16 updated savings after iteration 7

Savings	c1	c3	c5	c6:c8	c7:c14	c9	c12:c2	c13	c15	Quantity
c1		110.1	282.6	332.4		326.9		62.4	244.6	40
c12:c2										155
c3	110.1		216.8	0.1		122.3		219.3	1.5	34
c5	282.6	216.8		33.5		255.0		193.1	37.8	39
c6:c8	263.1	0.3	22.5			86.2		71.8	505.7	58
c9	326.9	122.3	255.0	105.6				71.5	103.9	48
c13	62.4	219.3	193.1	61.9		71.5			25.2	32
c7:c14										130
c15	244.6	1.5	37.8	518.2		103.9		25.2		36
Quantity	40	34	39	58	130	48	155	32	36	

Table 9.149 VRP16 updated savings after iteration 8

Savings	c1	c3	c5	c7:c14	c9	c12:c2	c13	c15:c8	Quantity
c1		110.1	282.6		326.9		62.4	244.6	40
c12:c2									155
c3	110.1		216.8		122.3		219.3	1.5	34
c5	282.6	216.8			255.0		193.1	37.8	39
c15:c8	263.1	0.3	22.5		86.2		71.8		94
c9	326.9	122.3	255.0				71.5	103.9	48
c13	62.4	219.3	193.1		71.5			25.2	32
c7:c14									130
Quantity	40	34	39	130	48	155	32	94	

the cells are shown as shaded. The updated savings matrix after iteration 9 is shown in Table 9.150.

The largest savings in the matrix corresponds to the shortcut from customer $c5$ to partial route $c1{:}c9$ with savings equal to 282.6. This cell is highlighted in Table 9.150. The same seven update operations are executed. The eliminated row corresponds to customer $c5$, the eliminated column corresponds to partial route $c1{:}c9$, the label of row $c1{:}c9$ is changed to $c5{:}c9$, the label of column $c5$ is changed to $c5{:}c9$, element on the intersection of row and column $c5{:}c9$ is cleared, and the quantities for row and column $c5{:}c9$ are changed to $39 + 88 = 127$. The combination of the other partial routes and customer $c3$ with route $c5{:}c9$ would violate the truck capacity of 160 and the savings in the cells corresponding to the other partial routes can customer $c3$ in row and column $c5{:}c9$ are cleared and the cells are shown as shaded. The updated savings matrix after iteration 9 is shown in Table 9.151.

Table 9.150 VRP16 updated savings after iteration 9

Savings	c1:c9	c3	c5	c7:c14	c12:c2	c13	c15:c8	Quantity
c12:c2								155
c3	110.1		216.8			219.3	1.5	34
c5	282.6	216.8				193.1	37.8	39
c15:c8		0.3	22.5			71.8		94
c1:c9		122.3	255.0			71.5		88
c13	62.4	219.3	193.1				25.2	32
c7:c14								130
Quantity	88	34	39	130	155	32	94	

Table 9.151 VRP16 updated savings after iteration 10

Savings	c3	c5:c9	c7:c14	c12:c2	c13	c15:c8	Quantity
c12:c2							155
c3					219.3	1.5	34
c15:c8	0.3				71.8		94
c5:c9					71.5		127
c13	219.3	193.1				25.2	32
c7:c14							130
Quantity	34	127	130	155	32	94	

The largest savings in the matrix corresponds to the shortcut from customer $c3$ to customer $c13$ with savings equal to 219.3. However, at this time already four partial routes exist and there are only four vehicles, so no new partial route can be created and only existing partial routes can be extended. The shortcut $c3{:}c13$ and its symmetrical shortcut of $c13{:}c3$ are not feasible. The next largest savings in the matrix corresponds to the shortcut from customer $c13$ to partial route $c5{:}c9$ with savings equal to 193.1. This cell is highlighted in Table 9.151. The same seven update operations are executed. The eliminated row corresponds to customer $c13$, the eliminated column corresponds to partial route $c5{:}c9$, the label of row $c13$ is changed to $c13{:}c9$, the label of column $c5{:}c9$ is changed to $c13{:}c9$, element on the intersection of row and column $c13{:}c9$ is cleared, and the quantities for row and column $c13{:}c9$ are changed to $32+127=159$. The combination of any partial route or singleton customer with route $c13{:}c9$ would violate the truck capacity of 160 and the savings in the cells in row and column $c13{:}c9$ are cleared and the cells are shown as shaded. The updated savings matrix after iteration 10 is shown in Table 9.152.

Table 9.152 VRP16 updated savings after iteration 11

Savings	c3	c7:c14	c12:c2	c13:c9	c15:c8	Quantity
c12:c2						155
c3					1.5	34
c15:c8	0.3					94
c13:c9						159
c7:c14						130
Quantity	34	130	155	159	94	

Table 9.153 VRP16 updated savings after iteration 12

Savings	c3:c8	c7:c14	c12:c2	c13:c9	Quantity
c12:c2					155
c3:c8					128
c13:c9					159
c7:c14					130
Quantity	128	130	155	159	

The largest savings in the matrix corresponds to the shortcut from customer $c3$ to partial route $c15:c8$ with savings equal to 1.5. This cell is highlighted in Table 9.152. The same seven update operations are executed. The eliminated row corresponds to customer $c3$, the eliminated column corresponds to partial route $c15:c8$, the label of row $c15:c8$ is changed to $c3:c8$, the label of column $c5$ is changed to $c3:c8$, element on the intersection of row and column $c3:c8$ is cleared, and the quantities for row and column $c3:c8$ are changed to $34 + 94 = 128$. The combination of the other partial routes with route $c3:c8$ would violate the truck capacity of 160 and the savings in the cells in row and column $c3:c8$ are cleared and the cells are shown as shaded. The updated savings matrix after iteration 12 is shown in Table 9.153.

There are no more feasible shortcuts in the savings matrix and the savings algorithm terminates. All the customers have been routed and four routes have been created, so the savings algorithm created a complete feasible solution. The statistics of the executed shortcuts and the partial routes are summarized in Table 9.154.

The route statistics are summarized in Table 9.155 and shown in Fig. 9.46. The total route length is 6,126.7.

GAP Heuristic The heuristic solution of the GAP is one of the algorithms that are strongly capacity oriented. This algorithm was first developed by Fisher and Jaikumar (1981). Recall that the heuristic first locates a seed point for each truck route in the problem area. It then computes the assignment cost of a customer to the route as the insertion penalty of the customer on the singleton routes from the depot to each of the seed points. Next, it solves the capacity GAP problem to determine the customer

Table 9.154 VRP16 parallel savings shortcut statistics

Step	Shortcut			Facilities							
	Points	Savings	Length	1	2	3	4	5	6	7	8
1	c11:c14	985.2	1,097.9	d1	c11	c14	d1				
2	c4:c10	970.4	1,607.8	d1	c4	c10	d1				
3	c16:c11	958.6	1,109.7	d1	c16	c11	c14	d1			
4	c12:c4	950.6	1,719.2	d1	c12	c4	c10	d1			
5	c6:c8	948.0	1,258.0	d1	c6	c8	d1				
6	c7:c16	834.8	1,230.2	d1	c7	c16	c11	c14	d1		
7	c10:c2	525.7	1,720.3	d1	c12	c4	c10	c2	d1		
8	c15:c6	518.2	1,263.2	d1	c15	c6	c8	d1			
9	c1:c9	326.9	919.6	d1	c1	c9	d1				
10	c5:c1	282.6	1,055.5	d1	c5	c1	c9	d1			
11	c13:c5	193.1	1,644.4	d1	c13	c5	c1	c9	d1		
12	c3:c15	1.5	1,531.8	d1	c3	c15	c6	c8	d1		

Table 9.155 VRP16 parallel savings routes

Route	Facility						Quantity	Length
	0	1	2	3	4	5		
1	d1	c7	c16	c11	c14	d1	130	1,230.2
2	d1	c12	c4	c10	c2	d1	155	1,720.3
3	d1	c3	c15	c6	c8	d1	128	1,531.8
4	d1	c13	c5	c1	c9	d1	159	1,644.4
Total							572	6,126.7

Fig. 9.46 VRP16 parallel savings routes

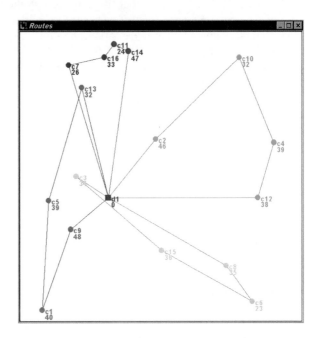

clusters. Finally, the customers in each cluster are sequenced by a TSP algorithm. Many GAP algorithm variations are possible depending on the methods to compute the initial location of the seed points and the assignment costs. The methods originally proposed by Fisher and Jaikumar are illustrated in the remainder of this section.

The location of the seed points is based on the notion of a pie-shaped truck zones or sectors. The tips of the sectors are located at the depot and the apertures of the sectors are such that the sectors contain customer whose quantities exactly sum up to the average vehicle load. In order to satisfy this load constraint with equality, splitting of the customers for the seed point location determination is not only allowed but is mandated, unless the customer can be included 100% by sheer accident. It should be noted that splitting customers in the third step of the algorithm, when the GAP is solved, is not allowed. The objective of the first step of the algorithm is the location of the route seed points.

The sector creation starts with a ray in a particular starting direction and rotation direction. This starting angle is an algorithm parameter and different starting angles may give different sectors, which in turn may lead to different routes. In this example, the starting angle is due east and the rotation direction is counterclockwise. Each customer has an associated cone with top point at the depot. The boundary rays are the bisectors of the rays through the preceding and succeeding customer, when the customers are sorted by polar angle. When a customer is traversed by the rotating ray, its demand is added to the vehicle load. When this addition process is continued, for a certain angle adding the next customer would violate the constraint that the sector quantity is less than or equal to the average vehicle load. Assume that customer i is the last customer that fit completely in the average vehicle load and customer j is the first customer that does not fit completely, where customers j follows customer i immediately, and customer h follows customer j immediately when customers are sorted by increasing relative polar angle to the starting direction.

To determine the sectors, the polar coordinates of the customers are computed and then the customers are sorted by increasing polar angle. The results are shown in the Tables 9.121 and 9.122. The first sector starts with customer $c12$ with polar angle equal to 0.000. The start angle of the first sector is then the bisector between customer $c12$ and customer $c8$, which is the customer with the largest polar angle. The angle of the bisector in radians is then computed with the following calculations:

$$\theta_1^{begin} = \frac{\theta_{c12} + \theta_{c8} - 2\pi}{2} = \frac{0.0 + 5.77 - 2 \cdot 3.14}{2} = -0.255$$

The starting angle for the first sector is equal to the end angle for the last sector. 2π, equivalent to one full circle, needs to be subtracted from the sum of the customer angles if the ray with an angle of zero radians is located in between the two customer rays.

Adding customers systematically by increasing polar angle, the sector quantity for customer $c10$ is 109 and the sector quantity for further adding customer $c2$ would be 155. This violates the sector load constraint of 143 and customer $c2$ will be split between sector 1 and sector 2. The fraction of customer $c2$ that is located in sector 1 and the boundary angle of sector 1 are computed with the following calculations.

$$\alpha_{c2} = \frac{143 - 109}{46} = \frac{34}{46} = 73.9\%$$

$$\theta_1^{end} = \frac{\theta_{c10} + \theta_{c2}}{2} + \alpha_{c2}\frac{\theta_{c14} - \theta_{c10}}{2} = \frac{0.805 + 0.874}{2} + 0.739\frac{1.429 - 0.805}{2} = 1.070$$

Sector 2 starts with customer $c2$ but only with its remainder load of 12 and at the end angle of sector 1, i.e. 1.070. Adding customers systematically by increasing polar angle, the sector quantity for customer $c16$ is 116 and the sector quantity for adding customer $c13$ would be 148. This violates the sector load constraint and customer $c13$ will be split between sector 2 and 3. The fraction of customer $c13$ that is located in sector 2 and the boundary angle of sector 2 are computed with the following calculations.

$$\alpha_{c13} = \frac{143 - 116}{32} = \frac{27}{32} = 84.4\%$$

$$\theta_2^{end} = \frac{\theta_{c16} + \theta_{c13}}{2} + \alpha_{c2}\frac{\theta_{c7} - \theta_{c16}}{2} = \frac{1.600 + 1.808}{2} + 0.844\frac{1.867 - 1.600}{2}$$
$$= 1.816$$

This process is repeated to determine all the remaining sectors. The calculations for sector 3 are given next.

$$\alpha_{c9} = \frac{143 - 104}{48} = \frac{39}{48} = 81.3\%$$

$$\theta_3^{end} = \frac{\theta_{c5} + \theta_{c9}}{2} + \alpha_{c2} \frac{\theta_{c1} - \theta_{c5}}{2} = \frac{3.189 + 3.832}{2} + 0.813 \frac{4.173 - 3.189}{2} = 3.910$$

The end angle for the last sector is equal to the starting angle for the first sector. 2π, equivalent to one full circle, needs to be added to the sum of the customer angles if the ray with an angle of zero radians is located in between the two customer rays.

$$\theta_4^{end} = \theta_1^{start} + 2\pi = -0.255 + 6.283 = 6.028$$

The angular polar coordinate for each seed point is on the center ray for each sector. The bisector or center angle for each of the sectors is then computed as the average of the two boundary angles. The angles for the four sectors are summarized in Table 9.156.

The second polar coordinate of each seed point is its radius. In the Fisher and Jaikumar heuristic, the seed radius in a cluster is the boundary radius where exactly 75% of the average vehicle load is contained inside the radius. This radius is computed next for each sector. To satisfy the 75% boundary at most one customer per sector may have to split between inside and outside the radius. In this example 75% of the average vehicle load is $0.75 \cdot 143 = 107$, when rounded to the nearest integer. The customers in each cluster, sorted by increasing radius per cluster, are shown in Table 9.157. Observe that the split customers from the previous calculations each appear in two sectors, with either a or b appended to their label. They have identical radius and angle in each sector but different quantities, equal to the split delivery quantities computed in the previous step.

The following calculations are for sector 1. When adding customers by increasing radius, the cumulative quantity is 72 for customer $c12$ and would be 111 for customer $c4$. This is larger than 107, so customer $c4$ will be split between inside and outside the boundary radius. The fraction of customer $c4$ inside the radius and the boundary radius are computed in the next calculations.

$$\beta_{c4} = \frac{107 - 72}{39} = \frac{35}{39} = 89.7\%$$

$$r_{s1} = r_{c12} + \beta_{c4} \cdot (r_{c4} - r_{c12}) = 531.0 + 0.897 \cdot (617.9 - 531.0) = 609.0$$

Table 9.156 VRP16 sector angles

Sector	Angles		
	Start	End	Center
1	−0.255	1.070	0.408
2	1.070	1.816	1.443
3	1.816	3.910	2.863
4	3.910	6.028	4.969

Table 9.157 VRP16 facilities by cluster sorted by increasing radius

Facility		Cartesian		Polar		Quantity
Type	Label	X-Coord	Y-Coord	Angle	Radius	
Customer	c2_a	480	371	1.070	263.4	34
Customer	c12	842	573	0.000	531.0	38
Customer	c4	899	383	0.313	617.9	39
Customer	c10	776	89	0.805	671.2	32
Customer	c2_b	480	371	1.070	263.4	12
Customer	c13_a	219	193	1.816	391.0	27
Customer	c16	297	88	1.600	485.2	33
Customer	c14	383	67	1.429	511.1	47
Customer	c11	332	43	1.531	530.4	24
Customer	c3	198	499	2.562	135.1	34
Customer	c9_a	179	682	3.910	171.2	39
Customer	c5	102	583	3.189	209.2	39
Customer	c13_b	219	193	1.816	391.0	5
Customer	c7	172	116	1.866	477.7	26
Customer	c9_b	179	682	3.910	171.2	9
Customer	c15	500	754	5.519	261.7	36
Customer	c1	79	961	4.173	452.1	40
Customer	c8	729	807	5.773	479.0	35
Customer	c6	822	931	5.672	623.9	23

These calculations are then repeated for each of the remaining sectors. For sector 2, when adding the customers by increasing radius, the cumulative quantity is 72 for customer $c16$ and 119 for customer $c14$. This is larger than the 75% percentage of the average load, so customer $c16$ will be split between inside and outside the boundary radius. The seed point radius is computed with the following calculations.

$$\beta_{c14} = \frac{107 - 72}{47} = \frac{35}{47} = 74.5\%$$

$$r_{s2} = r_{c16} + \beta_{c14} \cdot (r_{c14} - r_{c16}) = 485.2 + 0.745 \cdot (511.1 - 485.2) = 504.5$$

These calculations are repeated for the remaining sectors. The polar coordinates of each seed point are then transformed to Cartesian coordinates. The coordinates of the four seed points for this example are shown in Table 9.158. The locations of the seed points are illustrated in Fig. 9.47.

The cost of assigning a customer to a route is computed as the insertion penalty of the customer for the out-and-back route from the depot to the seed point. In

Table 9.158 VRP16 polar and cartesian coordinates for the seed points

Sector	Radius	Angle	X-Coord	Y-Coord
S1	609.0	0.408	870	668
S2	504.5	1.443	375	927
S3	204.4	2.863	114	483
S4	469.0	4.969	430	−27

Fig. 9.47 VRP16 facility and seed point locations

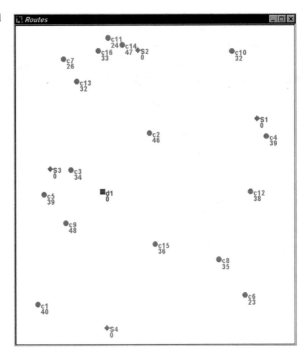

order to compute those insertion penalties, we need first to compute the distances from every customer to every seed point. The computed distances are shown in Table 9.159, displayed with one significant digit after the decimal point.

The assignment cost for customer $c1$ to seed point $S1$ is computed as the insertion penalty of customer $c1$ into route $(d1, S1, d1)$ as shown in the following calculations.

Table 9.159 VRP16 customer to seed point distances

Distance	S1	S2	S3	S4
c1	1,010.6	936.0	445.4	357.2
c2	392.0	316.0	394.1	657.9
c3	692.4	461.3	85.9	576.7
c4	58.7	608.8	796.4	796.7
c5	808.0	578.5	67.1	552.0
c6	600.9	967.5	820.2	403.6
c7	730.7	207.5	405.2	946.8
c8	495.5	814.9	679.9	371.2
c9	774.6	639.8	177.3	426.7
c10	260.6	401.3	788.3	999.8
c11	610.7	52.4	521.7	988.9
c12	242.6	684.2	730.2	613.1
c13	665.7	196.8	340.6	860.3
c14	554.4	10.0	524.3	961.2
c15	561.2	692.4	453.0	281.8
c16	622.8	79.4	466.4	948.4
d1	608.7	504.1	204.8	469.3

Table 9.160 VRP16 customer to seed point assignment costs

Cost	*S1*	*S2*	*S3*	*S4*
c1	853.9	884.0	692.7	339.9
c2	46.6	75.2	452.6	451.9
c3	218.8	92.3	16.2	242.5
c4	67.9	722.7	1,209.5	945.3
c5	408.5	283.6	71.5	291.9
c6	616.1	1,087.3	1,239.3	558.2
c7	599.6	181.1	678.0	955.2
c8	365.8	789.9	954.2	380.9
c9	337.0	306.9	143.7	128.5
c10	323.0	568.4	1,254.7	1,201.6
cll	532.4	78.8	847.4	1,050.0
c12	164.9	711.1	1,056.4	674.7
c13	447.9	83.7	526.8	781.9
c14	456.8	17.0	830.6	1,002.9
c15	214.2	450.0	509.8	74.2
c16	499.3	60.6	746.8	964.2

$$c_{c1,S1} = c_{d1,c1} + c_{c1,S1} - c_{d1,S1} = 452.1 + 1{,}010.6 - 608.7 = 853.9$$

The other assignment costs are computed in the analogue way. The assignment costs are shown in Table 9.160.

The GAP can now be solved using an integer programming (IP) solver. The GAP formulation can and will tend to yield fractional solutions if solved with a linear programming algorithm. The solver included in Excel will be used here, but other solvers can be used. The problem setup in Excel is shown in Fig. 9.48.

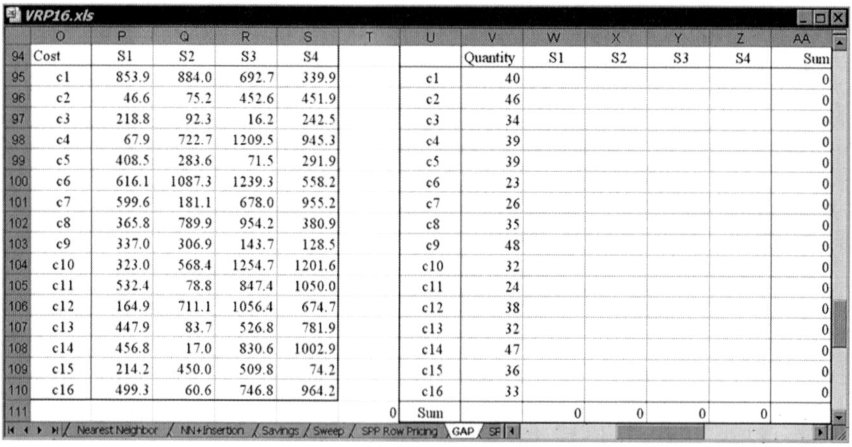

	O	P	Q	R	S	T	U	V	W	X	Y	Z	AA
94	Cost	S1	S2	S3	S4			Quantity	S1	S2	S3	S4	Sum
95	c1	853.9	884.0	692.7	339.9		c1	40					0
96	c2	46.6	75.2	452.6	451.9		c2	46					0
97	c3	218.8	92.3	16.2	242.5		c3	34					0
98	c4	67.9	722.7	1209.5	945.3		c4	39					0
99	c5	408.5	283.6	71.5	291.9		c5	39					0
100	c6	616.1	1087.3	1239.3	558.2		c6	23					0
101	c7	599.6	181.1	678.0	955.2		c7	26					0
102	c8	365.8	789.9	954.2	380.9		c8	35					0
103	c9	337.0	306.9	143.7	128.5		c9	48					0
104	c10	323.0	568.4	1254.7	1201.6		c10	32					0
105	c11	532.4	78.8	847.4	1050.0		c11	24					0
106	c12	164.9	711.1	1056.4	674.7		c12	38					0
107	c13	447.9	83.7	526.8	781.9		c13	32					0
108	c14	456.8	17.0	830.6	1002.9		c14	47					0
109	c15	214.2	450.0	509.8	74.2		c15	36					0
110	c16	499.3	60.6	746.8	964.2		c16	33					0
111						0	Sum		0	0	0	0	

Fig. 9.48 VRP16 excel GAP problem

Fig. 9.49 VRP16 excel GAP
solver parameters

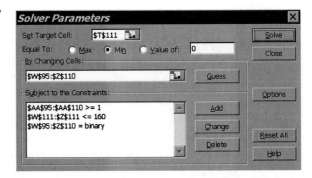

On the left, the two-dimensional matrix with the assignment costs is given in cells P95:S110. On the right, the two-dimensional matrix in cells W95:Z110 contains the assignment variables. Column AA contains the sum of the assignment variables for each customer, which must sum up to 1. Row 111 contains the sum of the quantities assigned to the respective routes. The cumulative quantity for seed S1 is computed in cell W111 and is computed with the Excel function SUMPRODUCT($W95:$W110,V95:V110). The vehicle capacity in this example is 160, so the cumulative quantities have to less than or equal to 160. Finally, the total assignment cost is stored in cell T111 and is computed with the Excel function SUMPRODUCT(P95:S110,W95:Z110). Initially, all the assignment variables, sums, and assignment costs are zero. The solver problem setup for this example is shown in Fig. 9.49.

The solver will minimize the contents of cell T111, which contains the sum of the assignment costs. The decision variables are stored in the rectangular matrix of cells W95:Z110. There are only three constraints for the problem. The first constraint is the assignment constraint, which ensures that the sum of the assignment variables for each customer is greater or equal to 1. The sums are stored in cells AA95:AA110. The second constraint is the capacity constraint, which ensures that the cumulative quantity on each route is less than the vehicle capacity. The cumulative quantities are stored in cells W111:Z111 and the vehicle capacity is 160. Finally, to avoid splitting customers among routes, the assignment variables in cells W95:Z110 are forced to be either zero or one, i.e., they must be binary.

The optimal solution value returned by the solver is 3,051.1. The assignment of customer to routes is shown in Table 9.161. It should be noted that at this time, this assignment only provides route clusters and that the customers have been routed yet. In this particular case, each route contains four customers and the depot.

Table 9.161 VRP16 GAP
route clusters

Route	Customers	Quantity
S1	c2,c4,c10,c12	155
S2	c7,c11,c14,c16	130
S3	c3,c5,c9,c13	153
S4	c1,c6,c8,c15	134

Table 9.162 VRP16 GAP facility routing

Route	Convex hull	Insertion	Final route	Length
S1	*c12,c4,c10,c2*		*c12,c4,c10,c2*	1,720.3
S2	*c14,c11,c7*	*c16*	*c14, c11 ,c16,c7*	1,230.2
S3	*c13,c5,c9*	*c3*	*c13,c3,c5,c9*	1,121.9
S4	*c1,c6,c8*	*c15*	*c1,c6,c8,c15*	1,847.4
				5,919.8

Table 9.163 VRP16 GAP route statistics

Route	Facility						Quantity	Length
	0	1	2	3	4	5		
1	*d1*	*c12*	*c4*	*c10*	*c2*	*d1*	155	1,720.3
2	*d1*	*c14*	*c11*	*c16*	*c7*	*d1*	130	1,230.2
3	*d1*	*c13*	*c3*	*c5*	*c9*	*d1*	153	1,121.9
4	*d1*	*c1*	*c6*	*c8*	*c15*	*d1*	134	1,847.4
Total							572	5,919.8

The routes are created by the convex hull algorithm for the TSP by cheapest insertion algorithm if necessary. The convex hull provides the optimal tour for the facilities on the convex hull and the optimal sequence of the facilities on any optimal route with additional facilities. Since each route has at most one facility not on the convex hull, the cheapest insertion creates a route with minimal length. The four vehicle routes created with the sequence of these two algorithms are guaranteed to be optimal for the given route clusters. This property is only valid for this case and not likely to be satisfied for larger problem instances. The total length of all the routes is 5,919.8. This is the best solution found for this problem, but this solution is not guaranteed to be optimal. The resulting routes are shown in Tables 9.162 and 9.163, Fig. 9.50.

VRP16.xls													
	O	P	Q	R	S	T	U	V	W	X	Y	Z	AA
94	Cost	S1	S2	S3	S4			Quantity	S1	S2	S3	S4	Sum
95	c1	853.9	884.0	692.7	339.9		c1	40	0.0	0.0	0.0	1.0	1
96	c2	46.6	75.2	452.6	451.9		c2	46	1.0	0.0	0.0	0.0	1
97	c3	218.8	92.3	16.2	242.5		c3	34	0.0	0.0	1.0	0.0	1
98	c4	67.9	722.7	1209.5	945.3		c4	39	1.0	0.0	0.0	0.0	1
99	c5	408.5	283.6	71.5	291.9		c5	39	0.0	0.0	1.0	0.0	1
100	c6	616.1	1087.3	1239.3	558.2		c6	23	0.0	0.0	0.0	1.0	1
101	c7	599.6	181.1	678.0	955.2		c7	26	0.0	1.0	0.0	0.0	1
102	c8	365.8	789.9	954.2	380.9		c8	35	0.0	0.0	0.0	1.0	1
103	c9	337.0	306.9	143.7	128.5		c9	48	0.0	0.0	1.0	0.0	1
104	c10	323.0	568.4	1254.7	1201.6		c10	32	1.0	0.0	0.0	0.0	1
105	c11	532.4	78.8	847.4	1050.0		c11	24	0.0	1.0	0.0	0.0	1
106	c12	164.9	711.1	1056.4	674.7		c12	38	1.0	0.0	0.0	0.0	1
107	c13	447.9	83.7	526.8	781.9		c13	32	0.0	0.0	1.0	0.0	1
108	c14	456.8	17.0	830.6	1002.9		c14	47	0.0	1.0	0.0	0.0	1
109	c15	214.2	450.0	509.8	74.2		c15	36	0.0	0.0	0.0	1.0	1
110	c16	499.3	60.6	746.8	964.2		c16	33	0.0	1.0	0.0	0.0	1
111						3051.1	Sum		155	130	153	134	

H ◄ ► H / NN+Insertion / Savings / Sweep / SPP Row Pricing \ GAP / SPP LP Pricing /

Fig. 9.50 VRP16 excel GAP solution

Table 9.164 VRP16 customer relative difficulty weights

Customer	Distance	Quantity	Weight
c1	452.1	40	18,082.8
c2	263.4	46	12,115.0
c3	135.1	34	4,592.4
c4	617.9	39	24,099.7
c5	209.2	39	8,160.4
c6	623.9	23	14,350.4
c7	477.7	26	12,419.4
c8	479.0	35	16,766.4
c9	171.2	48	8,217.1
c10	671.2	32	21,477.8
c11	530.4	24	12,730.1
c12	531.0	38	20,178.0
c13	391.0	32	12,511.4
c14	511.1	47	24,021.7
c15	261.7	36	9,420.8
c16	485.2	33	16,011.6

SPP Row Prices Heuristic The row price heuristic selects new routes with positive savings, or equivalently with negative reduced costs, based on a cost allocation of the current best feasible (incumbent) route cost. The best feasible route cost equals 5,919.9, based on routes generated by the GAP heuristic.

The route costs will be allocated to the customers according to relative weights that are computed as the product of the quantity and distance to the depot. The weights of the customers are shown in Table 9.164. A higher weight indicates a customer that is expected to be more expensive to deliver to.

The allocated cost for customer $c1$ is computed with the following calculations. The first calculation computes the total weight of all the customers on route R4, which contains customer $c1$. The second calculation computes the allocated delivery cost for customer $c1$. The allocated cost for all customers is summarized in Table 9.165.

$$W_{R4} = w_{c1} + w_{c6} + w_{c8} + w_{c15} = 18,082.8 + 14,350.4 + 16,766.4 + 9,420.8$$
$$= 58,620.4$$

$$c_1 = \frac{w_1 \cdot L_{R4}}{W_{R4}} = \frac{18,082.8 \cdot 1,847.4}{58,620.4} = 0.308 \cdot 1,847.4 = 569.9$$

Assuming that no more than four customers can be visited on a route, the number of possible routes with one, two, three, or four customers is computed with the following calculations. For example, the number of routes with three customers is equal to the number of variations of 16 customers in groups of three, but divided by 2 to eliminate the symmetrical routes since the Euclidean distances are symmetric.

Table 9.165 VRP16 allocated customer costs

Customer	Route	Total route		Individual facility	
		Cost	Weight	Weight	Cost
c1	4	1,847.4	58,620.4	18,082.8	569.9
c2	1	1,720.3	77,870.4	12,115.0	267.6
c3	3	1,121.9	33,481.2	4,592.4	153.9
c4	1	1,720.3	77,870.4	24,099.7	532.4
c5	3	1,121.9	33,481.2	8,160.4	273.4
c6	4	1,847.4	58,620.4	14,350.4	452.2
c7	2	1,230.2	65,182.8	12,419.4	234.4
c8	4	1,847.4	58,620.4	16,766.4	528.4
c9	3	1,121.9	33,481.2	8,217.1	275.3
c10	1	1,720.3	77,870.4	21,477.8	474.5
c11	2	1,230.2	65,182.8	12,730.1	240.3
c12	1	1,720.3	77,870.4	20,178.0	445.8
c13	3	1,121.9	33,481.2	12,511.4	419.2
c14	2	1,230.2	65,182.8	24,021.7	453.4
c15	4	1,847.4	58,620.4	9,420.8	296.9
c16	2	1,230.2	65,182.8	16,011.6	302.2

$$\# \ Routes \ = V_1^{16} + \frac{V_2^{16} + V_3^{16} + V_4^{16}}{2}$$

$$= 16 + \frac{1}{2}\left(\frac{16!}{14!} + \frac{16!}{13!} + \frac{16!}{12!}\right)$$

$$= 16 + \frac{1}{2}(16 \cdot 15 + 16 \cdot 15 \cdot 14 + 16 \cdot 15 \cdot 14 \cdot 13)$$

$$= 16 + 120 + 1,680 + 21,840 = 23,656$$

Instead of evaluating all these routes, we evaluate the routes generated by the parallel savings heuristic with the allocated cost based on the routes generated by the VAP heuristic. The evaluations are summarized in Table 9.166.

Routes 1 and 2 have zero savings or reduced cost. They are routes that are in the GAP solution route set and thus already in the SPP master problem. In general, routes with zero savings are equivalent routes with the same cost as routes already selected in the SPP master problem. They are either identical or alternative routes with the same cost to the current feasible route set. While they cannot improve the solution at this iteration, they may increase the flexibility of the master problem. The decision to include routes, that have zero reduced cost and that are not already in the SPP master,

Table 9.166 VRP16 route savings based on heuristic row prices

Route	Length	Customers	Cost	Savings
1	1,230.2	c7,c16,c11,c14	1,230.2	0.0
2	1,720.3	c2,c10,c4,c12	1,720.3	0.0
3	1,531.8	c3,c15,c6,c8	1,431.4	−100.4
4	1,644.4	c13,c5,c1,c9	1,537.9	−106.5

in the SPP master is an algorithm implementation choice. It is computationally easier not to include them, since then the algorithm does not have to check if they are already included in the master SPP problem. Routes 3 and 4 have negative savings and would thus not be added to the master SPP. Since no new routes were added to the SPP master problem, the optimal solution is given by the same set of routes with total length equal to 5,919.9 as generated by the VAP heuristic. The route statistics are given in Table 9.163 and the routes are shown in Fig. 9.50.

SPP with Linear Programming Based Pricing Problem The performance characteristics of the iterations of the linear programming–based pricing problem depend on the initial partition. This example starts with the routes generated by the parallel savings algorithm. Recall that the total length of those four routes is 6,127.7. The linear programming master problem starts off with those four routes only, and the value of the primal feasible solution and the objective function of the master problem are both equal to 6,127.7.

After four iterations, the pricing problem terminates because it can no longer generate routes with a negative reduced cost. The pricing problem generated 155 columns corresponding to desirable routes in the four iterations. The lower bound, generated by the linear programming relaxation is equal to 5,720.6. The optimal linear solution contained 11 routes, all of which had a fractional value. The routes and their execution value in the linear programming relaxation are shown in Tables 9.167 and 9.168. Recall that the total number of routes possible with either one,

Table 9.167 VRP16 iteration characteristics for the linear programming relaxation

Iteration	Routes		Primal	LP-Master
	# New	# Total		
0	4	4	6,127.7	6,127.7
1	34	38	5,919.8	5,919.8
2	80	118		5,811.4
3	20	138		5,811.4
4	17	155		5,720.6
			5,747.4	

Table 9.168 VRP16 optimal routes for the linear programming relaxation

Index	Value	Length	Quantity	Facilities						
2	0.75	1,720.26	155	d1	c12	c4	c10	c2	d1	
10	0.50	559.24	121	d1	c9	c5	c3	d1		
14	0.25	1,224.52	129	d1	c13	c7	c11	c14	d1	
17	0.75	1,847.42	134	d1	c1	c6	c8	c15	d1	
21	0.25	1,208.91	138	d1	c14	c16	c7	c13	d1	
29	0.25	1,181.05	150	d1	c16	c11	c14	c2	d1	
32	0.25	1,422.14	154	d1	c11	c16	c7	c13	c5	d1
124	0.25	1,845.21	146	d1	c9	c1	c6	c8	d1	
127	0.25	1,247.53	149	d1	c3	c13	c7	c16	c11	d1
151	0.25	1,952.77	156	d1	c12	c4	c10	c14	d1	
152	0.25	978.72	157	d1	c15	c9	c5	c3	d1	

Table 9.169 VRP16 optimal prices for the linear programming relaxation

Customers	Dual price
1	810.7
2	439.7
3	326.1
4	687.1
5	500.7
6	655.5
7	480.5
8	646.6
9	417.3
10	773.7
11	384.8
12	504.6
13	371.9
14	672.3
15	419.5
16	369.2
# Routes	684.9
Dual Obj.	5,720.6

two, three, or four customers was equal 23,656. Not all of these routes are feasible with respect to the vehicle capacity. In addition, a very small number of routes with five customers and feasible load exist. So the total number of possible routes for the pricing problem cannot be computed easily in advance but is expected to be no less than 23,656. The pricing problem generated thus 155 desirable routes out of at least 23,656 routes or 0.7% of possible routes.

The optimal dual variables for iteration 4 of the master problem are shown in Table 9.169. The dual variables for the customers represent the best estimate of the cost to serve each customer. The dual variable for the route count represents the best estimate of the savings for allowing one more vehicle and route.

The binary solution based on these 155 routes generated four routes with a solution value of 5,747.4. The gap for this solution is 26.8 or 0.5%. In other words, the length of these routes can never be more than 0.5% longer than the length of the optimal routes. In general, the lower bound could be further improved by a complete branch-and-price solution algorithm. However, implementing a full branch-and-price algorithm is a complex and extensive task. This programming effort is most likely not justified unless the routing decisions are very expensive or executed repeatedly. In this particular example, the gap is 0.5%, which is more than close enough to optimality for typical vehicle routing applications. The route statistics are given in Table 9.170 and the routes are shown in Fig. 9.51. Notice that in this case two routes overlap completely, which runs counter to the conventional wisdom that routes should not overlap and be shaped as the petals of a daisy flower.

The execution of the pricing problem in general depends on the starting feasible partition. The number of iterations, the number of candidate columns generated, and the primal integer solution all depend on the initial starting feasible partition.

Table 9.170 VRP16 integer SPP routes

Route	Facility							Quantity	Length
	0	1	2	3	4	5	6		
1	d1	c7	c11	c10	c4	c12	d1	159	2,148
2	d1	c3	c5	c9	d1			121	559.2
3	d1	c2	c14	c16	c13	d1		158	1,192.8
4	d1	c1	c6	c8	c15	d1		134	1,847.4
Total								572	5,747.4

Fig. 9.51 VRP16 GAP routes

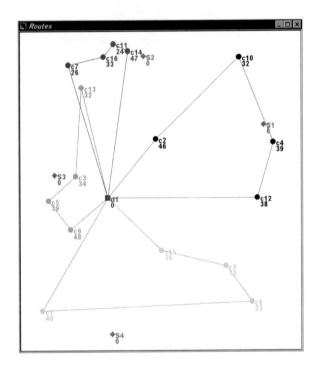

The statistics for the initial feasible partitions generated by the various construction algorithms are shown in Table 9.171. The routes of the starting partition are generated by the indicated algorithm. For each starting point, the pricing algorithm was run with candidates that do not and do allow multiple visits to the same customer facility. The primal length is the length found by either the linear relaxation of the master problem during the iterations or by the integer master problem at the end of the final iteration.

It can be observed that the two types of candidate routes with or without revisits consistently yield the same lower bound regardless of the starting point. The solution value of the integer master problem over the generated candidate routes, the number of iterations, and the number of candidate routes generated are dependent on the quality of the starting feasible partition. For this example and starting solution, the starting partitioning generated by the nearest neighbor algorithm had the

Table 9.171 VRP16 algorithm performance characteristics of the linear programming relaxation

Algorithm	Initial length	Revisits allowed	Primal length	Bound length	# Iterat.	# Cand.
GAP	5,919.78	No	5,919.78	5,720.59	5	221
	5,919.78	Yes	5,919.78	5,136.82	6	250
Savings serial	6,660.54	No	5,865.70	5,720.59	5	201
	6,660.54	Yes	6,660.54	5,136.82	8	381
Savings parallel	6,126.73	No	5,747.41	5,720.59	5	180
	6,126.73	Yes	6,126.73	5,136.82	6	333
Nearest neighbor	7,147.00	No	5,747.41	5,720.59	7	246
	7,147.00	Yes	6,550.65	5,136.82	7	324
Best	5,747.41	No	5,747.41	5,720.59	6	263
	5,747.41	Yes	5,747.41	5,136.82	6	225

Fig. 9.52 VRP16 integer SPP routes

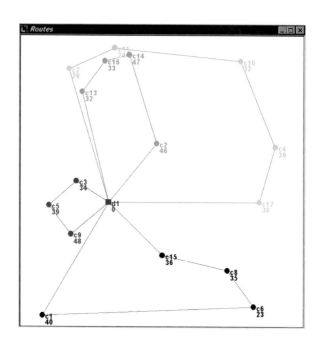

worst initial quality, but found the best primal feasible solution. For this particular example, the pricing problem variant that does not allow multiple visits to the same customer, always generates a primal integer solution that is better or equal to the one generated by the pricing problem variant that does allow multiple visits. In general, the performance impact of the different starting solutions cannot be predicted.

The following conclusions are based on anecdotal observations by author and not a systematic investigation on the use of vehicle routing algorithms. The performance of the various algorithms for this particular problem instance is consistent with algorithm performance for the standard VRP in general. The best primal feasible solution is most often found by a sequence of sophisticated optimization algorithms such as GAP followed by SPP with LP-based pricing problem. Most of these algorithms are not available to the practitioners. Even much simpler algorithms such as serial savings followed by route improvement algorithms are often avoided because of their computational complexity or because their software implementation is not available. The solution approach with very low complexity, such as nearest neighbor followed by or combined with visual inspection, is still widely used in practice. If the company has acquired a commercial truck dispatching application, then more sophisticated algorithms such as savings and 3-opt exchange improvement are often used.

References

Publications

ABC News. (2007). UPS figures out the 'right way' to save money, time and gas. http://abcnews. go.com/WNT/story?id=3005890.

Kearney, A. T. Inc. (1984). *Measuring and improving productivity in physical distribution.* Oak Brook: National Council of Physical Distribution Management (NCPDM).

Balas, E., & Padberg, M. (1976). Set partitioning: A survey. *SIAM Review, 18*(4), 710–760.

Ball, M. O., Magnanti, T. L., Monma, C. L., & Nemhauser, G. L. (Eds.). (1995). *Network routing.* Amsterdam: Elsevier.

Bazaraa, M. S., Jarvis, J. J., & Sherali, H. D. (2005). *Linear programming and network flows* (3rd ed.). Hoboken: Wiley.

Cullen, F., Jarvis, J., & Ratliff, H. (1981). Set partitioning–based heuristics for interactive routing. *Networks, 11*(2), 125–143.

Clarke, G., & Wright, J. (1964). Scheduling of vehicles from a central depot to a number of delivery points. *Operations Research, 12,* 568–581.

Deif, I., & Bodin, L. D. (1984). Extension of the Clarke–Wright algorithm for solving the vehicle routing problem with backhauling. In A. E. Kidder (Ed.), *Proceedings of the Babson conference on software uses in transportation and logistics management* (pp. 75–96) Babson Park.

Duhamel, C., Potvin, J.-Y., & Rousseau, J.-M. (1997). A Tabu search heuristic for the vehicle routing problem with Backhauls and time windows. *Transportation Science, 31*(1), 49–59.

Fisher, M. L., & Jaikumar, R. (1981). A generalized assignment heuristic for vehicle routing. *Networks, 11*(2), 109–124.

Fishetti, M., Toth, P., & Vigo, D. (1994). A branch-and-bound algorithm for the capacitated vehicle routing problem on directed graphs. *Operations Research, 42*(5), 846–859.

Gendreau, M., Laporte, G., & Hertz, A. (1997). An approximation algorithm for the traveling salesman problem with backhauls. *Operations Research, 45*(4), 639–641.

Golden, B., & Assad, A. (Eds.). (1988). *Vehicle routing: methods and studies.* North Holland: Elsevier.

Halse, K. (1992). *Modeling and solving complex vehicle routing problems.* Ph.D. Dissertation, Technical University of Denmark.

Or, I. (1976). *Traveling salesman-type combinatorial problems and their relation to the logistics of regional blood banking.* Unpublished Ph.D. Dissertation, Northwestern University, Evanston, IL.

Savelsbergh, M., & Goetschalckx, M. (1994). A comparison of the efficiency of fixed versus variable vehicle routes. *Journal of Business Logistics, 16*(1), 163–188.

Schrijver, A. (1990). *On the history of transportation and maximum flow problems.* Unpublished manuscript, Center for Wiskunde en Informatica (CWI), Amsterdam, the Netherlands, cwi. homepages.nl.

Toth, P., & Vigo, D. (1996). A heuristic algorithm for the vehicle rrouting problem with backhauls. In L. Bianco & P. Toth (Eds.), *Advanced methods in transportation analysis* (pp. 585–608). Berlin: Springer.

Toth, P., & Vigo, D. (1997). An exact algorithm for the vehicle routing problem with backhauls. *Transportation Science, 31*(4), 372–386.

Programs

Lineback. (1997). Marc Goetschalckx. http://www.isye.gatech.edu/people/faculty/Marc_Goetschalckx.

Chapter 10
Inventory Systems

Learning Objectives After you have studied this chapter, you should:

- Know the different types of inventory and their mathematical formulation in supply chain models.
- Know the different types of service levels and their computation methods.
- Know the different types of inventory policies and their characteristics.
- Know the properties and application of the Newsvendor model.
- Know the following continuous-review inventory policies:

  - Their assumptions.
  - The formulation of the long-term cost minimization problem and its simple solution algorithms.
  - The two-bin policy.

- Know the following fixed-period inventory policies:

  - Their assumptions.
  - The formulation of the long term cost minimization problem and its simple solution algorithms.
  - The min–max policy.

- Know the principles and material calculations of distribution resource planning.

10.1 Introduction

Inventory Definition The materials held in storage to satisfy a future demand are called *inventory*. The location where the inventory is held is most of the time stationary and is called a *warehouse*. However, small caches of inventory are sometimes held in the vehicles of repairmen or even in airplanes loaded with emergency service parts. The basic function of inventory is to act as a buffer between two subsequent processes. Often these processes are the production process and the demand process or different stages in the supply chain.

M. Goetschalckx, *Supply Chain Engineering,* International Series in Operations Research & Management Science,
DOI 10.1007/978-1-4419-6512-7_10, © Springer Science+Business Media, LLC 2011

Inventory Historical Perspective Historically, inventory was considered a sign of wealth. Before the twentieth century, a large warehouse filled with goods was a desirable characteristic of a manufacturer or merchant. Transportation and information systems were not very reliable and the goal was to have large inventories on hand as a buffer against unforeseen events. During the twentieth century this opinion of inventory changed. Systems to deliver goods became more reliable and alternative sources of goods became available. The goal was to minimize inventory. In the last few decades of the twentieth century, the image of inventory changed again. Inventory was seen as an expensive but necessary evil. The decision whether to hold inventory and how much inventory to hold was based on a balance between several costs such as production or purchasing, transportation costs, holding costs, and customer service requirements.

Inventory Goals and Associated Cost The overall objective of holding inventory is to satisfy the demand for the goods held in inventory with an acceptable service level. The inventory control system attempts to minimize the total system cost of providing this level of service. The total system cost traditionally consists of the costs associated with holding inventory, with ordering replenishment goods, and with unsatisfied demand. As an alternative to the cost of unsatisfied demand, a minimum service level may be used as a constraint on the inventory policy. Contemporary inventory control systems may also include the costs associated with delivering or transporting the goods from supplier to the inventory holding location and to the customer.

In traditional inventory systems the typical decisions involve the determination of the level of service to be provided, the frequency of or time between replenishments R, the order up to level S which determines how much to order, and the reorder point s which determines when in the cycle the order is placed. Depending on the conditions and assumptions of the inventory system, these values can be either parameters or variables and this has created many different types of inventory control policies. An inventory control policy is considered "optimal" if it minimizes the long-range or average total system cost. While this long-range average cost differs significantly from industry to industry and from product to product, 25% of the product value is often used as a first order approximation of the average cost for holding a product in inventory for 1 year.

The historical growth of the total value of goods held in inventory by business in the United States for the past 26 years is shown in Fig. 10.1. The business inventory value was 1857 trillion dollars and the inventory carrying rate was 24% in 2006. The data are based on the Annual State of Logistics Report produced by the CSCMP (Wilson 2007). The recent rise in the carrying rate is attributed to the rise short term interest rates from 2003 to 2006. The fraction of total logistics costs of 1305 trillion dollars attributed to inventory was approximately 34% in 2006. Transportation was responsible for 61% of total logistics costs, while the balance of 5% was consumed by administrative and shipper's costs.

Inventory Trends In recent times, the trend has been to decrease the amount of inventory by ordering more frequently in smaller quantities. In particular pull

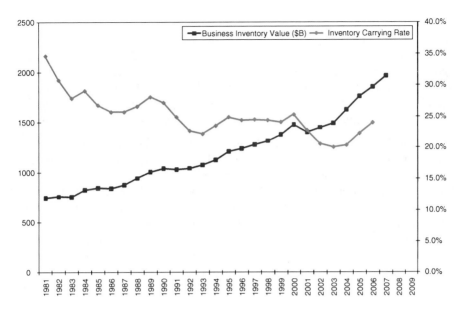

Fig. 10.1

inventory policies such as JIT are responsible for this trend. The work-in-process inventory in manufacturing has decreased dramatically. At the same time, the backroom inventory at retailers has been almost completely eliminated. Retail customers increasingly face the situation "what you see is what you can buy." As consequence, the transportation of goods has increased because of average size of a single order has decreased. At the same time, sophisticated sales tracking systems have been put into place so that goods sold can be reordered immediately and can be replenished quickly in order to keep the shelves filled and customer service levels high. This has led to dramatic increase in information technology systems and their associated costs in the management of supply chains.

10.1.1 Reasons for Inventory and Inventory Types

A large variety of reasons for holding inventory exist. Each of the reasons has yielded a corresponding type of inventory. The major types are described next.

Economies of Scale and Cycle Inventory Both manufacturing and transportation operations have significant economies of scale. Production operations have setup cost to start a new product or model as well as a learning curve for optimizing the production yield for each product. Transportation in full truckload or train carload quantities has significantly lower rates than less than truckload quantities or the same cost is paid for transporting a vehicle or container. In this case the unit cost is reduced by filling the vehicle or container as much as possible. In all of these cases, economic incentives exist to produce or transport in large quantities. But the corresponding demand may occur in much smaller quantities. The inventory that forms a buffer between these processes is called *cycle inventory*. Cycle inventory also is created when the production or supply process generates smaller quantities that are then transported in larger quantities. An example is the collection of cardboard at retailers or aluminum cans at a recycling center. On the main goals of the just-in-time (JIT) management system is to reduce cycle inventory of component parts.

Seasonal Processes and Seasonal Inventory Many processes in the agricultural sector and processes in the consumer sector have natural seasons. An example is the production and consumption of orange juice concentrate. The concentrate is produced is a relatively short period of time following the harvesting of oranges in that geographical area. The concentrate is consumed in a relatively steady process when it is converted to orange juice and sold to consumers. Similarly, the production of strings of Christmas lights is spread over a whole year, but the demand is concentrated in a relatively short period during the Christmas season. The producers can utilize equipment with a smaller capacity over an extended period at a steady rate and then satisfy demand in a burst mode. The inventory created through this interaction is called *seasonal inventory*.

Transportation and Pipeline Inventory *Pipeline inventory* is the inventory of goods currently being transported from the supplier to the customer. This inventory is sometimes also called *in-transit inventory*. The costs associated with pipeline inventory become only relevant for large transit times such as for sea cargo on intercontinental transportation. This inventory and its associated costs can be reduced by using faster transportation modes such as air cargo instead of sea cargo or by reducing the distance between supplier and customer.

Required Aging Processes and Work-in-Process Inventory Production process may include a necessary aging step before the product is ready for the next step. Prominent examples in agriculture are the required aging of cheese, wine, and spirits such as cognac and whiskey. The corresponding inventory is one type of work-in-process inventory. The inventory created by delays between the different processes and machines inside a manufacturing plant is also work-in-process inventory. It is often denoted by WIP. One of the main goals of the lean manufacturing management system is to eliminate WIP.

Hedging Against Price Changes and Speculative Inventory Speculative inventory is created when goods are purchased early at a lower price because it is anticipated that prices will be higher when the demand has to be satisfied. The goods are stored until the demand occurs. Speculative inventory may be created by a high inflation rate for a single-country supply chain or by an anticipated change in the exchange rates in a global supply chain.

Hedging Against Variability and Safety Inventory All of the inventory types described so far may be present even if the future characteristics of the demand and supply process were known with certainty. Safety inventory is the inventory held because the future conditions are not known with certainty. The main sources of uncertainty are future demand, replenishment lead time, and future supply. Uncertainty with respect to the future supply may include the yield of a manufacturing process and the production lead time. The uncertainty with respect to the replenishment lead time includes the variability of the transportation time. If all future conditions are considered to be known with certainty, i.e. are considered to be deterministic, then no safety inventory is required.

Response Time Constraints and Emergency Inventory Many systems have service level constraints that make it mandatory that inventory is stored close to the customer or demand process so that the demand can be satisfied within the allowable response time. An example is the inventory of service parts maintained in large cities for replacement of critical components of telephone switching centers. A military example is the storage of main battle tanks by the United States Army in locations in the middle east so that in times of conflict only the personnel has to be flown in to create a heavy armored capability. Personnel can be transported quickly by standard passenger aircraft, while transporting tanks requires specialized sea transportation, which may not be available and is comparatively slow. An example in disaster recovery operations is the pre-positioning of trucks with bottled water in the areas in the projected path of a hurricane. The strategic oil reserve of the United States is a national inventory of crude oil to be used in time of war or when oil imports are interrupted.

Inventory Materials The type goods held in inventory can be classified according to where they are held in the supply chain. Raw materials or supplies are goods entering the supply chain of the organization. Work-in-process inventory hold goods internal to the organization. Finally, finished goods and the corresponding inventory are goods ready to be sold to external customers of the organization. Of course the finished goods of the preceding step or organization in the supply chain become the supplies for the next step in the supply chain.

Depending on the degree of specialization towards the customer, products and their inventories can also be divided into commodities, standard products, and specialty products. Previously a commodity was identified as a product with no distinguishable characteristics between quantities of the same product manufactured by different producers. Examples of commodities are low-fat milk, gasoline, office paper, and polyethylene. Customers acquire commodity products solely on the basis of logistics factors such as price, availability, and convenience. A standard product has comparable and competing models from different suppliers that differ in functionality, quality, and availability. Examples are cars, personal computers, and fork lift trucks. Customers make acquisitions based on tradeoffs between functionality, value, price, and logistics factors. A specialty or custom product is produced to the exact and unique specifications of the customer. Typical examples are specialized machines, printing presses, fuselage sections for aircraft assembly, and conveyor networks. The product is defined by a technical specification and the supplier is selected by reputation, price, and logistics factors.

10.1.2   Inventory Planning

Inventory Decisions In an efficient supply chain, all inventories are created by a tradeoff between the costs of procuring a part early and holding until demand occurs versus procuring goods at the time the demand is realized. The cost tradeoff is made even more difficult because in reality future conditions are not known with certainty. In addition, the inability to satisfy the customer demand at an acceptable service level for a particular product may lead to lost sales of other products, loss of future sales of the same product, and even to the temporary or permanent loss of a customer. These cost impacts are extremely difficult to compute and are most often resolved by setting service level standards for the organization.

In designing and managing an efficient supply chain four types of questions have to be answered related to the holding of goods in the supply chain. The questions are: (1) what goods to store, (2) where to store the inventory, (3) when to place one or more orders for goods, and finally (4) how much to order. The analytical process to determine the answers to these questions assumes that the relevant supply chain conditions and data can be predicted with a quantifiable degree of certainty. The first and second questions are strategic or sometimes tactical decisions. These decisions determine the overall configuration and size of the supply chain. The third and fourth questions are operational decisions that use the configuration of the supply chain as constraints.

Inventory Performance Measures Recall that the overall objective of holding inventory is to satisfy the demand for the goods held in inventory with an acceptable service level. The inventory control system attempts to minimize the total system cost of providing this level of service. The three most common performance measures of an inventory system or policy are its cost, the provided service level, and the inventory velocity.

Inventory Costs All inventory calculations in the following inventory models and policies are expressed in economic terms and values for the organization holding and owning the inventory.

The *unit cost* or *unit value* ($/unit) represents the cost invested so far in a single unit of the product. This cost includes the total production cost, purchasing cost, transportation cost and any applicable duties. The unit value is not a direct inventory cost but is one of the factors in the inventory holding cost.

The *holding cost* or *carrying cost*, expressed as a cost per unit of inventory per unit of time ($/unit-year), represents all the costs associated with storing the inventory. This cost includes the costs associated with storage facilities, handling, insurance, pilferage, obsolescence, and the opportunity cost of capital. The *holding cost rate* is the ratio of the holding cost divided by the value of one unit of inventory ($/$-year). A holding cost rate of 25% of the unit value per year is a widely quoted average for the US industry.

The *reorder cost*, also called the fixed ordering cost or setup cost ($/order), represents all the costs incurred each time an order is placed. This cost includes the costs associated with preparing the purchase, receiving the order, paying the invoice, with equipment setups, or with transporting the order.

The *shortage cost*, expressed as a cost per unit of inventory ($/unit), represents all the costs associated with the delays and remedial actions when inventory was not available to satisfy customer demand. This cost includes emergency transportation costs, penalties, and loss of customer goodwill. The shortage cost is the most difficult to estimate accurately of the three inventory costs, especially the components related to loss of customer goodwill or the cost of lost sales of other items in the same customer order.

Finally, the *salvage value*, expressed as a cost per unit of inventory ($/unit), represents all the revenues or costs associated with removing the items from inventory. The costs are also called *disposal costs*. Salvage value may be created by selling the goods through a secondary, discount channel or by selling the goods to salvage operation, which disassembles the goods and sells the components or materials. Sometimes the goods have to be disposed of in landfill or dump and the disposal costs include transportation and landfill fees.

The total system cost is the aggregate of the cost components identified above. In the chapters on supply chain systems and supply chain modeling, the total system cost will include additionally the transportation costs and the network costs based on the installed facilities and information technology systems. The focus in this chapter is exclusively on the inventory costs.

Service Level Inventory systems are expected to satisfy an acceptable level of customer demand known as the *service level*. Three types of service levels are commonly used. The inventory decisions may apply to a single order and demand cycle or to a repetitive pattern of replenishment and demand cycles. The service levels are measured at the end of the cycle(s) or for the type 3 service level at the end of every period in the cycle. If a demand cannot be satisfied for a single cycle then it is typically lost, i.e., it is removed from the supply chain and is denoted by lost sales. For multiple repetitive cycles, the unsatisfied demand may either be lost or transferred to the next or subsequent cycles. If the demand is shifted then the products are said to be *backordered*. The degree of lost sales versus backorder depends on the competitive position of the product and the patience of the customers.

1. The α, P1, or type 1 service level is defined as the probability of not being out of stock per replenishment cycle. If only a single inventory cycle occurs it is the probability of having any inventory on hand at the end of the period. If multiple cycles occur, it is equal to the long-range fraction of cycles in which a stockout does not occur. This service level is also called the *cycle service level* or *in-stock probability*. This service level measures whether or not a lost sale or backorder occurs, but it is not concerned with the size of the lost sale or backorder.

2. The β, P2, or type 2 service level is defined as the long-range average fraction of demand delivered from inventory on the shelf. This service level is also called the *fill rate* (*fr*). The complement of the fill rate is the expected lost sales. This

service level considers not only the probability of a stock out but also the size of the lost sales or backorder.

3. There exist several different definitions of the third service level. The γ, P3, or type 3 service level is defined in Silver et al. (1998) as the fraction of the time during which there is inventory present on the shelf. This definition of the service level is also called the *ready rate* (*rr*). Schneider (1981) defines the (1 − γ) service level as the ratio of the long-run average cumulative unsatisfied demand per replenishment cycle divided by the average demand per replenishment cycle.

The first type of service level measures if there is a stockout, the second service level measures the size of the stockout, and the third service level measures the size and the duration of the stockout. Different types of products may require a different type of service level based in part on the competitive practices for the type of product. For expensive and highly specialized service parts for mining machinery, the appropriate service level may be of type one since the major cost is associated with the interrupted mining process and any shut down is to be avoided. The appropriate service level for a nonperishable item with a small profit margin in a grocery store such as chicken soup may be of type 2. Finally, the supply of medicines to victims of a terrorist attack using anthrax may have a service level of type 3 as defined by Schneider (1981). Since higher types of service level use more data to compute the customer service, it should come as no surprise that the determination of the optimal inventory policy becomes much more difficult when moving from the use of type α to β to γ. In addition, identical numerical values for α and β and γ indicate significantly different levels of customer service and the same inventory pattern may yield very different values for its α and β and γ service levels. This is illustrated by the following example.

Consider the on-hand inventory level over four replenishment cycles as shown in Fig. 10.2. Each replenishment cycle is ten time periods long and the average demand per period is 4 units or 40 units per cycle.

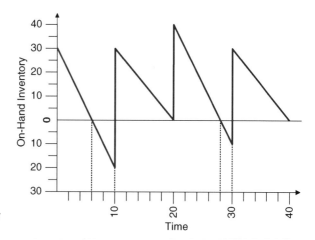

Fig. 10.2 On-hand inventory levels illustration

Two cycles out of the four experience backorders. While considering only four cycles is clearly not a long-run average, the α service level based on these four cycles is computed as:

$$\alpha = 1 - \frac{2}{4} = 0.5$$

The first cycle experiences 20 units backordered and the third cycle experiences a backorder of 10 units. The second and fourth cycles have no backorders. The β service level is then computed as:

$$\beta = 1 - \frac{20 + 10}{160} = 0.81$$

The cumulative amount of backordered units over time can be computed by measuring the backorder quantities at the end of each period. In the above example, the backorder quantities are 5, 10, 15, 20 in periods 7–10 of cycle one and 5 and 10 in periods 29 and 30 of cycle three. The cumulative amount of backordered units over time can then be computed as

$$\gamma = 1 - \frac{5 + 10 + 15 + 20 + 5 + 10}{4 \cdot 40} = 1 - \frac{65}{160} = 0.59$$

A continuous approximation of the cumulative amount of backordered units over time can be computed as the area below the zero inventory level or horizontal axis, or for the above example the areas of the two triangles below the zero inventory level

$$\gamma = 1 - \frac{40 + 10}{4 \cdot 40} = 1 - \frac{50}{160} = 0.69$$

The difference between those two values is caused by the small time offset when the backorder quantities are measured in each period. The continuous approximation measures the backorder amounts at the midpoint of each period, where the discrete computation measures the backorder amounts at the end of each period. The demand rates in the cycles with backorders are both equal to five units per period. The difference between the amount backordered at the midpoint or the endpoint of the period is half the demand during a period or 2.5 units. The difference between the discrete and continuous computation of the service level is then 2.5 units backordered for the six periods with backorders, or exactly the difference between 50 and 65 in the numerators of the above formulas.

Finally, the ready rate for this example is computed as

$$\gamma = \frac{6 + 10 + 8 + 10}{40} = 1 - \frac{4 + 0 + 2 + 0}{40} = 1 - \frac{6}{40} = 0.85.$$

If the demand pattern has a constant demand rate (d), then the ready rate is equal to the fill rate. The derivation of this equivalency is illustrated in Fig. 10.3 of a single inventory cycle. It is assumed that this cycle is repeated many times to yield the long-range averages.

Fig. 10.3 Ready rate and fill rate equivalency

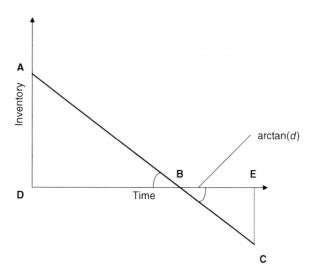

$$d = \frac{AD}{DB} = \frac{EC}{BE} = \frac{AD + EC}{DB + BE}$$

$$fr = \beta = \frac{AD}{AD + EC} = \frac{DB}{DB + BE} = \gamma = rr$$

The γ or type 3 service level is used to measure the performance of an inventory system for emergency situations such as hurricanes, flooding, health pandemic, famine crisis, or terrorist attack. In those cases it is assumed that the demand occurs in a single spike or relatively short time period at the beginning of the planning horizon.

Stock Turnover The stock turnover indicates the speed with which a single product moves through the distribution system. It is expressed in turns per year and is computed as the ratio of the value of the annual sales divided by the value of the average inventory of that product. Based on its analogy to the operating speed of an engine expressed in revolutions per minute (rpm), this performance measure is also called inventory velocity, even though inventory by definition is products held in storage. A higher level of stock turnover is more desirable since it indicates that more sales have been made for the amount of inventory in the system.

The average time in inventory for a product indicates on the average how long an item of the product is kept in inventory before it is sold. The average time in inventory is the inverse measure of the stock turnover and it is often expressed in years. This measure is also the called the *average inventory age*. Other time measures are also commonly used such as days of stock or DOS or months. For example, it was reported that the average inventory held by wholesalers in the United States decreased from 1.34 in January 2009 to 1.31 in February 2009, where the inventory was measured as the ratio of inventory to monthly sales (AJC 2009). This decrease was seen as a sign of improvement for the economy at that time. This ratio indicates how many months it would take to eliminate the inventory at the sales level of that month. The February ratio corresponds to $12/1.31 = 9.16$ turns per year (tpy).

10.1.3   Basic Inventory Policy Classes

An inventory policy basically provides the answer to two related operational questions when managing a product inventory: when and how much to order. The first answer determines how often the inventory levels are checked and when orders are placed. The second answer determines how much inventory is ordered, which is called the *order quantity*. If only a single ordering cycle is considered, then the first question is either non applicable or trivial. Depending on the answer to the two questions above, inventory policies can be divided into three classes.

The first class contains inventory policies that always order the same quantity. These are called *fixed order quantity policies*. These policies adjust the time between order placements depending on the demand. They are often used for products that have a small or irregular demand or for products that have significant savings for being replenished in a particular quantity. The second class contains inventory policies that check the current inventory at regular time intervals and place an order if needed. These are called *fixed-order frequency policies*. These policies adjust the order quantity, which may be zero. They are often used for item with high and regular demand. The third class contains inventory policies that adjust both the quantity ordered and time when the order is placed. These policies are denoted as *direct demand satisfaction policies*.

Inventory policies can also be classified as either *push* or *pull inventory policies*. In a push system, inventory is determined by a centralized planning tool simultaneously for all the inventory stocking locations in the system. Push systems use a top-down, centralized approach. The prime example of push systems are material requirements planning (MRP) in a production planning environment, and distribution resource planning (DRP) in a distribution environment. In DRP, based on the forecast of the sales to the end customer, the inventory at all the inventory locations is determined. In a pull inventory system, each individual inventory stocking location determines independently its orders. Pull systems use a bottoms-up, decentralized approach. One of the earliest pull systems in production planning was the kanban system implemented by the Toyota Motor Company. This led to the development of just-in-time (JIT) systems and contemporary lean production systems. Both fixed-order quantities and fixed-order frequency policies are controlled by the demand events and belong to the class of pull policies. Direct demand satisfaction policies can be either of the push or pull type.

Push and pull systems are philosophically different approaches. Both push and pull systems have advantages and disadvantages. Push systems rely very heavily on the quality of the forecast of the final sales. Push systems can adapt more easily to changing conditions if the change is forecasted accurately. This makes push systems more recommended for inventory control during sales promotions and the introduction of a new product. A single order inventory system must by definition also a push system. Push systems also have the capability to exploit coordination of different activities such as transportation. Push system also have the ability to allocate inventory equitable or according to management policies in shortage situations. Pull systems are based on the actual sales of the products to the end customer and this data can be assumed to be fully accurate. Pull systems replenish only the inventory that has been withdrawn by elements of the supply chain that are closer to the customer, so no unnecessary inventories are left orphaned in the supply chain because of incorrect forecasts. Pull systems are recommended for inventory of mature products with stable sales.

10.2   Independent Demand Systems

10.2.1   South Ascent Technical Parkas Inventory Example

The various inventory policies for independent demand systems that will be discussed below are illustrated by the same example. The description and data summary of the example are given next. Note that not all data items are used for every inventory policy.

The South Ascent (SA) is a manufacturer of premium camping, climbing, and adventure equipment. In addition to selling to stores and chains that specialize in camping equipment and clothing, it also sells directly to individual consumers through its web site. One of their most popular items is a mountain light parka, which is a lightweight, full-length, technical parka guaranteed to keep you dry even under the most extreme circumstances. There exist several competitors that offer similar high-end parkas. The business model of SA is to be the preferred retailer to individual consumers by providing a very high service level and by constantly updating the features and style of the parka while charging a high price to remain profitable. You are asked to determine the least cost inventory policy for this parka.

Demand data and sales forecast indicate that the weekly demand for the parka through direct sales can be approximated with sufficient accuracy by a normal distribution with mean of 450 and standard deviation of 127. The parkas are manufactured in China and there is a 6-week lead time for receipt at the SA warehouse that services the direct sales. SA has been using a 40% annual holding cost rate, since the parka model and colors are updated annually and models and colors of previous years have to be sold through a discount channel. The parkas cost $ 95 each, which includes the transportation cost to the warehouse and all applicable duties and tariffs, and the ordering cost is $ 3750 per order which includes all the administrative costs. The sales price to individual consumers for a parka is $ 390. Because of its customer service policies SA currently uses a 97% fill rate criterion. It is assumed that there are 52 weeks in a year and the weekly holding cost rate is

Table 10.1 South ascent technical parkas inventory example: data summary

Data item	Symbol	Value	Units
Purchase price	p	95	\$/unit
Lead time	lt	6	Weeks
Std. dev. lead time	slt	1.5	Weeks
Holding cost rate	hcr	0.0077	/week
Shortage cost	sc	150	\$/unit
Ordering cost	oc	3750	\$/order
Demand rate	d	450	units/week
Std. dev. weekly demand	sd	127	units
Probability no-stockout	$F(s)$	0.97	
Fill rate	fr	0.97	
Mean demand d. lead time	dlt	2700	units
Std. dev. demand d. lead time	$sdlt$	743	units

equal to $0.4/52 \approx 0.0077$. The data for the technical parka product is summarized in Table 10.1. The last two rows in the table hold derived values and their derivation will be explained below.

10.2.2 Supply Chain with Deterministic Parameters

In this section the costs of inventories are calculated, where the inventories are present in the supply chain assuming that the future conditions are known with certainty.

Pipeline Inventory Pipeline inventory is the inventory that is currently being transported from the supplier to the customer. In most contemporary supply chains the pipeline inventory cost is relatively small unless the transportation is intercontinental. For high-value products that are relatively light and small it may advantageous to use faster transportation modes such as air cargo instead of sea cargo. The following notation will be used.

PI pipeline inventory
D demand during the planning period (units/year)
TT transit time in planning periods (years)
PIC annual pipeline inventory cost
v unit value (currency/unit)
HCR holding cost rate (1/year)

Let v be the value of the product and let hcr be the holding cost rate expressed as a percentage of the value of the product for holding the product in inventory for one period, i.e., expressed in dollars per dollars per period. Let HCR be the holding cost rate for one year. The time units in the following equations must be consistent, i.e., if the demand and the transit time are expressed in years then the holding cost rate must also be computed per year and the result is the annual pipeline inventory cost. Other time horizons may be used provided they are used consistently throughout the calculations.

Fig. 10.4 Cycle inventory illustration for different cycle lengths

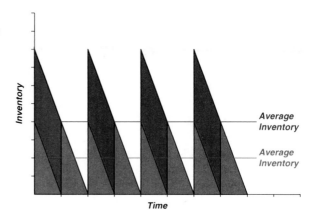

$$PI = D \cdot TT \qquad (10.1)$$

$$PIC = PI \cdot HCR \cdot v = HCR \cdot v \cdot D \cdot TT \qquad (10.2)$$

Cycle Inventory The cycle inventory is caused by the different batch sizes of the input and the output processes. Most typical is the transportation to the inventory stocking point in large batch sizes and the withdrawal of the goods from inventory in small quantities. These two patterns yield the characteristic saw-toothed pattern shown in Fig. 10.4.

The following notation will be used.

CI average cycle inventory
ci cycle inventory
d period demand rate (units/period)
ct cycle time (periods)
CT cycle time (years)
D demand rate (units/year)
CIC annual cycle inventory cost

Again the time units must be consistent in the following formulas. If the holding cost rate is computed per year, then the result is the annual cycle inventory cost. If an instantaneous replenishment and a constant demand rate are assumed as shown in the the previous figure, then the average cycle inventory is half the maximum cycle inventory, which in turn is equal to the replenishment quantity.

$$CI = \frac{D \cdot CT}{2} = \frac{d \cdot ct}{2} \qquad (10.3)$$

$$CI = \frac{1}{CT} \int_{0}^{CT} (D \cdot CT - Dt)dt = \frac{D \cdot CT}{2} = \frac{d \cdot ct}{2} \qquad (10.4)$$

In the previous figure, two inventory replenishment frequencies and their corresponding inventory patterns are shown. One pattern replenishes twice as often as the other pattern. This implies that its cycle time is also half the cycle time of the second pattern. As a consequence, the cycle inventory and cycle inventory cost are cut in half, even thought the annual demand is the same in both cases. The savings in cycle inventory cost corresponding to a higher frequency of replenishment must be carefully balanced against possible higher transportation costs now that the transportation quantities are also cut in half.

Seasonal Inventory Seasonal inventory is created during periods of lower demand and distributed during periods of high demand. This allows an organization to use a lower installed production capacity and still to meet all the customer demands. The reduced production capacity must be traded off with the inventory holding costs from period to period.

The following assumptions are usually made. The seasons in the cycle have equal duration. The value of the product does not change from season to season. The inventory buildup or withdrawal in a season occurs on the average at a constant rate, which is the difference between the constant production and constant demand rate for that season. This implies that in each season, the inventory change is linear. The inventory levels in a seasonal system are illustrated in Fig. 10.5. The solid thick line indicates the average inventory level based on average demand and production rates. The thin line illustrates the actual on-hand inventory which oscillates around the average inventory level. The on-hand inventory deviates from its average level because of the variations in actual demand. The following calculations will only use the constant rate per season since the supply chain conditions are assumed to be known.

The seasonal inventory costs can be computed in function of the seasonal inventory levels at the start and end of the different seasons.

I_t inventory level at the end of season t
I_0 initial inventory
$SeIC$ annual seasonal inventory cost

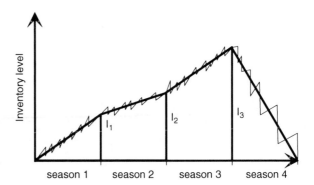

Fig. 10.5 Seasonal inventory levels

For cyclical systems, where the terminal inventory of the last period in the cycle is equal to the starting inventory of the first period, the seasonal inventory holding cost is given by the following formula. The holding cost rate hcr is computed per period. For example, if there are four equal seasons in a year, hcr would be computed as one fourth of the annual holding cost rate.

$$SeIC = hcr_s v \left(\sum_{t=1}^{N} I_t \right) \tag{10.5}$$

If the system is not cyclical, the seasonal inventory holding cost is given by

$$SeIC = hcr_s v \left(\frac{I_1}{2} + \sum_{t=2}^{N-1} I_t + \frac{I_N}{2} \right) \tag{10.6}$$

Finally, if the periods are not of equal length, then hcr is the holding cost rate for season i and the seasonal inventory cost is given by

$$SeIC = v \sum_{t=1}^{N} \frac{hcr_t (I_{t-1} + I_t)}{2} \tag{10.7}$$

Economic Order Quantity (EOQ)   One of the simplest logistics systems is the system in which the demand is constant. The models for constant demand can also be applied in situations with predictable demand, where the forecast error and uncertainty is small. Often there is a fixed setup cost for starting production or placing an order, which has to be balanced against an inventory holding cost which grows proportionally to the amount held in inventory. The economic order quantity finds the best tradeoff between the fixed and the variable cost assuming there is a constant demand rate. The following notation will be used.

TC	total cost per year
OC	cumulative ordering cost per year
hc	unit holding cost per year
oc	unit ordering cost
Q, Q^*	order quantity, optimal order quantity

The unit holding cost per year is the product of the holding cost rate per year and the product value.

$$hc = HCR \cdot v \tag{10.8}$$

The total annual cost is the sum of the annual inventory holding cost and the annual ordering or setup cost. The number of inventory cycles per year is given by the ratio of the annual demand divided by the ordering quantity of a single cycle, or D/Q.

$$\begin{aligned} TC(Q) &= CIC + OC \\ &= \frac{hc \cdot Q}{2} + \frac{D}{Q} oc \end{aligned} \tag{10.9}$$

The total cost is a nonlinear function of a single variable, namely the ordering quantity Q. The optimal ordering quantity can be found where the first derivative becomes zero, provided that the second derivative is positive indicating that the cost function is convex. Since a physical ordering quantity cannot be negative, the sign of the first derivative for a zero order quantity must be checked. The first derivative is negative at $Q=0$, so the total cost function has single optimal value for a non-negative Q. The indicated functions can be computed with the following formulas.

$$\frac{d\,(TC)}{dQ} = \frac{hc}{2} - \frac{D \cdot oc}{Q^2}$$

$$\frac{d^2\,(TC)}{dQ^2} = \frac{2 \cdot D \cdot oc}{Q^3} > 0$$

$$\left.\frac{d\,(TC)}{dQ}\right|_{Q \to 0} = -\left.\frac{D \cdot oc}{Q^2}\right|_{Q \to 0} = -\infty \tag{10.10}$$

$$\frac{d\,(TC\,(Q^*))}{dQ} = \frac{hc}{2} - \frac{D \cdot oc}{Q^{*2}} = 0$$

$$Q^{*2} = \frac{2 \cdot D \cdot oc}{hc}$$

$$Q^* = \sqrt{\frac{2 \cdot D \cdot oc}{hc}} \tag{10.11}$$

The value of the cost function at optimality can be expressed with the following closed form formula. At optimality, the annual inventory holding cost is equal to the annual ordering cost. The forces for decreasing and increasing the order quantity are at equilibrium.

$$TC\,(Q^*) = \frac{hc}{2}\sqrt{\frac{2 \cdot D \cdot oc}{hc}} + \frac{D \cdot oc}{\sqrt{\frac{2 \cdot D \cdot oc}{hc}}} \tag{10.12}$$

$$= \sqrt{2 \cdot D \cdot oc \cdot hc}$$

Technical Parkas Example Computing the optimal ordering quantity and the minimal weekly total cost for the example gives the following values. The graph for the total, ordering, and inventory holding costs is shown in Fig. 10.6. Observe that the minimal total cost is achieved when the annual cycle inventory cost is equal to the annual ordering cost. Further observe that the total cost curve is relatively flat around the optimal ordering quantity. This may indicate that a heuristic solution for the determination of the optimal order quantity is sufficient in practical situations.

$$Q^* = \sqrt{\frac{2 \cdot 450 \cdot 3750}{0.0077 \cdot 95}} = 2149$$

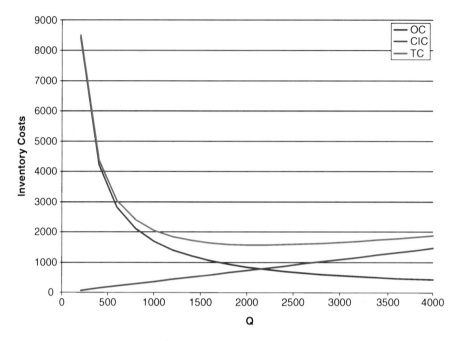

Fig. 10.6 Inventory example cost curves for known demand

$$TC\left(Q^*\right) = \frac{2149 \cdot 0.0077 \cdot 95}{2} + \frac{450}{2149}3750 = 1570.5$$

Economic Production Quantity From the marketing and sales department point of view, the best batch size is equal to one. This is equivalent to a *make-to-order* policy or demand driven production and gives the sales department the greatest flexibility. However, such small batch sizes might not be efficient for the manufacturing department if there are significant setup costs. For example, a customer could walk into a car dealership and "assemble" his own car from the available options. This would be acceptable to the customer with a manufacturing lead-time of 1 week and a delivery lead time of a week. Current realistic lead times for this scenario are much longer. Business corporations have identified the capability to manufacture on demand rather than to inventory as a major competitive advantage. This manufacturing philosophy is also called "mass customization."

Examples of both extreme points of the spectrum of manufacturing technology are given next. Henry Ford is attributed the quote that "the customer could order a car in any color he desired, as long it was black" illustrating the state of the art in the automotive assembly process of the Model T. This statement is a reflection that a single product is easier and more efficient to manufacture. On the other hand, Captain Jean-Luc Picard of the Starship *Enterprise* in "Star Trek: the Next Generation" can order a single cup of Earl Grey tea which is immediately delivered by the replicator in his quarters. This level of manufacturing flexibility and efficiency only exists in science fiction.

In computing the optimal batch size in production operations from the manufacturing point of view, we will use the following definitions:

CT production cycle time which repeats indefinitely expressed in years

RT production time per cycle and expressed in years for the product being evaluated

Q   production batch size for this product

MI maximum inventory of this product during the production cycle

d, D product demand rate, annualized product demand

p, P product production rate ($p > d$), annualized product production

CIC total annual cycle inventory cost

MC total annual manufacturing cost

TC total annual cost

hc inventory holding cost per year per product unit

fc fixed costs for starting production of a batch of this product

vc variable (marginal) cost for production of one unit of this product

ic inventory cost per unit

mc manufacturing cost per unit

tc total cost per unit

The inventory pattern over time is shown in Fig. 10.7.

We first compute the maximum on-hand product inventory. It should be noted that it is the maximum on-hand product inventory that influences the size of the storage facility or warehouse and its corresponding cost.

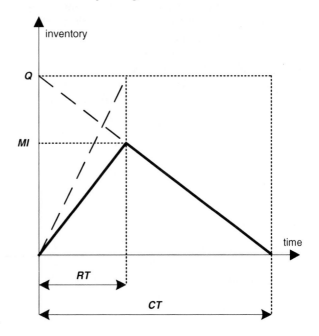

Fig. 10.7 Inventory pattern for finite production and demand rates

$$M = Q - D \cdot RT = Q - D \left(\frac{Q}{P} \right) = Q \left(1 - \frac{D}{P} \right) \qquad (10.13)$$

Next we compute the total annual costs. Note that the number of cycles per year is equal to D/Q and depends on Q.

$$
\begin{aligned}
TC &= CIC + MC \\
&= \frac{hc \cdot M}{2} + fc + vc \cdot Q \\
&= \frac{hc \cdot Q \cdot (1 - D/P) \cdot Q}{2} + fc + vc \cdot Q \qquad (10.14) \\
&= fc + vc \cdot Q + \frac{hc \cdot (P - D)}{2 \cdot P \cdot D} Q^2
\end{aligned}
$$

We then compute the unit costs:

$$TC = \frac{TC}{Q} = \frac{fc}{Q} + vc + \frac{hc \cdot (P - D)}{2PD} Q \qquad (10.15)$$

We find the optimal batch size by setting the first derivative equal to zero:

$$\frac{d(TC)}{dQ} = -\frac{fc}{Q^2} + \frac{hc \cdot (P - D)}{2PD} Q = 0 \qquad (10.16)$$

We establish that the first derivative is monotonically increasing by computing the second derivative, which is positive everywhere assuming the production rate is larger than the demand rate. Equivalently, minimizing the total cost by taking the first derivative and setting it to zero is valid, since the second derivative is positive and this proves that TC is convex with respect to Q.

$$\frac{d^2(TC)}{dQ^2} = \frac{2 \cdot fc}{Q^3} + \frac{hc \cdot (P - D)}{2PD} > 0 \qquad (10.17)$$

The optimal production quantity is then derived.

$$Q^* = \sqrt{\frac{2 \cdot fc \cdot D}{hc \cdot \left(1 - \frac{D}{P} \right)}} \qquad (10.18)$$

This is a generalization of the standard economic order quantity (EOQ) formula for which the production rate is infinite. The optimal batch size can then also be called the economic production quantity (EPQ) for a finite production rate.

The optimal total cost is then given by:

$$TC^* = \frac{hc(P-D)}{2P}\sqrt{\frac{2PD \cdot fc}{hc(P-D)}} + \frac{D}{\sqrt{\dfrac{2PD \cdot fc}{hc(P-D)}}}\left(fc + vc\sqrt{\frac{2PD \cdot fc}{hc(P-D)}}\right)$$

$$= D\left(\frac{2 \cdot fc}{\sqrt{\dfrac{2PD \cdot fc}{hc(P-D)}}} + vc\right)$$

(10.19)

Most of the factors in this equation are beyond the control of the production system. For example, the inventory holding cost hc is determined by the cost of capital and storage in the facility. The only way to reduce the optimal, efficient batch size is then to reduce the fixed or setup cost.

Note that the annual fixed cost is equal to the optimal annual inventory cost

$$FC(Q^*) = CIC(Q^*)$$

Economic Order Quantity with Replenishment Lead Time The inventory system is assumed to have a known annual demand D and constant demand rate d per period. The order product is replenished after a deterministic lead time lt. The reorder point s is the inventory position when an order is placed. The inventory position is equal to the sum of the inventory quantity on-hand and the on-order quantities. The latter are the product quantities that have already been ordered but not yet been delivered. The following notation will be used.

LT lead time expressed in years
lt lead time (expressed in time periods)
dlt demand during the lead time

$$s = dlt = D \cdot LT = d \cdot lt$$
(10.20)

If the lead time is longer than the replenishment cycle then the reorder point will be larger than the order quantity, which is equal to the maximum on-hand inventory. Note that this last equality is based on the assumption that there is no variability in the supply chain and hence there is no need for safety inventory.

Technical Parkas Example The calculations for the technical parkas are given next. Observe that the optimal ordering quantity and the total cost are the same as in the case of the zero lead time. In this case, the parkas are reordered when the inventory position reaches 2700.

$$Q^* = \sqrt{\frac{2 \cdot 450 \cdot 3750}{0.0077 \cdot 95}} = 2149$$

$$TC\left(Q^*\right) = \frac{2149 \cdot 0.0077 \cdot 95}{2} + \frac{450}{2149}3750 = 1570.5$$

$$s = 450 \cdot 6 = 2700$$

Since the reorder point is larger than the ordering quantity, the physical on-hand inventory will be $2700 - 2149 = 551$ parkas at the time orders are placed. Equivalently, because the lead time of 6 weeks is larger than the optimal reorder interval, which is equal to $2149/450 = 4.78$ weeks, the reorder point is larger than the ordering quantity. The maximum on-hand inventory will be 2149 units immediately after a replenishment order has been received, which again assumes that there is no safety inventory.

10.2.3 Stochastic Demand

In most logistics systems, the future conditions are not known with complete certainty but rather exhibit a significant amount of randomness. The future demand is often the parameter that is the most variable and is most often the first parameter for which variability is incorporated explicitly in the inventory models. In order to use scientific methods for the determination of the inventory policy, some information must be known about the future demand. Typically, either the complete demand distribution or at least the expected demand and the standard deviation of the demand are assumed to be known. In practice, either the demand distribution or its mean and standard deviation are based on forecasts. Inventory policies have to be determined for the cases when there is a single opportunity for ordering inventory or when there is a repetitive pattern of order, replenishment, and demand.

Single-Order Inventory Policies The inventory policies of this section apply to logistics systems where a single opportunity to order inventory exists to satisfy some future demand during a finite sales period. The demand is unknown at the time of ordering, but its cumulative demand distribution is assumed to be known. After the sales period has completed, there is no further demand for the product. Examples are the ordering of daily newspapers by the owner of a newspaper stand, ordering of perishable fruit and flowers by a street vendor, ordering of Christmas trees for a charity fund raiser, and the ordering of fashion products with particular styles and colors. In each case the sole decision to be made is how much inventory to order.

Each unit of inventory ordered has a constant purchase price. If not enough inventory has been ordered, a shortage occurs and the vendor could have sold more units during the sales period and made more profit. The potential extra profit per product unit is called the *shortage cost, underage cost*, or *marginal profit*. If too much inventory has been ordered, the vendor is left with excess units after the sales period and these units must be disposed of at a reduced rate, which is called the *salvage value*. The salvage value may even be negative, indicating that the vendor has to pay a third party to dispose of the remaining units. The difference between the purchase price and the salvage value is called the *excess cost, overage cost*, or *marginal loss*. It is the objective of the vendor to order the amount of inventory that minimizes the sum of the expected shortage and excess costs. This amount corresponds to the optimal trad-eoff between the cost of disposing excess items and the loss in profit caused by short-ages. There exist many applications in logistics systems with these characteristics, and as a consequence this problem has been studied extensively. It has been tradition-ally called the *newsboy problem* and is currently known as the *newsvendor problem*.

We will use the following notation

Q	amount of inventory purchased (items), also called ordering quantity
D	actual (unknown) demand during the single period (items)
$f(x)$	demand distribution
$F(x)$	cumulative demand distribution
$\bar{d}$	expected demand during the single period (items)
p	sales price ($/item)
c	purchase price ($/item)
s	salvage value ($/item)
$N(0, 1)$	standard normal cumulative distribution function with mean equal to 0 and standard deviation equal to 1
$N^{-1}(prob)$	inverse of the standard normal cumulative distribution function with mean equal to 0 and standard deviation equal to 1

The shortage cost (c_s), or marginal profit, and the excess cost (c_e), or marginal loss, are then computed as:

$$
\begin{aligned}
c_s = p - c && if\ Q \le D \\
c_e = c - s && if\ Q > D
\end{aligned}
\tag{10.21}
$$

To obtain realistic results, the cost parameters must satisfy the following sequence of inequalities, or equivalently, the shortage cost and excess cost must have positive values.

$$ p > c > s \tag{10.22} $$

If the salvage value were not smaller than the purchase price $(s \ge c)$, then the ven-dor would purchase an infinite inventory, since all unsold items can be disposed of without a loss. Similarly, if the purchase price were not smaller than the sales prices $(c \ge p)$, then the vendor would not purchase any inventory, since each item purchased and sold would cost the vendor money.

For an arbitrary demand distribution $f(x)$ the expected number of items short, called the expected shortage or $E[NS(Q)]$, and the expected number of units still on hand, called the expected excess or $E[NS(Q)]$, corresponding to an initial inventory of Q units are given by the following expressions, respectively.

$$E\left[NS\left(Q\right)\right] = \int_{Q}^{\infty} (x - Q) f\left(x\right) dx \qquad (10.23)$$

$$E\left[NE\left(Q\right)\right] = \int_{0}^{Q} (Q - x) f\left(x\right) dx \qquad (10.24)$$

The expected sum of shortage and excess cost is then given by the product of the unit shortage (excess) cost multiplied by the expected number of items short (in excess).

$$G(Q) = c_e E\left[NE\left(Q\right)\right] + c_s E\left[NS\left(Q\right)\right]$$
$$= c_e \int_{0}^{Q} (Q - x) f\left(x\right) dx + c_s \int_{Q}^{\infty} (x - Q) f\left(x\right) dx \qquad (10.25)$$

To compute the derivative of $G(Q)$ we use Leibniz's rule, which states that

$$\frac{d}{dy} \int_{l(y)}^{u(y)} h\left(x, y\right) dx = \int_{l(y)}^{u(y)} \left(\frac{\partial h\left(x, y\right)}{\partial y} \right) dx + h\left(u\left(y\right), y\right) \frac{du\left(y\right)}{dy}$$
$$- h\left(l\left(y\right), y\right) \frac{dl\left(y\right)}{dy} \qquad (10.26)$$

This yields for the expected sum of shortage and excess costs

$$\frac{dG\left(Q\right)}{dQ} = c_e \int_{0}^{Q} f\left(x\right) dx + c_s \int_{Q}^{\infty} -f\left(x\right) dx$$
$$= c_e F\left(Q\right) - c_s \left(1 - F\left(Q\right)\right) \qquad (10.27)$$

In order for the optimal value of Q to be found where the first derivative equals zero, the first derivative must be negative for an extreme left value of Q, such as $Q=0$, and the second derivative must be positive everywhere, indicating that the first derivative is increasing over the full region of Q.

$$\frac{d^2 G\left(Q\right)}{dQ^2} = (c_s + c_e) f\left(Q\right) \geq 0 \quad \forall Q$$
$$\qquad (10.28)$$
$$\left. \frac{dG\left(Q\right)}{dQ} \right|_{Q=0} = c_e F\left(0\right) - c_s \left(1 - F\left(0\right)\right) = -c_s < 0$$

Since $G(Q)$ satisfies these two conditions, it is a convex function and its globally optimal value can be found by setting its first derivative equal to zero.

$$\frac{dG\left(Q^*\right)}{dQ} = (c_e + c_s) F\left(Q^*\right) - c_s = 0 \qquad (10.29)$$

$$F\left(Q^*\right) = \frac{c_s}{c_e + c_s}$$

$$Q^* = F^{-1}\left(\frac{c_s}{c_e + c_s}\right)$$

(10.30)

Equilibrium theory states that at the optimal inventory level the expected profit of selling one more item equals the expected savings of reducing excess inventory by one item. For the inventory level equal to Q, the probability of selling more equals $1 - F(Q)$, while the probability of selling less equals $F(Q)$.

$$c_s \left(1 - F\left(Q^*\right)\right) = c_e F\left(Q^*\right)$$

$$F\left(Q^*\right) = \frac{c_s}{c_e + c_s} = \frac{p - c}{p - s}$$

(10.31)

The right-hand side of this equation is called the *critical ratio*. This is equivalent to stating that the optimal type-one service level for this system is again given by Eq. (10.31), where the type-one service level gives the probability that all demand in a period is satisfied immediately from on-hand inventory. In other words the critical ratio is equal to the expected in-stock probability at the end of the planning horizon.

If an additional cost (π) were associated with each unit of unsatisfied demand, this cost would be added to the shortage cost in expression (10.31). Additional costs may be caused by the loss of customer goodwill.

$$F\left(Q^*\right) = \frac{c_s}{c_e + c_s} = \frac{\pi + p - c}{\pi + p - s}$$

(10.32)

The optimal service level and corresponding optimal ordering quantity can also be determined by optimizing the expected profit. The profit achieved is a function of the quantity ordered before the sales period starts (Q) and the actual demand observed during the sales period (D). The expression for the profit is then:

$$Profit\,(Q, D) = \begin{cases} pD - cQ + s\,(Q - D) & Q > D \\ (p - c)\,Q & Q \le D \end{cases}$$

(10.33)

$$E\left[Profit\,(Q)\right] = p\int_0^Q x \cdot f\,(x)\,dx + s\int_0^Q (Q - x) \cdot f\,(x)\,dx$$

$$+ pQ\int_Q^\infty f\,(x)\,dx - cQ$$

(10.34)

The first two terms compute the revenue and salvage when the demand does not exceed the purchased supply of items; the third term computes the revenue when the demand exceeds the supply. In either case, the cost of items purchased, indicated by the fourth term $-cQ$, must be subtracted of the expected profit. The only unknown in the expression of the expected profit is the quantity of items purchased. To find the optimal quantity, we compute the derivative using again Leibniz's rule.

$$\frac{dE\left[Profit\left(Q\right)\right]}{dQ} = s \cdot F\left(Q\right) + p \cdot \left[1 - F\left(Q\right)\right] - c \tag{10.35}$$

$$\left.\frac{dE\left[Profit\left(Q\right)\right]}{dQ}\right|_{Q \to 0} = p - c > 0 \tag{10.36}$$

$$\frac{d^2 E\left[Profit(Q)\right]}{dQ^2} = (s - p)f\left(Q\right) < 0 \tag{10.37}$$

The first derivative is positive for $Q=0$ and the second derivative is negative everywhere. This proves that the profit function is concave. Maximizing the profit can then be achieved by setting the first derivative equal to zero and rearranging the terms yields again (10.31).

If the cumulative demand distribution has discrete breakpoints, the optimal Q^* is chosen so that the cumulative demand is no smaller than the computed ratio, i.e., we find the Q^* by rounding up. Alternatively, forward differences can be used to find the optimal inventory value. This technique was used to find the optimal fleet size in the Chap. 4.

If we assume that the demand is normally distributed, the optimal inventory level can be found based on tables of the normal distribution or using a spreadsheet with its built in functions for the inverse normal distribution or the inverse standard normal distribution. In Excel the inverse standard normal distribution function is called NORMSINV. Similar computations can be made for other continuous demand distributions, provided we can compute the mean, standard deviation, and inverse cumulative distribution. For tabular data, the optimal Q^* can be found as the smallest Q for which (10.31) holds.

$$z^* = N^{-1}\left(\frac{c_s}{c_s + c_e}\right) \tag{10.38}$$

$$Q^* = \bar{d} + z^* \cdot \sigma_D$$

Championship T-shirt Vendor Example The Cowpunchers are a football team that perennially wins the league championship title. A street vendor of championship T-shirts must order the T-shirts three days before game day and pay a purchase price of $ 5. The shirts can be sold for $ 15 on game day at the exit gate of the stadium. Based on his sales experience during the previous years, the vendor, who is a Georgia Tech student moonlighting as a street vendor, estimates that the average demand will be 100 shirts, is normally distributed, and that the standard deviation of the demand is 30 shirts. After the game day, the vendor returns to attending classes and donates all unsold shirts to charity.

The cumulative demand distribution at the optimal inventory level Q^* equals

$$F\left(Q^*\right) = \frac{(15-5)}{(15-5)+(5-0)} = \frac{10}{15} = 0.667$$

$$z^* = N^{-1}\,(0.667) = 0.431$$

$$Q^* = \bar{d} + k^*\sigma = 100 + 0.431 \cdot 30 = 112.9 \approx 113$$

The vendor should order 113 shirts.

If he could sell any remaining shirts for \$ 3 per shirt to another street vendor, who will continue selling the shirts on a street corner after game day, then his optimal inventory would increase to

$$F(Q^*) = \frac{(15-5)}{(15-5)+(5-3)} = \frac{10}{12} = 0.833$$

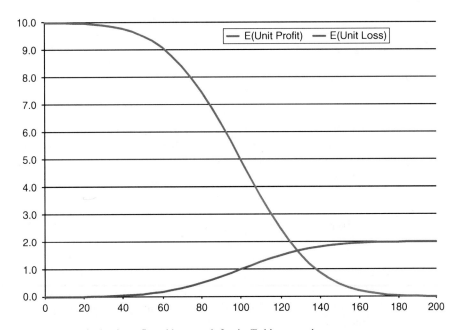

Fig. 10.8 Marginal unit profit and loss graph for the T-shirt example

$$z^* = N^{-1}(0.833) = 0.967$$

$$Q^* = \bar{d} + z^* \cdot \sigma = 100 + 0.967 \cdot 30 = 129.0 \approx 129$$

To further illustrate the critical ratio, the marginal profit and the marginal loss in function of the originally purchased inventory are plotted in Fig. 10.8 The two curves cross each other at the quantity corresponding to the critical ratio.

How to Test If a Distribution is the Normal Distribution The chi-square goodness-of-fit test was originally proposed by Pearson in 1900 to test if an observed frequency distribution conforms to another theoretical distribution by comparing the frequencies of experimental observations to the expected frequencies of the theoretical distribution. The frequencies in any of the intervals should not be less than 5. If this condition is not satisfied, several intervals can be combined to create frequencies not less than 5. The Kolmogorov–Smirnov goodness-of-fit test is preferred if the frequencies in the intervals are small and it can be used for very small frequencies, where the chi-square test does not apply. Hence, the Kolmogorov–Smirnov test is more powerful than the chi-square goodness-of-fit but it cannot be used for discrete distributions. If we are interested in establishing if the experimental data is conformant to the continuous normal distribution, so both test can be used if the frequencies are larger than 5. The following notation is used for the chi-square test.

f_i experimental frequency of interval i
π_i theoretical probability of interval i
N number of observations
K number of intervals

The chi-square test statistic is computed as

$$\chi^2 = \sum_{i=1}^{K} \frac{(f_i - N\pi_i)^2}{N\pi_i} \tag{10.39}$$

The computed chi-square has the value of zero for a perfect fit and is large when the fit is bad. If the computed chi-square value is smaller than the α percentile of the chi-square distribution with $K-1$ degrees of freedom, then the null hypothesis that the data has the theoretical distribution cannot be rejected with an α level of significance. Recall that the level of significance is the probability of a type one error, i.e., the probability of erroneously rejecting the null hypothesis. Finally, deviations from the normal distribution can be detected with the Anderson–Darling test.

Several other less rigorous tests can be used to investigate if the experimental data are conformant to a theoretical normal distribution. If any of the tests fail, then the experimental data is not conformant to a normal distribution. If the data pass all the tests below, then the chi-square goodness-of-fit test can be used to test conformity with a prescribed level of confidence. Such preliminary tests on the experimental data are:

- The coefficient of variation is less than 0.5.

- The probability of a negative demand is less than 2%.
- The probability that the demand is more than the mean plus two standard deviations is less than 2%.

The corresponding formulas are:

$$CV = \frac{\sigma}{\mu} \leq 0.5$$
$$P[x < 0] = F(0) \leq 0.02 \quad\quad (10.40)$$
$$P[x > \mu + 2\sigma] = 1 - F(\mu + 2\sigma) \leq 0.02$$

If the distribution of the cumulative demand is not known or if the inverse cumulative function cannot be easily computed, then the optimal order quantity can be found based on the interval description of the cumulative demand. The accuracy level of the optimal order quantity is then at the interval level but may be increased by interpolation if this is feasible for the inventory system. For instance, it may be possible to order a number of T-shirts different from the interval breakpoints, but it is not possible to order a fractional number of aircraft. If interpolating or rounding are not feasible, the optimal inventory quantity should be rounded up to the next largest feasible value. This property can be shown using the difference calculations. The use of an discrete interval table to describe the demand is illustrated in the following example.

PharmaCorp Flu Vaccine Example The PharmaCorp laboratories are one of the few remaining manufacturers of the annual flu vaccine. The production of the vaccine takes about 6 months and the vaccines are reformulated annually to combat the current mutation of the flu virus. The laboratories sell their vaccine to customers in the United States. The customer orders are received long after the decision on the vaccine manufacturing has been made. PharmaCorp has historical records on the quantities of vaccine ordered by customers in the United States, which includes quantities delivered as well as quantities not delivered. Based on those records, it

Table 10.2 Flu vaccine example demand data

Interval		
Lower bound	Upper bound	Probability
0	5	0.05
5	10	0.06
10	15	0.20
15	20	0.06
20	25	0.00
25	30	0.00
30	35	0.00
35	40	0.05
40	45	0.13
45	50	0.30
50	55	0.10
55	60	0.05

Table 10.3 Flu vaccine example solution

Interval			
Lower bound	Upper bound	Probability	Cumulative probability
0	5	0.05	0.05
5	10	0.06	0.11
10	15	0.20	0.31
15	20	0.06	0.37
20	25	0.00	0.37
25	30	0.00	0.37
30	35	0.00	0.37
35	40	0.05	0.42
40	45	0.13	0.55
45	50	0.30	0.85
50	55	0.10	0.95
55	60	0.05	1.00

has computed the following demand probabilities in Table 10.2. All demand quantities are expressed in millions of doses (Mu).

It costs PharmaCorp 4.87 € to produce one dose of vaccine. It sells one dose for 11.67 €. All unsold vaccine doses are destroyed at a cost of 1.18 € per dose.

The cumulative demand distribution at the optimal inventory level Q^* is given by the following calculation.

$$F\left(Q^*\right) = \frac{(11.67 - 4.87)}{(11.67 - 4.87) + (4.87 - (-1.18))} = \frac{6.80}{12.85} = 0.53$$

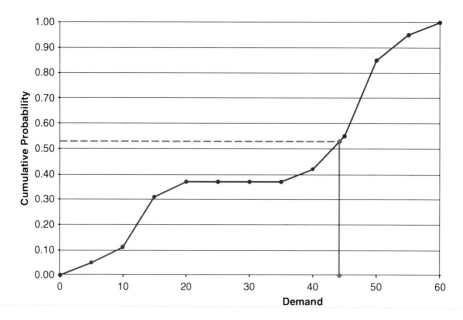

Fig. 10.9 Flu vaccine example cumulative demand and optimal manufacturing quantity

The cumulative demand distribution for the intervals is given in Table 10.3. The optimal number of doses to manufacture falls in the interval of 40–45 Mu.

If it is assumed that the demands inside an interval are equally likely or, equivalently, that the demand is uniformly distributed inside each interval, then the graph of the cumulative demand distribution is a concatenation of linear segments. The optimal number of doses can then be found by interpolation inside the interval and is equal to 44.2. The cumulative demand distribution and the optimal number of doses under this assumption are shown in Fig. 10.9. However, if the production can only occur in multiples of 5 Mu then optimal production quantity would be found by rounding up to the end point of the interval and would be equal to 45 Mu.

It has already been established that the critical ratio determines the type one service level using the inverse of the cumulative demand distribution. In the following the type two service level is derived for this inventory policy. Recall that the expected number of items short is equal to

$$ns\,(s) = E\,[NS\,(s)] = \int_{s}^{\infty} (x - s)f\,(x)\,dx \tag{10.41}$$

The above formula is valid for any continuous demand distribution $f(x)$. If the demand has the standard normal distribution $\phi(t)=N(0, 1)$, then the expected number of items short is denoted by the unit loss function $L(z)$.

$$L\,(z) = \int_{z}^{\infty} (x - z)\phi\,(x)\,dx \tag{10.42}$$

The unit loss function can be computed with the following formula, where $\Phi(z)$ is the cumulative standard normal distribution function.

$$L\,(z) = \phi\,(z) - z\,(1 - \Phi\,(z)) \tag{10.43}$$

This formula is derived next. The density function of the standard normal distribution is

$$\phi\,(t) = N\,(0, 1) = \frac{1}{\sqrt{2\pi}} e^{-z^2/2} \tag{10.44}$$

Differentiating this density function yields

$$\frac{d\phi\,(z)}{dz} = -z\frac{1}{\sqrt{2\pi}} e^{-z^2/2} = -z\phi\,(z) \tag{10.45}$$

The unit loss function is then equal to

$$
\begin{aligned}
L(z) &= \int_{z}^{\infty} (x - z)\phi\,(x)\,dx \\
&= \int_{z}^{\infty} x\phi\,(x)\,dx - \int_{z}^{\infty} z\phi\,(x)\,dx \\
&= -\phi\,(x)|_{z}^{\infty} - z\,(\Phi\,(\infty) - \Phi\,(z)) \\
&= \phi\,(z) - z\,(1 - \Phi\,(z))
\end{aligned}
$$

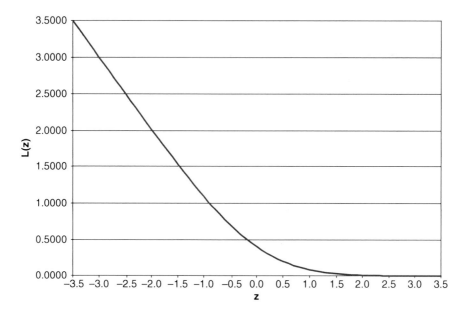

Fig. 10.10 Unit loss function

The unit loss function can thus be computed with the following Excel formula.

$$L(z) = Normdist(z, 0, 1, 0) - z * (1 - Normsdist(z)) \qquad (10.46)$$

The unit loss function $L(z)$ is shown in Fig. 10.10. Realistic arguments for the z-statistic will have positive values; otherwise the reorder point would be less than the expected demand during the lead time. A numerical table of the unit loss function for positive values of the z-statistic and a more detailed graph for positive z-statistic values is provided in the Appendix. Recall that the unit loss function assumes that the demand distribution is the standard normal distribution, which implies that negative normalized demand is possible. It is an intuitive result that given a reorder point of 3.5, the changes that the demand exceeds 3.5 are very small and thus the expected shortage is nearly zero. However, it is not nearly as intuitive that for a reorder point of 0, which implies that the reorder point is equal to the expected demand during the lead time, the expected shortage equals approximately 0.40. Note that the value at $z=$ of $\phi(z)$ is equal to 0.399 or approximately 0.4. For an initial inventory of 0, the probability that there will be a shortage is 0.5, but the expected value of that shortage is 0.40. Equivalently, for an initial inventory equal to zero and given that the demand is positive, the conditional expected value of that demand is 0.40.

If the demand is normally distributed, the expected shortage can be computed from the expected shortage of the standard normal distribution given by the unit loss function, through the following transformation.

$$ns(s) = sd \cdot L\left(\frac{s - d \cdot lt}{sd}\right) = sd \cdot L(z) \qquad (10.47)$$

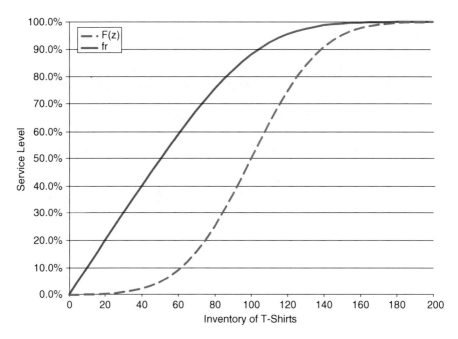

Fig. 10.11 Comparison of type 1 and type 2 service levels for the T-shirt example

Finally, we can compute the partial derivative of the expected shortage by applying Leibniz's rule. Details of that derivation are shown in the appendix. This yields the following expression for the derivative.

$$\frac{\partial ns\,(s)}{\partial s} = -\,(1 - F\,(s)) \tag{10.48}$$

The values of the two service levels in function of the initial inventory are given in Fig. 10.11 for the t-shirt example. For this figure a salvage value equal to \$ 3 was used. The type two service level is always larger than the type one service level. For this example, the expected demand was 100 T-shirts. If the initial inventory purchased is also equal to 100 T-shirts, then the type one service level is 0.5 since the vendor is just as likely to run out of T-shirts than to have any remaining inventory. However, the type two service level is approximately 88% when just ordering the expected demand.

The calculations to derive the fill rate for the initial inventory of 130, which corresponds to the critical ratio, are given next. Previously it has been determined that the optimal value of the z-statistic is 0.967.

$$L\,(0.967) = \phi\,(z) - z \cdot (1 - \Phi\,(z)) = \phi\,(0.967) - 0.967 \cdot (1 - \Phi\,(0.967)) = 0.083$$
$$NS\,(0.967) = L\,(z) \cdot \sigma = 0.083 \cdot 30 = 2.5$$
$$fr = 1 - \frac{NS}{\mu} = 1 - \frac{2.5}{100} = 97.5\%$$

The previous calculations assumed that the demand was normally distributed. If the demand distribution is different from the normal distribution or if the demand is given in an interval table, then a different method is required for computing $ns(Q)$. Any demand distribution can always be approximated by an interval table, so the method for an interval table covers both cases. The intervals are assumed to be sorted by increasing cumulative distribution values, i.e., it is assumed that the cumulative distribution is given for N intervals for with as upper bounds Q_1, Q_2, ... Q_N and that $F(Q_1) \leq F(Q_2) \leq ... \leq F(Q_N)$. $ns(Q)$ can be computed with the following initialization and recursive equations, where k indicates the interval in the table.

$$ns\,(0) = \bar{d} \tag{10.49}$$

$$ns\,(Q_1) = \bar{d} - Q_1 \tag{10.50}$$

$$ns(Q_{k+1}) = ns(Q_k) - (Q_{k+1} - Q_k) \cdot (1 - F(Q_k)) \tag{10.51}$$

The derivation of these equations is shown in Appendix A. Computing the $ns(Q)$ for the case of a discrete demand distribution is illustrated next using the flu vaccine example. Recall that the optimal type 1 service level is equal to 53%. To simplify the notation, the cumulative distribution function at the lower bound of the first interval will be denoted by $F(Q_0)$ and its value is by definition equal to zero. First the average demand will computed followed by the computation of the expected lost sales for the first interval and then recursively for the following intervals. Finally, the fill rate for each interval is calculated. The detailed calculations for the first two intervals are shown next. The calculations for all intervals are summarized in Table 10.4.

Table 10.4 Expected lost sales and type service level for the flu vaccine example	k	Q	F(Q)	ns(Q)	fr (%)
	1	5	0.05	31.4	13.7
	2	10	0.11	26.7	26.8
	3	15	0.31	22.2	39.0
	4	20	0.37	18.8	48.5
	5	25	0.37	15.6	57.1
	6	30	0.37	12.5	65.8
	7	35	0.37	9.3	74.5
	8	40	0.42	6.2	83.1
	9	45	0.55	3.3	91.1
	10	50	0.85	1.0	97.3
	11	55	0.95	0.2	99.3
	12	60	1.00	0.0	100.0

$$F(Q_0) = 0$$

$$\bar{d} = \sum_{k=1}^{N} Q_k \cdot (F(Q_k) - F(Q_{k-1})) = 36.4$$

$$ns(Q_1) = ns(5) = \bar{d} - Q_1 = 36.4 - 5 = 31.4$$

$$ns(Q_2) = ns(10) = ns(Q_1) - (Q_2 - Q_1) \cdot (1 - F(Q_k))$$
$$= 31.4 - (10 - 5) \cdot (1 - 0.05) = 26.7$$

$$fr(Q_2) = fr(10) = 1 - \frac{ns(Q_2)}{\bar{d}} = 1 - \frac{26.7}{36.4} = 0.268$$

If initially 45 Mu are manufactured, which corresponds to the interval that contains the critical ratio, then the type two service level is equal to 91%. These expressions for the loss function are also useful when the demand has a distribution that is very different of the normal distribution. A prime example is the demand for complex and specialized service or repair components, which are often requested infrequently and in small discrete quantities. Given those assumptions, the demand distribution is more accurately modeled by a discrete Poisson distribution. The probability mass function of the Poisson distribution is given by the following formula, where k is the number of occurrences and λ is the expected number of occurrences during a specific time interval. Based on the probability mass function the cumulative demand distribution and the loss function can then be computed. These calculations are typically organized in an interval table.

$$f(k, \lambda) = \frac{\lambda^k e^{-\lambda}}{k!} \tag{10.52}$$

Safety Inventory The safety inventory is inventory held to buffer against the variability of future conditions. In the following derivations of inventory policies it is assumed that both the future demand and the replenishment lead time are not known with certainty, but that information on their probability distribution is known. The inventory policies for these assumptions can be divided into continuous review and periodic review policies. Several optimal policies and one practical policy will be derived for each of the two classes.

Continuous Review Policies Continuous review policies monitor continuously the inventory position. When the inventory position equals or falls below the order point a fixed quantity is ordered. The two decision variables are the order point s and the fixed order quantity Q. Depending on the cost components that are to be minimized or on the type of service constraints that are to be observed, different expressions for the optimal s and Q are derived. These policies adjust the time between order placements depending on the demand. This type of continuous review with fixed-order quantity inventory policies are also referred to as (R, Q) policies in many publications. In this manuscript R will be used to denote the reorder time interval for fixed-order frequency policies.

Stochastic Lead Time Typically the first source of variability considered is the customer demand. In the following, the lead time before the replenishment arrives is also considered to be not known with certainty. In other words it is no longer considered deterministic but becomes a stochastic variable. There are now two sources of variability for the demand during the lead time and they interact. The first source is the variability of the demand per observation period; the second source is the length of lead time expressed in observation periods. If those two factors are independent, then the variance of the demand during the lead time is then given by the sum of the variances of all the contributing terms. The following notation will be used.

Var_x variance of stochastic variable x
s_x standard deviation of the stochastic variable x
CV_x coefficient of variation of the stochastic variable x
SI safety inventory
SIC safety inventory cost
AI average inventory
MI maximum inventory during the cycle
$N^{-1}(x)$ the inverse of the cumulative normal distribution function

The coefficient of variation is defined as the ratio of the standard deviation over the mean of a distribution. A larger coefficient of variation indicates higher variability. The coefficient of variation is a dimensionless measure and is often expressed in percent.

$$CV_x = \frac{\sqrt{Var_x}}{E[x]} = \frac{s_x}{\bar{x}} \qquad (10.53)$$

The mean and variance of a random variable that is the product of two other independent random variables can be computed in function of the mean and variance of the two factors. For inventory policies the demand during the lead time is the product of the demand during one observation period and the length of the lead time expressed in observation periods.

$$E[dlt] = E[d] \cdot E[lt] \qquad (10.54)$$

To simplify notation, the expected value operator $E[]$ will be omitted if there is no confusion possible.

$$dlt = \bar{d} \cdot lt \qquad (10.55)$$

$$Var_{dlt} = \sum_{lt} Var_d + \bar{d}^2 \cdot Var_{lt} = lt \cdot Var_d + \bar{d}^2 \cdot Var_{lt} \qquad (10.56)$$

Observe that all the terms in the previous formula have consistent dimensions equal to items-of-product squared since the lead time is considered a dimensionless scaling factor, i.e., lt is the number of observation periods whose duration add up to the lead time and $\bar{d}$ is the expected demand during one period with dimensions equal to items-of-product. Numerically the expected demand during one period $\bar{d}$ is equal to demand rate d and the symbols are often used interchangeably in equations. Compared to the case with a deterministic lead time, the standard deviation of the demand during the lead time and the corresponding safety stock level will increase.

$$SI = k \cdot \sqrt{lt \cdot Var_d + \bar{d}^2 \cdot Var_{lt}} \tag{10.57}$$

$$SIC = HCR \cdot v \cdot SI \tag{10.58}$$

Often the safety inventory is set to a multiple of the demand rate. For example, this practice may be stated as "the safety inventory is 3 weeks of demand." Using the coefficient of variation of the demand distribution, an expression for the safety inventory can be derived that captures this practice.

$$CV_d = \frac{\sqrt{Var_d}}{d} = \frac{s_d}{d}$$
$$Var_d = (CV_d \cdot d)^2 \tag{10.59}$$

$$SI = k \cdot \sqrt{lt \cdot CV_d^2 + Var_{lt}} \cdot \bar{d} \tag{10.60}$$

In the above expression for the safety inventory, the proportionality factor for the demand is equal to the product of the factor in function of the service level (k) and the factor in function of the variability of the demand during the lead time. The appropriate value of k will be determined for the various inventory policies.

(s, Q) Policies: Sequential Determination of Q and s Based on Type 1 Service Level A service level requirement of type 1 limits the probability that a stockout will occur during an inventory cycle. It achieves this service level by placing a

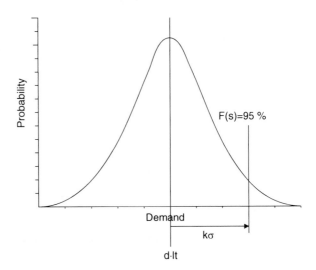

Fig. 10.12 Distribution of the demand during the lead time

replenishment order before the inventory drops to the level equal to the expected demand during the lead time plus a safety buffer depending on the required probability. The reorder point is thus larger than the expected demand for practical cases, where the required probability is larger than 50%. The higher the service level, the bigger the difference between the reorder point and the expected demand. This principle is illustrated in Fig. 10.12, where for illustration purposes a service level of 95% was required.

The inventory policy has to determine two parameters. For the classic (s, Q) policy, the parameters can be determined independently, i.e., one parameter after another or sequentially. In this sequential procedure, the optimal order quantity is first determined with the EOQ formula (10.11).

$$Q^* = \sqrt{\frac{2 \cdot D \cdot oc}{hc}} \tag{10.61}$$

The reorder point is then computed based on the variability of the demand during the lead time and required service level α of type one. In the following equations it is assumed that the demand is normally distributed but any other demand distribution can be used provided its inverse can be computed.

$$
\begin{aligned}
s_{dlt} &= \sqrt{lt \cdot s_d^2 + d^2 \cdot Var_{lt}} = d\sqrt{lt \cdot CV_d^2 + Var_{lt}} \\
z &= N^{-1}(\alpha) \\
s^* &= d \cdot lt + z \cdot s_{dlt}
\end{aligned} \tag{10.62}
$$

The average inventory in the system is now the sum of the cycle inventory and the safety inventory. The corresponding formulas for the average inventory and the total cost are shown next.

$$AI = CI + SI = \frac{Q}{2} + (s - d \cdot lt) \tag{10.63}$$

$$TC = \frac{D}{Q}oc + hc\frac{Q}{2} + hc \cdot (s - d \cdot lt) \tag{10.64}$$

It should be noted that the safety inventory is computed as the difference between the reorder point and the expected demand during the lead time. This expression is correct even if the reorder point is larger than the reorder quantity. In this case, the inventory on-order but not yet delivered is part of the inventory position, but it is not part of the safety inventory and so no inventory holding cost has to be paid for it.

Technical Parkas Example The inventory policy variables for the technical parkas are computed next, assuming a type 1 service level no less than 97%. First the reorder quantity is computed with the EOQ expression.

$$Q^* = \sqrt{\frac{2 \cdot 450 \cdot 3750}{0.0077 \cdot 95}} = 2149$$

In this particular example, because the lead time of 6 weeks is larger than the optimal reorder interval, which is equal to $2149/450=4.78$ weeks, the reorder point is larger than the ordering quantity. The maximum inventory (MI) will occur at the arrival of the replenishment order.

$$s_{dlt} = \sqrt{6 \cdot 127^2 + 450^2 \cdot 1.5^2} = 743.24$$
$$z = N^{-1}(0.97) = 1.88$$
$$s = 450 \cdot 6 + 1.88 \cdot 743.24 = 4098$$
$$SI = 4098 - 2700 = 1398$$
$$MI = 1398 + 2149 = 3547$$

$$TC(Q^*) = \frac{2149 \cdot 0.0077 \cdot 95}{2} + \frac{450}{2149} 3750 + (4098 - 2700) \cdot 0.0077 \cdot 95 = 2592$$

(s, Q) Policies: Sequential Determination of Q and s Using Shortage Costs This policy attempts to minimize the sum of the cycle inventory cost and safety inventory cost for a required service level of type 1. In addition, it evaluates the impact of choosing the reorder point by adding to the above inventory cost the shortage cost associated with items that could not be supplied in response to customer demand. The last cost component is called the shortage cost. In order to compute the shortage cost, we first need to compute the expected number of items short during a cycle corresponding to a reorder point s.

The expected shortage is the expected number of items short per replenishment cycle. To compute the shortage cost over the planning horizon we have to multiply the expected shortage by the unit shortage cost and by the number of cycles in the planning period. This yields the following expression for the total inventory cost, where z is the z-statistic corresponding to maximum no-stock out probability, i.e. the service level of type one. The equations assume that the demand is normally distributed.

$$TC(Q) = \frac{D}{Q}oc + hc\frac{Q}{2} + hc \cdot (s - d \cdot lt) + \frac{D}{Q}sc \cdot s_{dlt} \cdot L(z)$$
$$TC(s, Q) = \frac{D}{Q}(oc + sc \cdot ns(s)) + hc\left(\frac{Q}{2} + s - d \cdot lt\right)$$

(10.65)

Technical Parkas Example Southern Ascent estimates that the unit shortage cost for a technical parka equals \$ 150. The inventory policy variables for the technical parkas are computed next, assuming a type 1 service level no less than 97% and a unit shortage cost of \$ 150 and a normally distributed demand.

$$Q^* = \sqrt{\frac{2 \cdot 450 \cdot 3750}{0.0077 \cdot 95}} = 2149$$

$$s_{dlt} = \sqrt{6 \cdot 127^2 + 450^2 \cdot 1.5^2} = 743.24$$
$$z = N^{-1}(0.97) = 1.88$$
$$s = 450 \cdot 6 + 1.88 \cdot 743.24 = 4098$$
$$SI = 4098 - 2700 = 1398$$
$$MI = 1398 + 2149 = 3547$$
$$L(1.88) = 0.0116$$
$$ns(4098) = 0.0116 \cdot 743.24 = 8.635$$

$$TC\left(Q^*\right) = 0.0077 \cdot 95 \left(\frac{2149}{2} + (4098 - 2700)\right) + \frac{450}{2149} (3750 + 150 \cdot 8.635)$$

$$= 2863$$

(s, Q) Policies: Simultaneous Determination of Q and s Using Shortage Costs Up to this point the optimal ordering quantity and the reorder point have been computed sequentially because they were assumed to be independent. The introduction of the shortage cost component in the objective function made that assumption invalid. The previous sequential and heuristic policy optimizes the reorder point first so that the sum of the cycle inventory and ordering cost are minimized subject to the service constraint and then evaluates the impact of the reorder point with the sum of ordering, inventory, and shortage costs. The following policy attempts to minimize the sum of the ordering, cycle inventory, safety inventory, and shortage costs.

Recall that the total cost is given by Eq. (10.65). This equation has the same structure with respect to Q as the basic EOQ formula and thus the same convexity properties with respect to Q. We can minimize the total cost by setting the first derivative equal to zero.

$$\frac{dTC\,(s,Q)}{dQ} = \frac{hc}{2} - \frac{D\,(oc + sc \cdot ns\,(s))}{Q^2} \tag{10.66}$$

This yields the following optimal order quantity.

$$Q^* = \sqrt{\frac{2D\left[oc + sc \cdot ns\,(s^*)\right]}{hc}} = \sqrt{\frac{2D\left[oc + sc \cdot s_{dlt} \cdot L\,(z^*)\right]}{hc}} \tag{10.67}$$

The expression for the optimal order quantity includes the optimal reorder point, or equivalently, the z-statistic corresponding to the optimal safety stock, which is not known. The total cost is also a function of $ns(s)$ which also depends on the z-statistic.

The resulting problem is a nonlinear optimization problem in two decision variables Q and s, or equivalently, in Q and z. The optimal order quantity and optimal z-statistic can be computed with an iterative search algorithm. During each iteration, the optimal reorder quantity is computed first while the reorder point is held constant and then the optimal reorder point is computed next while the order quantity is held constant. This search method is called the *cyclical coordinates method* and corresponds to a sequence of perpendicular improvement steps along the reorder quantity and reorder point axes. The iterative procedure starts with the EOQ as initial value for the optimal order quantity.

$$Q^0 = \sqrt{\frac{2 \cdot D \cdot oc}{hc}} \tag{10.68}$$

The first derivative with respect to s of the total cost is equal to

$$\frac{dTC\,(s,Q)}{ds} = hc + \frac{D \cdot sc}{Q} \cdot \frac{dns\,(s)}{ds} \tag{10.69}$$

Recall that the derivative of the expected shortage is given by (10.48). Rearranging the condition that the first derivative of the total cost with respect to s equals zero yields the following expression.

$$\frac{dTC\,(s,Q)}{ds} = hc - \frac{D \cdot sc}{Q} \cdot (1 - F\,(s)) = 0 \tag{10.70}$$

This expression can be rearranged to yield the following expression.

$$F\,(s) = 1 - \frac{Q \cdot hc}{D \cdot sc} \tag{10.71}$$

Based on the inverse cumulative demand distribution, the z-statistic as well as the optimal reorder point can then be computed

$$z = F^{-1}\left(1 - \frac{Q \cdot hc}{D \cdot sc}\right) \tag{10.72}$$

$$s = d \cdot lt + z \cdot s_{dlt} \tag{10.73}$$

A new value for the optimal order quantity can then be computed in function of the reorder point.

$$Q = \sqrt{\frac{2D\left[oc + sc \cdot ns\,(s)\right]}{hc}} = \sqrt{\frac{2D\left[oc + sc \cdot s_{dlt} \cdot L\,(z)\right]}{hc}} \tag{10.74}$$

The algorithm iterates through these steps until there are no significant changes in the values of the order quantity or the reorder point.

Technical Parkas Example The following calculations correspond to the first iteration for the technical park as example. The nonnegative superscripts on the variables indicate the iteration; a superscript equal to negative one indicates the inverse function.

$$Q^0 = \sqrt{\frac{2 \cdot 450 \cdot 3750}{0.0077 \cdot 95}} = 2149.1$$

$$F^1\,(s) = 1 - \frac{Q^0 \cdot hc}{D \cdot sc} = 1 - \frac{2149.1 \cdot 0.0077 \cdot 95}{450 \cdot 150} = 1 - 0.0233 = 0.9767$$

$$z^1 = F^{-1}\left(1 - \frac{Q^0 \cdot hc}{D \cdot sc}\right) = N^{-1}\,(0.9767) = 1.9905$$

$$s^1 = d \cdot lt + z^1 \cdot s_{dlt} = 450 \cdot 6 + 1.9905 \cdot 743 = 4179.4$$

Table 10.5 Inventory example iterative algorithm for type 1 service level with shortage costs

Q	$F(s)$	z	s	$L(z)$	$n(s)$
2149.1	0.9767	1.9905	4179.4	0.0087	6.4725
2411.2	0.9739	1.9414	4142.9	0.0099	7.3730
2445.5	0.9735	1.9353	4138.4	0.0101	7.4919
2450.0	0.9735	1.9345	4137.8	0.0101	7.5075
2450.6	0.9735	1.9344	4137.7	0.0101	7.5095

$$L\left(z^1\right) = L\left(1.9905\right) = 0.0087$$

$$ns^1\left(s^1\right) = s_{dlt} \cdot L\left(z^1\right) = 743 \cdot 0.008 = 6.4725$$

$$Q^1 = \sqrt{\frac{2D\left(oc + sc \cdot ns^1\left(s^1\right)\right)}{hc}} = \sqrt{\frac{2 \cdot 450 \cdot \left(3750 + 150 \cdot 6.4725\right)}{0.0077 \cdot 95}} = 2411.2$$

The calculations for the next iterations are summarized in Table 10.5. After five iterations the values for Q and s have converged with sufficient accuracy. Finally, those values have to be converted to integer values, since the inventory and order quantity can only be in whole units. The optimal order quantity is thus 2451 and the optimal reorder point is 4138.

(s, Q) Policies: Sequential Determination of Q and s Based on Type 2 Service Level This policy attempts to minimize the sum of the cycle inventory cost and safety inventory cost, subject to the restriction that the fill rate must be no smaller than a given value. Previously, the expected number of items backordered at the end of a single cycle was defined as $ns(s)$. The expected number of cycles per year is equal to D/Q. The fill rate or long-range average ratio of the number of items delivered from inventory over the total demand is then equal to

$$fr = 1 - \frac{(D/Q)\,ns\,(s)}{D} = 1 - \frac{ns\,(s)}{Q} \tag{10.75}$$

The resulting problem is again a nonlinear optimization problem in two variables Q and s, or equivalently Q and z. If it is assumed that those variables can be determined independently then a sequential algorithm will suffice. In the sequential method, the order quantity is determined first with the EOQ expression. Based on the optimal order quantity and desired type 2 service level the reorder point is then determined.

$$Q = \sqrt{\frac{2 \cdot oc \cdot D}{hc}}$$

$$ns\,(s) = Q\,(1 - fr) \tag{10.76}$$

$$z = NS^{-1}\,(ns\,(s)) = NS^{-1}\,(Q\,(1 - fr))$$

$$s = d \cdot LT + z \cdot s_{dlt}$$

For general demand distributions, the inverse function of the expected shortage $NS^{-1}(x)$ may not available or easily computable. If it is assumed that the demand is normally distributed, then this inverse can be computed using the unit loss function.

$$Q = \sqrt{\frac{2 \cdot oc \cdot D}{hc}}$$

$$L(z) = \frac{Q(1 - fr)}{s_{dlt}} \tag{10.77}$$

$$z = L^{-1}\left(\frac{Q(1 - fr)}{s_{dlt}}\right)$$

$$s = d \cdot LT + z \cdot s_{dlt}$$

The average inventory and total cost are then computed with the same formulas used for the type 1 service level. Observe that these formulas do not include shortage costs, since the required service level is modeled as a constraint.

$$AI = CI + SI = \frac{Q}{2} + (s - d \cdot LT) \tag{10.78}$$

$$TC = \frac{D}{Q}oc + hc\frac{Q}{2} + hc \cdot (s - d \cdot LT) \tag{10.79}$$

Technical Parkas Example For the Technical Parkas example, the numerical values can then be computed as follows.

$$Q = \sqrt{\frac{2 \cdot 450 \cdot 3750}{0.0077 \cdot 95}} = 2149$$

$$L(z) = \frac{2149(1 - 0.97)}{743} = 0.0867$$

$$z = L^{-1}(0.0867) = 0.9786$$

$$s = 450 \cdot 6 + 0.9786 \cdot 743 = 3427$$

$$TC(Q^*) = 0.0077 \cdot 95\left(\frac{2149}{2} + (3427 - 2700)\right) + \frac{450}{2149} \cdot 3750 = 2102$$

(s, Q) Policies: Simultaneous Determination of Q and s Based on Type 2 Service Level The previous policy computes the optimal order quantity with the EOQ formulas and then derives the optimal reorder point based on that order quantity. This sequential determination of the optimal order quantity and order point assumes that those two decision variables are independent. The simultaneous determination of the optimal quantities yields two nonlinear equations in function of Q and s, where

Q depends on s and s depends on Q. The derivation of equation of optimal value of Q in function of s is shown in Appendix B. Since the independence assumption is invalid, the solution values generated by the sequential algorithm may be suboptimal. Assuming that the demand is normally distributed, the equations can be solved with the cyclical coordinates iterative search algorithm. The sequential algorithm is then identical to the first iteration of the iterative search algorithm.

$$Q^0 = \sqrt{\frac{2 \cdot oc \cdot D}{hc}}$$

$$ns(s) = Q\,(1 - fr)$$

$$L(z) = \frac{Q(1 - fr)}{s_{dlt}} \tag{10.80}$$

$$z = L^{-1}\left(\frac{Q(1 - fr)}{s_{dlt}}\right)$$

$$s = d \cdot lt + z \cdot s_{dlt}$$

$$Q = \frac{ns\,(s)}{1 - F\,(s)} + \sqrt{\frac{2 \cdot oc \cdot D}{hc} + \left(\frac{ns\,(s)}{1 - F\,(s)}\right)^2}$$

Technical Parkas Example The numerical calculations for the first iteration of the Technical Parkas example are given next. Again the nonnegative superscripts on the variables indicate the iteration and a superscript equal to negative one indicates the inverse function.

$$Q^0 = \sqrt{\frac{2 \cdot 450 \cdot 3750}{0.0077 \cdot 95}} = 2149.1$$

$$ns\,(s) = 2149.1 \cdot (1 - 0.97) = 64.47$$

$$L\left(z^1\right) = \frac{2149\,(1 - 0.97)}{743} = 0.0867$$

$$z^1 = L^{-1}\,(0.0867) = 0.9786$$

$$s^1 = 450 \cdot 6 + 0.9786 \cdot 743 = 3427.3$$

$$F\left(s^1\right) = N\left(z^1\right) = N\,(0.9786) = 0.8361$$

$$Q^1 = \frac{64.47}{1 - 0.8361} + \sqrt{\frac{2 \cdot 3750 \cdot 450}{0.0077 \cdot 95} + \left(\frac{64.47}{1 - 0.8361}\right)^2} = 2578.1$$

The calculations for the next iterations are summarized in Table 10.6. After four iterations the values for Q and s have converged with sufficient accuracy. Finally,

Table 10.6 Inventory example iterative algorithm for type 2 service level

Q	n(s)	L(z)	z	s	F(s)
2149.1	64.47	0.0867	0.9786	3427.3	0.8361
2578.1	77.34	0.1041	0.8804	3354.3	0.8107
2596.1	77.88	0.1048	0.8766	3351.5	0.8096
2596.8	77.90	0.1048	0.8764	3351.4	0.8096

those values have to be converted to integer values, since the inventory and order quantity can only be in whole units. The optimal order quantity is thus 2597 and the optimal reorder point is 3352.

The values of Q and s are then rounded to the nearest integer and the total cost is computed.

$$TC = 0.0077 \cdot 95 \left(\frac{2597}{2} + (3351 - 2700) \right) + \frac{450}{2597} \cdot 3750 = 2074.8$$

In practice, the optimal reorder quantity is typically rounded up to a multiple of the package size, which for this example may be 2600 units. This should be followed by the computation of the optimal z and s for that order quantity.

When the inventory policy is based on a service level constraint, the shortage cost is not used in the objective function. However, the resulting inventory policy corresponds to an implicit value of the shortage cost called the *derived shortage cost*. This derived shortage cost can be computed and used as a validation test for the service level that was required.

$$sc = \frac{Q \cdot hc}{D \cdot (1 - F(s))} \tag{10.81}$$

Technical Parkas Example For the Technical Parkas example, the derived shortage cost is then

$$sc = \frac{Q \cdot hc}{D \cdot (1 - F(s))} = \frac{2597 \cdot 0.0077 \cdot 95}{450 \cdot (1 - 0.8096)} = 22.15$$

For this particular example, the derived shortage cost is much smaller than the shortage cost estimated by the company. This would indicate that the required service level is set to low. Increasing the service level requirement would increase the total cost of the inventory policy, but this would be compensated for by a lower total shortage cost. In other words, the company would increase its profit from the sales of the parkas, if it set the service level requirement of the parkas to a higher fraction.

The optimal values of the optimal order quantity and reorder point for the different inventory policies are summarized in Table 10.7. It should be noted that the different inventory policies provide different service levels and different total costs through their choices of order quantities and reorder points. Given an imprecise requirement of a 97% service level without a type of service level qualifier, the

Table 10.7 Inventory example results summary

Type	Q	s	TC	SI	AI	F(s) (%)	fr (%)
Deterministic demand	2149	0	1570.5	0	1075	100.0	100.0
Det. demand + lead time	2149	2700	1570.5	0	1075	100.0	100.0
Type 1 service (indepedent)	2149	4098	2592.1	1398	2473	97.0	99.6
Shortage cost (sequential)	2149	4098	2863.3	1398	2473	97.0	99.6
Shortage cost (iterative)	2451	4138	2842.0	1438	2664	97.3	99.7
Type 2 service (sequential)	2149	3427	2102.1	727	1802	83.6	97.0
Type 2 service (iterative)	2597	3351	2074.8	651	1950	81.0	97.0

optimal total cost increases from \$ 2074.8 for a type 2 service level to \$ 2592.1 for a type 1 service level. This represents a 25% increase in the total cost for a single SKU. The total cost differential can be very large for companies with many hundreds of thousands of SKUs.

Two-Bin Policies as a Special Case of (s, Q) Policies The two-bin policy is a common inventory policy that has as its prime advantage that it is very easy to implement and manage. The items in stock are assumed to be stored in two identical bins. The current demand is withdrawn from one bin. As soon as that bin becomes empty, items are being withdrawn from the other bin and a replenishment order is placed for items sufficient to fill the first bin. The two-bin policy is a variant of the *(s, Q)* inventory policies where both the order quantity and reorder point are identical to the number of items in a bin.

$$Q = s \tag{10.82}$$

The two-bin policy is often used for items that are of lesser value or when there is no infrastructure to track withdrawals or forecast the demand. Typical examples are screws and nuts in manufacturing, packaging materials in distribution centers, and inexpensive office supplies such as pens. If the lead time exceeds the inventory cycle time, the inventory policy can be extended to a three-bin, four-bin, etc., policy. In these cases, $s = 2Q$ or $3Q$.

Periodic Review Policies

(R, s, S) Policies A second major class of inventory policies reviews the inventory position at regular intervals. If the inventory position is at or below the reorder point, an order is placed to bring the inventory position up to the order-up-to point. There are thus three decisions to be made: the frequency or time interval R, the reorder point s, and the order-up-to quantity S. Those policies are denoted by *(R, s, S)* policies. These policies adjust the amount order based on the observed demand during the interval. The simultaneous optimization of these three variables is extremely difficult. As a consequence, optimal *(R, s, S)* policies are almost never used in practice.

(s, S) Policies In real-world inventory systems, the choices for R are usually limited to a small number of discrete values. Deliveries typically occur with a natural fre-

quency, such as daily, once or twice a week, every 2 weeks, etc. The determination of the optimal R order interval can be easily achieved by complete enumeration over the feasible values. The determination of the optimal reorder level and order-up-to quantity for a given order interval R yields the class of (s, S) policies.

The (s, S) inventory policies then operate as follows every order interval, where i is the inventory position.

$$if \ (i \leq s) \ order \ (S - i)$$
$$if \ (i > s) \ do \ not \ order$$

Min–Max Policies as a Special Case of (s, S) Policies Even the determination of optimal values for s and S for a given reorder interval R is difficult. In practice, the optimal values are often approximated based on the optimal values for the fixed reorder quantity policies. This fixed reorder frequency policy with approximate values is called the Min–Max inventory policy. For a given cost objective and service constraints, first the optimal s and Q quantities for the fixed reorder quantity policy are determined. The reorder point min is set equal to the reorder point s. The order-up-to quantity max is equal to the reorder point plus the reorder quantity. The inventory position is examined with a fixed frequency and an order is placed when the inventory position is equal or falls below the reorder point (min). The amount ordered is equal to the difference between the target level (max) and the inventory position. The s and S values for a given reorder frequency are thus approximated by

$$Min = s \approx s$$
$$Max = S \approx s + Q \tag{10.83}$$

$$if \ (i \leq Min) \ order \ (Max - i)$$
$$if \ (i > Min) \ do \ not \ order \tag{10.84}$$

Base Stock or (S–1, S) Policies as a Special Case of (s, S) Policies The base stock policy is a variant of the periodic review inventory policies that reviews the inventory position every R time units. The inventory policy orders a number of items equal to the demand in the previous period. The inventory policy executes a one-for-one replacement of items. This is equivalent to setting the reorder point equal to $S-1$, which implies that an order is placed if there was any demand during the previous period, but no order is placed if there was no demand. S is the order-up-to level. The time interval, equal to R time units, is used as the fundamental period and the review periods are then indexed by subsequent integers. For example, if the inventory is measured every Monday morning, the fundamental time period would 1 week and the reviews and possible actions would be indicated by week or period 1, 2, … Assuming that the time period R is determined by the system constraints, the order-up-to level is the only variable that needs to be determined for this inventory policy. The value of S will determine the service level and the inventory costs of the inventory system.

The following assumptions are made to determine the optimal value of S. It is assumed that the inventory is checked at the beginning of every period and that an order could be placed at that time and that replenishment deliveries occur at the beginning of every time period. This implies that the only time the inventory can be observed is at the beginning of each period. The lead time, denoted by lt, is assumed to be an integer multiple of the fundamental time period and is expressed in periods. For example, if inventory is measured once week and the lead time for replenishment is 3 weeks then the lead lt would be equal to 3 and be a dimensionless quantity. Finally, it is assumed that all demand is eventually filled. If an order arrives and no inventory is available, the order is filled based on a first-in, first-out priority after one or more replenishments have arrived. So it is assumed that there are no lost sales or, equivalently, the backorder level is 100%.

Recall the following definitions.

d demand rate per period

OHI on-hand inventory, which is the physical inventory present in the warehouse. Its value is nonnegative.

BO backorder quantity, which is the quantity of items for which orders already have been received but that have not yet shipped. Back orders are kept in a first-come, first-served queue. The backorder quantity is nonnegative.

OOI on-order inventory, which is inventory that has been ordered from the supplier but that has not yet been received at the warehouse. Its value is nonnegative.

IL inventory level, which is the on-hand inventory minus the backorder quantity. Its value can be positive, zero, or negative.

i inventory position is equal to the sum of the inventory level and the on-order inventory

Q order quantity, which can change from period to period,

The following relationships between the various definitions and parameters of the inventory policy exist.

$$IL = OHI - BO \tag{10.85}$$

$$i = IL + OOI = OHI + OOI - BO \tag{10.86}$$

$$Q = S - i \tag{10.87}$$

Finally, it should be noted that the inventory position at the end of a period is equal to the inventory position at the beginning of the next period. Consider a system where the lead time is equal to three periods, or $lt = 3$. At the beginning of the fourth period the order quantity is equal to.

$$Q_4 = S - i_4 = S - IL_4 - OOI_4.$$

Immediately after the order has been placed the inventory position increases to S. The quantity on-order immediately after the replenishment order has been placed is then.

$$OOI_4 = S - IL_4$$

Since the lead time is equal to three periods, all the replenishment quantities of OOI_4 will have been received by the end of period 7 and observed by beginning of period 8. The replenishment will arrive sometime between the start of period 7 and the start of period 8, but will be observed at the start of period 8 when the inventory parameters are checked. The total demand during the time interval between the check at the start of period 4 and the check at the start of period 8 is equal to

$$d_{lt+1} = d_4 + d_5 + d_6 + d_7$$

This demand is based on the number of periods in the lead time plus one extra period. In the example the lead time is three periods and the demand is based on four periods. This relationship is indicated by the subscript $lt+1$. Note that the expected value of this demand is equal to

$$E\left[d_{lt+1}\right] = d\,(lt + 1) \tag{10.88}$$

The inventory level at the start of period 8 is equal to beginning inventory level at the start of period 4 plus all the replenishments received minus all the demands satisfied during the time interval from the start of period 4 to the start of period 8.

$$IL_8 = IL_4 + (S - IL_4) - \sum_{t=4}^{t=8} d_t = S - \sum_{t=4}^{t=8} d_t$$

The expected value, variance, and standard deviation of the inventory level can then be computed as follows.

$$E\,[IL] = S - E\left[\sum_{t=k}^{t=k+lt+1} d_t\right] = S - d\,(lt + 1) \tag{10.89}$$

$$Var\,[IL] = (lt + 1) \cdot Var\,[d] + d^2 \cdot Var\,[lt] \tag{10.90}$$

$$sd_{IL} = \sqrt{(lt + 1) \cdot sd_d^2 + d^2 \cdot sd_{lt}^2} \tag{10.91}$$

It should be noted that in the continuous review policies, the standard deviation of the inventory level was based on lt times the standard deviation of the demand per time period, but for the base stock level the standard deviation for the inventory level is $(lt + 1)$ times the standard deviation of the demand per time period. The equivalencies shown in Table 10.8 exist between these two inventory policies.

It should be noted that in the above formulas the reorder interval R and the lead time LT are expressed in the same time unit, such as 1 year. The optimal values can then be derived completely analogously to the case of the continuous review (fixed-

Table 10.8 Summary of equivalencies between continuous review and base stock inventory policies

Policy	(s, Q)	$(S-1, S)$	
Reorder point	s	$S-1$	
Order quantity	Q	$S-i$	(10.92)
Lead time	LT	$(lt+1)R$	

order quantity) policies, provided that the critical period is set to $(lt+1)R$ or $lt+1$ periods. The safety stock is intended to absorb the uncertainty of the demand during this critical period. An intuitive explanation that the length of the critical period for the base stock inventory policies is equal to $lt+1$ periods is based on the fact that first one time period has to pass before the inventory position is examined again and then followed by the lead time of lt periods for that replenishment order to arrive. In comparison, for the continuous review policies, as soon as the inventory position reaches the reorder point an order is placed and the replenishment occurs after the lead time LT.

The optimal value of the order-up-to level S can be determined subject to a service level constraint, be this either a no-stockout probability of type 1 or a fill rate constraint of type 2 in exactly the same way as for the case of the continuous review policy provided that the critical period is set to $(lt+1)R$ or $lt+1$ periods.

Finally, the safety stock level is based on a critical period of $(lt+1)R$ or $lt+1$ periods, but the in-transit or pipeline inventory is based on the transit time, which remains unchanged from the transit time in the case of the continuous review policies.

10.3 Dependent Demand Systems

In dependent demand systems, the production and shipment of components and raw materials is timed to meet the production planning requirements. The right amount of material is produced and delivered at the right time. The goal is to avoid carrying items as work-in-process (WIP) inventory or to find the best balance between inventory holding cost and production setup costs. This inventory control policy is often used for the scheduling of the high-value, custom-made items. It requires that the demand for the finished product is reasonably well known or can be forecasted with relatively small errors.

Characteristics, Advantages, and Disadvantages of Distribution Resource Planning Distribution requirement planning or distribution resource planning (DRP) uses the methodology and techniques of material requirements planning (MRP) applied to the distribution channel to achieve integrated materials scheduling throughout the entire supply chain from raw materials suppliers to the finished goods customers. DRP is based on a centralized, top-down, push philosophy of supply chain management. The basic DRP methodology assumes that the future is known with certainty and demand is deterministic. Supply chains using (Q, R) or (s, S) inventory policies generally manage products and retailers independently in a distributed, bottom-up, pull philosophy. These traditional reorder point policies explicitly incorporate uncertainty.

To a large extent, DRP will exhibit the same advantages and disadvantages of MRP. DRP has several advantages and benefits that derive from its centralized philosophy.

- DRP requires that similar and consistent data be collected throughout the entire supply chain. This in itself encourages integrated planning and enhances communication throughout the supply chain.
- DRP will show future shipments and deliveries of materials. This allows the management of the various facilities and transportation modes to anticipate their future requirements and enables them to better plan transportation, production, and warehousing activity levels.
- The requirements associated with new product introductions and sales promotions can be anticipated and the supply chain can be prepared for these sudden, irregular, or unusual requirements.
- When there is insufficient product inventory to satisfy all customer demand, the DRP system can allocate and distribute materials so that these shortages are more uniformly divided over the retailers. This prevents that one retailer may receive 100% of its demand and another retailer receives nothing depending on which one transmitted their order first.
- DRP incorporates all sources of demand, not just the sales observed or transmitted by the retailer. For instance, the materials required for a seasonal inventory buildup are included and these requirements can be distributed over time.
- The system view of DRP allows the balancing of materials and requirements over the whole supply chain system. The utilization of distribution centers and manufacturing facilities can be balanced.
- The systemwide view allows also the obsolescence control of the goods in inventory. This is especially important in industry dealing in perishable products such as fresh food and flowers.

DRP has the following disadvantages, which are caused by its strong dependence on the quality of the forecast for the final products.

- Errors in the forecast or changes in the forecast may create work-in-process inventory of intermediate components in the supply chain.
- DRP considers only an uncapacitated system and manufacturing and transportation resource limitations are not considered or incorporated.

DRP Mechanics DRP will compute required materials and orders backwards from the forecasted sale of the finished goods to the final customer. Based on given safety stock levels, lead times, shipping quantities, and the bill of materials (BOM), the forecasted sales are exploded backwards in time and through the supply chain. Forecasted demand is aggregated at the source facilities of the shipments.

The BOM gives the immediate components q required to produce one unit of product p. The BOM can be represented by a matrix A_{qp}, where the rows represent the various components and the columns represent the various intermediate and end products. The following notation will be used:

a_{qp} number of units of component q required to produce one unit of product p
$i_{p,t}$ on-hand inventory of product p during time period t
$d_{p,t}$ gross requirements (outflow) of product p during time period t
$s_{p,t}$ scheduled receipts (inflow) of product p during time period t
$r_{p,t}$ planned production receipts (inflow) of product p during time period t

The material requirements can then be computed with the following two equations. The first equation is a conservation of flow constraint for every commodity during every time period at every facility. The second equation translates the demand of a product at a particular time into demand for its components at the earlier time periods determined by the production lead time of the product. The flow balance is illustrated in Fig. 10.13. It should be noted that all of the circles in the diagram correspond to one facility, where product p is being manufactured, and that the rectangle represents a supplier facility, where the component q is being sourced from.

$$i_{p,t} = i_{p,t-1} - d_{p,t} + s_{p,t} + r_{p,t} \qquad (10.93)$$

$$d_{q,t-lt_p} = a_{qp}r_{p,t} \qquad (10.94)$$

The planned shipments at the various facilities and transportation modes are then used to generate the master production schedule and to update the safety stock levels and production and shipment quantity parameters. To schedule the production for products that have multiple demands, the EOQ equation, the heuristic algorithm developed by Silver and Meal (1973), or the optimal dynamic programming procedure by Wagner and Within (1958) may be used. To incorporate uncertainty

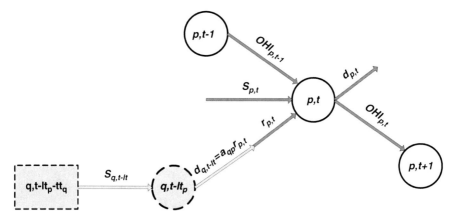

Fig. 10.13 Flow balance at a facility

of the demand quantities, the newsvendor algorithm may be used at each stage to determine safety inventories in the supply chain. The use of safety stock levels is an extension to the basic deterministic DRP method.

DRP is a simple but effective tool for multilevel distribution systems or supply chains for products with complex multilevel bill of materials. Such systems typically include two or more layers or echelons of facilities that are storing inventory. There exists an extensive theoretical literature on mathematical models for the management of multilevel inventory systems. However, most of these models are mathematically very complex or have significant simplifying assumptions that make their implementation and adaptation in large-scale industrial systems impractical.

10.4   Exercises

True/False Questions

1. A common measure of customer service is the long-range fraction of product delivered out of inventory. (T/F) _____
2. A fixed-order quantity inventory control system is more suitable for small irregular demand than for regular, high-quantity demand for a product. (T/F) _____
3. A just-in-time pull inventory system is best suited to regular demand patterns. (T/F) _____
4. A lower inventory turnover ratio is desirable. (T/F) _____
5. A mandated service level of 98% of the product delivered out of inventory will create higher levels of inventory than the mandated service level of the probability of no stockout more than or equal to 98%. (T/F) _____
6. DRP is an extension of MRP to allow integrated supply scheduling throughout the entire logistics channel. (T/F) _____
7. For a made-to-stock product the order cycle time for normal order fulfillment does not included the production time in the manufacturing plant. (T/F) _____
8. For an inventory system with a stochastic lead time, the safety inventory in a system with a larger coefficient of variation of the lead time will be less than or equal to than the safety inventory in a system with a smaller coefficient of variation of the lead time. (T/F) _____
9. If the coefficient of variation of the sample demand data is larger than one, then a normal distribution is a good approximation of the demand distribution. (T/F) _____
10. If the cumulative demand for the mean plus two standard deviations is less than 80% then the normal distribution is a good approximation of the demand distribution. (T/F) _____
11. If the future demand is known with perfect certainty, then there is no need to have inventory in the logistics system. (T/F) _____

12. If the marginal loss is larger than the marginal profit in a single-order inventory system, then the purchased inventory should be smaller than the expected demand. (T/F) _____

13. If the marginal profit is larger than the marginal loss in a single-order inventory system, then the purchased inventory should be larger than the expected demand. (T/F) _____

14. In a pull inventory system the replenishments are based on the forecasted demand of the final and intermediate products. (T/F) _____

15. In DRP the inventory levels of various components is dependent on the forecasted demand for the final finished good. (T/F) _____

16. One of the main reasons to hold product inventory in the supply chain is to decouple the sequence of processing steps in the supply chain. (T/F) _____

17. Response time constraints is one of the fundamental reasons to have warehousing and inventory. (T/F) _____

18. Safety stock is the inventory held for speculation beyond the foreseeable needs of the corporation. (T/F) _____

19. The aging or curing inventories used in the preparation of food products such as cheese and champagne can be modeled similar to pipeline inventory. (T/F) _____

20. The average inventory caused by the iterative determination of Q and R for the case of stochastic demand and shortage cost in the system and with a service level constraint of type 1 will be less than or equal to the average inventory caused by the single pass determination of Q and R for the same case. (T/F) _____

Landgate Landgate is a producer of a line of internal fixed disk drives for microcomputers. The drives use a 3.5-in. platter that Landgate purchases from an outside supplier. Demand data and sales forecast indicate that the weekly demand for the platters can be approximated with sufficient accuracy by a normal distribution with mean of 3800 and variance of 1,300,000. The platters require a 3-week lead-time for receipt at the disk drive assembly plant. Landgate has been using a 40% annual interest charge to compute the holding costs because of very short life cycle of the disk platters, since platters with higher data density are released frequently. The platters cost $ 18 each and the ordering cost is $ 3700 per order, which includes the transportation cost to the assembly plant by airfreight. Because of the extreme competitiveness of the industry, stockouts are very costly and Landgate uses currently a 99% fill rate criterion.

You have been asked to determine the inventory parameters for a continuous review inventory policy that minimizes the total cost associated with the inventory while satisfying the customer service constraints. First, give the numerical value of the problem parameters. Then compute the inventory policy parameters with the single-iteration algorithm. Next compute these parameters with the appropriate iterative algorithm, but compute only a single iteration starting from the solution of the single-pass algorithm. Specify the units for all variables. Round all numerical values related to platters (e.g., demand, standard deviation, and inventory) to the nearest integer number of platters. You can assume that there are 52 weeks in a year. Briefly discuss and explain the changes in average inventory and total cost between the one-pass and iterative algorithm.

Christmas Cards The deck-the-halls (DTH) Printing Company once a year prints a particularly richly decorated and ornate Christmas card and distributes the cards to department stores, stationery, and gift shops throughout the United States. It costs DTH $ 2.50 to print each card and ship the card to a shop. The company sells the cards for $ 12.50 a piece, which includes transportation. Each shop or store receives a single order before the start of the Christmas season. Because the cards have the current year printed on them and DTH wants to maintain the image of this particular signature card series, those cards that are not sold to the shops are destroyed. Based on past experience and forecasts of the current buying patterns, the probabilities of the number of cards to be sold nationwide for the coming Christmas season are estimated to be as shown in the next table.

Interval	Interval	
100,000	150,000	0.0625
150,001	200,000	0.1250
200,001	250,000	0.1875
250,001	300,000	0.2500
300,001	350,000	0.1875
350,001	400,000	0.1250
400,001	450,000	0.0625
		1.0000

Determine the number of cards that DTH should print this year. Summarize your calculations in a table, using a row for the computation of each relevant variable. In the first column, give the name of the variable you are computing; in the second column give the formula used to compute the variable; in the third column give the numerical value; and in the fourth column give the units of the variable. You cannot receive credit for the numerical value unless the units are specified.

A detailed analysis of the past data shows that the number of cards sold is better described by a normal distribution, with mean of 275,000 cards and standard deviation of 80,000 cards. Based on this sales forecast, how many cards should DTH print now? Again, summarize your calculations in a table, using the same conventions.

Beverage Mart The Beverage Mart Company is a discount store specializing in selling beverages such as water and house brand carbonated soft drinks in large quantities to individual consumers. Their typical sale is a case containing twelve 2-liter bottles of the single beverage of their house brand for a particular beverage type such as regular cola. Beverage Mart competes on price with regular grocery stores in their sales area. They have a set of products that have a heavily advertised low price and that are denoted as loss-leaders. However, the inventory for these loss-leader products may be insufficient to satisfy the demand. The business model of Beverage Mart assumes that the customer will buy a similar product that is not a loss-leader at the regular, but still competitive price. Because of their business model Beverage Mart uses currently a 75% fill rate criterion for loss-leader items. For one particular SKU of water, the weekly demand is assumed to be forecasted with sufficient accuracy by a normal distribution with mean of 1200 cases and standard deviation of 225 cases. The ordering cost is $ 145 per order. The lead for ordering this SKU is on average 1.5 weeks with a standard deviation of 0.2 weeks. The annual holding cost rate is 1000%. The average purchase price for a case is $ 6.

You have been asked to determine the inventory parameters for a continuous review inventory policy that minimizes the total inventory cost while satisfying the customer service constraints for regular water in 2-liter bottles and this SKU is considered to be a loss-leader. For all your calculations, use the notation developed in this book. Your answer should be summarized in two tables. The first table should contain a summary of the data. First, give the numerical value of the parameters in the first table. Give the formulas for the parameters that you had to compute in the third column of the table.

Data				
Parameters	Symbol	Formula	Value	Units
Ordering cost	oc			
Demand rate	d			
Demand rate std. dev.	sd			
Value	p			
Holding cost rate	hcr			
Leadtime	lt			
Std. dev. lead time	slt			
Average lead-time demand	dlt			
Std. dev. lead-time demand	$sdlt$			
Fill rate	fr			

Then compute the inventory policy parameters with the single-iteration algorithm. Give the formulas and numerical values for the single-pass algorithm in the second table. In the second table, the third column is for the formulas, the fourth column should contain the numerical values, and the fifth column must contain the units of the variable. If you do not specify the units, you cannot receive any credit for the numerical value! Indicate that values that are dimensionless by drawing a horizontal line in the corresponding cell of the column that contains the units. Round all numerical values related to product units (e.g., demand, standard deviation, inventory, and reorder point) to the nearest integer number of product units (cases). You can assume that there are 52 weeks in a year. If you determine the value of a variable by looking it up in a table, write "lookup" and then the distribution name in the formula cell.

One-pass algorithm

Variable	Symbol	Formula	Value	Units
Order quantity	Q			
Nonfilled items	$n(s)$			
Unit loss function	$L(z)$			
Standard deviation count	z			
Reorder point	s			
No stock-out probability	$F(s)$			
Average inventory	AI			
Ordering cost	OC			
Cycle inventory cost	CIC			
Safety inventory cost	SIC			
Total cost	TC			

A new purchasing manager has been hired by Beverage Mart and this manager wants to change the customer service policy to 75% probability of no stockout. Compute the continuous review inventory policy for this service level constraint. Give the formulas and numerical values for the single-pass algorithm in the next table.

Base stock period review with fill rate service level

Variable	Symbol	Formula	Value	Units
Order quantity	Q			
Standard deviation count	z			
Reorder point	s			
Average inventory	AI			
Ordering cost	OC			
Cycle inventory cost	CIC			
Safety inventory cost	SIC			
Total cost	TC			

Compute the continuous review inventory policy for the type 2 service level with the iterative algorithm. Give the formulas and the final numerical values for the iterative algorithm in the next table. Do not complete the shaded area of the table.

Iterative algorithm

Variable	Symbol	Formula	Value	Units
Order quantity	Q			
Nonfilled items	$n(s)$			
Unit loss function	$L(z)$			
Standard deviation count	z			
Reorder point	s			
No stockout probability	$F(s)$			
Average inventory	AI			
Ordering cost	OC			
Cycle inventory cost	CIC			
Safety inventory cost	SIC			
Total cost	TC			

Compute the derived shortage cost based on the values computed by the last inventory policy. Provide a brief discussion of the value of this derived shortage cost.

Appendix A: Expected Lost Sales for Discrete Distribution Function

Several alternative methods exist for the derivation of the expected lost sales for a discrete cumulative demand distribution. The approach taken in the following derivation approximates the continuous demand distribution by a single value in each interval. In an attempt to make this appendix self-contained several of the formulas shown previously in the chapter are repeated here. The intervals are assumed to be sorted by increasing cumulative distribution values, i.e., it is assumed that the cumulative distribution is given for N intervals for with as upper bounds $Q_1, Q_2, \ldots Q_N$ and that $F(Q_1) \leq F(Q_2) \leq \ldots \leq F(Q_N)$. To simplify the notation, the cumulative distribution function at the lower bound of the first interval will be denoted by $F(Q_0)$ and its value is by definition equal to zero.

For the first interval, the computation of the expected lost sales is given by the following two expressions.

$$
\begin{aligned}
ns\,(Q_0) &= \bar{d} \\
ns\,(Q_1) &= \bar{d} - Q_1
\end{aligned}
\tag{10.95}
$$

Recall that for a continuous demand distribution the expected number of lost sales is equal to the following.

$$
ns\,(s) = E\,[NS\,(s)] = \int_s^\infty (x - s) f\,(x)\,dx
\tag{10.96}
$$

The expected lost sales at the upper bounds of the intervals can then be computed as follows.

$$
\begin{aligned}
ns\,(Q_k) &= \int_{Q_k}^\infty (x - Q_k) f\,(x)\,dx = \int_{Q_k}^\infty x f\,(x)\,dx - Q_k \int_{Q_k}^\infty f\,(x)\,dx \\
&= \sum_{j=0}^{N-1-k} \left(\int_{Q_{k+j}}^{Q_{k+j+1}} x f\,(x)\,dx \right) - Q_k\,(1 - F\,(Q_k))
\end{aligned}
\tag{10.97}
$$

The integral in this expression calculates the expected demand in one interval. It is assumed that the only possible values of the demand in each interval is equal to the upper bound of that interval. The overall expected demand and the expected demand in a interval are then computed by the following two expressions. Recall that for discrete cumulative distribution functions, the critical ratio identifies the interval and the optimal value of the inventory is set to the upper bound of that interval.

$$\bar{d} = \sum_{j=1}^{N} Q_j \cdot \left(F\left(Q_j\right) - F\left(Q_{j-1}\right) \right) \tag{10.98}$$

$$\int_{Q_{k+j}}^{Q_{k+j+1}} xf(x)dx = Q_{k+j+1} \left(F\left(Q_{k+j+1}\right) - F\left(Q_{k+j}\right) \right) \tag{10.99}$$

The expected lost sales can then be expressed in quantities that only depend on interval values.

$$ns\left(Q_k\right) = \sum_{j=0}^{N-1-k} \left(Q_{k+j+1} \cdot \left(F\left(Q_{k+j+1}\right) - F\left(Q_{k+j}\right) \right) \right) - Q_k \left(1 - F\left(Q_k\right)\right)$$

$$\tag{10.100}$$

Next the difference between two values of the expected lost sales for adjacent interval end points is computed.

$$ns\left(Q_{k+1}\right) - ns\left(Q_k\right)$$
$$= \sum_{j=0}^{N-2-k} \left(Q_{k+j+2} \cdot \left(F\left(Q_{k+j+2}\right) - F\left(Q_{k+j+1}\right) \right) \right) - Q_{k+1} \left(1 - F\left(Q_{k+1}\right)\right)$$
$$- \sum_{j=0}^{N-1-k} \left(Q_{k+j+1} \cdot \left(F\left(Q_{k+j+1}\right) - F\left(Q_{k+j}\right) \right) \right) + Q_k \left(1 - F\left(Q_k\right)\right)$$

$$\tag{10.101}$$

The two summations in the above equation contain the same terms except that the second summation contains one extra term corresponding to the interval $[Q_{k+j}, Q_{k+j+1}]$. The expression can thus be simplified to the following.

$$ns\left(Q_{k+1}\right) - ns\left(Q_k\right)$$
$$= -Q_{k+1} \cdot \left(F\left(Q_{k+1}\right) - F\left(Q_k\right) \right) - Q_{k+1} \left(1 - F\left(Q_{k+1}\right)\right) \tag{10.102}$$
$$+ Q_k \left(1 - F\left(Q_k\right)\right)$$
$$= -\left(Q_{k+1} - Q_k\right)\left(1 - F\left(Q_k\right)\right)$$

This establishes the recursive relationship for the expected lost sales between subsequent intervals.

$$ns\left(Q_{k+1}\right) = ns\left(Q_k\right) - \left(Q_{k+1} - Q_k\right)\left(1 - F\left(Q_k\right)\right) \quad for\ k = 1 \ldots N - 1$$
$$\tag{10.103}$$

Appendix B: Optimal (s, Q) Policy for Service Level 2

In an attempt to make this appendix self-contained, several of the formulas shown previously in the chapter are repeated here. The objective is to minimize the total, long-range inventory cost subject to the fill rate service constraint. The total inventory cost includes the ordering cost and the holding costs for the cycle and the safety inventory. The optimization problem is thus:

$$\text{min} \quad TC = \frac{D}{Q}oc + hc\frac{Q}{2} + hc \cdot (s - d \cdot lt) \qquad (10.104)$$

$$s.t. \quad \frac{ns\,(s)}{Q} \le (1 - \beta) \qquad (10.105)$$

$$Q \ge 0$$

This is a nonlinear optimization problem with a single inequality constraint. Given that both the objective function and the constraint are convex in function of Q, the Karush–Kuhn–Tucker (KTT) conditions are sufficient conditions for a nonnegative Q^* to be the global optimum. The optimization problem can be written in the following standard form.

$$\begin{array}{ll} \text{min} & f\,(x) \\ s.t. & g\,(x) \le 0 \end{array} \qquad (10.106)$$

The sufficient KKT conditions for a feasible x^* to be the global optimum are then as follows, where $\nabla f(x)$ denotes the gradient of the function $f(x)$. The gradient has to be taken with respect to the two variables Q and s.

$$\nabla f\,(x^*) + \mu \cdot \nabla g\,(x^*) = 0 \qquad (10.107)$$

$$\mu \cdot g\,(x^*) = 0 \qquad (10.108)$$

$$\mu \ge 0 \qquad (10.109)$$

For the inventory problem, the sufficient KKT conditions can then be written as follows.

$$\nabla \left(\frac{D}{Q^*}oc + hc\frac{Q^*}{2} + hc \cdot (s^* - d \cdot lt)\right) + \mu\nabla \left(\frac{ns(s^*)}{Q^*} - (1 - \beta)\right) = 0 \qquad (10.110)$$

$$\mu \left(\frac{ns\,(s^*)}{Q^*} - (1 - \beta)\right) = 0 \qquad (10.111)$$

$$\mu \geq 0 \tag{10.112}$$

If μ equals zero, then the EOQ quantity provides the optimal solution to this problem and the safety inventory level is equal to zero. This can be interpreted as the case where the inventory level is computed using the EOQ formula while ignoring the service level requirement and this inventory level satisfies the service level. In other words, ordering enough inventory to cover the expected demand during the lead time satisfies the required service level.

$$Q^* = \sqrt{\frac{2 \cdot D \cdot oc}{hc}} \tag{10.113}$$
$$s^* = d \cdot lt$$

The remainder of the discussion treats the case where μ is strictly positive. In this case, the following equality must be satisfied.

$$ns\left(s^*\right) = Q^* \left(1 - \beta\right) \tag{10.114}$$

First we focus on the computation of the gradient constraint with respect to the reorder point s. This yields the following equality.

$$hc + \frac{\mu^*}{Q^*} \frac{dns\left(s^*\right)}{ds} = 0 \tag{10.115}$$

Recall that $ns(s)$ is the expected number of units short per cycle, or

$$ns\left(s\right) = E\left[NS\left(s\right)\right] = \int_s^\infty \left(x - s\right) f\left(x\right) dx \tag{10.116}$$

The derivative of $ns(s)$ with respect to the reorder point s can be computed with Leibniz's rule.

$$\frac{d}{dy} \int_{l(y)}^{u(y)} h\left(x, y\right) dx = \int_{l(y)}^{u(y)} \left(\frac{\partial h\left(x, y\right)}{\partial y}\right) dx + h\left(u\left(y\right), y\right) \frac{du\left(y\right)}{dy}$$
$$- h\left(l\left(y\right), y\right) \frac{dl\left(y\right)}{dy} \tag{10.117}$$

This yields the following substitutions:

$$y = s$$
$$h\left(x, y\right) = \left(x - s\right) f\left(x\right)$$
$$u\left(y\right) = \infty, \quad \frac{du\left(y\right)}{dy} = 0$$
$$l\left(y\right) = s, \quad \frac{dl\left(y\right)}{dy} = 1, \quad h\left(l\left(y\right), y\right) = \left(s - s\right) f\left(s\right) = 0$$
$$\frac{\partial h\left(x, y\right)}{\partial y} = \frac{\partial\left(x - s\right)}{\partial s} f\left(x\right) + \left(x - s\right) \frac{\partial f\left(x\right)}{\partial s} = -f\left(x\right)$$

$$\frac{dns\,(s)}{ds} = \int_s^\infty -f\,(x)\,dx = -F\,(x)|_s^\infty = -\,(1 - F\,(s)) \qquad (10.118)$$

Substituting this in the gradient equation (10.115) yields

$$hc + \frac{\mu^*}{Q^*}\left(-\left(1 - F\,(s^*)\right)\right) = 0 \qquad (10.119)$$

which can be rewritten as

$$F\,(s^*) = 1 - \frac{hc \cdot Q^*}{\mu^*}$$

The same equation can also be rewritten to determine the optimal value of μ^*.

$$\mu^* = \frac{hc \cdot Q^*}{1 - F\,(s^*)} \qquad (10.120)$$

Next we focus on the computation of the gradient constraint with respect to the reorder quantity Q. This yields the following equality.

$$-\frac{oc \cdot D}{Q^{*2}} + \frac{hc}{2} + \mu^*\left[-\frac{ns\,(s^*)}{Q^{*2}}\right] = 0 \qquad (10.121)$$

Multiplying all terms by $2Q^{*2}/hc$ and substituting for μ^* with (10.120) yields the following quadratic equation

$$-\frac{2D \cdot oc}{hc} + Q^{*2} - \frac{2 \cdot ns\,(s^*)}{1 - F\,(s^*)}Q^* = 0 \qquad (10.122)$$

The general quadratic equation

$$ax^2 + bx + c = 0 \qquad (10.123)$$

has the following two roots, which are two real numbers provided the discriminant, which is the expression under the square root sign in this equation, is positive.

$$x^* = \frac{-b \pm \sqrt{b^2 - 4ac}}{2a} \qquad (10.124)$$

Since for the quadratic equation given in (10.122) a is equal to 1 and c is negative, the discriminant for this equation is always positive. For the quadratic equation for the reorder quantity only the root value computed with the positive sign yields a root with a positive value and is thus feasible. The optimal reorder quantity is given by.

$$Q^* = \frac{ns\,(s^*)}{1 - F\,(s^*)} + \sqrt{\left(\frac{ns\,(s^*)}{1 - F\,(s^*)}\right)^2 + \frac{2D \cdot oc}{hc}} \qquad (10.125)$$

For a normal demand distribution, $ns(s^*)$ can be written in function of the unit loss function, which yields the following equation for z^*.

$$z^* = L^{-1}\left(\frac{Q^*\,(1 - \beta)}{s_{dlt}}\right) \qquad (10.126)$$

$$s^* = d \cdot lt + z^* \cdot s_{dlt} = d \cdot lt + s_{dlt} \cdot L^{-1}\left(\frac{Q^*\,(1 - \beta)}{s_{dlt}}\right) \qquad (10.127)$$

The optimal values of $ns(s^*)$ and $F(s^*)$ can then be determined from s^*.

The Eqs. (10.125) and (10.127) provide two equations for the optimal reorder quantity and the optimal reorder point. Because the variables are mutually dependent in the equations, they have to be solved for iteratively through the method of cyclical coordinates. Finally, the optimal value of μ^* can be computed with (10.120). Based on (10.71) and (10.120), the optimal value of μ^* can thus be interpreted as the penalty for having a shortage equal to the total annual demand.

$$\mu^* = sc \cdot D \qquad (10.128)$$

References

Schneider, H. (1981). Effect of service-levels on the order-points and order-levels in inventory models. *International Journal of Production Research, 19*(6), 615–631.

Silver E., & Peterson, R. (1985). *Decision systems for inventory management and production planning* (2nd ed.). New York: Wiley.

Silver, E. A., & Meal, H. C. (1973). A heuristic for selecting lot size quantities for the case of a deterministic time-varying demand rate and discrete opportunities for replenishment. *Production and Inventory Management, 14*, 64–74.

Silver, E., Pyke, D., & Peterson, R. (1998). *Inventory management and production planning and scheduling*. New York: Wiley.

Wagner, H. M., & Whitin, T. M. (1958). Dynamic version of the economic lot size model. *Management Science, 5*, 89–96.

Waters, C. (1992). *Inventory control and management*. New York: John Wiley.

Wilson, R. (2007). *18th Annual the state of logistics report: the new face of logistics*. CSCMP.

Zipkin, P. (2000). *Foundations of inventory management*. New York: McGraw-Hill.

Chapter 11
Supply Chain Systems

Learning Objectives After you have studied this chapter, you should be able to:

- Identify the major types of objectives for supply chain systems design.
- Know the major types of components in a supply chain system and their most important characteristics.
- Know how to apply, interpret, and use Pareto analysis.
- Know the types of strategic configuration of supply chains and their respective advantages and disadvantages.

11.1 Introduction

11.1.1 Definitions

Recall from the introductory chapter that a supply chain is a network of functional organizations that through their activities perform the logistics functions. These functions include procurement of materials, transformation of materials and intermediate products into intermediate and finished products, and distribution of finished products to the customers. Supply chains exist both in manufacturing and service organizations. Supply chains can differ greatly in complexity from industry to industry and from individual company to company. Because of the widespread prevalence and variety of supply chains, many alternative definitions of a supply chain exist. The term *supply chain* is somewhat of a misnomer because a supply chain is often not a single or simple chain but a complex network with many divergent and convergent flows. Because of the current focus of companies on their core competencies, there are usually many different organizations active in a supply chain. If all these organizations belong to the same (multinational) corporation, information flows usually are more comprehensive and engineering methodology based decision–making is easier. However, the fundamental nature of the supply chain does not change with the number of corporations involved. In other words, there is no difference in the definition of a supply chain depending on the fact if one

M. Goetschalckx, *Supply Chain Engineering,* International Series in Operations Research & Management Science 161,
DOI 10.1007/978-1-4419-6512-7_11, © Springer Science+Business Media, LLC 2011

or more corporations are responsible for executing the logistics functions. For an organization to become and remain part of a supply chain requires this to be a beneficial relationship or win–win situation in the long run for both this organization and for the other organizations in the supply chain.

There exist an enormous variety of supply chain implementations. In the manufacturing industries, examples are the manufacturing and distribution of consumer goods, the assembly of limited-quantity goods such as aircraft and locomotives, or the construction of telephone switching centers. In the service industries, supply chains take the form of hospital and provider networks, functionality and location of banking outlets, and hub-and-spoke networks by major airlines to offer seats on flights. In the defense organizations, supply chains correspond to personnel, equipment, and bases functions and locations. While many different manifestations and configurations exist, the underlying structure of any supply chain remains a network of capacitated production, storage, and transportation assets to provide customer service by the timely delivery of goods and services to the customers at the lowest possible cost. A supply chain schematic is shown in Fig. 11.1.

Some examples of the questions faced during the planning and design of supply chains are given next. This is by no means a comprehensive list.

- Where to purchase?
- Vendor selection and make-or-buy question?
- Where to produce?
- Plant location?
- Where to assemble?
- Final product configuration and duties?
- Where to hold in inventory?
- How to provide rapid response to customer demands and simultaneously smooth the status of the system?
- How to transport and deliver?
- Should tailored transportation modes and intermodal networks be used?
- How to expand or contract?
- Into Latin America from Miami or immediately establish a distribution center in Brazil?

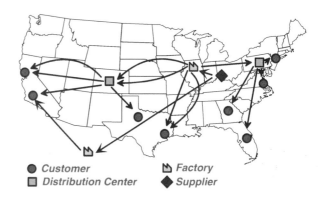

Fig. 11.1 Supply chain network schematic

● *Customer*   ◣ *Factory*
■ *Distribution Center*   ◆ *Supplier*

Fig. 11.2 Integrated nature of supply chain decisions

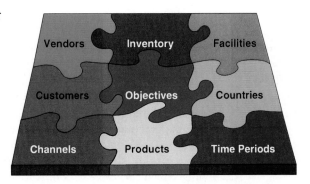

- Closing of railroad yards or old facilities?
- Recycling?
- How to observe the German 80% packaging law?

Historically, the marketing, purchasing, manufacturing, and distribution organizations in a supply chain have operated independently, where each organization has their own objectives, constraints, and reward system. These objectives often conflicted. Marketing strives to increase customer service, which tends to favor "manufacture and distribute on demand." Manufacturing strives to decrease unit production costs, which tends to favor long production runs of a limited variety of products. This policy may create large inventories in the distribution channels. The goal of the purchasing department to acquire materials at the lowest cost again may cause large order sizes and significant inventory in the acquisition channels. Supply chain management is the collection of planning tasks and policies that attempts to provide customer service at the lowest cost by integrating and coordinating the various plans and logistics actions across the whole supply chain. The integrated nature of supply chain management with respect to several prominent logistics components is illustrated in Fig. 11.2.

11.2 Supply Chain Design Objectives

The two main categories of supply chain design objectives are profit maximization and cost minimization. The profit maximization objective of a supply chain configuration project is the maximization of the cumulative, time-discounted, worldwide after-tax net cash flows over the planning horizon consistent with the risk preferences of the corporation. The total system cost minimization objective is to minimize the net present value of the time discounted costs of achieving the mission over the planning horizon. It is more restrictive than the profit maximization objective since it requires that a certain prescribed level of customer service has to be provided to all customers. The profit maximization may cause certain customers not to be served or to be served a lower service level, if these customers cannot be served over the planning horizon at a profit.

However, the primary objective of every actor in a supply chain is to optimize its own performance.

This self-ser ving behavior by each individual actor may lead to local optima rather than the global optimum of the overall supply chain performance. This phenomenon is denoted as performance or incentive conflicts. Such conflicts do not only exist when different corporations are supply chain components, but also if a corporation is the single component of a supply chain and it is organized around functional components such as purchasing, manufacturing, distribution, and marketing. These are often called *corporate silos* or *stove pipes* because of the vertical structure of the organization chart. One of the most difficult tasks for supply chain management is to structure the supply chain and its policies in such way that the behavior and policies of the participating actors are aligned and support the overall efficiency of the supply chain.

Costs are traditionally divided into three categories, depending on how they vary with the design decisions. Invariant costs are costs that are not significantly impacted by the decisions made during the supply chain design. They are also called *sunk costs* because they can no longer be changed by the design or management decisions. Typical examples are prior-service pension costs, which are the pension liabilities incurred by the corporation for labor already performed in its facilities, and preliminary engineering design costs, which are the cost already expended during this design project.The costs that are changed by the design and management decisions are further divided into fixed and variable costs. Fixed costs are costs that are incurred when the decision is made to execute an activity but these costs do not change with the intensity of the activity. Typical examples are the construction or leasing costs for facilities or the purchasing cost for vehicles in a fleet sizing problem. Variable costs change with the intensity of the activity. Typical examples are fuel consumption by vehicles or the cost of purchasing raw materials or components in manufacturing. Determining the type of a cost depends on the individual supply chain problem. For example, the labor cost in a distribution center may be either a fixed cost or a variable cost at the tactical planning level. If the number of workers remains constant throughout the year then their fully loaded base pay is considered a fixed cost. However, the cost of temporary labors hired to service the increased work load associated with the Christmas period or the overtime pay of the permanent laborers typically is categorized as a variable cost.

The data collection effort for a strategic supply chain design project is a time and resource intensive activity. It requires a large variety of cost data, which are usually computed and maintained by the finance department. But traditional accounting information is created with a different purpose, namely the creation of a corporate profit and loss statement on a corporate level. The costs are often adjusted or relocated to influence the profit and loss. On the other hand supply chain design needs performance and financial data on a mission-oriented basis. Activity-based costing (ABC) is a costing method that assigns all the direct and indirect costs to the activity that consumed them. This allows the determination of the resource cost and profitability of activities such as serving a particular customer group with a group of products. The existence of activity based cost data makes the data collection effort for supply chain planning and design much easier. Significant components of the required data typically only exist in the databases or spreadsheets of the functional departments. The collection and validation process to ensure a consistent data set for the overall supply chain design and planning is resource consuming and often incompatible with the organizational structure of the corporation(s).

Estimating the performance characteristics of a large and complex system that will be in operation for an extended period of time in the future requires some type of forecasting of the future conditions. Those conditions cannot be known with certainty and this uncertainty represents a risk to the corporation. Risk analysis and its associated graphs are used to support a large variety of capital investment and strategic decisions. A typical risk analysis graph is shown in Fig. 11.3. On one axis of the graph a measure of the central tendency of the yield of a system configuration is shown. Typical measures of central tendency of the yield are the expected total system profit or the expected total system cost. It should be noted that a better yield means larger numerical values if system profit is used but lower numerical values if system cost is used. On the second axis a measure of the dispersion of this yield is shown. Typical measures of dispersion are the standard deviation, the range, or the variance. Because of the many different alternatives for the central tendency and dispersion measures, multiple variations of the risk graph exist. The yield and dispersion may also be shown on the other axis, i.e., the graph is mirrored with respect to the 45° line. The following properties and analysis remain valid regardless which type of risk analysis graph is used provided the role and orientation of the axes in the graph are properly interpreted. In the following it is assumed that the dispersion is shown on the vertical axis and so lower value on the vertical axis is desirable.

The performance of each configuration is computed with respect to its central tendency and dispersion of the yield. The system configuration is then plotted or located in the risk analysis graph. The configurations can be divided into dominant and dominated groups. A configuration is dominant if no other configuration exists that has both a better yield and a better dispersion of the yield. Configurations that are not dominant are considered to be dominated. Risk graphs are used in the analysis of a large variety of systems. One example is the construction of a portfo-

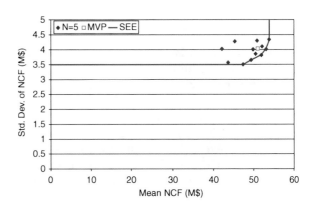

Fig. 11.3 Risk analysis graph of the net cash flow of different supply chain configurations

lio of stocks with optimal tradeoff between the yield and the risk or dispersion of the yield, where each stock has individual yield and dispersion characteristics. The design decision is to determine the amount of each stock to include in the portfolio. In this case, the design domain is continuous, since the amount of a particular stock in the portfolio can be changed in very small increments compared to the number of shares in the portfolio. The set of dominant portfolios or design configurations are called the *efficiency frontier*.

In the case of supply chain design, the design decisions cannot be changed in a continuous way since each represents a supply chain configuration that includes major binary decisions such as to build a plant in particular location or not. For the case of discrete decisions, i.e., design configurations, the efficiency frontier is not defined. However, an approximation of the efficiency frontier can be constructed. In the risk analysis graph for discrete design decisions a border can be constructed starting from the configuration with the best yield to the configuration with the lowest dispersion of the yield by systematically rotating a line in the graph. The initial rotation point is the configuration with the best yield and the rotation direction is toward the configuration with the smallest dispersion. Every time this line traverses another configuration, the rotation point is changed to this configuration and the rotation continues. This is the same procedure as used for constructing the convex hull of a set of points. The result will be piecewise linear curve connecting a number of dominant configurations. In other words, all configurations on this curve are dominant; however configurations that are not located on the curve but inside the curve may still be dominant.

Design configurations that lie on the curve or even close to it are considered to be desirable or efficient configurations. In general configurations are located far away from the curve tend to be dominated and are considered to be inefficient. The curve is denoted as the sample efficiency envelop or SEE. If all possible design configurations were plotted then the curve would be the lower efficiency envelop but typically the number of design configurations is so large, but finite, that only a fraction or a sample of them can be plotted. The curve is the lower efficiency envelope of the sample of configurations that has been plotted. Finally, if constraints on the design configuration can be plotted in the risk analysis graph, the corresponding curves may eliminate some design configurations, which are considered infeasible or failed.

One example of risk analysis given above is the construction of a portfolio of stocks. Another example in a completely different domain is given in Feldman (2003) reporting that movie studio executives produce more films containing sex and violence than family films because they want to avoid a career-killing flop and are thus very risk averse. While family films have a larger expected profit, sex-and-violence films are more likely to break even and thus have a smaller expected profit range and profit standard deviation.

Figure 11.3 shows the mean net cash flow (NCF) and the standard deviation of the NCF of different supply chain configurations of a global supply chain. The different configurations are indicated by diamonds. In this example, the configurations were optimized based on five scenarios, indicated by $N=5$. Configurations with better expected yield are located more towards the right and configurations with a better dispersion of the yield are located towards the bottom of the graph. The most desirable configurations are thus located in the right-bottom corner of the graph. The sample efficiency envelope is shown as the solid line connecting four dominant configurations and the envelope has a horizontal segment on the left and a vertical segment on the right. The configuration with the third lowest standard deviation is not located on the SEE but very close to it. This configuration is still dominant. One special configuration is indicated by MVP for the mean value problem and is indicated by a square. It corresponds to the optimal supply chain configuration for the expected value of all parameters. In other words, the best-guess value of all the parameters is used in a deterministic optimization formulation to find the optimal configuration.

It should be noted that for this example the MVP configuration does not lie on the SEE and is actually strictly dominated. This phenomenon can be rephrased in the following counterintuitive statement. "Using the best supply chain configuration for the best-guess values of the parameters may not be the best thing to do." Intuitively this property can be explained by the observation that the optimal configuration for a particular set of values will be highly targeted for that set of values. However, supply chains are configured long before all future conditions are known and the decisions for major assets such as the location of a manufacturing plant cannot easily be changed. If the configuration is too specific, it may not be able respond to changing conditions without incurring large extra costs. This phenomenon is also called fragility and is the opposite of supply chain robustness.

11.2.1 Customer Service

Recall that two of the major types of objectives for supply chain configuration are the minimization of total system cost or the maximization of total after-tax profit subject to customer service constraints. This is illustrated in the following figure where all the procedures and the configuration of the supply chain are determined in function of customer service level requirements. Any quantitative treatment requires then the definition of customer service and the development of methods and tools to measure it (Fig. 11.4).

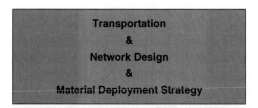

Fig. 11.4 Supply chain design

Many alternative definitions of customer service exist. Customer service is often described in a qualitative way since customer service has many components and stages. Service can be divided into pre-transaction, transaction, and post-transaction stages. Pre-transaction elements include declaration of policies and procedures and the amount of information available in real time to the customer. Transaction elements include the order cycle time, order accuracy, and ease and accuracy of the ordering and billing system and procedures. Finally, post-transaction components include maintenance and service, also known as sustainment, warranty service, and disposal service.

One component of customer service in the transaction stage is the order cycle time, which is often also called the *lead time*. The order cycle time is the length of time between the placement of the order and the receipt of the ordered products by the customer. The order cycle time includes order processing including credit verification, engineering design of the product, manufacturing, order assembly and order picking, packaging, and finally transportation to the customer, which may include customs clearing. Order cycle time and its different components can have vastly different values depending on the product and the supply chain. On one extreme, the cycle time may be nearly zero for ordering an electronic version of a song. On the other extreme, the order cycle time for highly engineered and customized capital equipment such as gas-fired generating units for electrical power may be up to 30 months.

It is commonly accepted that the sales revenue shows decreasing growth as the customer service level is increased. At the same time the cost of providing increasingly better service levels rises exponentially. The maximum profit for a supply chain is achieved at the customer service level where the sales revenue minus the supply chain cost is at its maximum. However, establishing the exact shape and values of these curves is extremely case dependent and determining these curves is very difficult to achieve even for a particular case. As a consequence, customer service are most often approximated by one or more of the following types of customer service constraints.

11.2.1.1   Service Constraints

Each of the following service level constraints is commonly used by itself or in combination with the other types. The long-term percentage of goods delivered out of on-hand inventory is often used in distribution centers and for repeated orders. Similarly is the long-term ratio of orders shipped or delivered within a certain time interval after order arrival. The configuration of a supply chain is often constrained by the maximum time or distance to a customer from the facility that services that particular customer. Single sourcing forces all the deliveries of a single product or of all products combined from a single facility to a customer, which reduces the number and complexity of the receiving operations at the customer.

11.3   Supply Chain Objects and Their Characteristics

As indicated earlier, there exists a nearly infinite variety of supply chains. However, all supply chains are composed of a limited number of fundamental components. In planning or designing a supply chain it is important to identify these components. The identification of these components or objects is necessary to structure or pose the design and management problem. Typically there are a large number of instances of each component type. Especially for supply chain design projects filtering the objects to focus on the important objects in a class is essential. Solving the design or management problem is the topic of the next chapter.

11.3.1   Products

11.3.1.1   Product Life Cycle

One of the essential requirements for designing and managing an efficient supply chain is establishing where the products are in their product life cycle. Product life cycle management of PLM is the process of managing the entire lifecycle of a product from its conception, through design and manufacturing, to sustainment and disposal. The typical product lifecycle in illustrated in Fig. 11.5. A product life cycle is usually divided into four phases, which typically have vastly different lengths.

During the introduction phase the availability of the product is limited and the products is available at a small number of sales points and sales channels. The supply chain for the product is often centralized because few supply chain assets have been put into place and the total volume of the product flow is small. During the growth phase the distribution of the product is expanded to more sales points and sales channels. Often the primary objective of the supply chain is to deliver the

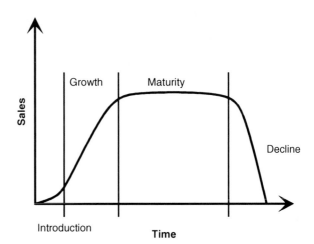

Fig. 11.5 Product life cycle graph

product to its customers rather than focusing on total system cost. The longest phase in the product life cycle is typically the maturity phase. During this phase a stable product volume is sold and often the product has competing products in the market place. The product is sold through a multitude of sales points and sales channels. Because of its competitive position, minimizing the total supply chain cost becomes an important objective. Finally, during the decline phase, the number of sales points and sales channels through which the product is distributed decreases. Because of the reduced volume often the supply chain has a centralized structure.

11.3.1.2 Pareto's Principle and Curve

In many supply chains and logistics systems a majority of the operations or of the economic impact is generated by relatively small fraction of the products. This differentiation and concentration phenomenon has become known as Pareto's principle. Vilfredo Pareto (1848–1923) observed at the end of the nineteenth century that about 80% of the wealth in Italy was concentrated into about 20% of the population. The Pareto principle states that a small subset of actors (the "vital few") affecting a common outcome tend to occur much more frequently than the remainder (the "useful many"). The concentration does not always have to be 80-20, but the 80-20 term has become associated with this concentration characteristic. The concentration can be graphically illustrated by the Pareto or 80-20 curve. The curve plots the cumulative effect, such as sales or transactions, versus the cumulative actors, such as customers. In Fig. 11.6 the Pareto curve is shown corresponding to the sales data in Table 11.1. Pareto bar charts provide an equivalent tool for visualizing the Pareto principle. Pareto analysis is an often used tool to identify or filter the most important components. A Pareto chart can be used to decide which subset of problems should be solved first, or which products deserve the most attention. In warehousing and logistics, products typically are classified as fast, medium, and slow movers based on the Pareto curve.

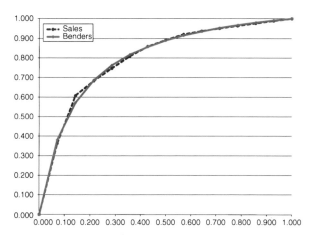

Fig. 11.6 Benders Pareto curve for product sales example

Table 11.1 Example of product sales data

Product	Cumulative products	Sales	Cumulative sales
1	0.071	5056	0.362
2	0.143	3424	0.607
3	0.214	1052	0.683
4	0.286	893	0.746
5	0.357	843	0.807
6	0.429	727	0.859
7	0.500	451	0.891
8	0.571	412	0.921
9	0.643	214	0.936
10	0.714	205	0.951
11	0.786	188	0.964
12	0.857	172	0.976
13	0.929	170	0.989
14	1.000	159	1.000
14		13,966	

Observe that the Pareto curve for this particular example in the above figure passes through the points (0.20, 0.65) and (0.35, 0.80), but not through the point (0.20, 0.80). Also observe that many different Pareto curves can all pass through the point (0.20, 0.80).

The Pareto curve can be described mathematically by several different formulas, such as the power, exponential, and Bender's formulation, given by formulas (11.1), (11.2), and (11.3), respectively. We will focus from now on the formulation originally proposed by Bender (1981), but the other formulations have analogue derivations.

$$Y = X^A \tag{11.1}$$

$$Y = 1 - e^{-AX} \tag{11.2}$$

$$Y = \frac{(1 + A)X}{A + X} \tag{11.3}$$

For each of the above formulations, the single A parameter needs to be computed in such way that the curve matches the observed data points as closely as possible. We can rearrange the Bender's curve formulation to derive the following explicit formula for the parameter A.

$$A = \frac{X(1 - Y)}{Y - X} \tag{11.4}$$

The value of A can then be based on one or more data points (X_i, Y_i). A better curve fit can be found by minimizing the sum of squared errors (SSE) between the actual data values (Y_i) and then data values derived from the curve $(\hat{Y}_i)$. The data values on the curve are computed with the following formula:

$$\hat{Y}_i = \frac{(1+A)X_i}{(A+X_i)} \qquad (11.5)$$

Setting the first derivative of SSE with respect to the parameter A equal to zero yields the least-squares estimator for the parameter A.

$$SSE = \sum_{i=1}^{N} \left(Y_i - \hat{Y}_i \right)^2 \qquad (11.6)$$

$$\frac{\partial SSE}{\partial A} = 0 \qquad (11.7)$$

$$\sum_{i}^{N} \frac{Y_i(X_i - X_i^2)}{(A+X_i)^2} - \sum_{i}^{N} \frac{(1+A)(X_i^2 - X_i^3)}{(A+X_i)^3} = 0 \qquad (11.8)$$

The smaller is the value of the A parameter, the more skewed is the curve becomes. If all products had equal sales, then the curve would be the diagonal line connecting the points (0.0, 0.0) and (1.0, 1.0) and the A parameter would be infinitely large. A skewed curve, which follows the Pareto principle, is pulled toward the top left area of the graph. The estimation of the A parameter based on a single point with formula (11.4) for an 80-20 and 90-10 curve is 0.0667 and 0.0125, respectively. Benders Pareto curves for different values of the A parameter are shown in Fig. 11.7.

How closely the curve fits the original data is typically quantified by the R^2 statistic, also called the *coefficient of determination*. This coefficient ranges between zero and one and the closer the coefficient is to one, the better the curve fit. The R^2 statistic is computed with the following formulas.

$$R^2 = 1 - \frac{SSE}{SST}$$

$$SSE = \sum_{i=1}^{N} \left(Y_i - \hat{Y}_i \right)^2$$

$$SST = \left(\sum_{i=1}^{N} Y_i^2 \right) - \frac{\left(\sum_{i=1}^{N} Y_i \right)^2}{N} \qquad (11.9)$$

If the A parameter has a large value, then the logistics strategy would be to treat the products identically. A highly skewed Pareto curve with a corresponding small value of the A parameter indicates that the products should be treated differently, e.g., by differentiated distribution. If the curve is strongly skewed, then we can establish product classes, typically called A, B, and C, or fast, medium, and slow movers. From this ABC classification, the curve derives its alternative name of ABC curve.

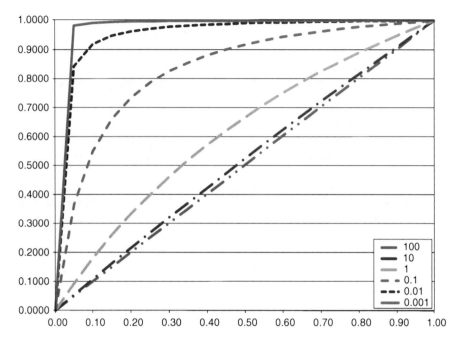

Fig. 11.7 Benders Pareto curves for different A parameter values

The exponential curve can be determined using the built-in GROWTH function of the Excel spreadsheet. Since the GROWTH function calculates the least squares fit through a set of points using the equation

$$CY = A^X$$

one must first compute the complement $CY_i = (1 - Y_i)$, fit the curve through the transformed data points (X_i, CY_i), and then finally take the complement $\hat{Y}_i = (1 - C\hat{Y}_i)$ again.

There exists considerable variation in the way the boundaries between the three classes are computed. In general, class A corresponds to the region where the curve has a strongly vertical slope. Class B corresponds to the region with the bend or knee of the curve. Class C corresponds to the region of the curve where the curve has a more horizontal slope. The classes are often constructed so that 80% of the cumulative effect is created by the products in class A, the next 15% of the cumulative effect is created by the products in class B, and the last 5% of the cumulative effect is caused by the products in class C. The more skewed is the curve, and the smaller is the A parameter, the easier it is to determine the dividing lines between the classes. For very large values of the A parameter, when the curve displays a single homogeneous population, the dividing lines between the classes are very hard to determine, very arbitrarily, and not very relevant.

The Pareto curve is an example of how raw sales data can be transformed into information, which is necessary for logistics knowledge and decisions. The information is the shape of the Pareto curve and the value of the A parameter. The logistics knowledge is based on the curve and will treat products identically or differently and divide the products into classes based on their location along the curve.

Benders Pareto Curve Example The detailed steps to compute the Benders formulation of the Pareto curve using the Microsoft Excel spreadsheet are given next. Figure 11.8 shows the spreadsheet with the initial data. The data are not sorted and are listed by part number. The objective is to construct the Pareto curve of the cumulative product sales in dollars in function of the cumulative number of products, where both cumulative values are normalized between zero and one.

The spreadsheet in Fig. 11.9 shows the same sales data after they have been sorted by decreasing dollar sales, i.e., by column D with heading Sales. The next four columns show the cumulative fraction of products (X), the cumulative fraction of sales (Y), the cumulative fraction of sales based on the Benders Pareto curve (BY), and the square of the deviation between the actual sales and the sales curve or squared error (SE). The following formulas are used to compute each SE and BY and then SSE.

$$BY_i = \frac{(1 + A)X_i}{(A + X_i)}$$

$$SE_i = (Y_i - BY_i)^2$$

$$SSE = \sum_{i=1}^{11} SE_i$$

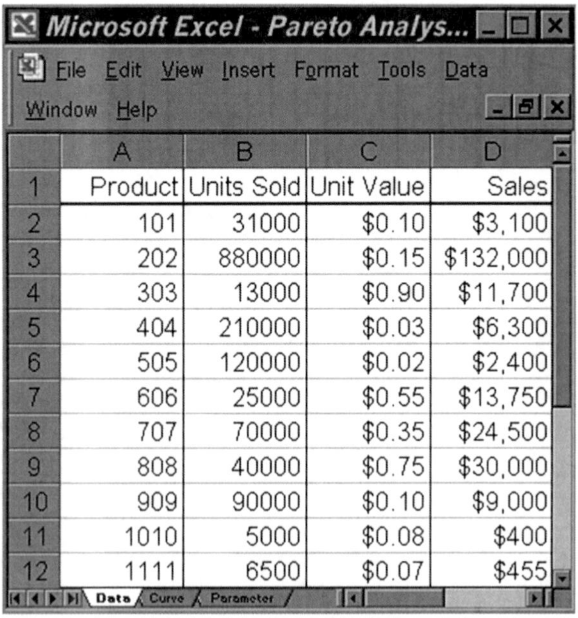

Microsoft Excel - Pareto Analys...

File Edit View Insert Format Tools Data

Window Help

	A	B	C	D
1	Product	Units Sold	Unit Value	Sales
2	101	31000	$0.10	$3,100
3	202	880000	$0.15	$132,000
4	303	13000	$0.90	$11,700
5	404	210000	$0.03	$6,300
6	505	120000	$0.02	$2,400
7	606	25000	$0.55	$13,750
8	707	70000	$0.35	$24,500
9	808	40000	$0.75	$30,000
10	909	90000	$0.10	$9,000
11	1010	5000	$0.08	$400
12	1111	6500	$0.07	$455

Data / Curve / Parameter /

Fig. 11.8 Excel spreadsheet with sales data

	A	B	C	D	E	F	G	H	I	J
								Benders		Exponent.
1										
2	Product	Units Sold	Unit Value	Sales	X	Y	BY	SSE	EY	SSE
3					0.000000	0.000000	0.000000		0.000000	
4	202	880000	$0.15	$132,000	0.090909	0.565056	0.538019	0.000731	0.433493	0.017309
5	808	40000	$0.75	$30,000	0.181818	0.693478	0.721292	0.000774	0.679070	0.000208
6	707	70000	$0.35	$24,500	0.272727	0.798356	0.813684	0.000235	0.818191	0.000393
7	606	25000	$0.55	$13,750	0.363636	0.857216	0.869363	0.000148	0.897004	0.001583
8	303	13000	$0.90	$11,700	0.454545	0.907301	0.906585	0.000001	0.941652	0.001180
9	909	90000	$0.10	$9,000	0.545455	0.945827	0.933223	0.000159	0.966945	0.000446
10	404	210000	$0.03	$6,300	0.636364	0.972796	0.953228	0.000383	0.981274	0.000072
11	101	31000	$0.10	$3,100	0.727273	0.986066	0.968804	0.000298	0.989392	0.000011
12	505	120000	$0.02	$2,400	0.818182	0.996340	0.981276	0.000227	0.993990	0.000006
13	1111	6500	$0.07	$455	0.909091	0.998288	0.991486	0.000046	0.996596	0.000003
14	1010	5000	$0.08	$400	1.000000	1.000000	1.000000	0.000000	1.000000	0.000004
15										
16				Sum			A	SSE	A	SSE
17				$233,605			0.093933	0.003001	6.250926	0.021214

Fig. 11.9 Excel spreadsheet to determine the optimal benders parameter

The next two columns show the cumulative fraction of sales based on the exponential Pareto curve (EY) and the squared error for the exponential curve fit. The following is formula used to compute EY:

$$EY_i = 1 - e^{-AX_i}$$

The sum of squared errors or SSE for the Benders curve is shown in cell H17. This sum depends on the value of the A parameter, which is shown in cell G17. The optimal value of the parameter A is found by minimizing the sum of squared errors with the help of the Excel Solver. The corresponding dialog window for the solver is shown in Fig. 11.10. The options for the Excel solver are shown in Fig. 11.11. The optimal value of the A parameter for the exponential curve was found with the Excel GROWTH function.

For the Benders curve, the total sum of squared errors is 0.003 for a parameter value of 0.0939. The sum of squared errors is very small, which indicates a very

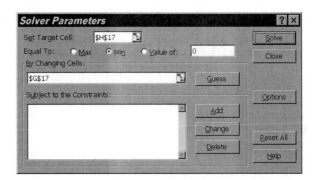

Fig. 11.10 Solver dialog window for determining the optimal Benders Pareto parameter

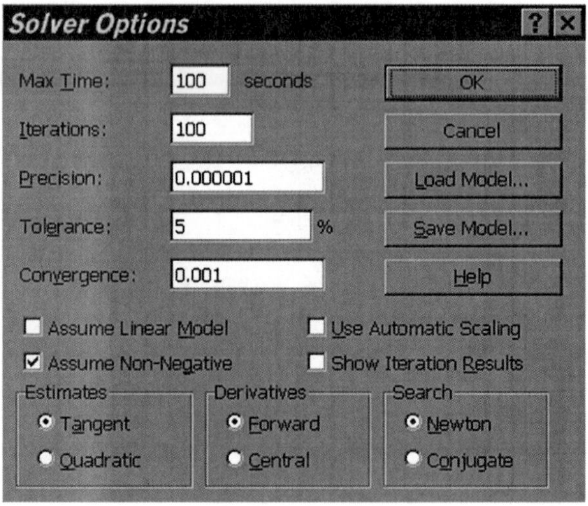

Fig. 11.11 Solver options dialog window for determining the optimal Benders Pareto parameter

good curve fit. In this particular example 27% of the products make up 80% of dollar sales. This curve is less skewed than the standard 80-20 curve, i.e., it takes more than 20% of the products to account for 80% of the dollar sales. For the exponential curve, the total sum of squared errors is 0.021 for a parameter value of 6.251. The sum of squared errors is still very small which indicates a good curve fit. The Benders approximation is preferred in this example because it has both a smaller SEE, and the Benders curve fits the sales data better for the leftmost section of the curve which corresponds to the products that contribute more to the annual sales. The actual cumulative sales and the computed cumulative sales curves are shown in Fig. 11.12. This chart can then be copied and pasted into other documents as illustrated in Fig. 11.6.

During the data analysis phase of a design project, often a large number of Pareto analyses are performed. One may want to identify the most important suppliers,

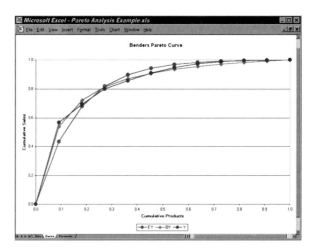

Fig. 11.12 Actual versus computed cumulative sales curves based on the Benders Pareto curve

the most important products, or the most important transportation channels. The measure investigated may be expressed in monetary units to determine the concentration with respect to sales revenue or transportation costs or the measure may be expressed in units of material flow to determine the concentration of activities. This data analysis effort is often denoted as profiling.

11.3.2 Suppliers and Vendors

Suppliers are providers of products to the supply chain from outside the supply chain. Purchases of product from suppliers may have price, availability, and time constraints, but suppliers are not under control of the supply chain management. Suppliers are sometimes also denoted as vendors. Customers are consumers of products from the supply chain. The customer demand for a product is not under control of the supply chain management. Depending on the scope of the supply chain design project both suppliers or customers may belong to the same corporation or be external to the corporation. At the opposite end of the design complexity spectrum, vendors or suppliers may belong to different corporate entities but considered to be part of the supply chain or the supply chain design project.

11.3.2.1 Strategies for Raw Material Procurement

The strategies for sourcing and transformation decisions in supply chain configuration and their respective advantages and disadvantages were summarized by Cohen and Lee (1989).

Centralization The centralization sourcing strategy purchases the total requirement of this raw material from a single vendor. The advantages are lower purchasing prices because economies of scale and lower purchasing overhead. This strategy has cost advantages of scale, however the supply system is not robust. The material management at various plants procured from a central location is complex compared to other strategies.

The fragility of a supply chain with a centralized structure is illustrated by the following example. In 2007, a strong earthquake struck Japan and damaged significantly the facilities of the Riker company, which manufactures piston rings used in the automotive engines used by many Japanese car manufactures. Piston rings fit around the head of the piston to create a seal that traps combustion gasses. According to Chozick (2007), due to the lack of four relatively small parts per car, each costing less than $ 1.50, 70% of the Japanese auto assembly plants were temporarily shut down.

Regionalization The regionalization strategy sources the raw materials and sub-components required by a plant from vendors in the same region. This allows improved communication between the plant and the vendors and quick response and just in item supply policies, which result in lower inventory costs. This strategy also has the advantage of reduced inbound transportation costs because transportation distances are smaller. Because the overall supply chain is divided in a number of autonomous regional supply chains, the smaller supply chains are also easier to manage and design. The combination of the regional supply chains is more robust than a single concentrated supply chain since even if the supplier in a particular region is incapacitated the suppliers in the other regions remain active and may even supply part of the distressed region.

Consolidation The consolidation strategy reduces the number of vendors on a worldwide basis. The smaller number of vendors allows for economies of scale, such as lower purchasing prices due to quantity discounts. The transportation costs for inbound materials may be higher than with regionalized supply chains because of the increased distances. One common consolidation strategy is called *dual sourcing*, since it establishes at minimum two suppliers in the world for every raw material or component. One extreme example of consolidation is called a *strategic alliance*, where a limited number of organizations jointly design, produce, and possible even jointly service a product. The supply chain is design and managed as a single entity and the costs and profits are shared. Such strategic alliances are used primarily for highly technological products because it allows for sharing of the high initial design cost. Examples are the B-787 aircraft model by the Boeing Company and the A-380 model by the Airbus Company. Both projects have been very difficult to manage because of the complexity of the product, the production process, and the business organization and processes.

Dispersion The dispersion or diversification strategy sources materials from a variety of vendors that are geographically dispersed. This strategy has diseconomies of scale and scope. The main advantage of the strategy is a more robust supply system that does not depend on the performance of a single vendor. This strategy also provides the opportunity to take advantage of currency exchange rate fluctuations. It may also have lower inbound transportation costs. Dispersion of the suppliers and the manufacturing sites also creates a large base of constituents that support the product. This strategy has been widely used by defense contractors and departments of defense to influence purchases of military equipment.

11.3.3 Transformation Facilities

The two main types of transformation facilities in a supply chain are manufacturing plants and distribution centers. The role of manufacturing plants is to produce the product while to role of the distribution centers is to efficiently satisfy the demand by customers from products held in inventory. Transformation facilities are typically the major physical assets of a supply chain. A manufacturing or assembly plant may have attracted a number of suppliers who have located a distribution center close to the manufacturing plant. Because of this clustering effect and of the investment cost for a new plant, manufacturing facilities are extremely difficult to relocate in a supply chain. The location of a new plant and the configuration of all the manufacturing facilities in a supply chain are some of the most strategic decisions with respect to supply chain design and planning.

11.3.3.1 Strategies for Manufacturing Network Configuration

Regionalization In a regionalization strategy, each manufacturing plant will serve all the customers in a particular geographical area with the full product assortment offered by the company. In essence, the global manufacturing network is divided into a number of local manufacturing networks with independent distribution to their assigned customers. This strategy enables a close link and cooperation between the manufacturing and the customers it serves. Each plant must be flexible and capable of producing all the products in demand in its area in the limited quantities corresponding to its area. This strategy suffers both diseconomies of scale and scope. This strategy has the advantages of enhanced customer service and the ease of decentralized decisionmaking. The distribution and transportation of finished goods is limited to a small geographical area. This strategy is also robust viewed from a global perspective since a catastrophic occurrence in one geographical area does not impact other areas. This strategy is, however, not robust at all viewed from the local perspective, since if production at the single plant serving the area is interrupted all products in the local market are no longer available. Finally, an important financial aspect of the regionalization strategy is that production costs are incurred and denominated in the same currency as the sales price to the customers which makes the supply chain performance less dependent on international currency exchange rates and their variations.

Consolidation In a consolidation strategy, all the production of all products for the entire world takes place at one or two places. Each manufacturing plant serves either the whole world or a very large section of the world. This strategy allows the plant economies of scale, such as product design, production design, and large production batches. However, the finished goods have to be distributed to large geographical areas. This strategy is not robust, since a catastrophic occurrence at the single plant would shut down production in the whole world. To avoid this situation, management often specifies as a strategic constraint that at least two plants in the world must produce or must be able to produce the products.

Product Focus In a product focus strategy, each plant specializes in the production of a single class of finished products. Each plant serves the whole world for that group of finished products. This strategy allows the plant economies of scale, such as product design, production design, and avoids diseconomies of scope, such as small production batches. The finished goods have to be distributed of large geographical areas. This strategy is not robust, since a catastrophic occurrence at the single plant would shut down production in the whole world for a limited number of finished goods.

Process Focus In process focus strategy, each plant specializes in a particular manufacturing process, which typically corresponds to a single step or stage in the overall manufacturing process. Examples are component production, assembly of subcomponents, or finished product assembly. This strategy also allows for economies of scale and economies of scope. The plant may use a higher level of automation or it may be located in a location with inexpensive manual labor. The disadvantage of this strategy is that it requires tight control integration among the different stages to ensure good production performance of the overall supply chain. This strategy also may require more transportation of work-in-process goods.

Dispersion In a dispersion strategy, plants are located at various locations geographically dispersed over the world. Each plant may have the capability to produce a limited number of products or execute a limited number of processing steps. The overall goal is to have overlapping coverage by several plants of the demand for various products in the world. This strategy tends to have both diseconomies of scale and of scope. However, it is considered to be very robust since for every product–customer combination there are at least two plants capable of servicing this demand and these plants are geographically not far from the customers. However, this strategy requires extensive coordination between the various plants to provide acceptable service to the customers while maintaining acceptable capacity utilization at the various facilities. Because the investment cost for manufacturing facilities is so large, this dispersion strategy is not often used.

11.3.3.2 Strategies for Distribution Network Configuration

Consolidation The consolidation strategy uses a single large distribution center to service most of the customers in the world with a large variety of products. The strategy has the advantage of the economies of scale. One specific effect is reduction of safety inventory since the demand uncertainty of many customers is pooled together to create a more stable aggregate demand. Another advantage is the reduced fixed facility costs. The disadvantages of a consolidation strategy are related to higher distribution cost of the finished goods and reduced robustness of the distribution system.

Customer Focus The customer focus strategy use a number of geographically dispersed distribution centers close to customer markets so that the transportation time to the customer is kept below a certain bound. This leads to faster response times and a higher level of service to the customer. However, demand pooling is much more limited and hence the total safety inventory in the system tends to be larger. Cycle inventories may also be larger than in the case of a consolidated warehouse, since the local demand may warrant less frequent replenishment. This strategy has diseconomies of scale and scope and higher fixed and operating costs are typical.

Co-location The co-location strategy places a distribution center next to every manufacturing facility so that the distribution center can perform some of the final value-added operations on the product. The distribution center functions as the finished goods storage location for that manufacturing plant. Operations at the distribution center may be performed by a third party logistics provider or by non-unionized labor and this may yield cost savings compared to labor force employed at the manufacturing plant.

11.3.3.3 Taxation, Duties, and Tariffs

The operational and financial performance of a supply chain may be significantly impacted when a supply chain crosses a national boundary. Each of the two governments may have regulations and taxation rules to influence the supply chain decisions. Complicated taxation and documentation requirements may also delay and change border crossing inside a country, e.g., supply chains crossing state boundaries in India. One strategy to avoid these complications and taxations is the establishment and use of free-trade zones. Most of the times duties, taxes, local content laws, and associated regulations cannot be directly set at the level of the individual corporation but rather function as constraints or impact the financial performance of supply chains. But many corporations are faced with the issue of setting transfer prices, which are the prices at which goods are sold between different national subsidiaries of the same global corporation.

Transfer Pricing In the *Economist* (2007) several cases are listed where major global companies are in negotiation with taxing authorities to determine the transfer prices for products and the associated tax impacts. This is in essence a grey area without hard rules on how to set the transfer prices and so many of the disputes end up in lengthy legal proceedings that typically involve a global corporation and two national governments.

Transfer pricing is to be optimized by a corporation within the limits set by the taxing authorities of the two countries involved. Most important is to determine those upper and lower limits and identify barriers that prevent the transfer price to go to either limit such as implicit or explicit minimum profit requirements in a country. Setting these lower and upper limits is usually performed by a multi-disciplinary team and involving the services of an international accounting firm. After the lower and upper bounds have been set, optimizing the value of the transfer price in a global supply chain requires calculations of the net cash flow in each country and for the global corporation.

A second major category of influence factors is the reward method for the subsidiaries. Transfer prices impact how the local management is rewarded and motivated. Typically setting transfer prices maximizes the financial performance of the overall corporation, which may involve disadvantaging some local subsidiaries. Hence bonus and reward policies have to be adapted.

11.3.4 Transportation Channels

So far the products and facilities components of the supply chain have been described. The components of the supply chain that move the goods between the various facilities are called transportation channels. A transportation channel between an origin and destination facility is defined by its combination capacity, costs, transportation mode, and the transportation frequency.

11.3.4.1 Strategies for Transportation Systems Configuration

One of the major driving forces in the configuration of transportation systems is the presence of strong economies of scale. Three of the major configurations strategies for transportation services and their associated infrastructure are hub-and-spoke, direct service, and opportunistic service.

Hub-and-Spoke Hub-and-spoke network are characterized by a large number of origins and destinations, denoted as suppliers and customers, and a large number of transportation activities, where each individual customer, supplier, or request occupies only a small fraction of the capacity of the transportation vehicle. Goods are transported to a consolidation center from the various origin facilities, which corresponds to spokes of the system. Then the goods are transported on the major transportation channels between the various hubs. Finally, the goods are distributed from a hub to the customers. The transportation hardware, infrastructure, and processes may be different for more localized spoke operations than for the more global backbone operations. Some of the largest hub and spoke networks are operated by the parcel and less than truckload transportation companies.

Direct Service The main characteristic of direct service is that a transportation cargo follows a direct route between its origin and destination facility. A typical example of direct service occurs in the supply chain for iron ore. The ore is mined in the interior of Australia or South America, transported by unit trains from the inland to the ocean port, transported by ore carriers to the destination port, and then again transported by train to the iron and steel plant. A very similar example is the transportation of coal to be used as fuel in electric power generation plants.

Opportunistic Service Transportation activities for opportunistic service do not have a fixed set of transportation routes but the transportation vehicles are routed to respond to demand of transportation requests. The vehicle may contain goods for a single transportation request or for multiple requests. An example of single transportation request is transportation by full truckload. After a carrier delivers a load, it searches for a new load for which the origin is near in space and time to its current location. An example of multiple loads sharing a carrier are the tramp ships which do have a fixed schedule but travel from port to port to satisfy individual requests.

11.4 Information Technology

11.4.1 Decision Support System Components

The information technology infrastructure for the tracking and reporting (execution) and planning at the operational level of supply chains has grown dramatically in the last decade. However, information technology for tactical and especially strategic planning of supply chains is much less developed. Information technology to support tactical or strategic decision making must have the following four components: data management, design or planning model, solution algorithm, and user interface. Data management is responsible for the collecting and processing of the date required for planning decisions. Many time this involves interacting with corporate databases and ERP systems to collect the raw data and then using Pareto analysis to synthesize the data. A model is a simplified representation of the real-world supply chain system that contains all the relevant components to make and evaluate planning decisions. A solution algorithm is a set of rules that determines the planning decisions in order to achieve the best possible performance of the supply chain system. Finally, the user interface is the collection of tools that allows the design engineer to pose a particular problem, obtain a set of planning decisions for the problem, and to communicate these decisions and their impact to the decision makers. If any of these four components is missing then the decision support system most likely will not be used consistently or frequently. The planning models and solution algorithms for transportation and inventory systems have described in previous chapters and the model and solution algorithms for supply chain planning and design are described in the next two chapters.

The application of supply chain engineering planning tools for the support of strategic design decisions has been more the exception than the rule. While the solution of large mixed-integer programming models has been one of the limiting factors on the implementation of optimization based techniques for the design of strategic logistics systems, the lack of easy interpretation and representation of the results has also contributed to the lack of acceptance by industry. Two dimensions of conflict exist for the application of planning systems. The first conflict dimension is need for standardization versus the need for specialization. Decision support tools can only be economically developed, supported, and deployed if they treat relatively standard problems. However, the variety of supply chains requires some degree of specialization for each individual project. The second conflict dimension is the need for ease of use versus transparency. Decision support tools will only be used repeatedly if they are easy to use and leverage the power of the human decision maker. This implies that computer tools will be used to automate many of the tasks. However, this introduces the danger that the tools will be used as a black box and the output of the tools will be used without critical evaluation of the assumptions, data used, or algorithms. In Fig. 11.14 a typical display of a supply chain configuration tool is shown. The facilities are displayed on a map and the transportation activities shown as lines between the various facilities, which leads to the typical "spider" graphs.

Because our model is generic, i.e. has standard components, we were able to develop a graphical representation of the problems. At the same time we were able to develop a relational database corresponding to the coefficients and parameters in our model. The relational database can be stored as a set of flat files or in a true relational data base manager (Fig. 11.13).

We selected the Microsoft Windows environment for our implementation because of its widespread acceptance and familiarity in industry. A sample screen of the CIMPEL program is shown in Fig. 11.14. The user can select in the standard

Fig. 11.13 CIMPEL component structure and flowchart

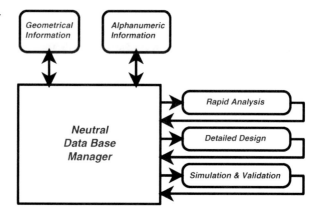

fashion the algorithms to be executed. After a solution has been obtained, the user can change through simple dialog boxes parameter values, force facilities open or closed, etc. For small or relatively simple cases the mixed integer programming solver can be called directly from within the CIMPEL program through a dynamic link library. For larger cases, the MPS file is generated, the solver is run in batch mode, and the solution file is read back into CIMPEL to display the results.

In our experience, the use of such a graphical front end is an absolute requirement for the adaptation of optimization-based techniques in the design of industrial logistics systems.

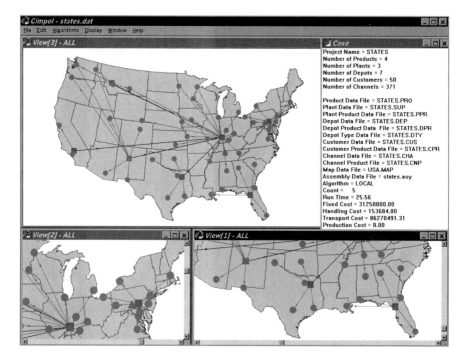

Fig. 11.14 Cimpel screen illustration

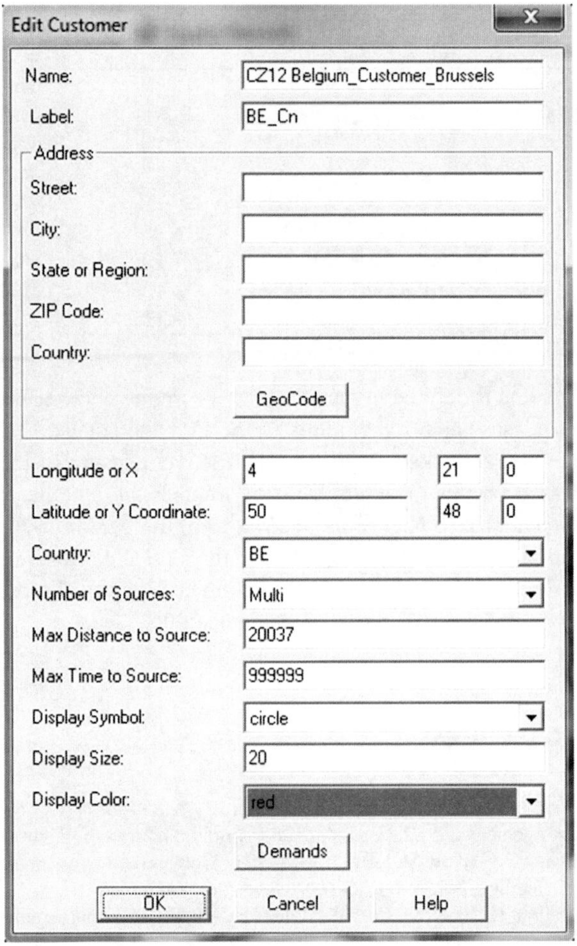

Fig. 11.15 Catenas edit customer dialog window

In Fig. 11.15 an example is shown of the data characteristics for a customer facility, including its required service levels. It allows for the definition of the location of the customer directly through is longitude and latitude coordinates or through the geocoding of its alphanumeric address.

11.5 Exercises

11.5.1 U.S. Household Income Trend

In an article in the *Atlanta Journal and Constitution* November 20, 2005 (Walker 2005), it was stated that the income gap between rich and poor households in the United States is getting larger. The income data is repeated in Table 11.2. Aggregate

Table 11.2 U.S. household shares of aggregate income by quintiles

Year	20%	40%	60%	80%	100%	Top 5%
2001	3.5%	8.7%	14.6%	23.0%	50.1%	22.4%
2000	3.6%	8.9%	14.8%	23.0%	49.8%	22.1%
1995	3.7%	9.1%	15.2%	23.3%	48.7%	21.0%
1990	3.9%	9.6%	15.9%	24.0%	46.6%	18.6%
1985	4.0%	9.7%	16.3%	24.6%	45.3%	17.0%
1980	4.3%	10.3%	16.9%	24.9%	43.7%	15.8%
1975	4.4%	10.5%	17.1%	24.8%	43.2%	15.9%
1970	4.1%	10.8%	17.4%	24.5%	43.3%	16.6%
1967	4.0%	10.8%	17.3%	24.2%	43.8%	17.5%

income is defined in the article as the money income before deductions of taxes and expenses and not including lump sum payments and capital gains.

You are asked to give a quantitative measure of the income gap over time and based on this measure to assert whether the income gap is getting larger. Finally, you are asked to forecast the shares of the U.S. households of aggregate income by quintiles and for the top 5% for the year 2005 at the 95% confidence level. Your presentation and report should contain a graphical representation of the shares over time and of the forecasted shares in 2005.

References

Arntzen, B. C., Brown, G. G., Harrison, T. P., & Trafton, L. L. (1995). Global supply chain management at digital equipment corporation. *Interfaces, 25*(1), 69–93.

Ballou, R. H., & Masters, J. M. (1993). Commercial software for locating warehouses and other facilities. *Journal of Business Logistics, 14*(2), 71–107.

Ballou, R. H., & Masters, J. M. (1999). Facility location commercial software survey. *Journal of Business Logistics, 20*(1), 215–233.

Bender, P. (1981). Mathematical modeling of the 20/80 rule: Theory and practice. *Journal of Business Logistics, 2*(2), 139–157.

Chozick, A. (2007). A key strategy of Japans car makers backfires. *Wall Street Journal,* 20-Jul-2007, B1.

Cohen, M. A., & Lee, H. L. (1989). Resource deployment analysis of global manufacturing and distribution networks. *Journal of Manufacturing Operations Management, 2,* 81–104.

Economist. (2007). Global companies have plenty of latitude to minimize their tax bills. *Economist,* February 22, 2007.

Feldman, J. (2003). Why Uma fights. *Money,* November 28, 2003.

Goetschalckx, M. (2009). *Catenas users manual.*

Miller, T. (2001). *Hierarchical operations and supply chain planning.* London: Springer.

Stadtler, H., & Kilger, C. (2000). *Supply chain management and advanced planning.* Heidelberg: Springer.

Walker, T. (2005). Rich control all, economist insists, out-of-mainstream theory holds that U.S. 'plutonomy' runs almost everything. *Atlanta Journal and Constitution,* 20 Nov 2005, Q1.

Chapter 12
Supply Chain Models

Learning Objectives After you have studied this chapter, you should be able to

- Know the characteristics of the major types of objectives for strategic models
- Know the tactical supply chain planning model
- Know how characteristics and differences between arc-based and path-based supply chain models
- Know the warehouse location model (WLP), the Geoffrion & Graves (G&G), and the multi-echelon strategic planning models
- Know the site relative cost factor and how to apply it

12.1 Introduction

As shown in the previous chapter, there exists a very large variety of supply chains. The management, planning, and design of these chains create a large number and diversity of decision support questions which in turn has yielded a large variety of models that have been created to assist in answering these questions. Some of these models were previously described in the chapters on transportation planning and inventory planning. This chapter will focus on models that describe the integrated supply chain. Supply chain design models are inherently the most complex of all supply chain decision models because they have to incorporate a multitude of factors such as purchasing, production, transportation, inventory, and facilities and supply chain structure. Global supply chain design models have the additional complexities of multiple currencies, different taxation systems, duties and tariffs, and transfer prices. Finally, the instance data for these models typically contain a very large number of supply chain objects, such as customers, products, and transportation channels. As a consequence the instance models, which incorporate both the model structure and the instance data, tend to be very large and the corresponding values of the decision variables can almost never be used directly in decision support. Faced with such large and complex engineering design problems, eight principles guide the engineering process in order to bring it to a successful completion.

12.1.1   Eight Principles of Supply Chain Design Projects

12.1.1.1   KISS

The first and most important principle is to keep the model and the instance data as simple as possible. It is commonly referred to as the KISS, or "keep it simple, stupid" principle. The goal of using a model in science and engineering has been to simplify the real world problem and to ease the manipulation of the corresponding data. This prime principle has been used over extended periods in a diverse variety of science and engineering disciplines. On the other hand, if structure or behavior exists in the system that impacts the design but is not included in the standard design models then the model has to be adapted and extended to include these additional factors. There will always remain a tradeoff between the need for the model to be simple and need for it to be comprehensive and detailed. The persistence of this tradeoff is illustrated by the following quotation attributed to Einstein "Things should be made as simple as possible, but not any simpler".

12.1.1.2   GIGO

The second principle is captured by the acronym GIGO which stands for "garbage in, garbage out". Engineering methodologies are data driven. If the data used in the decision support is of bad quality then the recommendations derived at after all the processing and design work may be faulty. Especially in strategic design projects where data has to be collected from a large variety of sources within and outside the supply chain organization, collecting, verifying, validating, and making the data internally consistent is a very time consuming but necessary process.

12.1.1.3   Festina Lente

The third principle is indicated by "festina lente", which is a Latin expression which means "hurry slowly" or proceed quickly but with caution. Because of the complexity of the engineering project and because strategic supply chain design is often done very infrequently, posing the problem, assembling the necessary data, and deriving the answers to decision support questions takes time. Design projects may take from three to six months. The shortest duration would be around six weeks. There is a very steep learning curve in supply chain design projects, so the following or follow-up projects would take much less time. Evaluating the impact of new supplier on a supply chain that has been previously modeled may only require a few hours.

12.1.1.4   Beware of the Spreadsheet Blob

In the 1958 classic science fiction movie "the Blob" a giant amoeba-like creature devours everything it comes into contact with. The use of spreadsheet models in decision support has similar characteristics to the blob creature. It has been often said that the most used and the most abused tool for decision support are spreadsheet models. Spreadsheet models are some of the most flexible tools, they are widely available, have a low startup cost, and can be easily adapted to individual needs. They are superior for producing graphs that communicate synthesis results from the models. Consequently, spreadsheet models have often grown organically in the organization over a period of time to answer specific needs. However, they are notoriously badly documented, difficult to understand, and often dispersed in an unstructured and unconnected way throughout the organization. The value of cells in the spreadsheet may be computed with very complicated formulas that refer to other cells so that their meaning is very difficult to understand. As consequence the models embedded in the spreadsheets have become black boxes and the model objectives, constraints, and limitations are not clearly understood, especially if the spreadsheet is no longer in use by its creator. Because supply chain design projects are so complex the resources used should be of "industrial" quality. This applies to software packages, modeling technology, and people.

12.1.1.5   Trust but Verify

The results generated by supply chain models are typically voluminous and require processing before they can be interpreted by the design team or decision maker. It is virtually impossible to look at the output of a model and determine if the configuration makes sense or not. It is not uncommon that wrong, i.e. infeasible, supply chain configurations are presented in academic journals even for very small educational examples. Errors in the model or more commonly in the data for real world sized problems can easily go undetected. On the other hand, the modeling results may be correct and the intuition of the design team or decision maker may be flawed. The validity of the model and the correctness of the data should be carefully validated through sensitivity analysis.

12.1.1.6   It's a Stochastic World

Supply chain planning models are typically used to determine the best actions or configurations in anticipation of future conditions, which are inherently not known with certainty. Often the stochastic nature of the input data for the models is ignored and only one or a very few deterministic cases are investigated. This ignores many of the risks for the supply chain. The impact of various risks on the performance of the supply chain should be examined through a large number of scenarios. Risks can be categorized as variations, hazards, and catastrophes. Variations are the changes in values of future conditions that can be anticipated and forecasted. One example is the variability of demand instances over time even though the demand distribution is constant. Hazards are uncommon events that are known to exist and have significant impact but whose timing and severity are difficult to predict. Examples are large winter storms or strikes by the labor force. Finally, catastrophes are exceedingly rare events that change the structure and behavior of the supply chain dramatically. Examples are influenza pandemics or global terrorist attacks.

12.1.1.7 There is No Single Best Design

For strategic design projects the expected yields and dispersion of the yields of various supply chain configurations can be shown in a risk analysis graph. One of the main benefits of this graph is to show that most often there is not a single "best" configuration or design. The graph provides an intuitive mechanism for executives to judge the risk of various decisions and to compare different decisions with respect to expected performance and risk. It allows matching the philosophy of the company to the characteristics of the configuration, i.e. risk adverse or risk seeking. The risk analysis graph was described in greater detail in the previous chapter.

12.1.1.8 Successive Refinement

Strategic supply chain design is a complex problem and providing decision support for the design is a challenging task. It is recommended that this decision support starts with some easier problems such as the tactical supply chain planning problem. This allows the organization to build up the data, modeling, solution algorithms, and engineering-based decision making culture gradually. This allows for the accumulation of confidence and trust in engineering based design and its components of mathematical modeling and solution algorithms.

During a typical supply chain design project, there are three phases with respect to the use of mathematical modeling as a decision support tool. Before the model is used, the problem is defined, overall objectives and constraints are determined, and set of feasible alternatives is constructed. Most of these activities are based on business goals and intuition and typically do not use any mathematics. During the middle phase, mathematical models and solution algorithms are employed to develop a limited number of desirable alternatives. During the final phase, the results of the mathematical models are again combined with many qualitative considerations to arrive at a final decision and design. The qualitative phases bracket the quantitative phase, like the two halves of the bun of a hamburger enclose the beef patty. At one time a presidential candidate asked during one of the presidential debates "where is the beef?" to cut through all the marketing and to get to the heart of the matter on a program proposed by one of his competitors. Similarly, mathematical models provide the objective and quantitative methods and tools to decide between various alternatives and to properly configure and size the design. So while mathematical models and solution algorithms form the central core of the decision process, they still make up only a small part of the overall design process. Experienced executives responsible for supply chain design and operation at leading companies typically state that between 6 to 10% of the time and resources of a supply chain design project are spent on the mathematical modeling and solution phase. A more in depth treatment of this topic can be found in Vidal and Goetschalckx (1996).

12.1.2 Model Characteristics

A single model for supply chain design does not exist. Rather a large variety of models have been developed. But these models have still some characteristics in common even if not all models may have all of the following characteristics. When a model is selected to provide a particular decision support function, it is useful to verify that characteristics listed next can be safely excluded from the model or should be included.

- The number of commodities in the model. Some models aggregate all material flows in the supply chain to a single product or commodity. But most products are made up out of several sub assemblies or raw materials. The relationships between the finished products and their components are given by a structured BOM which also describes the transformation processes.
- The number of echelons in the model. An echelon is defined as transformation process with its corresponding facility that are part of the supply chain and through which products must flow from external suppliers to external customers. Most supply chains are multi-echelon. If products flow directly from external suppliers to external customers the supply chain can be considered to have zero echelons. More commonly, the products are process in a production facility and delivered to the customer to a distribution center. Such a supply chain is said to have two echelons, one echelon of manufacturing facilities and one echelon of distribution facilities.
- The number of different countries in the model. Models can be single-country, also called domestic, or can be multi-country, also called global. A model may model multiple countries even if all of the supply chain is located in a single national country. Typical reasons for this are preferential tax treatments for certain areas of the country or free trade zones.
- Most strategic design models have a planning horizon of multiple years, where results in a single year determine the taxation values. The results from future years have to be discounted to the current decision moment with the capital discount rate which is company specific. Most tactical production planning models have multiple periods and inventories may be held between periods, but these planning periods are only fractions of a year such as month or a week. Strategic models may have to include such a detailed tactical planning if seasonal varia-

tions and seasonal inventories impact the decisions on strategic infrastructure location and capacity sizing.

- Nearly all supply chains have one or more facilities in which the commodities are processed. Most often these facilities have capacities, either for individual commodities or for joint-commodity resources. Processing the commodities may require fractions of the capacity per commodity for a fixed setup, a constant linear consumption rate, or a consumption rate with economies of scale. Facilities may also have a minimum quantity to be processed if the facility is used.
- Supply chains have transportation channels through which the commodities flow from facility to facility. The channels may have capacities, either for individual commodities or for joint-commodity resources and they may also a minimum quantity to be transported if they are used. If the channels deliver or pickup commodities in multi-stop routes then the route costs must be allocated to the commodities transported.
- The structure of the model that computes the financial performance of the supply chain. Financial models for the enterprise come in two basic varieties. The first variant focuses on the before-tax evaluation of operational investment or process improvements and results in the calculation of a before-tax return on investment or ROI. This model is most appropriately used for the evaluation of single equipment acquisitions and relatively localized process changes. The model ignores the time value of money and is not applicable if multiple time periods are involved. The second variant focuses on the after-tax evaluation of a major facility construction or acquisition for a global enterprise. The impact of the design or re-engineering on the time-discounted value of the net cash flow resulting of the global operations but expressed in the home currency is computed. Clearly the second variant is a much more complicated model but it has the capability to handle multi-period investment planning.
- The supply chain design model may have deterministic values of the parameters or multiple values for each parameter organized in scenarios. If multiple scenarios exist, the tradeoff between the central tendency and the dispersion of the performance of the supply chain has to be included in the model.

12.1.3 Model and Algorithm Hierarchy

While a very large number of supply chain models exist, a list of standard models is given next and their corresponding solution algorithms are discussed. The list is organized by increasing complexity of the supply chain model.

12.1.3.1 Display, Evaluate, and Benchmark

The simplest planning model for a supply chain is to compute the performance of the current supply chain and to display the current supply chain. The solution algorithm used is a very large summation of the various costs in the supply chain and this algorithm is typically implemented in a spreadsheet. The values are merely recorded from the real world system and are not optimized. The display is usually the network structure, where the transportation routes may follow the transportation network or show the connections between facilities in starburst diagrams. The display software is based on a geographical information system and may be used through a web service such as Google Maps. Since none of the planning decisions are optimized this is a descriptive model of the supply chain.

12.1.3.2 Distribution Channel Selection

One of the easiest prescriptive planning decisions is to decide on the transportation mode, with its corresponding frequency and transportation batch size characteristics, for a single commodity between a single origin and destination facility. Each of these decisions for a combination of commodity and origin and destination facility pair is made independently of the other similar decisions. The model will select the transportation mode and set the corresponding levels of cycle and safety inventory. The available facilities are assumed to be given and their total capacity may be computed but does not function as a constraint on the selection decisions. The decisions typically are implemented in a spreadsheet. This planning process works uses a bottom up approach and considers the resources in the supply chain to be without capacity constraints.

12.1.3.3 Tactical Supply Chain Model

The tactical supply chain model determines the purchasing, transportation, and delivery flows and the inventories in order to minimize the cost of satisfying customer demands for a number of periods in the planning horizon. It is assumed that the supply chain configuration with its facilities and their capacities is known and cannot be changed. The periods are typically weeks, months, or seasons in a year. The solution algorithm used is typically linear programming. If the demand is for a small number of discrete products a mixed integer programming solver may have to be used to avoid fractional product flows. The solver may be standalone application or an add-on to spreadsheet software, but because of the size of the problem instances a separate license for the solver typically has to be purchased.

12.1.3.4 Location-Allocation

The location-allocation model determines the location of the facilities in the supply chain in order to get the minimum cost tradeoff between transportation costs and facility costs for moving goods from external suppliers to external customers. The best number of facilities is often determined through a parametric design, i.e.

if one facility is established where is its best location, then if two facilities are used where are their best locations, etc... The transportation costs are proportional to the material flow quantities and to the distance between facilities which are computed with a distance norm. The cost of the facilities cannot be site dependent since the solution algorithm will locate the facilities in a continuous decision space. But the facilities may have different handling costs for processing flow through the facilities. The solution algorithms are heuristics to determine the continuous coordinates of the supply chain facilities. The accuracy of the location solution is low; typically the resolution is at the level of state, county or metropolitan area. The algorithms belong to the class of alternative generating algorithms since they determine the location coordinates of the facilities, while ignoring the underlying transportation network or the feasibility of location of the facility. The algorithms consist of specialized, non-linear optimization procedures combined with linear programming solvers and thus require significant programming effort to implement.

12.1.3.5 Supply Chain Design Models

The supply chain design models attempt to find the best supply chain configuration and the supply chain flows and inventories in order to minimize the supply chain costs or maximize the supply chain profit. The possible candidate supply chain configurations are based on a list of candidate facilities which may or may not be established in the supply chain solution. Since the candidates are selected from a list the algorithms belong to the class of alternative selecting procedures and site dependent costs can be included in the model. Because the status of a candidate facility is either established or not and the amount of product flow can change continuously, the solution algorithms belong to the class of mixed integer programming solvers. These solvers are almost always separate applications that may pull their data from either spreadsheets or databases. The supply chain design models can be further divided into major sub classes depending on the number supply chain components and the supply chain behavior that are optimized. In this chapter the P-Median and P-Center Problem, the Warehouse Location Problem (WLP), and the model by Geoffrion and Graves (1974) are discussed. In the next chapter on advanced supply chain models a comprehensive supply chain model, a global supply chain model with transfer prices, and a robust supply chain model with explicit consideration of supply chain risks are described.

12.1.4 Systems Modeling Language

A common task in the management and design of supply chain systems is the evaluation and modeling of the impact of a capital investment or process change on the financial performance of the supply chain or enterprise system. The financial model is typically embedded in a spreadsheet and may call separate sub models or evaluation techniques. While spreadsheets are a very common technology to implement this type of model, the spreadsheet technology has significant deficiencies. The main deficiency is the black box approach which allows the logic embedded in the spreadsheet to be obscured and the model to be internally inconsistent. A more structured, robust, and standardized modeling implementation is desirable. One example is the structured modeling language SysML, which has been implemented in several software applications. Further information on SysML can be found in Friedenthal et al. (2008). It should be noted that a particular variable may be used in several places in a SysML model but is only defined once and bounds on the valid values can be specified at its definition location. In addition, strict dimensional consistency is enforced. However, both approaches exhibit the same fundamental structure in that the final performance measure is computed by a set of cascading equations until all the required input variables for the equations are atomic, i.e. no longer dependent on other variables. Some of these equations are described in the following supply chain models. In general, the supply chain design models contain a large variety of parameters and variables and long variable names are used to facilitate the use and understanding by designers and managers.

12.2 Distribution Channel Selection

The distribution channel selection problem is one of the simplest supply chain planning problems. It determines the best distribution channel structure and transportation mode from a list of alternative modes between an origin and destination facility for a single commodity. The mode is selected based on the sum of inventory, transportation, and facilities costs. Each of these decisions for a commodity and origin and destination facility pair is made independently of the other similar decisions. This type of decision is typically revisited on a yearly or seasonal basis and belongs to the class of tactical planning decisions. A schematic of the different possibilities for the distribution channel between a manufacturing plant and a set of customers is shown in the next figure. The main principle of the solution algorithm is to add all the costs accumulated by moving the product from the origin to the destination facility for each of the channel alternatives. At the end the channel with the lowest unit cost is recommended (Fig. 12.1).

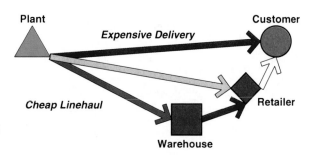

Fig. 12.1 Illustration of different distribution channel alternatives

12.2.1 *Distribution Channel Selection Model*

12.2.1.1 Notation

The distribution channel selection model contains a large number of parameters and decision variables. In the following notation symbols in upper case indicate total annual cost while symbols in lower case indicate cost per unit or cost rate. Two time units will be used. The first one is the long-term planning horizon and is referred to as the strategic time unit. It is most often a year. The second time unit is the time between demand observations at the destination facility and is referred to as the operational time unit. If the demand at the destination is known on a daily or weekly basis, then the second time unit would be a day or week. The number of operational time units equal to one strategic time unit also has to be specified, e.g. there are 52 weeks in a year or 364 days in a year.

12.2.1.2 Parameters and Variables

HCR	inventory holding cost rate (dollars per dollar of inventory per year). Since this is a rate the value is independent of the currency units but depends on the strategic time unit
D_p	annual demand for product p
v_p, v_{mpO}, v_{mpD}	value or accumulated cost of a unit of product p at different points in the supply chain indicated by the subscript, e.g. at arrival at the origin, at leaving the origin, and at arriving at the destination, respectively, and depending on the transportation mode m used by the product to get to this stage
pc_p	unit production or procurement cost of product p. This is the total landed unit cost for getting one unit of the product to the origin facility and this cost is assumed to be independent of the channel selection.
PC_p	total annual production or procurement cost for product p
TT_m	transit time of transportation mode m (expressed in years or strategic periods)
tc_{mp}	transportation cost for shipping one unit of product p with transportation mode m
TC_{mp}	total annual transportation cost for product p shipped with transportation mode m
TB_{mp}	transportation batch size of product p shipped with transportation mode m
slc_{pO}, slc_{pD}	storage location cost per unit of product p at the origin and destination facilities, respectively

$OFSC_{mp}, DFSC_{mp}$	total annual fixed storage cost in at the origin facility or at the destination distribution center for product p shipped with transportation mode m
sc_{mpO}, sc_{mpD}	annualized fixed storage cost per unit of product p shipped with transportation mode m at the two facilities, i.e., at the origin or destination facility respectively
$OCIC_{mp}, DCIC_{mp}$	average cycle inventory cost of product p shipped with transportation mode m at the origin facility or destination facility
$OCIC_{mp}, DCIC_{mp}$	cycle inventory cost of product p shipped with transportation mode m at the origin facility or destination facility
$ocic_{mp}, dcic_{mp}$	unit cycle inventory cost of product p shipped with transportation mode m at origin or destination facility, respectively
pic_{mp}	unit pipeline inventory cost of product p shipped with transportation mode m
PIC_{mp}	pipeline inventory cost of product p shipped with transportation mode m
d_p	average demand during one observable demand period, e.g. daily demand, of product p
Vd_p	variance of the demand during one observable demand period, e.g. daily demand, of product p
CVd_p	coefficient of variation of the demand during observable demand period, e.g. daily demand, of product p
lt_{mp}	average lead time for the delivery of product p using transportation mode m expressed in observable demand periods, e.g. days
Vlt_{mp}	variance of the lead time for the delivery of product p using transportation mode m expressed in observable demand periods, e.g. days
SI_{mp}	safety inventory of product p shipped with transportation mode m at the destination facility
DMI_{mp}, OMI_{mp}	maximum inventory of product p shipped with transportation mode m at the origin facility or at the destination facility, respectively
SIC_{mp}	safety stock inventory cost in destination facility of product p shipped with transportation mode m
TIC_p	total invariant cost for product p
TVC_{mp}	total variable cost for product p using transportation mode m
TFC_{mp}	total fixed cost for product p using transportation mode m
TAC_{mp}	total aggregate cost for product p using transportation mode m

A typical value of the holding cost factor or *HCR* is 0.25, i.e., 25 cents per dollar of inventory per year. To find the holding cost factor for another time period, we have to divide by the number of time periods in a year. A *HCR* equal to 0.25 per year equals a holding cost rate *hcr* of $0.25/364 = 6.868 \cdot 10^{-4} = 0.0006868$ per day.

12.2.2   Big Screen TV Company Example

The following example will be used to illustrate the calculations for the channel selection. The Big Screen TV Company manufactures projection TVs with screen sizes 55 inch and above for customers located in the continental United States. The manufacturing plant is located Japan and all units are imported through the container port of Newport Beach in California. There exists a large import warehouse near Newport Beach, which is assumed never to run out of inventory of TVs. The company operates a number of regional distribution centers, one of which is located in Atlanta, Georgia and serves the customers in the Southeast area of the United States. The goal is to select the least cost transportation mode between the import warehouse and the distribution center. The possible transportation modes are rail or truck. Various characteristics for each mode are given in the next table (Table 12.1).

The unit manufacturing and transportation cost to the import warehouse of an average projection TV is $3400, which includes all applicable duties and tariffs. TVs are imported on a bi-weekly schedule in intermodal containers that hold 160 units. Due to the annual feature and style changes in the TV models and the deep discounting of models of previous years, the aggregate holding cost for all inventories for one year is 60% of the product value, i.e., 60 cents per dollar per year. The total customer demand served from the Atlanta distribution center is 4160 projection TVs per year. It is assumed that the demand process has a constant average rate throughout the year. A year is equivalent to 52 weeks and 364 days. The weekly demand for TVs at the distribution center has a normal distribution with a mean of 80 TVs and a standard deviation of 40 TVs. The safety inventory for each mode in the distribution center is assumed to ensure a service level equivalent to a probability of 95% delivery out of inventory for the weekly demand of the projection TVs. The annualized fixed warehouse cost is equal to $200 per TV for the import warehouse in Long Beach and for the regional distribution center in Atlanta. All unit cost values will be computed in dollars and cents while all annual cost values will be computed in whole dollars. The best transportation mode based on the total cost for this distribution system is to be determined.

Table 12.1 Transportation mode selection data

	Rail	Truck
Unit Transportation Cost ($)	32	75
Channel Transit Time (days)	14	7
Transportation Batch Size	160	80

12.2.2.1 Cost Computations

Invariant Costs Invariant costs are costs that are incurred by the logistics systems but that do not depend on the selection of the distribution channel. Since it is assumed that the total demand does not depend on the selection of the distribution channel, the total production cost is a member of the invariant costs. The total production cost is computed as product of the yearly demand and the unit production costs.

$$PC_p = D_p \cdot pc_p \qquad (12.1)$$

$$TIC_p = PC_p \qquad (12.2)$$

For the Big TV example, the total invariant costs, which in this case are equal to the total purchasing costs, are computed as follows.

$$TIC_p = 4160 \cdot 3400 = \$14,144,000$$

If the costs are impacted by the channel selection they are called incremental or variant costs. Typically, incremental costs are further classified as fixed or variable costs. If the selection of the origin facility impacts the production or purchasing costs, then these costs are no longer invariant. Different costs may be moved to different categories if they depend on the selection decision or not.

Fixed Costs Fixed costs are costs whose magnitude does not change during the operation of the distribution channel. The fixed costs may be different from one distribution channel to another, but once a channel selection has been made, the fixed costs remain unchanged. In distribution channel design, the size of the warehouse remains unchanged for extended periods of time. Hence, the annualized cost per warehouse location or per cubic foot of warehouse volume is a component of the fixed costs. The space occupied by a product is typically computed as proportional to the maximum inventory of this product. The maximum inventory for each product is the sum of the cycle and safety inventory if inventory of that type is present. If the inventory cost at the origin are not borne by the corporation, then these costs should not be included in the incremental costs, since the size of the inventory at the origin facility does not impact the total logistics cost to the corporation. The inclusion of the storage costs in the fixed cost category rather than in the variable cost category is relatively arbitrary because facility costs in the supply chain have been traditionally considered as part of the fixed costs. Regardless in which category they are included the equations and the relative cost differential remains the same. The total fixed storage cost is then the product of the maximum product inventory and the annualized unit storage location cost for that product at that facility.

$$FSC_{mp} = OFSC_{mp} + DFSC_{mp} = OMI_{mp} \cdot sc_{pO} + DMI_{mp} \cdot sc_{pD} \qquad (12.3)$$

When shipping in transportation batches, there may be both an inventory build up at the source until the shipment occurs, and inventory depletion at the destination starting after a replenishment shipment arrives. This inventory is called the cycle inventory. If we assume a constant build up and depletion rate, then the average inventory follows the classic saw tooth pattern and the average inventory is half the maximum inventory or transportation batch size. If the product arrives at the origin facility at a fixed schedule and is shipped at the same fixed schedule, then there is no inventory at the origin facility since it is assumed that the product is cross docked and shipped out when it arrives. So the $OCIC$ term may have to be computed with different formulas or even not be present in the following calculations depending on the schedule of the product arrival and shipping at the origin facility and on the ownership of the inventory. In general, the selection of the correct formula depends on the operation details of the supply chain at either the origin or the destination of the channel and is thus instance and channel dependent. The general formula given above is transformed into the following specific formula based on the characteristics of the example.

$$FSC_{mp} = TB_{mp} \cdot sc_{mpO} + [TB_{mp} + SI_{mp}] \cdot sc_{mpD} \qquad (12.4)$$

$$TFC_{mp} = FSC_{mp} \qquad (12.5)$$

The unit storage cost at the origin is computed as the origin fixed storage cost divided by the total annual demand, i.e. the origin storage cost is considered as overhead and allocated uniformly to all the units of product that flow through the origin facility regardless if they are actually stored there or not.

$$sc_{mpO} = \frac{OFSC_{mp}}{D_p} \qquad (12.6)$$

In the case of rail transportation, the TVs arrive in batches of 160 units and are shipped in rail cars in batches of 160 units. So it is assumed that for rail transportation the TVs are cross docked and there is no cycle inventory at the import warehouse. In the case of truck transportation, the arrival batch size is 160 units, but the departure batch size is 80 units at the import warehouse. So, there is cycle inventory present at the import warehouse. 80 units are cross dock upon arrival and 80 units are stored for the next truck delivery. The maximum inventory per product is 80 units. Let the rail mode and the truck mode be indicated by index r and t, respectively. The fixed storage costs at the origin are then computed as follows.

$$OFSC_{rp} = \$0$$
$$OFSC_{tp} = TB_{tp} \cdot slc_{pO} = 80 \cdot 200 = \$16,000$$
$$sc_{rpO} = \$0$$
$$sc_{tpO} = \frac{OFSC_{tp}}{D_p} = \frac{16000}{4160} = \$3.85$$

Variable Costs The variable costs are costs that may change during the operation of the distribution channel. Typically these costs are a function of either the transfer batch size or order quantity and of the total annual demand.

The value of one unit of product is different at the origin and destination. At the destination the corporation has invested the sum of the production cost, the origin storage costs, the transportation cost, and the in-transit and origin cycle inventory cost in the product. The origin and destination cycle inventory and inventory costs depend on the replenishment and withdrawal processes at the origin and destination facility. If the warehouse at the origin facility is a finished goods warehouse fed by a manufacturing process, then the replenishment rate can be assumed to be constant and the withdrawal can be assumed to be instantaneous. The average cycle inventory is then half the maximum cycle inventory and computed as the product of half the transportation batch size, the holding cost rate, and the appropriate unit value.

$$OCI_{imp} = (TB_{mp}/2) \tag{12.7}$$

$$OCIC_{imp} = (TB_{mp}/2) \cdot v_p \cdot HCR = OCI_{mp} \cdot v_{pO} \cdot HCR \tag{12.8}$$

For the Big TV example, shipping by rail allowed a cross docking of the container and so no origin cycle inventory was created. When shipping by truck, the origin had a cycle inventory of 80 during the first week and no cycle inventory during the second week of the two-week cycle. The average origin cycle inventory is then 40 units.

$$OCI_r = 0$$
$$OCIC_r = 0$$
$$ocic_r = 0$$
$$OCI_t = 40$$
$$OCIC_t = 40 \cdot 3400 \cdot 0.6 = \$81,600$$
$$ocic_t = 81600/4160 = \$19.62$$

When the product leaves the origin warehouse, the corporation has invested the purchase or production cost, the origin storage cost, and the origin cycle inventory cost. This value will be used to compute the in-transit or pipeline inventory cost. The unit origin storage cost is computed as the origin fixed storage cost divided by the total annual demand, i.e. the origin storage cost is considered as overhead and allocated uniformly to all the units of product that flow through the origin facility regardless if they are stored there or not.

$$v_{mpO} = v_p + ocic_{mp} + sc_{mpO} \tag{12.9}$$

$$v_{rpO} = v_p = \$3400$$
$$v_{tpO} = v_p + ocic_{tp} + sc_{tpO} = 3400 + 19.62 + 3.85 = \$3,423.46$$

The pipeline inventory cost is computed as the product of the annual demand, the value of a single unit at the origin of the pipeline, the transit time for the flow to go through the pipeline, and the inventory holding cost rate.

$$PI_{mp} = D_p \cdot TT_m \tag{12.10}$$

$$PIC_{mp} = D_p \cdot v_{mpO} \cdot TT_m \cdot HCR = PI_{mp} \cdot v_{mpO} \cdot HCR \qquad (12.11)$$

$$pic_{mp} = \frac{PIC_{mp}}{D_p} = TT_m \cdot v_{mpO} \cdot HCR \qquad (12.12)$$

For the Big TV example, the value of a single unit at the start of the transportation is the sum of the production cost and the origin cycle inventory costs. Shipping by rail allowed a cross docking of the container and so no origin cycle inventory was created.

$$PIC_r = 4160 \cdot 3400 \cdot (2/52) \cdot 0.6 = \$326,400$$
$$pic_r = 3400 \cdot (2/52) \cdot 0.6 = \$78.46$$
$$PIC_t = 4160 \cdot 3423.46 \cdot (1/52) \cdot 0.6 = \$164,326$$
$$pic_t = 3423.46 \cdot (1/52) \cdot 0.6 = \$39.50$$

The total transportation cost is computed as the product of the annual demand and the unit transportation cost.

$$TC_{mp} = D_p \cdot tc_{mp} \qquad (12.13)$$

Now the destination cycle inventory cost can be computed, since all the unit costs incurred before the destination is reached in the supply chain have now been computed. The value at the destination facility is the sum of the purchasing, transportation, in-transit inventory, origin cycle inventory, and origin storage cost. If an instantaneous replenishment and a constant withdrawal rate are assumed then the average cycle inventory is half the maximum cycle inventory, which in turn is equal to the transportation batch size.

$$v_{mpD} = v_p + tc_{mp} + pic_{mp} + ocic_{mp} + sc_{mpO} \qquad (12.14)$$

$$DCIC_{imp} = (TB_{mp}/2) \cdot (v_p + tc_{mp} + pic_{mp} + ocic_{mp} + sc_{mpO}) \cdot HCR \qquad (12.15)$$
$$= (TB_{mp}/2) \cdot v_{mpD} \cdot HCR$$

$$DCI_r = 160/2 = 80$$
$$DCIC_r = 80 \cdot (3400 + 32 + 78.46) \cdot 0.6 = 80 \cdot 3510.46 \cdot 0.6 = \$168,502$$
$$dcic_r = 168502/4160 = \$40.51$$
$$DCI_t = 80/2 = 40$$
$$DCIC_t = 40 \cdot (3400 + 19.62 + 75 + 39.50 + 3.85) \cdot 0.6 = 40 \cdot 3537.96 \cdot 0.6 = \$84,911$$
$$dcic_t = 84911/4160 = \$20.41$$

Assuming single sourcing and a single transportation mode of the supply of each product at the distribution center, the safety inventory at the distribution center can then be computed as follows, where d is the expected demand during a single period and the lead time lt is expressed in observable demand periods.

$$SI = k \cdot \sqrt{lt \cdot Var_d + d^2 \cdot Var_{lt}} \tag{12.16}$$

$$CV_d = \frac{\sqrt{Var_d}}{d}$$
$$Var_d = (CV_d \cdot d)^2 \tag{12.17}$$

$$SI = k \cdot \sqrt{lt \cdot CV_d^2 + Var_{lt} \cdot d} \tag{12.18}$$

This formula quantifies the common practice in industry of keeping a safety stock level on hand equal to a number of demand periods. Policies that determine the safety inventory proportional to the demand are also called linear safety policies. The formula shows the relationship between the safety inventory and the customer service level based on probability of delivery out on-hand inventory, the average and variance of the lead time, and the average and variance of the demand. This formula ignores inventory costs at the origin facility and thus any pooling effect of distribution centers at the origin facility. Since the demand is determined by the customers and the service level is usually a mandate from corporate management, the only factors that can be influenced by the warehouse manager are the average and the variance of the lead time and the variance of the demand. Safety inventory can be reduced if the input and output flows, i.e., supply and demand, are kept as constant as possible and if the lead time for replenishments is reduced.

If a customer service level of type two is required and it is assumed that the demand is normally distributed, then the number of standard deviations can be determined using the unit loss function. The safety inventory cost is then computed as the product of the safety inventory level, the value for each unit, and the holding cost rate.

$$sd(dlt)_{mp} = \sqrt{lt_{mp}CV_{dp}^2 + Var_{lt,mp}d_p} \tag{12.19}$$

$$L(z) = TB_{mp}(1 - fr)/sd(dlt)_{mp} \tag{12.20}$$

$$z = L^{-1}\left(\frac{TB_{mp}(1 - fr)}{sd(dlt)_{mp}}\right) \tag{12.21}$$

$$SI_{mp} = z\sqrt{lt_{mp}CVd_p^2 + Vlt_{mp}d_p} = z \cdot sd(dlt)_{mp} \tag{12.22}$$

$$SIC_{mp} = SI_{mp} \cdot v_{mpD} \cdot HCR \tag{12.23}$$

For the Big TV example, the demand data are provided on a weekly basis. The calculations for the safety inventory and the total safety inventory cost are given next. In this example, the lead time is constant and thus the variance of the lead time is equal to zero.

$$CV_d = \frac{\sqrt{Var_d}}{d} = \frac{sd_d}{d} = \frac{40}{80} = 0.5$$

$$sd(dlt)_r = \sqrt{2 \cdot 0.5^2} \cdot 80 = 56.57$$

$$L(z)_r = \frac{(1 - 0.95)160}{56.57} = 0.141$$

$$z_r = L^{-1}(0.141) = 0.71$$

$$SI_r = 0.71 \cdot 56.57 = 40$$

$$SIC_r = 40 \cdot 3510.46 \cdot 0.6 = \$84,251$$

$$sd(dlt)_t = \sqrt{1 \cdot 0.5^2} \cdot 80 = 40$$

$$L(z)_t = \frac{(1 - 0.95)80}{40} = 0.100$$

$$z_t = L^{-1}(0.100) = 0.90$$

$$SI_t = 0.90 \cdot 40 = 36$$

$$SIC_t = 36 \cdot 3537.96 \cdot 0.6 = \$76,420$$

The only fixed costs included in the Big TV example are the fixed costs associated with the storage locations in the warehouses at the origin and destination facilities. The destination warehouse has to able to hold the sum of the safety and cycle inventory.

$$DMI_r = 160 + 40 = 200$$

$$DFSC_r = 200 \cdot 200 = \$40,000$$

$$TFC_r = DFSC_r = \$40,000$$

$$DMI_t = 80 + 36 = 116$$

$$DFSC_t = 200 \cdot 116 = \$23,200$$

$$TFC_t = OFSC_r + DFSC_r = 16,000 + 23,200 = \$39,200$$

The total variable cost is computed as the sum of the transportation cost, the pipeline inventory cost, the origin and destination cycle inventory costs, and the safety inventory cost.

$$TVC_{mp} = TC_{mp} + PIC_{mp} + OCIC_{imp} + DCIC_{jmp} + SIC_{jmp} \qquad (12.24)$$

For the Big TV example, the total variable costs by transportation mode are computed as follows.

$$TVC_r = 0 + 133120 + 326400 + 168502 + 84251 = \$712,273$$

$$TVC_t = 81600 + 312000 + 164326 + 84911 + 76420 = \$718,257$$

Finally, the total aggregate cost is computed as the sum of the total invariant, variable, and fixed costs.

Table 12.2 Channel selection comparison for the Big TV example

Category	Rail	Truck
Purchasing Cost	$14,144,000	$14,144,000
Total Invariant Costs	*$14,144,000*	*$14,144,000*
Transportation Costs	$133,120	$312,000
Transportation Batch Size	160	80
Maximum Origin Cycle Inventory	0	80
Origin Storage Cost		$16,000
Origin Unit Storage Cost	$0.00	$3.85
Average Origin Cycle Inventory	0	40
Origin Cycle Inventory Costs		$81,600
Unit origin cycle inventory costs		$19.62
Unit Value at Leaving Origin	$3,400.00	$3,423.46
In-Trans it Inventory Cost	$326,400	$164,326
Unit in-trans it inventory cost	$78.46	$39.50
Unit Value at DC	$3,510.46	$3,537.96
DC Max Cycle Inventory	160	80
DC Cycle Inventory Costs	$168,502	$84,911
Lead Time	2.00	1.00
St Dev Demand during Lead Time	56.57	40.00
L(z)	0.141	0.100
Z	0.71	0.90
DC Safety Inventory	40	36
DC Safety Inventory Costs	$84,251	$76,420
Total Marginal Costs	*$712,273*	*$719,257*
DC Maximum Inventory	200	116
DC Storage Cost	$40,000	$23,200
Total Fixed Costs	*$40,000*	*$39,200*
Total Variant Costs	*$752,273*	*$758,457*
Total Cost	*$14,896,273*	*$14,902,457*
Unit Value at Leaving DC	*$3,580.83*	*$3,582.32*

$$TAC_{mp} = TIC_p + TVC_{mp} + TFC_{mp} \qquad (12.25)$$

For the Big TV the total aggregate costs are computed as follows. The results for the Big TV example are also summarized in the previous table (Table 12.2).

$$TAC_r = 14144000 + 712273 + 40000 = \$14,896,273$$
$$TAC_t = 14144000 + 719257 + 39200 = \$14,902,457$$
$$\Delta = (712273 + 40000) - (719257 + 39200) = -\$6,184$$

In this particular example, the total annual costs of the two alternative transportation modes are nearly the same. The difference is only 0.82% of the logistics cost and only 0.04% of the total supply chain cost. The difference between the unit values of the product in function of the distribution channel when it leaves the distribution center is $1.49 per unit.

12.3   Tactical Supply Chain Planning

The tactical supply chain planning model is one of simplest models that considers the supply chain as an integrated system. It includes such decisions as supplier selection for the key components, transportation, and production planning, and deliveries to customer to satisfy the customer demands for each period during the planning horizon. The periods in the model are typically of intermediate durations such as weeks, months, or seasons in a year. Finished goods may be assembled using a limited number of sub assemblies or components. If such assembly process is present in the supply chain then the model is denoted as a bill of materials or BOM model. In this case component products that enter the supply chain from external suppliers typically do not leave the supply chain but are transformed in one or more facilities into finished goods. The finished goods usually do not enter the supply chain but are created by the transformation process and then leave the supply chain. Both the finished goods and its components are denoted as products. The model minimizes the total cost computed as the sum of the procurement (purchasing, acquisition), transportation, manufacturing (production, transformation), inventory, and backorder costs. The total demand of a customer has to be delivered, even though delivery may be delayed beyond the due date through backorders. The inventory cost at this time consists only of the holding costs at transformation facilities. The model incorporates a penalty for delayed delivery to customers, which is also denoted as the backorder cost. This model ignores the lead times for sourcing components of the various suppliers but it observes supplier capacities and transformation capacities. It is assumed that all the facilities are available during each period in the planning horizon, but the capacities can vary from period to period. The tactical supply chain planning problem is also called master planning. Further information can be found in Rohde and Wagner (2008).

The model is solved to optimality using a linear programming solver. If the demand is for a small number of discrete parts then a mixed integer programming solver has to be used to avoid fractional product flows. Even though the instance model may be large due to the presence of a large number of periods and other logistics objects, the solution times with a linear programming solver are typically modest and are in order of minutes.

12.3.1   Tactical Supply Chain Model

12.3.1.1   Components

The logistics objects in the tactical supply chain model are collected in the following sets.

S	Suppliers, indexed by i
P	Products, indexed by p (and v)
$1BOM_p$	Products in the single level bill of materials for product p, i.e. the immediate components in the BOM of product p
C	Customers, indexed by k
T	Periods, indexed by t (and u)
TR	transformation facilities or transformers, indexed by j
R	Resources required for product flows in supplier and transformation facilities, indexed by r
AR, IR	Resources required for product assembly and product inventory in transformation facilities, respectively
$O = S \cup TR$	Origin facilities, i.e. suppliers and transformation facilities
$D = TR \cup C$	Destination facilities, i.e. transformation facilities and customers
OD	Transportation channels, indexed by the combination of their origin and destination facilities

12.3.1.2 Decision Variables

The symbols for most decision variables related to material flows end on the letter q which indicates a quantity.

pq_{ipt}	amount purchased from supplier i of product p during period t
x_{ijpt}	amount of product p transported from facility i to facility j during time period t
$itq_{jpt},\ otq_{jpt}$	amount of product p transported into and out of facility j during time period t
iq_{jpt}	amount of product p stored (carried as inventory to the next period) at facility j from time period t to time period $t+1$
bq_{kptu}	amount of product p delivered to customer k during period t that is used to satisfy the demand of this customer for this product during time period u, where u is smaller than t. This is the backorder quantity.
aq_{jpt}	amount of product p assembled, i.e. manufactured or produced, at facility j during time period t
cq_{jpt}	amount of component product p used in assembly (manufacturing) at facility j during time period t
dq_{jpt}	amount of product p delivered to customer k during period t to satisfy the demand during this period and possible backordered quantities of prior periods. The presence of backordering allows the quantities delivered to be different from customer demand for a particular period

12.3.1.3 Parameters

The symbols for most unit cost parameters end with the letter (lower case) c which indicates the cost rate. Parameters related to capacities on flow start with the letter t, while capacities related to production and inventory start with the letters a and i. The latter two are only defined at transformation facilities.

$tcap_{jrt}$	aggregate capacity of resource r at supplier or at facility j during period t for all products combined. Note if the capacity is by product, supplier or facility capacity cap_{jpt} with three subscripts is to be defined and is no longer called aggregate.
$acap_{jrt}, icap_{jrt}$	aggregate capacity of resource r at transformation facility j during period t for all products combined produced or held in inventory, respectively. Note if the capacity is by product and transformation facility capacities $acap_{jrt}, icap_{jrt}$ with three subscripts are to be defined and are no longer called aggregate.
$tres_{jprt}$	units of resource r consumed by one unit of product p at facility j (be it either a supplier or transformer facility) during period t. The model can incorporate resource consumption rates that vary by period, e.g. to approximate learning curves.
$ares_{jprt}, ires_{jprt}$	units of resource r consumed by one unit of product p produced or stored at transformation facility j during period t. The model can incorporate resource consumption rates that vary by period, e.g. to approximate learning curves.
trc_{jrt}	unit resource cost for resource r at facility j during period t
arc_{jrt}, irc_{jrt}	unit resource cost for production or inventory resource r at transformation facility j during period t
dem_{kpt}	aggregate demand for product p at customer k during period t
pc_{ipt}	purchase cost for a unit of product p from supplier i during period t
tc_{ijpt}	unit transportation cost for a product p from facility i to facility j during period t
ac_{jpt}	assembly (production, manufacturing) cost for a unit of product p at facility j during period t
hc_{jpt}	unit holding (inventory) cost for a product p at facility j from time period t to the next period $t+1$
bc_{kptu}	unit delay cost, i.e. delay penalty or backorder cost, for delivering one unit of product p during period t to satisfy demand during period u at customer k
$lbom_{jpvt}$	number of units of component p required to assemble one unit of assembly v during period t in facility j where component p is an element of the single level bill of material of product v
$init\_inv_{jp}$	initial inventory of product p at facility j

12.3.1.4 Constraints

The model contains four types of constraints: supply capacity, transformation (production or assembly) capacity, demand satisfaction, and conservation of flow at the transformation facilities. The conservation of flow constraints may be by product or consider the BOM for the assembly process.

12.3.1.5 Model

The complete tactical production supply chain model is given next. The model can be further condensed by directly substituting variables, but it is given below in its more expanded form to clearer show its structure. Modern linear programming solvers will make the substitutions in their pre-solving phase, so this more expansive version does not increase solution time significantly.

Model 12.1. Tactical BOM Supply Chain Model

$$
\begin{aligned}
\min \quad & \sum_{i \in S} \sum_p \sum_t pc_{ipt} \cdot pq_{ipt} + \sum_{i \in O} \sum_{j \in D} \sum_p \sum_t tc_{ijpt} \cdot x_{ijpt} + \sum_{j \in TR} \sum_p \sum_t ac_{jpt} \cdot aq_{jpt} + \\
& \sum_{j \in TR} \sum_p \sum_{r \in AR} \sum_t arc_{jrt} \cdot ares_{jprt} \cdot aq_{jpt} + \sum_{j \in TR} \sum_p \sum_{r \in IR} \sum_t irc_{jrt} \cdot ires_{jprt} \cdot iq_{jpt} + \\
& \sum_j \sum_p \sum_{r \in R} \sum_t rc_{jrt} \cdot res_{jprt} \cdot tq_{jpt} + \\
& \sum_{k \in C} \sum_p \sum_{t \in T, t \geq 2} \sum_{u \in T, u < t} bc_{kptu} \cdot bq_{kptu} + \sum_{j \in TR} \sum_p \sum_t hc_{jpt} \cdot iq_{jpt}
\end{aligned}
\tag{12.26}
$$

$$
s.t. \quad \sum_p tres_{ip} \cdot pq_{ipt} \leq tcap_{it} \quad \forall i, \forall t
\tag{12.27}
$$

$$
pq_{ipt} \leq tcap_{ipt} \quad \forall i, \forall p, \forall t
\tag{12.28}
$$

$$
pq_{ipt} = \sum_j x_{ijpt} \quad \forall i, \forall p, \forall t
\tag{12.29}
$$

$$
\sum_i x_{ijpt} = itq_{jpt} \quad \forall j, \forall p, \forall t
\tag{12.30}
$$

$$
itq_{jpt} + aq_{jpt} + init\_inv_{jp} - iq_{jpt} - cq_{jpt} - otq_{jpt} = 0 \quad \forall j, \forall p, t = 1
\tag{12.31}
$$

$$
itq_{jpt} + aq_{jpt} + iq_{jpt-1} - iq_{jpt} - cq_{jpt} - otq_{jpt} = 0 \quad \forall j, \forall p, t = 2..T - 1
\tag{12.32}
$$

$$
itq_{jpt} + aq_{jpt} + iq_{jpt-1} - cq_{jpt} - otq_{jpt} = 0 \quad \forall j, \forall p, t = T
\tag{12.33}
$$

$$
\sum_k x_{jkpt} = otq_{jpt} \quad \forall j, \forall p, \forall t
\tag{12.34}
$$

$$cq_{jpt} = \sum_{v} lbom_{jpvt} \cdot aq_{jvt} \qquad \forall p \in 1BOM_v, \forall j, \forall t \qquad (12.35)$$

$$\sum_{p} ares_{jprt} \cdot aq_{jpt} \leq acap_{jrt} \qquad \forall j, \forall t, \forall r \qquad (12.36)$$

$$aq_{jpt} \leq acap_{jpt} \qquad \forall j, \forall p, \forall t \qquad (12.37)$$

$$\sum_{p} tres_{jprt} \cdot otq_{jpt} \leq tcap_{jrt} \qquad \forall j, \forall t, \forall r \qquad (12.38)$$

$$otq_{jpt} \leq tcap_{jpt} \qquad \forall j, \forall p, \forall t \qquad (12.39)$$

$$\sum_{p} ires_{jprt} \cdot iq_{jpt} \leq icap_{jrt} \qquad \forall j, \forall t, \forall r \qquad (12.40)$$

$$iq_{jpt} \leq icap_{jpt} \qquad \forall j, \forall p, \forall t \qquad (12.41)$$

$$\sum_{j} x_{jkpt} = dq_{kpt} \qquad \forall k, \forall p, \forall t \qquad (12.42)$$

$$dq_{kpt} + \sum_{t < u} bq_{kput} = \sum_{u < t} bq_{kptu} + dem_{kpt} \qquad \forall k, \forall p, \forall t \qquad (12.43)$$

$$pq, x, bq, iq, aq, cq \geq 0 \qquad (12.44)$$

The objective function computes the total cost as the sum of the individual unit costs multiplied by the corresponding quantities. The model has capacity constraints and conservation of flow constraints. Typically capacity limitations at suppliers are either for individual products or for all products combined. The model allows both simultaneously but usually either constraint (12.27), which models the joint capacity, or (12.28), which models the capacity for an individual product, are defined but not both. The equivalent is true for transformation capacities modeled by constraints (12.36), which models the joint capacity, or (12.37), which models the capacity for an individual product as well as for the throughput and inventory capacity constraints at the transformation facilities.

The remaining constraints are all conservation of flow constraints. Backorder flows can only occur at customers, inventory flows can only occur at transformation facilities. There are four types of conservation of flow constraints at the transformation facilities, indicated by space, space-time, creation-space, and creation-space-time, respectively. The flow diagrams for the four types are shown in the next figures (Figs. 12.2, 12.3, 12.4 and 12.5).

In its most general form, the conservation of flow constraint for a product in a period for a transformation facility has six flows. The three input flows are transportation receipts, inventory held from the previous period, and production during the period. The three output flows are transportation shipments, inventory held to

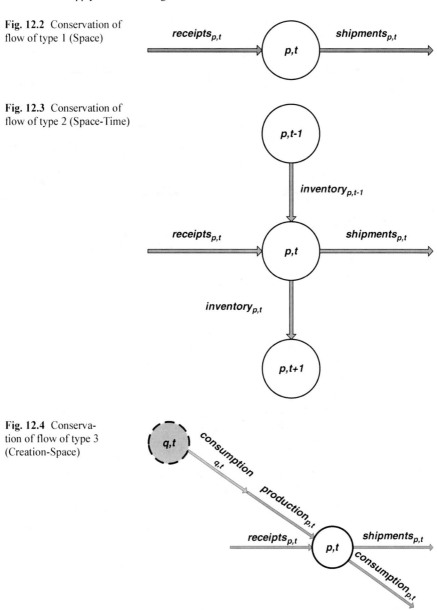

Fig. 12.2 Conservation of flow of type 1 (Space)

Fig. 12.3 Conservation of flow of type 2 (Space-Time)

Fig. 12.4 Conservation of flow of type 3 (Creation-Space)

the next period, and consumption of the product during the period when it is used as a component in the production process. The most general form has been used in the tactical model. The type of conservation of flow constraint used can be adjusted based on the requirements of the particular supply chain in question. If the time dimension is present, three variants of the conservation flow constraint need to be created since the equation is different for the first, intermediate, and last periods of the planning horizon. During the first period there is only the initial inventory which is a parameter and during the last period there is no inventory held to the next period.

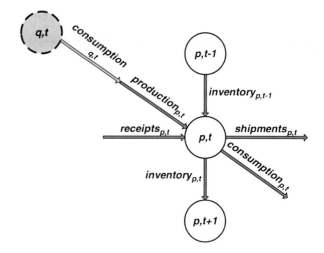

Fig. 12.5 Conservation of flow of type 3 (Creation-Space-Time)

Constraints (12.29) and (12.42) ensure that all the products purchased get transported from the suppliers and all finished goods produced get transported to the customers, respectively. Constraints (12.31) through (12.33) ensure the conservation of flow for a transformation facility for the first, intermediate, and last periods, respectively. The model uses a parameter for the initial inventory of a product at a facility. Constraint (12.35) ensures that the correct amount of component products is consumed in the assembly facility to be assembled into finished goods. Finally, constraint (12.43) ensures that the goods delivered to a customer and backorders from future periods are allocated to satisfy either the demand of that period or satisfy backorders in previous periods. The flow diagram for back orders for product p and customer k is shown in Fig. 12.6.

A rough calculation of the size of the instance model can be based on the following estimates. Assume there are 52 periods, 34 customers, 6 suppliers, and only

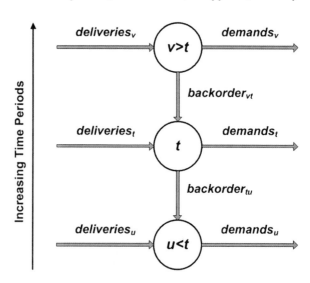

Fig. 12.6 Flow diagram for customer back orders

one product in the supply chain. The number of transportation decision variables would be $6*34*1*52=10,608$. The number of backorder variables would be $34*1*51*50=86,700$. For a larger supply chain instance, assume that there are 52 periods, 34 customers, 30 suppliers, and 6 products. The number of transportation decision variables would be $30*34*6*52=318,240$. The number of backorder variables would be $34*6*51*50=520,200$. For problem instances of this size, an automated way to generate the instance model has to available. Usually, a modeling language such as AMPL is used to store the model structure and a database is used to store all the model parameters and the values of the decision variables after the optimization has been completed. An industrial case of realistic size had 500,000 constraints and 1.8 million variables and was solved by a contemporary desktop computer in 30 s. The whole process of assembling the data, solving the instance problem, and storing the results required less than 3 min.

12.4 Continuous Location Model

12.4.1 Introduction

The strategic logistics design problem can be defined as follows: given a set of plants and customers with known characteristics, and the potential components of a logistics network, determine the number and location of warehouses, allocate of customers to warehouses, and select transportation channels such that customer requirements are met at the lowest possible cost.

Solution procedures for the strategic logistics system design problem can be divided into two types, each with different assumptions. Site generating procedures, such as location-allocation solution procedures, generate a set of new sites for the distribution centers, but do not consider whether to open or close distribution centers. That is, location-allocation procedures assume that each specified potential distribution center is open (though not necessarily used). Thus, to minimize total relevant costs, location-allocation procedures need only minimize the variable cost, which include at least the total transportation cost. To summarize, the location-allocation procedures minimize distribution cost by moving the distribution centers, while leaving their number unchanged. These procedures are further discussed in this section of this chapter.

The second class of solution procedures selects desirable distribution centers to open from among a list of possible candidate locations. They are called site selection procedures. The optimal solution algorithms of this type are based on Mixed Integer Programming (MIP) techniques. The MIP procedures determine the optimal number of distribution centers to open out of a set of candidate distribution centers. The candidate distribution centers are fixed in place. A mathematical model is constructed which captures all the cost and the solution is obtained by using a MIP solution program such as CPLEX or LINDO. To summarize, the MIP procedures minimize the distribution cost by opening and closing distribution centers, while leaving their location unchanged. These procedures are further discussed in the last section of this chapter.

The continuous location model focuses on the decision on where to locate one or more facilities that are elements of the supply chain and what are their incoming and outgoing material flows. The location of the facilities can be anywhere within a continuous area and influences the assignment and the transportation costs of the incoming and outgoing material flows. It is a fundamental assumption of this model that the different locations of the facility do not impact the fixed or variable cost inside the facility, but only the transportation costs in the supply chain. Clearly this is a very strong simplification of the real-world facility location decision and the results of this model should only be used for very aggregate and rough-cut decision making. If more accurate cost calculations are required, then a more complicated discrete location model has to be used. Some of these models are described in the next section and in the chapter on advanced supply chain models.

12.4.2 Location Problem

The location problem determines the best location of one or more facilities for given product flows. It is assumed that the facilities can be located anywhere within the area. The impact of the facility locations on the transportation costs is proportional to distance between the facilities to be located and other facilities with known locations. The distances are determined by a distance norm. In nearly all instances, the Euclidean distance norm is used.

12.4.2.1 Single Facility Location Problem

For this sub class of the location problem only a single facility has to be located. The following notation will be used, where subscript i is used if multiple new facilities have to be located and can be ignored if there is a single moveable facility.

(x_i, y_i) location coordinates of the facility to be located
(a_j, b_j) location coordinates of the facilities with fixed and known locations
w_{ij} interaction between moveable facility i and fixed facility j
d_{ij} distance between moveable facility i and fixed facility j computed by a distance norm

The facility location problem in the continuous space or FLP is then formulated as

$$\min \sum_{j=1}^{N} w_{ij} d_{ij}(x_i, y_i) \tag{12.45}$$

If the Euclidean distance norm is used, then formulation becomes

Model 12.2. Single Facility Location Model

$$\min \sum_{j=1}^{N} w_{ij} \sqrt{(x_i - a_j)^2 + (y_i - b_j)^2} \tag{12.46}$$

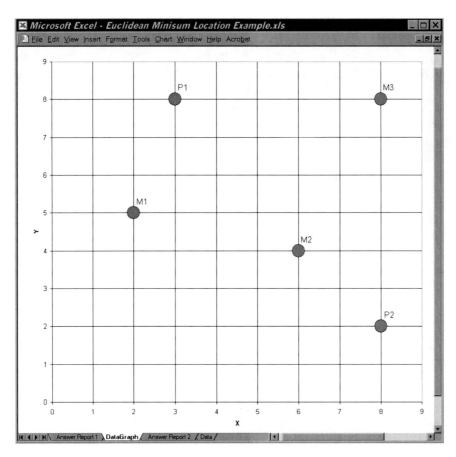

Fig. 12.7 Excel location data graph for single facility location

The above problem is a nonlinear unconstrained optimization problem in two continuous variables.

The solver in Excel can be used to determine the solution to this problem for small problem instances. Consider the following example, where a single facility has to be located while it interacts with five fixed facilities. The interaction is given as the product of V, the number of trips per year between the fixed and moveable facility, and the unit transportation cost R. The location of the fixed facilities is illustrated in the next figure and the coordinates of the fixed facilities, trips per year, and unit transportation costs in the second figure (Figs. 12.7 and 12.8).

In the above figure the cost of locating the new facility at the center of gravity of the existing facilities is also computed with the following formulas.

$$x_i = \frac{\sum_{j=1}^{N} w_{ij} a_j}{\sum_{j=1}^{N} w_{ij}}$$

$$y_i = \frac{\sum_{j=1}^{N} w_{ij} b_j}{\sum_{j=1}^{N} w_{ij}}$$

$$(12.47)$$

	A	B	C	D	E	F	G	H	I	J
1	Point	X	Y	V	R	W	W*X	W*Y	W*D0	W*D
2	P1	3	8	2000	0.050	100.0	300	800	355.2	350.8
3	P2	8	2	3000	0.050	150.0	1200	300	639.5	652.1
4	M1	2	5	2500	0.075	187.5	375	937.5	593.5	545.8
5	M2	6	4	1000	0.075	75.0	450	300	108.6	113.9
6	M3	8	8	1500	0.075	112.5	900	900	450.3	480.0
7	W0	5.16	5.18			625.0	3225.0	3237.5	2147.1	
8	W*	4.91	5.06							2142.5

Microsoft Excel - Euclidean Minisum Location Example.xls

File Edit View Insert Format Tools Data Window Help Acrobat

Answer Report 1 / LocationGraph \ Data

Fig. 12.8 Excel spreadsheet for single facility location

The sum of weights is computed in column F and equals 625.0, the weighted sum of the x and y coordinates is computed in columns G and H respectively. The center of gravity location for this problem instance is computed in row 7 and equal to (5.16, 5.18) and indicated by $W0$, where the 0 indicates the iteration subscript and in this case is an initial guess. The objective function value for this center of gravity location is computed in column I and is equal to 2147.1. The optimal location can be determined using the Excel solver. The objective function is computed in column J and the sum is computed in cell J8 by changing the location coordinates in cells B8 and C8. The optimal solution is indicated by $W*$. The corresponding solver dialog window is shown in the next figure. Note that the constraint area is empty (Fig. 12.9).

The necessary solver options are shown in the next figure. The check boxes for "Assume Linear Model" and "Assume Non-Negative" decision variable have to be cleared. The model is nonlinear because of the square root function and the decision variables do not have to be restricted to the first quadrant (Fig. 12.10).

The optimal objective function value is 2142.5. The solution location for this instance is shown in the next figure. The difference in the objective function values of the optimal solution and the center of gravity solution is 0.2% and the figure also shows that the locations are close to each other. Since the results of the continuous location problem are only to be used as a very approximate location for the facility, the center of gravity can be used as an approximate solution since it is even easier to compute than using the Excel solver (Fig. 12.11).

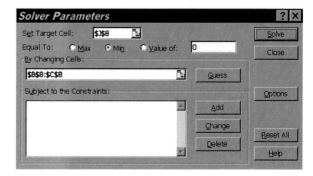

Fig. 12.9 Excel solver parameters for single facility location

Fig. 12.10 Excel solver
options for single facility
location

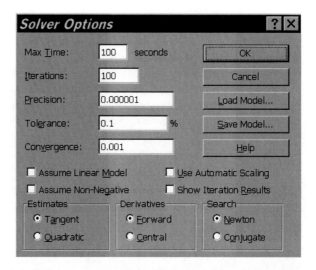

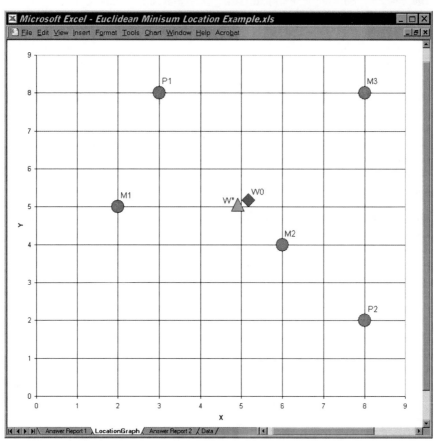

Fig. 12.11 Excel location graph for single facility location

12.4.3   Multiple Facility Location Problem

In this case more than one facility has to be located. Recall that the material flow interactions between the various facilities are given as parameters. If no interactions exist between the moveable facilities, then solving a multiple facility location problem is equal to solving a set of independent single facility location problems. If interactions between moveable facilities exist then the problem no longer decomposes by moveable facility. The joint location problem can be solved by an iterative nonlinear search algorithm using the gradients. This procedure is described in detail in the next section on location-allocation, where it is used as a sub procedure to solve that problem.

12.4.4   Location-Allocation Problem

The Location-Allocation Problem (LAP) determines simultaneously the location of one or more moveable facilities and the least-cost product flow between the fixed and moveable facilities. The fixed facilities are either plants (or suppliers) or customers. The plants have a maximum capacity and the customers have a demand that has to be met. The moveable facilities are either manufacturing plants or distribution centers and conservation of flow must be ensured at each facility. There exist two classes of decision variables: the location coordinates (x, y) and the product flows w. The objective function is the sum of their products. Multiple transportation modes may be possible between each pair of facilities, indicated by the subscript m, and each combination of facility pair and transportation mode may have an individual unit transportation cost c. The LAP formulation is given next, where the appropriate distance norm formula is used to compute the distances d in function of (x, y).

Model 12.3. Location-Allocation Model

$$\min \sum_{i=1}^{M} \sum_{j=1}^{N} \sum_{m=1}^{L} c_{ijm} d_{ijm} w_{ijm} \tag{12.48}$$

$$s.t. \sum_{i=1}^{M} \sum_{m=1}^{L} w_{ikm} = dem_k \quad k \in Customers \tag{12.49}$$

$$\sum_{j=1}^{N} \sum_{m=1}^{L} w_{ijm} \le cap_i \quad i \in Plants \tag{12.50}$$

$$\sum_{i=1}^{M} \sum_{m=1}^{L} w_{ijm} - \sum_{k=1}^{N} \sum_{m=1}^{L} w_{jkm} = 0 \quad j \in Depots \tag{12.51}$$

$$d_{ij} = \sqrt{(x_i - a_j)^2 + (y_i - b_j)^2} \quad \forall ij, \forall jk \ combinations \qquad (12.52)$$

$$w_{ijm} \geq 0$$

This LAP problem is a difficult to solve nonlinear optimization problem. Since the solution can only be used as a very approximate location of the facilities, this problem is only solved heuristically in practice. One heuristic proposed by Eilon and Watson-Ghandi exploits the bi-level structure of the problem by alternatingly holding the variables of one of the classes constant while solving for the other class of variables. This approach is similar to the cyclical coordinates search algorithm, but applied to classes of decision variables rather than to individual decision variables.

12.4.4.1 Eilon-Watson-Ghandi Iterative Location-Allocation Algorithm

This heuristic procedure attempts to find a good set of locations for the distribution centers by repeatedly executing the following steps:

1. Allocate customers to depots and depots to plants based on current facility locations and distances
2. Relocate depots to minimize transportation costs of the current allocations.
3. Repeat steps 1 and 2 until done.

The allocation phase is solved via a network flow algorithm. The location phase is solved by the Weiszfeld algorithm with hyperbolic approximation. Further details are given below.

The network flow model considers plant, customers and depots. It determines the location of the distribution centers and the allocation of customers to distribution centers based on transportation costs only. The distribution centers are capacitated and flows between the distribution centers are allowed. In addition, more than one transportation mode and flow between two facilities is allowed.

Allocation Phase The algorithm starts with an initial solution in which the initial location of the distribution centers is specified. This initial location can be random, specified by the user, or the result of another algorithm. Based on this initial location, the network flow algorithm computes transportation costs and then assigns each customer to the nearest distribution center or plant with sufficient capacity by solving the following network flow problem.

M	the total number of source facilities, which is equal to the number of plants plus the number of depots
N	the total number of sink facilities, which is equal to the number of depots plus the number of customers
L	the number of transportation modes. The modes are indexed by the subscript m
w_{ijm}	flow from facility i to facility j by mode m

c_{ijm} the cost per unit flow per unit distance for transportation from facility i to facility j by mode m

d_{ijm} the distance from facility i to facility j by mode m

dem_k the demand of customer k

cap_i the capacity of plant i

Further information on solving the network flow problem can be found in the chapter on multiple flow routing.

Location Phase After all the customers have been allocated to the nearest distribution center with available capacity, a second sub-algorithm locates the distribution centers so that the sum of the weighted distances between each source and sink facility is minimized for the given flows. This problem is formulated as a continuous, multiple facility weighted Euclidean minisum location problem.

$$Min \ f(x, y) = \sum_{i=1}^{H} \sum_{j=1}^{G} \sum_{m=1}^{L} c_{ijm} w_{ijm} \sqrt{(x_i - a_j)^2 + (y_i - b_j)^2}$$

$$+ \sum_{i=1}^{H} \sum_{j=1}^{G} \sum_{m=1}^{L} c_{ijm} v_{ijm} \sqrt{(x_i - x_j)^2 + (y_i - y_j)^2} \qquad (12.53)$$

A preprocessing step combines all modes (L) between a pair of facilities into one aggregate mode:

$$Min \ f(x, y) = \sum_{i=1}^{H} \sum_{j=1}^{G} c_{ij} w_{ij} \sqrt{\left(x_i - a_j\right)^2 + \left(y_i - b_j\right)^2}$$

$$+ \sum_{i=1}^{H} \sum_{j=1}^{H} c_{ij} v_{ij} \sqrt{\left(x_i - x_j\right)^2 + \left(y_i - y_j\right)^2} \qquad (12.54)$$

H the set of movable facilities, i.e. the distribution centers

G the set of fixed facilities which is composed of plants and customers

w_{ij} the flow from moveable facility i to fixed facility j

v_{ij} the flow from movable facility i to moveable facility j

(x_i, y_i) the variable location of the distribution center i

(a_j, b_j) the fixed location of customer j or of plant

The distance between centers is assumed to be proportional to the straight line Euclidean distance.

This problem can no longer be solved with the center of gravity algorithm because of the material flow between moveable facilities since the location of one moveable facility depends on the location of the other moveable facilities. If no flow between moveable facilities exists then the problem decomposes by moveable facility and can be solved with repeated application of the center of gravity method. In practice, the equivalent condition is that no cross shipping of products between distribution centers is allowed. For the general problem, when flows between moveable facilities are allowed, the following nonlinear optimization algorithm can be used. To minimize $f(x, y)$ the partial derivatives with respect to x and y are calculated and set to zero which yields the following recursive expressions for x and y. First, define the following two functions:

$$g_{ij}(x_i, y_i) = \frac{c_{ij} w_{ij}}{\sqrt{(x_i - a_j)^2 + (y_i - b_j)^2 + \varepsilon}} \qquad (12.55)$$

$$h_{ij}(x_i, y_i) = \frac{c_{ij} v_{ij}}{\sqrt{(x_i - x_j)^2 + (y_i - y_j)^2 + \varepsilon}} \qquad i \neq j \qquad (12.56)$$

$$h_{ii}(x_i, y_i) = 0$$

Note that the denominators are adjusted by the (small) positive constant ε. This prevents the denominators from ever being zero when the two facilities are co-located. Without the ε term, these functions would be undefined whenever a distribution center was located at the same site as a customer or plant and the algorithm would terminate prematurely because of numerical instability. This adjustment method is called the Hyperbolic Approximation Procedure or HAP. Further details can be found in Francis and White (1974) and Love et al. (1988).

Now, the set of locations (x^k, y^k) is determined as follows:

$$x_i^k = \frac{\sum_{j=1}^{G} a_j g_{ij}(x_i^{k-1}, y_i^{k-1}) + \sum_{j=1}^{H} x_j h_{ij}(x_i^{k-1}, y_i^{k-1})}{\sum_{j=1}^{G} g_{ij}(x_i^{k-1}, y_i^{k-1}) + \sum_{j=1}^{H} h_{ij}(x_i^{k-1}, y_i^{k-1})} \qquad (12.57)$$

$$y_i^k = \frac{\sum_{j=1}^{G} b_j g_{ij}(x_i^{k-1}, y_i^{k-1}) + \sum_{j=1}^{H} y_j h_{ij}(x_i^{k-1}, y_i^{k-1})}{\sum_{j=1}^{G} g_{ij}(x_i^{k-1}, y_i^{k-1}) + \sum_{j=1}^{H} h_{ij}(x_i^{k-1}, y_i^{k-1})} \qquad (12.58)$$

The recursive formulas require an initial location (x^0, y^0) as input and then the procedure uses an iterative improvement scheme to get the next estimation. The superscript k denotes the iteration number. The iterative procedure continues until a stopping criterion has been satisfied, be it either a maximum number of iterations or maximum error gap.

Since the overall algorithm iterates between allocation and location algorithm and the location algorithm itself is iterative, large problem instances may take a significant amount of computation time. Several enhancements for the algorithm have been developed that reduce the computation time. Details on these enhancements are described in the appendix on continuous Euclidean location. The location-allocation problem is not convex which means that the algorithm can only assure convergence to a local optimum. In general the local optimum depends on the starting locations used for the moveable facilities. Several strategies for determining these starting locations have been proposed. One can think of this problem of finding an equilibrium location in the three dimensional space for a number of balls which correspond to the new facilities and that are connected with springs to each other and to the existing facilities. The material flow between them is proportional to the spring constant which measures the strength of the spring. All the new facilities can initially be located in a single location which is equivalent to pushing all the balls together. The iterative algorithm will spread out the locations of the new facilities just as the springs would push the balls away from each other. A second initial location strategy would locate all new facilities at the perimeter of the problem area. The iterative algorithm will concentrate the location of the new facilities just as the springs would pull the balls together.

12.5   Discrete Supply Chain Models

In the previous section, the new facilities could be located anywhere within the boundaries of the feasible domain but the facilities were assumed always to be available for use. The previous location and location-allocation problems are site-generating problems. In this section, the new facilities can only be located at the site of existing facilities or at finite set of candidate locations. These problems belong to the class of site-selecting problems.

12.5.1   P-Median and P-Center Problems

In the class of discrete supply chain problems, the discrete P-Median and discrete P-Center problems have the simplest structure. As before, the P-median problem has as objective minimizing the sum of the assignment distances or cost between existing facilities and their closest servicing facility, while the P-center has as objective minimizing the maximum of the assignment distances or cost between existing facilities and their closest servicing facility. The servicing facilities that are to be located are called the medians or clusters in the P-median problem and the centers in the P-Center problem. The discrete variants of these problems are often used when there are a large number of existing facilities that cover relatively uniformly the feasible domain or when there is a finite list of feasible locations.

The P-Median and the P-Center problems are classic examples of the minisum and minimax classes of optimization problems, respectively. The minisum objective consists of the sum of the individual cost components and the objective is thus to optimize the overall or average performance. This objective is appropriate and used in business systems and is also called economic efficiency. This problem is also called the median problem on networks. In general, the objective function for the minisum problem can then be written as

Fig. 12.12 Median versus center illustration

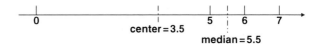

$$\min_{X} \left\{ \sum_{j} C_j(X) \right\} \tag{12.59}$$

where X indicates the coordinates of the new object to be located, j is the index of the existing and fixed objects and $C_j(X)$ denotes the cost of locating the new object at X with respect to the existing object j.

The minimax objective consists of the largest individual cost component of an existing facility and the objective is thus to optimize the worst-case behavior. This objective is often used in military, emergency, and public sector systems and is also called economic equity. This problem is also called the center problem on networks. The objective function for the minimax problem can then be written as

$$\min_{X} \left\{ \max_{j} C_j(X) \right\} \tag{12.60}$$

For example, assume 4 points located on a line at positions 0, 5, 6 and 7, respectively. Assume further that the cost of serving each of these points is strictly proportional to the distance between these points and the new facility. The optimal location of the new facility with respect to the minisum objective is the median of these points, i.e. $X^* = 5.5$, so that as many points are to the left as to the right. Actually, the line segment between five and six contains an infinite number of alternative optimal median locations. The optimal location with respect to the minimax objective is the center of these points, i.e. $X^* = 3.5$, so that the distance to the leftmost and rightmost point is equal (Fig. 12.12).

Observe that the optimal median location would not change if the leftmost point was located at -1000 rather than at 0. For this particular example, where the location domain is a line, the order of the fixed locations is important rather than their actual location. Also observe that the optimal center location would not change if an additional 1000 points were located between coordinates 5 and 6. The center location is always determined by a number of "extreme" locations and the number and location of all the other "interior" objects does not matter.

12.5.1.1 Notation

The formulation of the P-Median problem is given below using the following notation:

y_j 1 if a new facility or cluster is located at facility j, 0 otherwise
x_{ij} 1 if existing facility i is assigned to new facility j, 0 otherwise

c_{ij} cost of assigning existing facility i to new facility j, this cost is often the product of the weight or importance of facility i multiplied by the distance between facilities i and j, $c_{ij} = w_i \cdot d_{ij}$. The cost typically is computed outside the model and the model retrieves it from a table. This makes it possible to use the Euclidean or great circle distance norms in this model even though they have nonlinear expressions.

P the maximum number of new facilities that can be established

12.5.1.2 Discrete P-Median Problem

Model 12.4. P-Median Model

$$\min \ z = \sum_{j=1}^{N} \sum_{i=1}^{N} c_{ij} x_{ij} \tag{12.61}$$

$$s.t. \ \sum_{j=1}^{N} x_{ij} = 1 \quad \forall i \tag{12.62}$$

$$x_{ij} \le y_j \quad \forall i, \forall j \tag{12.63}$$

$$\sum_{j=1}^{N} y_j \le P \tag{12.64}$$

$$y_j \in \{0, 1\}, x_{ij} \ge 0 \tag{12.65}$$

The objective is to minimize the sum of the assignment costs. The first set of constraints ensures that each existing facility is assigned to a new facility or cluster. The second set of constraints ensures that a facility is only assigned to a cluster if this cluster is established. Constraints of this type are called the linkage or consistency constraints. Finally, the third constraint ensures that at most P clusters are established. The formulation needs to include this upper bound on the number of clusters; otherwise a cluster would be established at every existing facility. There are two types of decisions, the first one selects which medians will be established, and the second one assigns existing facilities to the established medians. Observe that the assignment variables are unconstrained non-negative continuous variables that will automatically take on the values of either zero or one in the optimal solution. However, the location decisions must be explicitly defined as binary. The problem thus belongs to the class of mixed-integer linear programming problems (MILP or MIP) since it has both discrete and continuous variables and thus requires the use of a MILP solver. A standard algorithm for solving this type of problems is branch-and-bound using linear relaxation.

12.5.1.3 Discrete P-Center Problem

Occasionally the objective is to design the supply chain which has smallest possible worst-case assignment costs. The objective is thus of the minimax type. This problem is known as the P-Center problem. For example, one may be interested in determining the largest distance between a customer and the distribution center that services this customer in function of the number of distribution centers. In the above formulation the assignment cost would then be the transportation distance between the corresponding facilities. By systematically increasing P, the monotonically non-increasing maximum service distance z in function of P can be determined.

Model 12.5. P-Center Model

$$\min\ z \tag{12.66}$$

$$s.t.\ z \geq c_{ij}x_{ij} \quad \forall i,\ \forall j \tag{12.67}$$

$$\sum_{j=1}^{N} x_{ij} = 1 \quad \forall i \tag{12.68}$$

$$x_{ij} \leq y_j \quad \forall i,\ \forall j \tag{12.69}$$

$$\sum_{j=1}^{N} y_j \leq P \tag{12.70}$$

$$y_j \in \{0,1\},\ x_{ij} \geq 0 \tag{12.71}$$

A generalization of the P-Median problem is the Warehouse Location Problem or WLP, where there is a cost associated with establishing a new facility, which is denoted as cluster or warehouse, but where there is no upper bound on the number of new facilities that can be established. This model is described in the next section.

12.5.2 Supply Chain Example

A common example will be used to illustrate the different supply chain design models. A geographical figure and a schematic of the supply chain are shown in the next two figures. The data for a supply chain are inherently large and an attempt was made to reuse as many of the data as possible. Not all models will use all of the components or echelons of the supply chain and associated their data and as consequence different models may generate different optimal solutions. The supply chain has two echelons corresponding to manufacturing and warehousing (distribution), respectively. There is one external supplier. In ad-

Fig. 12.13 Map of the supply chain example

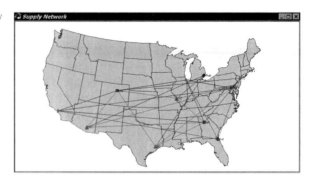

Fig. 12.14 Schematic of the supply chain example

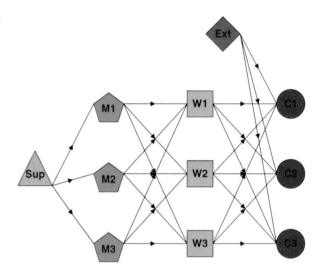

dition, products can also be delivered to the customers directly from an external outsourcing supplier. Direct shipping is not allowed, so products are manufactured in the supply chain must pass through the distribution centers (warehouses) (Figs. 12.13 and 12.14).

In the following table all the data for the supply chain example are shown in 12 sections. The type of data in each section is indicated at the top of each section and the data in each section is of the same type and units (Table 12.3).

12.5.3 Warehouse Location Problem (WLP)

12.5.3.1 Warehouse Location Problem Definition

The goal of the warehouse location problem is to determine the number and location of a set of warehouses and of the customer zones serviced by each warehouse

Table 12.3 Supply chain example data

Fixed Cost	
M1	650000
M2	950000
M3	550000
W1	250000
W2	400000
W3	200000

Transporation Cost		W1	W2	W3
P1	M1	1.8	5.8	7.8
P1	M2	4.8	2.8	6.8
P1	M3	8.8	6.8	1.8
P2	M1	1.6	3.6	5.6
P2	M2	4.6	2.6	5.6
P2	M3	6.2	4.6	1.6

Transporation Cost		C1	C2	C3
P1	W1	5.6	4.2	6.6
P1	W2	2.8	1.8	3.2
P1	W3	6.2	5.2	4.2
P2	W1	2.6	1.6	3.6
P2	W2	4.0	3.0	3.2
P2	W3	5.6	4.6	3.6

Production Cost	P1	P2
M1	7.2	5.0
M2	5.2	2.8
M3	7.8	6.0

Handling Cost	P1	P2
W1	3.2	4.6
W2	1.8	2.8
W3	4.8	3.8

Max Capacity		
M1	M2	M3
340000	480000	288000

Max Capacity		
W1	W2	W3
330000	516000	308000

Resource Rate	P1	P2
M1	2	3
M2	1	2
M3	2	4

Resource Rate	P1	P2
W1	2	3
W2	1	2
W3	1	3

Demand	C1	C2	C3
P1	75750	62700	101625
P2	21000	26220	39000

Unit Revenue	C1	C2	C3
P1	44.0	44.0	52.0
P2	40.0	56.0	56.0

Outsource Cost	P1	P2
C1	44	62
C2	44	60
C3	44	62

so that the total cost for servicing customer demands from these warehouses is minimized. There are no external suppliers in the model, so the warehouses are assumed to generate the flows in the supply chain. The customer demands are assumed to be known and deterministic. The total cost is the sum of the fixed costs to establish a warehouse in a particular location and of the variable transportation costs. The transportation costs have a constant marginal cost rate so the total cost function is thus a concave. The number of warehouses to be established is based on the cost tradeoff between fixed facility costs and variable transportation costs. Establishing an additional facility yields higher fixed facility costs but lower variable transportation costs. Since there is a single assignment variable indicating if a customer is serviced from a particular warehouse, the WLP implicitly enforces the single sourcing service constraint for each customer. The number of echelons in the WLP is open for interpretation. The model determines one level of facilities in the supply chain, which indicates a single echelon model. But the model determines only the transportation flows from the warehouses to the customers, which indicates a zero echelon model. It is assumed that the warehouse have no throughput capacity restrictions. The classic WLP has only a single commodity, but it can be easily expanded to multiple commodities since there are no capacity limitations in the problem and the customers have no single sourcing service constraint. The WLP has only a single planning period. The classic WLP can be easily extended to incorporate warehouse handling costs. Since all parameters are known with certainty the WLP belongs to the class of deterministic problems.

The constraints that ensure that a customer is only serviced from an established warehouse are called consistency or linkage constraints. The constraints can be written for every customer individually or for all the customers serviced from a warehouse. The corresponding variants of the WLP are called the aggregate and disaggregate WLP, respectively.

The following additional notation will be used.

f_j fixed cost for establishing a warehouse in location j
c_{ij} transportation cost for servicing the total demand of customer i from warehouse j

Model 12.6. Aggregate WLP

$$\min z = \sum_{j=1}^{N} \left(f_j y_j + \sum_{i=1}^{M} c_{ij} x_{ij} \right) \tag{12.72}$$

$$s.t. \sum_{j=1}^{N} x_{ij} = 1 \quad \forall i \tag{12.73}$$

$$\sum_{i=1}^{M} x_{ij} - M y_j \leq 0 \quad \forall j \tag{12.74}$$

$$y_j \in \{0, 1\}, x_{ij} \geq 0 \tag{12.75}$$

Model 12.7. Disaggregate WLP

$$\min \ z = \sum_{j=1}^{N} \left(f_j y_j + \sum_{i=1}^{M} c_{ij} x_{ij} \right) \tag{12.76}$$

$$s.t. \ \sum_{j=1}^{N} x_{ij} = 1 \quad \forall i \tag{12.77}$$

$$-x_{ij} + y_j \geq 0 \quad \forall i \forall j \tag{12.78}$$

$$y_j \in \{0, 1\}, x_{ij} \geq 0 \tag{12.79}$$

The second formulation is said to be disaggregated because there is one consistency or linkage constraint for each assignment variable. The first formulation is said to be aggregate since there is one linkage constraint per facility status variable. The number of constraints in the disaggregate formulation is much larger. The number of linkage constraints is M, i.e. the number of customers, times larger in the disaggregate than in the aggregate model. The aggregate and disaggregate formulations of the WLP have the same optimal solution. However, the optimal solutions to their respective linear relaxations may not be the same. A formulation is said to be weak or weaker if there is a larger difference between the solution values of the mixed-integer program and its corresponding linear relaxation. The linear relaxation is obtained by substituting the requirement that the facility status variables only have zero or one values by the requirement that the facility status can take any real value between zero and one. The weak and strong attribute are thus based solely on the values of the optimal solutions of the corresponding linear relaxations. Any solution to the linear relaxation of the disaggregate formulation will also be a feasible solution to the linear relaxation of the aggregate formulation, but the reverse is not true. The disaggregate linear relaxation is thus a more restrictive formulation and is also denoted as the "strong" formulation. As indicated above the disaggregate formulation contains also many more constraints. The number of linkage constraints increases from N for the aggregate formulation to $M*N$ for the disaggregate formulation, which is a significant difference for problem instances of industrial size. Even though the disaggregate formulation contains more constraints, in the past disaggregate formulations could be solved in a shorter amount of computation time by the mixed-integer solvers or, equivalently, larger problem instances could be solved in a given amount of time. However, contemporary mixed-integer solvers have the capability to recognize the structure of the WLP and the disaggregate formulation no longer yields an advantage in solution times.

12.5.3.2   Linear Programming Relaxation and Lower Bound

The linear relaxation of the aggregate formulation is given next. The solution of this problem provides a lower bound value on the optimal solution of the WLP.

Model 12.8. Linear Relaxation of the Aggregate WLP

$$\min \ z = \sum_{j=1}^{N} \left(f_j y_j + \sum_{i=1}^{M} c_{ij} x_{ij} \right) \tag{12.80}$$

$$s.t. \ \sum_{j=1}^{N} x_{ij} = 1 \quad \forall i \tag{12.81}$$

$$\sum_{i=1}^{M} x_{ij} - M y_j \leq 0 \quad \forall j \tag{12.82}$$

$$y_j \geq 0, x_{ij} \geq 0 \tag{12.83}$$

At optimality, the linkage constraints will be satisfied at equality, since otherwise the value of the y variable could be reduced which would reduce the total cost and contradict the assumption of optimality. At optimality the linkage constraints can then be written as follows.

$$\sum_{i=1}^{M} x_{ij}^* = M y_j^* \tag{12.84}$$

Substituting this expression for y_j^* in the aggregate relaxation formulation yields the following condensed relaxation formulation.

Model 12.9. Condensed Linear Relaxation of the Aggregate WLP

$$\min \ z = \sum_{j=1}^{N} \sum_{i=1}^{M} \left(\frac{f_j}{M} + c_{ij} \right) x_{ij} \tag{12.85}$$

$$s.t. \ \sum_{j=1}^{N} x_{ij} = 1 \quad \forall i \tag{12.86}$$

$$x_{ij} \geq 0 \tag{12.87}$$

This relaxation can be solved optimally with a greedy algorithm. Each customer is assigned to the distribution center with the minimum expanded cost for that customer. After the customers have been assigned, any distribution to which one or more customers were assigned is established exactly enough to satisfy the linkage constraint. The resulting solution is optimal for the linear programming relaxation and but most often the y variables have fractional optimal values. The fractional solution can be converted to a binary solution by rounding any y variable with value larger than zero up to one. This guarantees only a heuristic solution to the WLP.

12.5.3.3 WLP Example

Several of the algorithms used to solve the WLP will be illustrated on the following example. The example has eight customer facilities and five candidate warehouse locations. This example was described originally in Erlenkotter (1978) to illustrate a very efficient special purpose algorithm to solve the WLP. At the current time, standard MIP solvers are used since they can find the optimal solution in a reasonable amount of time without any specialization or user programming. This specific example is used here because the supply chain example defined above generates the same solution for all the variants of the WLP and thus cannot illustrate the differences between the variants. The assignment costs and the fixed warehouse costs for the WLP-specific are given in the next table. If an assignment or transportation cost is infinite then the customer cannot be served from that warehouse (Table 12.4).

In the next table, the updated assignment costs and the solution constructed by the greedy algorithm are shown. For each warehouse (column) the original assignment costs are increased by one eight of the fixed cost of the warehouse. For example, the assignment cost of customer one to warehouse one is computed as $120+(100/8)=132.5$. Each customer assigned to a warehouse adds one eight to the value of the corresponding warehouse variable. The optimal solution to the linear programming relaxation is highly fractional. The sum of the fixed costs is 88.75. The sum of the assignment costs is 970. The total solution cost for the linear relaxation is thus 1058.75. This value provides a lower bound on the optimal solution value for this example (Table 12.5).

Rounding up the fractional warehouse variables creates a solution that has all warehouses open or established. This solution is a primal feasible solution. The fixed cost increases to 420 and the total cost increases to 1390. This small problem

Table 12.4 WLP example data		1	2	3	4	5
	1	120	210	180	210	170
	2	180	∞	190	190	150
	3	100	150	110	150	110
	4	∞	240	195	180	150
	5	60	55	50	65	70
	6	∞	210	∞	120	195
	7	180	110	∞	160	200
	8	∞	165	195	120	∞
	f_j	100	70	60	110	80
	f_j/M	12.50	8.75	7.50	13.75	10.00

Table 12.5 Greedy solution to the relaxed aggregate WLP

	1	2	3	4	5
1	132.50	218.75	187.50	223.75	180.00
2	192.50	∞	197.50	203.75	160.00
3	112.50	158.75	117.50	163.75	120.00
4	∞	248.75	202.50	193.75	160.00
5	72.50	63.75	57.50	78.75	80.00
6	∞	218.75	∞	133.75	205.00
7	192.50	118.75	∞	173.75	210.00
8	∞	173.75	202.50	133.75	∞
f_j	100.00	70.00	60.00	110.00	80.00
f_j/M	12.50	8.75	7.50	13.75	10.00
1	1				
2					1
3	1				
4					1
5			1		
6				1	
7		1			
8				1	
y_j	0.250	0.125	0.125	0.250	0.250

can be easily solved to optimality with an MIP solver and the optimal solution value equals 1235.

12.5.3.4 Shadow Prices and Site Relative Costs

If we relax the assignment constraints using Lagrangean multipliers u, the resulting objective function is given by the next equation.

$$\min \; z_{LAR} = \sum_{j=1}^{N}\left(f_j y_j + \sum_{i=1}^{M} c_{ij} x_{ij}\right) + \sum_{i=1}^{M} u_i \left(1 - \sum_{j=1}^{N} x_{ij}\right) \tag{12.88}$$

The Lagrangean relaxation formulation is then given next.

Model 12.10. Lagrangean Relaxation of the WLP

$$\min \; z_{LAR}(U) = \sum_{j=1}^{N}\left(f_j y_j + \sum_{i=1}^{M} \left(c_{ij} - u_i\right) x_{ij}\right) + \sum_{i=1}^{M} u_i \tag{12.89}$$

$$s.t. \; -x_{ij} + y_j \geq 0 \quad \forall i \forall j \tag{12.90}$$

$$y_j \in \{0, 1\}, x_{ij} \geq 0 \tag{12.91}$$

Observe that the objective function of the Lagrangean relaxation is a lower bound to the objective function of the original problem, or

$$z_{LAR}(U) \leq z^* \tag{12.92}$$

We can condense this formulation by introducing a site's relative cost factor.

u_i Current cost for servicing customer i, U is the collection (vector) of the individual u_i

$\rho_j(U)$ Site relative cost for opening warehouse j based on the current customer service cost u_i. Note that both u_i and c_{ij} are the cost for servicing the total demand of a customer for a particular product.

The site relative cost factor computes the additional cost associated with opening a warehouse at that site. This additional cost has two terms, the first one is the additional fixed cost for the warehouse, and the second term computes the savings in the transportation cost if this customer can be serviced at a lower cost from this warehouse instead of from its current servicing warehouse. Larger savings have a more negative value. So an efficient warehouse location will have a large negative site relative cost factor.

$$\rho_j(U) = f_j + \sum_{i=1}^{M} \min\left\{0, c_{ij} - u_i\right\} \tag{12.93}$$

The condensed Lagrangean relaxation is given next. This problem is an unconstrained optimization problem, aside from the constraints that force the y variables to have binary values. Since the solution is found for a particular set of values for the u_i variables and the formulation is based on Lagrangean relaxation, this problem is also denoted as the Lagrangean subproblem.

Model 12.11. Lagrangean Subproblem of the WLP

$$\min \quad z_{LAR}(U) = \sum_{i=1}^{M} u_i + \min \sum_{j=1}^{N} \rho_j(U) y_j \tag{12.94}$$

$$s.t. \quad y_j \in \{0, 1\}$$

This problem can be easily solved to optimality by computing the $\rho_j(U)$ and setting the corresponding y variable to one if the $\rho_j(U)$ is negative, which implies that opening that warehouse will yield savings larger than its fixed cost. The optimal x values are then found by setting the x variables equal to one for the warehouse j with the lowest assignment cost among the open warehouses.

The above solution for the sub problem is computed in function of the Lagrangean multipliers u. Kuehn and Hamburger (1963) developed three heuristic adjustment procedures for the Lagrangean multipliers, based on the systematic closure or establishment of the facility with the largest positive or negative site relative cost, respectively. Contemporary mixed-integer programming solvers have sufficiently improved in their solution speed that the use of the drop-add-swap heuristic is no longer warranted. The optimal solution to the WLP can be found in a few minutes for problem instances of industrial size. However, the site relative cost factor still is a relevant measure to rank either existing distribution centers or potential candidate distribution centers. The AMPL implementation of the WLP is shown in the Appendix 12.B.

12.5.3.5 WLP Supply Chain Example

For the WLP, the manufacturing plants are not included in the model and the only facility decisions are related to the warehouses. Internal material handling costs inside the warehouses are also not included in the model. The objective is to minimize the sum of transportation cost between warehouses and customers and the warehouse facilities cost while the external outsourcing option is not available.

The optimal solution establishes only warehouse W2 and satisfies all customer demands from this warehouse. The total facilities cost is 400,000 and the total transportation cost is 937,620 for a total system cost of 1,337,620. The solution to the linear relaxation generates automatically binary values for this example.

Since the linear relaxation provides the optimal integer solution, the values of u are given by the dual variables of the assignment constraints. The dual variables and the calculations for the site relative cost factor (r) are shown in the next table (Table 12.6).

The cost factor for warehouse W2 equals zero since this warehouse determines all the costs in the current solution. The cost factors for the other warehouses are positive, and so opening these warehouses would increase the cost of the supply chain and warehouse W3 would be a slightly less bad selection than warehouse W1 to open up. When the optimal solution is found with the linear programming relaxation, the site relative cost factor is equal to the reduced cost of opening a warehouse. In the example, the site relative cost factor of W2 has to be zero since it is open in the optimal solution and the site relative cost factors of warehouse W1 and W3 are positive.

Table 12.6 Site relative cost factor for the supply chain example

u	C1	C2	C3	
	429,433	324,853	583,333	
savings	C1	C2	C3	r
W1	49,367	−19,561	227,792	507,597
W2	−133,333	−133,333	−133,333	0
W3	157,817	121,799	−16,108	463,507

12.6 Geoffrion and Graves Distribution Model

12.6.1 Model Characteristics

Geoffrion and Graves (1974) developed a supply chain model that takes more factors in consideration compared to the WLP. The model, denoted here by G&G, corresponds to a supply chain that has a single echelon between external suppliers and customers, corresponding to warehouses or distribution facilities. Because of the external suppliers, the supply chain model contains two transportation steps, one from suppliers to warehouses and one from warehouses to customers. In addition, there is a handling cost for each unit of material flow processed through the different warehouses. The model has multiple products. The suppliers are assumed to be available, i.e. determining their status is not part of the problem, but have a supply constraint for each individual product. The warehouses also have throughput capacity constraints that bound the total amount of material flow processed through a warehouse from below and above. The lower bound constraint eliminates supply chain configurations that establish warehouses which are used very little. The planning horizon contains only a single planning period. The model assumes that all parameters are known with certainty and is thus a deterministic formulation. The objective is to minimize the total system cost consisting of facilities cost, the cost of two transportation steps, and the handling cost in the warehouses while satisfying all customer demands. The decision variable for the material flows models the material flow for a particular product from a supplier, through a warehouse, to the final customer. Because there is a single variable indicating if a customer is serviced from a warehouse, the model implicitly enforces the single sourcing service constraint. The linkage or consistency constraints are for all commodities combined, so this model has the aggregate form. Finally, the model can be easily extended by linear configuration constraints in the facility status variables and the assignment variables.

12.6.2 G&G Model

12.6.2.1 Notation

y_{jk} status variable indicating if customer k is serviced from warehouse j or not

x_{ijkp} amount of product p flowing from supplier i through warehouse j to customer k. This variable is expressed in flow units (not in fractions of the total demand) and thus usually is much larger than one

c_{ijkp} transportation cost rate for a unit of product p flowing from supplier i through warehouse j to customer k

h_j handling cost rate for processing a unit of material flow through warehouse j

S_{ip} maximum amount of product p available from supplier i

TL_j, TU_j lower and upper bound on the amount of material that can be processed through warehouse j, respectively

12.6.2.2 G&G Model

Model 12.12. Geoffrion and Graves (G&G) Model

$$\min \sum_{ijkp} c_{ijkp} x_{ijkp} + \sum_j \left(f_j z_j + h_j \sum_{kp} dem_{kp} y_{jk} \right) \tag{12.95}$$

$$s.t. \sum_{jk} x_{ijkp} \le S_{ip} \quad \forall i, \forall p \tag{12.96}$$

$$\sum_i x_{ijkp} = dem_{kp} y_{jk} \quad \forall j, \forall k, \forall p \tag{12.97}$$

$$\sum_j y_{jk} = 1 \quad \forall k \tag{12.98}$$

$$TL_j z_j \le \sum_{pk} dem_{kp} y_{jk} \le TU_j z_j \quad \forall j \tag{12.99}$$

$$z, y = \{0, 1\}, x \ge 0 \tag{12.100}$$

The objective function (12.95) contains three terms: the transportation cost, the facilities fixed cost, and the warehouse handling cost. Constraint (12.96) ensures that capacity of supplier for a particular product is sufficient. Constraint (12.97) models the conservation of flow in a warehouse on a customer by customer and product by product base by ensuring that for every customer serviced by this warehouse the total flow arriving from all suppliers into this warehouse destined for this customer of this product is equal to the demand of this customer for this product. Constraint (12.98) ensures that every customer is assigned exactly to one warehouse. Constraint (12.99) ensure that the flows through the warehouse fall between minimum and maximum bounds, provided the warehouse is established. This constraint ensures thus both the capacity constraint and the linkage constraint for the warehouse, since demand for a customer can only be shipped through the warehouse if the warehouse is established. The model has three sets of variables. The facility status variables and the customer to warehouse assignment variables are binary. The flow variables for each of the flow paths from suppliers to customers are standard continuous and nonnegative variables.

Geoffrion and Graves (1974) developed a solution procedure based on Benders' Decomposition that was much more efficient than solving this formulation with branch and bound using its linear relaxation. As a consequence much larger problem instances could be solved in a reasonable amount of time. However, contemporary MIP solvers have significantly improved in capability and speed so that currently the G&G model can be solved without requiring any custom programming except for the largest industrial problem instances. The AMPL implementation of the G&G is shown in the Appendix 12.C.

12.6.2.3   G&G Model for the Supply Chain Example

For the G&G, the manufacturing plants are included in the model as suppliers, whose status does not have to be determined by the model. The only facility decisions are related to the warehouses. The internal material handling costs inside the warehouses are specified on a product by product basis. The supplier capacity for each product is computed as the total supplier capacity divided by the resource rate of that product. This implies that each product has the full capacity of the supplier available. The resource rate for each product in the warehouses is identical, i.e. each product consumes at an equal rate the warehouse capacity. These adjustments were made in order to use the same data for the supply chain example. The lower bound on the warehouse throughput was set to zero for each warehouse. The objective is to minimize the sum of transportation cost from suppliers to customers, the warehouse handling cost and the warehouse facilities cost while the external outsourcing option is not available. The transportation cost for the flow path from supplier to customer is computed as the sum of the transportation cost between supplier and warehouse and between warehouse and customer, respectively.

The optimal solution established only warehouse W2 and sourced all products from supplier M2. The flow variables for the products on the flow paths from supplier to customer are thus equal to the corresponding demand for the product by the customer. The total system cost was 2,907,553 with the costs for facilities, transportation, and handling equal to 400,000, 1,834,000, and 673,551, respectively.

12.7   Multi-Echelon Supply Chain Model

Up to this point the models have considered either a direct transportation from the material suppliers to the customers, i.e. a zero echelon supply chain, or a single intermediate echelon between suppliers and customers. The following models allow an arbitrary number of echelons between suppliers and customers and are denoted as multi-echelon models. There are three types of facilities in the supply chain: customers, internal facilities, and suppliers. Prime examples of internal facilities are manufacturing plants and distribution centers. Multiple products are considered. The products are jointly subject to capacity constraints in the facilities but the models in this chapter do not allow the transformation of products in the internal facilities. Such models will be considered in the next chapter. The facilities are connected by transportation processes. The possible source facilities of transportation are the union of suppliers and internal facilities. The possible destination facilities of transportation are the union of internal facilities and customers.

12.7.1 Arc Versus Path Based Formulations

Two basic modeling paradigms exist for multi-echelon supply chain models. In the first class of models, there exists a decision variable for every transportation process between an origin and destination facility. This class of models will be called arc-based, because there is a decision variable for every transportation arc and product combination. In the second class of models, there exists a decision variable for every flow path from supplier to customer. This flow path may traverse zero, one, or more internal facilities. This class of models will be called path-based. The two principles for modeling the product flows are shown in the next schematics. The arc-based model has two subscripts for a flow decision variable indicating the origin and destination facility. The path-based model has one additional subscript for each echelon between suppliers and customers. In other words a single echelon model will have three subscripts to the flow variables and a two echelon model will have four subscripts. Multiple products, multiple periods, and multiple scenarios each would add another subscript to both the arc and path based models (Fig. 12.15).

Each of these two modeling approaches has its advantages. The arc-based models have the advantage that adding a new echelon between suppliers and customers does not change the decision variables except for the echelon to be added. However, conservation of flow constraints have to be added for every facility (and product) in the new echelon. Adding an echelon to the path-based models requires changing all the flow decision variables. Path-based models can be used to optimize the flow from a supplier to the customer and can accommodate constraints on this flow path such as a maximum length or duration.

Recall that the WLP had no intermediary facilities between flow source and sink facilities and thus had only one transportation step. The number of echelons in the WLP is considered to be zero and the arc-based or path-based formulations for this model are equivalent. The G&G had a single intermediary echelon between suppliers and customers. It traced flow from a supplier, through a distribution center, to the customer and it thus belongs to the class of path-based formulations.

Fig. 12.15 Arc and path based model illustrations

12.7.2 Arc-Based Multi-Echelon Supply Chain Model

The WLP can be easily extended to include multiple echelons and multiple products in the supply chain. The supply network contains three types of nodes: suppliers, intermediate facilities or transformers, and customers. The suppliers are the source of any material flowing through the supply chain and have an available supply for each product. The customers are the sinks of material flowing through the supply chain and have a demand for each product. The transformers neither generate nor consume flow. While multiple products can be flowing through the supply chain and the products may have joint capacity constraints in the transformation facilities, no transformation between products is included. In other words, this model does not treat the case where there are bill of materials constraints.

The model contains two types of decision variables. The first type is the status variable of the transformation facilities. The supplier and customer facilities are assumed always to be active or available in the model. The second type of variable is the transportation flow between facilities and the throughput flow in a facility. Note that in this model the variable is expressed in flow units and is no longer expressed as a fraction of the customer demand for that product and thus is no longer an assignment variable.

The following notation will be used.

y_j the status of transformation facility j, equal to one if the facility is established, zero otherwise
x_{ijp} amount of flow being transported directly from facility i to facility j of product p
v_{jp} amount of flow throughput through facility j of product p
pc_{ip} cost rate for purchasing one unit of product p from facility i
tc_{ijp} cost rate for transporting one unit of product p from facility i to facility j
hc_{jp} cost rate for handling or processing one unit of product p through facility j
res_{jp} resource consumed by one unit of product p when it is processed through facility j

The arc-based supply chain model is then as follows.

Model 12.13. Arc-Based Multi-Echelon Supply Chain Model

$$\min z = \sum_j^N f_j y_j + \sum_i^M \sum_p^P pc_{ip} x_{ijp} + \sum_i^M \sum_j^M \sum_p^P tc_{ijp} x_{ijp} + \sum_j^N \sum_p^P hc_{jp} v_{jp} \quad (12.101)$$

$$s.t. \sum_j^M \sum_p^P x_{ijp} \le sup_i \quad i \in Suppliers \quad (12.102)$$

$$\sum_i^M x_{ijp} = v_{jp} \quad j \in Transformers, \forall p \quad (12.103)$$

$$\sum_{k}^{M} x_{jkp} = v_{jp} \quad j \in \textit{Transformers}, \forall p \tag{12.104}$$

$$\sum_{p}^{P} res_{jp} \cdot v_{jp} \le cap_j \cdot y_j \quad j \in \textit{Transformers} \tag{12.105}$$

$$\sum_{k}^{M} x_{jkp} = dem_{kp} \quad k \in \textit{Customers}, \forall p \tag{12.106}$$

$$y_j = \{0, 1\}, x_{ijp} \ge 0 \tag{12.107}$$

The objective (12.101) is the minimization of the total system cost, which consists of the facility fixed costs, the purchasing costs, transportation costs, and the throughput costs in the facilities. The model contains only two classes of constraints. The first class of constraints ensures the conservation of flow. For each combination of transformation facility and product the total inflow is equal to the throughput flow (12.103) and is also equal to the total outflow (12.104). Meeting the required customer-product demands is formulated as a conservation of flow constraint (12.106), where the outflow from a customer facility is its required demand. The second type of constraints ensures the linkage and capacity limits. Each transformation facility has a resource capacity limit provided the facility is established (12.105) and products consume this resource capacity at an individual product rate. The model has only a single resource per facility, but it could be extended readily to multiple resources. The supply limitations are also formulated as a capacity constraint (12.102). Finally, the status variables are binary variables and the flow variables are continuous nonnegative variables.

12.7.2.1 Arc-based Model for the Supply Chain Example

The arc-based supply chain model in the AMPL or Mathprog modeling language is given in Appendix D of this chapter. The data for the supply chain example instance is also listed in the appendix. Solving this model for the supply chain example instance problem yields the supply chain configuration in which only the W2 and M2 transformation facilities are established. The total cost is equal to 5,347,359. The facilities, transportation, production, handling, purchasing, and outsourcing cost are 1,350,000, 1,834,000, 1,489,810, 673,551, 0, and 0, respectively. The total number of variables was 62, 6 of which were binary, and the total number of constraints was 33.

12.7.3 Path-Based Multi-Echelon Supply Chain Model

Since there are two echelons of intermediary facilities between the supplier(s) and the customers in the supply chain example, any flow path will have three transportation steps and will be based on four facilities, including the source and sink facilities. The flow variables will have four subscripts related to the facilities plus one subscript for the product type for a total of five subscripts. In general, the number of subscripts for facilities for the flow variables will be equal to the number of echelons of intermediary facilities plus two, corresponding to the source and sink facility. The number of subscripts and the number of flow path variables is so large that only models with a very limited number of echelons can be considered for industrial sized problems.

The following changed notation will be used in addition to the notation developed for the arc-based model. The amounts of product supplied by a particular supplier and flowing through a particular transformation facility are accumulated through substitution constraints. The aggregate variables will be substituted for by contemporary solvers before the actual solution search starts, so they can be eliminated from the model through substitution. Their use does not increase the solution time but increases readability for the user.

x_{ijklp} amount of flow being transported directly from supplier i through facilities j and k to customer l of product p

pq_{ip} amount of flow being supplied by supplier i of product p

tc_{ijklp} cost rate for transporting one unit of product p from supplier i through facilities j and k to customer l

Model 12.14. Path-Based Multi-Echelon Supply Chain Model

$$\min z = \sum_{j}^{N} f_j y_j + \sum_{i}^{M} \sum_{p}^{P} pc_{ip} pq_{ip} + \sum_{i}^{M} \sum_{j}^{N} \sum_{k}^{N} \sum_{l}^{C} \sum_{p}^{P} tc_{ijklp} x_{ijklp}$$
$$+ \sum_{j}^{N} \sum_{p}^{P} hc_{jp} v_{jp} \tag{12.108}$$

$$s.t. \sum_{j}^{N} \sum_{k}^{N} \sum_{l}^{C} x_{ijklp} = pq_{ip} \quad \forall i \in Suppliers, \forall p \in Products \tag{12.109}$$

$$\sum_{p}^{P} pq_{ip} \leq sup_i \quad i \in Suppliers \tag{12.110}$$

$$\sum_{i}^{M} \sum_{k}^{N} \sum_{l}^{C} x_{ijklp} = v_{jp} \quad j \in Transformers\ Echelon\ 1, \forall p \tag{12.111}$$

$$\sum_{i}^{M}\sum_{j}^{N}\sum_{l}^{C} x_{ijklp} = v_{kp} \quad k \in \textit{Transformers Echelon } 2, \forall p \qquad (12.112)$$

$$\sum_{p}^{P} res_{jp} \cdot v_{jp} \leq cap_j \cdot y_j \quad j \in \textit{Transformers} \qquad (12.113)$$

$$\sum_{i}^{M}\sum_{j}^{N}\sum_{k}^{N} x_{ijklp} = dem_{lp} \quad l \in \textit{Customers}, \forall p \qquad (12.114)$$

$$y_j = \{0, 1\}, \ x_{ijklp} \geq 0 \qquad (12.115)$$

The first two constraints compute the amount of flow shipping from a supplier and enforce the supplier capacity constraint. The next two constraints model the computation of the amount of flow flowing through a facility in the first and second echelon, respectively. If more than two echelons of transformation facilities are present, then the number of constraint sets would be increment. Constraint (12.113) models the capacity and linkage constraint for each transformation facility. The last constraint ensures that all the demand for a product by a customer is delivered to that customer.

12.7.3.1 Path-based Model for the Supply Chain Example

The path-based supply chain model in the AMPL or Mathprog modeling language is given in Appendix D of this chapter. The data for the supply chain example instance is also listed in the appendix. Solving this model for the supply chain example instance problem yields the same supply chain configuration as for the arc-based model with the same solution values. In this instance there are 54 flow variables in addition to 6 outsourcing flow variables. The total number of variables was 74, 6 of which were binary, and the total number of constraints was 21. The number of variables is larger and the number of constraints is smaller than for the corresponding arc-based model. The problem instance is too small to make any meaningful statements about the difference in execution times.

12.8 Conclusions

In this chapter a sequence of increasingly complex models for the planning and design of supply chains was presented. With each increase in complexity come additional requirements for data and usually for more sophisticated solution algorithms with their corresponding increasing computation times. One of the most important tasks in a supply chain planning project is determining what the appropriate level of complexity is in order to support the planning decisions that have to be made. Similarly, it is an important task to determine what the cost versus benefit ratio is of applying a more sophisticated solution algorithm. The models in this chapter can still be solved in a reasonable amount of time with standard MIP solvers for most industrial problem instances. This no longer holds true for the models presented in the next chapter on advanced models.

At the same time, the increasing complexity of supply chain planning problems makes solving them by intuition or by trial and error nearly impossible. The number of variables and constraints in the models grow quickly into the thousands or even hundreds of thousands. Only a rigorous modeling and solution approach can find the most desirable configurations and efficient plans.

12.8.1   Costs Calculations

One of the most difficult aspects of strategic distribution models is the determination of the correct values of the cost parameters. If transportation services are rendered using a dedicated carrier, such as in the full truckload mode, then the cost calculations are typically straightforward. However, if the transportation services are executed in a multi-stop vehicle routing mode, then the allocation of the route cost to the individual customers is difficult to compute. At the strategic level determining the proper fixed cost for large capital-intensive assets such as facilities, buildings, and major machining lines is also difficult since most of the cost information is stored in the corporate accounting database. A further complication is the interaction between corporate accounting and the taxing authorities of all the countries involved in the supply chain and their taxation rules. While in many operational and tactical decision support systems the impact of taxes can be ignored, this is no longer the case for strategic decisions. This topic will be further explored in the chapter on advanced supply chain models.

12.9   Exercises

True-False Questions

1. An advantage of the path-based formulation over the arc-based formulation is that the addition of an additional echelon between source and sink does not dramatically increase the number of required variables, (T/F) _____(1).
2. For the design of strategic logistics systems the site generating algorithms are especially good at incorporating site dependent costs, (T/F)_____(2),
   while the site selecting algorithms are primarily strong at trading off fixed versus variable costs, (T/F)_____(3).

Table 12.7 Transportation mode selection data

Characteristic	Rail	Piggyback	Truck	Air
Unit Transportation Cost ($)	1	1.5	2	14
Channel Transit Time (days)	21	14	5	1
Transportation Batch Size	1500	360	360	50

3. In the Add heuristic for the discrete warehouse location problem, the warehouse or depot with the most negative site dependent cost is evaluated next for possible establishment (addition), (T/F)_____(4).
4. It is the recommended practice that the first supply chain design project in a corporation should be for the strategic design of the supply chain, (T/F) _____(5).
5. The Geoffrion and Graves model for strategic logistics systems design enforces customer single sourcing service constraints, (T/F)_____(6), and is an arc-based formation, (T/F)_____(7).
6. The Kuehn and Hamburger model for strategic logistics systems design enforces customer single sourcing service constraints, (T/F)_____(8).

ColorJet Company The ColorJet Company manufactures color inkjet printers. The manufacturing plant is located on the West Coast of the United States and the company operates a regional distribution center on the East Coast. You are responsible for selecting the least cost transportation mode between the manufacturing plant and the distribution center. The possible transportation modes are rail, piggyback (truck trailer on rail), truck, and air. Various characteristics for each mode are given in the next table (Table 12.7).

The unit manufacturing cost of the printers is $300. The aggregate holding cost for all inventories for one year is 30% of the product value, i.e., 30 cents per dollar per year. The total customer demand served from the distribution center is 18,000 printers per year. It is assumed that both production and demand processes have a constant rate throughout the year. A year is equivalent to 365 days. The daily demand for printers at the distribution center has a coefficient of variation equal to two. The safety inventory for each mode in the distribution center is sufficient so that the probability of stock-out during the lead-time is less than 5% for that transportation mode. The annualized fixed warehouse cost is equal to $250 per storage location and each storage location can hold 10 printers.

Determine the best transportation mode based on the total cost for this production-distribution system. Show your results in a clear table (alternatives versus costs) and compute all costs on an annual basis. Be sure to indicate the units for all numerical results.

Million Bubbles Company The Million Bubbles Company manufactures Jacuzzi baths for customers in the continental United States and Alaska. The manufacturing plant is located in Macon, Georgia, on the East Coast of the United States and the company operates a regional distribution center in Seattle, Washington on the West Coast of the United States. You are responsible for selecting the least cost

Table 12.8 Transportation mode selection data

Characteristic	Rail	Truck
Unit Transportation Cost ($)	18	160
Channel Transit Time (days)	15	5
Transportation Batch Size	20	6

transportation mode between the manufacturing plant and the distribution center. The possible transportation modes are rail or truck. Various characteristics for each mode are given in the next table (Table 12.8).

The unit manufacturing cost of the Jacuzzi baths is $1,500. Due to the annual style and color changes in the Jacuzzi models, the aggregate holding cost for all inventories for one year is 90% of the product value, i.e., 90 cents per dollar per year. The total customer demand served from the distribution center is 360 Jacuzzi baths per year. It is assumed that both production and demand processes have a constant average rate throughout the year. A year is equivalent to 360 days. The daily demand for baths at the distribution center has a normal distribution with a mean of one bath and a standard deviation of 0.33 baths. The safety inventory for each mode in the distribution center is assumed to ensure a service level equivalent to a probability of 99.5% delivery out of inventory for the daily demand of Jacuzzi baths. The annualized fixed warehouse cost is equal to $125 per bath.

Determine the best transportation mode based on the total cost for this production-distribution system. Show your results in a clear table (alternatives versus costs) and compute all costs on an annual basis. Be sure to indicate the units for all numerical results.

One-Echelon Supply Chain Design Consider a single echelon supply chain with two plants, two distribution centers, three customers, two products, and one time period. The data for the single echelon supply chain are given in the next table. The data for this design problem are assumed to be known with certainty. Find the minimum cost supply chain configuration and flows for this supply chain. Show your solution in a clear and concise format and provide a summary of the costs in this supply chain. Report which solution method or solution software you have used (Table 12.9).

Euclidean Minisum Exercise 1 Consider the following Euclidean minisum multi-facility facility location problem. The location of the four existing facilities is given in Table 12.10. The interaction between the three new facilities and the four existing facilities is given in Table 12.11. The interaction between the three new facilities is given in Table 12.12.

Solve in the most efficient way for the optimal location of the new facilities and compute the objective function value. While solving for the optimal locations, show in a clear table your initial locations and the initial objective function. Then, execute *one* iteration of the iterative algorithm, if necessary. Show again in a clear table the locations of the new facilities and the objective function value. Describe clearly the assumptions and steps you have made in this algorithm.

Table 12.9 Supply chain data

Cost Data								
Transportation Step 1 (Plant-Warehouse)				Transportation Step 2 (Warehouse-Customer)				
	Cost	Destination			Cost	Destination		
Product	Origin	W1	W2	Product	Origin	C1	C2	C3
P1	P1	2	4	P1	W1	5	4	6
	P2	4	2		W2	6	4	5
P2	P1	3	5	P2	W1	6	3	4
	P2	6	3		W2	5	4	5

Production			Handling			Facility Costs	
Product	Plant	Cost	Product	Warehouse	Cost	Facility	Cost
P1	P1	4	P1	W1	4	W1	100000
	P2	2		W2	2	W2	400000
P2	P1	5	P2	W1	3		
	P2	3		W2	1		

Capacities					
Warehouse Capacity (Throughput)			Production		
Facility	Capacity		Product	Facility	Capacity
W1	250000		P1	P1	60000
W2	500000			P2	400000
			P2	P1	50000
				P2	300000

Customer Demands			
Product	C1	C2	C3
P1	25000	35000	55000
P2	45000	110000	35000

Table 12.10 Existing facilities locations

j	a_j	b_j
1	1	2
2	2	4
3	3	3
4	4	1

Table 12.11 New to existing facilities interaction

	P_1	P_2	P_3	P_4
X_1	4	2	3	1
X_2	2	3	1	2
X_3	11	1	2	2

Table 12.12 New to new facilities interaction

	X_2	X_3
X_1	1	2
X_2	–	4

Fig. 12.16 Minimax problem
with infeasible region

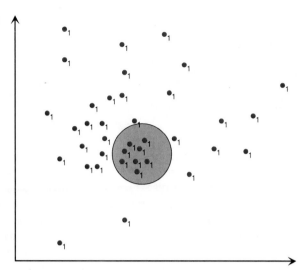

Minimax Location Exercise Consider the problem of finding the location of the Euclidean minimax center of a number of points with equal weight with the additional constraint that excludes certain regions for the location of the minimax center. For this particular case the gray circle represents the infeasible region for the center. The location of the points is given in the Fig. 12.16.

Power Buy The Savvy Customers (SC) chain of warehouse stores has been offered the opportunity for a special deal by a national manufacturer of laundry detergent. If SC purchases the expected sales quantity for the following quarter in one order and takes delivery of the complete quantity of the detergent at the beginning of the quarter, the manufacturer is offering a 25% discount on the purchase price. This practice is commonly known as a "power buy". For the traditional, staggered purchases and deliveries, the only practical transportation mode between the manufacturing plant and the distribution center of SC is by truck. When the complete quantity is transported and delivered as a single quantity, transportation by rail has become an additional possible transportation mode. As the junior industrial engineer employed by SC you are asked to evaluate the three alternatives and make a recommendation based on which alternative has the lowest total cost.

The various quantities of detergent are given in pallets. The quarterly demand is 3000 pallets. The purchasing price when ordering in multiple orders is $120 per pallet. The holding cost rate is 25 cents on the dollar per quarter. The cost per pallet location in the warehouse is $16 per quarter. The warehouse stores have an explicit "quantities are limited" customer service policy and the stores nor the distribution center keep any safety inventory. The traditional periodic purchases occur once a week. You can assume that there are 12 weeks and that there are 90 days in a quarter. The transportation cost and transportation times for each of the three alternatives are given in the next table.

	Powerbuy Rail	Powerbuy Truck	Multibuy Truck	Units
Unit Transportation Cost ($)	4	20	24	$/pallet
Channel Transit Time (days)	14	5	5	days
Unit Purchasing Cost			$120.00	$/pallet

Summarize your calculations in a table using the traditional cost categories. Clearly separate and sum different aggregate cost categories such as invariant, variable, and fixed costs. The costs in each category must sum to the aggregate cost of the category. The sum of all aggregate costs must be equal to the total cost. You can use rows of the table to perform intermediate calculations if this clarifies your cost calculations. In the first column give the title of the cost, intermediate variable, or cost category, in the second column give the formula you used to compute this cost, in the next three columns give the computed cost for each of the three alternatives, and in the last column give the units for the variable or cost in that row. You must specify the units to get credit for the numerical answers in that row. Execute and display all cost calculations in whole dollars.

Chemical Arsenal A military depot is responsible for storing chemical weapons and needs to establish sites for emergency response equipment in case of a chemical accident. The emergency equipment is very expensive and so the depot wants to install as few of these quick response sites as possible. The chemical weapons are stored in bunkers and the emergency site responsible for a particular bunker cannot have a travel time of more than 6 min. to that bunker. For simplicity, assume that the only possible locations for the emergency sites are next to an existing bunker. Different space constraints at the bunkers generate different costs for establishing the emergency sites. All bunkers must be assigned to an emergency site and no emergency site can be responsible for more than three bunkers. The costs of establishing an emergency site at each of the bunkers are given in Table 12.13. The travel times in minutes between the various locations on the transportation network are given in Fig. 12.17. Find the minimum cost configuration for the emergency sites.

State Institute of Technology The State Institute of Technology is in the process of creating a campus master plan. The growing student population and the removal of existing parking areas due to new building construction make it necessary to construct a number of multilevel parking decks. The planning committee has made the promise to the faculty and staff that no academic area will be farther than 5 min. walking or 800 feet removed from the nearest parking deck. There exist eight major academic areas on campus and ten possible parking deck locations are being con-

Table 12.13 Cost of emergency equipment sites

Site	1	2	3	4	5	6	7	8	9
Cost	105	130	145	125	70	80	110	115	75

Fig. 12.17 Traveling times between chemical storage bunkers

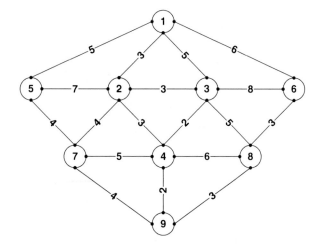

sidered. Each of the major academic areas requires a number of parking spaces to accommodate its faculty, staff, and students. The construction costs for each parking deck location are different due to different the different sizes of the decks and due to rock removal and other civil engineering considerations. The following table shows the required number of parking spaces per academic area, the cost of building a parking deck at a location, and the satisfaction matrix, whose elements are equal to a one if a parking deck is within the promised distance to an academic area and zero otherwise. The objective is to build parking decks at the locations that minimize the overall cost and so that the distance constraints are satisfied (Table 12.14).

Solve this problem in the most efficient way with the standard greedy heuristic. Show the computations and the sequential decisions that you made. Summarize your solution and compute the total cost of your solution.

The planning committee decided to allocate the construction cost of a particular parking deck to the various academic areas served by this deck proportional to the number of parking spaces required by the academic areas. Compute and show the

Table 12.14 Parking data

Academic area	Parking deck location									
	Spaces	1	2	3	4	5	6	7	8	9	10
1	300	1	1	0	1	0	0	1	1	0	0
2	400	1	1	1	1	0	0	1	1	1	0
3	700	1	1	1	0	1	0	1	1	1	0
4	800	1	1	1	1	1	1	1	0	0	0
5	400	0	0	0	0	1	0	0	0	0	0
6	500	0	0	1	1	1	1	1	1	1	1
7	200	0	0	0	1	1	1	1	1	1	1
8	600	0	0	0	0	0	1	1	1	1	1
	Cost	380	240	480	450	350	250	850	750	450	175

Table 12.15 Additional
parking deck location data

Academic area		Deck
	Spaces	11
1	300	1
2	400	0
3	700	1
4	800	0
5	400	1
6	500	1
7	200	0
8	600	1
	Cost	460

allocated cost for each academic area. After the planning phase has been completed, a new parking deck location had become available. The data for this new location are given in the previous table. Determine if this new location should be added to the list of ten initial locations and the solution process should be repeated. Justify your answer numerically (Table 12.15).

BRAC-99 Reduced tensions in the world have led to a reduced military force for the United States. This reduced military requires a smaller number of support bases and significant costs can be saved if some bases are closed. The Base Realignment and Closing Commission for the fiscal year 1999, (BRAC-99), is in the process of determining which bases to close down. The bases that remain open must be able to provide military support for potential operations in various areas of the world. The world has been divided in ten areas of operations. The following table shows which bases can support operations in which areas of the world and the annual cost in millions of dollars to keep each base open. The objective is to build enough bases so that all areas are covered and to minimize the total cost of the open bases (Table 12.16).

Table 12.16 Military base covering data

World areas	Base locations														
	1	2	3	4	5	6	7	8	9	10	11	12	13	14	15
1	1	1	0	1	0	0	1	1	0	0	0	1	0	0	1
2	1	1	1	1	0	0	0	0	1	0	0	1	1	1	0
3	1	1	1	0	1	0	1	0	1	0	0	0	0	0	1
4	1	1	1	1	1	1	1	0	0	0	0	0	0	0	0
5	0	0	0	0	1	0	0	0	0	0	0	0	0	0	0
6	0	0	1	1	0	1	1	1	1	1	1	1	1	1	0
7	0	0	0	1	1	1	1	0	1	1	1	0	1	0	1
8	0	0	0	0	0	1	1	1	1	1	1	0	1	0	1
9	0	0	0	0	0	0	0	1	0	0	0	0	0	0	0
10	0	0	0	0	0	0	0	0	0	1	1	1	1	1	1
	800	750	650	450	350	250	1050	750	650	450	350	750	550	500	850

Table 12.17 Additional base data

World areas	Base
	16
1	1
2	1
3	1
4	1
5	0
6	0
7	0
8	0
9	1
10	0
	800

Solve this problem in the most efficient way with the standard greedy heuristic. Show the computations and the sequential decisions that you made. Summarize your solution and compute the total cost of your solution.

The planning committee wants to provide insight in how much it costs to support military operations in a certain area of the world. For simplicity, all world areas are assumed to require the same amount of support from the base that supports it. If a world area can be supported by more than one open base, the support function is allocated in equal parts to all the open bases that can support this area and the total cost for this world area is the sum of its costs allocated to the bases that can support it. Compute and show the allocated cost for each world area.

After the planning phase has been completed, the powerful senator and chairperson of the armed services committee wants to establish a new base in his district and uses the argument that it will reduce the overall base cost without reducing support coverage. The data for this new base are given in Table 12.17.

Determine if this new base should be added to the list of potential bases to remain open and if the decision process should be repeated. Justify your answer numerically.

Automotive Emission Inspection Stations The State of Georgia requires an annual emission inspection of all non-commercial automobiles. The CLEANAIR company has agreed to establish enough inspection stations in a particular service area so that the average waiting time is kept below a limit of 5 min. It has been determined that 38 possible station locations exist in the service area. Furthermore, the customer demand data has been aggregated into the same 38 locations. Based on the number of cars in the customer zone associated with each location, the contribution of each location to the average waiting time has been computed. It is assumed that the waiting times of the individual customers zones assigned to an inspection station can be added to determine the waiting time of the inspection station. The geographical location of each location is illustrated in Fig. 12.18. The coordinates of each location and its associated contribution to the average waiting time is given in Table 12.18.

Fig. 12.18 Customer locations

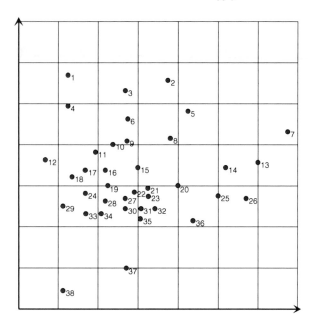

Determine the minimum number of inspection stations, their locations, and their associated customer zones, i.e. customer assignments, and the radius of the customer zones with a greedy heuristic. Copy the above Fig. 12.18 and draw the solution.

Determine the optimal solution with a mathematical programming solver programming solver such as LINGO, MathLab, or Mathematica. Copy the above Fig. 12.18 and draw the solution.

Compare the solution quality and solution times for both procedures. Give a brief assessment of modeling assumptions made for this study

Develop a mathematical programming model that more closely represents the real-world system described above. Clearly list its assumptions, objectives, and constraints. What data are missing to solve this new model? Solve this model with a mathematical programming solver. Discuss the differences between the prior solution and this solution.

Appendices

Appendix 12.A Continuous Point Location Based on the Euclidean Distance Norm

The objective of this location problem is to determine the best location for one or more facilities so that the sum of the transportation costs for goods being supplied to and being delivered from these facilities is minimized. The transportation cost is assumed to be proportional to the product of the flow between two facilities multiplied by the distance between the two facilities. Since the location of the facilities is not known in advance an efficient method is required to compute the

Table 12.18 Customer data

#	x	y	r	#	x	y	r
1	1.250	5.687	3.89	21	3.250	2.937	3.84
2	3.750	5.562	0.36	22	2.938	2.812	2.79
3	2.688	5.312	4.22	23	3.125	2.750	1.46
4	1.250	4.937	3.34	24	1.688	2.812	3.99
5	4.250	4.812	4.60	25	5.000	2.750	0.15
6	2.750	4.625	3.86	26	5.813	2.687	3.21
7	6.750	4.312	2.18	27	2.750	2.687	3.77
8	3.875	4.125	1.11	28	2.188	2.625	4.72
9	2.688	4.062	1.32	29	1.215	2.500	1.68
10	2.375	4.000	2.68	30	2.688	2.437	2.90
11	1.938	3.812	3.83	31	3.063	2.437	0.53
12	0.813	3.625	0.88	32	3.313	2.437	0.61
13	6.000	3.562	0.34	33	1.813	2.312	3.18
14	5.188	3.437	1.94	34	2.063	2.312	4.21
15	3.000	3.437	1.86	35	3.063	2.187	4.15
16	2.188	3.375	3.64	36	4.375	2.125	1.01
17	1.813	3.375	1.03	37	2.750	1.000	0.82
18	1.500	3.250	0.96	38	1.125	0.437	0.77
19	2.250	3.000	0.01				
20	4.000	3.000	0.99				

distance between any two locations. In most logistics and supply chain design problems the distance between two points can be approximated by the Euclidean distance between the facilities multiplied by a constant adjustment factor. Finally, in the classic variant of this problem the facilities can be located anywhere within the area of interest to the problem. The location of the facilities that minimizes the distance score may inside an infeasible region such as a ocean, lake, or mountain range. The role of this design problem is thus not to determine the final location of the facility at a very detailed level, but rather to identify the general region where the facilities should be located. Prior, an approximate method for solving this problem based alternating between the solutions of two sub problems has been described. If the problem instance becomes large, the following algorithm can be used. The greater efficiency of this algorithm comes at a cost of greater complexity but it also allows the calculation of a lower bound on the objective value of the location sub problem.

The development of the algorithm starts with an investigation of the properties of the distance calculation using the Euclidean norm. The optimal solution of the nonlinear problem is then found with an iterative procedure. Finally, the properties are derived that allow the computation of a lower bound on the objective function. This material requires knowledge of continuous optimization methodology.

Euclidean Distance Norm

The calculation of the travel distance between two points is one of the two factors in the objective function terms. In order to find the optimal location for the location problem, the properties of the Euclidean distance norm which is used to calculate the distance have to be established. It will be shown that the Euclidean distance is continuous, convex, but not differentiable in the problem domain.

Definition

A distance norm is the formula for computing the distance between two points in the plane. Let d_{ij} denote the distance between two points i and j in the plane with coordinates (x_i, y_i) and (a_j, b_j), respectively. The Euclidean norm is then computed as

$$d_{ij}^E = \sqrt{(x_i - a_j)^2 + (y_i - b_j)^2} \qquad (12.116)$$

The superscript E denotes the Euclidean distance norm. The **Euclidean** distance is also called the straight-line travel and is frequently used in national distribution problems and for communications problems where straight line travel is an acceptable approximation. The actual over-the-road distances in national distribution problems can then be approximated by multiplying the Euclidean distance with an appropriate factor, e.g. 1.2 for continental United States or 1.26 for the South Eastern United States.

Euclidean Norm Properties

Since it is a proper distance norm, the Euclidean norm satisfies the four properties of any distance norm:

Non-Negativity

$$d^E(X) \geq 0 \quad \forall X \tag{12.117}$$

Equality to Zero

$$d^E(X) = 0 \Leftrightarrow X = 0 \tag{12.118}$$

Homogeneity

$$d^E(kX) = |k| d(X) \quad \forall X \tag{12.119}$$

This property is sometimes also called scalability.

Triangle Inequality

$$d^E(X) + d^E(Y) \geq d^E(X + Y) \quad \forall X, \forall Y \tag{12.120}$$

A fifth property can be derived from the homogeneity property using $k = -1$.

Symmetry

$$d^E(-X) = d^E(X) \quad \forall X \tag{12.121}$$

In addition to the general distance norm properties, the Euclidean norm satisfies the following properties.

Continuous

A function is said to be continuous at point a if the following condition holds

$$\forall \delta > 0 \rightarrow \exists \varepsilon > 0 : if \|x - a\| < \varepsilon \Rightarrow \|f(x) - f(a)\| \leq \delta \tag{12.122}$$

The Euclidean norm is continuous.

Convex

A function is said to be convex if the chord or line segment connecting any two points on the graph of the function never lies below the graph of the function, i.e., if the following condition holds.

$$d^E(\lambda X_1 + (1 - \lambda)X_2) \le \lambda d^E(X_1) + (1 - \lambda)d^E(X_2) \quad \lambda \in [0, 1] \quad (12.123)$$

If the second derivative of the function is defined everywhere in the domain of the function, then a function is said to be convex if the second derivative is nonnegative everywhere in the domain of the function. The Euclidean norm is convex.

A function is said to be strictly convex if the above inequality holds as a strict inequality for any pair of distinct X_1 and X_2 and any $\lambda \in (0, 1)$. In other words, strictly convex means that the line segment lays strictly above the graph of the function except at the two endpoints of the line segment. The Euclidean distance norm is not strictly convex.

A level set is the collection of points in the domain of a function where the function value is less than or equal to a certain value or level, or

$$S(\alpha) = \{x \mid f(x) \le \alpha\} \quad (12.124)$$

A set is convex if any point on the line segment connecting two points in the set is also in the set, or

$$\lambda \cdot P_1 + (1 - \lambda) P_2 \in S \quad \forall P_1, P_2 \in S \text{ and } \lambda \in [0, 1] \quad (12.125)$$

The level sets of a convex function are convex sets. A convex and non-convex function and their corresponding level sets are shown in figure (Fig. 12.19).

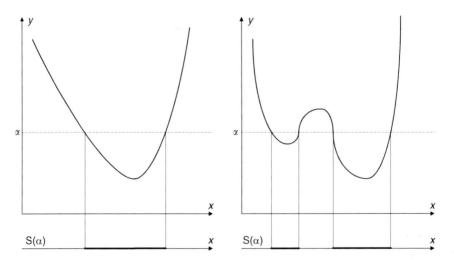

Fig. 12.19 Convex and non-convex function and corresponding level sets

Differentiable except at the fixed facilities

The gradient of the Euclidean distance is given by

$$\frac{\partial d^E(X)}{\partial x_i} = \frac{(x_i - a_j)}{\sqrt{(x - a_j)^2 + (y - b_j)^2}}$$

(12.126)

$$\frac{\partial d^E(X)}{\partial y_i} = \frac{(y_i - b_j)}{\sqrt{(x - a_j)^2 + (y - b_j)^2}}$$

This gradient is not defined at the location of the existing facilities (a_j, b_j). Equivalently, the left and right derivatives at the location of existing facilities are not equal to each other. For a one-dimensional problem the Euclidean distance function has a V shape, with the tip of the V located at the coordinate a and with left and right derivatives at the coordinate a equal to -1 and $+1$, respectively. This is illustrated for the one-dimensional case in Fig. 12.23.

Single Facility Minisum Location

Introduction

Varignon Frame

Weber (1909) published his treatment of industrial location and in an appendix the use of the *Varignon Frame* was described as a way to solve the single facility minisum Euclidean location problem. The Varignon Frame is illustrated in Fig. 12.20.

The optimal location of the knot can be found based on the principles of kinematics. The position of the knot is such that the (vector) sum of all forces on it equals zero. Projecting the force vectors on the x and y axes gives us two equations. The variables are illustrated in Fig. 12.21.

To determine the equilibrium position, the horizontal and vertical components of the forces need to be balanced. The projection of the force vectors on the horizontal and vertical axis are based on the point coordinates. This is illustrated in Fig. 12.22.

$$X_1 = V_1 \cos \theta_1$$
$$Y_1 = V_1 \sin \theta_1$$

(12.127)

$$X_1 = \frac{w_1(a_1 - x)}{\sqrt{(x - a_1)^2 + (y - b_1)^2}}$$

$$Y_1 = \frac{w_1(b_1 - y)}{\sqrt{(x - a_1)^2 + (y - b_1)^2}}$$

(12.128)

Fig. 12.20 Varignon frame

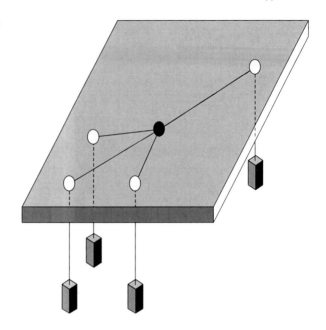

The stationary position of the knot requires that the force components are balanced, i.e., sum up to zero.

$$\sum_j X_j = 0$$
$$\sum_j Y_j = 0$$

$$(12.129)$$

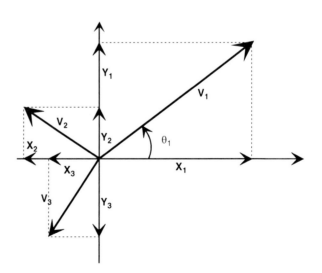

Fig. 12.21 Varignon force schematic

Fig. 12.22 Varignon force
projection

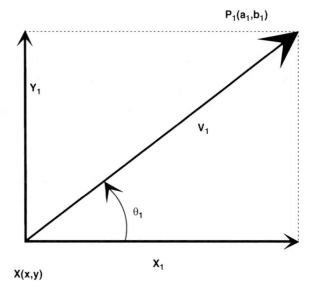

With the Euclidean distance norm explicitly expressed, this equivalent to the following two equations.

$$\sum_j \frac{w_j(x - a_j)}{\sqrt{(x - a_j)^2 + (y - b_j)^2}} = 0$$

$$\sum_j \frac{w_j(y - b_j)}{\sqrt{(x - a_j)^2 + (y - b_j)^2}} = 0$$

(12.130)

The equations that ensure that the forces are at equilibrium are equal to the gradient optimality conditions for the Euclidean distance minisum problem.

$$z = \sum_j w_j \sqrt{(x - a_j)^2 + (y - b_j)^2}$$

$$\frac{\partial z}{\partial x} = \sum_j \frac{w_j(x - a_j)}{\sqrt{(x - a_j)^2 + (y - b_j)^2}} = 0$$

$$\frac{\partial z}{dy} = \sum_j \frac{w_j(y - b_j)}{\sqrt{(x - a_j)^2 + (y - b_j)^2}} = 0$$

(12.131)

Hyperboloid Approximation

To avoid the singularities of the derivative at the existing facilities, the distance norm can be perturbed by adding a small constant ε. The size of ε is based on a tradeoff between numerical accuracy and numerical stability. Larger values of ε increase the stability of the gradient computation but obscure more of the original problem data. A reasonable value of ε lies between 10^{-4} and 10^{-6} of the diameter of the problem domain.

$$d^E(X_i, P_j) = \sqrt{(x_i - a_j)^2 + (y_i - b_j)^2 + \varepsilon} \qquad (12.132)$$

$$\varepsilon \approx 10^{-6} \cdot \max_{i,j} d^E(P_i, P_j) \qquad (12.133)$$

The function defined by the ε-approximation is called a hyperboloid and it is illustrated in the next figure for a one dimensional problem. The figure is for illustration purposes only and is not numerically accurate (Fig. 12.23).

The partial derivatives of the distance for a single existing facility are then given in the next equations.

$$\frac{\partial d}{\partial x_i} = \frac{(x_i - a_j)}{\sqrt{(x_i - a_j)^2 + (y_i - b_j)^2 + \varepsilon}} \qquad (12.134)$$

$$\frac{\partial d}{\partial y_i} = \frac{(y_i - b_j)}{\sqrt{(x_i - a_j)^2 + (y_i - b_j)^2 + \varepsilon}}$$

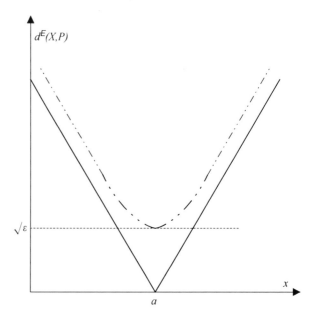

Fig. 12.23 Illustration of the hyperboloid approximation

The partial derivatives of the objective function for a multiple existing facilities with different sizes are then given in the next equations.

$$\frac{\partial z}{\partial x_i} = \sum_j \frac{w_j(x_i - a_j)}{\sqrt{(x_i - a_j)^2 + (y_i - b_j)^2 + \varepsilon}}$$

$$\frac{\partial z}{\partial y_i} = \sum_j \frac{w_j(y_i - b_j)}{\sqrt{(x_i - a_j)^2 + (y_i - b_j)^2 + \varepsilon}}$$

(12.135)

Weiszfeld's Iterative Procedure

Finding the optimal location is achieved by setting the partial derivates equal to zero. This yields two nonlinear equations in two unknowns (x_i, y_i). The solution can be found by an iterative search algorithm. To simplify the notation the following function is defined.

$$g_{ij}(x_i, y_i) = \frac{w_{ij}}{\sqrt{(x_i - a_j)^2 + (y_i - b_j)^2 + \varepsilon}}$$

(12.136)

The optimality conditions can then be rewritten as follows.

$$\sum_j (x_i - a_j) \cdot g_{ij} = 0$$

$$\sum_j (y_i - b_j) \cdot g_{ij} = 0$$

(12.137)

The optimal values of the unknown can be found by rearranging these equations.

$$x_i \sum_j g_{ij} = \sum_j a_j \cdot g_{ij}$$

$$y_i \sum_j g_{ij} = \sum_j b_j \cdot g_{ij}$$

(12.138)

Finally, the notation can be further simplified by defined the following function λ.

$$\lambda_{ij}(x_i, y_i) = \frac{g_{ij}(x_i, y_i)}{\sum_j g_{ij}(x_i, y_i)}$$

(12.139)

This function has the following properties.

$$0 \le \lambda_{ij} \le 1$$

$$\sum_j \lambda_{ij} = 1$$

(12.140)

The optimal values of the location can be written as follows.

$$x_i = \sum_j \lambda_{ij}(x_i, y_i) \cdot a_j$$
$$y_i = \sum_j \lambda_{ij}(x_i, y_i) \cdot b_j$$
(12.141)

In the above expression, the variables to be optimized still appear to the left and right of the equation sign. An iterative method is used to determine the optimal values.

$$x_i^{k+1} = \sum_j \lambda_{ij}^k \left(x_i^k, y_i^k\right) \cdot a_j$$
$$y_i^{k+1} = \sum_j \lambda_{ij}^k \left(x_i^k, y_i^k\right) \cdot b_j$$
(12.142)

Properties

Two properties can be used to find the optimal location of the facility without the iterative method developed above. In the multi-facility case it can be used to identify facilities whose location at be determined a priori and thus reduces the overall problem size. The third property limits the area for the optimal location of the facility to the convex hull of the know facilities.

Majority Property (Scalar Sum)

A sufficient but not necessary condition for the location of an existing facility k to be the optimal location of the Euclidean single facility minisum problem is

$$\left.\begin{array}{l} w_k \geq \dfrac{W}{2} = \dfrac{\sum\limits_{j=1}^{N} w_j}{2} \\[3mm] w_k \geq \sum\limits_{j=1, j \neq k}^{N} w_j \end{array}\right\} \Rightarrow P_k = X^*$$
(12.143)

This property can be interpreted based on the mechanical analog of the Varignon frame. An existing facility k is the optimal location if the vector sum of all the forces to the other existing facilities is smaller than the affinity with facility k, even if all the other existing facilities fall on a line through facility k. This property is only based on the size of the forces, not on their direction. Given the name of the next property, the majority property could then also be called the scalar sum property (Fig. 12.24).

This property can be realized in practice when there is only a single upstream facility, i.e. a single supplier, and the unit transportation cost rates into the moveable facility are equal to the transportation cost rates from the moveable facility to its downstream

Fig. 12.24 Scalar sum property illustration

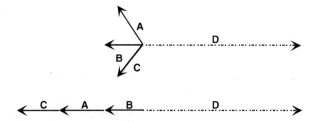

customers. A practical example of this may be when both incoming and outgoing material flows are executed with full truckload carriers. Given overall flow balance for the moveable facility, half the material flow occurs with the single upstream facility and this upstream facility is then the optimal location for the distribution center.

Vector-Sum Property

The location of an existing facility k is the optimal location of the Euclidean single facility minisum problem if and only if the following inequality holds.

$$\sqrt{\left(\sum_{j=1, j \neq k}^{N} \frac{w_j(a_k - a_j)}{\sqrt{(a_k - a_j)^2 + (b_k - b_j)^2}}\right)^2 + \left(\sum_{j=1, j \neq k}^{N} \frac{w_j(b_k - b_j)}{\sqrt{(a_k - a_j)^2 + (b_k - b_j)^2}}\right)^2}$$
$$\leq w_k \Rightarrow P_k = X^* \tag{12.144}$$

This is a necessary and sufficient condition. This property can be interpreted based on the mechanical analog of the Varignon frame. An existing facility k is the optimal location if the vector sum of all the forces to the other existing facilities is smaller than the affinity with facility k (Fig. 12.25).

This property allows checking all the existing facilities for optimality before entering the iterative procedure, which then never has to consider or visit the existing facilities, where its derivative is undefined.

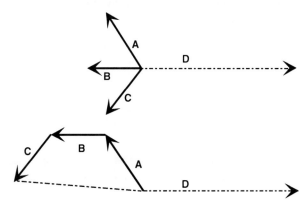

Fig. 12.25 Vector sum property illustration

Fig. 12.26 Convex combination illustration on the line

In practice, this condition may be satisfied for facilities that are located centrally in the problem domain. Even if the transportation rates to the supplier are smaller than the rates to the customers, if the supplier is located centrally with respect to the customers, then the supplier location may be the optimal location for the distribution center.

Convex Hull Property

The convex hull property restricts the optimal location of the moveable facility to be within the convex hull of the fixed facility locations. This restriction limits the location for the starting point of the iterative search algorithm and may eliminate some of the early iterations. Next the equations for the location of a point in the convex hull on the line and in a general coordinate space are shown. The equations are identical to (12.140) and (12.141) which proves that the optimal location must fall within the convex hull of the existing locations (Fig. 12.26).

The first pair of equations defines the line segment between points $[a_1, a_2]$ or in other words the convex hull of the points a_1 and a_2.

$$x = \lambda a_1 + (1 - \lambda)a_2$$
$$0 \le \lambda \le 1 \tag{12.145}$$

The preceding pair of equations is equivalent to the following three equations, which are the convex hull equations.

$$x = \lambda_1 a_1 + \lambda_2 a_2$$
$$\lambda_1 + \lambda_2 = 1 \tag{12.146}$$
$$0 \le \lambda \le 1$$

Figure 12.27 shows the convex hull in the two-dimensional plane, followed by the convex hull equations for a general n-dimensional space, which includes the two-dimensional plane.

$$X = \sum_j \lambda_j P_j$$
$$\sum_j \lambda_j = 1 \tag{12.147}$$
$$0 \le \lambda \le 1$$

Lower Bounds

Several properties have to be established in order to develop an expression for the lower bound of the optimal solution (objective) value.

Fig. 12.27 Convex combination illustration in the plane

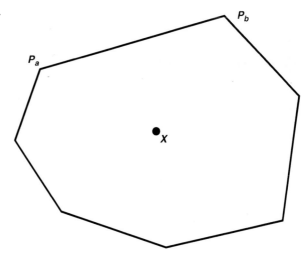

Lower and Upper Bounds based on the Rectilinear Norm

The following notation is used.

$z_K(X)$ objective function value computed using distance norm K = {R (rectilinear), E (Euclidean), RX (Y component of the rectilinear norm), RY (Y component of the rectilinear norm)} at point X.

X_K^* optimal solution location for problem K, where K is defined as above

The following upper and lower bounds can be established for the optimal solution value of the Euclidean location problem through a sequence of inequalities based on optimality and triangle inequality conditions. The three terms are illustrated in Fig. 12.28.

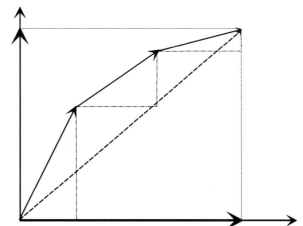

Fig. 12.28 Geometrical illustration of the rectilinear norm based lower bound

$$z_R(X_R^*) \geq z_E(X_E^*) \geq \sqrt{z_{RX}^2(X_{RX}^*) + z_{RY}^2(X_{RY}^*)} \tag{12.148}$$

The disadvantage of this lower bound is that it requires the optimal solution to another location problem. Luckily, solving the rectilinear point location problem is easy. The advantage of this lower bound is that it does not require the determination of the vertex points of the convex hull of existing facilities like the lower bound derived below and that it needs only to be computed once.

Lower Bound Based on Convex Function Support

A convex function z has the following property which states that is completely located above the linear support in any of its points X^k. This property is graphically illustrated in Fig. 12.29.

$$z(X) \geq z(X^k) + \nabla z(X^k) \cdot (X - X^k) \quad \forall X \tag{12.149}$$

Since the above property is valid for any X it is also valid for the optimal location X^* even though this optimal location is unknown until the algorithm completes successfully. Through a sequence of inequalities the lower bound can be expressed in function of the known locations of the fixed facilities. In the last (rightmost) expression all the quantities are either given parameters or can be computed for a given point X^k.

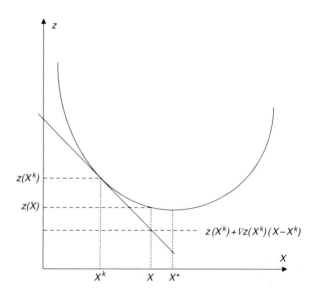

Fig. 12.29 Convex function support

Fig. 12.30 Vector sizes inside the convex hull

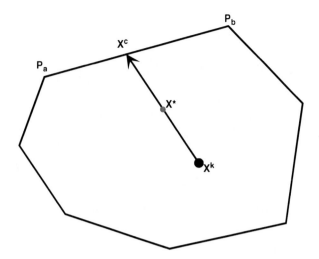

$$z(X^*) \quad \geq z(X^k) + \nabla z(X^k) \cdot (X^* - X^k)$$
$$\geq z(X^k) - \left| \nabla z(X^k) \cdot (X^* - X^k) \right|$$
$$\geq z(X^k) - \left\| \nabla z(X^k) \right\| \cdot \left\| X^* - X^k \right\| \quad (12.150)$$
$$\geq z(X^k) - \left\| \nabla z(X^k) \right\| \cdot \max_j \left\| P_j - X^k \right\|$$

In the sequence of the inequality the following property is used, which is also graphically illustrated in the next figure. Note that it has been established that X^* must fall inside the convex hull of the fixed facilities and that X^k can be restricted to this convex hull. In that case, the point X^c on the intersection of the vector from X^k through X^* with the boundary of the convex hull always exists (Fig. 12.30).

$$\left\| X^* - X^k \right\| \leq \left\| X^c - X^k \right\| \leq \max \left\{ \left\| P_a - X^k \right\|, \left\| P_b - X^k \right\| \right\} \leq \max_j \left\| P_j - X^k \right\|$$
$$(12.151)$$

Location Algorithm

The complete location algorithm is summarized below. Three possible choices for the initial location are the center of gravity location, the location of the largest fixed facility, or the solution to the corresponding rectilinear location problem.

Algorithm 12.1 Euclidean Location with Lower Bound

1. *Problem Reduction*
   Majority Theorem
   Vector Sum Theorem

2. *Initial Starting Point*
   Center of Gravity or
   Largest Fixed Facility or
   Optimal Rectilinear Location
3. *Check Stopping Criteria*
   Compute Lower Bound
   Stop if Gap within Tolerance or Iterations exceed Maximum Number
4. *Compute Next Location*
   Weiszfeld's Method—Hyperboloid Approximation
   Go to Step 3

Multiple Facility Minisum Location

In this case multiple moveable facilities exist. If there are no flows or relationships between the moveable facilities, then this problem decomposes in a sequence of single facility problems, which can be solved by the algorithm derived above or even very approximately by the center of gravity method. In the general case there are material flows between the moveable facilities and an iterative search procedure must be used. The following notation will be used.

H	the set of movable facilities
G	the set of fixed facilities
w_{ij}	the affinity or flow from moveable facility i to fixed facility j
v_{ij}	the affinity or flow from movable facility i to moveable facility j
(x_i, y_i)	the variable location of the moveable facility i
(a_j, b_j)	the location of the fixed facility

The multi-facility Euclidean minisum problem is then given by.

$$Min\ z = \sum_{i=1}^{H} \sum_{j=1}^{G} w_{ij} \sqrt{(x_i - a_j)^2 + (y_i - b_j)^2}$$

$$+ \sum_{i=1}^{H} \sum_{j=i+1}^{H} v_{ij} \sqrt{(x_i - x_j)^2 + (y_i - y_j)^2} \tag{12.152}$$

To minimize z the partial derivatives with respect to x and y are calculated and set to zero, which yields the following recursive expressions for x and y.

$$\frac{\partial z}{\partial x_i} = \sum_{j}^{G} \frac{w_{ij}(x_i - a_j)}{\sqrt{(x_i - a_j)^2 + (y_i - b_j)^2}} + \sum_{j, j \neq i}^{H} \frac{v_{ij}(x_i - x_j)}{\sqrt{(x_i - x_j)^2 + (y_i - y_j)^2}} = 0$$

$$\frac{\partial z}{dy_i} = \sum_{j}^{G} \frac{w_{ij}(y_i - b_j)}{\sqrt{(x_i - a_j)^2 + (y_i - b_j)^2}} + \sum_{j, j \neq i}^{H} \frac{v_{ij}(y_i - y_j)}{\sqrt{(x_i - x_j)^2 + (y_i - y_j)^2}} = 0$$

$$\tag{12.153}$$

First, define the following two functions:

$$g_{ij}(x_i, y_i) = \frac{w_{ij}}{\sqrt{(x_i - a_j)^2 + (y_i - b_j)^2 + \varepsilon}} \tag{12.154}$$

$$h_{ij}(x_i, y_i) = \frac{v_{ij}}{\sqrt{\left(x_i - x_j\right)^2 + \left(y_i - y_j\right)^2 + \varepsilon}} \qquad i \neq j \tag{12.155}$$

$$h_{ii}(x_i, y_i) = 0$$

Note that the denominators are adjusted by the (small) positive constant ε. This prevents the denominators from ever being zero. Without the ε term, these functions would be undefined whenever a moveable facility was located at the same site as a fixed facility. This adjustment method is called the Hyperbolic Approximation Procedure or HAP. Further details can be found in Francis and White (1974) and Love et al. (1988).

Now, the set of locations (x^k, y^k) is determined as follows:

$$x_i^k = \frac{\sum_{j=1}^{G} a_j g_{ij}(x_i^{k-1}, y_i^{k-1}) + \sum_{j=1}^{H} x_j h_{ij}(x_i^{k-1}, y_i^{k-1})}{\sum_{j=1}^{G} g_{ij}(x_i^{k-1}, y_i^{k-1}) + \sum_{j=1}^{H} h_{ij}(x_i^{k-1}, y_i^{k-1})} \tag{12.156}$$

$$y_i^k = \frac{\sum_{j=1}^{G} b_j g_{ij}(x_i^{k-1}, y_i^{k-1}) + \sum_{j=1}^{H} y_j h_{ij}(x_i^{k-1}, y_i^{k-1})}{\sum_{j=1}^{G} g_{ij}(x_i^{k-1}, y_i^{k-1}) + \sum_{j=1}^{H} h_{ij}(x_i^{k-1}, y_i^{k-1})} \tag{12.157}$$

The recursive formulas require an initial location (x^0, y^0) as input and then the procedure uses an iterative improvement scheme to get the next estimation. The superscript k denotes the iteration number. The iterative procedure continues until a stopping criterion is satisfied. Examples of stopping criteria are the location of all moveable facilities falls within the relative tolerance of their previous location, the objective function is within an acceptable tolerance of a lower bound on the objective function, or the maximum number of iterations has been reached.

Appendix 12.B AMPL Model for the WLP

The formulation for the WLP in the AMPL and Mathprog modeling languages is given next. The formulation incorporates multiple products. There is a single objective and two types of constraints, the assignment and the linkage constraint sets, respectively. This model can be used for problem instance irrespective of the instance size. Only the statements following the data statement would have to be changed to solve for another instance.

Model 12.15. AMPL Model for the WLP

```
# Warehouse Location Model (WLP)
#
# notes
#
# allows for multiple commodities (products)
#
# sets
#
set products;
set customers;
set warehouses;
#
# parameters
#
param demand {products, customers} >= 0;
param facility_cost {warehouses} >= 0;
param transport_rate {warehouses, customers, products} >= 0;
#
# variables
#
var facility_status {warehouses};
var assignment {warehouses, customers} >= 0;
#
# objective
#
minimize total_cost:
        sum {j in warehouses} facility_cost[j] * facility_status[j] +
        sum {j in warehouses, k in customers}
                ( sum{p in products} transport_rate[j, k, p] * demand [p, k]) * assignment[j, k];
#
# constraints
#
subject to satisfy_demand {k in customers}:
        sum {j in warehouses} assignment[j, k] = 1;

subject to consistency {j in warehouses}:
        (sum {k in customers} assignment[j, k]) <= card (customers) * status[j];

solve;

display facility_status;
display assignment;
```

The data corresponding to the supply chain example are given next.

```
# Data for the supply chain example for the WLP model
#
# data
#
data;
set products := P1 P2;
set customers:= C1, C2 ,C3;
set warehouses:= W1, W2, W3;

param facility_cost:=
        W1 250000
        W2 400000
        W3 200000;

param demand: C1 C2 C3:=
        P1 75750 62700 101625
        P2 21000 26220 39000;

param transport_rate:=
        [*, *, P1]: C1 C2      C3:=
                W1      5.6     4.2     6.6
                W2      2.8     1.8     3.2
                W3      6.2     5.2     4.2
        [*, *, P2]: C1 C2      C3:=
                W1      2.6     1.6     3.6
                W2      4.0     3.0     3.2
                W3      5.6     4.6     3.6;
```

Appendix 12.C AMPL Implementation of the G&G Model

The formulation for the G&G model in the AMPL and Mathprog modeling languages is given next. The formulation incorporates multiple products. The objective is to minimize the sum of the transportation, facility, and handling costs. There are four types of constraints. The first one is supplier capacity, the second is conservation of flow in and out a warehouse on a customer by customer base, the third is the customer assignment, the fourth one is the warehouse capacity and linkage constraint. This model can be used for problem instance irrespective of the instance size. Only the statements following the data statement would have to be changed to solve for another instance.

Model 12.16. Geoffrion and Graves (G&G) Model

```
#
# notes and variants
#
# the path transportation costs are computed as the sum of the two arc transportation costs
# the handling costs are computed by product
#
# sets
#
set products;
set customers;
set warehouses;
set suppliers;
#
# parameters
#
param demand {customers, products} >= 0;
param facility_cost {warehouses} >= 0;
param transport_WC_rate {warehouses, customers, products} >= 0;
param transport_SW_rate {suppliers, warehouses, products} >= 0;
param handling_rate {warehouses, products} >= 0;
param supplier_capacity {suppliers, products} >= 0;
param warehouse_capacity {warehouses} >= 0;
param warehouse_minthroughput {warehouses} >= 0;
#
# variables
#
var facility_status {warehouses} binary;
var assignment {warehouses, customers} binary;
var flow {suppliers, warehouses, customers, products} >= 0;
#
# objective
#
minimize total_cost:
        sum {j in warehouses} facility_cost[j] * facility_status[j] +
        sum {j in warehouses}
                (sum {k in customers} (sum{ p in products}
                        demand [k, p] * handling_rate[j, p]) * assignment[j, k]) +
        sum {i in suppliers, j in warehouses, k in customers, p in products}
                flow[i, j, k, p] * (transport_SW_rate[i , j, p] + transport_WC_rate[j , k , p]);

# constraints
#
subject to supply_capacity {i in suppliers, p in products}:
        (sum {j in warehouses, k in customers} flow[i, j, k, p]) <= supplier_capacity[i, p];

ıbject to Warehouse_flow_balance {j in warehouses, k in customers, p in products}:
        (sum {i in suppliers} flow [i, j, k, p]) = demand[k, p] * assignment[j, k];

ıbject to satisfy_demand {k in customers}:
        sum {j in warehouses} assignment[j, k] = 1;

ıbject to warehouse_upperbound {j in warehouses}:
        (sum {k in customers, p in products} assignment[j, k] * demand[k, p]) <=
                warehouse_capacity[j] * facility_status[j];

subject to warehouse_lowerbound {j in warehouses}:
        (sum {k in customers, p in products} assignment[j, k] * demand[k, p]) >=
                warehouse_minthroughput[j] * facility_status[j];
```

```
solve;

display facility_status;
display assignment;
display flow;

end;
```

The data corresponding to the supply chain example are given next.

```
#
# data
#
data;
set products := P1 P2;
set customers:= C1, C2 ,C3;
set warehouses:= W1, W2, W3;
set suppliers:= M1, M2, M3;

param facility_cost:=
        W1 250000
        W2 400000
        W3 200000;

param demand: P1 P2:=
        C1 75750 21000
        C2 62700 26220
        C3 101625 39000;

param transport_SW_rate:=
        [*, *, P1]: W1 W2       W3:=
                M1      1.8     5.8     7.8
                M2      4.8     2.8     6.8
                M3      8.8     6.8     1.8
        [*, *, P2]: W1 W2       W3:=
                M1      1.6     3.6     5.6
                M2      4.6     2.6     5.6
                M3      6.2     4.6     1.6;

param transport_WC_rate:=
        [*, *, P1]: C1 C2       C3:=
                W1      5.6     4.2     6.6
                W2      2.8     1.8     3.2
                W3      6.2     5.2     4.2
        [*, *, P2]: C1 C2       C3:=
                W1      2.6     1.6     3.6
                W2      4.0     3.0     3.2
                W3      5.6     4.6     3.6;

param handling_rate: P1 P2:=
        W1 3.2  4.6
        W2 1.8  2.8
        W3 4.8  3.8;

#
# supplier capacity is given as total capacity divided by resource rate
# this gives each product the total supplier capacity
#
param supplier_capacity: P1 P2:=
        M1      170000 113333
        M2      480000 240000
        M3      144000  72000;

#
# warehouse resource rate is assumed to be one for each product
# so all products have equal resource consumption rates
#
param warehouse_capacity:=
        W1      330000
        W2      516000
        W3      308000;

param warehouse_minthroughput:=
        W1      0
        W2      0
        W3      0;
```

Appendix 12.D AMPL Implementation of the Multi-Echelon Model

Arc-Based Model

The arc-based model for the multi-echelon supply model in the AMPL and Math-prog modeling languages is given next. The formulation incorporates multiple products. The objective is to minimize the sum of the purchasing, transportation, facility, production, handling, and outsourcing costs. There are three types of constraints. The first set of constraints consists of substitution constraints, i.e. they define and compute the total cost for a cost category in function of its elements. An example is total production cost. The next set of constraints consists of conservation of flow constraints. There is a constraint for every combination of facility and product. The third set of constraints contains constraints that simultaneously model capacity and linkage. There is a constraint for every transformation facility. This model can be used for problem instance irrespective of the instance size or of the number of echelons in the supply chain. Only the statements following the data statement would have to be changed to solve for another instance.

Model 12.17. Arc-Based Multi-echelon Model

```
#
# SC_MinCost
#
# supply chain configuration example
# deterministic mean value problem
# cost minimization
#
# sets
#
set customers;
set plants;
set warehouses;
set facilities := plants union warehouses;
set suppliers;
set products;
#
# variables
#
var facilities_cost;
var transport_cost;
var production_cost;
var handling_cost;
var purchasing_cost;
var outsourcing_cost;
var facility_status {f in facilities} >= 0.0, <= 1.0 binary;
var purchase {s in suppliers, p in products} >= 0;
var outsourcing{c in customers, p in products} >= 0;
var flow1 {s in suppliers, m in plants, p in products} >= 0;
var flow2 {m in plants, w in warehouses, p in products} >= 0;
var flow3 {w in warehouses, c in customers, p in products} >= 0;
```

```
#
# parameters
#
param facility_cost {f in facilities};
param demand   {c in customers, p in products};
param purchase_cost {s in suppliers, p in products};
param plant_capacity {m in plants};
param produce_cost {m in plants, p in products};
param produce_use {m in plants, p in products};
param warehouse_capacity {w in warehouses};
param handle_cost {w in warehouses, p in products};
param handle_use {w in warehouses, p in products};
param move_cost1{s in suppliers, m in plants, p in products};
param move_cost2{m in plants, w in warehouses, p in products};
param move_cost3{w in warehouses, c in customers, p in products};
param outsource_cost{c in customers, p in products};
#
# objective
#
minimize total_cost: transport_cost + production_cost + handling_cost + purchasing_cost +
                     facilities_cost + outsourcing_cost;
#
# constraints
#
# cost component calculations
#
s.t.   tfc: facilities_cost - sum {f in facilities} facility_cost[f] * facility_status[f] = 0;
       tac: purchasing_cost - sum {s in suppliers, p in products}
                  purchase_cost [s, p] * purchase [s, p] = 0;
       thc: handling_cost -
              sum {m in plants, w in warehouses, p in products}
                  handle_cost [w , p] * flow2 [m, w, p] = 0;
       tpc: production_cost -
              sum {m in plants, w in warehouses, p in products}
                  produce_cost [m , p] * flow2 [m, w, p] = 0;
       ttc: transport_cost
              - sum {s in suppliers, m in plants, p in products}
                  flow1 [s, m, p] * move_cost1 [s, m, p]
              - sum {m in plants, w in warehouses, p in products}
                  flow2 [m, w, p] * move_cost2 [m, w, p]
              -  sum {w in warehouses, c in customers, p in products}
                  flow3 [w, c, p] * move_cost3 [w, c, p] = 0;
       toc: outsourcing_cost - sum {c in customers, p in products}

                  outsource_cost [c, p] * outsourcing[c, p] = 0;
#
#      conservation of flow
#
       fcs{s in suppliers, p in products}:
             purchase [s, p] - sum{m in plants} flow1[s, m, p] = 0;
       fcp{m in plants, p in products}:
             sum{s in suppliers} flow1[s, m, p] = sum {w in warehouses} flow2 [m, w, p];
       fcw{w in warehouses, p in products}:
             sum {m in plants} flow2 [m, w, p] - sum{c in customers} flow3 [w, c , p] = 0;
       fcc{c in customers, p in products}:
             sum {w in warehouses} flow3 [w, c, p] + outsourcing[c, p] - demand[c, p] = 0;
#
#      capacity constraints
#
       pc{m in plants}: sum {w in warehouses, p in products} flow2 [m ,w, p] * produce_use [m, p]
             - plant_capacity[m] * facility_status[m] <= 0;
       wc{w in warehouses}: sum {c in customers, p in products} flow3 [w, c, p] * handle_use [w, p]
             - warehouse_capacity[w] * facility_status[w] <= 0;
#
```

The data corresponding to the supply chain example are given next.

```
data;
#
set customers := C1 C2 C3;
set plants := M1 M2 M3;
set warehouses := W1 W2 W3;
set products := P1 P2;
set suppliers:= Sup;
#
param facility_cost :=
M1      650000
M2      950000
M3      550000
W1      250000
W2      400000
W3      200000;
#
param demand: P1 P2 :=
            C1  75750 21000
            C2  62700 26220
            C3 101625 39000;
param plant_capacity:=
            M1    340000
            M2    480000
            M3    288000;
param purchase_cost: P1 P2 :=
            Sup  0 0;
param outsource_cost: P1 P2 :=
            C1    44 62
            C2    44 60
            C3    44 62;
param produce_cost: P1 P2 :=
            M1  7.2  5.0
            M2  5.2  2.8
            M3  7.8  6.0;
param produce_use: P1 P2 :=
            M1  2  3
            M2  1  2
            M3  2  4;
param warehouse_capacity:=
            W1    330000
            W2    516000
            W3    308000;
param handle_cost: P1 P2 :=
            W1  3.2  4.6
            W2  1.8  2.8
            W3  4.8  3.8;
param handle_use: P1 P2 :=
            W1  2  3
            W2  1  2
            W3  1  3;
param move_cost1:=
       [*, *, P1] : M1 M2 M3 :=
            Sup   0  0  0
       [*, *, P2] : M1 M2 M3 :=
            Sup   0  0  0;
param move_cost2 :=
       [*, *, P1] : W1 W2 W3 :=
            M1    1.8  5.8  7.8
            M2    4.8  2.8  6.8
            M3    8.8  6.8  1.8
       [*, *, P2] : W1 W2 W3 :=
            M1    1.6  3.6  5.6
            M2    4.6  2.6  5.6
            M3    6.2  4.6  1.6;
param move_cost3 :=
       [*, *, P1] : C1 C2 C3 :=
            W1    5.6  4.2  6.6
            W2    2.8  1.8  3.2
            W3    6.2  5.2  4.2
       [*, *, P2] : C1 C2 C3 :=
            W1    2.6  1.6  3.6
            W2    4.0  3.0  3.2
            W3    5.6  4.6  3.6;

end;
```

Path-Based Model

The path-based model for the multi-echelon supply model in the AMPL and Math-prog modeling languages is given next. The formulation incorporates multiple products. The objective is to minimize the sum of the purchasing, transportation, facility, production, handling, and outsourcing costs. There are three types of constraints. The first set of constraints consists of substitution constraints, i.e. they define and compute the total cost for a cost category in function of its elements. An example is total production cost. The next set of constraints consists of conservation of flow constraints. There is a constraint for every combination of facility and product. The third set of constraints contains constraints that simultaneously model capacity and linkage. There is a constraint for every transformation facility. This model can be used for problem instance irrespective of the instance size or of the number of echelons in the supply chain. Only the statements following the data statement would have to be changed to solve for another instance.

Model 12.18. Path-Based Multi-echelon Model

```
#
# SC_MinCost
#
# supply chain configuration example
# deterministic mean value problem
# cost minimization
# path-based flows
#
# sets
#
set customers;
set plants;
set warehouses;
set facilities := plants union warehouses;
set suppliers;
set products;
#
# variables
#
var facilities_cost;
var transport_cost;
var production_cost;
var handling_cost;
var purchasing_cost;
var outsourcing_cost;
var facility_status {f in facilities} >= 0.0, <= 1.0 binary;
var purchase {s in suppliers, p in products} >= 0;
var outsourcing{c in customers, p in products} >= 0;
var flow {s in suppliers, m in plants, w in warehouses, c in customers, p in products} >= 0;
#
# parameters
#
param facility_cost {f in facilities};
param demand   {c in customers, p in products};
param purchase_cost {s in suppliers, p in products};
param plant_capacity {m in plants};
param produce_cost {m in plants, p in products};
param produce_use {m in plants, p in products};
param warehouse_capacity {w in warehouses};
param handle_cost {w in warehouses, p in products};
param handle_use {w in warehouses, p in products};
#param move_cost {s in suppliers, m in plants, w in warehouses, c in customers, p in products};
param move_cost1{s in suppliers, m in plants, p in products};
param move_cost2{m in plants, w in warehouses, p in products};
param move_cost3{w in warehouses, c in customers, p in products};
param outsource_cost{c in customers, p in products};
#
# objective
#
```

```
minimize total_cost: transport_cost + production_cost + handling_cost + purchasing_cost +
facilities_cost +
        outsourcing_cost;
#
# constraints
#
# cost component calculations
#
s.t.    tfc: facilities_cost - sum {f in facilities} facility_cost[f] * facility_status[f] = 0;
        tac: purchasing_cost - sum {s in suppliers, p in products}
                purchase_cost [s, p] * purchase [s, p] = 0;
        thc: handling_cost -
                sum {s in suppliers, m in plants, w in warehouses, c in customers, p in products}
                handle_cost [w , p] * flow [s, m, w, c, p] = 0;
        tpc: production_cost -
                sum {s in suppliers, m in plants, w in warehouses, c in customers, p in products}
                produce_cost [m , p] * flow [s, m, w, c, p] = 0;
        ttc: transport_cost
                - sum {s in suppliers, m in plants, w in warehouses, c in customers, p in products}
                flow [s, m, w, c, p] *
                (move_cost1 [s, m, p] + move_cost2 [m, w, p] + move_cost3 [w, c, p]) = 0;
        toc: outsourcing_cost - sum {c in customers, p in products}
                outsource_cost [c, p] * outsourcing[c, p] = 0;
#
#        conservation of flow
#
        fcs{s in suppliers, p in products}:
                purchase [s, p] - sum{m in plants, w in warehouses, c in customers}
                flow[s, m, w, c, p] = 0;

        fcc{c in customers, p in products}:
                sum {s in suppliers, m in plants, w in warehouses} flow[s, m, w, c, p] +
                outsourcing[c, p] - demand[c, p] = 0;
#
#        capacity constraints
#
        pc{m in plants}: sum {s in suppliers, w in warehouses, c in customers, p in products}
                flow [s, m, w, c, p] * produce_use [m, p] - plant_capacity[m] * facility_status[m] <= 0;
        wc{w in warehouses}: sum {s in suppliers, m in plants, c in customers, p in products}
                flow [s, m, w, c, p] * handle_use [w, p] -
                warehouse_capacity[w] * facility_status[w] <= 0;
```

References

Benders, P. (1962). Partitioning procedures for solving mixed-variables programming problems. *Numerische Mathematik, 4*, 238–252.

Canel, C., & Khumawala, B. M. (1997). Multi-period international facilities location: An algorithm and application. *International Journal of Production Research, 35*(7), 1891–1910.

Cohen, M. A., & Huchzermeier, A. (1999). Global supply chain management: A survey of research and applications. In S. Tayur et al. (Eds.), *Quantitative models for supply chain management* (pp. 669–702). Boston: Kluwer.

Cohen, M. A., & Lee, H. L. (1985). Manufacturing strategy: Concepts and methods. In P. R. Kleindorfer (Ed.), *The management of productivity and technology in manufacturing* (pp. 153–188). New York: Plenum Press.

Cohen, M. A., & Lee, H. L. (1988). Strategic analysis of integrated production-distribution systems: Models and methods. *Operations Research, 36*(2), 216–228.

Cohen, M. A., & Lee, H. L. (1989). Resource deployment analysis of global manufacturing and distribution networks. *Journal of Manufacturing Operations Management, 2*, 81–104.

Cohen, M. A., & Moon, S. (1991). An integrated plant loading model with economies of scale and scope. *European Journal of Operational Research, 50*(3), 266–279.

Cohen, M. A., & Kleindorfer, P. R. (1993). Creating value through operations: The legacy of Elwood S. Buffa. In R. K. Sarin (Ed.), *Perspectives in operations management (Essays in honor of Elwood S. Buffa)* (pp. 3–21). Boston: Kluwer.

Cohen, M. A., Fisher, M., & Jaikumar, R. (1989). International manufacturing and distribution networks: A normative model framework. In K. Ferdows (Ed.), *Managing International Manufacturing* (pp. 67–93). Amsterdam: North-Holland.

Dogan, K., & Goetschalckx, M. (1999). A primal decomposition method for the integrated design of multi-period production-distribution systems. *IIE Transactions, 31*(11), 1027–1036.

Drezner, Z. (1995). *Facility location: A survey of applications and methods.* New York: Springer.

Erlenkotter, D. (1978). A dual-based procedure for uncapacitated facility location. *Operations Research, 26*(6), 992–1009.

Feldman, E., Lehrer, F. A., & Ray, T. L. (1966). Warehouse location under continuous economies of scale. *Management Science, 12,* 670–684.

Fisher M. L. (1985). An applications oriented guide to lagrangian relaxation. *Interfaces, 15*(2), 10–21.

Francis, R. L., McGinnis, L. F., & White, J. A. (1992). *Facility layout and location: An analytical approach* (2nd ed.). Englewood Cliffs: Prentice-Hall.

Friedenthal, S., Moore, A., & Steiner, R. (2008). *A Practical Guide to SysML.* Amsterdam: Morgan Kaufman OMG.

Geoffrion A. M., & Graves, G. W. (1974). Multicommodity distribution system design by Benders decomposition. *Management Science, 20*(5), 822–844.

Geoffrion A. M., & McBride. (1978). Lagreangean relaxation applied to capacitated facility location problems. *Operations Research, 10*(1), 40–47.

Geoffrion, A. M., & Powers, R. F. (1995). 20 years of strategic distribution system design: An evolutionary perspective. *Interfaces, 25*(5), 105–127.

Geoffrion, A. M., & Powers, R. F. (1980). Facility location analysis is just the beginning (if you do it right). *Interfaces, 10/2,* 22–30.

Geoffrion, A. M., Graves, G. W., & Lee, S. J. (1982). A management support system for distribution planning. *INFOR 20, 4,* 287–314.

Geoffrion, A. M., Graves, G. W., & Lee, S. J. (1978). Strategic distribution system planning: A status report. In A. C. Hax (Ed.), *Studies in operations management* (pp. 179–204). Amsterdam: North-Holland.

Geoffrion, A. M., Morris, J. G., & Webster, S. T. (1995). Distribution system design. In Z. Drezner (Ed.), *Facility location: A survey of applications and methods.* New York: Springer.

Goetschalckx, M. (2000). Strategic network planning. In H. Stadtler & C. Kilger (Eds.), *Supply chain management and advanced planning.* Heidelberg: Springer.

Goetschalckx, M., Nemhauser, G., Cole, M. H., Wei, R. Dogan, K., & Zang, X. (1994). Computer aided design of industrial logistic systems. In *Proceedings of the Third Triennial Symposium on Transportation Analysis* (TRISTAN III), Capri, Italy, pp. 151–178.

Kuehn, A. A., & Hamburger, M. J. (1963). A heuristic program for locating warehouses. *Management Science, 9,* 643–666.

Lasdon, L. S. (1970). *Optimization theory for large systems.* New York: McMillan.

Lee, C. (1991). An optimal algorithm for the multiproduct capacitated facility location problem with a choice of facility type. *Computers and Operational Research, 18*(2), 167–182.

Lee, C. (1993). A cross decomposition algorithm for a multiproduct-multitype facility location problem. *Computers and Operational Research, 20*(5), 527–540.

Love R. F., Morris, J. G., & Wesolowsky, G. O. (1988). *Facilities location.* New York: Elsevier.

Mirchandani, P. B., & Francis, R. L. (1990). *Discrete location theory.* New York: Wiley.

Moon, S. (1989). Application of generalized Benders decomposition to a nonlinear distribution system design problem. *Naval Research Logistics, 36,* 283–295.

Nemhauser G. L., & Wolsey, L. A. (1988). *Integer and combinatorial optimization.* New York: Wiley.

Park, C. S., & Sharp, G. P. (1990). *Advanced engineering economics.* New York: Wiley.

Rohde, J., & Wagner, M. (2008). Master planning. In H. Stadtler & C. Kilger (Eds.), *Supply chain management and advanced planning* (4th ed., pp. 161–180). Berlin: Springer.

Schmidt, G., & Wilhelm, W. E. (2000). Strategic, tactical, and operational decisions in multinational logistics networks: A review and discussion of modeling issues. *International Journal of Production Research, 38*(7), 1501–1523.

Schrage, L. (1986). *Linear, integer, and quadratic programming with LINDO.* Palo Alto: The Scientific Press.

Stadtler, H., & Kilger, C. (2008). *Supply chain management and advanced planning*. Berlin: Springer.

Tayur, S., Ganeshan, R., & Magazine, M. (Eds). (1999). *Quantitative models for supply chain management*. Boston: Kluwer.

Thomas, D., & Griffin, P. M. (1996). Coordinated supply chain management. *European Journal of Operational Research, 94*, 1–15.

Van Roy, T. J., & Erlenkotter, D. (1982). A dual-based procedure for dynamic facility location. *Management Science, 28*, 1091–1105.

Van Roy, T. (1983). Cross decomposition for mixed integer programming. *Mathematical Programming, 25*, 46–63.

Van Roy, T. (1986). A cross decomposition algorithm for capacitated facility location. *Operations Research, 34*(1), 145–163.

Verter, V., & Dasci, A. (2001). The plant location and flexible technology acquisition problem. *European Journal of Operational Research*, (to appear).

Vidal, C., & Goetschalckx, M. (1996). The role and limitations of quantitative techniques in the strategic design of global logistics systems. CIBER Research Report 96-023, Georgia Institute of Technology. Accepted for publication in the special issue on Manufacturing in a Global Economy of the Journal of Technology Forecasting and Social Change.

Vidal, C., & Goetschalckx, M. (1997). Strategic production-distribution models: A critical review with emphasis on global supply chain models. *European Journal of Operational Research, 98*, 1–18.

Vidal, C., & Goetschalckx, M. (2000). Modeling the Impact of Uncertainties on Global Logistics Systems. *Journal of Business Logistics, 21*(1), 95–120.

Vidal C., & Goetschalckx, M. (2001). A global supply chain model with transfer pricing and transportation cost allocation. *European Journal of Operational Research, 129*(1), 134–158.

Whitaker, R. A. (1985). Some Add-Drop and Drop-Add interchange heuristics for non-linear warehouse location. *Journal of Operational Research Society, 36*, 61–70.

Chapter 13
Advanced Supply Chain Models

Learning Objectives After you have studied this chapter, you should be able to:

- Know the characteristics of the major types of objectives for strategic models.
- Know the characteristics and differences of single-country versus global logistics models.
- Know the definition of transfer prices and know the major transfer pricing heuristics.
- Know how to measure the robustness of a supply chain.
- Know the characteristics and differences of deterministic versus stochastic strategic models.

13.1 Introduction

13.1.1 Current Trends in Supply Chain Models and Algorithms

In Chap. 12, three main models were developed for the planning and design of supply chains. The first model supported the selection of the transportation process for a single origin–destination link in the supply chain. Because of its focused scope the model could be highly detailed. The second model supported tactical planning. It accommodated multiple products with a bill of materials structure, multiple echelons, and multiple periods. The third major model supported strategic supply chain decisions. It accommodated multiple echelons and multiple periods, but not bill of materials relationships. In general, the models became more aggregate when their scope and time horizon expanded. In this chapter, more advanced models are introduced that accommodate specific complicating features of the supply chain. The model used in the decision support for a specific supply chain instance may include some, but most likely not all, of these expansions. Increasing the complexity of the model requires more detailed data, more sophisticated algorithms, and longer computation times.

M. Goetschalckx, *Supply Chain Engineering,* International Series in Operations Research & Management Science 161, DOI 10.1007/978-1-4419-6512-7_13, © Springer Science+Business Media, LLC 2011

The trend towards more comprehensive decision support models is based on two developments. On the one hand, there is a growing acceptance among practitioners and corporations of the necessity for an integrated view of the supply chain. One aspect of this integrated view is the consideration of the entire supply chain from the suppliers of raw materials to the customer of the finished goods. This is often denoted as the cradle-to-grave view. A second trend is the inclusion of more corporate functions. At the basic level this implies including inventory in the supply chain model in addition to purchasing, transportation, and production functions. At a more advanced level, this includes sophisticated contracts between the corporations collaborating in a supply chain based on performance based logistics or even an integrated view of the initial production and the long-term sustainment phase of the products. A second development is the ever-increasing capabilities of the information technology infrastructure for supply chain management. This includes the growing use of enterprise resource planning software (ERP), the inclusion of more mathematical models (APS) in the ERP software, and the growing capabilities of mathematical programming solvers (MIP). The application of the models, however, is strongly oriented towards operational and tactical planning.

As a consequence, more and more supply chain planning models are developed by practitioners and the owners of the supply chains and these models are growing in complexity and realism. At the same time, the solution techniques and software have become more generic and multipurpose and are often sold or licensed in a "shrink-wrapped" form.

However, there remain a number of significant challenges for supply chain planning and especially for the strategic decision support models. In a response to growing competitive pressures, markets and products are changing much more rapidly. This implies that products will have a growth, maturity, and decline phase in a strategic planning horizon. The corresponding strategic model has to become a dynamic, multi-period model. Most supply chains have components located in different countries, which implies that the models have to incorporate local differences such as taxation and local content requirements. Finally, supply chain risk and risk mitigation strategies such as strategic safety stock and dispersion requirements for supply chain infrastructure have to be included in strategic models. Modeling risk mitigation fundamentally requires stochastic decision support models. The linear deterministic models that arise naturally in the framework of tactical planning can be solved routinely for large problem instances. The very large problem instances generated by stochastic strategic planning models may not be solvable with the general purpose algorithms implemented in commercial solvers. The instance sizes of nonlinear problems that can be solved in a reasonable amount of time are several orders of magnitude smaller. As a consequence, nonlinear effects such as safety inventory or robust configurations are often approximated to yield mixed-integer linear models.

The remainder of this chapter develops the models for specific enhancements to the strategic model. The enhancements are collected into three classes: single-country, multiple-country, and robustness. The model used for a specific supply chain may contain several of these enhancements simultaneously.

13.2   Strategic Single-Country Supply Chain Design

13.2.1   Economies of Scale

One of the most common effects in both transportation and production costs are economies of scale, which assume that the cost per unit transported or produced decreases as the total transportation or production quantity increases. If the cost reduction effect is valid for the full quantity then they are denoted as full quantity discounts. Alternative names are all-units and all-inclusive quantity discounts. If the cost reduction only affects the additional quantities beyond certain breakpoints, then they are denoted as incremental discounts. Incremental discounts have concave total cost curves and the total cost curves for full-quantity discounts may have discontinuities. The two types of cost curves are shown in Fig. 13.1.

13.2.1.1   Notation

Both discounts can be included in cost models for supply chain planning and design. The submodels for just the economies of scale are shown next. Both use the following notation

c_i marginal transportation cost rate for discount class i

e_i offset (intersection with the y axis) of the total cost line of discount class i (incremental discounts only)

$MaxQ_i$ maximum quantity transported in discount class i and quantity breakpoint at which discount rate $i + 1$ becomes effective

x_i quantity transported (or produced) at discount rate i

z_i status variable indicating if discount rate i is the lowest cost rate used

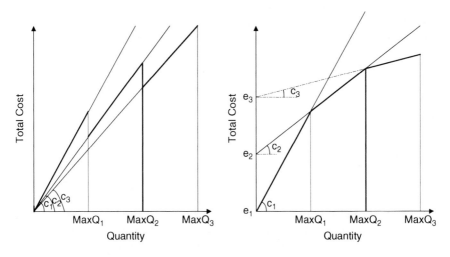

Fig. 13.1 Total cost curves for full-quantity and incremental discounts

TC total cost of the quantity transported
$ReqQ$ required transportation quantity

Quantity discounts imply that $c_1 > c_2 > c_3$,—in other words, the cost rate is strictly decreasing by increasing quantities in the discount classes.

13.2.1.2 Full-Quantity Discount Cost Model

Model 13.1   Full-Quantity Discount Model

$$\min \quad TC = \sum_i c_i x_i \tag{13.1}$$

$$s.t. \quad MaxQ_{i-1} \cdot z_i \leq x_i \qquad \forall i \tag{13.2}$$

$$x_i \leq MaxQ_i \cdot z_i \qquad \forall i \tag{13.3}$$

$$\sum_i z_i = 1 \tag{13.4}$$

$$\sum_i x_i \geq ReqQ \tag{13.5}$$

$$z_i \in \{0, 1\}, x_i \geq 0 \tag{13.6}$$

In the full discount case, only one transportation rate is active and the total quantity is transported at that rate. The total cost is equal to the total quantity transported at the active rate. The first two constraints ensure that the quantity transported in the active discount class falls between the lower and upper quantity bounds for that class and that the quantities in all other discount classes are equal to zero. Constraint (13.4) ensures that only one discount class is active. Finally, constraint (13.5) ensures that the sum of all quantities in the discount classes satisfies the material flow requirement. When this submodel becomes part of a larger supply chain model, the parameter $ReqQ$ may be replaced by a flow variable indicating a particular flow in the supply chain.

The model belongs to the class of mixed-integer programming models since it contains binary variables for the selection of the discount class and continuous variables for the quantity transported in the corresponding class. This makes this submodel or any model that contains this submodel much harder to solve than a model with the standard linear cost equation. Since typically a large number of transportation channels exist in a supply chain design model, a large number of additional binary variables and constraints are created when economies of scale are modeled. For example, assuming there are 40,000 transportation channels and five discount classes for each channel, this would result in 200,000 extra binary variables and 440,000 extra constraints. Clearly, increasing the model complexity in such significant manner should only be done if it is essential for the validity of the model. Constraint (13.4) is a typical example of a clique constraint or a special ordered set constraint of type 1 (SOS1), which ensure that exactly one element from a set of elements is chosen or activated. Some MIP solvers can exploit the clique or SOS1 structure and significantly reduce the solution time for the model.

13.2.1.3 Incremental Discount Cost Model

This model has the same constraints as the full discount model, but the objective function has a different equation. In this case, more than one discount class can have a nonzero quantity transported at its corresponding cost rate. Consider the case where the material flow requirement is such that discount class 2 has the lowest transportation rate among the used classes. The total cost is then given by

$$TC = c_1 MaxQ_1 + c_2 (x_2 - MaxQ_1) = c_2 x_2 + (c_1 - c_2) MaxQ_1$$

and thus

$$e_2 = (c_1 - c_2) MaxQ_1$$

Now consider the case where the material flow requirement is such that the discount class 3 has the lowest transportation rate among the used classes. The total cost is given by

$$TC = c_1 MaxQ_1 + c_2 (MaxQ_2 - MaxQ_1) + c_3 (x_3 - MaxQ_2)$$
$$= c_3 x_3 + (c_2 - c_3) MaxQ_2 + (c_1 - c_2) MaxQ_1$$

and thus

$$e_3 = (c_2 - c_3) MaxQ_2 + (c_1 - c_2) MaxQ_1$$

The general expression for the offset is then

$$e_i = \sum_{k=2}^{i} (c_{k-1} - c_k) MaxQ_{k-1} \quad i \geq 2 \tag{13.7}$$

All offset values can thus be computed before the model is solved. The general expression for the objective function is then

$$\min \quad TC = \sum_i (c_i x_i + e_i z_i) \tag{13.8}$$

This problem is also a mixed-integer optimization problem and the comments made for the case of the full quantity discounts are also valid for this case. The incremental discount model does not include the clique constraint of the full-quantity discount model since multiple cost rates can be used simultaneously.

13.2.2   Facility Technology or Capacity Selection

Two of the most common decisions in the strategic configuration of supply chains
are the determination of the most economical technology to be implemented in a
facility and the determination of the most economical capacity for a facility. The
choices for either technology or capacity are assumed to be selected from a list of
available technologies or capacities. These problems belong to the class of alternative selection problems. In many cases the selection problem it is a more realistic
than the corresponding alternative generation problem which would determine the
best value of the capacity within a feasible range. A second fundamental assumption
is that only one technology or one capacity level can be implemented at the facility.
The choice is modeled using the notions of facility site and facility type. In general,
each potential facility site can be occupied by one of several types of facilities. For
example, small, medium, and large may be three possible types of facilities. The
notion of multiple facility types, each with a linear cost structure, allows a nonlinear
(but piecewise linear) cost structure for each potential facility site.

Such a piecewise linear cost curve generated by the cost curves of three different
technologies is illustrated in Fig. 13.2. There is a facility site binary status variable
for each possible facility location as well as binary variables for each possible alternative of either technology or capacity level included in the model. Finally, a binary
decision variable allows the model to select the closure of an existing facility. The facility cost of each facility includes a cost proportional to storage capacity, a cost proportional to the amount shipped through or manufactured at the facility, and a fixed
cost to either operate a facility or to close a warehouse. The fixed cost to operate a
facility accounts for the overhead, capital, and other costs that are not considered to
be proportional to storage capacity or throughput. The cost to close an existing facility accounts for the various expenditures needed to cease operations at a particular
site. Each of these costs is defined in terms of a facility site and a facility type.

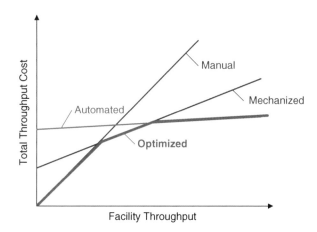

Fig. 13.2 Piecewise linear
technology cost curves for a
facility

13.2.2.1 Notation

The following notation will be used to model this decision. When this model component is included in a complete model there will be many types of variables and parameters. To avoid confusion, the parameters use long parameter names.

Sets

D	set of facility sites, indexed by j
C	set of customers
$L(j)$	set of possible facility types for the facility at site j, indexed by l
$M(j, k)$	set of transportation mode channels connecting facility j (origin) with facility k (destination), indexed by m

Parameters

$FacFixedCost_{jl}$	fixed cost to establish at facility of type l at site j
$FacClosingCost_{jc}$	fixed cost to close down facility at site j, zero if no facility currently exists
Vol_p	volume of product p
$FacStorageCap_{jl}$	storage capacity of facility type l at site j, units consistent with Vol_p
$FlowResUnit_{jlp}$	unit resource consumption rate for product p through facility type l at site j
$FacFlowCap_{jl}$	throughput capacity of facility type l at site j

Variables

y_j	1 if a facility at site j is established
y_{jl}	1 if the type l of facility site j is established, 0 otherwise
y_{jc}	1 if a facility is *not* established at site j, 0 otherwise
v_{jlp}	throughput flow of product p through facility type l at site j
miq_{jlp}	maximum inventory quantity of product p stored at facility type l at site j
x_{jkmp}	transportation flow of product p from facility j to facility k using mode m

13.2.2.2 Model

The volume of all products is assumed to be expressed in the same volume units, e.g., pallets, boxes, trucks, or cubic meters. All the facility storage capacities and facility storage costs are expressed in terms of the same volume units.

Each potential facility (site) either can be established as exactly one type or not be established.

$$\sum_{l \in L(j)} y_{jl} = y_j \qquad j \in D \tag{13.9}$$

If there is cost of closing an existing facility, the following equation has to be added to the model. The right-hand side equal to one can be interpreted as the initial status of the facility at that site.

$$y_j + yc_j = 1 \qquad j \in D \tag{13.10}$$

The warehouse fixed and closing costs are terms in the objective function

$$\sum_{j \in D} \left(\sum_{l \in L(j)} FacFixedCost_{jl} y_{jl} + FacClosingCost_j \, yc_j \right) \tag{13.11}$$

The following constraint enforces that the flow through a facility cannot exceed the maximum throughput capacity for each facility type. This constraint can be generalized to a general resource consumption proportional to the flow and resource capacity constraint for a facility type. The parameters in the constraint would have an additional subscript indicating the resource and there is a capacity constraint for every resource defined at this facility.

$$\sum_{p \in P} FlowResUnit_{jlp} v_{jlp} \leq WhseFlowCap_{jl} y_{jl} \quad j \in D, l \in L(j) \tag{13.12}$$

The following constraint ensures that the amount of product p flowing through a facility is equal to the product flow leaving that facility through the various transportation channels. This constraint models the conservation of flow on the outbound side of the facility.

$$\sum_{l \in L(j)} v_{jlp} = \sum_{k \in C \cup D} \sum_{m \in M(j,k)} x_{jkmp} \qquad j \in D, p \in P \tag{13.13}$$

The maximum inventory of product p stored in the facility of type l at site j is determined by a set of equations related to the inventory in the facility and the supply chain. Those equations will be developed below. The following constraint enforces the required facility storage capacity for each facility type. The storage capacity constraint can usually not be written as a general resource constraint based on the facility throughput because the maximum inventory (miq_{jlp}) is not proportional to the facility throughput (v_{jlp}). β is the ratio of the aggregate inventory in the warehouse for all products divided by the sum of the maximum inventories of all the products that flow through this warehouse. Its value has to be estimated experimentally and is further discussed in the section on the inventory in transformation facilities.

$$\beta \left(\sum_{p \in P} Vol_p miq_{jlp} \right) \leq WhseStgCap_{jl} y_{jl} \qquad j \in D, l \in L(j) \tag{13.14}$$

The warehouse variable operating costs terms are given next. If the facility is a warehouse, then the second cost component is usually the warehouse handling cost, but it can be generalized to any resource and cost proportional to the throughput flow.

$$\sum_{j \in D} \sum_{l \in L(j)} \left(WhseStgCost_{jl} \sum_{p \in P} Vol_p miq_{jlp} + \sum_{p \in P} WhseFlowCost_{jlp} v_{jlp} \right) \tag{13.15}$$

Constraints on the minimum and maximum number of established facilities can be specified and belong the class of extraneous constraints. The following is an example of such a constraint similar to the constraint in the P-median problem.

$$\sum_j y_j \leq P \tag{13.16}$$

13.2.3   Transportation Channel Costs

At the strategic level the transportation between facilities, also called *trunking*, and local delivery to the final customers are assumed to be executed by direct shipment and vehicle routing planning is not considered. If routing cost estimates are available, then the local delivery costs can be based on these estimates. At the strategic and tactical planning level the total amount of product shipped through a transportation channel during a planning period is assumed to be much larger than the size of a single carrier used on that channel. Thus, integrality requirements for the number of carriers used on a channel are often ignored. The transportation costs for a channel are calculated as the sum of the variable cost proportional to the number of carriers used and the variable cost proportional to the amount of weight units shipped. If one of those two cost drivers is not applicable then it can be safely removed from the model. Similarly to the technology selection decision for a facility, multiple alternative transportation channels are possible between an origin and destination facility. Alternative channels may be generated by different transportation modes, such as truck and rail transportation, different carrier vehicles, such as standard trucks versus giant trucks, or by different frequencies and transit times. Each channel alternative has its own values for transportation mode, vehicle size, frequency, transit time, and cost and capacity parameters. Since the alternative channels have the same origin and destination facility they are also called parallel channels. The alternative channels are indexed by m and the model will select the channel that contributes to most to the overall supply chain performance. Because of the number of available transportation modes, vehicle sizes, transit times, and frequencies, the number of parallel channels for a single origin-destination pair can be quite large. Five to twenty alternative or parallel channels is not unusual. Typically, the channel data is by far the largest component of the instance data for a particular planning problem.

13.2.3.1 Notation

The following notation will be used.
Sets

$M(i, j)$	set of available (parallel) channels from origin facility i to destination facility j, indexed by m

Parameters

$CarrierCost_{ijm}$	cost for transportation of a single carrier vehicle from facility i to facility j using alternative channel m
$TranUnitCost_{ijmp}$	transportation cost rate for transporting one unit of product p from facility i to facility j using alternative channel m
$TranFixedCost_{ijm}$	fixed cost for a shipment from facility i to facility j using alternative channel m
$Value_{jp}$	value of on unit of product p which is equal to the total amount invested in one unit of product p when it is located at facility j
r	corporate capital discount rate. This rate is based on the corporate weighted average cost of capital or *wacc* and reflects how the corporation has to pay to have capital available to them during the planning horizon
$TransitTime_{ijm}$	total time required to transport products from facility i to facility j using alternative channel m expressed in planning periods. Since the strategic planning period is often a year, the transit time would be expressed as the fraction of a year which may yield numbers that are very small. For example, if the transit time is 3 days and the strategic planning period is one year, then the transit time would be equal to $3/365 = 0.008219$. Other time units can be used as long as the consistency between variables and constraints using the different units has been assured.
R_{ijm}	time interval expressed in planning periods between subsequent transportation activities from facility i to facility j using alternative channel m, i.e., the inverse of the channel frequency. For example, if the transportation frequency is once a week and the strategic planning period is a year, then the channel frequency is 52 and the time interval is $1/52 = 0.01923$.
$MinCarriers_{ijm}$	minimum number of carrier vehicles to be used per time interval R_{ijm} in the channel from facility i to facility j using alternative channel m
$MaxCarriers_{ijm}$	maximum number of carrier vehicles to be used per time interval R_{ijm} in the channel from facility i to facility j using alternative channel m
Vol_p	volume of one unit of product p
Wt_p	weight of one unit of product p
$CarrierVolCap_{ijm}$	volume capacity of one vehicle used to transport goods from facility i to facility j using alternative channel m

$CarrierWtCap_{ijm}$ weight capacity of one vehicle used to transport goods from facility i to facility j using alternative channel m

Decision Variables

w_{ijm} number of carrier vehicles sent from facility i to facility j using alternative channel m during the planning horizon, e.g., trucks per year

z_{ijm} 1 if the channel alternative m facility i to facility j is used, zero otherwise

s_i 1 if supplier i is activated, i.e., available to be used, zero otherwise

13.2.3.2 Model

The channel transportation cost is given by the following expression. The fixed cost incurred per transportation shipment is assumed to occur every R_{ijm} periods or $(1/R_{ijm})$ times per period (year). Similarly to requiring a certain minimum number of carriers per transportation channel if the channel is used, modeling the fixed cost per channel requires a large number of binary variables. This significantly increases the computational burden of the solution algorithm and the addition of this complexity to the model should be considered carefully.

$$\sum_{i \in B \cup D} \sum_{j \in C \cup D} \sum_{m \in M(i,j)} \left[CarrierCost_{ijm} w_{ijm} + \sum_{p \in P} TranUnitCost_{ijmp} x_{ijmp} \right. $$
$$\left. + \frac{TranFixedCost_{ijm}}{R_{ijm}} z_{ijm} \right] \qquad (13.17)$$

Each unit shipped through channel ijm spends $TransitTime_{ijm}$ time in-transit while travelling from i to j. The total inventory costs associated with being in transit are then given by the following equation. These inventory costs are also called in-transit or pipeline inventory costs. Note that the value of a product at a particular facility in the supply chain is assumed to be independent on how that product arrived that this facility, i.e., independent of its supply chain history. In the tactical channel selection model developed above, the value of a product was considered dependent on the channel used. Because that model each channel is considered independently, the complexity of the calculations to track the supply chain history of a product is manageable. In the strategic planning model, only an aggregate value is used, which is clearly a simplifying approximation. If the dependency of the value of a product in a facility on its supply chain history has to be modeled, then the value of a product in a particular facility becomes a model variable instead of a model parameter. This significantly increases the data and solution time requirements. For complex industrial supply chains it is not unusual to have the value of a product considered to be a parameter that is updated periodically, such as once or twice a year, and that is identical irrespective of where in the supply chain this product is located. The value is computed as an average over the locations of the product and reflects the most current supply chain history for that product.

$$\sum_{i \in B \cup D} \sum_{j \in D} \sum_{m \in M(i,j)} \sum_{p \in P} r \cdot Value_{ip} \cdot TransitTime_{ijm} x_{ijmp} \qquad (13.18)$$

Each alternative transportation channel may have a required minimum and maximum number of carriers used per time interval on that transportation channel provided the transportation channel is used at all. The minimum requirement avoids channels that are hardly used at all and the maximum requirement may reflect a limit on the availability of transportation vehicles. The minimum number, which may be zero, is the enforced by the following constraint. Note that number of vehicles per strategic planning period (w_{ijm}) is divided by the channel frequency or equivalently multiplied by the channel time interval (R_{ijm}) to satisfy the bounds on the number of vehicles per time interval.

$$R_{ijm} w_{ijm} \geq MinCarriers_{ijm} z_{ijm} \qquad (13.19)$$

Each transportation channel has a limited maximum allowable number of carriers used per order interval. The maximum number, which may be infinity, is enforced by the following constraint. This constraint also ensures the consistency between the use of carriers in a channel and the use of the channel itself.

$$R_{ijm} w_{ijm} \leq MaxCarriers_{ijm} z_{ijm} \qquad (13.20)$$

For example, assume that 100 trucks are available to satisfy transportation requests throughout the year (the strategic planning period) for a particular channel. Furthermore, assume that frequency of the truck service is once a week, i.e., the trucks can execute one round trip in no more than a week. The time interval between truck arrivals is then $1/52 = 0.0192$. The maximum number of truck transports per year available for this service on this channel is then $52.100 = 5,200$.

$$\left(\frac{1}{52}\right) w_{ijm} \leq 100 \cdot z_{ijm}$$

If either constraint on the minimum or maximum of carriers is present or if fixed cost is incurred with every shipment, then a binary variable for every combination of origin-destination pair and alternative transportation channel has be defined and this typically yields a very large number of binary variables. For example, assume that there are 20 possible origin facilities, 200 customer facilities, and 10 alternative channels, this would create 40,000 binary variables to model the transportation channels. The impact on the complexity of the model and the increase in corresponding solution times have to be very carefully considered, before this type of constraints is included.

The number of carriers that have to used during a planning period may depend on the weight of the products to be transported or on the volume of the product. The weight constraint typically is binding for the transportation of bulk and liquid products, but the volume constraint is often the binding constraint for the transportation of piece goods that are packaged in boxes or stacked on pallets. The packaging materials used to protect the goods during transportation may lower the average density of the shipment sufficiently or the fragility of the product may prevent stacking pallets on top of each other. Each carrier vehicle has a weight capacity, enforced by the following constraint.

$$\sum_{p \in P} W t_p x_{ijmp} \le Carrier WtCap_{ijm} w_{ijm} \tag{13.21}$$

Each carrier vehicle has a volume capacity, enforced by the following constraint.

$$\sum_{p \in P} Vol_p x_{ijmp} \le Carrier VolCap_{ijm} w_{ijm} \tag{13.22}$$

The preceding two constraints also ensure the consistency between the product flow on a channel and the number of vehicles used to carry that product flow. Finally, the consistency between the use of a transportation channel and the establishment of either the origin or destination facilities is modeled by the following constraints. Note that customers are considered to be always present, but that establishment of transformation facilities and the use of suppliers is a decision to be optimized.

The following constraints require that transportation channels to and from a potential transformation facility site are usable only if a transformation facility is actually established at that site.

$$z_{ijm} \le \sum_{l \in L(j)} y_{jl} \tag{13.23}$$

$$z_{jkm} \le \sum_{l \in L(j)} y_{jl} \tag{13.24}$$

The following constraint requires that transportation channels from a supplier are usable only if the supplier has been activated.

$$z_{ijm} \le s_i \tag{13.25}$$

13.2.4 Facility Inventory

In this section the equations that model the inventory and compute the inventory costs in a supply chain are developed. The strategic planning model assumes that no inventory is held at the supplier and the customer facilities in the supply chain. If there is inventory present at those facilities, then it is not controlled by the supply chain plan and the corresponding inventory cost does not impact the supply chain

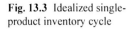

Fig. 13.3 Idealized single-product inventory cycle

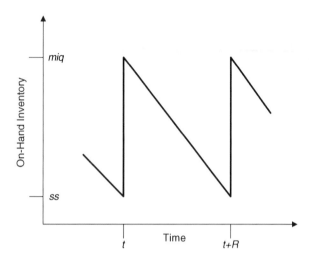

performance. So the only location where inventory is relevant in the planning model is at the transformation facilities. The equations presented next describe the operations of a warehouse that functions as a distribution center in the supply chain for products with a repetitive demand. It is assumed that the warehouse operates under periodic review policy and every R days places an order for a product.

The schematic in Fig. 13.3 shows an idealized inventory cycle for a single product. The warehouse placed an order and after the lead-time the order is received at time t. At that time the on-hand inventory level is at its maximum level and equal to miq. Both the facility site and facility type index and the product index are suppressed here for notational simplicity, but remain present in the model. The cycle repeats, a new order is placed R time after the previous order is placed and the next order will be received at time $t+R$. The safety stock level ss is the amount of inventory on hand just before the replenishment occurs.

On average the maximum on-hand inventory is given by the following expression.

$$miq = ss + DemandRate \cdot R \qquad (13.26)$$

In the chapter on inventory systems the expression for the safety inventory in function of the lead time and the product demand process were developed. However, during the strategic planning problem the demand for a product in a facility is a decision variable. Furthermore, the order interval is assumed to be the same as the shipping interval of the transportation channel from that source facility supplying the warehouse and this interval depends on the supply transportation channel selected, which is also a decision variable.

$$DemandRate_{jlp} = \sum_{k \in D \cup C} \sum_{m=M(j,k)} x_{jkmp} \qquad (13.27)$$

It is assumed that the supply chain is operating in steady state, so the quantity of product leaving the warehouse during the planning period must be equal to the quantity arriving at the warehouse. If necessary, seasonal and strategic inventory can be considered and this would lead to more complex conservation of flow constraints. In this development the simple conservation of flow, which requires that inflow equals outflow, will be used. The cycle inventory is equal to the demand of product during a replenishment cycle.

$$\sum_{i \in B \cup D} \sum_{m \in M(i,j)} x_{ijmp} = \sum_{k \in D \cup C} \sum_{m=M(j,k)} x_{jkmp} \tag{13.28}$$

$$Cycle\_Inventory_{jp} = \sum_{i \in B \cup D} \sum_{m \in M(i,j)} R_{ijm} \, x_{ijmp} \tag{13.29}$$

The safety inventory required to provide the service level is approximated by a linear safety inventory level that is proportional to the throughput. This corresponds to a common practice that the safety inventory is proportional to the demand rate, e.g., the safety inventory is 3 weeks of demand in a distribution center. This approximation always overestimates the true required safety inventory and thus will yield a better actual service level than the required service level and is thus a conservative estimate. This approximation ignores the pooling effect created by the summation of the demands of facilities and customers supplied from the warehouse. It is a property in statistics that the standard deviation of a sum of independent random variables is less than the sum of the standard deviations of the individual random variables. Many times the theoretical equations for the calculation of safety inventory assume independent demand behavior of the customers but this assumption is often violated in practice. For example, if high temperatures increase the demand for soft drinks at one store, then the demands at all the stores in the same area will also be likely to be higher. The following equation for the safety stock can be interpreted as assuming that the customer demands are 100% correlated. The value of the safety factor depends on the required service level through the choice of k and on the replenishment interval and is computed as shown below and in the chapter on inventory systems and is used as parameter in the strategic planning model. The coefficient of variation (CV) of the demand rate for product p in facility j has to be estimated based on historical data.

$$ss_{jlp} = \sum_{i \in B \cup D} \sum_{m \in M(i,j)} SSFactor_{ijmp} \, x_{ijmp} \tag{13.30}$$

$$SSFactor_{ijmp} = k \cdot \sqrt{lt_{ijm} \cdot CV^2_{DemandRate} + Var_{lt_{ijm}}} \tag{13.31}$$

The following expression for the average inventory in the warehouse models incorporates the four most important factors: (1) the average demand, (2) the impact of the cycle interval of the replenishment process and transportation channel used for the replenishment process, and (3) the impact of the lead time and (4) the required service level on the safety inventory. This equation is a conservative, linear approximation of the true average inventory required in the facility to ensure the desired service level.

$$Average\_Inventory_{ijmp} = \sum_{i \in B \cup D} \sum_{m \in M(i,j)} \left(SSFactor_{ijmp} + \frac{R_{ijm}}{2} \right) x_{ijmp} \qquad (13.32)$$

Thus, the warehouse inventory cost for warehouse j is given by the following expression.

$$\sum_{p \in P} \sum_{i \in B \cup D} \sum_{m \in M(i,j)} r \cdot Value_{jp} \left(SSFactor_{ijmp} + \frac{R_{ijm}}{2} \right) x_{ijmp} \qquad (13.33)$$

Finally, the total required storage capacity of the warehouse is less than the sum of the maximum inventory levels of each of the product in the warehouse, since usually not all products are replenished at the same time. The required storage capacity depends on the interactions of the demand and replenishment processes of all the products flowing through this warehouse. This aggregate maximum inventory is difficult to compute with a closed form expression. If the warehouse has different storage sections, such as for frozen, refrigerated, and room temperature products, then this maximum inventory has to be estimated for each section. In the strategic planning model, the aggregate maximum inventory is assumed to be a fraction of the sum the maximum inventories of each product. The value of the fraction depends on the number of products in the warehouse and on how coordinated the replenishment processes for the different products are. This value is often estimated to be between 0.8 and 0.9. A value of 1.0 corresponds to the worst possible case in which all product orders are replenished simultaneously and the warehouse has to be large enough to hold this peak inventory. The required warehouse storage capacity is modeled by the following constraint, where β is the fraction of the aggregate inventory divided by the maximum inventory of all products.

$$\beta \left(\sum_{p \in P} Vol_p \cdot \left(\sum_{i \in B \cup D} \sum_{m \in M(i,j)} r \cdot Value_p \left(SSFactor_{ijmp} + \frac{R_{ijm}}{2} \right) x_{ijmp} \right) \right)$$
$$\leq WhseStorCap_{jl} \cdot y_{jl} \qquad (13.34)$$

It is clear from the above development that computing the required inventory in a distribution center for products distributed from this facility and computing the required warehouse storage capacity depends on variety of factors that most likely are not known during the strategic planning process. The expressions have been simplified to make them linear and contain safety factors that can only be determined with simulation for a particular instance. During the design phase these factors have to be estimated based on professional engineering practice. Using approximate formulas with significant safety factors that are very risk averse is a standard practice in many engineering design disciplines.

13.2.5 Modeling Customer Service

13.2.5.1 Single Sourcing

Customers are the ultimate destination facilities for all the material flow in the supply chain. Customer facilities are assumed to be always established and customer facilities cannot hold inventory or transform products. Specific customer service requirements often dramatically change the overall configuration of a supply chain. Customers may require that all the goods delivered to them arrive from a single facility because this reduces the number of vehicles coming to their receiving dock. This service constraint is called single sourcing.

Notation. The following notation will be used.

Sets

C set of all customers

Parameters

$Distance_{jkm}$ distance from facility j to customer k using transportation mode m
$MaxDistance_k$ maximum distance to customer k from the facility that services it
$MaxTime_k$ maximum transit time to customer k from the facility that services it

Decision Variables

q_{ik} 1 if customer k is serviced from facility i, zero otherwise

Model. The most common service constraint for a customer is that its demand gets satisfied or delivered by the supply chain. The first equation below models the simple demand satisfaction constraint.

$$\sum_{j \in B \cup D} \sum_{m \in M(j,k)} x_{jkmp} = Demand_{kp} \tag{13.35}$$

The next two equations model the case when there is a single sourcing requirement for that customer. It requires the use of a binary assignment variable that assigns the service of customer k to facility j.

$$\sum_{m \in M(j,k)} x_{jkmp} = q_{jk} Demand_{kp} \tag{13.36}$$

$$\sum_{j \in B \cup D} q_{jk} = 1 \tag{13.37}$$

The following linkage constraints ensure that a customer is only serviced from a facility, be it a supplier facility or a transformation facility, respectively, if that facility is established.

$$q_{ik} \leq s_i \tag{13.38}$$

$$q_{jk} \leq \sum_{l \in L(j)} y_{jl} \tag{13.39}$$

The next constraint requires that transportation channels from a source facility to a customer are available only if that customer is serviced from or assigned to that source facility. The constraint links the usage of a channel to the existence of a customer service relationship.

$$z_{jkm} \leq q_{jk} \tag{13.40}$$

The next two constraints ensure that a customer is within a specified maximum travel distance and maximum travel time from the facility that services it.

$$Distance_{jkm} z_{jkm} \leq MaxDistance_k \tag{13.41}$$

$$TransitTime_{jkm} z_{jkm} \leq MaxTime_k \tag{13.42}$$

13.2.5.2 Single Sourcing by Order

For highly engineered products the supply chain is not only responsible for the production of the product, but also for the sustainment during the total product life cycle. Consider the case of a manufacturing corporation that sells highly engineered products to industrial customers in a make-to-order system. A typical sale to a customer consists of a batch of units, e.g., between 12 and 60 units. Many configurations and customizations for a final product may exist, but all the finished product units in a single order are identical. The products have a multi-level bill of materials with hundreds to thousands of parts. One of the additional customer service requirements is "single sourcing by order," or SISBO. In order to reduce maintenance burdens during the life time of the product, SISBO requires that all the equivalent parts in the units of one order come from a single supplier. For example, assume that a final product contains four electric actuators. If the order consists of 50 units, then the 200 actuators in the units of that order all have to come from the same supplier. Modeling this service constraint requires the definition of one additional product for every part in every order that has the SISBO requirement.

Notation. The number of products is expanded for the previous notation and the following additional notation is used.

pq_{iq} amount purchased from supplier i of product q

BOM_{qp} the number of component products q included in one finished goods product p. Note that this quantity is more general than $1BOM_{lqp}$ previously defined since BOM_{qp} is defined for all components of product p, not just components used in the immediate assembly of product p.

u_{iq} 1 if product q is procured from supplier i, zero otherwise, where q belongs to the products and parts included in the BOM of a SISBO order

The following two constraints ensure that only one supplier is used for every part in a SISBO order.

$$pq_{iq} \leq BOM_{qp} \cdot u_{iq} \tag{13.43}$$

$$\sum_{i \in S} u_{iq} = 1 \tag{13.44}$$

While the structure of these two constraints is relatively simple, the presence of SISBO orders significantly increases the data and computational burdens, because now all the parts included in all the SISBO orders have to tracked and modeled separately. This also implies that physically the parts and work in process inventory in the supply chain are dedicated to a specific final order. This typically is implemented through a barcode or RFID tag. If the SISBO requirement only applies to the immediate components of product p, i.e., the level-one components just below the finished product in a hierarchical BOM or work breakdown structure (WBS), then this service constraint is relatively easy to implement. In this case BOM_{qp} holds the same data as $IBOM_{qp}$, except that $IBOM_{jlqp}$ depends on the transformation facility site and type where the assembly or production occurs. Usually for complex final products and level-one components the number of components does not depend on the assembly site.

13.2.6   Computational Characteristics in Case Studies

A comprehensive model that includes the appropriate modeling components described above has been applied in a variety of industrial case studies. Typically the number of variables is in the order of tens of thousands and less than 100,000. The number of binary variables is in the order of tens or hundreds and less than 500. The number of constraints is again in the order of tens of thousands and less than 100,000. The models can be solved to optimality with an optimality gap of 0.01% in a few minutes and always in less than 30 min on contemporary workstations or desktop computers. Either the CPLEX solver by ILOG or the open source solver GLPSOL have been used. A large fraction of the total time required to obtain a solution is spent extracting the data from the instance database and storing the optimal values of the decision variables back into the database. If the database has a standardized structure then reports and graphs can be generated without customized programming for every individual case.

13.3   Strategic Global Supply Chain Design

Most supply chains have infrastructure components that are located in different countries. The presence of different political or taxation authorities that govern elements of a supply chain make the planning and design of the supply chain significantly more difficult. The infrastructure components may even be located in the same country but because of taxation regulations still needed to be treated in a different manner. For example, a facility in a particular site may enjoy special treatment of its income for the first 5 years of its existence because of favorable conditions negotiated with the local government. In most cases the government forgoes initial taxation or invests in general infrastructure such as roads and sewer in order to gain long-term taxation and job creation benefits.

13.3.1   Local Content Requirements

Especially for products that are paid for by public funds, there is often a requirement that a certain fraction of the value of the product is created in the country of the purchaser. This value may be created through purchasing of components or through transformation of products. Such requirements are denoted as "local content requirements." The difficulty of including local content requirements in a supply chain planning or design model depends on the level of accuracy that is required. If the value of the delivered product is based on the sales price and if the local content of the components of the product is known, i.e., given as parameters, then a simple equation can be added to the models.

13.3.1.1   Notation

The following notation will be used. It is assumed that the parameters remain constant during the different time periods in the planning horizon. If this assumption is not valid, the model can be extended in a straightforward manner.

Sets

$IBOM_p$	set of all the immediate component products included in the final product p
$c(k)$	country c in which customer k is located

Parameters

$SalesPrice_{pk}$	sales price for one unit of product p to customer k
$Localvalue_{qc}$	fraction of the value of one unit of product q created in a country c
γ	required local content fraction

The next five equations have already been described as part of the tactical model in the previous chapter and express the relationship between the product flows and the component flows in a supply chain when the final product has a bill of materials.

$$itq_{jpt} + aq_{jpt} + init\_inv_{jp} - iq_{jpt} - cq_{jpt} - otq_{jpt} = 0 \quad \forall j, \forall p, t = 1 \tag{13.45}$$

$$itq_{jpt} + aq_{jpt} + iq_{jpt-1} - iq_{jpt} - cq_{jpt} - otq_{jpt} = 0 \quad \forall j, \forall p, t = 2..T \tag{13.46}$$

$$\sum_{k} x_{jkpt} = otq_{jpt} \quad \forall j, \forall p, \forall t \tag{13.47}$$

$$cq_{jpt} = \sum_{v} 1bom_{jpvt} \cdot aq_{jvt} \quad \forall p \in 1BOM_v, \forall j, \forall t \tag{13.48}$$

$$\sum_{j} x_{jkpt} = dq_{kpt} \quad \forall k, \forall p, \forall t \tag{13.49}$$

The following equation ensures that the local content summed over the immediate components of the final product is larger than the minimum required fraction. Note that the product $LocalValue_{qc} \cdot Value_{jq}$ remains a parameter and can be computed in advance for all required combinations of the subscripts.

$$\sum_{j} \sum_{t} \sum_{q \in BOM_p} (LocalValue_{qc} \cdot Value_{jq}) \cdot cq_{jqt}$$
$$\geq (\gamma \cdot SalesPrice_{pk}) \cdot dq_{kpt} \quad \forall c(k) \tag{13.50}$$

However, modeling the local content requirement becomes significantly more difficult if the value of a component or local content fraction is no longer a given parameter but is a decision variable whose value is determined by the supply chain optimization. In the section on the distribution channel selection problem, the value of the product was determined by the model by systematically adding all incurred costs along the supply chain steps for that product. The local content fraction of a component may depend on the source for that component which is determined by the supply chain planning. If either of both cases occurred the dependency would make the previous equation quadratic since it multiplies the product quantity by its value or the product quantity by the local content fraction to compute the monetary equivalent flow. If both dependencies occur the equation would have the product of three variables. In either case, standard mixed-integer linear programming solvers can no longer be used. The same quadratic modeling and algorithm complications occur when the model has to determine the transfer prices of the products in a supply chain. A transfer price is the internal sales price for a product between two subsidiaries of the same corporation. Designing and planning a supply chain if transfer prices have to be determined is further developed in the next section.

13.3.2 Transfer Pricing

Because the transfer price is an internal sales price controlled by the corporation that wholly owns the selling and the buying subsidiaries, the corporation has certain latitude in setting its value. This is especially the case for highly engineered, specialized, and customized products for which no public market and market prices exist. The value of the transfer price will influence the allocation of the total profit of the supply chain between the different subsidiaries of the corporation. If the selling and the buying subsidiaries are located in countries with different tax rates then the transfer price impacts the overall after-tax profit of the corporation and the taxes paid in both countries. This is of concern to the taxation authorities in the countries on both sides of the sales transaction since they want to avoid that the corporation manipulates the transfer price in order to minimize taxable profits in their respective jurisdictions. As a consequence transfer prices have been heavily regulated and transfer prices are a major component of tax compliance for an international corporation.

13.3.2.1 Introductory Example

Consider the following extremely simplified example of a global supply chain that spans two countries and consists of a single company with a subsidiary in each of the countries. The first manufacturing step occurs in country A and the final manufacturing and sales occur in country B. The relevant data for both countries are shown in Table 13.1.

Based on taxation regulations and accounting data, the allowable range for the transfer price has been set to the interval from $60 to $80. Three obvious rules for determining the transfer price exist: lower bound, upper bound, and midpoint of the transfer price interval. A fourth rule is called the *tax rate heuristic*. It sets the transfer price to the lower bound if the tax rate in the destination country is lower than in the origin country, otherwise the transfer price is set to the upper bound. Formally, the tax rate heuristics is given below, where tr is the constant marginal tax rate for a country and tp is the transfer price between two countries. In this example the tax rate is lower in the destination country and higher in the origin country, so the goal is to realize the least amount of profit in the origin country and thus the transfer price is set to the lower bound.

Algorithm 13.1. Transfer Price Tax Rate Heuristic

$$\begin{aligned} if \quad tr_{dest} < tr_{orig} \quad & then \quad tp = LB \\ & else \quad tp = UB \end{aligned} \qquad (13.51)$$

Table 13.1 Transfer price illustration data

Category	Country A	Country B
Sales price		$100
Tax rate	35%	15%
Production cost	$50	$10

Fig. 13.4 Tax rate step function

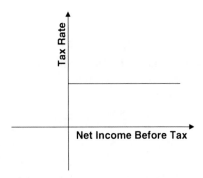

Figure 13.4 illustrates the corporate tax rate function considered for all countries. No tax credit for losses is included in the initial analysis. When the corporate tax rate function is more complex, i.e.: when it has more "steps" and breakpoint values, additional analysis is necessary. However, for large companies the function considered here is realistic and valid in most countries.

The *net income after tax* (NIAT) is computed with the following sequence of calculations and based on the *net income before taxes* (NIBT):

$$NIBT = Revenues - Costs \tag{13.52}$$

$$Taxes = NIBT \cdot TaxRate \tag{13.53}$$

$$NIAT = NIBT - Taxes = (Revenue - Cost) \cdot (1 - TaxRate) \tag{13.54}$$

The calculations for the total NIAT for corporation for the four transfer price heuristics are shown in Table 13.2.

The NIAT for the corporation in this example ranges from 28 to 32, which represents a gap of approximately 14%. The corporation could theoretically increase its profit margin by 14% by just changing an internal accounting value without making any change to its supply chain configuration or operation. It is exactly because of this ease of change that transfer prices are so heavily regulated. It should also be noted that the NIAT in the different countries, i.e., for the different subsidiaries, changes dramatically depending on the value of the transfer price. In this example,

Table 13.2 NIAT calculations for various transfer price heuristics

	Lower bnd.	Upper bnd.	Midpoint	Tax rate
Transfer Price	60	80	70	60
NIBT(A)	10	30	20	10
Taxes (A)	3.5	10.5	7	3.5
NIAT (A)	6.5	19.5	13	6.5
NIBT (B)	30	10	20	30
Taxes (B)	4.5	1.5	3	4.5
NIAT (B)	25.5	8.5	17	25.5
NIAT (total)	32	28	30	32

the NIAT in both countries changes by a ratio of 300% depending on the transfer price. The corporate reward structures may have to be adjusted to reflect this.

In the above example the total sales amount was held constant and both subsidiaries made a profit for all values in the allowable range of the transfer price. If the fixed costs for facilities are included in the total supply chain costs and if subsidiaries are allowed to realize a loss, then the overall corporate profit will depend on the amount of product sold between the subsidiaries, on the transfer price for the internal sale, and on the interaction of the amount sold and the transfer price. Note that if a subsidiary makes a loss before taxes during a tax year then its taxes will be zero for that year, but it is assumed that no tax credit will accrue. To derive the general function of the global NIAT in this example, four disjoint regions for the NIBT have to be considered: (1) both subsidiaries make a profit, (2) only the selling subsidiary makes a loss, (3) only the buying subsidiary makes a loss, and (4) both subsidiaries make a loss. Figure 13.5 illustrates the possible values of the global NIAT versus the transfer price t for different values of the material flow x for an example that allows losses and when the sales quantities are changed as part of parametric design. Obviously, for the NIAT to be bounded, there must exist an upper bound on the flow x from selling to purchasing subsidiaries. This bound may be determined by a limited capacity of one or the two subsidiaries, by a limited demand, and/or by other flow constraints imposed on the system. Notice that the optimal solution to the problem depends on both the possible flows in the supply chain and the bounds of the transfer price. The optimal transfer price may be equal to its lower bound, its upper bound, or may fall strictly between the two.

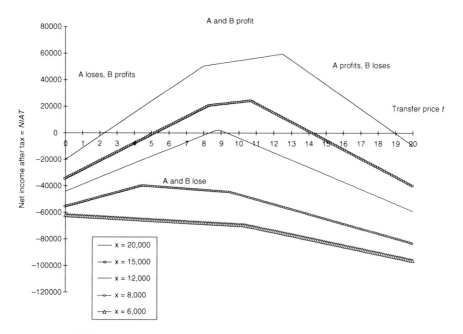

Fig. 13.5 NIAT for the two-country supply chain example

The model to determine the optimal value of the transfer prices is developed next. The focus will be on the differences between this model and the strategic model described above. Since the taxation authorities in general disallow the use of different transfer prices for the same product to different destinations but allow different transportation costs, the transportation costs must be modeled separately for every combination of origin, destination, and commodity. The allocation proportion p models what fraction of the total transportation cost each subsidiary will pay for.

The NIAT is modeled traditionally by substituting two nonnegative variables, representing the profit and loss of subsidiary. The NIBT of that subsidiary is modeled by a free variable, i.e., a variable that can be either negative, zero, or positive. In the resulting model, for every flow the product of the transfer price multiplied by the material flow quantity, denoted by tx, appears in the two equations that determine the NIBT of the origin and destination country. The detailed expression for the net income before tax of distribution centers located in countries where duties are charged on the FOB value and the full model for the determination of transfer prices and transportation cost allocation can be found in Vidal and Goetschalckx (2001).

This model will be denoted as $P(x, t, p)$. $P(x, t, p)$ is a nonconvex optimization problem with a linear objective function, a set of linear constraints, and a set of bilinear equality constraints created by the products of flow quantities and transfer prices and product flows and transportation cost fractions. All computational results reported in the research literature on global and bilinear optimization for this problem correspond to relatively small instances of this problem. However, applying $P(x, t, p)$ to global supply chains yield usually medium to large-scale problem instances for which none of the global optimization approaches reported in the literature appear to work satisfactorily. For this reason, and given the structure of the problem, an optimization-based heuristic procedure using successive linear programming solutions has been developed. An optimization algorithm with a prescribed maximum optimality gap and a metaheurstic have also been developed for this problem. The numerical experiment given after the description of the heuristic indicates that the solution quality generated by the successive linear programming heuristic algorithm is sufficient in practical applications.

The proportion of the transportation cost charged to either subsidiary can be set by the corporation based on the destination and on the used transportation mode.

13.3.2.2 Notation

The following notation will be used.

$transpc_{jkmp}$ transportation cost rate for product p from facility j to facility k by transportation mode m

$transprop_{jkmp}$ fraction of the total transportation cost for transporting product p from facility j to facility k by transportation mode m charged to the origin facility j

$OrigTransCost_{jkmp}$, $DestTransCost_{jkmp}$ total transportation cost for transporting product p from facility j to facility k by transportation mode m charged to the origin facility j or the destination facility k, respectively

13.3.2.3 Model

Consequently, the bilinear terms in x and p can be linearized by using the following substitution. The allocated transportation costs will be subtracted from the *NIBT* for the origin and destination facilities. The resulting problem will be denoted as $P(x, t, TC)$.

$$OrigTransCost_{jkmp} = transprop_{jkmp} \cdot transpc_{jkmp} \cdot x_{jkmp}$$
$$DestTransCost_{jkmp} = \left(1 - transprop_{jkmp}\right) \cdot transpc_{jkmp} \cdot x_{jkmp}$$

We can use the same approach to linearize the bilinear terms in x and t, provided a set of constraints is added that make the transfer prices t from one origin j to all destinations h the same. This can be thought of as the transfer price being determined based on production costs, and therefore there is no reason to allow it to be different for different buyers.

$$TransferSalesPrice_{jkmp} = t_{jkmp} \cdot x_{jkmp}$$

$$\frac{TransferSalesPrice_{jkmp}}{x_{jkmp}} = \frac{TransferSalesPrice_{jhmp}}{x_{jhmp}} \qquad \forall h$$

This substitution eliminates all remaining bilinear constraints from the model. Note that the *TransferSalesPrice* is added to the NIBT for the origin country and subtracted from the NIBT for the destination country. The new model is denoted as $P(x, TRP, TC)$ and includes all the ratio equality constraints introduced above. When those ratio constraints are relaxed the model is denoted as $P_R(x, TRP, TC)$ and it is a linear programming formulation. Its optimal solution also provides an upper bound on the objective of the original $P(x, TRP, TC)$ and is used to determine the maximum optimality gap in the numerical experiment described below.

    If the flow variables x are fixed in problem $P(x, t, TC)$ then this problem becomes linear in t and vice versa. These problem will be donated by $P(x, t, TC | x)$ and $P(x, t, TC | t)$, respectively. The successive linear programming solution heuristic iteratively fixes one set of variables and solves the remaining linear program for the other set. This is similar to the cyclical coordinates search procedure but applied to two classes of variables rather than to two individual variables. The process is terminated when the change in the objective function value becomes negligible. The difficulty in solving the original problem $P(x, t, TC)$ to optimality is its multiextremaltiy characteristics, i.e., it has multiple local optimal. Consequently, the local solution obtained by the heuristic is highly dependent on the starting point. The performance of different algorithms to determine the starting point was examined in the following numerical experiment.

The first starting point is generated by the solution of problem $P_R(x, TRP, TC)$ and taking the optimal set of flows x. A second starting point is generated by taking the solution of problem $P_R(x, TRP, TC)$ and taking the optimal set of transfer prices t. If one of these transfer price values is not feasible then nearest boundary value of the feasible interval for that transfer prices is selected. If there is no flow from some origins, then value of the transfer price is not meaningful in the solution and the transfer prices is set to its lower bound to start the process. In addition, four procedures based on the lower and upper bound of the feasible transfer price intervals were also examined. All transfer prices were set either to their lower bound (LB) or to their upper bound (UB), to the middle of the interval, that is, equal to (LB + UB)/2, or to the value determined by the tax heuristic.

The successive linear programming heuristics was implemented using AMPL and solved with CPLEX. Two problem instances of different sizes were tested. All instances were carefully generated to approximate the costs and constraints of real-world instances as much as possible. Further details can be found in Vidal and Goetschalckx (2001).

The computational experiments with various starting point procedures yielded optimality gaps of less than 2.2%. For most of the instances, the best solutions were obtained when the starting points are either the optimal flows or the optimal transfer prices from the relaxed problem. The iterative procedure tends to quickly converge to a high-quality solution and then improvements level off. The user can limit the allowed computation time as an alternative stopping criteria. It should be observed that the user has no control over the achieved optimality gap. If the optimality gap of a solution is unacceptable, the only thing the user can do is to try one or more different starting points. Only the global optimization procedure developed by Vidal (1998) can guarantee that the prescribed optimality gap is satisfied.

To measure the impact of the simultaneous determination of the transfer prices and the material flows in the international logistics systems, its results were compared with procedures that set the transfer prices first based on the bounds of their feasible intervals and then determine the optimal product flows. The savings gener-

Table 13.3 NIAT performance of the integrated versus the sequential transfer price procedures for the medium instances

Transfer Price heuristics				
Medium instance	Middle point	Tax rate	Lower bound	Upper bound
1	2.4	0.2	0.8	4.1
2	23.2	12.1	17.1	29.2
3	22.6	30.2	39.9	16.2
4	45.6	65.0	95.2	32.1
5	2.3	0.2	0.7	3.9

Increase in NIAT profit by the integrated procedure expressed in percent

ated by the integrated procedure as compared with the four sequential procedures are given in Table 13.3 For the six instances of the medium problem instance, the average profit increase was 17.3% and ranged from as small as 0.18% – 95.2%. There was not an a priori characteristic that predicted the savings for a particular instance. Clearly, significant savings could be achieved, depending on the individual logistics systems data, by using the integrated procedure as compared to state-of-the-art sequential procedures.

The above instances in the numerical experiment assumed that the locations and status of facilities were known. However, corporations may be interested in determining the optimal configuration of international supply chains to test the economic feasibility of new configurations and new products simultaneously with the determination of their transfer prices. The successive linear programming heuristic can be extended so that the $P(x, t, TC \,|t\,)$ problem not only determines the product flows but also the status of the facilities. In this case the heuristic solves a sequence of MIP formulations.

13.4   Strategic Robust Supply Chain Design Incorporating Uncertainty

13.4.1   Modeling Techniques with Explicit Consideration of Uncertainty

In this section several models for the strategic design of supply chains are presented that incorporate the uncertainty regarding future conditions and parameters explicitly. In the deterministic case, two major classes of objectives can be distinguished. The first class focuses on cost minimization and typically has constraints that ensure the satisfaction of the demand of all customers. The second class focuses on profit maximization and the available demand of the customers becomes an upper bound or capacity constraint on the sales to the customers. In the second class not all customer demands have to be satisfied. The same two major classes of objectives exist for the stochastic strategic supply chain design models that incorporate uncertainty. However, for each of the classes several variants of formulations and objective functions exist depending on how the uncertainty is modeled and evaluated.

Several optimization techniques are used for the design of systems when explicitly considering the stochastic nature of the data. Six commonly used techniques are briefly reviewed and some of their advantages and disadvantages are highlighted.

1. **Deterministic mean value formulation**. One of the most popular methods in stochastic optimization is the expected or mean value method. This method starts by finding the expected value of each stochastic cost coefficient, capacity, and demand parameter based on its individual probability distribution function. Then, a deterministic model is created to solve the optimization problem with the expected values of the parameters. This model is called the *mean value problem* (MVP). The stochastic characteristics are investigated through sensitivity analy-

sis. This method is widely used, especially to find a first-cut solution. However, as indicated before, the MVP solution is believed to be very fragile or nonrobust with respect to changes in the values of the parameters.

2. In **scenario-based optimization** a limited number of deterministic scenarios or sample sets are constructed to represent the range and combinations of values of the parameters and coefficients consistent with their probability distributions. A single robust solution is found for the deterministic equivalent problem (DEP), which includes all scenarios simultaneously weighted by their respective scenario probabilities. This method has several shortcomings. First, it is very difficult to construct a limited number of deterministic scenarios that represent all the combinations and full range of the stochastic values of the parameters. Especially, when the stochastic parameters have continuous probability distributions the number of scenarios becomes infinite. Second, it is common practice to scale all similar parameters up or down by a fixed ratio, e.g., determine a supply chain configuration for the expected demand, the optimistic case, and the pessimistic case. Scenarios in which the parameter values are 100% correlated may be unrealistic and do not allow an accurate assesment of the risks associated with a particular configuration. Finally, it is very difficult to determine accurately the probabilities of the constructed scenarios.

3. **Sampling-average approximation (SAA) scenario optimization.** A third method for stochastic optimization is based on random sampling, and the details of this method for the design of robust supply chains are described in the next section. This method has the advantage that only the probability distributions of the individual parameters need to be estimated. The scenarios are then created by random sampling from the parameter distributions and are assumed to be equally likely. A large number of scenarios are required and created to approximate the underlying stochastic process. Because of the random sampling, this method cannot incorporate the occurrence of catastrophic events that have a very low probability, such as earthquakes, flooding, and fires, but that may be very important in the overall design of the supply chain. Scenarios incorporating such rare events have to be created separately.

4. **Robustness optimization.** This method determines a single robust solution or supply chain configuration, whose performance is the best with respect to all possible scenarios. This method requires that an optimal robust configuration and the optimal configurations for each scenario be found. Another disadvantage is that the robustness constraint considers all scenarios to be equally important. So, a single very pessimistic but very unlikely scenario may determine the supply chain configuration. This procedure is considered to be excessively conservative.

5. A fifth method is **change-constrained optimization**, but to our knowledge this method has been applied only occasionally—e.g. to model supplier reliability; see Vidal and Goetschalckx (2000)—in the strategic design of supply chain systems.

6. Finally, stochastic systems are often designed using **digital simulation of a limited number of parameterized configurations**. However, since simulation is a descriptive and not a normative method the optimality or optimality gap of the obtained solution is unknown.

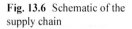

Fig. 13.6 Schematic of the supply chain

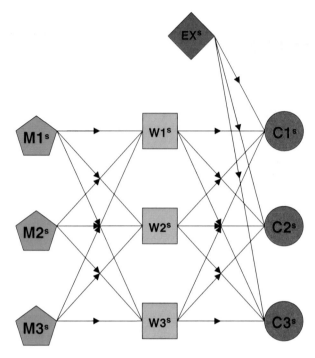

13.4.2 Supply Chain Scenario Example

The various formulations and objective functions and their corresponding supply chain configurations will be illustrated based on the following small example.

The goal is to design the supply chain configuration for the Packaging Printing Corporation (PPC), which operates in the continental United States. PPC sells two major products. The supply chain for these products consists of two stages: a manufacturing and a distribution stage. There are three candidate manufacturing facilities and three candidate warehousing facilities. In addition, the finished products can also be acquired from an external source. There are three customers. Each customer has demand for the two products. The demands are not known with certainty at the current time. This uncertainty is modeled by using three possible scenarios, each with an associated probability of occurring. Scenarios are indicated by the superscript in the following schematic of the supply chain structure.

Most of the parameters are stochastic, i.e., they differ between scenarios, but the fixed cost of the facilities is assumed deterministic because it is based on decisions made before the scenarios are realized. The resource consumption rates are the same in the different scenarios. The manufacturing facilities have a joint-commodity production capacity and the warehousing facilities have a joint-commodity material handling capacity. Production and handling of the products requires resources and incurs a cost. Transportation of the products between the various facilities and to the customers also incurs a cost but the transportation

Table 13.4 Scenario probabilities

Probability	
S1	0.55
S2	0.4
S3	0.05

Table 13.5 Customer demands

Demand		C1	C2	C3
S1	P1	50000	100000	75000
S1	P2	20000	30000	60000
S2	P1	120000	18000	150000
S2	P2	10000	9300	0
S3	P1	5000	10000	7500
S3	P2	120000	120000	120000

Table 13.6 Sales revenues

Unit revenue		C1	C2	C3
S1	P1	40	40	48
S1	P2	36	52	52
S2	P1	50	50	58
S2	P2	46	62	62
S3	P1	40	40	48
S3	P2	36	52	52

Table 13.7 External supply cost rates

Outsource cost		P1	P2
S1	C1	41	61
S1	C2	42	59
S1	C3	40	60
S2	C1	49	64
S2	C2	47	62
S2	C3	50	65
S3	C1	41	61
S3	C2	42	59
S3	C3	40	60

channels are assumed to be uncapacitated. The relevant cost and capacity data are summarized in Tables 13.4–13.16.

The following four formulations can be solved for the strategic supply chain design: (1) the mean value problem, indicated by *mvp*, where the expected value or best guess of each stochastic parameter is used; (2) the expected value problem over all scenarios, indicated by *exp*; (3) the robust problem, indicated by *rob*, where first the configuration is determined that maximizes the minimum profit for all the scenarios and then each scenario is optimized for this configuration; and finally, (4) the weighted sum of the optimal solutions for each independent scenario, indicated by *ind*. This last formulation yields an upper bound on the profit maximization since in essence it assumes that the decision maker knows what will happen in the future before the configuration decision has to be made, even though the future is still sto-

Table 13.8 Manufacturing–warehouse transportation cost rates

Transportation cost			W1	W2	W3
S1	P1	M1	1	5	7
S1	P1	M2	4	2	6
S1	P1	M3	8	6	1
S1	P2	M1	2	4	6
S1	P2	M2	5	3	6
S1	P2	M3	7	5	2
S2	P1	M1	3	7	9
S2	P1	M2	6	4	8
S2	P1	M3	10	8	3
S2	P2	M1	1	3	5
S2	P2	M2	4	2	5
S2	P2	M3	5	4	1
S3	P1	M1	1	5	7
S3	P1	M2	4	2	6
S3	P1	M3	8	6	1
S3	P2	M1	2	4	6
S3	P2	M2	5	3	6
S3	P2	M3	7	5	2

Table 13.9 Warehouse–customer transportation cost rates

Transportation cost			C1	C2	C3
S1	P1	W1	4	3	5
S1	P1	W2	2	1	2
S1	P1	W3	5	4	3
S1	P2	W1	3	2	4
S1	P2	W2	4	3	4
S1	P2	W3	6	5	4
S2	P1	W1	8	6	9
S2	P1	W2	4	3	5
S2	P1	W3	8	7	6
S2	P2	W1	2	1	3
S2	P2	W2	4	3	2
S2	P2	W3	5	4	3
S3	P1	W1	4	3	5
S3	P1	W2	2	1	2
S3	P1	W3	5	4	3
S3	P2	W1	3	2	4
S3	P2	W2	4	3	4
S3	P2	W3	6	5	4

chastic as expressed by the different scenarios and their probabilities. In stochastic programming terminology this formulation is a relaxation of the original problem and the corresponding solution may violate the nonanticipativity constraints. The *exp* formulation is used in stochastic linear programming and for strategic supply chain design the deterministic equivalent problem (DEP) is solved. For the first three formulations, the variance and standard deviation of the objective function values with respect to the three scenarios can be computed. Clearly, the variance

Table 13.10 Production costs

Production cost		P1	P2
S1	M1	6	3
S1	M2	4	2
S1	M3	5	4
S2	M1	9	8
S2	M2	7	4
S2	M3	12	9
S3	M1	6	3
S3	M2	4	2
S3	M3	5	4

Table 13.11 Production capacities

MaxCapacity			
	M1	M2	M3
S1	300000	400000	180000
S2	400000	600000	450000
S3	300000	400000	180000

Table 13.12 Production resource rates

ResourceRate		P1	P2
S1	M1	2	3
S1	M2	1	2
S1	M3	2	4
S2	M1	2	3
S2	M2	1	2
S2	M3	2	4
S3	M1	2	3
S3	M2	1	2
S3	M3	2	4

Table 13.13 Warehousing costs

Handling cost		P1	P2
S1	W1	2	3
S1	W2	1	2
S1	W3	4	3
S2	W1	5	7
S2	W2	3	4
S2	W3	6	5
S3	W1	2	3
S3	W2	1	2
S3	W3	4	3

Table 13.14 Warehousing capacities

Handling cost		P1	P2
S1	W1	2	3
S1	W2	1	2
S1	W3	4	3
S2	W1	5	7
S2	W2	3	4
S2	W3	6	5
S3	W1	2	3
S3	W2	1	2
S3	W3	4	3

Table 13.15 Warehousing resource rates

ResourceRate		P1	P2
S1	W1	2	3
S1	W2	1	2
S1	W3	1	3
S2	W1	2	3
S2	W2	1	2
S2	W3	1	3
S3	W1	2	3
S3	W2	1	2
S3	W3	1	3

Table 13.16 Facilities fixed costs

Fixed cost	
M1	650000
M2	950000
M3	550000
W1	250000
W2	400000
W3	200000

calculation is highly degenerate since only three scenarios exist that make up the complete scenario population. In real-world supply chain design projects there will typically exist many hundreds or even thousands of scenarios.

13.4.2.1 Notation

The following notation will be used for these formulations:

s	cenario index, $s = 1, ..., S$, $S = 3$ in the example
p_s	probability of scenario s
y	binary configuration decision variable, in the example there are six configuration variables
y_s	optimal binary configuration variables for the independent scenario s
x	continuous flow decision variables

$z_{exp}, z_{mvp}, z_{rob}, z_{ind}$ optimal objective function values for the formulation variant as identified by the subscript

z_s optimal objective function value of the independent scenario s

z_0 optimal objective function value of the mean value problem, i.e., a single "scenario" deterministic model with the best-guess value for each of the parameters

$z_s(y_k)$ optimal objective function value of the independent scenario s for the given configuration y_k, in other words the solution to a linear network flow problem where only the continuous flow variables x are optimized

The *mvp* formulation is the standard deterministic formulation as discussed in the previous chapter. For the *mvp* the uncertainty is incorporated in the calculation of the parameters in the formulation, for the other formulations the uncertainty yields different formulation structures and objectives. The objective function of the *mvp* is computed as follows:

$$y_{mvp} \leftarrow \max_{y} z_0(y)$$
$$z_{mvp} = \sum_{s} p_s \cdot z_s(y_{mvp}) \tag{13.55}$$

The objective functions of the *exp*, *rob*, and *ind* formulations are then computed as follows:

$$z_{exp} = \max_{y} \sum_{s} p_s \cdot z_s(y) \tag{13.56}$$

$$y_{rob} \leftarrow \max_{y} \min_{s} z_s(y)$$
$$z_{rob} = \sum_{s} p_s \cdot z_s(y_{rob}) \tag{13.57}$$

$$z_{ind} = \sum_{s} p_s \cdot \left(\max_{y_s} z_s(y_s) \right) = \sum_{s} p_s \cdot z_s \tag{13.58}$$

The optimal solution of the various formulations yields the following optimal configuration variables and optimal objective function values.

The independent objective provides an upper bound on the expected value of the profit. The robust configuration achieves 97.4% of the bound and the expected value configuration achieves 99.5%, respectively. Note that the determination of the objectives for the mean value problem case and the robust case requires a two-phased approach. In the first phase the single robust configuration is determined that maximizes the minimum profit over all the scenarios. To enable profit maximization for the robust configuration, the flows are optimized for every scenario given the robust facility configuration. The weighted average of those scenario objective functions is used as the robust objective and shown in Table 13.17. The same approach is used to

Table 13.17 Optimal configurations and objective values for the supply chain scenario example

Formulation	Configuration	Objective(thousasds)				
		S1	S2	S3	Expected	Std.Dev.
mvp	0,1,0,0,1,0	$9,122.5	$9,709.7	$6,456.3	$9,224.1	695.0
rob	1,1,0,1,1,0	$9,645.0	$8,809.7	$8,699.6	$9,263.6	422.3
exp	0,1,0,0,1,1	$9,662.5	$9,509.7	$6,996.3	$9,468.1	571.8
ind	S1: 0,1,1,0,1,1	$9,645.0	$9,709.7	$6,456.3	$9,511.4	701.6
	S2: 0,1,0,0,1,0					
	S3: 0,1,0,0,1,0					

determine the values for the mean value problem. In the first phase, the single *mvp* configuration is determined that maximizes the profit for the expected value of the parameters. This is a deterministic problem that is also denoted as the best-guess problem. In the second phase, the flows are optimized for every scenario given the *mvp* configuration. The weighted average of those scenario objective functions is used as the *mvp* objective and shown in Table 13.17.

The expected value configuration has a larger standard deviation than the robust configuration. The configurations are placed in a standard risk analysis graph with as coordinates their expected profit and profit standard deviation. The graph is shown in Fig. 13.7 The standard deviation is typically used as a proxy for the risk associated with a configuration. The risk analysis graph allows the tradeoff between two performance measures of a configuration, i.e., the maximization of the expected profit and the minimization of the standard deviation of the profit.

Following the classic risk analysis definitions, supply chain configurations for which no other configuration exists that has both a larger expected value and a

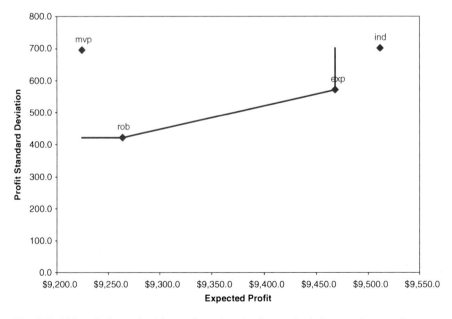

Fig. 13.7 Risk analysis graph of the configurations for the supply chain scenario example

smaller standard deviation are said to be Pareto-optimal, efficient, or nondominated. All the configurations for a supply chain can be classified as being either efficient or dominated. The efficient frontier is the envelope of the configurations that are non-dominated. It is a continuous approximation and graphical representation of the set of efficient configurations. It should be noted however that points on the efficiency frontier may not represent supply chain configurations. Similarly, configurations may be located inside, i.e., to the left and above, the efficiency frontier and still be non-dominated. Configurations inside and far removed from the efficiency frontier are usually dominated by another configuration and should only be selected as candidates after careful consideration. Constructing the efficiency frontier requires the identification of all Pareto-optimal configurations for the supply chain. Usually only a subset of the efficient configurations is known.

A piecewise linear lower convex envelope of the sample solutions can be drawn to give an estimation of the efficiency frontier. This sample-based lower efficiency envelope will be denoted by SLE. If more efficient configurations become known, then the SLE may have to be updated. Note that the sample solutions were generated by optimizing with respect to the expected value only. The corporation can then select a preferred configuration based on its risk tradeoffs from the efficient configurations. The indifference curve for a particular decision maker with a particular risk tradeoff behavior is the line that connects alternatives with expected value and standard deviation coordinates that are judged by the decision maker to have the same desirability or utility. The SLE for this example at this time connects the robust and the expected value configurations and is indicated by the solid line in the risk analysis graph. The *ind* configuration is not part of the efficiency frontier since it only represents an upper bound and is not a real configuration. A corporation may choose to implement either the average or robust configuration depending on their risk profile. For the small example, the mean value configuration is located inside and far from the SLE and is dominated by both the expected value and the robust configurations. It should not be selected as a configuration candidate for further investigation. This leads to the following observation that runs contrary to conventional wisdom: the optimal supply chain configuration for the best-guess values of the parameters is an inferior supply chain configuration, in the sense that it is Pareto-dominated. This observation is often true for real-world supply chain designs.

It is possible to efficiently identify all configurations that are Pareto-optimal with respect to the mean-standard deviation objective. The overall algorithm is a branch-and-reduce algorithm extended from Ryoo and Sahinidis (1996) where for each interval a quadratic-objective mixed integer programming formulation has to be solved. This optimization algorithm is beyond the scope of this book. For the small example there is one additional Pareto-optimal configuration identified by the branch-and-reduce algorithm and it is located close to the line connecting the expected value and the robust configuration. The SLE will have to be adjusted based on this additional Pareto-optimal configuration.

The accurate assessment of the risk associated with a strategic supply chain configuration requires the use of a large number (hundreds or thousands) of scenarios. At the same time, increasing the number of scenarios in the DEP yields unacceptable computation times. Next, an algorithm is described that integrates a recently proposed sampling strategy—the sample average approximation scheme—with an accelerated Benders decomposition algorithm to solve the strategic supply chain design problem with continuous distributions for the uncertain parameters, and hence a theoretical infinite number of scenarios. The design objective of the model is to maximize the expected value of the profit. The standard deviation of the scenario profits is used as the proxy for risk of a configuration and is computed in a second phase.

The two-stage stochastic optimization formulation for the strategic design of supply chains is approximated with its deterministic equivalent problem based on randomly sampled scenarios. The algorithm is described for a minimization formulation as is customary in the literature.

Model 13.2   Stochastic Expected Value Master Problem

$$
\begin{aligned}
Min \quad & cy + \mathrm{E}\left[Q(y,\xi)\right] \\
s.t. \quad & Hy \le g \\
& y \in \{0,1\}
\end{aligned}
\tag{13.59}
$$

Where the second stage or inner optimization problem is defined as

Model 13.3   Stochastic Expected Value Sub Problem

$$
\begin{aligned}
Q(y,\xi) = \quad Min \quad & d(\xi)x \\
s.t. \quad & F(\xi)x \le h(\xi) + E(\xi)y \\
& x \ge 0
\end{aligned}
\tag{13.60}
$$

with:

y	binary facility, size, and technology status variables
x	continuous material flow and storage variables
c	fixed facility cost vector
$d(\xi)$	operational cost vector consisting of variable transportation, purchasing, production, and inventory costs
$h(\xi)$	right-hand side of the technological constraints
$E(\xi) F(\xi)$	technology and conservation of product flow and storage matrix
H	relationships between facility status variables
g	right-hand side of the facility relationship constraints
$E[v]$	expected value of random variable v
ξ	randm vector

In the SAA method, a random sample of N realizations (scenarios) of the random vector ξ is generated, and the expectation $E\left[Q(y,\xi)\right]$ is approximated by the sample average function $\frac{1}{N}\sum_{n=1}^{N} Q(y,\xi_n)$. Consequently, the original stochastic problem is approximated by the following deterministic equivalent problem (DEP) containing N scenarios

$$DEP_N \; : \; \min_y \left\{ \hat{f}_N(y) \equiv cy + \frac{1}{N} \sum_{n=1}^{N} Q(y, \xi_n) \right\}. \tag{13.61}$$

Model 13.3   Stochastic Expected Value Deterministic Equivalent Model

$$\begin{aligned}
Min \quad & cy + \sum_{s=1}^{N} p_s d_s x_s \\
s.t. \quad & Hy \leq g \\
& y \in \{0, 1\} \\
& -E_s y + F_s x_s \leq h_s \\
& x_s \geq 0
\end{aligned} \tag{13.62}$$

with

s scenario index, $s = 1,2,\ldots N$

p_s probability of scenarios s, in the SAA method $p_s = 1/N$

The focus is on modeling and the solution characteristics of the strategic supply chain design model. In order to find the solution in a reasonable amount of time, several algorithm extensions and accelerations have to be used. The impact of these extensions will be shown here, but further details on the algorithm can be found in Santoso et al. (2003) and Santoso (2002).

After the probability distributions of the stochastic parameters have been determined, the algorithm executes the following steps:

Algorithm 13.1. Sample Average Approximation Algorithm for Strategic Supply Chain Design

1. Repeat steps 2–4 for $i = 1..M$ replications.
2. Create N scenarios by random sampling from the parameter distributions.
3. Solve the DEP with N scenarios to within a specified optimality gap, yielding solution y_i.
4. Evaluate solution y_i by computing the solution to the recourse problem for N' new random samples from the parameter distributions, record the mean μ_i, standard deviation σ_i, and range ρ_i of the solution value distribution.
5. Place the y_i solutions in a mean versus standard deviation risk analysis graph and identify all non-Pareto-dominated y_i solutions.
6. Select a preferred configuration y^* from among the non-Pareto-dominated y_i solutions based on the risk preferences of the corporation.

Steps 1–4 of the above algorithm contain the sample average approximation (SAA) method, and steps 5 and 6 correspond to the classic risk analysis method. Kleywegt et al. (2002) have shown that the SAA method converges to the optimal solution and solution value. Based on the solutions y_i a lower bound to the original minimization problem and an incumbent feasible solution to the original problem can be computed. From these the optimality gap can then be derived. Further details can be found in Santoso et al. (2003) and Kleywegt et al. (2002). Finally, the SAA algorithm uses an exterior sampling method, since the samples can be generated independently of the optimization method. This independence allows a modular structure of the overall algorithm, so that different optimal and heuristic methods can be used to solve the problem. The evaluation of a given configuration in step 4 requires the solution of a large number of recourse problems that are themselves large multi-commodity network flow problems with identical network structure. Typically, N' is chosen much larger than N. However, the most time-consuming step in the algorithm remains the solution of the DEP problem with a large number of scenarios. A specialized MIP algorithm based on accelerated Benders decomposition was used to solve the DEP for industrial problems in a reasonable computation time. The details of this algorithm are shown in Appendix 12.A.

Two case studies based on industrial projects will be used to illustrate the results obtained by the enhanced algorithm to solve the expected value problem described above. The first case study focuses on the minimization of the before-tax costs in a single country assuming that customer demand has to be satisfied. It will be referred to as the domestic model. The second model focuses on the maximization of the after-tax net cash flow (NCF) of a global corporation operating in multiple countries. In this case the customer demands are upper bounds on the amount of goods that can be sold to the customers. This model will be referred to as the global model. In both models all the right hand side parameters, constraint coefficients, and objective function coefficients are stochastic, i.e., they have known continuous probability distributions.

The domestic model is an extension of the model presented in Dogan and Goetschalckx (1996) through the inclusion of scenarios and similar to other models in the literature. The supply chain has multiple echelons between the suppliers and the customers. The supply chain of the industrial case study has two manufacturing stages for the production of cardboard packages used in breweries and soft drink bottling plants, which are the external customers. Only the single peak period is considered, ignoring the seasonality patterns in the customer demands. The first stage binary variables correspond to the opening or closing of facilities (major binary variables) and the installation of the number and different types of manufacturing lines or machines in the facilities (minor binary variables). The continuous recourse variables correspond to the production and transportation material flows in the supply chain. All customer demands must be fully satisfied, so the for this case the cost minimization model is equivalent to the profit maximization model. Raw materials and intermediate products quantities, requirements, and costs are modeled in function of finished products delivered to the customers, so only finished products are flowing through the supply chain. All costs are expressed in function of a single currency. The fixed costs for the establishment of facilities and machines correspond to the annualized equivalent before-tax costs. All transportation and production costs are linear functions of the quantities produced or transported. Each machine has a single resource capacity expressed in production hours and the various products have different resource consumption rates on the different machines expressed in hours per ton. A subset of the transportation channels has capacity restrictions, which are binding for the optimal solution.

To model the stochastic nature of the real-world deterministic data it was assumed that customer demands and production and transportation capacities are uncertain with continuous lognormal probability distributions. The mean of the distributions equaled the deterministic mean and the standard deviations were set to certain fractions of the mean to model different degrees of uncertainty. The use of the lognormal distribution assures the nonnegativity of the demand and capacity values and recent evidence provided by Kamath and Pakkala (2002) shows that lognormal distributions are well-suited for modeling economic stochastic variables such as demands. The supply chain solution configuration and used transportation channels for the domestic and global problem are presented in Figs. 13.8 and 13.9, respectively. The main characteristics of these two networks are presented in Table 13.18.

The global model is an extension of the model presented in Vidal and Goetschalckx (2001) through the inclusion of scenarios, but the transfer prices, transportation cost allocations, and duties and other international commercial terms (INCOTERMS) are constant parameters, i.e. not decision variables. The supply chain has two manufacturing stages for the production of consumer paper tissues. The customers are the regional wholesale distribution centers for the products in various countries in South America. The model considers a single time period. As in the domestic cast, the first-stage binary variables correspond to the opening or closing of facilities (major binary variables) and the installation of the number and different types of

Fig. 13.8 Domestic supply chain solution

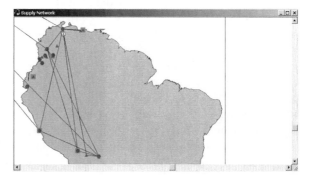

Fig. 13.9 Global supply chain solution (partial map)

Supply chain components	Domestic	Global
Product families	13	29
Raw materials		13
Intermediate materials		8
Finished products		8
Total Facilities	142	87
Internal suppliers	2	6
Manufacturing plants	8	8
Machines	28	10
Finishing facilities	9	10
Finishing machines	93	36
Warehouses	2	17
Customers	238	17
Transporation channels	1559	239
Countries	1	7
Planning periods	1	1

Table 13.18 Domestic and global characteristics

manufacturing lines or machines in the facilities (minor binary variables). The continuous recourse variables correspond to the production and transportation material flows in the supply chain. The finished products have a two-stage bill of materials (BOM) and there are different production cost rates and conversion ratios for converting a source product to an output product on a particular machine in a particular facility. Scrap flows are not included in the model. There are possible facilities and customers in seven different countries and all costs are converted to a single currency of the global corporation. The customer demand is an upper bound on the amount of products that can be sold to respective customers. The objective is the maximization of the worldwide after-tax net cash flow (NCF) of the corporation. It is assumed that the local subsidiaries in each country have sufficiently large and profitable operations so that they are subject to constant country-dependent marginal tax rates. In addition, the subsidiary in each country has a positive lower bound constraint on their NCF, which implies that losses and negative tax credits are not allowed in any country. The NCF is computed according to the generally accepted accounting principles (GAAP) and consistent with corporate financial reporting.

It is commonly accepted that increasing the number of scenarios in the DEP increases the robustness of the solution, but at the cost of significantly increasing the computational burden. In Table 13.19 the number of variables and constraints in the DEP are shown for the two test cases in function of the number of scenarios included in the DEP.

The numerical experiment supports four propositions: (1) the accelerated Benders decomposition scheme can solve industrial-sized problems with a large number of scenarios in a reasonable amount of computation time, while standard solution algorithms cannot; (2) the solutions generated by the SAA algorithm, based on multiple samples of the DEP each with many sampled scenarios, Pareto-dominate the solutions of the mean value problem; (3) the solutions to the DEP become increasingly robust with respect to the variability of the data with increasing number of

Table 13.19 Domestic and global deterministic equivalent model sizes

Domestic formulation problem statistics				
Scenarios	1	20	40	60
Constraints	7,822	156,440	312,880	469,320
Inequality constraints	3,498	69,960	139,920	209,880
Equality constraints	4,324	86,480	172,960	259,440
Variables	21,052	418,380	836,620	1,254,860
Continuous variables	20,912	418,240	836,480	1,254,720
Binary variables	140	140	140	140
Global formulation statistics				
Scenarios	1	10	20	60
Constraints	1,467	14,670	29,340	88,020
Inequality constraints	402	4,020	8,040	24,120
Equality constraints	1,065	10,650	21,300	63,900
Variables	6,894	68,310	136,550	409,510
Continuous variables	6,824	68,240	136,480	409,440
Binary variables	70	70	70	70

scenarios in the DEP; and (4) the stochastic solutions based on the SAA method tend to establish more facilities and machines at a higher configuration cost but with a significantly reduced operational recourse cost compared to the MVP solution. Further details to support each these conclusions are given next.

The optimality gap for the domestic case was set to 0.01% and to 1% for the domestic and global case, respectively. Solving the mean value problem to optimality using a Pentium II 400 MHz computer and CPLEX 7.0 as the MIP solver required 42 s and 200 s for the domestic and global case, respectively. The computation times by a standard MIP procedure of a commercial solver (CPLEX MIP), by the standard Benders decomposition algorithm, and by the accelerated Benders decomposition algorithm for the domestic and global case in function of the number of scenarios in the DEP are shown in Fig. 13.10. The global model requires significantly more computation time. For the domestic model, the standard MIP algorithm based on branch-and-bound and linear programming relaxation is superior to the standard implementation Benders decomposition up to 60 scenarios. For the global case, standard Benders decomposition becomes more efficient than the MIP algorithm for more than 15 scenarios. Both standard algorithms are strongly dominated by accelerated Benders, especially for large number of scenarios in the DEP. The time ratio is 7.9 for the domestic case and 60 scenarios and 50 for the global case and 20 scenarios. For the global case the accelerated Benders is the only algorithm that can solve the DEP in a reasonable amount of time for more than 20 scenarios.

The number of recourse optimizations N' to determine the mean and standard deviation of the objective function associated with a particular configuration was set equal to 1000. The values of the mean and standard deviation converge within less than 500 recourse optimizations. However, to remain consistent all experiments were run with $N' = 1000$. The solutions to the stochastic formulation were compared with the solution to the deterministic MVP in the classic risk analysis framework.

Fig. 13.10 CPU times for
the two cases in function of
the number of scenarios in
the DEP

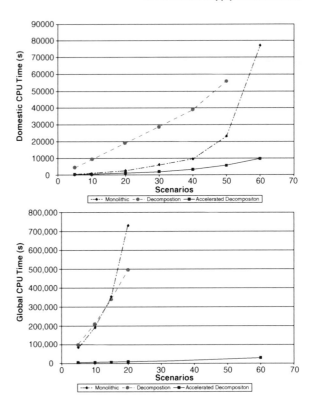

Their characteristics are shown in Fig. 13.11 More detailed statistics are provided in Table 13.20.

Note that S1 and S2 do not indicate the same configuration in problems with different number of scenarios in the DEP. S1 is always the configuration with the best expected value and S2 is always the configuration with the best (smallest) range.

Both the figures and the tables show that the solution of the MVP is Pareto-dominated by the best solutions to the DEP, i.e., there exist solutions to the DEP that have both a better expected value and a lower variability (either standard deviation or range) than the MVP solution.

If the objective of the stochastic formulation is changed to a linear combination of the expected value and a measure of the variability or dispersion such as the standard deviation, variance, or absolute deviation from the mean, i.e.,

$$Max \quad cy + E\left[Q(y,\xi)\right] - \alpha E\left[\left|Q(y,\xi) - E\left[Q(y,\xi)\right]\right|\right] \quad (13.63)$$

then the efficiency frontier for a range of values of α can be determined. The efficiency frontier for this discrete configuration problem may not be a concave or continuous function. However, if either the standard deviation or the variance are used as the dispersion measure as shown in the next formula then the objective function is a concave function.

Fig. 13.11 Risk analysis graph for domestic configurations ($N=5$ or 60, $N' = 1000$)

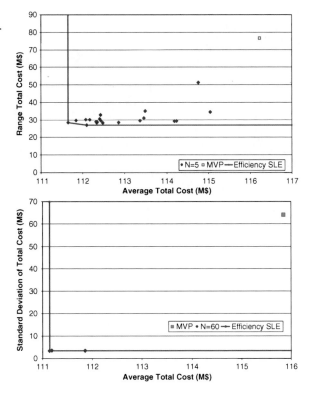

$$Max \quad cy + E\left[Q(y,\xi)\right] - \alpha STDEV\left[Q(y,\xi)\right] \qquad (13.64)$$

In the two cases studies investigated, the MVP solution has a much larger range and worse worst-case objective, i.e., the maximum cost for the domestic case or the minimum NCF for the global case, which supports the assertion that MVP solutions are much more "fragile" or less robust than DEP solutions.

Table 13.20 Statistics for various solutions to the domestic problem ($N'=1000$)

	MVP	S1	S2
$N=5$			
Avg.	116.2	111.7	112.1
Max	173.7	129.1	127.9
Min	96.8	100.6	100.8
Range	76.9	28.5	27.1
Std. D.	14.3	4.2	4.2
$N=60$			
Avg.	115.9	111.1	111.1
Max	162.5	123.3	123.3
Min	98.6	100.7	100.7
Range	64.0	22.7	22.7
Std. D.	9.8	3.5	3.5

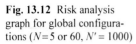

Fig. 13.12 Risk analysis graph for global configurations ($N=5$ or 60, $N' = 1000$)

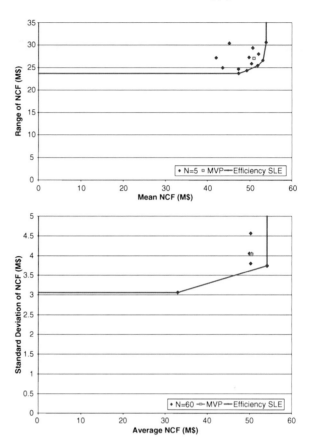

The risk tradeoff preferences of the corporation are modeled through the parameter α. However, the value of α is usually only known approximately. The standard deviation versus expected value risk analysis graph can determine the boundary values of ranges of α for which a particular configuration is preferred. $1/\alpha$ equals the slope of the tangent to the efficiency SLE identifying the preferred configuration in the standard deviation versus expected value graph.

To further investigate the robustness of solutions to the DEP the variability of the data was varied as indicated in Table 13.22.

The following two graphs in Fig. 13.13 show the behavior of the range of the objective in the function of the data variability for the domestic and global case, respectively. Solution S2 with minimum range was selected from all the solutions generated by the SAA algorithm, which corresponds to a high value of α for the risk preference parameter of the corporation.

For both cases, the MVP solution has larger range and the range grows faster than for the DEP solutions when the variability of the data increases. The mean values, worst-case objective, and the standard deviations of the solutions all show the same behavior. For the domestic case the DEP solution is slightly better and for the

Table 13.21 Statistics for various solutions to the global problem (N'=1000)

	MVP	S1	S2
N=5			
Avg.	51.0	53.9	47.3
Min	37.8	38.5	36.7
Max	64.9	69.2	60.4
Range	27.1	30.6	23.7
Std.D.	4.0	4.3	3.5
N=20			
Avg.	51.0	54.0	32.3
Min	35.2	43.1	23.7
Max	64.3	69.4	44.0
Range	29.0	26.3	20.3
Std.D.	4.0	3.9	3.0
N=60			
Avg.	51.0	54.1	32.3
Min	31.4	46.5	23.7
Max	67.0	68.1	44.0
Range	35.6	21.5	20.3
Std.D.	4.0	3.8	3.0

global case the DEP solution is significantly better when the number of scenarios increases from 20 to 60. Regardless of the number of scenarios, the DEP solutions are more resistant to variability in the data than the MVP solutions for both the domestic and global case.

The supply chain configuration of the MVP solutions was also compared to the configuration of the DEP solutions. For both the domestic and the global case, the DEP solution uses almost always more machines than the MVP solution. The DEP solutions also establish the same number or more facilities than the MVP solutions. This implies that the fixed cost for the DEP solutions is higher than for the MVP solution. However, the corresponding additional capacity allows the supply chain to respond to larger customer demands without resorting to outsourcing from external suppliers. In other words, installing more capacity is a risk mitigation strategy for the supply chain. The fixed and operational costs of the MVP and the best DEP solutions are compared in Table 13.23.

The small configuration example and the industrial domestic and global supply chain configuration projects have shown that explicit incorporation of uncertainty in the data yields significantly more robust supply chain configurations. In all of the examples from the literature and industrial projects the optimal configuration of the mean value problem with the best-guess values of the data was always Pareto-

Table 13.22 Coefficient of variation (CV) statistics of problem data variability

Problem variability	Customer demand Coeff. variation	Other parameters Coeff. variation
Low	15%	5%
Medium	30%	10%
High	40%	20%

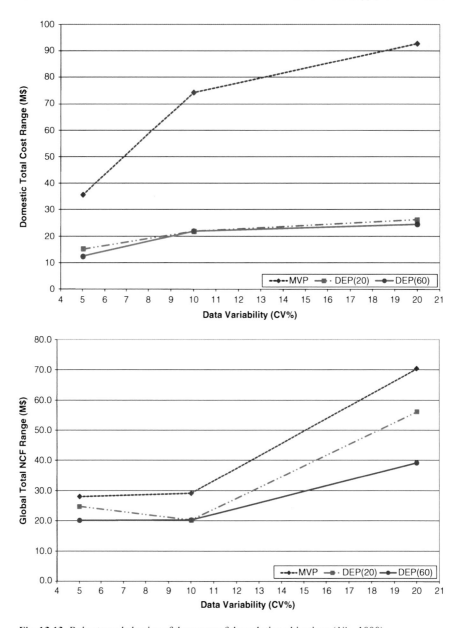

Fig. 13.13 Robustness behavior of the range of the solution objectives ($N' = 1000$)

dominated by configurations derived based on multiple scenarios. It did not matter if the standard deviation, the mean absolute deviation, or the range was used as the measure of dispersion of the objective value and the risk analysis graph. The objective function used was the expected value of the performance criteria, be it either cost minimization or profit or NCF maximization.

Table 13.23 Fixed versus operational costs (N=20)	Domestic		Global	
	MVP	DEP	MVP	DEP
Fixed cost	3.8	4.7	11.6	13.9
Operational cost	113.0	106.3		
NCF without fixed cost			62.6	67.9
Total cost or NCF	116.8	111.0	51.0	54.0
(M$/year)				

It should be noted that including more scenarios creates larger problem instances. Hence including more scenarios improves the configuration quality but a significant increase in computational burden. The number of scenarios to include corresponding to the best tradeoff between solution quality and computational burden depends on the size and the structure of the supply chain. Given the significant financial impact of supply chain configurations, a value of 50 appears to be a reasonable number of scenarios. Computational power and the power of off-the-shelf mixed integer programming solvers continue to increase. The implementation of a targeted algorithm such as Benders decomposition appears to only be needed for the largest problem instances.

13.5 Conclusions

In this chapter, a collection of models for the strategic design of supply chains was presented. The model extensions for several real-world considerations such as safety inventory, bill-of-materials relationships between products, local content requirements, and data uncertainty were developed. For some of these extensions the basic solution methodology of mixed integer programming still can yield solutions within acceptable computation times. However, large problem instances or models incorporating uncertainty require specialized algorithms. Knowledge of such specialized algorithms is almost never available within the corporation that is designing the supply chain. The supply chain configuration provided at a particular time by an external consulting group may be difficult to adapt to the changing business conditions. The strategic design of a supply chain is most successful if it is executed as a continuous effort and part of a core business planning function. The ongoing data collection, model creation, solution generation, and result presentation requires in house expertise and tools. The necessary resources have to be made available for the original creation and the support of these decision support tools.

There will always be a tradeoff between a general purpose tool and a narrowly focused and specific decision support tool. The continuously growing power of standard computing resources has made the development of design environments possible. These design environments can contain a richer variety of models and of solution algorithms and can still be used by supply chain professionals rather than by supply chain, modeling, and algorithm specialists. Without doubt, there will be design problems where the proposed model is not sufficiently accurate or detailed. A prominent example is the assumption that the production ___t and resource requirements for producing a particular product at a manufacturing plant are independent of the production quantity or the product mix produced at this plant. Also, the treatment of safety inventory is very simplistic but conservative and realistic. At the same time, the execution times of the algorithms described above will be larger than that of specialized models and solution techniques when designing systems of comparable size.

But the goal was to reduce the time required to design a supply chain system for a company without extensive prior experience in this area. The predefined structure of the model allows the company to focus on the data collection and sensitivity analysis parts of the design task. The algorithm enhancements allow the strategic model to be solved for these real life cases in a fraction of the time of a general purpose solver, if the general purpose solver can reach a solution at all. At the same time, the modeling environments have been of significant help in communicating models and solution algorithms with industrial companies and with students in undergraduate, graduate and continuing education classes. It is my belief that there is a place for generic but domain specific design models, algorithms, and modeling environments that bridge the gap between multipurpose algebraic modeling languages and one-of-a-kind specialized models and associated solution algorithms.

13.6 Exercises

13.6.1 Strategic Model Extension: Assembly Operations in Warehouses

Consider the strategic model for the design of strategic production–distribution systems. Assume that some assembly operations can be performed in the last warehouse before the products reach the customers. There are two intermediate products, denoted by A and B, and there are two final products, denoted by C and D. The assembly equations for the final assembly are:

$$\begin{cases} 2A + 3B = C \\ 2B + 5A = 2D \end{cases}$$

In other words, the first assembly equation states that two units of product A plus three units of product B are required to make one unit of product C.

Assembling one product C takes 9 min; assembling two units of product D takes 24 min. The handling of one unit of product C from receiving through shipping takes 3 min. The handling of one unit of product D from receiving through shipping takes 7 min. The handling of an assembled unit of product C takes 1 min. The handling of an assembled unit of product D takes 2 min. All assembly and handling has to be done by a team of ten equivalent workers. Each works 480 min per shift. The cost per minute of labor spent on either handling or assembling products C and D is equal to \$1. Assembling product D requires the presence of a particular machine. This presence is denoted by variable $Machine_N$, equal to 1 if the machine is present, zero otherwise. The fixed cost per shift for Machine N is equal to \$100.

1. Clearly define all your variables and parameters consistent with the tactical model and list the legend.
2. Write down explicitly the flow conservation equations for the last warehouse before the products reach the customers (i.e., without summation signs and with numerical values for all parameters).
3. Write down explicitly the capacity constraint for the total throughput of products C and D through this final warehouse (i.e., without summation signs and with numerical values for all parameters).
4. Write the linkage or consistency constraints for assembly of product D and Machine N
5. Write the cost function for the handling and assembly of products C and D.

13.6.1.1 Recycling Operations

Consider the integrated model for the design of strategic logistics systems. The following questions are related to extending this strategic logistics model to incorporate for various additional constraints, commonly encountered in practice. In your answers, clearly indicate the bounds of any summations signs you might have used and the number of constraints of that particular type.

Using the notation developed in class for the strategic model, write down the most compact constraint which assures that at most one transportation channel between an origin facility i and destination facility j is used, assuming there are many alternative or parallel transportation channels available between the origin and destination facility. These alternatives are indexed by m. Give a clear definition of the variables and parameters used in this constraint. Will there be many or few constraints of this type in the extended model?

Assume that if a warehouse is used, then it must have a minimum throughput or material flow through this warehouse. This minimum throughput is denoted by $MinFlow_{jl}$ for a warehouse of type l at site j. Write down the most compact constraint which assures that if the warehouse of that type at that site is used it will have at least the required minimum throughput. Give a clear definition of the variables and parameters used in this constraint. Will there be many or few constraints of this type in the extended model?

Consider the case where a raw material vendor i ships raw material p to a manufacturing plant j. The production process at the manufacturing plant creates a finished product q and scrap material t. The finished product is shipped to distribution center k. The scrap material is returned to the vendor from which it came to be recycled at the raw material vendor. All shipments occur at a weekly frequency. The amount of all material flows is expressed in tons per week. The production process at the plant has a 20% scrap rate, i.e., 20% of the incoming raw material is scrapped. All material flows are carried by identical, company owned trucks which carry exclusively company materials. The materials are heavy so all trucks are constrained by their weight capacity only. The company can use or deploy at most V trucks. Write down all the required constraints to ensure that the design model will find a feasible solution. Use the notation developed in class and extend it in a logical fashion when required. Write the most compact constraints. Give a clear definition of the variables and parameters used in this constraint. The formulation for this case depends strongly on the detailed assumptions that are made regarding transportation. List clearly all your transportation assumptions.

13.7   Appendix 13.A   Benders Decomposition Algorithm for the stochastic strategic supply chain design model

The DEP is a large mixed integer programming problem with block angular structure and joining binary configuration variables. Such problems lend themselves to primal Benders decomposition schemes, originally proposed by Benders (1962), which are also known as L-shaped decomposition methods in the stochastic programming literature, see, e.g., Van Slyke and Wets (1969).

Algorithm 13.2. Original Benders Primal Decomposition Algorithm

Step 1: Initialization: set the iteration counter $k = 0$ and solve the initial master problem

$$
\begin{aligned}
min \quad & cy + \varphi \\
s.t. \quad & Hy \leq g \\
& y_f \in \{0, 1\} \qquad \forall f
\end{aligned}
\tag{13.65}
$$

Let y^0 be the optimal solution and let $LB = cy^0$ be current lower bound and let $UB^{-1} = \infty$ be the feasible upper bound (which does not exist at this time).

Step 2: Subproblem solution:

$$
\begin{aligned}
Min \quad & \sum_{s=1}^{S} p_s d_s x_s \\
s.t. \quad & F_s x_s \leq h_s + E_s y^k \\
& x_s \geq 0
\end{aligned}
\tag{13.66}
$$

Let (x^k, λ^k, μ^k) be the optimal primal and dual solution variables and let $z^k = cy^k + \sum_{s=1}^{S} p_s d_s x_s^k$ be value of current primal feasible solution

Step 3: Convergence Test: compute the upper bound (incumbent primal feasible solution value)

$$UB^k = min\left\{UB^{k-1}, z^k\right\} \tag{13.67}$$

and compute the relative optimality gap

$$gap^k = \frac{UB^k - LB^k}{LB^k}, \; gap^k = \infty \quad if \quad LB^k = 0 \tag{13.68}$$

if $gap^k \leq \varepsilon$ terminate with the (y^k, x^k) as the optimal solution, otherwise increment the iteration counter $k = k + 1$ and go to Step 4

Step 4: Master Problem Solution: add the feasibility cut based on the dual variables (λ^k, μ^k) and solve the expanded master problem

$$
\begin{aligned}
min \quad & cy + \varphi \\
s.t. \quad & Hy \leq g \\
& \varphi + \sum_f \sum_s \left(\mu_{fs}^l \cdot e_{fs}\right) y_f \geq \sum_c \sum_p \sum_s \lambda_{cps}^l \cdot h_{cps} \quad l = 1...k \tag{13.69} \\
& y_f \in \{0, 1\} \quad \forall f
\end{aligned}
$$

where e_{fs} and h_{cps} are the corresponding elements of the matrix E and vector h. Let y^k be the optimal solution and let $LB = cy^k + \varphi$ be current lower bound and go to Step 2.

While these schemes are theoretically guaranteed to converge, very large gaps during the initial iterations and poor convergence behavior during the final iterations limit the straightforward application of this primal decomposition method in practice. Several acceleration techniques have been implemented that dramatically reduce the computation times and allow for the solution of realistically sized DEP in a reasonable amount of computation time. The acceleration techniques are briefly described below and further details of the acceleration techniques and their effectiveness can be found in Santoso et al. (2003) and Santoso (2003).

In the standard implementation of the Benders algorithm, the early iterations have a very large optimality gap because the master problem contains very few primal cuts and the corresponding solutions close most of the facilities. Logistics constraints are additional constraints in the master problem that must be satisfied in order for a feasible solution to exist. One example is the constraint that ensures that each echelon in the supply chain has sufficient capacity in the open facilities to satisfy the total customer demand or the average customer demand. The logistics constraints have the following general form, where x_s is a vector of parameters with realized values.

$$-E_s y \leq h_s - F_s x_s$$
$$\text{or} \qquad\qquad\qquad\qquad\qquad\qquad\qquad (13.70)$$
$$E_s y \geq F_s x_s - h_s$$

References

Benders, P. (1962). Partitioning procedures for solving mixed-variables programming problems. *Numerische Mathematik, 4,* 238–252.

Canel, C. & Khumawala, B. M. (1997). Multi-period international facilities location: An algorithm and application. *International Journal of Production Research, 35*(7), 1891–1910.

Cohen, M. A. & Lee, H. L. (1985). Manufacturing strategy: concepts and methods, Ch. 5 In P. R. Kleindorfer (Ed.), *The management of productivity and technology in manufacturing,* (pp. 153–188) New York: Plenum Press.

Cohen, M. A. & Lee, H. L. (1988). Strategic analysis of integrated production–distribution systems: models and methods. *Operations Research, 36*(2), 216–228.

Cohen, M. A. & Lee, H. L. (1989). Resource deployment analysis of global manufacturing and distribution networks. *Journal of Manufacturing Operations Management, 2,* 81–104.

Cohen, M. A. & Moon, S. (1991). An integrated plant loading model with economies of scale and scope *European Journal of Operational Research, 50*(3), 266–279.

Cohen, M. A. & Kleindorfer, P. R. (1993). Creating value through operations: The legacy of Elwood S. Buffa. In R. K. Sarin, (Ed.), *Perspectives in operations management (Essays in Honor of Elwood S. Buffa)* (pp. 3–21). Boston: Kluwer Academic.

Cohen, M. A., Fisher, M., & Jaikumar, R. (1989). International manufacturing and distribution networks: a normative model framework. In K. Ferdows (Ed.), *Managing international manufacturing* (pp. 67–93). North-Holland: Amsterdam.

Cohen, M. A. & Huchzermeier, A. (1999). Global supply chain management: A survey of research and applications. In S. Tayur et al. (Eds.), *Quantitative models for supply chain management* (pp. 669–702). Boston: Kluwer Academic.

Dogan, K., & Goetschalckx, M. (1999). A primal decomposition method for the integrated design of multi-period production-distribution systems. *IIE Transactions, 31*(11), 1027–1036.

Drezner, Z. (1995). *Facility location: a survey of applications and methods.* New York: Springer-Verlag.

Erlenkotter D. (1978). A dual-based procedure for uncapacitated facility location. *Operations Research, 26*(6), 992–1009.

Feldman, E., Lehrer, F. A., & Ray, T. L. (1966). Warehouse location under continuous economies of scale. *Management Science, 12,* 670–684.

Fisher, M. L. (1985). An applications oriented guide to lagrangian relaxation. *Interfaces, 15*(2), 10–21.

Francis, R. L., McGinnis, L. F., & White, J. A. (1992). Facility layout and location: An analytical approach. (2nd ed.) Englewood Cliffs: Prentice-Hall.

Geoffrion, A. M., & Graves, G. W. (1974). Multicommodity distribution system design by Benders decomposition. *Management Science, 20*(5), 822–844.

Geoffrion, A. M., Graves, G. W., (1978) Strategic distribution system planning: A status report, In A. C. Hax (Ed.), *Studies in Operations Management*, Amsterdam: Elsevier.

Geoffrion A. M., & McBride (1978). Lagreangean relaxation applied to capacitated facility location problems. *Operations Research, 10*(1), 40–47.

Geoffrion, A. M., & Powers, R. F. (1980). Facility location analysis is just the beginning (if you do it right). *Interfaces, 10*(2), 22–30.

Geoffrion, A. M., Graves, G. W. & Lee, S. J. (1982). A management support system for distribution planning. *INFOR, 20*(4), 287–314.

Geoffrion, A. M., Morris, J. G., & Webster, S. T. (1995). Distribution system design. In Z. Drezner (Ed.), *Facility location: a survey of applications and methods*. New York: Springer-Verlag.

Geoffrion, A. M., & Powers, R. F. (1995). 20 years of strategic distribution system design: An evolutionary perspective. *Interfaces, 25*(5), 105–127.

Goetschalckx, M., Nemhauser, G., Cole, M. H., Wei, R., Dogan, K. & Zang, X. (1994). Computer-aided design of industrial logistic systems. In *Proceedings of the Third Triennial Symposium on Transportation Analysis* (TRISTAN III), Capri, Italy, pp. 151–178.

Goetschalckx, M. (2000). Strategic network planning. In H. Stadtler & C. Kilger (Eds.), *Supply chain management and advanced planning*, Heidelberg: Springer-Verlag.

Kuehn, A. A., & Hamburger, M. J. (1963). A heuristic program for locating warehouses. *Management Science, 9,* 643–666.

Lasdon, L. S., (1970). *Optimization Theory for Large Systems.* New York: MacMillan.

Lee, C. (1991). An optimal algorithm for the multiproduct capacitated facility location problem with a choice of facility type. *Computers and Operational Research, 18*(2), 167–182.

Lee, C. (1993), A cross decomposition algorithm for a multiproduct-multitype facility location problem. *Computers and Operational Research, 20*(5), 527–540.

Love, R. F., Morris, J. G., & Wesolowsky, G. O. (1988). *Facilities location*. New York: Elsevier.

Mirchandani, P. B., & Francis, R. L. (1990). *Discrete location theory*. New York: Wiley.

Moon, S. (1989). Application of generalized Benders decomposition to a nonlinear distribution system design problem. *Naval Research Logistics, 36,* 283–295.

Nemhauser, G. L., & Wolsey, L. A. (1988). *Integer and combinatorial optimization*. New York: Wiley.

Park, & Sharp, G. P. (1990). *Engineering Economics*.

Schrage, L. (1986). *Linear, Integer, and Quadratic Programming with LINDO*. Palo Alto: The Scientific Press.

Schmidt, G., & Wilhelm, W. E. (2000). Strategic, tactical, and operational decisions in multi-national logistics networks: a review and discussion of modeling issues. *International Journal of Production Research, 38*(7), 1501–1523.

Stadtler, H., & Kilger, C. (2000). *Supply chain management and advanced planning*. Heidelberg: Springer-Verlag.

Tayur, S., Ganeshan, R., & Magazine, M. (Eds.). (1999). *Quantitative models for supply chain management*. Boston: Kluwer Academic.

Thomas, D. & Griffin, P. M. (1996). Coordinated supply chain management. *European Journal of Operational Research, 94,* 1–15.

Van Roy, T. J., & Erlenkotter, D. (1982). A dual-based procedure for dynamic facility location. *Management Science, 28,* 1091–1105.

Van Roy, T. (1983). Cross decomposition for mixed integer programming. *Mathematical Programming, 25,* 46–63.

Van Roy, T. (1986). A cross decomposition algorithm for capacitated facility location. *Operations Research, 34*(1), 145–163.

Verter, V., & Dasci, A. (2001). The plant location and flexible technology acquisition problem. *European Journal of Operational Research* (to appear).

Vidal, C., & Goetschalckx, M. (1996). The role and limitations of quantitative techniques in the strategic design of global logistics systems, CIBER Research Report 96-023, Georgia Institute of Technology. Accepted for publication in the special issue on Manufacturing in a Global Economy of the *Journal of Technology Forecasting and Social Change*.

Vidal, C., & Goetschalckx, M. (1997). Strategic production-distribution models: A critical review with emphasis on global supply chain models. *European Journal of Operational Research*, *98*, 1–18.

Vidal, C., & Goetschalckx, M. (2000). Modeling the impact of uncertainties on global logistics systems. *Journal of Business Logistics*, *21*(1), 95–120.

Vidal, C. & Goetschalckx, M. (2001). A global supply chain model with transfer pricing and transportation cost allocation. *European Journal of Operational Research*, *129*(1), 134–158.

Appendix A: Standard Distributions

A.1. Cumulative Normal Distribution

Figure A.1 and Table A.1 show the cumulative standard normal distribution in function of z, i.e., $P[x \le z]$ in function of z, where $x = N(0,1)$. The values can also be computed with the NORMSDIST function in the Excel spreadsheet.

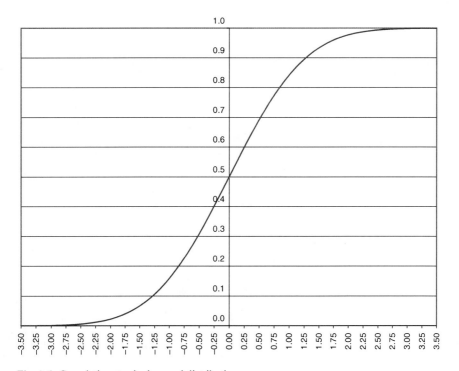

Fig. A.1 Cumulative standard normal distribution

M. Goetschalckx, *Supply Chain Engineering,* International Series in Operations Research & Management Science 161, DOI 10.1007/978-1-4419-6512-7, © Springer Science+Business Media, LLC 2011

Table A.1 Cumulative standard normal distribution

z	F(z)	z	F(z)	z	F(z)	z	F(z)	z	F(z)
-3.50	0.000233	-2.10	0.017864	-0.70	0.241964	0.75	0.773373	2.15	0.984222
-3.45	0.000280	-2.05	0.020182	-0.65	0.257846	0.80	0.788145	2.20	0.986097
-3.40	0.000337	-2.00	0.022750	-0.60	0.274253	0.85	0.802337	2.25	0.987776
-3.35	0.000404	-1.95	0.025588	-0.55	0.291160	0.90	0.815940	2.30	0.989276
-3.30	0.000483	-1.90	0.028717	-0.50	0.308538	0.95	0.828944	2.35	0.990613
-3.25	0.000577	-1.85	0.032157	-0.45	0.326355	1.00	0.841345	2.40	0.991802
-3.20	0.000687	-1.80	0.035930	-0.40	0.344578	1.05	0.853141	2.45	0.992857
-3.15	0.000816	-1.75	0.040059	-0.35	0.363169	1.10	0.864334	2.50	0.993790
-3.10	0.000968	-1.70	0.044565	-0.30	0.382089	1.15	0.874928	2.55	0.994614
-3.05	0.001144	-1.65	0.049471	-0.25	0.401294	1.20	0.884930	2.60	0.995339
-3.00	0.001350	-1.60	0.054799	-0.20	0.420740	1.25	0.894350	2.65	0.995975
-2.95	0.001589	-1.55	0.060571	-0.15	0.440382	1.30	0.903200	2.70	0.996533
-2.90	0.001866	-1.50	0.066807	-0.10	0.460172	1.35	0.911492	2.75	0.997020
-2.85	0.002186	-1.45	0.073529	-0.05	0.480061	1.40	0.919243	2.80	0.997445
-2.80	0.002555	-1.40	0.080757	0.00	0.500000	1.45	0.926471	2.85	0.997814
-2.75	0.002980	-1.35	0.088508	0.05	0.519939	1.50	0.933193	2.90	0.998134
-2.70	0.003467	-1.30	0.096800	0.10	0.539828	1.55	0.939429	2.95	0.998411
-2.65	0.004025	-1.25	0.105650	0.15	0.559618	1.60	0.945201	3.00	0.998650
-2.60	0.004661	-1.20	0.115070	0.20	0.579260	1.65	0.950529	3.05	0.998856
-2.55	0.005386	-1.15	0.125072	0.25	0.598706	1.70	0.955435	3.10	0.999032
-2.50	0.006210	-1.10	0.135666	0.30	0.617911	1.75	0.959941	3.15	0.999184
-2.45	0.007143	-1.05	0.146859	0.35	0.636831	1.80	0.964070	3.20	0.999313
-2.40	0.008198	-1.00	0.158655	0.40	0.655422	1.85	0.967843	3.25	0.999423
-2.35	0.009387	-0.95	0.171056	0.45	0.673645	1.90	0.971283	3.30	0.999517
-2.30	0.010724	-0.90	0.184060	0.50	0.691462	1.95	0.974412	3.35	0.999596
-2.25	0.012224	-0.85	0.197663	0.55	0.708840	2.00	0.977250	3.40	0.999663
-2.20	0.013903	-0.80	0.211855	0.60	0.725747	2.05	0.979818	3.45	0.999720
-2.15	0.015778	-0.75	0.226627	0.65	0.742154	2.10	0.982136	3.50	0.999767
				0.70	0.758036				

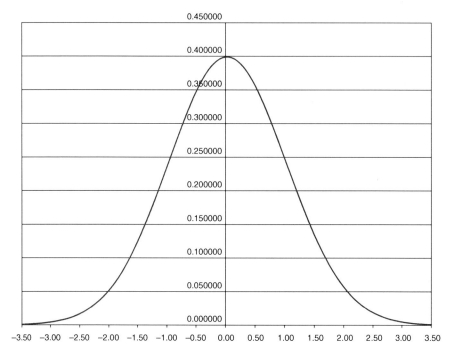

Fig. A.2 Standard normal distribution

The standard normal density function with mean equal to zero and standard deviation equal to one is shown in Fig. A.2.

A.2. Unit Loss Function

Figure A.3 and Table A.2 show the unit loss distribution in function of z. The unit loss function is defined as $L(z) = \int_z^\infty (t-z)\phi(t)dt$, where $\varphi(t)$ is the standard normal density function. The unit loss function can be computed with the Excel formula NORMDIST(z,0,1,0)-z*(1-NORMDIST(z)).

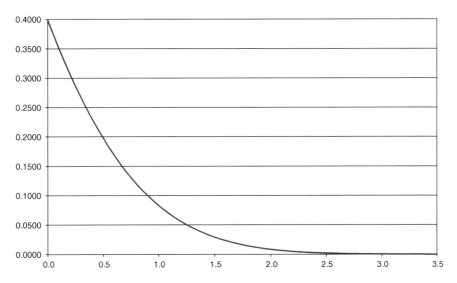

Fig. A.3 Unit loss function

Table A.2 Unit loss function

z	L(z)	z	L(z)	z	L(z)	z	L(z)	z	L(z)
0.00	0.3989								
0.05	0.3744	0.75	0.1312	1.45	0.0328	2.15	0.0056	2.85	0.0006
0.10	0.3509	0.80	0.1202	1.50	0.0293	2.20	0.0049	2.90	0.0005
0.15	0.3284	0.85	0.1100	1.55	0.0261	2.25	0.0042	2.95	0.0005
0.20	0.3069	0.90	0.1004	1.60	0.0232	2.30	0.0037	3.00	0.0004
0.25	0.2863	0.95	0.0916	1.65	0.0206	2.35	0.0032	3.05	0.0003
0.30	0.2668	1.00	0.0833	1.70	0.0183	2.40	0.0027	3.10	0.0003
0.35	0.2481	1.05	0.0757	1.75	0.0162	2.45	0.0023	3.15	0.0002
0.40	0.2304	1.10	0.0686	1.80	0.0143	2.50	0.0020	3.20	0.0002
0.45	0.2137	1.15	0.0621	1.85	0.0126	2.55	0.0017	3.25	0.0002
0.50	0.1978	1.20	0.0561	1.90	0.0111	2.60	0.0015	3.30	0.0001
0.55	0.1828	1.25	0.0506	1.95	0.0097	2.65	0.0012	3.35	0.0001
0.60	0.1687	1.30	0.0455	2.00	0.0085	2.70	0.0011	3.40	0.0001
0.65	0.1554	1.35	0.0409	2.05	0.0074	2.75	0.0009	3.45	0.0001
0.70	0.1429	1.40	0.0367	2.10	0.0065	2.80	0.0008	3.50	0.0001

Index